HISTORIC BUILDINGS IN EASTERN SU

RYE REBUILT

REGENERATION AND DECLINE WITHIN A SUSSEX PORT TOWN, 1350-1660

David and Barbara Martin
with
Jane Clubb and Gillian Draper

2009

Published 2009 by domtom publishing ltd on behalf of The Romney Marsh Research Trust

ISBN 978-1-906070-11-3

The Romney Marsh Research Group and the authors are greatly indebted to The Marc Fitch Fund, Sussex Archaeological Society (a Margary Research Grant) Colyer Fergusson Trust and the Hawkins Trust for generous grants towards the cost of this publication. They also acknowledge the generous permission granted by the various institutions acknowledged within this volume for allowing the reproduction of illustrations held by them.

CONTENTS

FOREWORD

This is one of two volumes arising from an integrated research project co-ordinated and managed by the Romney Marsh Research Trust. The idea of an interdisciplinary project centred on the town of Rye was first proposed by the then Chair of the Executive of the Trust, Helen Clarke, in 2004. Subsequently two strands developed, work on the history of Rye, which has been published as *Rye: a History of a Sussex Cinque Port to 1660*, by G. Draper with contributions by D. Martin, B. Martin and A. Tyler (Phillimore) and *Rye Rebuilt* which places the domestic built heritage of Rye in the context of the town's history. For *Rye Rebuilt*, the Trust funded the writing and publication costs and the costs of additional work to complete a buildings survey of Rye started by David and Barbara Martin in 1977. The 'Rye and hinterlands Project' was overseen by a Steering Committee comprising Martyn Waller (Chair), Terry Burke (Secretary), David Williams (Treasurer), Luke Barber, Caroline Barron, Gillian Draper, Barbara Martin, David Martin, Caroline Thackray and Alan Tyler. The research underpinning the Rye and hinterlands Project and the publication of the two volumes was enabled by very generous donations from the Colyer Fergusson Trust and the Hawkins Trust. The publication costs for *Rye Rebuilt* were supported with additional grants from The Marc Fitch Fund and the Sussex Archaeological Society (a Margary Research Grant).

The Romney Marsh Research Trust exists to promote, co-ordinate and disseminate research into the historical, social, economic and physical development of Romney and Walland Marshes and their immediate hinterlands. The Trust receives, raises and holds funds to meet grant applications to support and publish research into the Marsh and invites individuals to become Friends of the Romney Marsh Research Trust and to participate in lectures, conferences, field visits and research projects. Details of the Trust and membership are available on the web-site www.rmrt.org.uk.

Martyn Waller,
Chair of the Executive,
Romney Marsh Research Trust

PREFACE

INTRODUCTION

In the late 1960s and early 1970s scholars such as Maurice Barley, Eric Mercer and Stuart Rigold were actively encouraging programmes of detailed regional analyses into vernacular buildings. In south-east England the principal promoters of this form of systematic and detailed study were Roy Armstrong (founder of the Weald and Downland Open Air Museum) and Reg Mason (author of *Framed Buildings of the Weald* published in 1964). It was they who encouraged us to embark upon the long-term study of the 250 square mile region of eastern Sussex called the 'Rape of Hastings'. This study became known as the 'Rape of Hastings Architectural Survey' (hereafter RoHAS).

The Rape of Hastings includes 36 rural parishes (plus substantial parts of three others) and the four towns of Battle, Hastings, Rye and Winchelsea. Discounting two areas of largely unoccupied marshland, the rape is located entirely within the heavily wooded and undulating High Weald geological region. In terms of settlement pattern and the agrarian regimes practised historically, the High Weald and the adjacent area known as the Low Weald are very similar: both are areas of dispersed settlement comprising a mosaic of small-acreage holdings. In contrast, the Greensand and Downland areas which surround the Weald were once dominated by nucleated settlements and open-field farming augmented by communal sheep downs. Despite the differences in settlement background between the Wealden and Downland areas, in terms of domestic architecture (size, plan form and constructional details) the study area is representative of the historical houses which survive over a large part of the counties of Kent and East and West Sussex. Many of those which survive in the Downland areas are now encased in flint, whilst those within the Weald are today largely tile hung and brick underbuilt, but these differences represent relatively recent modifications. On account of their number, age, and quality of finish, collectively the surviving historic houses and farm buildings of the region form a nationally significant concentration. They make a very important contribution towards the area's distinctive character. The houses in the eastern and northern parts of Kent and in the western half of West Sussex are somewhat different, as are those of the county of Surrey.

Between 1967 and 1991 approximately 1150 individual building surveys were undertaken within the Rape of Hastings. Running in tandem with these was a programme of historical analysis aimed at compiling historical profiles of the tenements within the rape. This work was considered essential in order that sufficient data would be available to place the buildings into their social and historical context in a later phase of the analysis. In 1982 sufficient work had been completed to commence thematic analysis, and by 1991 syntheses of farm buildings (Martin & Martin, 1982; *see also* Martin & Martin, 2006), as well as the constructional details of walls, windows and doorways in houses (Martin & Martin, 1989; Martin & Martin, 1991) had been completed and published.

The research had been carried out on a voluntary basis which came to an end in 1991 when we entered employment with the University College London Field Archaeology Unit as Historic Buildings Officers, principally carrying out commercial commissioned work on the analysis of individual buildings in south-east England.

Most of the work between 1991 and 1998 was either planning or conservation related, though some research relevant to the original project was possible. However, in the main, analytical research relating to the buildings which survive in the Rape of Hastings was put on hold, with the archive in storage at East Sussex Record Office (hereafter ESRO HBR) where it remains publicly accessible upon request (within defined limitations regarding use). Copyright on all material remains with the persons responsible for compiling the records, principally with us. Initiatives since 1998 have allowed analysis to be carried out in respect of the four towns within the rape (*see* below).

THE RYE REPORT

This analysis of Rye's built environment has been written as a companion volume to similar studies, funded by English Heritage, currently in progress in respect of the historic houses within the towns of Hastings and Battle. A detailed synthesis of the fourth town within the Rape of Hastings, Winchelsea, was completed in 2004 as part of another project funded principally by English Heritage (Martin & Martin *et al*, 2004).

It is accepted that an adequate knowledge of the historical context of Rye and its houses is the key to understanding the layout of the town and its surviving domestic buildings. In this we, as students of architecture, have been fortunate. The Tudor period — the period of Rye's greatest prosperity — was the subject of separate detailed analyses carried out by documentary-based historians, Graham Mayhew and Stephen Hipkin, both of whom wrote on the subject during the last quarter of the 20th century. Despite published accounts by the 19th-century antiquarian, William Holloway, the 20th-century local historian, Leopold Vidler, and a useful summary compiled by William Page for Volume **9** of the Victoria County History of Sussex, published in 1937, until now the medieval period has been less well served. This disadvantage has been corrected by the work undertaken by the historian, Gillian Draper, in the preparation of 'Rye History', which forms the primary element of the Romney Marsh Research Trust's Rye project. The content of this present study into the historical built environment of the town has benefitted greatly from the work of these scholars, a point which will be only too evident from the many references to their work.

A Note on Dating the Surviving Buildings

If the buildings used in any synthesis have not been dated with reasonable accuracy, then the results of any analysis based upon that sample must be suspect. In this respect, it must be borne in mind that a little over half the surveys used in this present study were carried out before 1987, at a time when scientific dating by means of dendrochronological analysis (tree-ring dating) was neither widely available nor affordable. Furthermore, funds have not been available as part of the present project to tree-ring date any of the buildings contained within this present study. Given this fact, it would be useful to include here a brief account of the dating methods used and the checks included to confirm, as far as is possible, the accuracy of the dates allocated.

In 1987 all buildings which had been surveyed within the Rape of Hastings up to that date (including those in Rye) were subjected to a rigorous dating check and re-calibration. All phases in the development of each house had been allotted dates at the time of initial survey and it is these dates which appear in the archive reports lodged at ESRO as part of the HBR record. However, these relied upon the experience of the authors at the time of survey and, having been carried out over a period of 20 years, it was inevitable that the allotted dates were subject to inconsistencies. To rectify this, in 1987 the 137 houses which incorporate dated works (including two from Rye) were extracted and carefully studied. A selection of these was published in *Historic Buildings in Eastern Sussex* Volume 4. The next step was to re-date the entire sample by impression derived from our experience of over 1000 surveys, fortified by the results of the dated-buildings study. This was followed by a more systematic attempt in which date ranges were allocated to a series of features. In association with Don Clark, these were then considered in relation to each of the 137 known dated buildings and a date range established for each, from which a mid-date could be calculated. Throughout the process the buildings were referred to only by their survey number, thereby maintaining an anonymity which was essential if unbiased results were to be obtained. The calculated mid-dates were then compared with the known dates for each of the 137 buildings. Eighty-three per cent of the sample were dated accurately to within a range of +/- 25 years, the principal area of error being the late 17th and early 18th centuries where the ranges given to all late features had been terminated at 1750. In effect this prevented any calculated mid-date from approaching the year 1750 and placed the dates of these houses far too early. With this adjusted, the chart was utilized to acquire a mid-date and date range for all undated building works. The results were compared with those acquired by 'experience' and in those instances where discrepancies were found, the facts were again examined and a compromise arrived at. At this point the agreed mid-dates were entered upon the Survey's database, together with an acceptable date range, typically +/- 25 years, but occasionally greater.

Because the sample of dated buildings included few houses of medieval origin, as an additional check the Kent office of the then Royal Commission on the Historical Monuments of England (now subsumed into English Heritage) agreed to set a test based upon eleven Kent houses successfully dated by dendrochronology undertaken by Nottingham University Tree-Ring Dating Laboratory. This would allow any necessary adjustments to be made to the allotted medieval dates prior to commencement of analysis. With a date span 1371-1533, the chosen Kent sample was well spread chronologically. The conditions throughout were strictly controlled under the auspices of Sarah Pearson. In the event, the results proved the success of the technique outlined above — nine of the eleven buildings were dated to within 15 years and the mid-dates of all but one of the eleven houses were accurately dated to within 20 years of the estimated felling date. The exception showed few datable features and at the time was given a range of +/-75 years, a range within which the estimated felling date lay — but only just!

The same dating methods as outlined above have been used to ascribe dates to those Rye houses which have been surveyed since 1987. Although the methods of dating described above can only ever be regarded as a poor substitute for the true date of each building, they are essential in the absence of more reliable information. Inevitably some errors exist, but sufficient safeguards have been incorporated in the methodology to ensure that their effect upon any conclusions reached should be minimal.

The Illustrations

A prime objective throughout this publication has been to keep the illustrations as clear and uncomplicated as possible so as to transmit maximum information without the need to spend time analysing the individual drawings. In order to achieve this end it has been necessary in some instances to firm up details where doubts of interpretation exist. For this reason, it is recommended that if the contents of this volume are used for research purposes, specific examples contained within these pages are not relied upon without first consulting the relevant full archive report deposited at ESRO. Reference details are given at the end of each individual entry contained within the gazetteer in Chapters 10 to 14. Likewise, in the interest of clarity the reconstruction drawings contained within this publication make no attempt to differentiate between surviving and evidenced fabric. The positions of doorways are shown only where good evidence for their locations exist. As a result, the plans of some houses do not show the method of access from the exterior, and likewise some rooms are illustrated with no visible means of access. All plans, sections and elevations contained within the gazetteer section (Chapters 10-14) are reproduced to a consistent scale in order to aid comparison between buildings. Except for some details and cross sections (where larger scales have been necessary in order to maintain clarity) a common scale has likewise been used for the architectural reconstruction drawings reproduced in the overviews given in Chapters 3, 4, 6 and 7 of this study. The drawings in these chapters are deliberately small scale in order to allow a relatively large sample of buildings to be reproduced in a single illustration. The scales used are identical to those adopted within the companion studies into the towns of Battle and Hastings.

ACKNOWLEDGEMENTS

It goes without saying that a project of the scope of this present synthesis, in which the background research has been carried out over a period in excess of 30 years, has involved commitment by many more people than the two principal authors listed. We turn first to our debts built up during the data-collection phase involving on-site research. Many of the early surveys were carried out with the help of Alan Dickinson and his late wife, Jean, and, although not personally involved in subsequent surveys, Alan has continued to give valuable advice throughout. Introductions to the owners of houses within the town were on most occasions arranged by local residents and, in this respect, we would in particular like to extend our warmest thanks to Kenneth and Margaret Bird, Terry Burke, Jo Kirkham and Vera Proctor for individually shouldering the lion's share of this essential activity — we, after all, are strangers to the town. Our most sincere thanks must, of course, go to the residents of Rye for so warmly welcoming us into their homes and business premises. Our apologies to those whose buildings we saw back in the 1970s and 1980s for having to wait so long to see the results of our work in published form.

And so to the synthesis stage of the project. Our wholehearted thanks go to Rye's historians, Gillian Draper, Stephen Hipkin and Graham Mayhew: their published works underpin so much of what we have done (for which *see* 'Bibliography'). All have readily discussed issues with us as and when they have arisen and have made available unpublished data used by them during their researches. In addition, as the list of authors on the cover of this volume acknowledges, Gillian Draper has contributed directly to the present publication.

The second listed contributor, Jane Clubb, is currently a trainee building recorder and analyst with whom we have had the privilege of working as part of an English Heritage training scheme. Although the main thrust of her work has lain elsewhere, her involvement in the synthesis stage of the Rye project has been substantial. Not only has she actively engaged in lively discussions regarding interpretation, and drafted substantive sections of the text, she also single-handedly took on the re-drafting of the entire second part of the study, following comments by Sarah Pearson on the format of our initial draft.

This brings us neatly to the enormous debt we owe to those who have given their time to discuss, advise, comment upon and — above all else — criticize early drafts of the text. As those who have undertaken similar exercises will know only too well, such a job is always a thankless task. What is required at that stage in the production of any work of this type is constructive criticism, with no holds barred. It must be admitted that, at the time, such criticism is not always welcomed by the authors, but is necessary if the end product is to be improved. In the words of Stephen Hipkin, as spoken during the presentation of a recent paper given at Bodiam Castle, 'this is a subject over which, believe me, I have agonized long and hard'. For us, how true that has been in the case of Rye! The infliction of that 'necessary pain' has in this instance been shared around and (in alphabetical order) we most sincerely thank Terry Burke, Gillian Draper, Casper Johnson, Jo Kirkham, Adam Longcroft, Sarah Pearson, Alan Tyler and Christopher Whittick for carrying out what must, for each of them, have been a difficult task. It is our hope that we have in some way recompensed them by giving a more worthwhile end product than would otherwise have been the case. All errors and shortcomings which remain are entirely our responsibility.

On a more general note, our thanks are extended to the successive curators at Rye Museum and to the staff of the East Sussex Record Office for making available maps and documents relating to the town, Frank Palmer and Pauline Kingswood for bringing to our attention early photographs and manuscript documents, Hugh Moseley for assistance relating to the church, and, above all, the volunteers of the Romney Marsh Research Trust for their assistance throughout. As always, Christopher Whittick — the third member of the old RoHAS team — has acted as 'trouble shooter' throughout, including double-checking the wording of problematic documents and catalogue entries, as well as correcting the worst of our poor grammar! Caroline Barron has given invaluable assistance on specific issues relating to ward structure, as has Gerald Moody in respect of the Austin Friary.

Finally, this publication would not have been possible without the support and funding of the Romney Marsh Research Trust, in particular the individual members of the project's Steering Group. We thank them most sincerely for their confidence in our endeavours. It has been the Romney Marsh Research Trust's hard work in raising funds and setting deadlines which has allowed the labours of our earlier work to be brought through to publication. Their own acknowledgements to outside funding bodies are given in the foreword to this volume.

Most of the illustrations contained within this publication have been generated by the authors, or are old photographs and prints in the public domain. Every effort has been made to seek permission to reproduce those images whose copyright does not reside with the authors, and we are grateful to the individuals and institutions who have assisted in this task. Any omissions are entirely unintentional.

David and Barbara Martin
May 2009

1 INTRODUCTION

Rye, located near the eastern end of Sussex on the south coast of England, is a compact town, the historic part of which occupies a small, low hillock with the parish church at its highest point. The island-like site, today somewhat colourfully known by the local residents as 'The Citadel', stands adjacent to the south-eastern extremity of one of the heavily wooded Wealden ridges, to which in historical times it was linked by a vulnerable, low land link.

In most towns the surrounding geographical features can be regarded as fixed points of reference, but the shoreline in the vicinity of Rye has undergone such radical changes that the coast of today provides no guidance to its various forms and alignments during the medieval period (*see* below): only the contours of the upland should be regarded as relatively unchanging (Figure 1.1). The marshes to east, south and west were once tidal estuary — simply referred to in documents of the 17th century and before as 'the sea' — whilst St. Mary's Marsh (the band of low land which separates the town from the hill to the north) has until relatively recent times been liable to periodic flooding by salt water. It is now mostly built over.

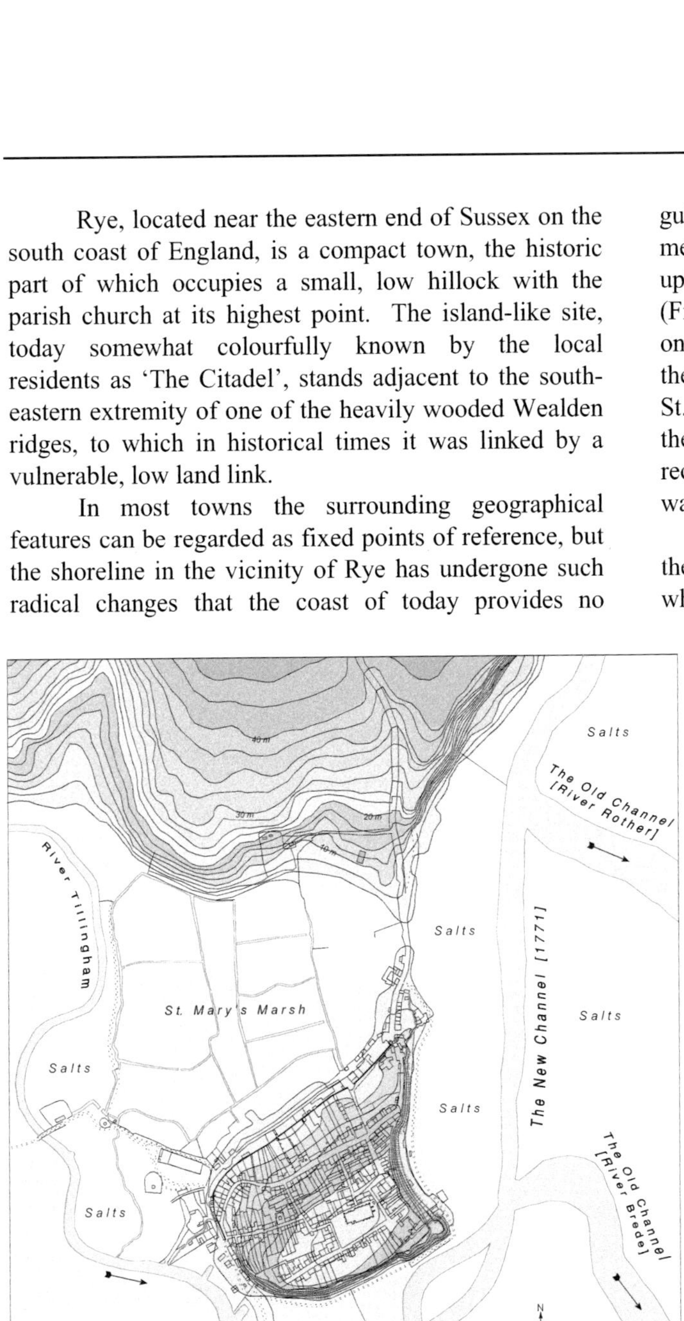

Today the diminutive River Tillingham skirts to the west of the town, meeting the slightly larger Brede which passes close under the low, *c*.15-metre (*c*.45-feet) southern cliffs before converging with the largest of the trio — the Rother — making its way through Walland Marsh to the east of the town, flowing down from the heartland of the Weald. The great expanse of Romney Marsh lies beyond, to the east. It was the lesser of the three rivers — the Tillingham — which provided the town its late medieval and Tudor quayside strand, though additionally there were minor quays to the east, served by the Rother, and in the 13th and early 14th centuries these may have been of greater significance.

Fig. 1.1
Contours superimposed upon a base map of the town and its immediate environs as in 1771
[Outline map based upon town plan of 1771]

The Brede river's broad, flat-bottomed valley, delineated on its southern side at this point by nothing more than grass-covered shingle ridges, stretches away towards Rye's sister town of Winchelsea only two miles (3km.) to the southwest. Between the two is Camber Castle which originally occupied the head of a shingle spit jutting out into the estuary mouth (*see* Figure 1.2). Initially built in the late 1480s as an isolated tower defending the two port towns, this squat structure was transformed into a substantial coastal fort under Henry VIII.[1]

The sister town of Winchelsea has not always occupied its present site: it was moved to its current location late in the 13th century after its original site — here called (Old) Winchelsea — was in imminent threat of being overwhelmed

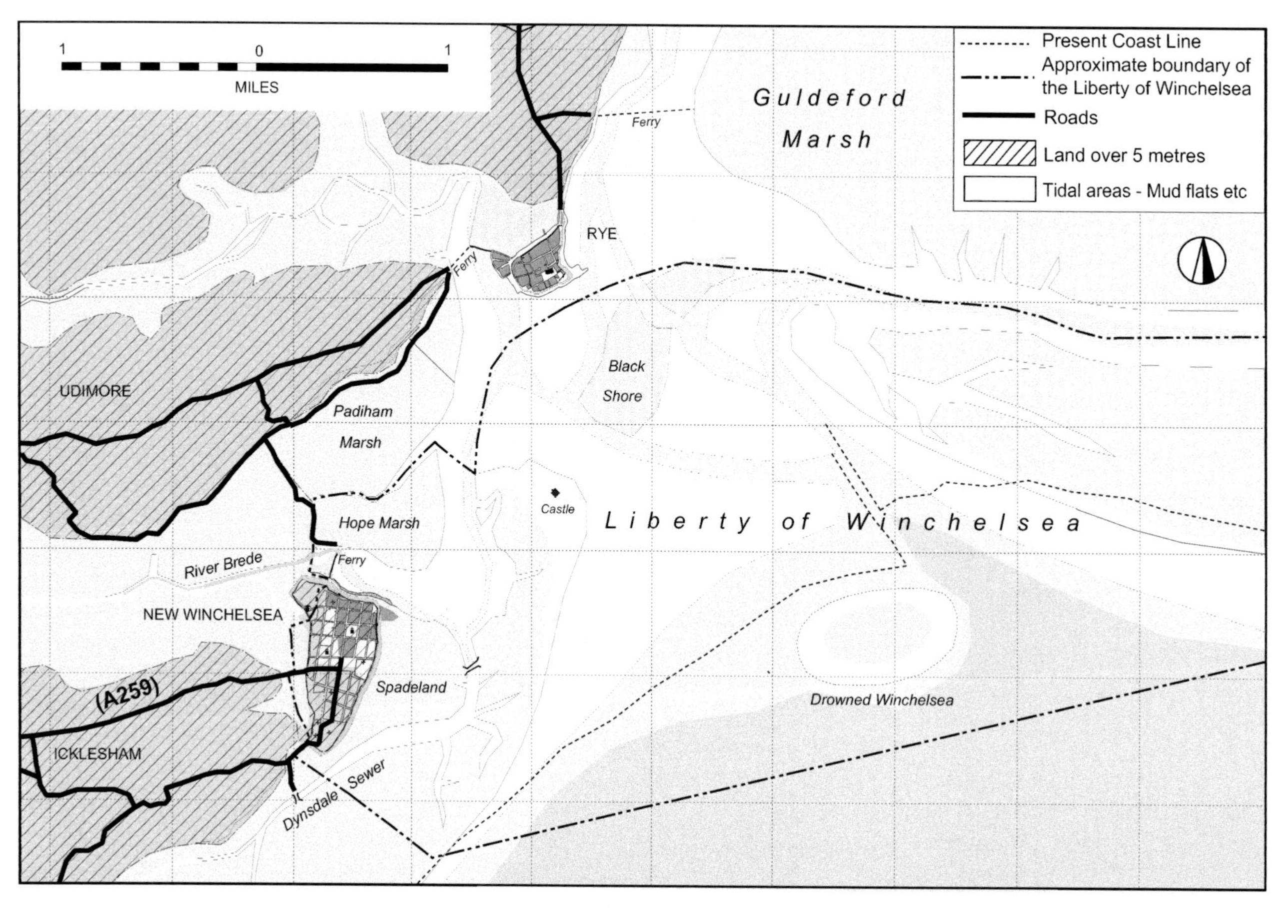

Fig. 1.2
The immediate environs of the town in the mid 16th century showing access roads, ferry etc.

by the sea. That initial site was about 2½ miles (4km.) distant from Rye, a little to the east of south in what is now Rye Bay (Figures 1.2 and 1.3). Winchelsea's present location occupies a comparable though much larger and more prominent site to that of Rye, on a peninsula at the extremity of another Wealden ridge.[2] A third ridge, originally accessible from Rye only by boat, stretches away to the west towards Robertsbridge on the Rother and the ridge-top town of Battle eleven miles (nearly 18km.) distant, the latter overlooking the headwater streams of the Brede (Figure 1.4).

Now two miles (about 3km.) inland from the sea (Figure 1.3) throughout the medieval period the port town of Rye fulfilled a significant, but secondary role to that of its much larger sister town of Winchelsea, which enjoyed very considerable prosperity as a seaport in the 13th and early 14th centuries. Both towns owed their importance to their shared, protected natural harbour and to their strategic position near the shortest crossing of the English Channel to Normandy.

More than any other feature, it was the ever changing character of the river estuary which most affected the prosperity of the two towns, both of which were forced to make considerable adaptations during periods of rapid change. Three of these periods were

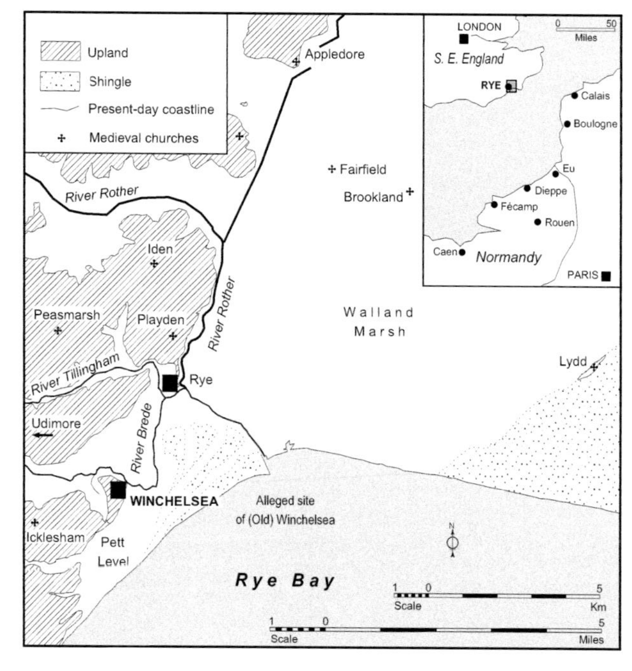

Fig. 1.3
The location of Rye and its present surroundings, including modern-day coastline. The inset map shows the relationship of the town to the coast of France.

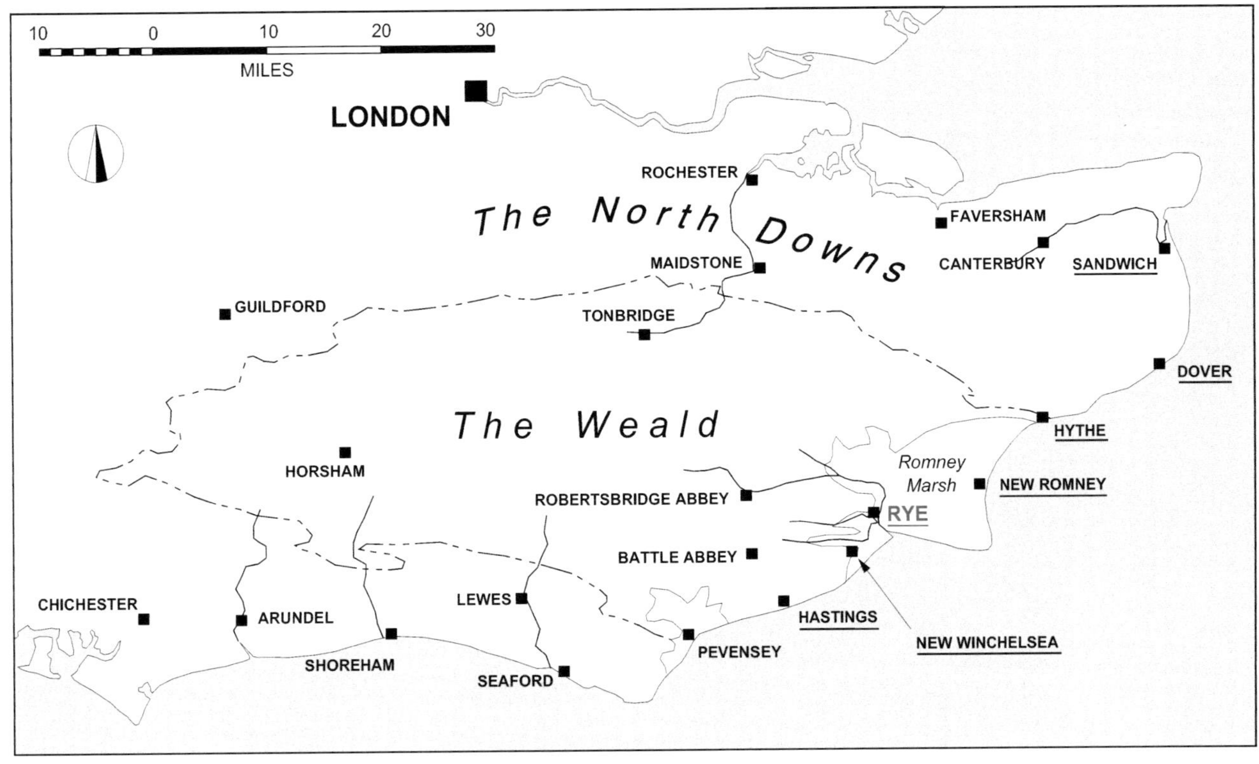

Fig. 1.4
The south-east of England showing the medieval coastal ports and selected other towns. The Cinque Ports and the 'Two Ancient Towns' are shown underlined.

pivotal. The first occurred in the second half of the 13th century and resulted in Winchelsea's forced move to its present site. The second was in the early years of the 16th century when continued silting in Brede channel finally prevented all but the smallest of ships reaching Winchelsea, allowing Rye to usurp that town's seaborne trade. As a result, Winchelsea collapsed and became near deserted, whilst Rye experienced meteoric growth both in terms of population and prosperity. But Rye's period of greatness was very short, for within less than a hundred years the problems which befell Winchelsea were visited upon it too, causing the third of the three great changes. During the final decade of the 16th century and throughout the following century Rye was forced to accept the role of a local market town, much reduced in both size and wealth.

MEDIEVAL RYE - A SECONDARY ROLE

From the 11th century onwards shipping in the English Channel increased and a number of small ports grew up, based on fishing and a developing cross-Channel trade. The sister towns of Rye and (Old) Winchelsea were most probably two of these ports, although nothing specific is known of their origins. Even at this early stage the two towns appear to have shared a common harbour, though whereas (Old) Winchelsea occupied an exposed coastal location, Rye's site appears at this time to have been more protected, perhaps occupying the landward side of the combined Tillingham and Brede river estuary, partly protected from the sea by a shingle barrier. Both towns were located within the bounds of the sprawling Saxon manor of Rameslie which King Canute had already granted to the Norman Abbey of Fécamp by *c*.1017. Rameslie covered a large, though probably scattered area at the eastern end of Sussex. Based in the Hundred of Guestling, it stretched eastwards from Hastings and amounted to 20 hides, re-assessed 17½ hides following the Conquest. In addition to 99 villeins and five churches, Domesday Book (1086) recorded that it included a *Novus Burgus* containing 64 burgesses valued collectively at £7 18s 0d. The debate as to the identity of this new town is inconclusive: the favoured candidate is Rye. Even if Rye is not the new borough, it probably already existed as a non-incorporated settlement by 1086, served by one of the five churches mentioned. Evidently the manor also included extensive salt marshes, for the Domesday entry mentions 100 salt pans; an exceptionally high, if nominal, number.[3]

Both Rye and (Old) Winchelsea were already ports of some significance by the middle years of the 12th century: they are mentioned in the Pipe Rolls for 1131 and 1164-5. The earliest surviving charter to the two towns dates from 1191, but confirms liberties which had been granted to them earlier, in the reign of Henry II (1154-89). By 1190 they had joined the association of the Cinque Ports as limbs of Hastings, each contributing two ships towards Hastings' quota. At that stage their shipping was still inferior to that of their head port.[4] The two towns seem to have risen to prosperity in the late 12th century and thereafter rapidly outstripped Hastings, though they were not formally elevated to the level of the other ports within the confederation until the 14th century, from which time onwards they were given the title 'the Two Ancient Towns'.[5]

Already by the end of the 12th century Rye seems to have been lagging considerably behind (Old) Winchelsea. The Pipe Roll of 1204 includes a financial document which, although incomplete, records a taxation of one fifteenth on merchants at seaports. Whereas the merchants of (Old) Winchelsea paid £62.2s.4d. in tax, placing that port at the head of the second rank of ports (behind only London and Southampton in the southeast) the merchants of Rye contributed only £10.13s.5d., suggesting only moderate participation in overseas trade at this period.[6] Later documents portray a similar imbalance between the two towns (*see* below) and this continued to be the case throughout the medieval era, long after Winchelsea had moved to its present site.

In 1247 Henry III claimed back from Fécamp the two port towns in exchange for manors in Gloucestershire and Lincolnshire: the King no doubt felt it undesirable to allow the French to retain command of two front-line English ports. Despite the exchange, the abbey was allowed to keep the residue of its old Saxon manor of Rameslie, by then transformed into the manor of Brede. Furthermore, with regards to Rye the boundary of the lands exchanged was drawn tight around the town, allowing the abbey to retain most of its rural property within the parish — the northern rural part of the parish is still known as 'Rye Foreign'.[7]

The mid 13th century not only heralded a period of change for the two towns with regards to ownership. As already noted, the natural surroundings within which they were located were in the process of being transformed. Whereas the climate up to the early 13th century seems to have been relatively tranquil, 1236 heralded a period of exceptional storms which continued for at least the next half century, breaking down sea defences, converting hard-won productive marshlands back into tidal salt flats, and threatening the futures of both towns. Already by 1261 the estuary of the Rother had widened sufficiently, at the expense of the flanking marshlands, for it to be described as an 'arm of the sea'. Furthermore, the boundary clause given in the 1247 Royal exchange suggests that this was already the case by that date.[8]

(Old) Winchelsea, built adjacent to a breach in the shingle barrier which stretched from Fairlight in the southwest to Lydd and beyond, was especially vulnerable to the changes which were occurring. Under threat from 1244 onwards, by 1280 it had become clear that the town could not be saved. As a result its Royal owner, Edward I, took steps to acquire a replacement site. Evidently the relocation was achieved in the nick of time, for in 1287-88 three great storms occurred within the space of 14 months. The final destruction of the old town was swift and total: the only known reference to it after 1292 is a quitclaim of 1294/5 relating to properties 'within the new and old towns of Winchelsea'. It would seem that the storms swept away a considerable length of the shingle barrier in the area where Winchelsea had stood, giving the Brede, Tillingham and Rother a remodelled combined outlet to the sea, exposing Rye to the tides in a way it had not previously experienced.[9]

Being located upon a hill, Rye itself seems to have escaped debilitating damage from the storms, but over the next century serious losses were experienced along its eastern fringe. Low-lying properties in the area were lost through inundation during the first half of the 14th century. Evidence of erosion at Rye is suggested by a petition to the Crown which preceded a murage grant in 1348, and in the wording of a grant to the Austin friars in 1363 of two acres of low-lying land upon which had stood five messuages, destroyed by the sea.[10] Reference at this time to the sea as a primary destructive force may have been exaggerated for effect, for a return of decayed rents dated 1351 gives only 18 houses as 'drowned by the sea', the vast majority of the decay being attributed to burning by the French, probably during the known French raid of 1339. However, the inundation of these low lands allowed the sea to wash against the foot of the cliff on this eastern side of the town. In this respect it cannot be coincidence that in the early 15th century an elevated populated area of the town known as 'The Ness' (implying a peninsula) ceases to be mentioned in the town records.[11] Erosion along this side of the hill continued through to the end of the 16th century, and perhaps a little beyond.

More destructive for the town than the sea were the maraudings of the French. The attack in 1339 destroyed at least 52 houses and a mill (this was the total not rebuilt and thus recorded as decayed rents twelve years after the raid) and another successful attack was made in 1377. An alleged burning in 1448-9 is unsupported by evidence.[12]

Medieval Economy [13]

Few urban communities in medieval England were as thoroughly orientated to the sea as the three East

Sussex Cinque Port towns of Rye, Winchelsea and Hastings. Their common geography dictated broadly similar economic interests bound by access to the English Channel. Their Wealden hinterland functioned as something of a barrier to inland transportation, though movement was possible via the ridge-top highways and — in the case of Rye and Winchelsea — by barge along the rivers Rother and Brede. This limited access into the relatively under-populated and agriculturally poor hinterland forced the residents of all three towns to concentrate on the sea. As Sylvester and others have pointed out, this maritime orientation was the defining characteristic of these urban coastal towns: their townsfolk were almost totally reliant upon the sea and were thus exceptionally vulnerable to changed circumstances. Their principal activities were trading, fishing, and shipping, both commercial and naval. In 1440 it was said that the people of all three towns 'care nothing for agriculture but employ themselves solely in fishing and sea works'.

Together with the other towns of the Cinque Ports Confederation, Rye was a collection centre for regional commodities shipped to London and for the distribution of goods transferred into the Weald from the capital and elsewhere. Representatives of the ports regularly attended London's markets and participated in a well-established coastwise trade, exporting the Weald's staple resource — bulky, low-value wood for fuel and timber for construction. Meat products and by-products from the region's woodland pastures were also of importance, as initially was salt produced from the marshlands around the town. In exchange, cereals and general goods were imported.

Perhaps even more than trade, the sea's natural resource — fish — was the town's staple. The first mention of the fishery is in a 12th-century agreement with the Abbey of Fécamp which required each Rye vessel engaged in fishing to render a 'share' (percentage) of its catch to the Abbot, based upon the size of the vessel.

There can be no doubt that Rye's medieval fishing industry was smaller than that of Winchelsea: in 1267, for instance, fish shares collected at Rye were approximately a sixth of those collected at its sister town. Even so, the extent to which the town relied upon the industry is indicated by a petition dated 1305 in which the Rye barons requested that the date of their fair be changed from the Nativity of the Blessed Virgin Mary to that of the Assumption because at the former date 'all the people of the country are at sea engaged in fishing'. As with the other Cinque Ports, the most important fishery for the town was the herring catch in the North Sea, based at Great Yarmouth in East Anglia each autumn. Here the confederation held special privileges, including the right to occupy the shore, dry their nets, and sell their catch without charge. In the late 13th century Rye ships attending the fair numbered half the average of 15 vessels sent by Winchelsea. However, in considering these figures it should be borne in mind that Rye was small in comparison to Winchelsea, emphasizing just how important this fishery was to the town. In addition to supplying the town's own needs, fish from Rye were sold to residents of the hinterland, a particularly valuable customer being the Benedictine abbey at Battle.

By no means all the fish landed at Rye were destined for local consumption: from the 13th century, and perhaps before, Rye supplied fish to the royal household, and this trade continued through to Tudor times. Moreover, despite the distance from London, a healthy over-land trade in fresh fish developed with the capital, supplied by rippiers equipped with pack horses. Despite the industry's importance to the town, there is no trace of a fishing guild within the port during the medieval period, though a practice of collective bargaining was in force.

Beyond their own needs and those of the ordinary local rural population, the three East Sussex port towns of Rye, Winchelsea and Hastings serviced the households of the local gentry (of whom very few were of more than local significance) and acted as important markets for the great Benedictine monastery at Battle and the much smaller Cistercian house at Robertsbridge. Unlike Dover, Sandwich and Faversham (all of which served as outports for Canterbury) the catchment area of neither Rye, Winchelsea nor Hastings contained inland urban centres of any size — the small town of Battle was by far the largest. Thus, the hinterlands of all three towns were of only limited importance: of far greater significance was the role of the towns' ships as carriers of goods for others.

Occasionally foreign trade extended as far as Spain. For instance, in 1364 Rye vintners were 'licensed to go to Spain to buy wine, provided a certain amount of it was bought in exchange for cloth'. Rye was involved in the importation of wine on other occasions too, as indicated by the losses suffered by wine-merchants of Rochelle during the capture and re-taking of Rye in 1216, or the 42 casks of wine taken by the French when they sacked the town in 1377. Not all wine carried by Rye ships was destined for the port — in 1212 Ypres and Ghent merchants brought 120 tuns of wine into neighbouring Winchelsea aboard the ship of Geoffrey, son of Michael de Rye.

Despite these references and the existence within the town of vaulted cellars (*see* Chapter 6) in comparison to that of Winchelsea, Rye's involvement in the wine trade was minor. In all probabilities the majority of wine brought into the town was intended for domestic consumption.

Most of Rye's economic connections to the continent were to Flanders and eastern Normandy, as evident in the medieval documentary record. Like Winchelsea, the port was used extensively by travellers (including pilgrims) passing between England and the north coast of the continent. This cross-channel activity — both cargo and passenger — should not be allowed to overshadow the importance of coastal trade with other English ports: in this respect it is worth bearing in mind that such trade constituted 80 per cent of all traffic coming into late 14th-century Hythe. Furthermore, as Sylvester points out, coastal trade was less subject to disruptions caused by international disputes, less risky than long-distance cross-channel voyages, and provided a more accessible investment option to a wider group of port town residents.

As with the other Cinque Ports, Rye's involvement in the carrying trades and fishing provided ships and experienced mariners of considerable use to the crown. In exchange for their extensive privileges the Cinque Ports were required to contribute a substantial number of ships and mariners to the royal fleets. As established in 1229, Rye was required to provide a quota of 5 ships — Dover was called to send 21, Winchelsea 10, Hastings 6, and (like Rye) Sandwich, Romney, and Hythe 5 each, though contributions above the quota were commonly made for payment.

Throughout the late 13th century and first half of the following century Winchelsea consistently provided well above its allotted quota, as indicated by an analysis of national ship surveys and summonses spread over the period between 1300 and 1347. The analysis, which includes over 1700 vessels from 180 different port towns, shows Winchelsea to have been a first-rate provider, second only to Great Yarmouth. Its total contribution was just higher than that for Dartmouth and substantially greater than the contributions from Fowey, Southampton and Plymouth. In comparison, Rye's involvement was more modest. During seven campaigns between 1282 and 1347 Rye contributed a total of 31 ships, ranking it fourth within the Cinque Ports confederation, behind Winchelsea (102), Sandwich (58), and Dover (43), but ahead of Hastings (26), Hythe (21), and Romney (20).[14]

Rye's contribution should not be belittled — in 1336 it was home to the largest ships in the Cinque Port squadron, supplying the 240-ton *la Michel* and the 170-ton *la Edmund*. Although all of Winchelsea's vessels were in excess of 100 tons, the largest was only 160-tons. An assessment of English and Welsh ships participating in the larger naval expeditions during three important stages of the Hundred Years' War indicates that Winchelsea, Rye and Sandwich together provided 6.6 per cent of all shipping in 1336-1346, 4.5 per cent in 1377-1395 and 9.4 per cent in 1439-1450. But by the late 15th century the importance of the Cinque Ports quota was well past its prime and dwindled still further subsequently. The Cinque Ports provided only six ships to the English fleet that confronted the Armada.

Regardless of the form it took, seafaring provided employment for substantial numbers of Rye sailors and a whole range of allied service occupations such as shipbuilders, sail-makers, corders and the like, not to mention victuallers.

Apart from the production of salt, manufacturing industries played little part in the life of medieval Rye. One important exception was that of ship-building. In the 13th and 14th centuries galleys were frequently built and repaired there. Indeed, in the early 13th century Winchelsea and Rye were specifically mentioned as home ports for the king's galleys and sites of royal dockyards and storehouses. The only known industry of note not allied to the sea was an important, though localized pottery manufactory at Rye Hill to the north of the town — it was operational from the 13th century to the middle of the 14th century.[15]

Signs of change - the late 14th and 15th centuries [16]

Declaration of war with France in the 1330s resulted in trade embargoes and prolonged periods of ship service. Seaborne trade was further weakened by rampant privateering in the Channel and by coastal raiding at the hands of the French. The raid on the town in 1337 was particularly savage, causing extensive destruction, leaving 52 houses destroyed and still un-tenanted more than a decade after the event. Other properties were no doubt damaged in the raid, but were repaired or rebuilt with little delay. The Black Death of 1348 followed, reducing population and trade opportunities generally. Coupled with this, the 14th century saw a general westward shift in commercial shipping to ports better positioned to exploit changing trade patterns, marginalizing the south-eastern ports. The mid century also witnessed a serious decline of the Great Yarmouth herring fishery in favour of other locations where the Cinque Ports Confederation did not hold special privileges. The combined effect of all these factors seriously weakened the south-eastern ports. It was during this period, following devastating raids in 1360 and 1380, that Winchelsea faded from national to regional importance.

Despite a second serious attack in 1377, Rye seems to have fared somewhat better than Winchelsea and, as a result, the inequality in respect of size and economic wealth which had existed between the two sister towns lessened. Even so, Rye still remained the smaller, less important of the two towns throughout the 15th century and in 1449 was sufficiently impoverished to require the incorporation of Tenterden as a limb of the

Cinque Ports in order to assist it in meeting its quota for ship service.

Expressed in general terms, for Rye as for many other south-coast port towns, the late 14th and 15th centuries should be seen as a period of contraction, both with regards to population and economy. Yet it would be very wrong to give a blanket impression of poverty. Yes, in 1449 Rye needed the help of Tenterden to meet its obligation to the Cinque Ports Confederation — though political manoeuvring within the confederation needs to be taken into account before the formal wording of Tenterden's incorporation is taken at face value. Although it must certainly have been true that for many Rye residents life was hard, their lot was perhaps not so very different from earlier times when the town's population was higher. Despite Rye's alleged depressed state in 1449, there are limited indications of gradual economic improvement as the century progressed. A number of substantial repairs were carried out within the church, money was found to undertake work on the defences (albeit in response to French invasion threats) and, to judge from surviving domestic buildings, the number of good-quality houses under construction — or perhaps reconstruction — was increasing, albeit slowly. Furthermore, the borough accounts show a modest increase in corporate revenue from £34 in 1450 to £55 in 1480.[17]

A sesse (local tax) raised in 1491/2 makes clear that there was a wealthy resident urban elite. The 13 or 14 men (seven per cent of taxpayers) who headed the town's hierarchy contributed almost two-thirds the total assessment. These men were exceptional, though it is worth stressing that no fewer than 36 taxpayers were valued at £30 and over. It is surely safe to assume that these men lived comfortably. Financially, a number of others were not far behind, but, as was normally the case, the bulk of the population survived on very meagre resources (*see* Chapter 2).

TUDOR BOOM, 1490s to 1570s [18]

Despite the hints of revival in the town's fortunes during the second half of the 15th century, in 1489-91 Rye's customs revenues amounted to only a fifth of those of Winchelsea. These statistics, however, are misleading in that they demonstrate the relative strength of Winchelsea rather than the weakness of Rye. In this respect it is surely relevant that the combined revenues of the two towns were more than double the combined revenues collected from the seven other south-coast ports between Chichester in the west and Folkestone in the east.[19] As during previous centuries, the combined estuary of the Rother, Brede and Tillingham continued to serve as the principal harbour along this stretch of the south coast.

The town would, no doubt, have remained in the shadow of its larger neighbour had Winchelsea's hill-top site been more favourably placed — a little closer to the sea with better tides to serve it. As it was, the sea, which had so nearly destroyed it two hundred years earlier when the site of (Old) Winchelsea was washed away, now deserted the replacement site. There was insufficient depth of water remaining in the Brede channel to maintain an adequate draught for shipping, even at high tides. The estuary had been becoming more shallow for years, but it now reached the point where only the smallest of vessels could easily reach the town. The end, when it came, was swift. Equally swift, it would seem, was the shift in maritime trade across the estuary to neighbouring Rye which, being located nearer to the sea, was at this time largely unaffected by the silting.

Already by 1513/14 the customs revenues collected from the two towns were equal, Rye's take-off date apparently having occurred during the mid 1490s.[20] By 1528-32 the position of 40 years earlier had been reversed with Rye's customs revenues sixfold those of Winchelsea. Furthermore, in monetary terms Rye's total was by this time three times that of Winchelsea forty years earlier, suggesting not just a transfer of trade from one port to the other, but real economic growth. A large part of this was apparently brought about primarily by servicing England's last continental outpost, Calais.[21]

Populations follow shifts in economic activity. Already by 1529 houses in the centre of Winchelsea were described as 'pulled down', 'fallen down', 'fell into decay' and 'standing void', indicating that by the late 1520s decay was affecting even the commercial core.[22] No such descriptions are to be found at this period in respect of Rye. On the contrary, from the end of the 15th century onwards vacant land was being granted out for development by the corporation, and private individuals were building houses — for sale and rent — on those parts of their properties which incorporated undeveloped frontages. The rate of development accelerated as the 16th century progressed, with an ever-increasing tendency for houses to be divided into tenements as the town struggled to keep pace with rising population (*see* Chapters 2, 5 and 7).

Resident foreigners within a coastal port town are always a good barometer of its vitality. The shift in economic activity from Winchelsea to Rye is well illustrated by the number of resident foreigners within each of the two towns in 1524/5. Only 18 aliens are recorded in Winchelsea, whereas Rye had 55, excluding a further eight who could not be found and three who had then recently died. Where nationality is given most were French, but Scots were also present, as was one Italian. By 1538 the number of resident aliens within the town had risen to over a hundred.[23]

It seems likely that Rye's initial population growth can be accounted for by a transfer of families from Winchelsea, but with an exceptionally high mortality rate within the town, Rye must increasingly have relied upon immigration both from its hinterland and further afield in order to maintain, let alone increase its population. Even so, as Brent, Mayhew and Hipkin have independently concluded, Rye's population did grow, and rapidly. Accurate estimates are difficult to establish, but a doubling, and perhaps a figure closer to a tripling, occurred in under a century.

It is not hard to see why the town was such a magnet. To quote Mayhew, during the middle years of the 16th century it 'was easily the largest and most prosperous town in Sussex and [in economic terms] can claim to rank amongst the foremost provincial towns [of the day] in England.[24] Hipkin suggests that by the 1560s it ranked equal in population to provincial centres such as Canterbury, whilst, as Mayhew points out, expressed in terms of the tonnage of its merchant vessels, Rye ranked eleventh in England in 1571-2, being on a par with Bristol and ahead of south-eastern ports such as Southampton and Sandwich.[25] Admittedly Sandwich was at this time facing depression, with, in 1565, a reduced population which — expressed in terms of households — amounted to just over three quarters that of Rye, this despite a major influx of Dutch families into Sandwich since 1560.[26]

That Rye was flourishing is beyond doubt. However, Mayhew's claim that in 1523-5 it ranked 'amongst the top 20 English towns after London' depends upon the validity of comparing potentially dissimilar sources of data — being a Cinque Port, there is no detailed 1524/5 lay subsidy return for the town, though Mayhew argues that a 1523 benevolence represents a reliable substitute.[27] Even if such a comparison proves invalid, other sources confirm the pre-eminence of the town within the counties of Kent and Sussex. In 1545, for instance, despite massive expenditure on its defences, Rye contributed almost two-thirds of the total tax payments made by the Sussex ports 'and more than any of the Sussex Rapes with the exception of Chichester Rape, which included the city.' '... in the 1540s, Rye would seem to have been taxed at approximately three times the rate of Chichester, including the Cathedral close ...'.[28]

Despite its new-found dominant role within the area, the town either felt it unnecessary or was unable to widen its economic base — as was the case at Winchelsea, it continued to rely to an unhealthy degree upon its port as the source of its wealth. Admittedly, given the weak economic base of its Wealden hinterland, this was probably inevitable. It is worth re-emphasizing just how reliant the town was upon its port, and, in this respect, to reiterate the similarity with Winchelsea at an earlier period. In 1565, about half a century after Winchelsea's spectacular collapse following desertion by the sea, that town had just 12 resident mariners/fishermen and but 12 boats, averaging amongst them 7 tons capacity. At this time only 109 inhabited houses remained in Winchelsea. Subsequently, in the 17th century, that total reduced still further to perhaps as few as 30 houses.[29]

Rye, in 1565, was already five times the size of Winchelsea with a reported 530 households and an [?adult] population of 2,468 excluding strangers (aliens). These totals did not peak for probably another decade. The town's exceptional reliance upon the sea is well

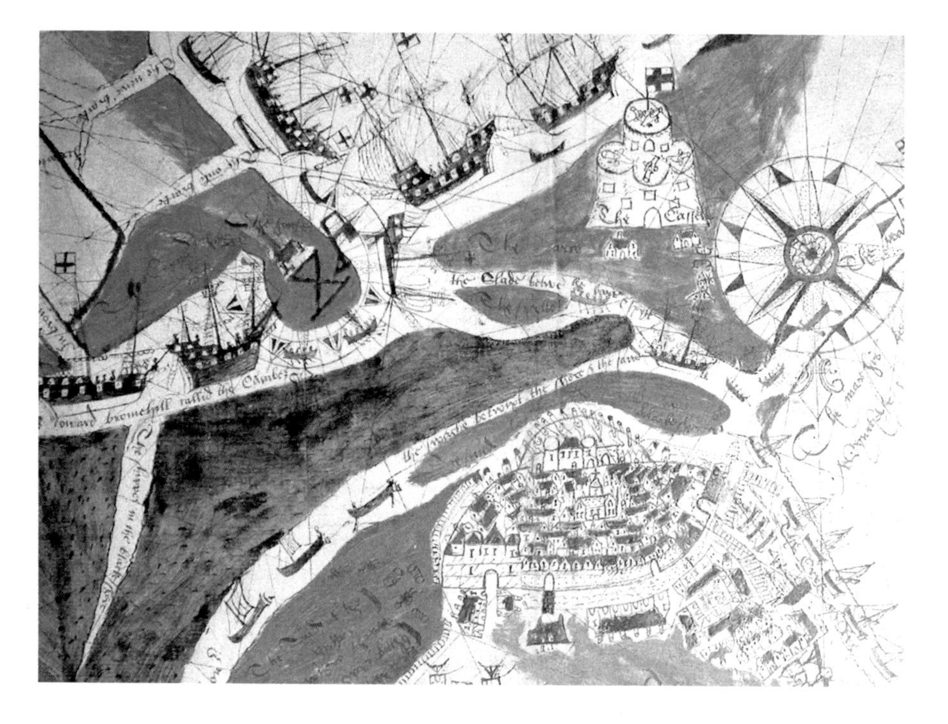

Fig. 1.5
Detail from map of Rye Harbour by John Prowze, 1572, showing the town of Rye with ships moored at the Strand (bottom right), Camber Castle (top right) with larger ships standing off in the bay (top) and moored in The Camber (centre left). Note the smaller vessels sailing The Rother to the right of the town and the barrels, boats etc lying on the mud between the river and the town gate. North is towards bottom left. [TNA MPF 1/212]

illustrated by the proportion of its population who in 1565 were employed as fishermen and mariners — over half (54 per cent) of households were headed by fishermen and mariners, whilst if 'servants of fishermen' and 'young men engaged with the sea' are included the average number involved in seafaring was a phenomenal 1.5 men per household. At Hastings the percentage of households headed by fishermen and mariners was not that dissimilar — 58 per cent — but it had considerably fewer young and servant seafarers, resulting in almost half the percentage seafarers at Rye, with 0.85 men per household. Furthermore, with only 280 households in total, Hastings was half the size of Rye. In comparison, the other ports in eastern Sussex hardly figure. At that date there were, apparently, no fishermen or mariners resident in Pevensey (64 households), only 0.2 men per household were so employed at Seaford (38 houses), 0.1 per household at Winchelsea (109 houses), and 0.08 per household at Eastbourne (141 houses).[30] Other data for Rye suggests that by the 1570s the number of households headed by seafarers may have dropped to just over 40 per cent. The residue of the population were primarily engaged in servicing the town and its (relatively) sparsely populated rural hinterland, providing food and drink, clothing, building trades and distribution services.[31]

The loss of Calais by the English to the French in 1558 dealt a major blow to the port — three-quarters of Rye's export trade had been Calais based — though in the short term the opening up of alternative maritime opportunities served as a welcome cushion (*see* below).[32] In fact, both Mayhew and Hipkin agree that not only the 1550s, but also the 1560s saw Rye at its economic peak, with little change detectable during the opening years of the 1570s. Even so, whereas the corporation had been able to invest in infrastructure at a level on a par with the western port city of Exeter during the 1540s, by the 1550s investment by Exeter's Corporation was rising faster, this despite increased expenditure at Rye. By the 1570s Rye's corporate expenditure had stagnated at £356 per annum, compared to £536 per annum for Exeter.[33] The closing years of the 1570s saw Rye's fortunes begin to decline, a decline which thereafter accelerated through time. In contrast, Exeter's economy, like those of most other western ports, continued to expand. As Mayhew has remarked, the two towns are a clear example of the differing fortunes of the east-coast and west-coast ports during the late 16th century. For Rye in particular, other factors worsened the situation still further (*see* below).

The fact that Rye's population continued to rise during the late 1560s and 1570s, despite challenging economic circumstances, probably had more to do with the town's religious allegiances than economic success. In common with most successful port towns, it had always had resident populations of alien merchants and traders, but immigration by foreigners now took a new form — French protestants fleeing religious persecution. What more obvious place to seek sanctuary than within a staunchly protestant port such as Rye, just across the channel? Over 500 such refugees fled to the town during the initial troubles in 1562. Many — probably most — returned home with little delay, but renewed violence in July 1568 resulted in a second wave. In March the following year there were still 83 refugee households resident within the town.[34]

Not surprisingly, the largest influx of refugees followed the St. Bartholomew's Day massacre on 24th August 1572 and, unlike in earlier years when the refugees fleeing to the town tended to be wealthy, these included many poor and destitute families. A high proportion stayed until the end of the troubles in the early 1590s, with a reported 1,534 French refugees resident within the town in 1582. Most seem to have quickly integrated into everyday Rye life, pursuing their crafts and trades, and some rose to hold positions of authority within the town. However, one aspect of their life remained separate — they were served by their own religious leaders who were allowed the use of the parish church at specified times for this purpose.[35]

Undoubtedly, during the 1570s and 1580s a high proportion of Rye's population comprised French immigrants. In this respect the town must have mirrored some English towns and cities during the present century. No doubt the debates of the day as to whether such a high percentage of immigrants within the population served to enhance or hold back the town's economic and social development were similar to those of today. Historians have yet to address the effect the religious refugees had on the next phase in Rye's development and to assess how things may have been different had they not settled within the town.

LATE 16TH AND 17TH CENTURY DECLINE AND BEYOND [36]

When in the closing decades of the 16th century Rye's economy stalled and its population began to drift away, the residents and corporation alike had no doubts as to the cause — as at Winchelsea less than a century earlier the approaches to Rye's quayside were becoming choked with silt. In local dialect, the harbour was becoming '*all slubbed up*'. The catalyst in the minds of Rye residents was beyond dispute: large-scale inning of the extensive salt marshes which fringed the river estuary was preventing the tides from scouring the channel. So convinced were the corporation of this that they embarked upon a cripplingly expensive and — as it turned out — futile engineering project aimed at diverting the course of the Rother past The Strand so as to add its flow to that of the Tillingham.

Harbour silting was undoubtedly a major — probably *the* major — factor behind the town's growing problems, but as Hipkin has pointed out, to lay all the blame at that particular door is to accept an over-simplistic explanation. If the sole cause of the town's difficulties had been the choking of its harbour, how is it that it experienced a decade of economic revival based upon maritime trade during the 1630s? Furthermore, how could a commission held in 1652 report (apparently without challenge) that 'there may lie afloat at low water 15 or 20 sail of ship . . . . and at the same time, further up in the channel may ride afloat at low water 50 or 60 sail'. It seems more likely that the real cause of Rye's problems was a cocktail of factors, of varying severity, which triggered a sequence of events from which the town's port was unable to recover. These contributory factors are fully examined by Hipkin in his paper 'The Maritime Economy of Rye, 1560-1640'. Only the briefest of summaries need be given here.

Rye had grown not only as a result of the collapse of Winchelsea, but also due to other factors. One of these was the strength of its revitalized fishing fleet, which in addition to meeting local needs succeeded during the early Tudor period in developing its existing role as a supplier to the ever-expanding Royal Court and London markets, becoming a lead player. The trade was served by rippiers who transported the fish overland by pack horses. A second factor was growing trade with the Netherlands and France, notably Dieppe and, above all, the English outpost of Calais. The town's fleet had the advantage over those of some other ports in being exceedingly versatile — as demand dictated its vessels and their crews commonly switched between fishing and carrying activities, both coastal and overseas. The loss of Calais by the English in 1558 dealt the town a severe blow, but one from which, in the short term, it was able to recover by exploiting new markets, most notably by serving as an outport to London in the capital's two-way trade with Rouen and northern France. In this it was able to take advantage of the new trade routes which were developing to replace older routes blocked by continental warfare. Unfortunately, for a number of reasons this source of trade was not sustained and effectively collapsed during the 1590s and 1600s as the Port of London increasingly dealt direct with its trading partners. A separate factor was the virtual loss at the close of the 16th century of the town's wood-fuel export trade to the Netherlands, partly as a result of government restrictions on export at times when domestic supply was low. This resulted in a serious loss of work for local labour handling the cargo, though most of the cargo itself was carried in Netherlandish vessels. Far more serious for Rye's fleet was (as mentioned above) weakening trade with the Norman ports. Unlike the wood-fuel trade, this had largely relied upon Rye vessels for transshipment.

The combined effect of these disruptions was a reduction in the profitability of the Rye fleet. Simultaneously, the fleet was experiencing competition in its traditional fishing grounds, not just from foreign vessels, but from the Essex and North Kent ports and expanding beach-based fleets at Hastings and Brighton. These aggressive fleets not only had lower harbour-based costs — the costs at Rye were rising steeply as the corporation attempted to keep its harbour free of silt — but adopted more efficient, though controversial methods of fishing. The Rye fleet was either unwilling to adopt these new methods, or was unable to invest in the equipment necessary to do so. As a result, at the close of Elizabeth's reign these other fleets, particularly those from Essex and the north Kent coast, rapidly usurped Rye's coveted hold on the London market. They were also able to transport their catch to the capital quicker than Rye's rippiers, who were, in any case, increasingly disadvantaged by deteriorating road conditions. Rye's fish were no longer regarded in high esteem, the joke in government circles being that stale news was like Rye's fish — unfit for consumption.

With the dual disadvantages of rising maintenance and operating costs Rye's fleet became increasingly uncompetitive in its fishing activities and unprofitable as a carrier of cargoes. As Rye's economic tide ebbed, the fleet no longer attracted the new, young blood it so desperately needed in order to compete. Good sailors looked elsewhere for more profitable employment. Inevitably, as opportunities evaporated the Rye-based fleet shrunk in size, from 66 vessels in 1565, to 51 in 1580, 45 in 1587, 35 in 1596 and just 16 by the mid 1620s, at which reduced level it stabilized. Whereas during the early Elizabethan period the strength of Rye's fleet had guaranteed it a solid level of external investment, underpinned by a reasonable assurance of profits, by the mid 1620s outside investors had forsaken the town through lack of confidence. Even native investors spread their risk more widely than previously, taking increasingly small shares in individual vessels.

As Elizabeth's reign ended and the Stuart era opened, Rye was experiencing spiralling economic decline as circumstances conspired to drag the town under. By this time the corporation was near to bankruptcy, crippled by its well intentioned, but unwise attempt to 'save' its harbour. In order to remain solvent the ruling elite took the inept short-term decision to sell most of the corporation's capital assets, seriously undermining any hopes of a secure income in the future.

Probably more than any other factor, the crippling cost of the abortive 'harbour improvements' had seriously disadvantaged the economic viability of both the fleet and the general population. Lack of profitability within the seafaring sector — by far the most important element of Rye's economy — inevitably had an adverse effect upon all sectors of the town's economy. Any ambitious seafarers, and those residents of similar ilk who serviced them, increasingly drifted away in order to secure better opportunities elsewhere. An increasing proportion of those who stayed were seriously impoverished. As the town's population fell, so demand for goods slumped still further. The only elements of trade which saw growth during the early years of the 17th century were the importation of sea coal from Newcastle and Sunderland (which almost tripled between the 1580s and 1640) and an increase in the exportation of iron from the Weald. The latter gave little employment to Rye vessels, though the trade in sea coal provided a much-valued return cargo for those Rye vessels still partaking in the summer fishing expedition to Scarborough.

The collapse of Rye during the forty-year period from *c.*1590 is well illustrated in the records of the period, and not only by the major slump in births, marriages and deaths recorded within the parish registers (*see* Chapter 5). The fall in population resulted in the virtual abandonment of the poorest part of town — The Wishe — with a corresponding major reduction in household density elsewhere. A large percentage of those residents who chose to stay, or had nowhere else to go, were becoming increasingly impoverished.

A marked upsurge in economic activity during the 1630s resulted in a short-term labour shortage and promised a revival in the town's fortunes. It was during this short respite that the Grammar School was founded and built — a very up-to-date structure with a stylish brick facade of 1636 (Figure 1.6). It is one of very few buildings constructed within the town during the first half of the 17th century. In the event, the outbreak of civil war stopped Rye's revival in its tracks, and the town returned to its early Jacobean depressed state.

Fig. 1.6
The Grammar School, High Street, built 1636

As has already been emphasized for the 15th century, despite the pessimistic picture painted above regarding the post-Elizabethan period, it would be wrong to overstate the troubles experienced by the town. Throughout the period there remained a minority — albeit small — who were able to make a good living, and it is surely significant that, despite the virtual absence of house reconstruction, minor low-key additions and modifications continued to be made to the existing building stock. Furthermore, very few of the many medieval and Tudor houses which remain show obvious signs of neglect. This impression of an adequately maintained existing building stock — at least amongst those which have survived — is reinforced by the sketches made by Van Dyck in the 1630s, none of which give the impression of a seriously run-down town (*see* Figures 2.3, 3.15 and 6.29).

As always tends to be the case following a period of economic boom, observations regarding the 'current' state of the town tend to be influenced by the then recent past. Poverty is relative: without a memory of the town's period of economic success, Rye may have been regarded by contemporaries in a very different light. After all, it had the advantage of a sound and recently rebuilt (or, at worst, refurbished) housing stock which, with adequate but limited maintenance, was capable of surviving for centuries. It should also be remembered that, unlike the situation at Winchelsea a century earlier, the sea did not totally desert the port, which was able to stabilize at a much reduced size. In fact, it remains a viable local port even today.

The town had another distinct advantage over its neighbour. Whereas in its hour of need failing Winchelsea was unable to contend with a rapidly rising nearby rival — Rye — Rye itself had no such local competition and was able to sustain itself as a local market centre. Seen in this light the oft-quoted 'collapse of Rye' takes on a new light. By the 1660s Rye was no longer the largest town in the area: that role fell to a new rising star — or rather a rejuvenated old one — Hastings. As Rye's population fell during the first half of the 17th century, Hastings grew from 280 households in 1565 to approximately 400 in 1670. Even so, in 1660 Rye remained a town of no mean size with 290 households, more than double that of the next largest local town, Battle, and not that far behind the county town of Lewes.[37]

A poll tax of the inhabitants made in 1660 allows a reconstruction to be made of the town's occupational

Fig. 1.7
Lamb House, West Street, built by James Lamb, c.1723

Fig. 1.8
The Town Hall, rebuilt 1742-3

structure at that time.[38] It demonstrates how this had adjusted itself to take into account the town's much reduced reliance upon the sea. Whereas in 1565 54 per cent of households had been headed by seafarers (*see* above) by 1660 that total had reduced by 174 households, whilst very few of those who remained were described as fishermen. Many of the seafarers were exempt from paying the hearth tax on account of poverty. Despite this reduction in numbers, more than 100 households within the town were reliant upon the sea for their livelihood: a reminder of the continued importance of the port to the town, even in the mid 17th century. Most of the non-seafaring households concentrated on servicing the town and its rural hinterland (*see* Chapter 5).

Unlike Winchelsea, and despite what has been written in the past, Rye was never in serious danger of wholesale desertion, nor of shrinking to the size of a small village. True, Rye's short period of prosperity as the premier south-eastern port was indeed followed by a prolonged period of depression during which it underwent the painful process of adjusting to its new role within the local economy. However, once through this phase, Rye was able to settle comfortably into its function of local market town served by a small riverside quay. Despite high levels of poverty (resulting in a high proportion of householders being exempt from hearth tax in the 1660s) the 1660 poll tax return reminds us that a good living was possible for some — 47 households (16 per cent) are listed in the poll tax return as having either real estate valued at £5 per annum or above, or personal estates worth £100 or more, or a combination of both. The majority of these households (85 per cent) were concentrated either in the commercial north-eastern corner of the town or in Middle Street (Mermaid Street). This emphasizes the depressed state of the traditional seafaring wards of Strandgate, Baddings, and Watchbell and Wishe.

From the closing years of the 17th century and throughout the 18th and 19th centuries an increasing proportion of the town's merchants and traders were able to maintain a good standard of living. Whilst some built new storehouses and rebuilt their houses in the latest fashion (Figure 1.7) most took advantage of the solid 15th- and 16th-century structures they inherited and simply re-fronted them, modifying their internal layout to suit the requirements of the day.

By 1742-3 the town government had sufficiently recovered from its financial difficulties of a century-and-a-half earlier to embark upon the reconstruction of the town hall in a style befitting a moderately successful local borough (Figure 1.8). The water cistern built in the churchyard in 1733-5 is further proof of the town's moderate success in its new reduced role. During this period too the then principal inn of the town, The George in High Street, was remodelled. Subsequently, in 1818, it had a spacious assembly room added to its western end.

For us in the 21st century Rye's varied and often turbulent past has resulted in a compact and picturesque historic townscape which deserves to be cherished, studied, and learnt from.

2 THE INFRASTRUCTURE - Topography, Street Pattern and Public Spaces

GENERAL TOPOGRAPHY OF THE SITE

Regardless of whether deliberately planned or the result of organic growth, a town's infrastructure — in particular its street pattern — is arguably the most important component in forming the character of a settlement. It represents the skeleton upon which all else fits. An adequate knowledge of the infrastructure, and the factors instrumental in its development is therefore an essential of any urban study. It leads to a consideration of how and when the town grew, and whether its development was in any sense 'planned'.

Inevitably, the site's natural geography has an important part to play in determining layout, especially where, as at Rye, features such as river estuaries, cliffs, salt marshes and sea shore have had a major confining influence. Figures 1.1 and 2.2 not only show the contours of the site, but depict the configuration of the marshland and waterscape as it existed at two points in time: 1667 and 1771. It should be borne in mind that, during the historical period, all land below the five-metre contour (and especially below equinoxial high tide of about four metres above Ordnance Datum) has been prone to periodic flooding and, at times, very rapid changes.[1] For this reason, the five-metre contour can conveniently be taken as defining the island-like hill upon which Rye sits. It is tiny, amounting to 14.6 hectares (36 acres) — no more than the size of a small Tudor farm. The longest diagonal, measured across the site from northeast to southwest, is only

Fig. 2.1
Rye viewed from the NNW, c.1851, following construction of the railway which skirts the northern edge of town. Note St. Mary's Marsh, visible between the town and the upland in the foreground, the River Tillingham meandering through the marshland, and Camber Castle and windmills on the extreme right. [Engraving by John Hughes]

690 metres (0.4 of a mile), whilst the distance from northwest to southeast averages a mere 340 metres (0.2 of a mile).

The island hill was once part of a low spur which jutted out south-westwards from the upland into low-lying flatlands. During geological times, prior to the last Ice Age, this became cut off from the main block of uplands due to marine erosion. The erosion line presents itself in the landscape as an interrupted arc of degraded cliffs which defines the eastern side of Rye town and curves gently around for a distance of 20 miles (32 km) before meeting the sea at Hythe in the east (*see* Figure 1.4). These cliffs effectively form the 'northern' edge of Romney and Walland Marshes.

As with the eastern side of the hill upon which Rye is built, sea action during geological times has remodelled the southern and southwestern sides of the site, cutting them back to a low sandstone cliff *c.*15 metres (*c.*49 feet) high at its greatest extent. The line of erosion stops short of the former spur's crest, which reaches a flat-topped summit at the church, 24 metres (about 79 feet) above O.D. To the south of the crest the ground slopes imperceptibly down to the cliff top. At the south-eastern corner of the hill the erosion has eaten back less markedly into the slope, probably due to an underlying outcrop of harder rock. Here for a short length the original slope of the hillside is more intact, though nonetheless subjected to some remodelling. At this point the cliff is virtually non-existent and until quite recently the underlying harder substrata appeared as a

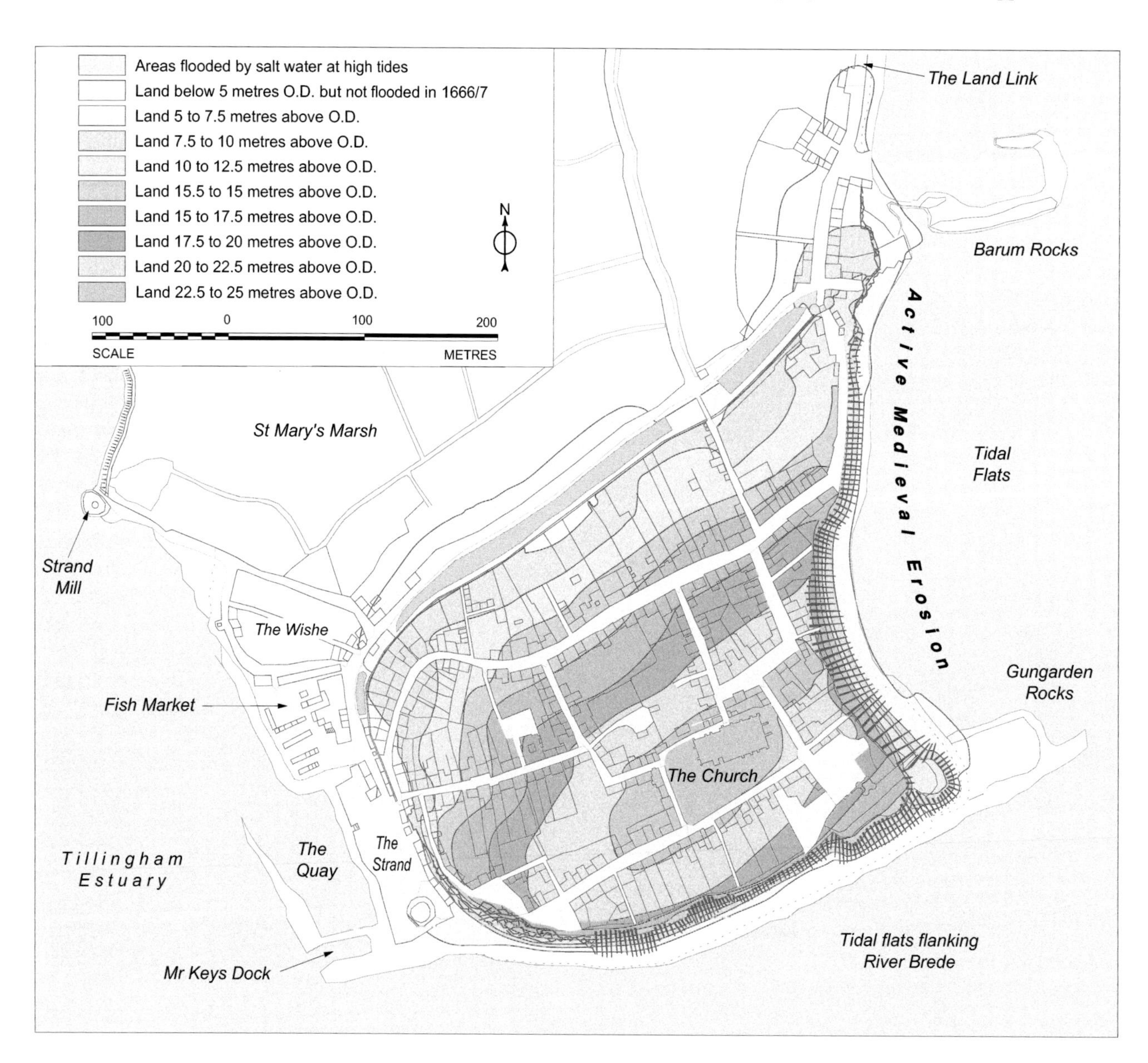

Fig. 2.2
Outline plan based upon the Jeake map of 1667 with ground-level contours superimposed

nose of rocky outcrops called 'Gungarden Rocks', projecting eastwards into the mudflats (Figure 2.2).[2]

Extending northwards from this outcrop, the hill's eastern cliff curves gently around, linking to another outcrop of harder rock at the north-eastern corner of the town, at Landgate. Here too a series of disjointed rocks, known in the 17th century as the 'Barum Rocks' jutted out into the mudflats, rising above the Rother estuary as a series of imposing stone monoliths. Shown extant in the Jeake plan of 1667 and in a number of 17th-century and later topographical views of the town from the north (for instance, Figures 2.3 and 2.4), the last vestiges of these were blown up in the 19th century.[3] The low cliffs in this area (to the east of Landgate) show a near-vertical sandstone face where eroded and cut back. In contrast, the remainder of the eastern cliff is very degraded, having more the appearance of a steep clay bank than a cliff. There is known to have been active erosion/slippage along this stretch in historical times (*see* below).

Unlike the eastern, southern and south-western sides of the hill, the north-western and northern slopes have not been subjected to marine erosion. Instead, in this area the ground slopes gently down to the Tillingham estuary and northern valley inlet known as St. Mary's Marsh (Figures 2.1 and 2.2).

Throughout the late Medieval, Tudor and Stuart periods water lapped close under the hill on the east, south and west sides at each tide. The town map shows that even in 1771 these areas were unimproved 'salts', and as such subject to regular inundation at high tides. Although limited reclamation occurred under the south cliff in the 18th century, it was not until 1834 that a sea wall was built from the then Fishmarket (southeast of the town) to Pollards Wharf, finally excluding the tides from the Town Salts and North Salts on the eastern side of town. Even afterwards, the houses in Landgate Square were flooded following an exceptional high tide in 1875.[4]

For the period prior to the great storms of the late 13th century the situation on the eastern side of the town is far from clear and is still much debated (*see* below). There is more certainty regarding St. Mary's Marsh, immediately to the north of the town. By the early 13th century this area was valuable marshland and was still much valued in 1247, though subsequently — probably as a result of the late 13th-century storms — the defences were broken and the area had become a brackish tidal creek. By the close of the 14th century it had been fully reclaimed, protected from the tides on the western side by a high earthen wall. In November 1571 the sea once more broke through the defences and the area reverted to salt marsh, before being reclaimed at the end of the century.[5]

LINKS TO THE SURROUNDING AREA

Whilst many towns owe their existence to the service needs of a major establishment — a cathedral, monastery, castle or great mansion — others grew up to take economic advantages of transport routes, being sited at a strategic river crossing, the intersection of important roadways, or a convenient access point to a navigable river or to the open sea. In yet other instances the impetus was access to an exploitable natural resource, especially where the value of that resource could be enhanced by processing or manufacturing to give a more valuable end-product. The most successful towns usually combined a number of these functions, making them less vulnerable to external influences.

Seen in this light, Rye was relatively undeveloped in economic terms in the medieval period. As demonstrated in Chapter 1, the principal reason for its existence — and what made it a place of some significance — was its port, served by the protected natural harbour it shared with Winchelsea. Both towns developed a versatile fleet of ships which could be used for both fishing and trade, for war, and for transport of royalty, troops and messages. When the opportunity arose these were further augmented by privateering. This versatility and adaptability was vital to the success of the town, for the principal exports from the immediate Wealden area were bulky and of low-value, consisting mostly of wood, timber and (during the post-medieval period) iron. Furthermore, whereas some port towns were fortunate in serving as an outport for a large local land-locked town, there were no such centres within Rye's undeveloped terrestrial hinterland to the west which, in any case, it shared with both Winchelsea and Hastings. New Romney served the Romney Marsh hinterlands across the estuary to the east of the town, and this remained the case even after the damaging storms of the mid to late 13th century. Despite these apparent economic disadvantages, the naturally defensive, dry, raised, 'island' location of the site, with its protected access to the sea, made Rye an obvious location for colonisation and development.

Whatever the reasons for a particular town's existence, its long-term success depended to large extent upon its transport links to the wider world. For this reason, access points to a town had an important influence upon internal layout. Conversely, the existing street layout of a town can in itself give clues to former routes which have fallen into partial or total disuse: it can also hint at routes which have developed late, or been subjected to radical modification.

In historical times Rye had but two principal access points to the outside world: from at least the early 14th century both were protected/controlled by town gates. One of these, at the north-eastern corner of the

Fig. 2.3
Rye viewed from the north, by an unknown artist working in the school of Hendrick Danckaerts. The land link is visible in the foreground with the Wool Warehouse (dated 1674) visible on the left, at the end of Landgate suburb and, to the left of the warehouse, one of the upstanding needles of the Barum Rocks. Unless retouched, the painting cannot predate 1736 as the 'triple-M' roof of 8-10 High Street is depicted. Note the masts of ships moored at the Strand (middle right). [© Rye Castle Museum]

'island' site, provided the only dry long-distance route into town from the adjacent upland. Even this was via a low, narrow and vulnerable land-link protected from the salt water on the east in post-medieval times by a series of groins, depicted in the Jeake map and in Van Dyck's view of the town from the north (Figure 2.4). The second, on the western side of town, gave direct access to the Strand, and thus to the sea.

There were other pedestrian routes, all of which are of uncertain date. For example, by 1667 at least one path descended the eastern cliff to the shore beneath, with another at the south-eastern corner, whilst by 1771 another path descended the cliff to The Strand from the south-western corner of the site.[6]

On the northern side, a postern gate in the town wall gave access over the town ditch to the low land to the north of the town, called variously St Mary's Marsh (16th/17th C), St Mary's Croft [Marsh] (15th C) or, in the mid 13th century, North Marys/North Marays [Marsh]. Jeake's map of 1667 shows a straight track (now Rope Walk) extending out from the gate, crossing St. Mary's Marsh to Queen Elizabeth's Well (alternatively known as Dodes Well or Blikewell) — one of the town's water sources at the foot of the northern uplands. There are much earlier documentary references to this track.[7] The postern gate was reached from the town centre via its own street, now called Conduit Hill and formerly called 'The Friars' on account of the Austin Friary which was moved to this part of the town in 1378.

There is the possibility of another pedestrian gate through the town wall at The Mint, opposite the end of Ferry Road in the area where the wall skirts around the north-western corner of the town (*see* Chapter 3). The location of this possible gate is of some relevance: it is shown where a public alley — Needles Passage — today links to The Mint. One possible explanation for the silence in the records is that the passage did not become a public right of way until much later. If this is so, the gate shown by Prowze (*see* Figure 2.19) was most likely a private entrance through the wall.

Excepting the unproven pedestrian gate, it is surely significant that there was no direct route into town from the Wishe suburb which occupied the low land beside the Tillingham to the north-west of the town. What makes this fact even more significant is that by the 16th century the road from the Town Ferry (otherwise West Ferry) entered through The Wishe.[8] This is the ferry which crossed to the under-cliff track to Winchelsea Ferry and to the important Udimore and Brede ridgeway leading towards Battle (*see* Figure 1.2). The implication of this must be that both the suburb and the ferry road developed after — perhaps long after — the town's street pattern became firmly established. People entering town from this direction were forced to utilize the existing access points. To understand the

Fig. 2.4
Rye from the north as depicted by Van Dyck August 1633. Note the land link (protected by breakwaters on the seaward side) leading to Landgate suburb with, on the left, the Barum Rocks.

level of inconvenience this caused it must be realized that the nearest gate — The Strand Gate — faced south onto The Strand, and to use it from the direction of The Wishe meant a tight 180-degree turn.

To suggest that Rye had no ferry link to the important Udimore/Brede ridgeway until a relatively late date seems untenable: the two must surely have been linked from early times. What the street pattern suggests is that the route into town from the ferry was relatively new in the 16th century. If this was so, it seems likely that in earlier times the westward ferry link to both the end of the ridgeway and the under-cliff track which ran along the southern edge of the ridge towards the ferry from Udimore to Winchelsea, was direct from The Strand.

The ferry across the Tillingham was not the only one which existed in the 16th century: as Figure 1.2 indicates, there was a second, across the Rother estuary to the east. It would be logical to suggest that this developed as a 'fixed' route only after 1478, following the foundation of a settlement called East Guldeford on the estuary's eastern shore by inning 1,300 acres of salt marsh. However, there must have been some form of earlier route in this direction as there are references in the town accounts to ferry costs for officials going to the Cinque Ports Courts at New Romney *etc.* prior to the foundation of East Guldeford.[9] In the 16th century the Guldeford ferry crossed from a point half a mile (0.8 km) to the north-north-east of the town, at the eastern end of Saltcote Street in Playden parish.

STREET PATTERN

Layout as existing in the 16th and 17th centuries

Given the small size of the 'island' site, it is hardly surprising that a network of streets was adopted in order to accommodate the town's population. In general the layout is rectilinear, with the streets intersecting at right angles, giving a 'planned' feel. That the layout does not consist of a grid in which the streets in both directions run continuously across the site is clear from Figure 2.5.[10]

The town is dominated by three principal east-

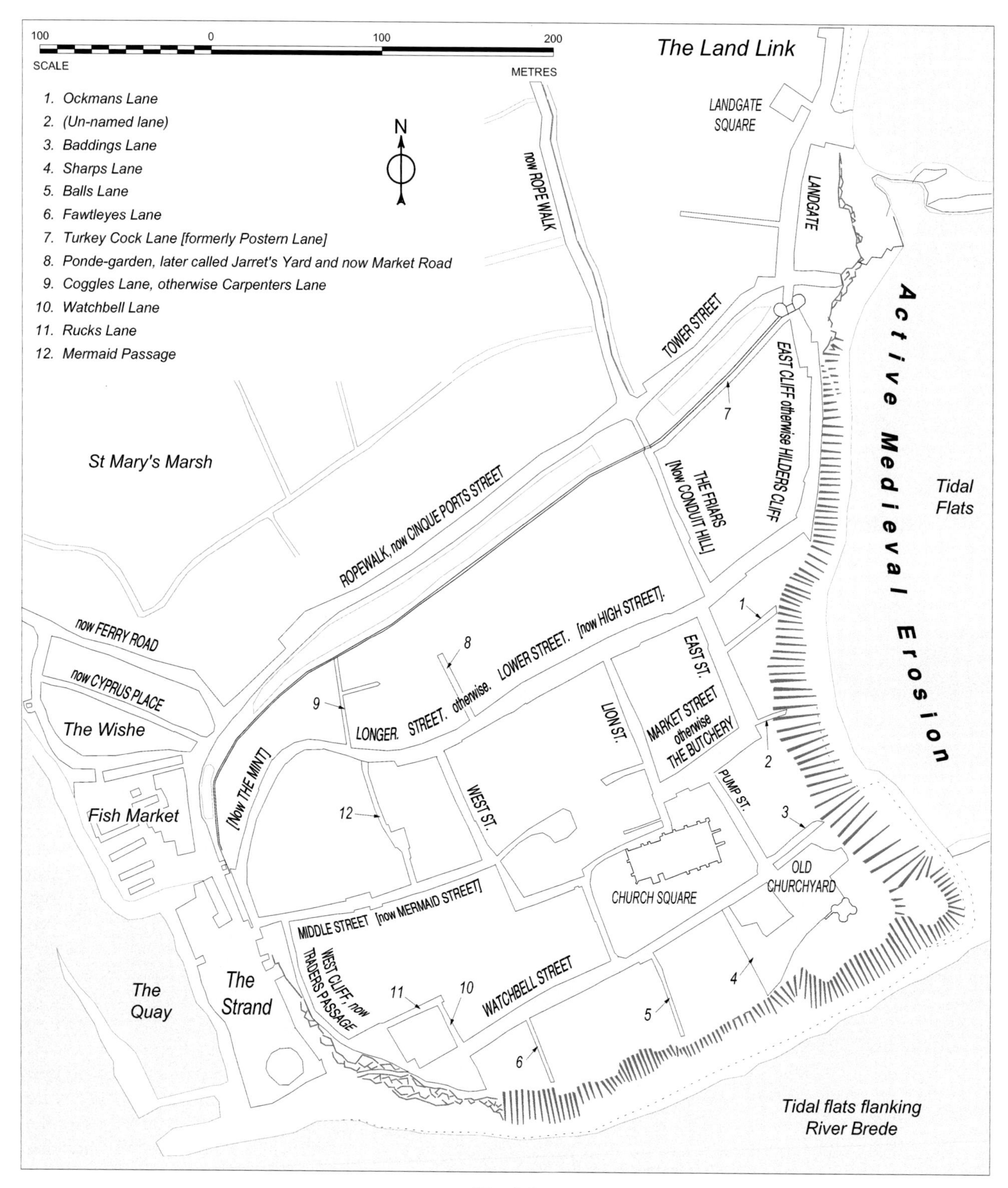

Fig. 2.5
Outline plan of town as in 1667 showing street pattern and street names

west aligned streets, giving two rows of *insulae* varying in width from 65 metres to 90 metres (213 feet to 295 feet). In the north is Longer Street otherwise Lower Street (now High Street and The Mint): across the centre, in two disjointed sections, stretches Market Street otherwise The Butchery and the steeply climbing Middle Street (now Mermaid Street): to the south, extending along the crest of the hill is Watchbell Street, the eastern half of which is included within the area now called Church Square. Crossing these at right angles are short randomly placed lesser streets. East Street, Lion Street and West Street climb southwards from present-day

High Street to link with Market Street and Mermaid Street, whilst Market Street and Mermaid Street are themselves linked to Watchbell Street by the eastern side of Church Square (part of which is alternatively known as Pump Street) and by the western side of Church Square, linking to a dog-legged continuation of West Street. None of these north-south streets are mentioned by name in 16th- and 17th-century deeds, being identified instead by reference to the streets they link (*e.g.* the highway or street between Longer Street and The Butchery, or between Longer Street and the church, or Longer Street and Middle Street, *etc*).

None of these streets can be described as either overly narrow or overly wide — perhaps the best term for them is 'average'. Mermaid Street, West Street and the lower end of High Street (in The Mint) contain sections which measure as little as *c*.5.5 metres (*c*.18 feet) between the houses, but widths of 6 to 7 metres (19 feet 8 inches to 23 feet) are more typical. At its widest, along the eastern half, High Street is almost double the narrowest widths, at 10 metres (*c*.33 feet). At its greatest expanse Market Street is about 13 metres (42 feet 8 inches) wide, but this is meant to have been the site of the town's market (but *see* below).[11] In fact, in comparison to neighbouring Winchelsea, all the streets appear to be of mean proportions. There the principal north-south streets were laid out to be 12.6 metres (41 feet 4 inches) in width, whilst even the minor east-west streets were mostly 10.0 metres (*c*.33 feet).[12] But Winchelsea is well known for the spaciousness of its layout: despite this comparison, none of Rye's main streets should be considered narrow by the standards of the time.

The network described above communicates well with the town's quayside (The Strand) which was reached through Strand Gate at the point where gently sloping High Street/The Mint and the much steeper Mermaid Street converge at the foot of the hill. A narrow lane (now called Traders Passage but formerly known as West Cliff) climbs the edge of the south-western cliff to link the foot of Mermaid Street to the western end of Watchbell Street.

Except for traffic entering the town from The Strand, the entire street network was (and, because of the present one-way traffic flow, for all practical purposes still is) accessed from the surrounding area by a single road (East Cliff *otherwise* Hilders Cliff) which enters the town through Land Gate and climbs gently along the top of the eastern cliff, linking to the eastern end of High Street. True, there was an alternative minor pedestrian route, which entered through the postern gate in the wall a short distance to the west of Land Gate before climbing steeply up Conduit Hill to High Street, and over time other 'unofficial' pedestrian routes developed (*see* below and Chapter 3).

Although the route into town from Land Gate gives easy access to High Street, the procedure by which the other two principal east-west streets were reached was (and still is) more tortuous. Market Street/Mermaid Street could be arrived at only by turning south part-way along High Street, whilst Watchbell Street was similarly reached from Market Street. The possible reasons for the inconvenient layout on the eastern side of town are discussed below, as is the age and development of the street system. But before considering these important issues mention should be made of other, more minor elements of the historical street layout, as well as the town's two suburbs.

The best source of information regarding the arrangement of the minor lanes is Jeake's town plan of 1667 (copied in 1728) upon which the outline of streets shown in Figure 2.5 is based.[13] On the east and south sides short, narrow lanes extended out to the cliff edge: Ockmans Lane (1), a very short un-named lane (2), and Baddings Lane (3) on the east; Sharps Lane (4), Balls Lane (5) and Fawtleyes Lane (6) on the south. Others, not shown in the 1667 plan, are known from both the documentary and architectural record — presumably these had been abandoned by the mid 17th century.

There were also lanes extending out to the edge of town on the northern side — all these terminated at the town wall. Conduit Hill, running down to the Postern Gate west of Land Gate, has already been referred to. Its northern end was (and still is) linked to the Land Gate by a narrow lane (7) extending along the back of the town wall: it is known today as Turkey Cock Lane, but was called 'Postern Lane' in 1667. There is no evidence to suggest a continuation westwards, running along the inside of the remaining length of the town wall. Westwards of Conduit Hill Jeake illustrates two further lanes. Ponde-garden (8) stopped short of the defences, but by 1683 had a flight of steps — known as 'Robert Brown's Stairs' — giving access over the wall.[14] Subsequently called Jarret's Yard, the lane was widened and extended across the line of the town defences to become Cattle Market Road in 1859 and was still so called in 1934, despite the market having moved in 1871. It is now called Market Road.[15] Beyond this, in the area now known as The Mint, was Coggles Lane otherwise Carpenters Lane (9) which not only extended up to the wall but also incorporated a short spur street running back towards Ponde-garden. It is possible that the two were once linked.[16]

In addition to the lanes around the periphery of the town, Jeake shows short spurs in the market area immediately to the north of the church, and there is documentary and architectural evidence of other lanes in this vicinity (*see* 'The Town Centre – Church, Market and Court Area' below). The only other street within the walls which requires mention is a dog-legged street called Watchbell Lane (10) and Rucks Lane (11) on the northern side of Watchbell Street, near the west cliff. Jeake indicates (in somewhat sketchy form) a narrow path extending from the bend in this lane through to Mermaid Street, and the existence of this minor thoroughfare seems to be confirmed by the western boundary clause of a deed dated 1652 relating to a house on the southern side of Mermaid Street. In this it is referred to as 'lane called Mr Ruckse Lane', suggesting that this was a continuation of the street of that name at its southern end, though the precise location of this 'lane' has yet to be ascertained: for this reason it is not depicted in Figure 2.5.[17] A second passage (12) is shown on the opposite side of the street, running northwards to connect to The Mint. Unlike its counterpart, this survives and is now known as Mermaid Passage. Mermaid Passage uses the carriage entrance to The Mermaid Inn and from the depiction on the map it seems likely that the now lost southern path likewise utilized a carriage entrance within the street's built-up frontage. Sharps Lane on the south side of Watchbell Street/Church Square was similarly accessed through a carriage entrance.[18]

Documentary sources name several medieval streets and lanes in Rye, the locations of which are unknown. These include The Pygge Lane (1316 and 1321), Schytbourglane (1365), a lane leading towards M[i]lnerstrete [*ie* Miller Street] (1347), Merstret (1307) and Potepirie Lane (1363).[19] The Pygge Lane was outside the north gate (Landgate), whilst Potepirie Lane was undoubtedly associated with the 'tenement potepirie' where Paul, son of Robert Paulin [the bailiff], lived in the reign of Edward I. There are mentions of several more lanes and streets without specific names (*e.g.* 'a small lane from land called Courton').

The Suburbs

Because of its low-lying surroundings, Tudor and Stuart Rye possessed but two extra-mural suburbs of which one — Landgate — consists of nothing more than a short street climbing very gently up to the town gate from the land-link to the mainland. Perhaps in the 16th/early 17th centuries there was limited overspill from this towards the postern gate, along a minor track which skirted the northern bank of the town ditch, but, if so, the area had been abandoned by 1667.[20] At its western end the ditch-side track (now Tower Street and Cinque Ports Street) linked to the larger of the two suburbs — The Wishe — built along two low-lying streets known today as Ferry Road and Alma Place/Cyprus Place. At their far end these two streets are linked by a short return section of Cyprus Place: this may have been nothing more than a footway. A third street is shown by Jeake, curving back along the Tillingham estuary to the large Fishmarket at the southern end of the suburb with, beyond the Fishmarket, The Strand.

Development of the town plan and street layout: origin of the street pattern

Towns based upon a rectilinear street pattern are often assumed to have been planned at a single point in time with, apart from minor amendments, little or no subsequent modification. As plan analysis of the rectilinear street layouts at such places as Ludlow, Shropshire, and, more recently, at Rye's fellow Cinque Port town of New Romney, Kent, has demonstrated, such an assumption can be erroneous. Recent historical and archaeological work suggests that New Romney was not a planted Anglo-Saxon town laid out on a rectilinear plan as Beresford had suggested. Instead there was a simple early layout including a beach trackway (or 'old high street') and two roads surrounding the first market place, the early guildhall (pre-1234), and two early churches. Another road led to the leper hospital of *c.*1180. In the mid 13th century a new high street and second market place were set out, with surrounding plots of the types usually denoted 'burgage plots'. Secondary streets subsequently developed giving a rectilinear appearance, into which fitted the third church, the second town hospital, the alien priory, the fair site, and the civic buildings. The early boat beach with associated maritime and fishing activities was supplemented by quays and wharves in the harbour area, separate from the boat beach, to accommodate the larger vessels of the 13th century.[21]

At another Cinque Port town — Hastings, to the west of Rye — the reverse appears to have been the case. Here, when a new Norman town (New Hastings: now known as the Old Town) was laid out on the opposite side of the castle to the Saxon town a tight 'grid' of streets seems to have been used, occupying the floor of a narrow valley behind the boat beach. Later this was supplemented by development along two long streets extending up the valley, aligned parallel to one another, perhaps replacing houses within the southern part of the grid which had been washed away by storms. By this date Hastings was in decline.[22] New Romney exemplifies how the development of a medieval town with an apparent early grid-plan must be carefully examined, whilst Hastings demonstrates the need to show caution when using as a model the developments found in other towns. This especially applies to ports such as Rye which occupy sites on changing coastlines and estuaries.

Given the very limited below-ground archaeological excavations at Rye, any observations regarding the development of the street layout must rely on limited documentary evidence and a consideration of the layout of the street pattern, together with the strands, defences and access points. In this way the plan of the Tudor/Stuart town can be better understood and some tentative views formulated regarding the origins of the layout.

Excepting the possibility of an initial, small, unplanned community, perhaps pre-Conquest in date, the earliest known developments were the church, the market functions, and (if Rye is the 'New Borough' mentioned in Domesday Book) the existence of 64 burgage plots.[23] If these developments did not form part of a single planned plantation, it is difficult to determine the order in which they were established, and thus which influenced the location of the others. Regardless of whether the Borough was established before Domesday or soon afterwards, the burgesses (called 'Barons' within the Cinque Ports Confederation) would have needed a location in which to dwell and trade. It is possible that these early burgage plots were laid out adjacent to the church and market place, which is known from later evidence to have been next to the church. In this area too was land reserved for courts and, perhaps, an official local headquarters of the seigniorial lord (*see* below). Another likely candidate for early settlement is the highway which led along the slope to the western landing point on the Tillingham: that is, along the curved part of present day High Street — the part now known as 'The Mint' (*see* Figure 2.5).[24] This latter area would have provided a natural route leading from the northern upland, via the land link, to the potential early landing place beside the river.

There are other difficulties in attempting an interpretation of the early layout of the town. Already by the late 13th century there were two beach/quay areas — a western and an eastern — and there is no way of knowing which of the two developed first. Furthermore, the eastern edge of the town has been subjected to an uncertain degree of loss through inundation, erosion, and slippage (*see* below). It is impossible to know how extensive this was, or how much remodelling of the street pattern was necessary as a result. It has to be accepted that the street layout within these lost areas cannot be reconstructed, though some useful observations are possible. In this area was a strand (*la Estronde*) sited below a cliff-top promontory (*la Nesse*). Here there were tenements, mills and a salt house (*see* below).

Already by the early 1340s some of the tenements and mills on this eastern side of Rye had been washed away by the action of the sea and within the next hundred years both the East Strand and the Nesse disappear from the records — a ward within the town was still called '*La Nesse*' in 1415, suggesting that part of this area still remained at that time.[25] From this date onwards no prefixes were included in documents to differentiate between the two strands: logic suggests that this was because only one survived and that from this time onwards any mention of 'The Strand' refers to what had earlier been called 'West Strand'.

During the early period the inhabitants of Rye obviously needed access to their two strands. In the case of the since lost East Strand this would have required a way down the east cliff. It should also be borne in mind that from at least the early 14th century the defences of Rye would have had an effect upon the medieval street layout. These both provided and prevented access at various points. Being upon a hill-top 'island' site largely surrounded by salt water, the town effectively had no 'on site' supply of drinking water. Thus, an essential for the inhabitants of Rye was access to a reliable water supply, which was taken from natural springs (sometimes known as wells) some distance to the north, beyond St. Mary's Marsh and the land-link. By or during the 14th century an important spring known as 'Blikewell' was accessed from the town via the steep street later known as Conduit Hill, through the Postern Gate, across the town fosse and along a causeway which crossed the reclaimed St. Mary's Croft in St. Mary's Marsh. Other springs existed at the foot of the cliffs to the northeast of the town, adjacent to Playden parish, and to the northwest near a place called Leasam (*see* 'Water Supplies' below).

The eastern cliff

Essential to any attempt at understanding the evolution of Rye's street layout is a consideration of an anomaly evident along the eastern cliff of the town. Why is there no direct route up from Land Gate to the central and southern streets? Holloway quotes Jeake who, writing in the mid 17th century, refers to this part of town as 'where by the flux and reflux of the tides, have been washed away some streets, the Badding's Gate, and wall leading therefrom to the Land Gate'.[26] Whether this was based upon folk memory or documentary evidence is unclear. The statement is arguably supported by the petition which preceded the murage grant of 1348 in which reference is made to 'a great part of the town' having been 'consumed by the sea and in other ways'.[27] What cannot be told from the petition is whether this alleged destruction was caused through inundation of low-lying land, or by erosion of the hill, though other evidence suggests it was a combination of both — inundation of reclaimed land, followed by erosion and slippage once the base of the cliff had become exposed to the tides.

Although the *Nesse* place-name and the references to associated cliffs are strong circumstantial evidence, the first certain proof that cliff erosion/slippage had occurred along the eastern edge of the town comes from much later — the late 15th century. In 1482 money was spent on repairs to a jetty near the Land Gate, followed the same year by expenses in picking up the wreckage from it, whilst just four years later there were further payments for saving and taking up the timber from the jetty without the Land Gate 'when the great water broke in'.[28] A series of grants relating to land on the southern side of High Street, near its eastern end, are sufficient to reconstruct this area at this period (Figure 2.6). They indicate the existence of a 'common way near the cliff', extending southwards from the end of High Street. This turned along the southern edge of the land being granted, linking to Ockmans Lane which therefore, unlike now, extended through from East Cliff to East Street. Jeake's map indicates that by the mid 17th century the eastern end of Ockmans Lane had slipped down the cliff.[29] Today the eroded cliff in this area lies very close to the backs of the High Street houses and shops. Another deed, of 1491, refers to three parcels and a cottage on the south side of the lane, abutting the cliff on the east, and by 1569 seven dwellings had been built upon this property, again implying a greater expanse of land than now exists.[30]

There is other evidence of cliff falls/slips in this general area. During the middle years of the 16th century the corporation, Christopher Scales and John Ford made exchanges of small plots of land at East Cliff, at least some of which (and perhaps all) were associated with re-aligning the street away from the vulnerable cliff top.[31] A kink in the alignment of East Cliff, just inside the Land Gate, no doubt reflects in part this re-alignment of the street. In the early/mid 16th century slippages of the cliff further north were also expected — clauses were included in deeds to cover the possibility of re-aligning the highway adjacent to the lands called 'Montes' (now Mountsfield) immediately north of the land link should the need arise.[32] The problems evidently continued into

Fig. 2.6
Vacant land on south side of High Street granted out by the corporation in the late 15th century (above) with the same area as shown in 1909 (below).

the late 16th century. Plans were made in late 1572 to build a substantial sea wall of stone at a distance of ten feet (3 metres) from the base of the cliffs, 140 feet (about 43 metres) long and 12 feet (3.7 metres) high, in an attempt to arrest erosion in the area immediately outside the Land Gate. The work was put in hand the following year, but was delayed part way through by a visit to the town by Elizabeth I, requiring a '*bushgroyne*' to be built to protect the wall during the winter, until work could start again in March. In the words of a letter sent by the Mayor and Jurats to the Lord Warden on 18th September 1573 concerning the delays 'which not being done our Landgate will shortly away and not be made again for 1000li'. Whether the Land Gate was under serious short-term threat is doubtful, but some erosion evidently continued, for just three years later discussions were in progress to consider how the old bastion at wall's end could be prevented from falling over the cliff.[33] Today the Land Gate stands close to the cliff edge, but this reference, taken with the quantity of building work carried out on the town wall to the east of the gate in 1545, suggests that the length of wall shown projecting eastwards from the gate in the late 16th-century birds-eye view reproduced in Figure 3.1 may not be an exaggeration.[34]

It seems almost certain that this series of slips and feared slips represented late phases in a sequence of subsidence which had been occurring along this edge of town ever since the adjacent low-lying land became inundated by salt water in the late 13th and/or early 14th centuries. That would explain why the townsfolk were so worried in 1348. The cliff top is so close to East Cliff that the danger is still obvious today. What is less obvious from within the town, because the buildings block the view, is how very close to the cliff is the south side of High Street and the eastern side of East Street, particularly at the junction of East Street with Market Street. The area is still prone to slippage, the most recent being in the early 1980s, behind Ypres Tower garden, which necessitated the long-term evacuation of a terrace of houses beneath the cliff. Given what had happened at (Old) Winchelsea in the late 13th century, it is understandable that the Barons of Rye should be so concerned by active slippage in this area.

Despite these observations, the point should not be over-emphasized. Geomorphologists consider that the circumstances which existed in the medieval period, as currently understood, did not lend themselves to large-scale erosion in this area — the depth of sea water was too slight. Furthermore, the cliff was in the lee of the prevailing winds. Rather than active erosion, the problems were more likely caused by gradual slippage and slumping of the soft clay cliff face, perhaps exacerbated at times by storms blowing in from the southeast, especially when these coincided with high tides.[35]

Probably the quite considerable area of lost hill top conjectured by Vidler in his published reconstruction of Rye represents an exaggeration of the true circumstances. Despite the desirability of a regular arrangement of streets on this side of town, the pattern adopted in reality had to take into account the alignment of the cliffs as they existed at the time the streets were laid out. Indeed, an irregular, rather than a regular outline is to some extent implied by the early place-names within the town. For example, in this general area was the elevated land known as '*la Nesse*' (*ie.* headland or nose) where in 1358 stood a 'windmill situated on the cliff next to the sea harbour (*portum maris*) on the south'. Furthermore, as has been pointed out, this area gave its name to one of Rye's medieval wards.[36] The Nesse was evidently a built-up part of the town, for in 1341 an agreement was made to take down a house there and rebuild it elsewhere: it was described as being between two other houses.[37] The mention of the harbour on the south is the only hint as to location. One possibility for *la Nesse* is the degraded outcrop of rocks known in the 17th century as 'Gungarden rocks' which projected eastwards from the south-eastern corner of town; another is the degraded outcrop known as 'Barum Rocks' further north, with the harbour (centred on East Strand) occupying a small sheltered 'cove' between the two outcrops. It may have been in this general area that the eighteen tenements mentioned in 1351 as inundated by the sea were sited, effectively giving a small 'low town', though these are equally likely to have stood on the western side of the land link, beside St. Mary's Marsh, as too could the first site of the friary. Beyond these comments, the location of the Nesse, of East Strand and the associated *portum maris* remain speculation.

All the above suggests an irregular eastern edge to the town, perhaps not too unlike the cliff configuration of today, but a little further out. Despite this likely lack of regularity, a lost cliff-top street linking East Cliff to the end of Market Street, and possibly extending as far south as the eastern end of Watchbell Street, seems highly likely. Such an arrangement would make a great deal of sense of the existing street pattern. Most likely the 'common way' mentioned earlier which extended southwards from East Cliff in 1490, intersecting with Ockmans Lane, represented the last remnants of this street. Whatever the arrangement may have been, the physical evidence has been destroyed and there are no known documents to either confirm or deny 'folk memory' dating back to at least the mid 17th century.

The above conjectural issues are important if the evolution of Rye's layout is to be understood. However, with a few exceptions (principally a small number of accessible vaulted cellars, for which *see* Chapter 6) the present arrangement of streets on the eastern side of town had already been established by the time the oldest surviving houses were being constructed.

THE 'TOWN CENTRE' AREAS

From at least the late 14th century the town's principal activities were concentrated in two distinct areas, though it should be stressed that because of Rye's compact nature, these two *foci* were very close to each other. The church, administrative court and market were located on the highest point of the hill, with a second commercial area (including The Strand and a substantial Fishmarket) outside the town walls on the Tillingham waterfront to the west. As has already been noted, documents indicate the former existence of a further centre of activity — East Strand — but this ceases to be mentioned after the middle years of the 14th century, having probably been destroyed through inundation (*see* above). The other two centres have experienced significant modification over time and therefore, if the nature of the medieval and Tudor town is to be understood, both require consideration.

Church, Market and Court Area (Figure 2.7)

In the central area, around the church, the problems relate to the size and significance of the market, the changing nature of the site set aside for the courts, and the mechanism by which the central street may have became severed into two quite distinct and unconnected parts — Market Street and Mermaid Street.

There was, no doubt, a market within the town from earliest times: 10d was paid for 'four shamels in the market place' in 1272 and it is mentioned in a rental and deeds of the early 14th century. There are references to properties next to the market place in 1306 and 1312, whilst other houses (including at least one 'principal tenement') are described as 'in the market' in the early rental and 'in the market place' in deeds of 1325 and 1354.[38] Whether any significance should be placed on the reference to 'in' (as opposed to 'next to', 'by', or 'near') the market place is debatable — although rare, such early encroachments upon market places are not unheard of. None of these early references give any clues as to the location of the market place at this time, but by 1374 it is known to have been immediately north of the church, in the vicinity of present-day Market Street (*see* below). There are no reasons to suspect an early change of location.

If the conjecture regarding a lost eastern cliff-top street is correct, access from Land Gate to the combined church, court and market area would have been both easy and intuitive, whereas today (and from at least the late 15th century) this area needs to be sought out by turning off High Street part-way along its length. Both the documentary and architectural evidence for the area help unravel its development, but are insufficient to allow an accurate reconstruction to be made for any point in time prior to the mid 17th century.

The earliest extant visible work within the present parish church is within the transepts and lower stages of the central tower: they seem to belong to no earlier than the mid 12th century.[39] It was planned from the outset as a substantial cruciform structure, suggesting that the settlement was already of some size and/or importance by that date. To judge from the remnant of Norman work incorporated within the eastern wall, the chancel was surprisingly long. Whether (as seems likely) the church replaced an earlier building and, if so, whether it was located upon the same site is not known.[40] What is clear is that the present nave and side aisles were not constructed until late in the 12th century, perhaps suggesting the progressive reconstruction of an earlier building upon this site, or alternatively the replacement of an initial temporary nave.

Immediately to the north of the church was an open area called 'Courton' set aside (as the name implies) for the holding of courts. In 1348 part of it, described as 'of ancient times ordained there for a dwelling of the parsons of that church' was granted by the Crown to the parson of Rye. The remainder of the land, 'where the pleas affecting the town are now held, adjoining the churchyard ...' is described as measuring 200 feet by 43 feet (61.0 metres by 13.1 metres). This residue was 'to remain to the commonalty [of Rye] in perpetuity ... whereon a house can be built in which future pleas pertaining to the King can be pleaded ... and other business affecting the commonalty of the town can be made'.[41] This is the land upon which the Town Hall, on the southern side of Market Street, now stands.

Even as rebuilt in its enlarged form in 1742-3, the Town Hall occupies only a small part of the land reserved for the courts. The dimensions given in 1348 allow the boundaries of 'Courton' to be identified with considerable accuracy: it was bounded on the south by the churchyard and on the east by Pump Street (part of Church Square). Based upon the town layout as it existed in 1667, logic would suggest that the western side was formed by that part of Lion Street which continues up to the north transept of the church, with the northern edge defined by Market Street. But this area represents less than half the site as it existed in 1348, for whilst the distance across the plot from the churchyard to Market Street equates to the stated width, the distance from Pump Street to the southern end of Lion Street is only *c.*97 feet (*c.*29.6 metres). The distance from Pump Street to the boundary of the Old Vicarage, on the other hand, is *c.*194 feet (*c.*59.1 metres) — very close to the 200 feet (61 metres) mentioned in 1348. Given that Old

Vicarage is known to have been ancient glebe and part of Courton was granted to the church in 1348, it makes sense that this boundary represents the western edge of the lands reserved for the use of the town (Figure 2.7).

Fifteen years after the grant, the patronage of Rye Church was given by Edward III to the Cistercian Abbey of Stanley, Wiltshire.[42]. They seem not to have installed a resident rector, relying instead upon a vicar to serve the parish — a common arrangement and one which is known to have already been in place within the town by 1291, with a further specific reference in 1304. Even later, when rectors were installed they were rarely resident.[43] This explains the vicarage sited at the western end of Courton. Stanley Abbey did not allocate all of their land within the town to the use of their vicar, for in 1443 a deed made by the corporation granting out two tenements next to the market place gave the owner of one of the two western abutting properties as the vicar of Rye [*ie* The Vicarage] and the northern abutment as land of Stanley Abbey.[44] Stanley Abbey's property probably represented the rectorial (as opposed to the vicarial) glebe. After the dissolution, in 1551 the rectory (but not the vicarage) was appropriated to the bishopric of Winchester, which still held it in 1682 when the bishop leased the Rectory to the vicar for 21 years at £9.10s. per annum, saving to the vicar the £12.10s. previously paid to him. By 1860 the property had passed into lay hands.[45]

Given that Courton (excluding the part reserved to the town) was granted to the parson of Rye and that subsequently Stanley Abbey became the rectors of the parish — delegating a vicar (with a vicarage) to serve the congregation — it seems logical to suggest that not only the site of present-day Old Vicarage, but also the property owned by Stanley Abbey in 1443 had once formed part of Courton.

It is evident from the wording of the 1348 grant that the part of Courton not given to the parson was intended to become the property of the corporation, with the expectation that a court house would be erected upon it. Part of Courton apparently remained open land in 1443, for the southern boundary of the two tenements granted out by the corporation in that year was described as 'a small lane from *land* called Courton', but already by 1374 plots had been sold off and were being built upon. In that year privately owned shops flanked the eastern and western sides of a plot of land in which

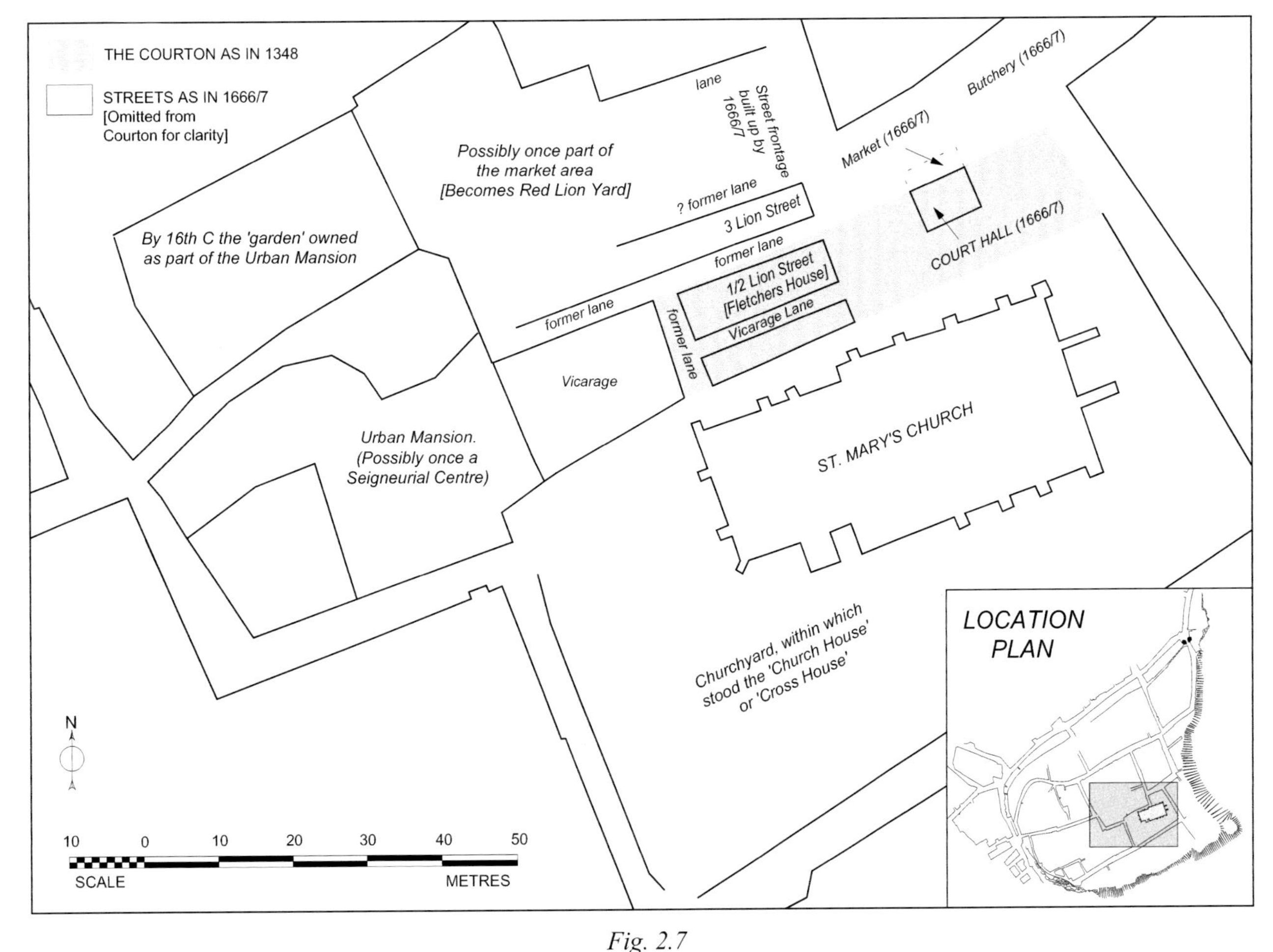

Fig. 2.7
The central area showing location of features mentioned in the text.

Robert Stoneherst of Rye quitclaimed his interests. The plot abutted south onto the cemetery of the church and north onto the 'market place of the lord King'.[46] In 1348 all three of these properties must have formed part of Courton for, as has been suggested, at that date Courton extended the entire length of the churchyard from Pump Street to the Vicarage. What is not clear from the 1374 document is whether the piece of land and the shops which flanked it were on the eastern half of Courton (between Lion Street and Pump Street) or the west part (between Lion Street and the Vicarage).

The generally accepted location for Rye's medieval and Tudor market is Market Street, with the street itself serving as the market place. This was certainly the situation in 1667: Jeake annotates the eastern end of Market Street as 'Butchery' with the western end — in front of and under the Court Hall — as 'Market' (*see* Figure 2.8).[47] Based solely upon this evidence, the three properties mentioned in 1374 should have been on the eastern half of the site, for on the north they abutted the market place. But such a solution is simplistic. Firstly, the 1443 deed by which the corporation granted out two tenements abutting lands of Stanley Abbey and the vicar (and therefore on or near the western end of Courton) gives the eastern abutment as the market place. Secondly, a further grant by the corporation just three years later relating to a piece of empty ground gives its boundaries as the wall of the cemetery on the south and a path from the market place to the cemetery on the west: the deed is endorsed in a 16th-century hand 'in the Vicarage Lane' which — as Jeake shows on his map — extended westwards from Lion Street towards the vicarage.[48] There was a cottage and a piece of land on the east, but on the north was a 'lane [Vicarage Lane] between the premises and the Town Butchery'.[49]

These two documents raise important issues. Not only do they suggest that in the medieval period the market place extended west of Lion Street, but at that time the Butchery was not where Jeake depicts it in 1667, but further west within this (suggested) subsequently enclosed part of the market. In fact, given this, is it safe to assume that the market place as initially laid out included the area known today as Market Street, or is it possible that it expanded into this street only later and remained there, in residual form, when the (assumed) western part became enclosed? Is it coincidence, for instance, that of the early deeds which relate to enclosures upon Courton and which give abutments onto the market place, none have abutments to the Court House, despite the small size of the eastern part of Courton upon which the Court House (for a short time in the late 16th century called the Guildhall and now the Town Hall) stands?

The two deeds quoted above are insufficient evidence upon which to base an argument for a substantial now lost area of market place. Luckily, they are not the only evidence available. One significant piece of data comes from the 1635 Glebe Terrier which, in giving the boundaries of the Vicarage, refers to what was apparently a dog-legged lane extending along the east side and part way along the north side of the Vicarage: it is described as a 'lane giving into the butchery'.[50] In fact the late medieval deeds indicate a complex of lanes and shops in this general area, and although some of these may have been located on the eastern part of the Courton, others were in what is argued to have been the now lost western part of the market place. In 1395, for example, a vacant plot in the market place was described as having a highway (?Lion Street) on its east, the market place on its north and west, and shops (plural) on the south. Eighty years later, in 1476, a property containing shops (again plural) and a small stable was conveyed — it was bounded on the west by another shop, on the north by the market place, on the east by a minor way described as 'a lane leading from the cemetery to the market place', and on the south by 'another lane'.[51]

Although no buildings in this western part of the Courton and market place predate the late 15th century, those which remain confirm the existence of the narrow lanes. Fletchers House (1-2 Lion Street), for instance, is jettied on its southern, eastern and northern sides and stood upon a plot bounded on these three sides by lanes. As already noted, the southern of these was Vicarage Lane, to the south of which was a narrow row of plots (now occupied by 68, 70, 72 Church Square) filling the gap up to the cemetery.[52] The lane on the northern side divided off 3 Lion Street, a structure built end-on to the street, most likely representing the eastern end of another row, probably with either another lane or the open market place to its north. Both these buildings are in the general area described in 1446 as the 'Town Butchery'. It was across the western ends of these 'rows' that the lane flanking the vicarage ran, linking the cemetery to the western part of the market

What the combined documentary and architectural evidence suggests for this area is a gradual replacement during the 14th, 15th and early 16th centuries of temporary market stalls by permanent structures and enclosures, resulting in a complex of small buildings, plots, and narrow lanes colonizing Courton and the (assumed) south-western part of the medieval market place. East Sussex has never been a strong area for markets: the norm during the late medieval and early modern period seems to have been for the markets to shrink in area to such an extent that their sites are hardly detectable within the modern town plan — as indeed is the case at Rye today.[53] The likely general reason for this trend was the increased use of household space for shops, allowing some of the former market functions to become permanently located within properties away from the market centre. This procedure was doubtless accelerated at Rye by the fact that during the late 15th and the 16th centuries the town's second market centre, on the Strand, was rapidly growing in importance at the expense of the general market. As a result, the conjectured colonisation of the market place's western end appears already have been well advanced by the mid 16th century. The decline was doubtless exacerbated subsequently by the town's significant reduction in population which started during the closing decades of the 16th century and persisted throughout the next century.

The deed evidence indicates that during the medieval period the corporation conveyed at least some of the market plots into private hands, often reserving a rent resolute to the corporation. A town rental of 1575 includes five entries for rents on property in the Butchery — one for shops (plural), another for a shop, one for a messuage, and two for tenements, including one with a stable behind it.[54]

As the extract from Jeake's map reproduced in Figure 2.8 shows, the final enclosing of the (conjectured) western part of the open market area was already complete by 1667 and, to judge from the wording of a deed relating to a property in the area, it had probably already come about by 1642.[55] The final demise appears to have been marked by the formation on the residual part of an extensive property later known as 'The Red Lion' (now destroyed). The erection of this building, fronting onto Lion Street, formed a barrier at the western end of Market Street, effectively 'completing' the built-up western frontage of Lion Street. The conjectured former market area became a substantial yard to the rear of the inn.

Despite the fact that by the early 18th century the complex of narrow market lanes had mostly been stopped up for the best part of a century, and that the Butchery (together with most of the butchers) had long moved to the opposite end of Market Street, it may be significant that even in 1723 a slaughter house remained at the rear of 3 Lion Street (then owned by a butcher and occupied by his son) in the area of the former Town Butchery. It may also be significant that Fletchers House immediately to its south was also owned by the same butcher. The slaughter house was at that date reached via a right-of-way through Red Lion Yard.[56] Perhaps equally relevant to the former market-place site are the four houses which in 1860 extended back at right angles to the rear of 4-6 Lion Street, along the northern side of Red Lion Yard.[57] Were these the last vestiges of properties which once faced onto the old open market?

Whilst both the importance of the market relative to the economy of the town and variations in the town's wealth and population levels must have had an inevitable influence on the size and character of the market area, they were not the only defining factors. As has already been discussed, part of what became the market area was initially an open area for the holding of courts, and this continues to be the site of the town administration up to the present day. Now much depleted in their scope, in the past these administrative functions were many and varied. They included courts dealing with administration (including the annual election of officials) and law (both civil and criminal). Areas were set aside for the regulation of the market and the collecting of market tolls, as well as regulation of the harbour and the collection of customs. The administrative buildings incorporated other necessities too, such as the safe

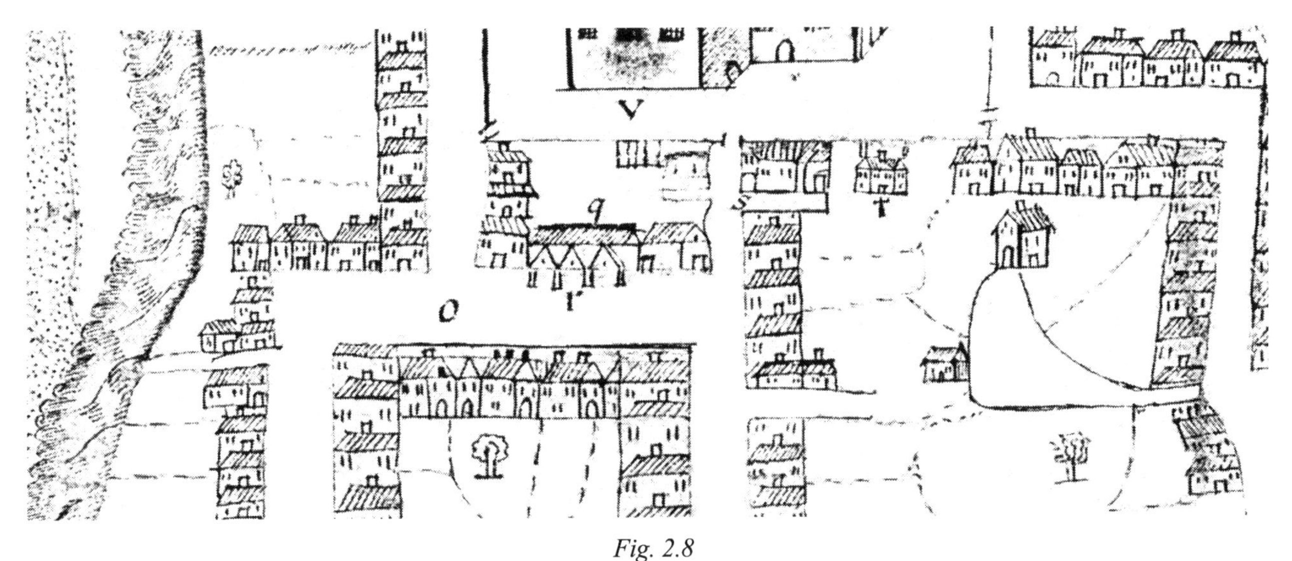

Fig. 2.8
Extract from the 1728 copy of Jeake's town map, dated 1667 [ESRO RYE 132/15]. South is to the top of the picture. [o = Butchery, q = Court Hall, r = Market, s = Vicarage Lane, t = Vicarage ho., v = Church.]

custody of the town's muniments.

The town's administration in general has been discussed in detail by others.[58] What is of concern here are the spaces and buildings required to fulfil these varied activities. There is a tendency to regard these as unchanging — carried out on the same site(s), within the same building(s) over long periods of time. This assumption is encouraged by the fact that those documents which mention both the activities and the relevant sites/buildings do not describe form and location — they were written by, and intended for, people who knew the circumstances well. As a result, there has been a tendency in the past for local antiquarians to assume stability without question.

Some activities, such as the regulation of the harbour and the collection of customs, were carried out away from the central area, down by the Strand and Fishmarket, and thus the facilities required for these will be considered later. The locations of some other activities are known to have migrated over time (and in this respect it is possible that some of those associated with the harbour migrated to Strand from East Strand after the latter's destruction). An example of migration is the criminal court and town goal. From at least 1507 (and perhaps from the 1480s or a little before) Baddings Tower *otherwise* Ypres Tower, located in the south-eastern corner of the town, was used for this purpose. This had also been the case in the 14th and early 15th centuries, prior to its sale by the corporation in 1430 to a private individual, John de Iprys, who put it to domestic use (*see* Chapter 3). Thus, during the middle years of the 15th century both the criminal courts and the prison must have been located elsewhere within the town, most likely within the court hall erected on Courton.[59]

The date at which the first court hall was built on Courton is unclear: the wording in the 1348 document implies that it did not exist at that date, but was nonetheless anticipated. It is possible that at this early date Ypres Tower served not only in criminal cases but also as a civil court hall and administrative centre, just as is likely to have been the case with the court hall on Courton subsequently. Courton had been Fécamp property and, from 1247, Crown property. An undated early 14th-century rental of the town (Vidler says *c.*1317) describes it as a *placea* (open space, site, plot, or square) and shows it at that date farmed to the king's bailiff, Robert Paulyn, at a rent of 5 shillings.[60] This open space was the location for the open-air hundred courts and, probably therefore, also the annual election of the mayor. The earliest extant Customal (mid 15th century) indicates that by then the mayoring took place in open hundred at a cross in the churchyard,[61] but, as has already been demonstrated, by then Courton had been enclosed and partly sold off by the corporation, and was part built over. This action by the corporation would (arguably) have obliged the hundred courts to transfer into the adjacent churchyard.

The court hall on the Courton was reconstructed in 1514/15 and at the same date the accounts include repairs to the stairs and roof of 'the cross' — evidently a two-storeyed building — to work on 'the newe crosse', including four locks for the doors (plural) and 'for 12 days working in making the partition of the crosse in the market place'.[62] Evidently these entries relate to more than one building, including at least two buildings called crosses, but how many is unclear. One possibility is that the new building referred to in 1514/15 was a combined structure and had the court hall on the first floor with the market area beneath. If so, the whole building may have been known as the 'newe crosse' and the reference to the new court house may simply have referred to its upper storey. This could also explain the wording of the entry relating to the [old] cross in the market place — it was being partitioned to suit new uses. Both Vidler and Mayhew concluded that the Court Hall and the Market Cross were different buildings, but Vidler goes further and specifically states that in 1742 the separate buildings called the old court hall and the market place were pulled down to make way for the new town hall and that the material from them were sold to the mayor for £38 10s 0d.[63] If this last comment of Vidler's is correct, why is only one building — the court hall — shown in the copy of the Jeake map? It seems to be depicted with an open arcade towards the street on the ground floor and flanked on east and west by other buildings (*see* Figure 2.8, 'q' and 'r') though an alternative interpretation is that the open-fronted part represents a separate structure standing in the street, in front of the Court Hall.

Unlike the Butchery, there are no known reasons for suggesting that, once built, the court hall moved location — the reconstruction in 1514/15 appears to have been upon the original site, as was certainly the case in 1742, though the 1742 rebuild was larger than its predecessor, extending over property to the west. There is, on the other hand, evidence to indicate that some of the uses to which the court hall was put changed over time. Whilst the building seems to have functioned as a civil administrative centre and court throughout its life, and was where all but specified muniments of the corporation were housed, in a chest, in 1590,[64] it seems to have lost its role as a court house for criminal cases, as too its role as a prison. That function moved, or perhaps returned, to Ypres Tower. On the other hand, the evidence presented above suggests that it probably gained a role as the location for the provisions market which, according to Mayhew, had previously been held 'by the market cross, in the Butchery', *ie* in the Town Butchery, further west.[65] The situation regarding the various crosses is further muddied by a deed of 1529 in which Robert Oxenbridge quitclaimed to the corporation 'land with the house called Highcross at the Woolwarehouse (*canisterio*)' which had belonged to his father, Thomas. According to one source, this was located in the Flesh Market, though the deed is endorsed 'Court hall'.[66] Thus far, therefore, early 16th-century references are known to buildings called 'the cross', 'the newe crosse', 'the cross in the market place' and 'the High Cross at the Woolwarehouse'. To these must be added yet another; that which stood within the churchyard — apparently on the south side of the church — where the mayoring took place. This is the cross which is referred to by Vidler and others (without giving reasons) as the 'Saxon Cross', though if this is what it was, by the 16th century it too had developed into a two-storeyed structure.[67]

It is highly unlikely that early 16th-century Rye contained five buildings known as crosses in the vicinity of the parish church and market, though three such structures do seem likely. Two of these, it is argued, had fulfilled the same function, with one becoming redundant in 1514/15 when the other was rebuilt, perhaps merged with the court hall. When in 1567 the brick and timber-framed building in the churchyard was repaired it was described as 'the Church House in the churchyard' though the entry is endorsed 'cross house'. Its demolition was ordered in July 1603, by which date the structure had become 'so ruinous that the same is ready to fall down, and ... has become so odious, loathsome and noisome, that no person is able to endure or come near the place'.[68]

As will be clear from the above, there is little firm evidence upon which to base a reliable detailed interpretation of the market area and associated public buildings, but that which exists is sufficient to call seriously into doubt the notion of stability and lack of development in the area during the late medieval and Tudor periods. These likely modifications to the townscape are of importance when considering the final challenge relating to the development of this central area — why at a relatively early date (and certainly by *c.*1500) was the central of the town's three main streets apparently severed into two separate parts (Market Street and Mermaid Street) thereby seriously disrupting east-west communications across the central part of town?

The effect of this apparent modification was to divert the street southwards around a small block of properties which included the vicarage and what in the early 16th century — and perhaps for long before — was a substantial urban mansion with letting units against the street. It was held by Sir John Shurley, king's bailiff of Rye from before 1501 until 1524. What appears to have been the stopped-off remains of the old street, extending eastwards from West Street though a gatehouse at a point directly opposite the top of Mermaid Street, still survived as a private access road leading to the mansion until 1695 when this part of the property was sold off separately.[69] The lane (but not the gatehouse) is shown clearly on the Jeake map of 1667 (*see* Figures 2.7 and 2.8).

It would be wrong to imply that the mechanism by which the (assumed) diversion was achieved is understood. A likelihood is that it in some way relates to the acquisition by the mansion's owner of what was (or became) 'amenity land' on the opposite (northern) side of the (assumed) old street alignment, and his desire to consolidate both parts into one. The history of the mansion prior to Shurley's 'ownership' is uncertain: it is possible Shurley inherited it from his father-in-law, John Grauntford, who was likewise at one time bailiff of the town. Given the mansion's location close to the church, market, and the monarch's open-air court (the Courton), it is even possible that the mansion was once Crown demesne, and that, as such, it served as the official home/headquarters of the bailiff on those common occasions when the town was farmed out. This remains speculation, as too does a second possibility — that the 'amenity land' which was laid into the mansion was once part of the market place, effectively extending the market along the entire northern side of the 'lost' section of street, from Lion Street to West Street. If there is any merit in these possibilities — and they have much to commend them — it would have made the task of extinguishing part of an important existing town-centre street and the acquisition of an unwanted area of market place much less difficult.

It has to be accepted that there is yet another possible interpretation regarding the central street and market area, a possibility which, if correct, has implications for the town's initial layout. It is normally assumed that the central street originally extended through, linking Market Street to Mermaid Street. But it is possible that this assumption is incorrect and that the two streets were not originally linked, at least, not by a public thoroughfare. In this alternative hypothesis both the mansion and the ground to its north represent the urban centre of the seigneurial lord — initially Fécamp Abbey and subsequently the King — with the church, Courton and market deliberately clustered at its eastern gate. As far as is known, there is no evidence which can be cited in support of this hypothesis, yet it has a strong logic and deserves serious future consideration.

The Waterfront – Strand, Fishmarket and The Wishe

The second and, from an economic point of view, more important of Rye's late medieval and early modern *foci* was the extra-mural area to the west and northwest of the town. Here, on the Strand, was the trading heart

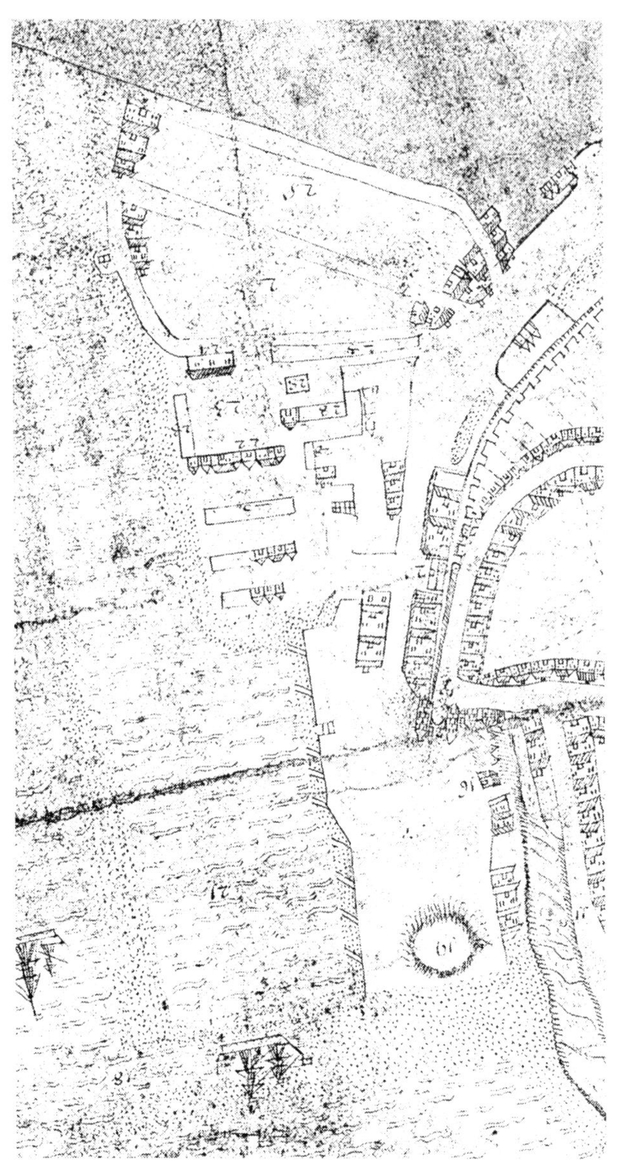

Fig. 2.9
Extract from Jeake's town map (1667, copied 1728) [ESRO RYE 132/15]. The plan is rotated with north to the top to allow ease of comparison with Figure 2.10.

of the community and here too, just to the north, was the second and more important of Rye's two markets — the Fishmarket. Further north still, stretching along the peninsula of low-lying land which had formed between the sea wall protecting St. Mary's Marsh and the tidal edge of the Tillingham, grew up the suburb of Wishe (not to be confused with other local areas which incorporated within their name the element 'wishe').[70] On account of its low-lying nature — all of it lies at less than 4.5 metres (14 feet 9 inches) above O.D. — Wishe tended to be an unhealthy area and as a result was largely occupied in the 16th and early 17th centuries by the

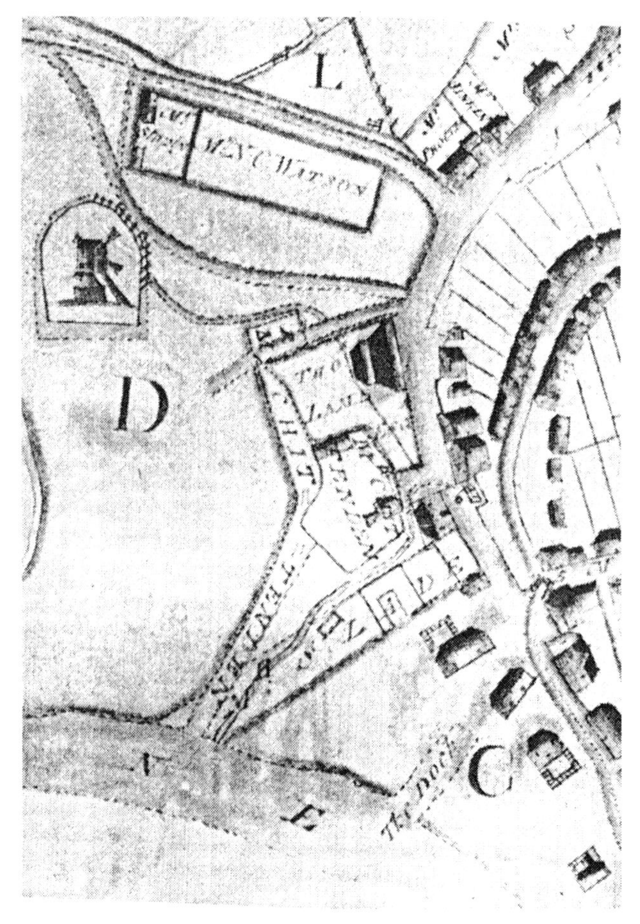

Fig. 2.10
Extract from town plan of 1771 showing the same area as in Figure 2.9. [© Rye Castle Museum]

urban poor. As population decreased after *c.*1600 the area became all but abandoned and was not re-colonized until the 19th century. It is now Ferry Road, Alma Place and Cyprus Place.

This former waterfront area of the town — Strand, Fishmarket and Wishe — is the part of Rye which has altered most. Some of the changes are historic, including gradual, but relentless land reclamation, pushing ever further out into the estuary. Others, very recent, include the cutting of the present A259 across the Fishmarket and Strand in the 1960s and the subsequent redevelopment of much of the Fishmarket area. Tragically, no serious archaeological investigations were undertaken when these works were carried out.[71]

As a result of this short-sightedness, almost all information regarding the riverside relies upon documentary sources. As with the core area of town, the best starting points for interpreting the development of the individual areas are the town plans of 1667 and 1771 (Figures 2.9 and 2.10). Evidence from deeds and accounts, augmented by relatively small-scale late 16th-century pictorial maps of the area (such as that by

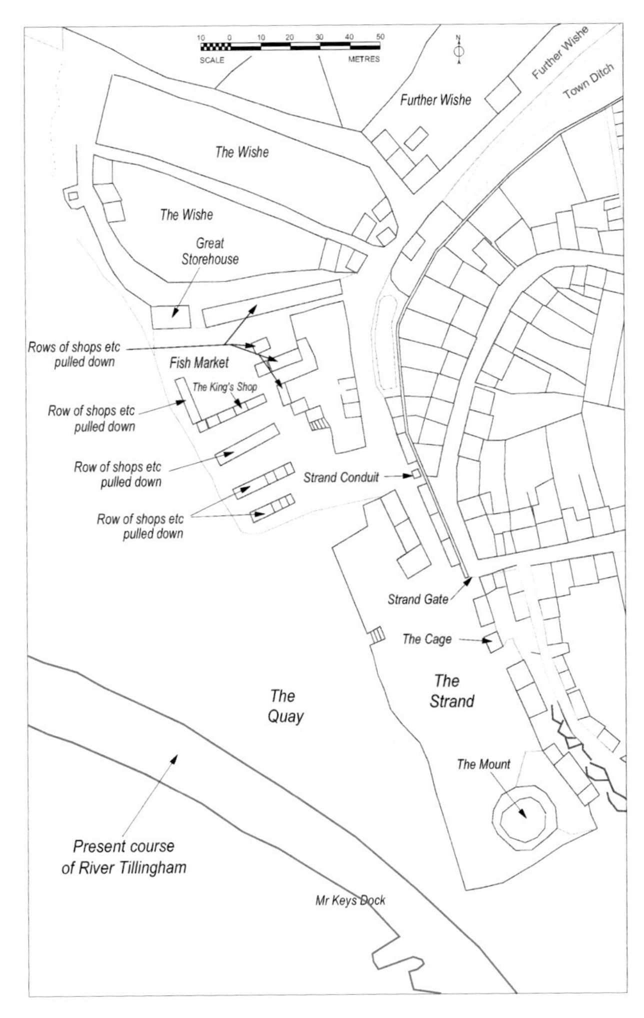

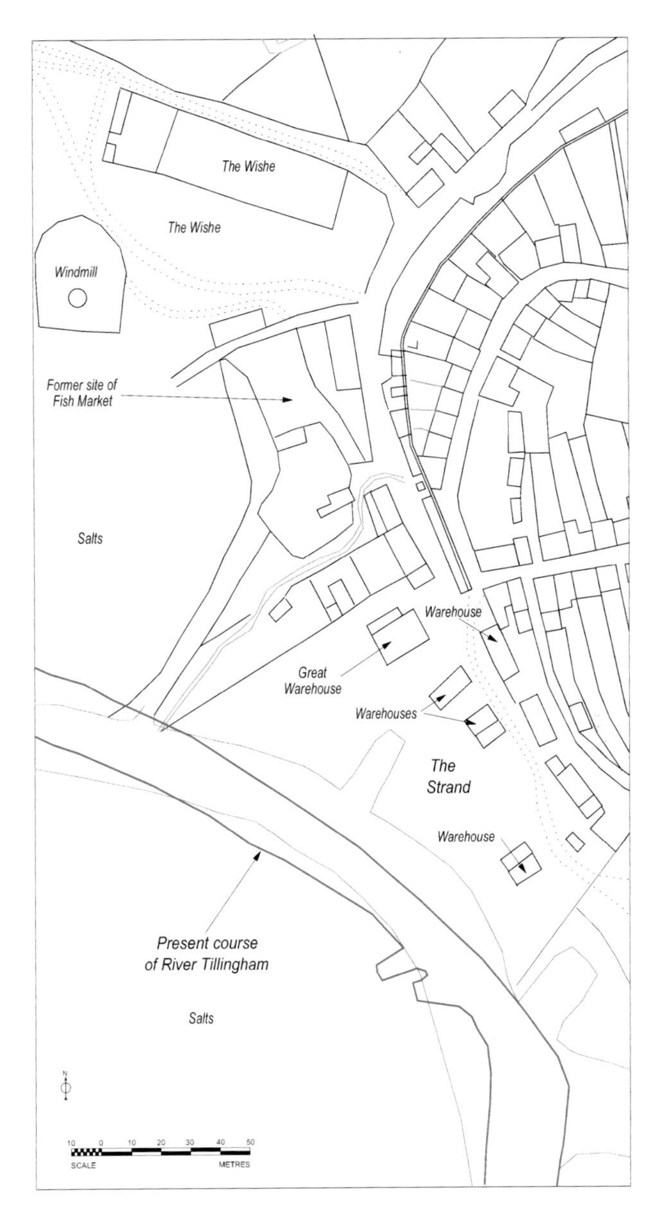

Figs. 2.11 (above) and 2.12 (right)
Details shown on Jeake's map of 1667 (above) and town plan of 1771 (right) redrawn to scale for ease of comparison. Course of modern river shown red.

Prowze produced in 1572, for which *see* Figure 2.19) allow some useful deductions to be made regarding each of the three areas as they existed in the 15th and 16th centuries.

The Strand (also known as The Quay)

The Jeake map shows the Strand as an open, rectangular area of land which was considerably narrower than today — as Figure 2.11 illustrates, the river wall now runs at an angle to the earlier alignment and, particularly at its northern end, is much further west. At this northern end the townward side of the Strand was flanked by the town wall, whilst the rest was bounded by West Cliff otherwise Baldwins Cliff. Strand Gate, once known as 'South Gate' or 'Water Gate', separated these two parts and faced south — the gate is clearly shown in Figure 2.14. It gave direct access from Strand to High Street and, via a ninety-degree turn, to Mermaid Street. Jeake shows a small defensive fort called 'The Mount' (otherwise known as 'The Platform') adjacent to the shelving foreshore at the southern end of Strand. For further discussion of Strand Gate and The Mount *see* Chapter 3.

A little to the south of Strand Gate, under West Cliff, a small isolated building is marked as 'The Cage' ('16' in Figure 2.14). This was a minor lock-up used to exhibit townsfolk — particularly women — for behavioural offences. It had existed in this area from at least the 16th century and is specifically mentioned in a deed of 1587. Close by were the ducking stool and 'collar', but in the 16th century other means of punishment, such as the pillory, stocks and whipping post, were located in the town-centre market place. However, already by 1587 the stocks had been moved down to 'the town's house' near the cage.[72] Further

Fig. 2.13
Aerial photograph of c.1940 showing The Strand viewed from the south prior to construction of the new relief road. The bridge taking the A259 over the River Tillingham is visible top left. Compare this view with the plans shown in Figures 2.11 and 2.12.

south on this eastern side of Strand, extending up to the southern boundary, Jeake shows a number of houses built hard under the cliff, and these (or rather their plots) are referred to in grants of 1557, 1561, 1565, 1587, 1599 and 1609. Indeed, under the head of 'Strandgate Ward', the 1576 town sesse makes specific mention of 'the new buildings without the said [Strand] gate, under the west cliff'.[73]

The western, seaward side of Strand is delineated in the Jeake plan by a quay wall, a revetment which the Chamberlains accounts indicate was constructed part in timber and part stone. Part way along its length (roughly opposite Strand Gate) was incorporated an in-set flight of steps leading down to the sea bed. Groynes (built 1545) projected westwards out into the channel from the southern end of the quay, not only protected the inner basin of the harbour (called 'The Key' in 1667) but also a dock, rather confusingly known at that time as 'Mr Key's Dock' after the merchant of that name whose property it was. By 1701 the dock was merely called 'Keys Dock'.[74] Houses are depicted to the north of Strand Gate, standing against the outer face of the town wall. These fronted on to the street now known as 'Wishe Ward', which at this point intruded into the north-western corner of Strand, being divided from it to south and west by a row of houses.

By 1771 the Strand had pushed further westwards, giving the river its (approximate) present alignment (*see* Figure 2.12) with a narrow dock or 'float' extending eastwards, at right angles to the river, up to the approximate line of the mid 17th-century quayside. By this time the central part of the row of houses between Strand and Wishe Ward appears to have been demolished and The Mount at the southern end of Strand had been removed. Perhaps the most marked difference which had occurred over the ensuing century, however, was the construction of five warehouses on the eastern edge of the Strand — four are shown as being isolated freestanding structures and one, at the foot of West Cliff, backed on to the cliff itself. The southernmost of the isolated buildings occupies the site of The Mount, whilst the northernmost — The Great Warehouse — stands in line with the bottom of Mermaid Street. The latter is a substantial building with an 'M' roof, constructed by the

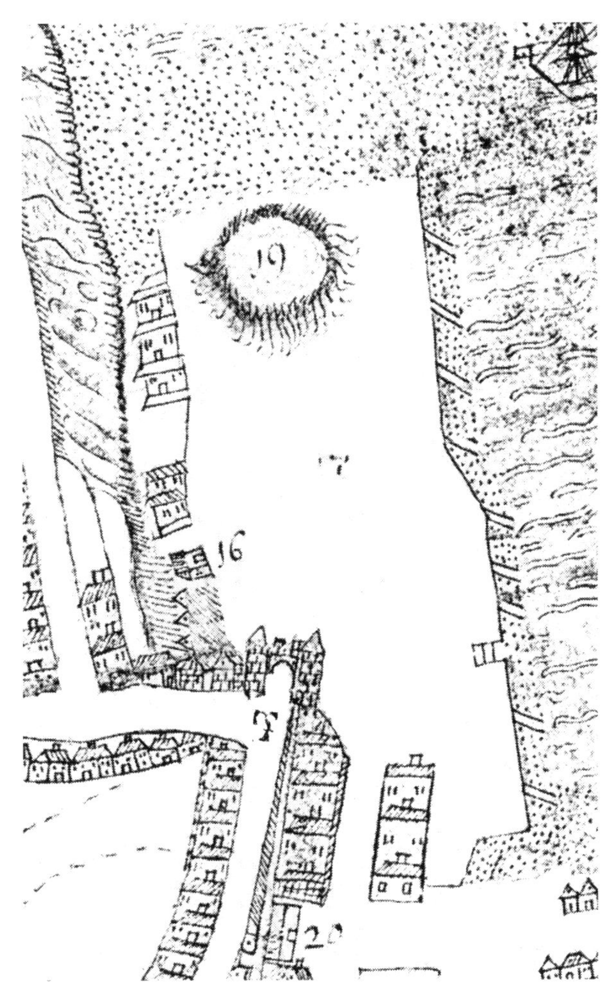

Fig. 2.14
Extract from the 1728 copy of Jeake's town map, dated 1667 [ESRO RYE 132/15]. The plan is reproduced here to the orientation drawn, with south at the top. [16 = The Cage, 17 = Strand, 18 = Mr Key's Dock, 19 = The Mount, 20 = Strand Conduit].

Fig. 2.15
The Great Warehouse (c. 1736) viewed from the east in the early 20th century.

Fig. 2.16
Warehouse which formerly stood beneath West Cliff., viewed from the north-west with Borough Arms (formerly The London Trader) elevated on the town wall to the left.

corporation *c.*1736 (Figure 2.15; for location *see* Figure 2.12). It seems to have been the earliest of the Strand warehouses. Even so, to judge from a photograph of a warehouse (Figure 2.16) which stood against West Cliff, between Strand Gate and The Cage, taken prior to its demolition, this building too seems to have been of similar date.[75]

The construction of these buildings — preempted by Samuel Jeake the younger with his storehouse built in Mermaid Street in 1689 and by Thomas Fagg when he obtained land to the south of Keys Dock, against Watchbell Cliff, for the construction of storehouses and buildings — marks Rye's emergence from a long period of economic depression.[76] These are, as far as is known, the first storehouses/warehouses ever built upon this southern part of the Strand, though it should be stressed that a similar building (or buildings) had existed in the 16th century further north, near the Fishmarket (*see* below). This, therefore, seems to reflect a change in focus, brought about by the abandonment of the Fishmarket area after 1667 (*see* below). It should not, however, be assumed that no early buildings existed on this southern part of the Strand: in 1545 'the old shops' in this area were pulled down to make room for 'a railed way from Strand Gate' built as part of defences being erected.[77]

Fishmarket (regarded as part of the Strand in the 16th century)

In his map Jeake makes a clear distinction between the open quayside which he calls 'Strand' and the area further north which he refers to as 'Fish Market'. The Strand lay to the south of Strand

Conduit (one of the town's water supplies) whilst the Fish Market with its associated rows of shops lay to the north. The two areas were separated from one another by a dock-like inlet, perhaps the 'common dok' mentioned in a deed of 1489.[78] At the eastern end the two areas were linked by the street which is today called Wishe Ward. The northern boundary of the Fishmarket area was a street which, in its present enlarged and extended form, is Wish Street. This separated the Fishmarket from the northernmost of the three areas, labelled by Jeake as 'The Wishe'.

Deeds of the late 15th and early 16th centuries make clear that at that time the Strand was considered to extend further north than indicated by Jeake and was deemed to include the Fishmarket and the adjacent rows of shops. Although most of the buildings in this area are referred to in documents of the time as 'shops', the term had a much broader usage than now — it meant shop/workshop/storage area *etc* — and some (perhaps most) of the shops included above them separately occupied lofts and garrets. Some of these lofts were used as domestic accommodation and subsequently a number of the buildings were converted into rows of tenements (*see* below).

Shops were being built at the Strand from at least 1448 when the town accounts begin, though these could have been on that part of the Strand to the south of this area.[79] However, already in the mid 1480s the corporation were building shops by the quayside in this part of the Strand, whilst deeds from that time onwards (particularly the period 1506-1518) show that a number of plots in this part of the Strand were granted out by the corporation for the construction of similar buildings.[80]

These shops were commonly referred to in the plural. That this is no accident of grammar is confirmed by other sources. For example, the strand-side plot of William Mede contained four shops when he died in 1543, whilst that of John Fletcher accommodated eight at his death just two years later.[81] So many such buildings were being newly erected during the closing years of the 15th and opening years of the 16th centuries that this part of the Strand must previously have been either undeveloped open ground or had very few structures upon it.

Construction of new shops was not confined to this initial flurry. In 1544 the corporation erected two new rows of such buildings for letting, and others were put up in 1551.[82] The two rows were still in corporation ownership in the 1570s. One contained 5 shops, each rented out at 16 shillings, over which were 9 lofts separately rented at 8 shillings, a loft and 'garret on the loft' rented at 16 shillings and a further garret for which no rent is stated. The configuration within the second row was similar, but with an additional shop (?half the size) at 8 shillings and an additional loft and garret (?over the extra shop) at 6 shillings.[83] The impression given is that over each shop were two lofts which, given their smaller rental value, were probably each half the size of the shops, with a garret over one loft (?the central one). The extra shop, loft, and garret in the second row may have been an addition.

By the 1570s the other properties on the Strand were privately owned, but nonetheless owed a rent to the corporation. The rent roll includes five persons who each paid for an individual shop, nine persons paying for shops (plural), one entry for a stable at the Strand, and

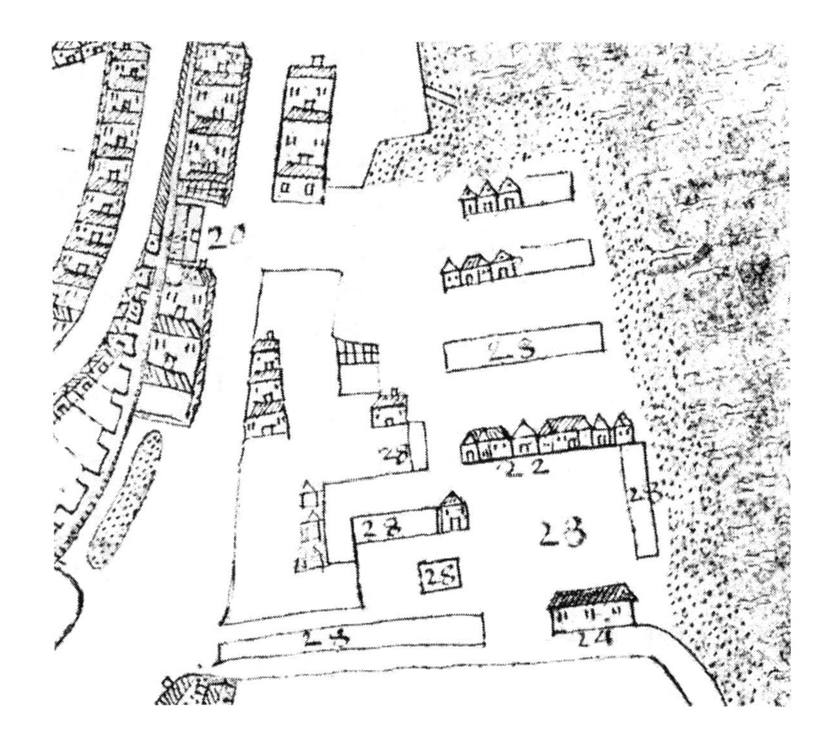

Fig. 2.17
Extract from the 1728 copy of Jeake's town map, dated 1667 [ESRO RYE 132/15]. The plan is reproduced here to the orientation as drawn, with south at the top. [20 = Strand Conduit, 22 = The King's Shop, 23 = Fish Market, 24 = Great Storehouse, 28 = Rows of shops etc pulled down].

another for a privately owned storehouse (perhaps that for which deeds survive). Further entries were for 'ground' and 'tenements' 'at the Strand on the New Quay' and an entry for a 'void piece of ground at the Strand adjoining to the Customs House'. There are other entries for shops in the rental for which the locations are not given — they could have been on the Strand, or at the Butchery in the town centre, or elsewhere.[84]

As the enlargement of Jeake map in Figure 2.17 shows, not only the town's shops but many of the others too were arranged in detached rows. Two of these rows flanked the southern and western sides of the Fishmarket itself. Incorporated within the southern of these was 'the King's Shop', out of which the royal purveyor of fish operated.[85]

In addition to their shops, the corporation owned other infrastructure upon the Strand. For example, the customs office was kept in a building by the quayside — no doubt the Customs House mentioned in the 1570s rentals. In 1587 the town leased part of it out, reserving the 'room wherein the searcher's office is kept' and 'the chamber wherein the office of the Custom House is now kept'. There was a further chamber at the northwest end which was already let to Richard Wowan. The part to be leased was described as being the garret over all the aforesaid rooms, the cellars and the parlour at the northwest end, together with the backside. This gives some indication of the size of the building.[86] Subsequently the customs office was moved elsewhere and in 1602 the building was sold by the corporation into private hands. It was described at that time as a 'tenement called the Customs House, with two chambers or lofts, at the Strand ... abutting south and west on the quay and the channel', and upon tenements (specified) to east and north.[87] Other official buildings in the same area included woodhouses (mentioned in 1545 and used in association with the town's Wealden wood trade) and the town's storehouse (No. 24 — the Great Storehouse' — in Figure 2.17). This latter structure was built in 1555 in the north-western corner of the Strand, on a site north of the Fishmarket and next to the quay. It cost just under £100 and had iron grates set in brick window surrounds, heavy wooden doors, lead gutters, tiled roof, and stone paving to its floors and courts. A gallery was incorporated, as too was a weigh beam. A quay-side crane (modelled upon that at Sandwich) was added adjoining the storehouse the following year, and six years later this was supplemented by a second.[88]

In addition to buildings, the corporation put considerable investment into The Strand itself. A new quay had already been built in the area in 1480. In 1551 and 1569 new jetties were erected, followed in 1571 by a stone quay 90 feet (27.4 metres) long and 12 feet (3.65 metres) high, and a further timber quay just three years later. Whether these were within the southern part of the Strand or in the area near the Fishmarket is unclear, but the presence of the cranes in the latter area, near the Town Storehouse, make it likely that at least one was in the latter area. References in the 1575/6 (and subsequent) town rentals to 'tenements on the New Quay' and 'ground on the New Quay' (both of which commanded high rents) imply that the works involved the reclamation of ground, or at least the conversion of existing ground (perhaps foreshore or salt marsh) to commercial use.[89] Away from the quayside itself, on the eastern edge of the Strand, in 1573 the corporation conveyed to the newly formed fishermans' guild a piece of land 54 feet (16.5 metres) long 'under the town wall at the Strand' for them to lay their masts.[90]

Rapid decline of the northern Strand area in the 1590s reflects economic depression suffered by the town at the same period. From 1592 onwards half the corporation tenants of the warehouses and shops on the Strand defaulted on their rents.[91] Poor investment in

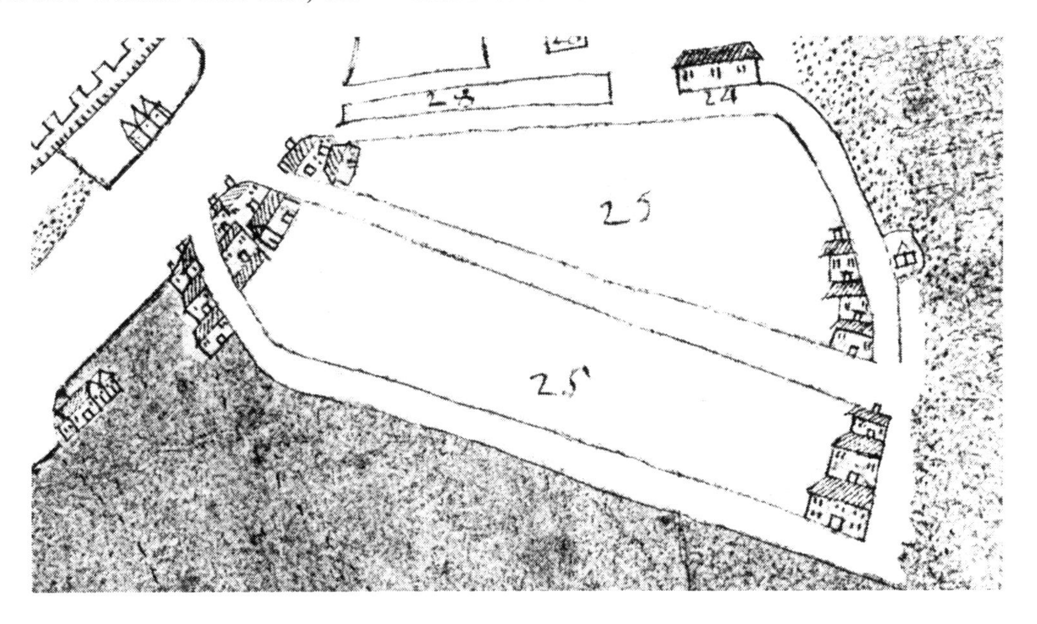

Fig. 2.18 Extract from the 1728 copy of Jeake's map, dated 1667 [ESRO RYE 132/15]. The plan is reproduced here to the orientation as drawn, with south at the top. [25 = The Wishe].

Fig. 2.19
Detail from map prepared by Prowze in 1572 viewed from the north (i.e. south to the top of the picture). The extract shows the quay (centre right) with the Fishmarket and Wishe Suburb at the bottom of the picture, below and to the left of the quay. Note the main part of the town (top left) clustering within the town walls. [TNA MPF 1/212]

ambitious, ill-conceived harbour improvements throughout the 1590s brought the corporation to near bankruptcy. Their solution to their problems was the sale of Town property during the period 1600-1602. This included the two rows of shops at the Strand (conveyed in 1602 and by 1619 described as '32 cottages called the Fish Shoppes'), the town's storehouse there (also conveyed 1602 and by 1619 described as a 'messuage called Townes Store House') and (as already noted above) the Customs house.[92] The Store House (by then called the 'Great Storehouse') was still standing in 1667, as too were the shops on the southern side of the Fishmarket and a few other isolated shops, but many of the building had been demolished: Jeake specifically marks six plots (some very long) as 'Rows of Shops _ _ &c Pulled Down'[93] Two other rows appear to be shown as truncated. As Figures 2.10 and 2.12 show, by 1771 the area had been all but abandoned with only one or two isolated buildings remaining.

Wishe Suburb

The third and northernmost of the three linked extra-mural 'areas' west of the town is assumed to represent estuary reclamation. Its location, on the estuary side of the sea wall protecting St. Mary's Marsh (which wall was already in place by 1428) suggests that it represents reclamation subsequent to the inning of St.

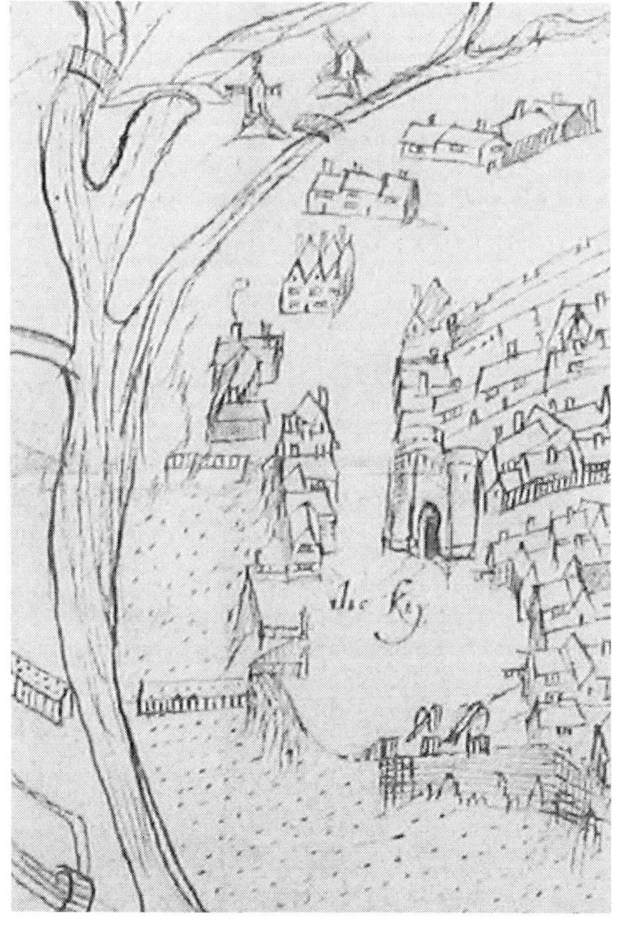

Fig. 2.20
Detail from 16th-century plan showing with the Fishmarket and Wish Suburb beyond. [TNA MPF 1/3]

Mary's Marsh. The wall itself became utilized as a road leading to the west ferry, forming the north-eastern perimeter of The Wishe.

The name 'wishe' suggests that initially this was meadow. By 1489 there was at least one house in the area — it is the subject of a conveyance of that year when it was separated from its adjacent lands, reserving a right of way from the street to the house, across the retained lands. The wording of the deed suggests that the southern end of Wishe may already by that time have been taken over as an extension to the Strand, for the property is described as being 'at the Wisshe at the Strond'. The southern abutment is given as thc 'Common Dok'.[94] Both parties to the deed were to be responsible for repairing their parts of the sea wall.

By 1667 there were three roads crossing The Wishe, radiating out from the road which skirted beneath the town wall (Figure 2.18). Roads still follow these alignments: Ferry Road follows the line of the northern sea wall, Cyprus Place/Alma Place crosses the centre, and Wish Street defines the southern boundary, against the Fishmarket. A further road, located hard against the foreshore and no longer extant, is depicted curving northward from the end of present day Wish Street to join the end of Cyprus Place, and this appears to extend through to Ferry Road, but without a defined edge against the foreshore, so perhaps at this point it was only a footway. A small group of houses are depicted clustered along the landward side of the foreshore road, with a further cluster at the opposite end, near the town wall, but in 1667 the rest of The Wishe is shown deserted. Most of the houses shown had been destroyed by 1771 (*compare* Figures 2.9 and 2.10).

Despite the picture painted by the town maps of 1667 and 1771, in the 16th century Wishe was a populous, though poor suburb. Prowze shows houses and streets occupying this area in his 1572 map, and even shows further houses extending some distance eastwards from present-day Ferry Road, opposite the town ditch (Figure 2.19). These latter are probably the 15 houses built on the edge of St. Mary's Marsh since 1555 which were threatened by high tides following breaches in the sea walls in 1571[95] Other late 16th-century small-scale maps, such as that reproduced in Figure 2.20, illustrate a similar picture, whilst in 1583 no fewer than 27 of the inhabitants of Wishe Ward were presented for throwing their filth into the 'Highway that goes to the ferryway (*i.e.* Ferry Road). In the 1570s Watchbell Ward was described as extending 'through the Fish market, the old wishe on both sides the same street, with all the new buildings along the town dyke.[96]

Even the tidal land beyond the sea defences which protected The Wishe was used: in 1567 the corporation leased out to a shipwright for 99 years an area of 'vacant ground, 60 feet (18.3 metres) by 60 feet (18.3 metres), 'now drowned by salt water in the Wishe'. The 'seawall of the Wishe' lay to the east with [assumed tidally drowned] town land to the north, south and west. A proviso was made that if the lease was assigned to anybody other than a shipwright a licence would be needed. Perhaps not surprisingly, the ground to the north was likewise leased to a shipwright.[97]

In fact, it seems likely that ship building and ship breaking had been carried on here for some time, for in 1963 the remains of two substantial vessels (one carvel built) were found at the western end of Cyprus Place, 84-90 feet (25.6-27.4 metres) from Ferry Road. The vessels were encountered at a depth of 0.6 metres and 2.15 metres (2 feet and 7 feet) below O.D. respectively, buried deep below the road surface. Another vessel (or perhaps part of the same vessels) had been discovered in the same area a hundred years earlier, in 1866.[98] Clearly, when the vessels were left there the road (and presumably the houses shown standing by the road in the Jeake 1667 plan) did not exist. The ages of the ships could not be ascertained, though the use of carvel construction suggests a date subsequent to the late 14th/early 15th century.[99]

Landing facilities on the east of the town

Despite the fact that from at least the late 14th century Rye's main quay had been at The Strand on the western side of town, some waterborne traffic evidently continued to use the 'waterfront' beyond the Landgate suburb, beside the land link from Playden, even after destruction of the East Strand and *portum maris* on this side of the town. An idea of the activities carried on in this vicinity in the mid 17th century is given by a drawing of that period depicting the town viewed from near the end of Saltcote Street in Playden (*see* Figure 2.21). It shows the tide partially out, revealing the edge of the mudflats adjacent to the suburb and land link. A cluster of small single-masted sailing ships are shown moored at the end of the Barum Rocks, which jut out into the estuary from the Landgate cliffs, with two other vessels close by, in the bay. The shore in the foreground of the picture is the end of a sand spit, marking the point from which the Saltcote Ferry crossed to East Guildeford on the other side of the Rother: a similar 17th-century view by an unknown artist shows a rowing boat docking at this point — perhaps it was the ferry boat!

There is no guarantee that the vessels depicted in this and the other illustration are an accurate representation, but these are not the only sources to indicate waterborne commerce in this area. Why else, for instance, would a wool warehouse be built beneath the Landgate cliffs in 1674! In his book 'A Maritime History of Rye' John Collard notes that 'Another form of harbour revenue was derived from charging fishing vessels for using a dock called The Graven Place or Gravel Ground on the bank of the Rother not far from Land Gate. The charge in 1706 for cleaning or caulking a vessel at this place was one shilling per tide and in the same year receipts and payments of expenses balanced out at £124.19s.0d.'.[100] Nor was this use of the Landgate waterfront only a 17th-century and later phenomenon — in 1486 a new jetty 'outside the Landgate' was completed at an outlay to the town of £12.7s.2d.[101] Prowze's map of the harbour made in 1572 shows the navigable channels, and thus shows the course of the Rother as being some distance from the shore at Landgate (*see* Figure 1.5). Like the other areas of shingle, mud flats and sands, the flats between the Rother and the Landgate suburb and land link are coloured brown. Two small boats, five people and three barrels stand on the flats in this area, which is annotated 'The sand at the gutte where the ships boats fetch [..] across'. The meaning is clear — it is where boats ferry

Fig. 2.21
Drawing of Rye viewed from the north-east, from Point Hill, by Jacob Esselens (1626-1687)
[© Reproduction by permission of the Syndics of the Fitzwilliam Museum, Cambridge. Accession Number: PD.298-1963]

goods and people from ships anchored further out in the Rother channel.

In the 17th century the area of mudflats to the south of the Barum Rocks was evidently used to lay up vessels, for in 1677 it was agreed that mooring posts should be placed between the Gungarden and Barum Rocks for the convenience of vessels laid up during the winter. In the 18th century the Gungarden Rocks area became a centre for the Rye fishermen and their boats, leading to the disuse of the old Fishmarket area on the Strand, which had been abandoned by 1771 when the new town plan was prepared.

HEALTH AND HYGIENE

Street Paving and lighting [102]

Already by the 16th century householders were responsible for paving the section of street outside their individual tenements and were presented if they did not do so. The corporation, on the other hand, were responsible for maintaining those sections of street away from houses. Thus, it was the town who, at the townsfolk's expense, maintained the Kings Highway and its land link which led into town from Playden to Landgate, as well as the Market Place and The Strand. In 1512 and 1514, for instance, the town's expenditure includes payments for paving the market, as well as 'gravelling' the way at the Strand. They also made payments for gathering stones from beneath the cliff in order that the 'pavers of London' could pave a street on the Strand. The latter sounds very much like the collection of water-worn cobbles from the foreshore. Even today Rye is famous for its cobbled streets, a feature which adds so much to the character of the town. This use of cobbles contrasts markedly with the procedure at neighbouring Winchelsea, further up the estuary, away from the foreshore, where all known early paving makes use of stone slabs, mostly Tilgate stone pitched on edge.[103] By no means all the streets in Winchelsea seem to have had adequate paving. That the same applied to Rye is suggested by the banning of wheeled vehicles in the town in poor weather because they rutted the roads. This also brings into question

Fig. 2.22
Rye from the north at high tide in 1823, by William Daniell.

whether paving, where it existed, extended the full width of the street or whether, in some instances, it was restricted to the margins only.

To judge from an entry in the accounts for 1549/50, individual paving schemes could be extensive — this particular entry relates to 489 [?square] yards (409 M^2) of street paving against 'Mr Wood's shops'. The terms of specific labour requirements placed upon townsfolk prior to the mid 16th century are uncertain, but from 1555 onwards householders were required to work four days a year on the highways, and in 1563 this was increased to six days. Householders (or, at least, those with the ability to do so) also had a responsibility to light the street outside their houses. In the 1570s, from 1st November until 1st February they were required to hang a lantern at their windows for the two hours from 6 to 8 o'clock in the evening when there was no moon. In 1577 this was increased by an hour to 5 o'clock and clarification was made that the lanterns were not to be set in the window, but hung out of them. The end time of 8 o'clock might seem surprising, but night came early in town — at 8 o'clock in winter (9 o'clock in summer) the inns and taverns ceased serving.

Water Supplies [104]

In historical times, towns which occupy hill-top sites were prone to problems with water supply. This was particularly the case in places like Rye which are small in area and largely surrounded by sea, adding the risk of pollution by salt water to the digging of wells. Indeed, the 1:500 Ordnance Survey map of the town prepared in 1871-2 marks not a single well within the town walls, whereas tanks (for the storage of rainwater) are not uncommon. As at Winchelsea, the town relied principally upon springs (called 'wells' — a simple corruption of the Saxon word 'wealle' for spring) at points where clean water percolated out from the base of the upland. At Winchelsea they ringed the edge of the town,[105] but at Rye they were located along the foot of the upland mass across the marsh to the north of the town. Perhaps the earliest of these 'wells' was Budgwell, at the foot of Playden Hill, across the link from the Landgate. Water was carried into town in water budges (casks on wheels), almost certainly indicating how this particular well obtained its name.[106] Even so, from quite an early date — just how early is uncertain — a piped conduit was installed from Budgwell, running across the land link and around the edge of the marsh to a 'conduit house' just outside the postern gate at the foot of Conduit Hill. The conduit then continued along the town ditch to the Strand. In the late 1540s a second conduit — the new conduit — was built. It ran from a spring head called Blikewell (later known as Queen Elizabeth's Well) at the base of Leasham Hill, across the marsh along the line of what is now known as Ropewalk, to the Conduit House. Evidently pumps and water pipes were installed at about this time, allowing water to be supplied to a cistern up in town, near the Chantry Stables, perhaps near the point where a new combined water tower and cistern was built in 1735. New pipes were installed to the Strand cistern in 1570.

Most residents relied upon collecting their water from the communal town storage cisterns, but as early as the 1550s a few houses which stood near the water supply had water piped direct to their property. Prior to 1556 Thomas Birchett, jurat, had made an arrangement with the corporation to have 'pipes laid in the High Street from the old conduit to his house'. Later, in 1597, Thomas Lashinden was granted the right to lay a small pipe from the main water pipe to his tenement, probably just outside Landgate, on condition that he shut off his water cock to avoid waste when he had drawn sufficient water.

Not surprising, the cost of maintaining the system of water pipes and pumps was high, but it was a payment worth the meeting. Despite the superstructure of the conduit house outside the postern gate being shown in a dilapidated, ruinous state in a drawing of the 1630s (Plate 3.15), it is clear that in general terms the system was well maintained and was still operational in 1735 when the improved storage cistern was built by the corporation just beyond the east end of the church.

Waste Disposal [107]

Waste disposal within any town was always an issue, particularly one built upon such a confined site. Despite this, Rye's location, hemmed in by the sea on three sides, was probably something of an asset in that it provided an area for general disposal — the sea. For instance, in September 1540 a timber 'pulpit' (platform) was built by the corporation on the East Cliff 'to cast over dung there' and other payments were made for cleaning the pulpit and 'hurling over the dung'. How much of this refuse reached the sea is open to question, for recent studies, designed to ascertain why the section of cliff a little to the north of Ypres Tower was slipping, found deep deposits of tipped rubbish.[108] Other methods of disposing of rubbish over the cliffs were less official and had to be curtailed. John Fagg, jurat, simply threw his filth into Rucke's Lane by the West Cliff. In 1580 Francis Christmas was given permission to set up a pale to prevent the poorer inhabitants of the area throwing filth over the cliff onto his house and backside, whilst in 1583 a total of 27 of the inhabitants of the suburb of Wish were presented for throwing their filth into the Horseway leading to the Ferry. In 1583, Richard Dardowne was presented for habitually 'hurling of dirt out of a chamber window' in the market place where he dwelt and making a dunghill there. Areas of vacant land seem commonly to have become places to pile rubbish. For instance, in 1583 a void plot against Robert Farley's house beside the Friars 'now a dunghill' was granted to him for 31 years at 18d on condition it was fenced off. The gun platform down on the Strand was likewise fenced off 'for the better keeping of the people from throwing dung, soil or filth there'. More controlled, beneficial dumping could on occasions be carried out down on the Strand where refuse was deposited to reclaim land and infill behind new quays. In similar vein, in 1581 the corporation conveyed a piece of ground behind the almshouse in Landgate to the trustees stating that 'the donage and offal of the town shall be here laid [to make up the ground level] and then to be enclosed'. The plot was intended to serve as a new garden for the almshouse.

The above entries give some general indication of methods used for disposing of rubbish. That people were presented for such nuisances suggests that they were the minority and that most residents took steps to dispose of their waste responsibly. Certainly the corporation tried to keep the town tidy. For instance, they paid for the removal of dunghills and for general tidying up of the town in 1487, though admittedly this was in preparation of a visit by Henry VII. But this is not the only example. Men were paid to keep the market and Strand clean. In 1574 pumps were made for the cleansing of the streets and in the same year it was ordered that twice a week the four brewers 'shall let go a barrel of water in such convenient places in the streets as to them shall be assigned for the sweeting of the streets and to continue the same during the heat of this summer'. The residents seem usually to have taken responsibility for keeping clean the area in front of their houses, though the impression is that sometimes this was to the detriment of their neighbours. In 1584 it was decreed that when householders or their servants sweep the 'streets and gutters before their houses ... it is to be taken up and carried away and not swept the same down to their neighbours'.

Very little is known about the means of disposing of human (as opposed to general) waste within the town. The only confirmed garderobes (toilets) which have been recorded within the town's buildings are at Ypres Tower. Land Gate, and The Mermaid, Mermaid Street [72] (Figure 12.57), but privies built over cess pits in the back gardens must have been common, if not ubiquitous. Mayhew notes that the larger houses in Lower Street [High Street] built privies by the town wall with a hole running through into the town ditch, whilst one Richard Jacobs was fined for making a privy under his stairs by the fish market.

The purpose of this chapter on infrastructure has been to set the framework within which the houses of the town were built and functioned. However, one important element of Rye's layout — the defences which encircled and protect it — has yet to be considered. It is these defences which will be discussed in the next chapter.

3 TOWN DEFENCES

INTRODUCTION

By no means all medieval towns were defended: less than a quarter of the 600 or more English towns possessed walls and/or gates, and in some instances these were as much for trade control and civic pride as for defence. It might be expected that all the vulnerable south-eastern coastal ports, and, in particular, the seven head ports of the Cinque Ports confederation, would be amongst those that were defended. Yet there appear to have been no early defences at Hythe and, except for a single mention of a *foveam Fortem* (strong ditch) none at New Romney either. The two towns of Old and New Hastings were dominated by the hill-top castle which separated them, but here too the only mention of town defences prior to the 16th century is a contract to cut a defensive ditch through the marsh below Hastings Priory in 1439 in order to protect the subsequently abandoned site of Old Hastings. The first known reference to defences at New Hastings (the present Old Town) is in 1556. Even then the wall was restricted to a seaward length spanning the valley mouth, extending between two small forts.

The other towns in the confederation — Sandwich, Dover, Rye and Winchelsea — had defences from an earlier date.[1] The majority of their gates have been destroyed: easily the most impressive of those which survive is the Land Gate at Rye.

Being built upon a hill and largely surrounded by sea, in many ways the site upon which Rye is built was naturally defended against enemy attack, being protected on its eastern, southern and south-western sides by a cliff, albeit in places somewhat degraded. Additional protection would always have been desirable at the south-eastern corner where the cliff is less defined, but the principal weak zone was the northern and north-

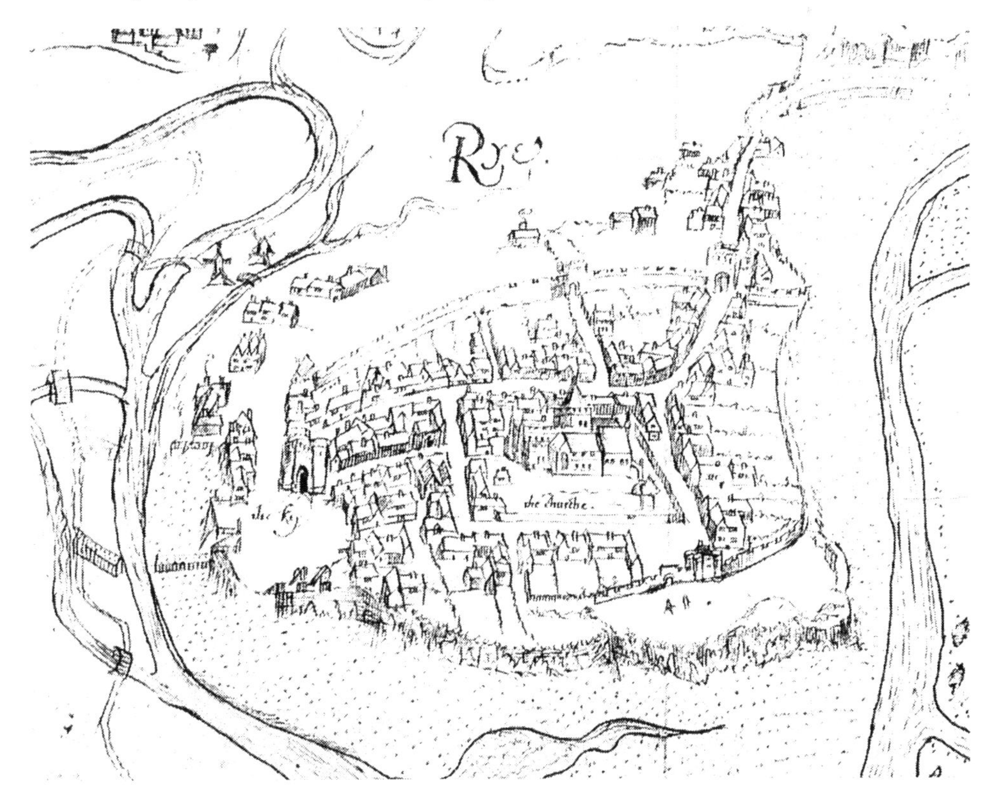

Fig. 3.1
Rye from the south, L 16th C, showing the defences
[TNA MPF 1/3]

western edge where the hill slopes naturally down to the flatlands. This weak area accounted for approximately 43 per cent of the total perimeter (Figure 3.1).[2]

HISTORICAL BACKGROUND

(For location of defensive features see Figure 3.3)

The first definite indication of the intention to raise military (as opposed to sea) defences at Rye is found in 1226 when Henry III opened negotiations with Fécamp Abbey for an exchange of the town: one reason given was that the king wished to build a castle there. It took another 21 years before a mutually acceptable agreement was reached and although the final document mentions as a reason for the transfer that the abbot and monks 'are not able to fortify them [Winchelsea and Rye], without danger to the realm in time of war', no mention is made in the document of a castle at either town. Nevertheless, it has been argued by Derek Renn that by 1247 a castle at Rye 'was probably complete'. His reasoning seems to be that in 1243 the king's galleys were transferred to the town and were ordered 'to be placed in our building at Rye made for their storage'.[3] Renn considers that if the king had built a store (presumably defended) for his galleys, he would also have had a castle there. Furthermore, he argues that a grant of certain revenues made to the king's uncle, Peter of Savoy, in 1249 does not suggest the foundation of a new castle, but merely building works to an existing structure.[4] Others take another interpretation. The intention of the 1249 grant was that Savoy should use the revenues to 'cause the Castle [at Hastings] to be fortified . . . . and if there should be anything over, then La Rye also'.[5] Given that two years later Savoy surrendered the revenues to the king, it is doubtful whether any work was carried out at Hastings, let alone at Rye. As no further documentary mention can be found to a castle at Rye, even by those who have methodically researched the 'History of the King's works', it seems safe to conclude that, even if built, the life of any such Royal castle – whether finished or not – was of short duration.[6]

Based upon the 1226 and 1249 documentary references, the Ypres Tower which occupies an exposed location in the south-eastern corner of the town is usually considered to be Rye's castle and is therefore attributed to the 13th century, despite its lack of closely-datable architectural features. As will be argued subsequently, although a 13th-century date cannot be totally dismissed, it seems more likely that this tower was built in the 14th century, probably during the second half. Regardless of date, its military role seems to have been that of a blockhouse attached to an isolated length of town wall which protected this vulnerable part of the hill. At this initial period the tower may also have doubled as the town's courthouse and prison, as was certainly the case later.

Even if the King did not fulfil his desire to erect a castle within Rye, having acquired the town from Fécamp he evidently wished to see it adequately protected against enemy attack, for on 30th June 1246 the following instruction was issued: 'Of the making of walls it is notified to Bertram de Croyl that where it is necessary he makes repairs to the walls around the towns of Rye and Winchelsea'. Furthermore, he was instructed to entrust the guarding of the towns to those whom he believed effective and faithful.[7] This is the earliest known document which makes specific reference to existing fortifications at Rye. However, it should not be taken as proving the existence of stone-built town walls: it could relate to earthen ramparts and/or timber palisades similar to those described at adjacent New Winchelsea late in the same century. That there was a length of stone wall in existence at Rye by the 1270s is indicated from documentary references, though it is unclear from these references whether the wall was defensive.[8] Certainly during the middle decades of the following century (1327x1377) an un-dated memorandum prepared on the state of the defences at Rye, Winchelsea and Hastings and the areas around noted that whereas the defences at Winchelsea were satisfactory, those at Rye and Hastings were poor.[9]

Effectively the responsibility for making and maintaining Rye's town defences against both enemy attack and the sea had been transferred from the Crown to the mayor and commonality when the town was incorporated in *c.*1289, though the crown continued to take an active interest inasmuch as the overall defence of the realm was affected.[10] It seems likely that already by *c.*1300 a town gate protecting the landward link had been built (*see* below). From 1329 onwards successive grants of murage were made the better to enable the town to contend with its twin enemies, the sea and the French. Following the commencement of the Hundred Years War, the French successfully attacked Rye in 1339 when they burned at least 52 houses and a mill (*see* Chapter 2). Soon afterwards a further 18 houses were claimed by the sea. After mentioning that the sea surrounded the town on all sides, a petition which preceded a further murage grant made in 1348 states that by then a great part of the town had been consumed by the sea and in other ways, and that total destruction was feared unless the same be speedily strengthened.[11] It is worth noting that the tenor of this petition is targeted towards sea defences rather than fortification against attack.

Even if previous work had been undertaken in stone, it is not known whether any work undertaken on the 'town walls' in response to these early murage grants was carried out using this material. Such an interpretation would be consistent with a reference in 1378 to the strategic section of town defence extending westwards from Land Gate (in the north-east of the town) as a 'fosse' (ditch/embankment). The reference occurs in a grant to the Austin Friars by the mayor and commonality of The Halton, reserving a competent space by the fosse 'for the building of the wall of our town', as well as 'a way for going to (*adeundo*) the wall'.[12] Work at this date on the erection of new walls (probably, in this instance, of stone) is entirely understandable, for the previous year the French had carried out a successful attack.

It was during the final third of the 14th century that an apparent shift can be detected on the part of the corporation away from sea defences and towards defence against enemy attack, no doubt prompted by the successful raids on neighbouring Winchelsea in 1360 and 1380 and – more so – by the attack and burning of Rye in 1377. Already by 1372 the profits of the town and bailiwick had been made over to the mayor and commonalty to assist them with their defences (type unspecified) though the success of the 1377 attack suggests that the resulting work was perhaps focused upon sea defences: alternatively, either insufficient progress had been made on the walls, or the chosen design was inadequate. Perhaps any work carried out on the town walls at this time had not been in stone, but in timber.

The corporation's intention in 1378 to build a more substantial defence was ratified three years later by the issue of a Royal charter instructing the building of a wall of stone and lime. At this time the farmer of the bailiwick was ordered to pay the town £18 per year for two years because 'they have begun to enclose the town with a wall of stone and lime against attacks of the enemy, who lately have utterly burnt the same, and they are not sufficient to complete it without the king's aid.' The following year, in 1382, a renewal of the murage grant was issued on condition that they enclosed the town with a stone wall within three years under penalty of £100. In this they failed, but the fine was halved due to their poverty.[13] The extent of this failure is uncertain.

Given that the 1382 instruction was to 'enclose' the town, and that, as far as is known, none of the cliff-top parts of the perimeter have ever been protected by a stone wall (excepting the area adjacent to the Ypres Tower) it may have been at this period that the town made the decision to restrict their stone wall primarily to the most vulnerable area, extending from the northern end of West Cliff, around the north-western edge and along the northern side to 'Walls End' at the East Cliff beyond Land Gate. In the main the line of this seems to have followed that of the earlier fosse. Even so, there is archaeological evidence which suggests the opportunity was taken to straighten the central section of the fosse in order to alleviate a slight indent in the contours of the land (*see* below). Furthermore, rather than curving to meet West Cliff, it is possible – perhaps even likely – that the western end of the early fosse extended straight out so as to meet the estuary, as was the case at neighbouring Winchelsea.[14]

By 1385 a French invasion of England was considered a very real possibility. In the circumstances the King was forced to accept that an entire circuit of stone, completed within the near future, was beyond the town's capabilities. This view may have been taken on the advice of his commissioners appointed on 14th January in response to 'information that the French are scheming to seize and fortify Rye'. Their commission was 'to examine said town and see how it may best and most speedily be fortified, to summon the better sort of men of the town and parts adjacent, explain to them the imminent danger, treat with and if necessary compel them, each according to his estate, to contribute to the fortification and safe keeping of the same'. On 6th February the commissioners were ordered to fell trees in the woods of the alien abbot of Fécamp, 'and bring to Rye as many trees as may be necessary for the walling and fortification of Rye' with, on 16th February, a further order to fell 200 trees in Crowhurst Park (demesne of the Rape of Hastings, then in Royal hands) 'and bring them to Rye for its fencing and fortification'.[15]

Although it is not known whether the earlier fosse incorporated a ditch, the improved defences did, for in 1428 it is mentioned as a southern boundary to a property in St Mary's Croft. The attack expected in 1385 did not materialize, but, with its ditch and mixed defences of stone and timber in place, it seems likely that the town thereafter saw less urgency in replacing in stone the newly erected sections of timber wall. This may explain the several building campaigns, of varying quality, recognizable within the extant length of northern stone wall (*see* below).

By 1430 the town appears to have felt sufficiently relaxed about the threat of attack to sell the Ypres Tower into private hands, though in taking this action the corporation's apparent poverty and the need to liquidate assets may have been an important factor. They were sufficiently prudent to write a re-entry clause into the sale should the building be required for defensive purposes (*see* below). The town's economic circumstances did not, apparently, improve: nineteen years later, in 1449, Tenterden was incorporated into the Cinque Ports Confederation in order to assist Rye which had 'fallen into devastation, destruction, waste and impoverishment, not only of lands and tenements, but also of inhabitants'.[16]

The sale of the tower into private hands came at

the end of more than a decade in which England's hold on French territory seemed relatively secure, following Agincourt (1415) and the Treaty of Troyes (1420). But already by 1430 the appearance of Joan of Arc had begun to turn the tide in favour of the French, and slowly the south-coast ports were once again put under threat. By 1453 Calais was all that remained of the English possessions in France. In response to these changed circumstances the Rye accounts make clear that the town governors anxiously kept their defences in readiness against anticipated French attacks. An alleged burning of the town by the French in 1448-9 is unsupported by evidence, but the corporation was clearly expecting such an attack, for guns were at this time provided for the defences of the town. Later, in 1457-8 a gun was brought to Baddings, presumably to overlook the estuary from the south-eastern corner of the hill top where the town's permanent gun garden was later established. French attacks were once more feared in 1459, at which time works were carried out 'about the edifices of the north tower, called 'Landgate tower'', whilst labourers were paid for making wooden hurdles 'to put on top of the tower over the water-gate (Strand Gate), for men to stand there in defending the town' and cartloads of stone missiles were collected on the town walls in readiness, the latter action repeated in 1474.[17]

With the increased use of artillery on board ship, coupled with the town's meteoric growth in population and rise in local importance during the closing decade of the 15th and early 16th centuries — brought about as a result of neighbouring Winchelsea's collapse — a rethink of the defences was inevitable. The change appears to have been piecemeal, reacting to threats as they presented themselves. Already by the early years of the Tudor dynasty the town seems to have possessed

Fig.3.2
Detail from Prowze map of 1572 showing Ypres Tower with Baddings Gate to the right and the gun garden beyond.
The top of the picture is toward the south.
[TNA MPF 1/212]

at least three and possibly four pieces of ordnance, including a great serpentine for which new wheels were made in 1491. In 1493 two more guns were purchased from Adam Oxenbridge, a leading baron of the town and onetime mayor, and in 1513 a further two serpentines were acquired, each with three chambers and forelocks. At this time an arsenal of at least four guns was stored at Baddings (*otherwise* Ypres) Tower, which by this date had been bought back by the town. Further purchases and loans meant that in 1515, at the end of Henry VIII's first war with France, the town must have had ten or eleven guns at its disposal.[18]

It was during this general period that the Crown showed interest in assisting the towns of Rye and Winchelsea by taking steps to protect the mouth of their shared harbour. With Henry's French war in mind, and the inevitably heightened threat to the south coast, between 1511 and 1514 Sir Edward Guldeford received £1,300 from the crown towards making 'a bridge and tower' in Iham Marshes, on the end of a shingle spit at the entrance to the estuary. Sir Edward's father, Sir Richard, had been granted the lordship of Iham twenty years earlier, in 1486, on condition that he maintained a tower to be built in the marshes there within the next two years for the defence of the port: the payments in 1511-1514 suggest that this had not been done. Further, it seems likely that even in 1514 the work remained incomplete, for in 1521 the corporation sent one of their leading barons, Mr Wymond, 'to sue for the same [blockhouse] to be finished'.[19]

During the first half of the 16th century the new artillery defences within the town became concentrated in two locations: a gun garden on the cliff to the south of the Ypres Tower (Figure 3.2) and a bulwark at the southern end of The Strand (*see* Figures 3.3 and 3.25). Both were strategic locations for defence of the harbour estuary. Some form of bulwark probably already existed on the Strand by 1491-2 when a 'sege house' was built by the town at a cost of £5.5s.5d.: certainly the bulwark existed by 1513 when money was expended upon it. It was rebuilt as a 'new fortress' in 1544-5, in which year major improvements were also made to the Gungarden at Ypres Tower. These included the construction of further bulwarks called the 'lower fortress' (i.e. The Lower Gungarden) and the making of a gate, called Baddings Gate, in the town wall adjacent to the tower so as to improve access. The work undertaken 1544-5 was under the direction of a Royal Commission. In order to store the munitions required by the ordnance, as well as storing other weapons and armaments, a former chantry chapel in the parish church was taken over as a store.[20]

The improvements to the town's defences were considerably augmented by the completion in 1544 of Henry VIII's new artillery fort — Camber Castle (initially known as Winchelsea Castle) — on the end of

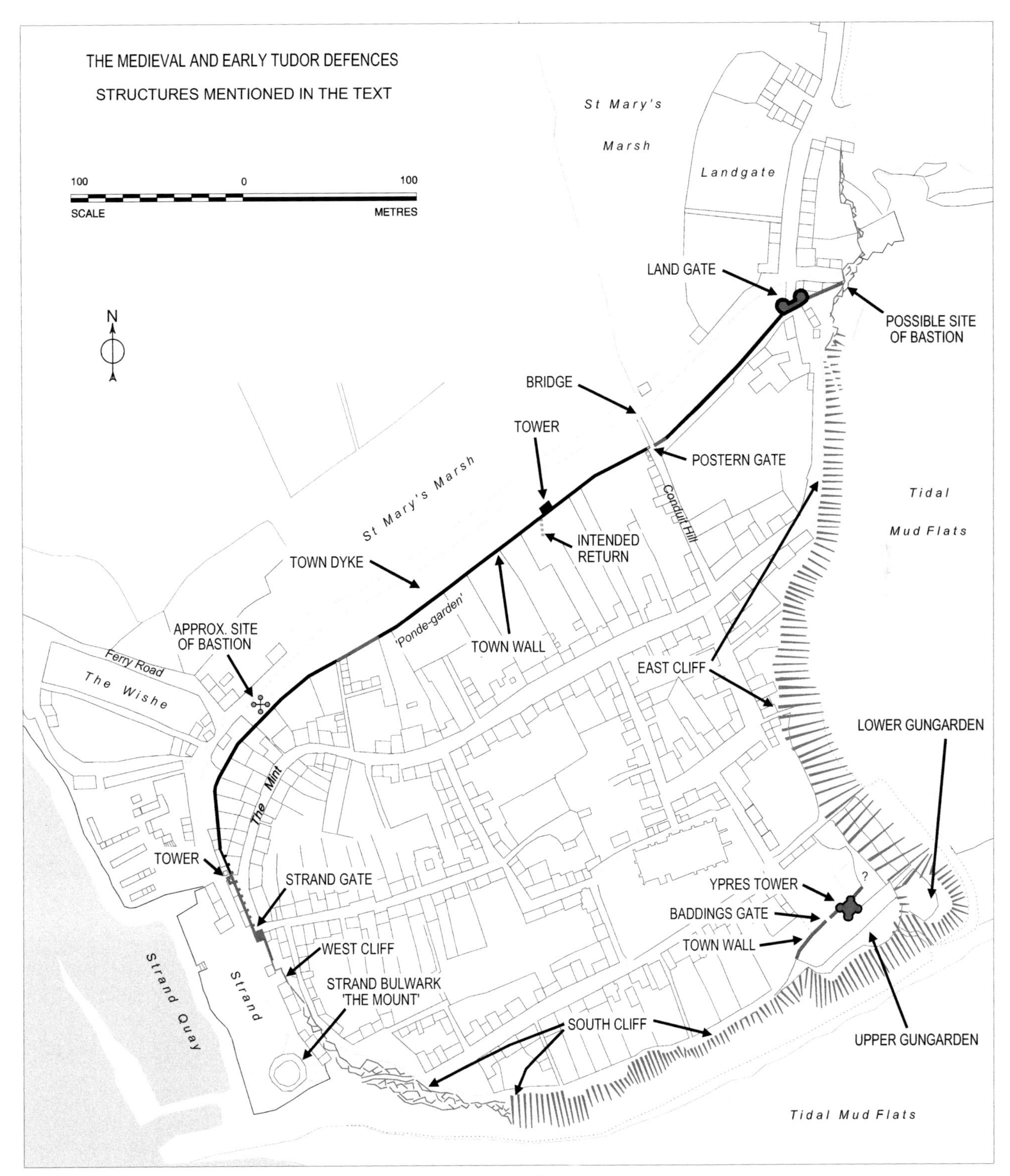

Fig. 3.3

the shingle spit at the entrance to the estuary, greatly improving upon the earlier blockhouse which had been built there by the Guldeford family. The Guldefords' earlier blockhouse was incorporated into the central tower of the new fort.[21]

Even with the substantial arsenal the town had at its disposal by the 1520s, it was nevertheless vulnerable. In 1528 it was reported that 'ships could lie at a stone cast from the town wall and the town would not be able to resist them'.[22] The chief area of concern must have been the creek to the west of the town, adjacent to the Strand and Wishe. Here, once past the ordnance stationed at the Ypres Tower and Strand Bulwark, enemy ships could sail into the inner harbour and, potentially, wreak havoc. On account of the wide inter-tidal zone, the eastern edge probably gave less concern, but nonetheless was considered in need of some extra protection.[23] In response to these problems, a series of stone-filled wooden groynes and jetties, in some instances with thorns as extra protection, were built in the inner harbour area and, in 1544-5, against the link to the mainland. In 1558-9 palisade fencing was added on the seaward side of the link, extending up to the Land Gate, presumably to give protection against enemy fire to people using this route. There was a further expense for similar fencing in 1562. In the case of the groynes and jetties it is often difficult to differentiate within the accounts between harbour improvements, sea defences, and defence against enemy action, though peaks in expenditure during periods of know threat give some guidance. A pair of groynes built across the inner harbour so as to narrow the entrance probably served a dual, even multiple function.[24]

Despite the ever-increasing reliance upon artillery and its inevitable focus towards the harbour mouth to the south, Rye's north-facing wall and associated gates were nevertheless regarded as being of importance throughout the late 15th and early 16th centuries and were maintained accordingly. In 1501, for example, the town wall was white limed; the sum of 2s. being paid for so treating the length between the 'Friars and the Bulwark'.[25] This concern for maintenance was not merely a mark of civic pride and a desire to control entry to the town for economic reasons. In 1489-90 the town ditch running along the base of the northern wall was scoured at a cost of £11.6s.8½d. and monies were spent on repairs to the wall itself. This work was evidently a response to a specific threat, for in the areas linking the ends of the wall to the cliff temporary post-and-rail barricades surmounted by bundles of thorns were erected: a similar arrangement was put in place at the end of the town ditch. In addition, areas of the cliff were pared back to make them more steep. The removal of fallen detritus and slippages from the cliff in order to make them sheer at the base was probably the usual way of strengthening these parts of the town's defensive circuit in times of threat.

The section of the town ditch immediately to the west of the Land Gate was still in water in 1511.[26] Sections of the wall which had fallen into the ditch were rebuilt in 1513, at which time the top of the Land Gate was defoliated and repaired. Major works were under way on the wall in 1544, showing that even at this late date not all the town's efforts were directed towards its artillery. This work included the section of wall to the east of Land Gate, extending up to wall's end, for which material left over from building Camber Castle was used, as was stone from redundant buildings in destitute Winchelsea, including stone salvaged from St. Giles' Church. One area of wall was evidently strengthened to carry ordnance: this may have been at the rear of Mr Easton's property where it is known ordnance was placed.[27]

Two pieces of ordnance were sited at the Land Gate in 1557-8, whilst new portcullises were fitted to both the Land Gate and Strand Gate in 1559. These activities were part of what appears to have been a major programme of repairs to the town wall and ditch, which work included 'digging out' (i.e. cleaning, and perhaps deepening) the town ditch. At the height of the work 51 men were employed on the ditch with a further 18 masons and 14 labourers working on repairs to the town wall.[28]

In 1588, during the Armada scare, both the Gungarden and Strand Fortress were repaired using over 240 tons of timber, and at this time 'gunholes' arched with brick were made through the walls of the Land Gate and work was undertaken to 'hedge in the flanker there'.[29] But generally from this time onwards concern for defence at Rye diminished. Already by 1576 'new buildings' had been erected 'along the town ditch', in the area near the Wishe. During the twelve-year period between 1582 and 1594 no less than 319 feet of the ditch was granted out as plots extending out 14 to 33 feet (4.25 to 10.00 metres) from the wall, and such grants continued thereafter.[30] The drawing by Van Dyke reproduced in Figure 3.15 indicates that by the early 1630s the section of town ditch to the west of Land Gate had largely been filled in and in this area the wall had lost its crenellations, this despite their depiction in the Jeake plan of 1667.[31] In the 1630s the section of wall to the west of the postern gate still retained its crenellations (*see* Figure 2.3).

Much of the wall still remains to this day, reduced in height and now mostly hidden by later buildings, but

Fig. 3.4
Ypres Tower (13th or 14th century)
viewed from the town

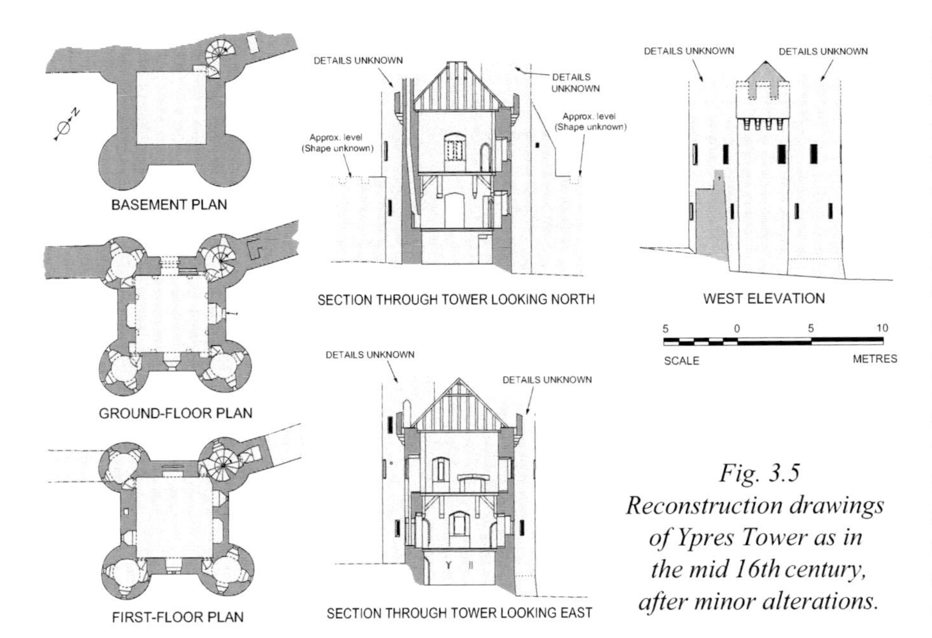

Fig. 3.5 Reconstruction drawings of Ypres Tower as in the mid 16th century, after minor alterations.

a section near Market Road was demolished soon after 1766 and the length against The Mint, extending northwards from Strand Gate, was totally rebuilt in the 19th century as the eastern wall of a new building. The Gungarden Gate otherwise Baddings Gate (which had been punched through an isolated section of town wall in 1545) was pulled down in 1734/5 and the Postern Gate at the bottom of Conduit Hill was threatened with removal in 1736, but evidently managed to survive until soon after 1819, despite an opening having been cut through the wall adjacent to it. Strand Gate (the arch of which had been taken down in 1767) was totally demolished in 1815. A bastion which projected from the wall near Ferry Road was taken down in the mid 19th century.[32] In addition to the sections of wall which survive, Land Gate and Ypres Tower likewise remain. Of the Tudor defences, the bulwark/fort on the Strand survived as an earthwork (called The Mount) in 1667, but was subsequently removed to make way for a warehouse.[33] Limited earthworks are visible at Gungarden.

THE DEFENSIVE CIRCUIT

Ypres Tower and adjacent lengths of town wall [34]

The tower as built

Ypres Tower otherwise Baddings Tower, located on elevated ground at the extreme south-eastern corner of the town, is a small, square, three-storeyed structure with corner turrets. It was originally attached to and projected forward from an isolated length of town wall which cut off a stubby spur at a point where the steepness of the cliff is much less pronounced than elsewhere. The only means of access was from the town, by means of a doorway set centrally within the northern wall. This was protected by a small portcullis. Because of the ground slope, the doorway was elevated well above the medieval ground surface and led into the central of the three storeys. Ignoring the small cell-like spaces within three of the four turrets on the ground and first floor, each storey housed but a single room. The lowest, originally accessible only by a spiral staircase in the north-eastern turret, was always wholly above ground on its western, southern and eastern sides, but as it originally incorporated neither windows nor external doorways, it is best regarded as a basement. The rooms on all three storeys are small, the basement being 4.85 metres x 4.85 metres (15 feet 11 inches square) and the first-floor chamber 5.30 metres x 5.30 metres (17 feet 4 inches square). The floors and roof have been adjusted since initial construction, but the original levels are ascertainable. The storey height of the basement was *c.*2.35 metres (7 feet 8 inches), compared to a generous *c.*3.65 metres (*c.*12 feet) on the ground floor and 4.15 metres (13 feet 8 inches) on the first floor. In stark contrast to the basement, both the ground-floor room and first-floor chamber were well lit and each was heated by a fireplace. The existence of four windows serving the first-floor chamber (of which at least one was of two lights) suggests this was the principal space within the building.

The north-eastern turret accommodates the spiral staircase which originally climbed from basement to parapet level. Rising above the town wall and projecting out from the turret is a buttress-like 'cabin' housing a garderobe. Although this served the entire tower, it was particularly convenient for use by the occupants of the first-floor chamber. The other three turrets are solid at basement level, but house tiny cell-like rooms on the other two floors. Each is accessed direct from the main room and chamber. In drawings of the building by Van Dyck (1634) and S. H. Grimm (1784/5) the stair turret is shown rising high above the then partially-extant parapets, allowing access to the battlements. The turret was at that time capped by a semi-conical roof. The other three turrets rise much lower.

The walls of the tower are of coursed rubble

Fig. 3.6
Ypres Tower from the SE, as drawn by Van Dyck,1634
[©Foundation Museum Boijmans Van Beuningen, Rotterdam. Inventory No: V 18.]

Fig. 3.7
Ypres Tower from the SW, as drawn by Van Dyck, 1634
[©Reproduction by permission of the Syndics of the Fitzwilliam Museum, Cambridge. Accession Number: PD.282-1963]

masonry, mostly of iron-stained sandstone, and roughly finished. They are not particularly thick, measuring 1.40 metres (4 feet 7 inches) at the base, reducing to 1.15 metres (3 feet 9 inches) at roof level. At an average of 800 mm to 950 mm (2 feet 7 inches to 3 feet 1 inch) the walls of the turrets are thinner still. There is no reason to doubt that the adjacent sections of town wall and the tower are of one build: the remnants of the town wall are fully bonded to the turrets and the windows of the north-western and north-eastern turrets are spaced so as to avoid the alignment of the town wall. Externally many stones show traces of lime mortar on their faces, but whether this indicates former neatly-finished rendering or a rough mortar wash is unknown.[35] The internal surfaces of all walls were once neatly rendered and lime-washed. Structural evidence and the Van Dyck drawings of 1633 and 1634 show that the wall tops incorporated corbelled machicolations which carried a projecting parapet (Figures 3.6 and 3.7).

The external arch of the entrance doorway in the north wall was replaced in the 15th or early 16th century, though the original internal elements survive. It is uncertain whether the associated portcullis is an original feature — the likelihood is that it is. All surviving doorways which are original to the initial build have two-centred arches, continuously chamfered on their principal face with the chamfers stopped just above floor level. Where they survive, the stops are of pyramidal type. In plan the ground-floor doorway which leads to the spiral staircase is set at a slightly canted angle, whereas all others are set flush with the walls, being positioned so tight into the corners of the chambers that shallow wall recesses were necessary in order to accommodate the doors when open.

Being square-headed and plainly chamfered externally, all original windows are very simple in nature. Except where repaired, they are of coarse brown ironstone with a very rough external finish. The windows increase in size as they rise through the building, indicating design for defence, as does the absence of any openings at basement level. Derek Renn makes the point that, taken collectively, the windows are positioned so as to fully cover the ground around the tower, both outside and inside the town.[36] Internally the openings are exceptionally plain, being capped by flat stone lintels. Except where altered, they are designed as shallow walk-in recesses, thereby reducing the wall thickness in order to give the defenders ease of use. For the same reason, although the side jambs of the shallow recesses are set square, the jambs of the openings themselves are widely splayed to allow maximum sideways vision. Because of their awkward locations, some are irregular in plan.

Although the designers had to take into account the need for defence, the windows serving the two chambers (ground and first floor) provide a good level of light. The ground-floor entrance chamber was the least well provided in that it was served by two windows only — one each set centrally within the south and east walls. The corresponding locations within the north and west walls were occupied by the main entrance doorway and fireplace respectively.[37] Internally the southern window is narrower than that in the eastern wall. The window surround is intact. Although much repaired, it has a square-headed single-light chamfered opening, unglazed, originally protected by an iron grille (now replaced) and closed by hinged shutters. The window is approached via a recess, with square-set, un-chamfered jambs and a chamfered segmental rear-arch, but the visible features strongly suggest that the recess was not originally of walk-in type.

The first-floor chamber was served by a square-headed, chamfered window in each of its four walls. Those in the east and west walls are each of one light and are off-centred so as to avoid the fireplace and the flue to the ground-floor fireplace respectively. They are generally constructed as on the floor below, but in this instance the internal jambs always extended down to

Fig. 3.8
Ypres Tower from the townward side as drawn by S. H. Grimm in 1784.
[© The British Library Board. Add Ms 5670 f.15 [28]]

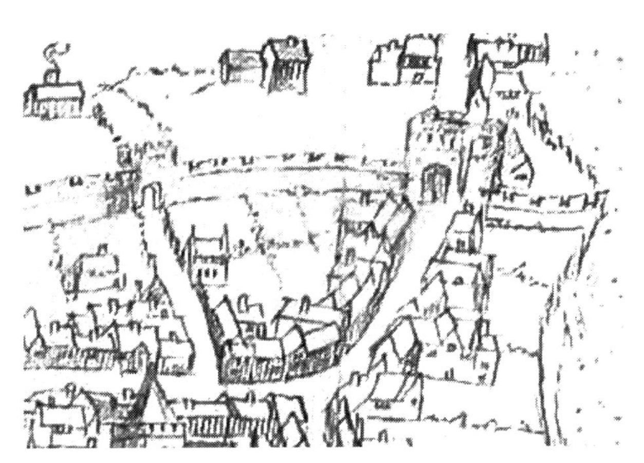

Fig. 3.9
Detail from a L 16th C plan showing Land Gate with the town wall extending to East Cliff on the right. Note Postern gate on the left. [TNA MPF 1/3]

floor level. The window in the north wall has been much modified: formerly its recess accommodated the slot for the portcullis which protected the entrance below. It was from here that the portcullis was operated. As on the floor below, the windows were un-glazed, but were fitted with iron grilles and hinged shutters.

Two snapped-off corbels built into each of the four walls of the ground-floor chamber evidently supported wall-posts rising to ceiling beams. The posts no doubt supported braces which helped carry the ceiling beams.

The two chambers of the building are each served by a fireplace: an unusual and sophisticated feature for its period. That which heated the ground-floor chamber is set centrally within the western wall, whilst the first-floor chamber was served by an off-centred fireplace within the eastern wall. Both were originally of similar design, being flush-fronted and surprisingly low. Each had un-chamfered jambs and was capped by a massive stone lintel (in two sections) incorporating a segmental chamfered arch. The lintel to the ground-floor fireplace survives, but that on the first floor was removed when a timber lintel was inserted at a higher level. Both fireplaces must be contemporary with the building, for their flues rise within the thickness of the walls and are neatly constructed. It would have been impossible to insert them later without rebuilding large sections of the external wall.

Dating and use

Based upon inconclusive documentary evidence of a possible castle at Rye (*see* above) Ypres Tower is usually said to be 13th century.[38] However, the building's architecture is notoriously difficult to date. Its doorways and windows are so plain in their detail as to be equally at home during either the 13th or the 14th centuries. Arguably the tower's most datable features are the corbels just below the wall heads, which once supported machicolations. Renn points out that corbelled machicolations occur from the end of the 12th century onwards, but gives Héliot as his example. If Renn knows of British examples he does not quote them — machicolations do not appear to have been used in any early/mid 13th-century English or Welsh castle: they seem to have been used first at Conway, and then only sparingly. Even if earlier examples can be cited, it is beyond dispute that only during the 14th century did their use became widespread. Unfortunately there is no guarantee that those at Ypres Tower do no represent a later improvement.

Another architectural feature which appears to have a dating significance is the design of the fireplaces, with their flush monolithic lintels. Most 13th-century fireplaces were fitted with projecting canopied hoods and this type remained the norm during the first half of the 14th century. The earliest fireplaces known locally which are of the type found in Ypres Tower are the exceptionally early examples in the undercroft and hall at Blackfriars Barn, a ruined late 13th- or early 14th-century stone house in nearby Winchelsea.[39]

Also at Winchelsea is the Strand Gate of *c.*1300, a building which in its basic plan — square tower with corner turrets — closely mirrors the plan of Ypres Tower. A further analogy with a local building can be made: the Land Gate in Rye itself. The lower two storeys of the gate are attributed to the early 14th century, but Bloe considers the upper parts to represent a repair or heightening of *c.*1380-5 (*see* 'Land Gate' below). It may be no coincidence that the masonry of this later work closely resembles that of the Ypres Tower, as too do the square-headed windows and corbelled machicolations which link the tops of the two towers.

One further point is worth making. A feature of Ypres Tower is the crude nature of the building's finish, in particular the inaccuracy of the setting out with regards the turrets. Such work is more likely to have been carried out in the 14th century by an impoverished provincial town than by the State, which had been responsible for Rye's defences in the 13th century.

It will be clear from the above that based upon current knowledge no definitive date can be given for the tower, though the weight of evidence seems to favour it having been constructed in the 14th century as part of the town's programme of defence. In this respect it is perhaps worth noting that in 1392 a bond for the large sum of £120, probably relating to a building contract, was made between John Baddyng and three stonemasons from Kent. The name of the Baddyng family was often associated with the tower. Richard Baddyng was a ship owner and mayor, MP and bailiff of Rye between 1352 and 1371, and the John Baddyng mentioned above — his immediate descendant — fulfilled the same roles between 1386 and 1407, as well as that of churchwarden in 1399.[40] Given the historical association of the family name with the tower, is it too far-fetched to suggest that the bond relates to the building's initial construction?

Despite the available evidence which points to a 14th-century date, it has to be acknowledged that a 13th-century date for Ypres Tower is not impossible.

Subsequent use and alterations

By 1421 the corporation of Rye appears to have been utilizing the tower as a court hall, for in that year it was ordered that 'all offenders summoned to the Tower and not attending at the hour assigned' were to pay a fine of 12d.[41] It is perhaps significant that the structure is referred to in the document as 'the Tower', not as 'the Castle'. Vidler argues that the earlier Court Hall had been destroyed during the French raid of 1377, hence the use of 'the Tower' for this purpose in 1421. It seems equally possible that this had been one of its uses from the outset. Vidler further argues that a new Court Hall was constructed upon the Courton soon afterward. This seems an entirely plausible suggestion, for in 1430 the town granted to a resident of the town, John de Ypres, a 'certain tower in the town embattled, with reasonable way from the highway with horses, carts and wains, and reasonable ground on the south of the tower as far as the cliff, of the same breadth as the tower, or more'. The grant was subject to the corporation's right to re-enter for the defence of the town (bringing their own victuals) in time of hostilities or war.[42] There can be no doubt that this grant refers to Ypres Tower and represents the date at which it was transferred into private ownership. It was subsequently acquired by James Hyde (also a Rye resident) whose heirs sold it in 1477.[43]

It is usually assumed that during this period the tower was in use as a private house, but it should be pointed out that it incorporates only two usable rooms (excluding the basement and small turrets) and neither includes cooking facilities. It is possible, therefore, that it served as a separate camera block attached to another building. In this respect, it may be relevant that by 1452 the deeds include reference to a tenement with cellar beneath, near the town wall. It remains unclear whether this building was located near the tower, but Mayhew thought it was.[44] The Van Dyck and subsequent illustrations show a low house extending northwards from the tower's north-east turret. The southern end of this survived until severely damaged during World War II. Photographs taken after the bombing show it as a false-fronted timber-framed structure with a steeply-pitched roof and heavy framing. They are too indistinct to allow accurate dating, but a 15th- or 16th-century date seems likely, and thus it could have been used in conjunction with the tower.

In 1477 Ypres Tower was acquired by Lord Stanley, Steward of the King's Household, and for the next two decades it can be assumed that the building was leased out. It was conveyed by Stanley to John Newbury (another outsider) in 1492 and he in turn conveyed his interest to the corporation in 1495.[45] In fact, it seems likely that even prior to its acquisition by Lord Stanley the town was already the leaseholder, for the accounts for 1475-7 contain several references which seem to relate to it, including the mayor and his brethren meeting and dining in 'the tower'.[46] Although it is conceivable that Land Gate could have been referred to by that name, the exceedingly small size of it rooms makes this highly unlikely. Even after Stanley's acquisition, the accounts continue to include similar payments, including the purchase in 1481 of new keys for the door of 'the tower', 'for [the] Sergeant to go in and out with prisoners'.[47] What is certain is that by the early 16th century the corporation was using the tower as the town gaol and as a courthouse for criminal cases (not to be confused with the court hall, which was located elsewhere).[48] Presumably the cells were at this time located within the corner turrets and basement. Only subsequently was the building made over to sole use as a gaol, as it continued to be into the 19th century.

Few alterations can be attributed to the late 15th and 16th centuries. One of the most significant was the reconstruction of the external door surround (and portcullis groove) to incorporate a four-centred arched head. Another was the replacement of the earlier roof by the fully-hipped pitched roof which survived until damaged by bombing during the Second World War.[49] Photographs taken following bomb damage indicate it to have been of paired-rafter-and-collar construction of a type in common use during the late-medieval and transitional period. This was, no doubt, the 'new roof ... for the Courthouse' built in 1552. New floors were made at the same time, the whole costing £5.[50]

Baddings Gate and adjacent town wall

Extending out from Ypres Tower to east and west was a short length of town wall built at the same time as the tower to protect a weak point in the natural defences formed by the cliff. Only the stub ends of the wall now remain, projecting short distances from the tower's north-eastern and north-western turrets. It measured *c.*2.15 metres in thickness and on its extra-mural side rose to a height of just over 5 metres (excluding parapet). Because of known changes in ground level on the townward side, the height on this side is uncertain.

When the wall and tower were first built the town appears not to have been accessible from this side, but in 1545 a gate was cut through adjacent to Ypres Tower.[51] Its purpose, as its alternative name of 'Gungarden Gate' implies, was to give access to the gun garden which was at that period being developed on the hill-top slope to the south of Ypres Tower. The gate is shown in the maps of Prowze (1572) and Jeake (1667), but the best views are in two sketches made by Van Dyck in the 1630s. The details in all are consistent, showing a simple arched opening cut through the wall roughly on the alignment of the present public footpath. A short section of the wall was deliberately raised in height in order to accommodate the top of the arch (*see* Figure 3.7). The gate and the section of wall in which it was located were taken down in 1735.

The Town's Northern Defences

Although only one short *c.*60 metre (196 feet 10 inches) length of town wall is today easily visible (and even this has had its upper parts rebuilt as a garden wall) two thirds of the *c.*575 metres (1,886 feet) of wall which formerly linked the two ends of the cliff survives to some extent in visible form, whilst on the extra-mural face much of this still stands to between two and three metres high. These remains have been little studied and as a result much of their early topographical context and subsequent evolution remains uncertain. Archaeological investigations undertaken during redevelopment along the central section between 1981 and 2005 allow this part to be better understood: the results alert historians to the complexity of the wall's evolution, warning against dogmatic interpretation.

Within the overview which follows the northern and north-western defences will be divided into sections, working from east (where the wall was elevated atop the east cliff at a height of 10 metres (*c.*33 feet) above O.D.) to its south-western end (where it blends gradually and seamlessly into the west cliff as the cliff rises out of the flatlands of the estuary). Close to the two ends stood the town's two principal gates — Land Gate (otherwise North Gate) near the eastern end of the northern length, and Strand Gate (otherwise South Gate, Sea Gate or Water Gate) close to the wall's south-western end. Between those two points were at least one, possible two, postern gates and apparently three projecting towers/bastions. For most of its length the side of the wall facing away from the town was protected by a town ditch or 'dyke'.

East Cliff to Land Gate

As it exists today the length of defence from East Cliff to Land Gate is very short — about 20 metres (*c.*65 feet 6 inches). This section of wall is shown in a late 16th century drawing of the town, but to judge from the Grimm drawing made of Land Gate in the 1780s (*see* Figure 3.12) by then it had either been totally demolished or was so low that it was hidden from view by a boundary wall flanking the street.[52]

Finishing as it did atop the cliff, this section must always have been vulnerable to erosion: even today the base of the cliff in this area can be seen to be worn smooth by wave action. There is known to have been cliff loss in this area and this continued into the late 16th century when, in 1573, the future of Land Gate itself was threatened (*see* Chapter 2). The cliff-top end of the wall may have terminated in a tower or bastion, for in 1575 the corporation appointed six men to 'view the house of old bastion and to make report what way is best to help the same from falling over the cliff'. Work is known to have been carried out on this section of wall a century prior to these concerns, for in 1483 purchases relating to repairs or alterations included 4,200 bricks purchased for the bulwark of the wall at Land Gate. Further major rebuilding here was undertaken in 1544.[53] What is surprising — but is made very clear by the exposed face of the cliff — is that in this area there was no ditch to protect the extra-mural face of the wall, this despite the existence of a ditch extending westwards from Land Gate.

Land Gate

Land Gate presents an impressive north-facing elevation to visitors, but is far more austere on its townward side and has very little depth viewed sideways on. Planned as an entrance arch flanked by two round towers which project forward on the extra-mural face and rise from stepped, two-tiered plinths, it is a three-storeyed structure faced in mixed Tilgate and brown ironstone rubble. Despite the fact that properties are described as 'outside the gate' in the undated rental of Edward I (1272-1307) and deeds refer to property 'outside the gate' in 1323 and 1325 and 'within the North Gate' in 1335, the lower part of the present structure is usually attributed to *c.*1340 which, if correct, imply it replaced an earlier gate.[54] Initially it stood very much in isolation, having nothing more than a fosse (perhaps topped by a timber palisade) abutting it to the west. As such it must have dominated the approach to the town. Even afterwards the wall at this point was low, leaving the gate towering above it. Perhaps initially the structure was not quite as dominant as appears in Figures 3.12 and 3.15, for the top storey is convincingly argued by J. W. Bloe to be work of *c.*1380-5, possibly associated with a heightening.[55] Although the parapets have been lost, the string-course and corbelled machicolations still remain within the extra-mural face. Projecting forwards from the western tangent of the west tower, forming the end-wall of the adjacent 19th-century terrace, is an old-looking masonry wall incorporating 'medieval-style' openings, but contrary to comments by Bloe, this wall is the same date as the terraced housing.[56]

Fig. 3.10
North (extra-mural) elevation of Land Gate as in 2007

Fig. 3.11
South (townward) elevation of Land Gate as in 2007

The entrance through the gate is in three parts: an outer arch, a main arch with door rebate and rear arch, and beyond this on the townward side, a deep inner arch supporting intra-mural chamber-like 'passages' linking the towers at first-floor and second-floor level. The chamfered outer archway, which is set back from the upper storeys within a chamfered square-headed recess, stands before the narrower and lower principal doorway. This gives the entrance a deeply recessed appearance. In the spandrels is a pair of small bull's-eye piercings, perhaps associated with the lifting mechanism for the bridge which stood in front of the gate. The gate's principal arch is of two chamfered orders supporting a four-centred head reminiscent of the arches at Bodiam Castle, built under licence dated 1385, perhaps indicating the extent of the argued late 14th-century alterations to the structure. In contrast, the rear arch of the opening is semi-elliptical – again, not a typical early 14th-century profile. Between the outer archway and the main entrance is a portcullis slot and associated grooves. Like the jambs of the arch, the grooves terminate well above the present road surface, indicating the extent to which the street was lowered when the former entrance bridge in front of the gate was removed. This bridge had been renewed in 1480/1: the portcullis — together with that protecting the Strand Gate — was replaced in 1559 by a new one (since destroyed).[57] A pair of heavy doors/gates (evidenced by two of four hinge pintles) closed the main archway on the townward side. The inner archway supporting the intra-mural linking passage was formerly flanked by south buttresses, though that on the west is today evidenced only by a wall scar. Like the rear arch of the entrance, the inner arch is semi-elliptical. Built into each of the jambs are short passages containing steps which ascend

Fig. 3.12
N. elevation of Land Gate. Drawn by S. H. Grimm, 1784.
[© The British Library Board. Add Ms 5670 f.16 [30]]

Fig. 3.13 Interior of Land Gate's eastern tower, 1784. Note the gun ports at the base of the wall, the arch-headed rear arches of the windows on the next two storeys, and the square-headed windows in the upper storey. [© The British Library Board. Add Ms 5670 f.16 [29]]

to two-centred doorways which in turn lead into the ground-floor rooms of the side-towers. In the roofs of the passages are small vertical shafts, or murder holes, rising within the wall thickness.

The floors, roofs and parapets of the two towers had already been removed when S. H. Grimm illustrated the gate in the 1780s, as too had the second floor and roof over the linking passages above the inner arch, though the pitched roofs are depicted intact in Prowze's map of 1572, and likewise appear to be shown in Van Dyck's illustrations of half a century later (*see* Figure 2.3). The upper storeys of both towers were originally reached via a spiral staircase built into the thickness of the wall adjacent to the removed western buttress, the staircase being accessed from inside the doorway leading from the street to the western tower. The first-floor doorway leading off the staircase is blocked, whilst that on the second floor now has an arched head of brick. The stair continues up, rising above the main walls as a small octagonal watch-tower.[58] Each of the two upper storeys of the eastern tower was reached via the chamber-like passages which cross the building above the inner arch of the entrance, and it was from these too that the portcullis was operated and, no doubt, the bridge also. Doorways with chamfered jambs link the passages to the towers: three of these have shouldered lintels, but the fourth, leading into the second-floor chamber in the east tower, now has a four-centred arch, probably a repair. The first-floor passage is lit by a pair of small single-light trefoil windows in each wall, front and back. In contrast, the passage above has a window with an ogee head (with trefoil cusping) positioned centrally in the north wall, looking out of town, with a similar window west of central in the south wall. The corresponding position in the east half of the south wall is occupied by a fireplace. A two-centred doorway at the east end of the wall leads

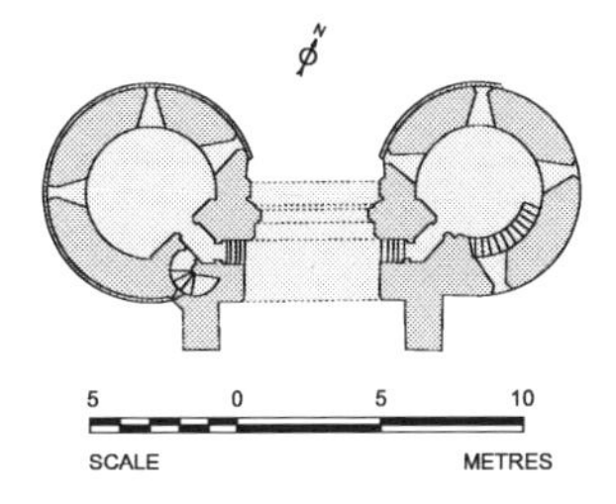

Fig. 3.14 Reconstructed ground-floor plan of Land Gate as built.

to a garderobe in the south-east buttress: this has a loop-light in its east side.

Reflecting the westward, downward slope of the site, there was a basement-like area beneath the western tower's ground-floor chamber but, apparently, no corresponding basement beneath the eastern tower. Ignoring this, the lower two storeys within each tower were served by narrow, irregularly spaced arch-headed slit-like windows, now remade externally, but shown un-restored in early photographs. There are three each to the ground and first floors of the west tower and four to the east tower. All these have ashlar dressings to the inner splays and segmental pointed rear-arches. In the third storey the embrasures are square headed, less tall and are evenly spaced: five in the west tower and seven in the east. They have rough rubble splays and flat rear lintels and appear to be later in date than those on the storeys below. Certainly representing insertions are the gun ports cut through the upper tier of the plinth, immediately below the ground-floor windows. There are two in the west tower, one pointing northwards down Landgate, the other (now hidden by terraced housing) facing west along the town ditch. Two of those in the east tower are visible in Grimm's drawing of the interior (*see* Figure 3.13). The wide external surrounds of the gun ports are assumed to indicate external visibility splays, but the detail is now hidden by later blocking. In all probability these are the 'gunholes' for which bricks were bought to make the arches in 1588, though guns were already stationed here in 1548 when Ordnance at the Landgate was made ready for a salute for a visit by the Regent.[59]

The wall between Land Gate and Postern Gate

The *c.*100 metre (about 330 feet) length of wall which extends westwards from Land Gate to the site of the former postern gate at the foot of Conduit Hill is backed on its rear (townward) side by Turkey Cock Lane, sloping down from Landgate to the foot of Conduit Hill.[60] It is this section of defence which was described in 1378 as a fosse, along the line of which the Corporation at that date intended to build a wall (*see* above) and this section too which is shown in an undated drawing attributed to Van Dyck and assumed to have been made in the 1630s (*see* Figure 3.15). The

Van Dyck view looks east along what is today Tower Street and shows the Land Gate standing prominently. A horse on the extreme right of the picture appears to be on a track exiting the town through the postern gate (out of picture) at the bottom of Conduit Hill. The town wall is shown stripped of its crenellations and reduced on the townward side (against Turkey Cock Lane) to the height of a low boundary wall. Between it and the residual ditch is what at first sight appears to be a relatively steep, rough bank, but this is more likely to represent dense foliage — shrubs and bushes — reducing the visible height of the town wall.[61] There is a hint in the drawing of a shallow, much silted ditch (marked as a line of shadow) between the highway and the (assumed) scrub, but by this date the ditch was of minimal depth.

Assumed to have been built soon after 1378, the wall in this area survives as a high retaining wall extending along Turkey Cock Lane, to the rear of the houses which front Tower Street. The superstructure could never have been of sufficient width to have incorporated an elevated walkway and is therefore likely to have been low: probably a crenellated parapet only two metres or so in height at the merlons. This would have been sufficient to give protection to defenders and townsfolk using the lane which, in 1557, was described as a 7-feet (2.15 metre) wide footway. Bearing in mind the extensive height of the lower retaining element on the extra-mural side, such a low wall on the townward side would not have been a problem from the point of view of defence. Walls of similar design are found in other local towns, as for instance within the sister ports of Winchelsea and Hastings.[62]

The only archaeological section so far cut across the town dyke was located in this area, approximately 15 metres (around 50 feet) to the east of Conduit Hill.[63] As Figure 3.16 shows, a horizontal deposit of dark grey silt was encountered at the bottom of the excavation.[64] In the mid 18th century (dated by a George II coin) pebbles were used to infill the dyke above the silt, with further ground raisings subsequently. Although there is no specific statement within the excavation report to indicate that the bottom of the archaeological trench represented a change in layer, this is the implication. Neither does the text state whether any trial excavations were carried out below the general base of the trench in order to ascertain whether any archaeological deposits lay buried at a greater depth, though the wording of the text suggests that no such investigations were made. It is therefore possible that even if a clean, natural-looking layer was found beneath the silt deposit at the bottom of the trench, this could have represented re-deposited material used to deliberately backfill the lower parts of a ditch. The silt layer contained part of a late 17th-century candlestick holder, so this is likely to represent the ground surface as shown in the 1630s Van Dyck illustration. For safety reasons the archaeological trench could not be extended up to Tower Street, and thus the archaeologists had no opportunity to ascertain the width of the ditch, nor was it possible to obtain early road levels within Tower Street.[65] In 1511 this section of the town ditch was specifically described as 'the water ditch' (*see* above) so there must have been some form of bank extending along the northern edge of the ditch in order to retain the water.

On the townward side of the 17th-century silt deposit the archaeologists encountered a wide, low, flat-topped berm.[66] It is from this berm that the town wall rises (Figure 3.16). Given the position at which the post-1378 town wall meets the Land Gate, and the wording of the 1378 grant of The Halton to the Austin Friars, it seems reasonable to suggest that at this point the town wall follows the line of the fosse's townward crest. If this is so, it probably explains the reason for the flat top to the berm, for it would have been necessary to cut into the upper part of the earlier bank in order to establish a firm foundation for the wall, at the same time ensuring the wall was of sufficient height to serve as a defensive obstacle. Even with this conjectured extra height to the earlier bank, unless topped by a timber palisade the pre-1378 earthwork could have been of neither sufficient

Fig. 3.15
Drawing of 1630s attributed to Van Dyck, looking east along present-day Tower Street. [Private collection]

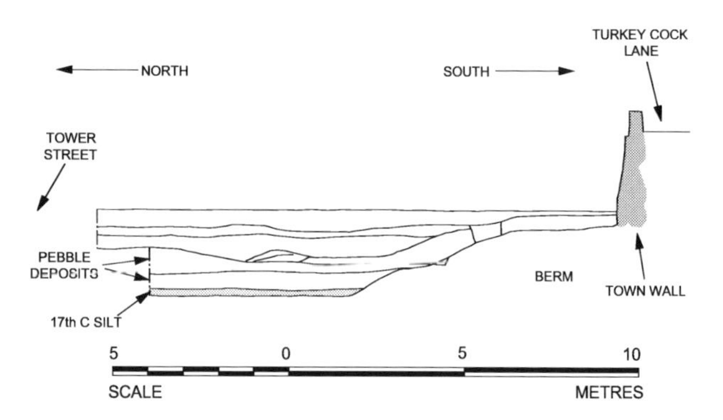

Fig. 3.16
*Section through town wall and ditch. [After SAC **119**, 223, Figure 11]*

height nor steepness to have served as anything more than a minor defence or boundary marker.

Postern Gate

Very little is known about the Postern Gate which stood at the bottom of Conduit Hill. Clark, writing in 1861, states that it was removed in 1736, but Vidler corrects this, stating that some people within the town wished it to be preserved and made a counter suggestion that a way be knocked through the wall to its west. This, however, was found to endanger an adjacent section of wall and the idea was therefore left in abeyance. According to Vidler the gate still stood in 1767 when a section of wall immediately to its east was pulled down to enable carriages to come into town that way: he adds that 'some years after this the Postern Gate was put into a good state of repair'. It was, he says, finally taken down soon after 1819.[67] If this was so, presumably the large gap in the wall shown in the town plan of 1771 relates to the section demolished in 1767 immediately to the gate's east.[68] Although a long section of crenellated wall to the west of the gate is visible in Van Dyck's 1633 sketch of the town from the north, the gate is hidden from view by buildings. It is, however, shown in a 16th-century sketch map of the town from the south (*see* Figure 3.9) as well as in Prowze's map of 1572 and Jeake town map of 1667.[69] All these depictions are at thumbnail size. The former is the only one to show the top of the gate upstanding above the crenellations of the town wall. All show the opening as a simple archway built into the wall, without either towers or other associated structures.[70] Prowze indicates a bridge crossing the town ditch immediately to the north and this is referred to in documents. For instance,

Fig. 3.17
Base of interval tower in Cinque Port Street car park. The structural join in the town wall is to the right.

it was taken up and rebuilt in 1588 when the town ditch was cleaned. Mayhew specifically states that it was a 'removable wooden bridge', further adding that the gate was for the use of foot passengers.[71] Even so, the horse shown apparently leaving the gate in the Van Dyck sketch suggests that by that time it may also have been accessible to pack animals (Figure 3.15). Perhaps it is significant that by this date the bridge appears to have been removed and the relevant section of ditch infilled, a configuration also indicated by the Jeake map of 1667.

The wall between Postern Gate and the interval tower in Cinque Ports Street car park

To the west of Conduit Hill the ground on the townward side of the wall once more rises and here too the wall doubles as a substantial retaining wall.[72] In common with the areas to west and east, both Prowze (1572) and Jeake (1667) indicate that the extra-mural side of the wall was fronted by the town dyke, now entirely backfilled.

Although no interval towers are shown in any known cartographic source, the base of a substantial tower nonetheless survives within the Cinque Port Street car park, at a distance of about 70 metres (*c*.230 feet) to the west of Conduit Hill. The tower, now topped by a much later gazebo, measures 6.85 metres (22 feet 6 inches) wide and projects 3.75 metres (12 feet 4 inches) from the wall (Figure 3.17). A further 4 metres (13 feet 1 inch) to the west is a very obvious vertical joint in the external face of the wall, indicating a break in construction. A similar break in the opposite (townward) face was found during archaeological investigations. It is associated with toothings for an intended (but apparently never built) *c*.1.50 metre (*c*.5 feet) thick wall returning southwards. As with the extant length of wall to the east, the lower part of this intended wall seems to have been designed to retain the ground behind.[73] The implication is that the section of town wall which includes the interval tower once terminated at an intended very pronounced kink in the wall's alignment. In the event, when the next phase came to be built the intended kink was abandoned and the existing alignment was projected westwards.

Wall from the interval tower to Ferry Road

The section of wall extending westwards from the joint adjacent to the interval tower was built to a different design to those parts to its east. Whereas the latter doubled as a retaining wall, this section was wholly freestanding, crossing a gently curving indent in the side of the hill slope. This probably explains the intended but abandoned kink in the wall – in all probability the original plan was to follow the contour of

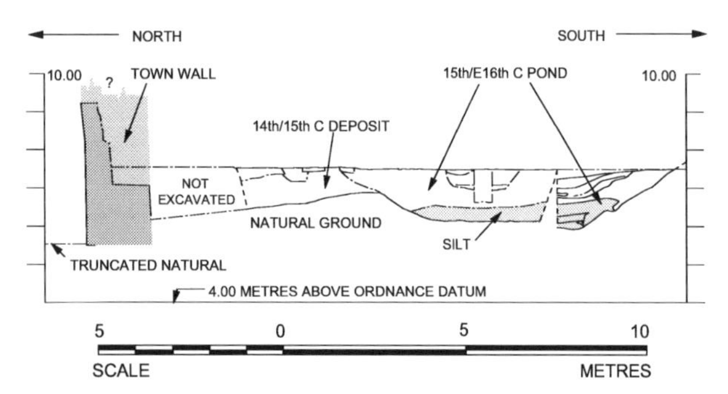

Fig. 3.18
Composite section through town wall and intra-mural deposits at a distance of 17 to 20 metres west of interval tower.

the hill, thereby maintaining the same retaining-wall design as used elsewhere. Because it was built freestanding and was considerably taller than the height of a man, the 1.5 metre (*c*.5 feet) thick wall in this area must have incorporated a narrow walkway, protected on its extra-mural face by the crenellated parapet shown in Van Dyck's 1630s illustration (for which *see* Figure 2.3).

Adjacent to the abandoned wall toothings the approximate medieval ground level on the townward side of the wall had already dropped considerably and this downward slope continued so that by 20 metres (approximately 66 feet) to the west of the interval tower the ground level was virtually the same on both sides of the wall (Figure 3.18). Despite this, the wall in this area was evidently built with very little depth of foundation.[74] Most of the town wall along the 65 metre (*c*.213 feet) length from this point westwards, up to and including Market Road, was demolished to ground level sometime after 1766. It should be borne in mind that until the late 18th or early 19th century Market Road had been a cul-de-sac (initially known as 'Pongarden' and later as Jarret's Yard) which stopped short of the wall on the townward side.[75] The medieval ground levels continued the downward slope so that, at a point half-way between the interval tower and Market Road undisturbed natural ground lies less than 4.70 metres (15 feet 5 inches) above ordnance datum and is overlaid by a build-up of deposits which predate the construction of this part of the town wall — the foundation is cut into and rests upon the deposits.[76]

The freestanding wall in the area between the interval tower and Market Road is not of one date but was built in short lengths over a number of campaigns, the breaks not only being indicated by structural joints but also by marked variations in quality of construction. For example, the 20 metre (approximately 66 feet) length of extant wall to the west of the wall scar is of two builds, with the western part more poorly constructed. Beyond this the quality again improves, suggesting yet another phase of construction. However, this improvement does not last, for further west excavations have revealed a very distinct break. The eastern part is well built and has a substantially founded base, whereas that to the west is very poor, incorporating a kink in its alignment and an insubstantial foundation. The joint between the two demonstrates that the poorly-built section of wall is of later date: its foundation is cut into and built upon medieval fill which includes 15th-century material and thus, at the earliest, could not have been built until that time.

The general east to west downward trend in medieval ground levels noted above did not continue to the west of Market Road. By 60 metres (about 197 feet) west of the road the 13th/14th-century ground surface had risen significantly and, furthermore, this 13th/14th-century ground surface had structures built upon it. Levels established between this point and Market Road are consistent with a gradual east to west rise in ground, with the lower part of the wall once again serving to retain the land on the townward side.[77]

As was the case with the archaeological section taken across the town ditch immediately to the east of Conduit Hill, the below-ground investigations along this entire central length of town wall were able to show that on the extra-mural side the wall was built off a wide earthen berm. At the points investigated the berm incorporated a gentle slope down towards the town ditch, but at no point was it possible to investigate the nature of the ditch itself. At one location limited probing suggested that the bottom of the ditch might at that point be located at a depth of 3.45 metres (11 feet 4 inches) above ordnance datum.[78]

What the above demonstrates is that when the alignment of the stone defensive circuit was laid out it did not follow the meandering marsh-edge contour (as appears initially to have been the intention) but instead took a direct route across the indentation. Given the documentary references to timber defences erected in response to the 1385 scare (*see* above) the construction of this length of stone wall over a series of short building campaigns would be consistent with the piecemeal replacement of the 1385 timber defence, each campaign being designed to replace a relatively short length of timber palisade. In this way the vulnerability of the town could be minimized during the construction work. If this hypothesis is correct, it indicates that the timber wall likewise took the short route across the contours and suggests that the structural joint and abandoned wall toothings immediately to the east of the interval tower in Cinque Ports Street car park may indicate the point to which the stone town wall had been constructed by 1385.

It is possible that at one point along its length the

alignment of the 13th-century or earlier fosse meandered partially across this later alignment of the town wall. This may, for instance, explain the low-lying medieval deposits encountered in the area of the poorly-built section of wall, though it would be dangerous to place too much reliance on this without additional evidence. Another possibility is that the new wall cut into the edges of small projecting spurs of slightly raised land on either side of the indentation, explaining why the lower parts of the defence in these areas act as a retaining wall.

One effect of the wall's straightened alignment appears to have been to trap water (perhaps only seasonally) in the trough of low land on the intra-mural side of the wall, presenting the townsfolk with an obvious location to tip unwanted soil and waste. It seems a fair assumption that it was this wet, pond-like area which gave rise to the area occupied by Market Road and Meryon Court (behind 25-27 High Street) becoming known as 'Ponde-garden'. Whether the pond thus formed was accidental or deliberate, and whether it was put to a purposeful use has yet to be demonstrated. Vidler considered it to have been both deliberate and purposeful.[79] He gives no hint as to its intended use, though it is worth noting that recent archaeological investigations have shown that during the 15th or early 16th century a substantial pit/pond was deliberately dug into the rising ground in the area immediately to the east of the interval tower, presumably in association with some form of industrial activity. Thus, ponds were being deliberately formed in this general area. Mayhew confirms that the town wall had a number of drains through it, but makes no reference to the making of the ponde-garden. [80]

The wall from Ferry Road to Strand Gate

The length of wall extending from the end of Ferry Road to Strand Gate has not been subjected to below-ground investigations, though there has been limited above-ground recording. Furthermore, one important section extending north-eastwards from Strand Gate, against The Mint, is depicted largely extant in a 1784 illustration by the artist S. H. Grimm. As elsewhere along the line of the wall, the present extra-mural ground level is quite flat.[81] On the intra-mural side the ground slopes gently down to the junction of The Mint and Mermaid Street adjacent to the site of Strand Gate — at this point the ground on the intra-mural side of the wall is virtually level with that on the outside. Although it needs to be confirmed by archaeological investigation, this gradual downward slope on the townward side of the wall appears to follow quite closely the buried medieval ground surface. Thus, despite the fact that to the west of Market Road the lower 3 metres (roughly 10 feet) or so of the wall acts as a retaining wall, this retaining section gradually reduces as the internal ground level falls away.

In his map of 1572 Prowze illustrates a postern gate opposite the end of Ferry Road, though whether this gate ever existed has still to be confirmed. What neither Prowze nor the other cartographers show – but is known to have existed – is a bastion which until *c.*1850 stood

Fig. 3.19
Cellar beneath Sharpes Pottery, The Mint, showing the remains of the town wall (right) and the wall of an interval tower (left). Note the recess in the wall of the interval tower and the start of a substantial arch built into the town wall, with 19th-century brickwork to the right. Beyond this, out of picture, the face of the town wall remains intact.

Fig. 3.20
Cellar beneath Sharpes Pottery, The Mint, showing one of four arches incorporated into the west wall, on the opposite side of the cellar to the town wall. All four arches are blocked with brickwork. They appear to represent the remains of an arcade which supported the side of the street which, at this point, appears to be built intruding partially over the town ditch.

close to this point. Concerning this, Holloway writing in 1847 says that it stood 'in the north wall, about 200 feet [*c*.61 metres] from the north-west corner of the same'. By that date its top had been reduced to the same level as that of the town wall which at this point, he informs us, stood 6 or 7 feet (1.8-2.1 metres) high. He describes the bastion as a half circle in plan with embrasures for cannon similar to those in the Land Gate 'and which are about 9 feet (2.75 metres) above the upper level of the ditch', suggesting the lower part of the structure was built solid. He goes on to say that 'The inside diameter of the building [above the solid base] is 29 feet (8.85 metres), and its projection from the face of the wall into the ditch is 15 feet (4.60 metres). About 6 feet (1.80 metres) above the ditch was a round hole cut through a solid stone: but for what purpose does not appear'.[82] It should be noted that, unlike the rectangular-plan tower visible in the public car park in Cinque Ports Street to the east, the front face was semi-circular in plan. Given that it appears to have been designed for cannon, it is possible that the tower/bastion was built as part of the known extensive improvements made to the town defences in the 1540s (*see* above).

The 'north-west corner' of the wall referred to by Holloway relates to the point where the town wall curves southwards so as to skirt the eastern edge of the Strand before meeting Strand Gate. The nature of the town wall in this area was different. It was in this area too that the town ditch was first backfilled and built over: both Prowze (1572) and Jeake (1667) depict houses squeezed into the space between the wall and the street, whilst the 1576 town sesse makes specific reference to 'all the new buildings along the town ditch'. Despite this, a short isolated length of the ditch is shown remaining in Jeake's 1667 plan. Whereas further to the east an earthen berm separated the ditch from the wall, here the street squeezed the ditch hard against the town wall, which in consequence rose sheer from it. This much is clear from a 12.5-metre (41 feet) exposed length of wall visible in the basement beneath Sharpes Pottery,

Fig. 3.21
Strand Gate and town wall looking north, S. H. Grimm, 1784.
[© The British Library Board. Add Ms 5670 f.17 [31]]

Fig. 3.22
The same view as in Fig. 3.21 showing present appearance, 2007.

Fig. 3.23
Extra-mural face of town wall incorporated into rear wall of 54 The Mint. The right-hand half was raised in height when the upper storey of the house was extended over it, but the left-hand part stands to near original height, but with the parapet removed. Note how the roof gable of 54 The Mint is set back at this point to respect the original alignment of the wall walk. The brick building (extreme right) is Sharpes Pottery and the barrel-vaulted structure (foreground) is the top of the Strand Conduit, a water cistern built into the backfilled town ditch.

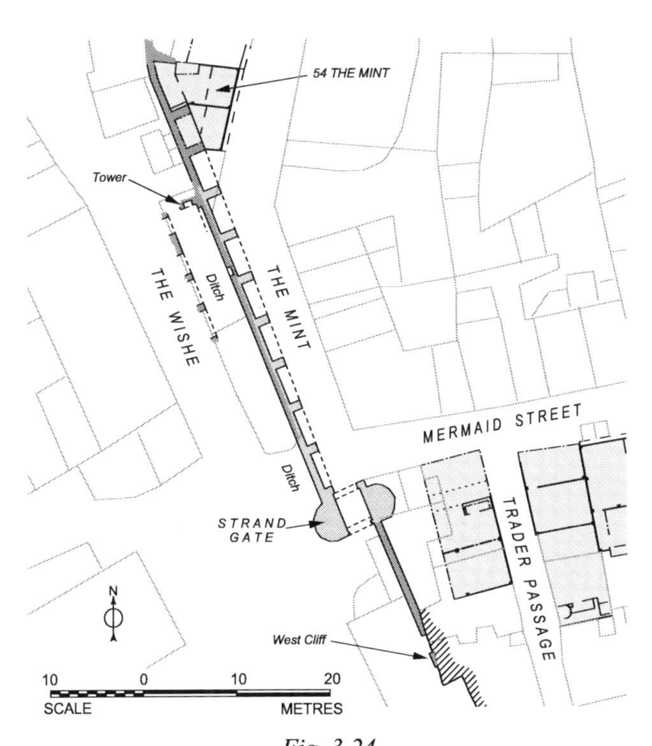

Fig. 3.24
Reconstruction plan showing section of town wall from 54 The Mint to West Cliff. Size and footprint of Strand Gate are conjectural.

Fig. 3.25
Detail from late 16th-century plan showing Strand Gate from the south. Note the fort ('The Mount') at south end of Strand. [TNA MPF 1/3]

either constructed or rebuilt in the 19th century over the town ditch on a 5-metre (16 feet 5 inches) plot between The Mint and Wishe Ward. The wall is faced down to the basement floor located at *c*.3.00 metres (*c*.10 feet) O.D., but how much of the ditch is buried below the modern floor is unknown. At the northern end of the basement, roughly 34 metres along the wall from the site of Strand Gate, can be seen the remains of what must be the base of yet another interval tower – apparently quite small – projecting out from the town wall. Like that in Cinque Ports Street car park, it was rectangular in plan. Whether the visible face represents the interior or exterior of the tower is uncertain, for the evidence is contradictory. Built into it is an arched recess (? the base of a garderobe chute) whilst immediately to the south the town wall itself incorporates the broken remains of a substantial arch (*see* Figure 3.19). The tower appears to have projected only 2 metres (6 feet 7 inches) from the wall. These are not the only features of interest within the basement, for whereas the cellar's eastern wall is formed by the town wall, the western side (likewise of rubble masonry) incorporates four wide arched openings, now blocked with brickwork (*see* Figure 3.20). The impression is that the adjacent street has encroached into the town ditch and is supported at this point by an arcade.[83]

Although the lower, retaining-wall element of the town wall survives, from this point southwards (extending up to the site of Strand Gate) the superstructure has been destroyed. This is the part shown by Grimm in his illustration of 1784. As Figure 3.21 illustrates, he depicts the wall standing to near full height, backed on the townward side by a blind arcade of seven bays, with probably an eighth extending up to the building in the background. Each is capped by a gothic two-centred arch supporting a wide parapet walkway. The arcade continues into 54 The Mint where fragments of two further bays are still incorporated within the rear wall. The section contained within No. 54 is arguably the best preserved part of Rye's town wall in that it still stands to a height of 6.0 to 6.5 metres (19 feet 8 inches to 21 feet 4 inches) above Wishe Ward on its extra-mural side, suggesting that at this point, even without its parapet (now lost) it rose at least 8 metres (26 feet 3 inches) above the base of the town ditch (Figure 3.23).[84] Despite this impressive height, the superstructure element of the wall is vcry thin, measuring only c.1.00 metres (*c*.3 feet 3 inches), though this increases markedly at the piers of the arcade. Thus, the purpose of the blind arcade becomes clear: it was an economy incorporated at the design stage in order to give strength to the wall whilst at the same time supporting the elevated walkway. A variation of this theme is to be found at Southampton where the facade of a Norman building was incorporated into the 14th-century town defences, except in that instance the arcade is on the exterior and the work is of more than one date.[85] A more precise parallel was the section of

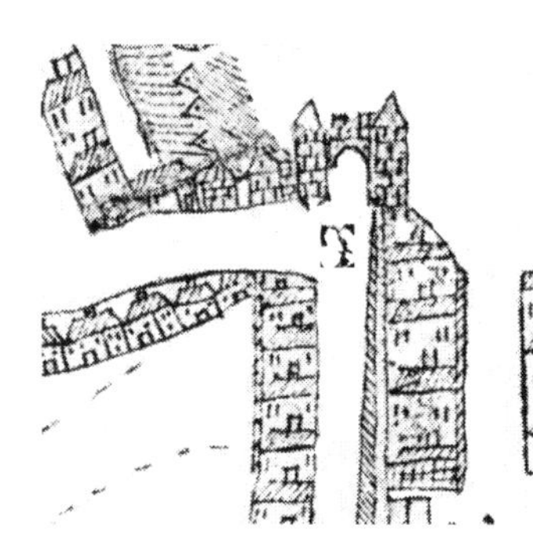

Fig. 3.26 (left) Detail from Jeake Map of 1667 showing Strand Gate viewed from the north. [ESRO RYE 132/15]

town wall which skirted the western side of the port town of King's Lynn.[86]

Strand Gate and the town wall linking to West Cliff

No doubt access to the wall-walk mentioned above was gained from the upper part of Strand Gate, the arch of which were removed in 1767: the gatehouse itself was finally demolished in 1815 (*see* above). Thumbnail sketches of dubious accuracy are shown in a number of small-scale 16th-century representations of the town, as well as on the Jeake map of 1667. Most are consistent in that they show the gate aligned to The Mint with its main arch facing south onto the Strand, and this is confirmed by Grimm's illustration. Evidently it was a simple tower gatehouse consisting of a passage on the ground floor, flanked by turrets and having either a parapetted roof platform or perhaps a chamber above. The arcaded section of town wall referred to above extended northward from the north-western corner, whilst a short southern section of wall extended southwards from the opposite corner so as to plug the gap between the gate and West Cliff.

In its relationship to the town walls the gate closely resembled that of neighbouring Winchelsea's Pipewell Gate, largely rebuilt c.1400 following damage by the French. As with Pipewell Gate, a plaque was incorporated into the front wall, over the arch. That at Winchelsea bore a heart-like shield decorated with a beast (said to be a squirrel) with, above it, the name of the serving mayor, John Helde. The Rye plaque is today reset in the wall of a house at the corner of Mermaid Street and bears the port's arms. Unlike the Pipewell Gate, Strand Gate incorporated a portcullis, known to have been renewed in 1559 (*see* 'Land Gate' above).

Rising to the south of Strand Gate is West Cliff, a vertical face of sand rock which already reaches a height in excess of 4 metres (over 13 feet) at a point 20 metres (about 65 feet) south of Mermaid Street. The short section of wall which extends south from the site of Strand Gate blends seamlessly into the rock face in order to fill the gap between gate and cliff. On average it measures only 820 mm (2 feet 8 inches) thick and stands to a height of about 4 metres (approximately 13 feet) above the modern ground level on the extra-mural side. The townward side is today occupied by an 18th-century extension to Trader Cottage etc: a medieval building fronting Trader Passage. The addition (now a separate building called 'The Borough Arms') is elevated over three metres (roughly 10 feet) above the Strand, from which it is reached via a flight of steps built against the face of the town wall. From this point southwards the cliff served as a natural defence. Where its face was weak or needed building forward, the fissures were infilled with masonry (Figure 3.27).

Fig. 3.27
Rock face of West Cliff visible in background within a modern building constructed against the cliff just beyond the southern end of the town wall. Note the masonry infilling to fissure in foreground.

With the gates defining the entrances to the town and the northern length of town wall forming a distinct edge to the built-up core, there is no doubt that the medieval defences did much to define the town's character. True, during the 16th century limited growth spilled outside the defences, particularly in the Wishe suburb to the northwest of the town, and here, during the second half of the century the visual impact of the wall began to be diminished as houses were built in the town ditch, partially hiding the wall. Arguably, the only medieval structures which had a greater impact upon the town's visual character were the religious buildings. It is to these that we will turn in the next chapter.

4 RELIGIOUS, EDUCATIONAL AND WELFARE BUILDINGS

INTRODUCTION

Despite having been founded by a great, albeit absentee Norman abbey — Fécamp — Rye as a town was somewhat poorly served by religious establishments. True, it does have a larger than average church, prominently sited on the highest point within the town. Even so, it is unusual for a Cinque Port in that it had only one parish church. Later in the medieval period it was similarly poorly served by friaries, never having had more than one simultaneously — firstly the small and very short-lived Friary of the Sack (dissolved by 1307) and subsequently, from 1364, a small Austin friary. Lastly, from an early date, there was a hospital — St Bartholomew's — founded by Fécamp some distance outside the town, beside the landward route leading in from the north.

The effects and influences these establishments had on the lives of the town's inhabitants have been adequately discussed by others elsewhere: there are chapters devoted to this topic in Gill Draper's companion volume, 'Rye History', and another, relating to the later period of the town's religious history, in Graham Mayhew's 'Tudor Rye'.[1] In similar manner, the parish church of St Mary and the surviving medieval buildings at the Friary of the Sack (site not proven, *see* below) and the Austin Friary have been fully covered by others. Although the Trust for Thanet Archaeology has recently been engaged in archaeological work on the site of the Austin Friary,

Figure 4.1
Parish church of St Mary. Exterior from south west.

Figure 4.2
Parish church of St Mary. Eastern end wall.

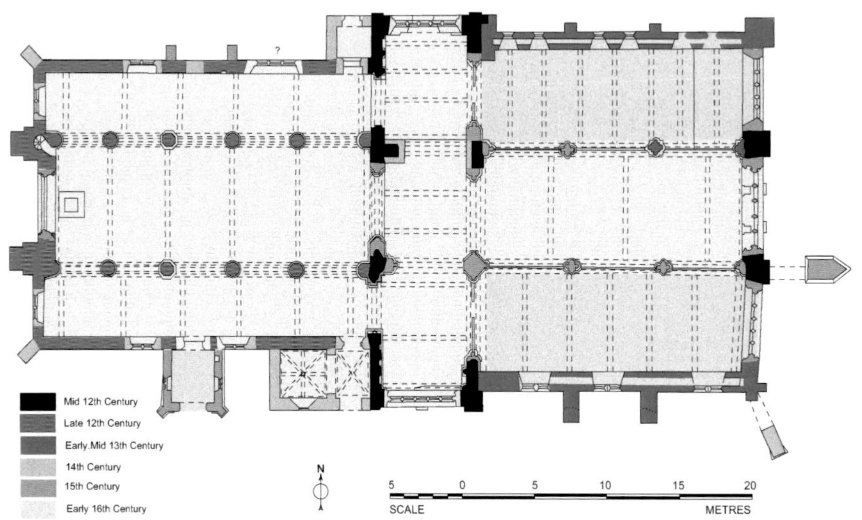

Figure 4.3
*Parish Church of St Mary. Reconstructed plan as in the early 16th century showing phases of development. [After a plan by W. H. Godfrey, reproduced in VCH **9**]*

Figure 4.4
Parish Church of St Mary. Respond to nave arcade adjacent to the opening to wall passage.

which promises to lead to new insights into the buildings there, research since the late 1930s has to date added nothing significant to the accounts of these three buildings given in Volume 9 of the Victoria County History of Sussex published in 1937. Because of this past coverage, all that is needed here is a brief, illustrated summary of the religious buildings, sufficient to give a flavour of their size and form to those unfamiliar with these monuments. Those wishing a more complete account are directed to the publications mentioned above.

PARISH CHURCH OF ST MARY
(Figures 2.3, 2.4, 4.1-4.22 and 6.29)

Not unusually, the parish church is easily the largest building within the town, measuring 47.50 metres (156 feet) long internally and 23.8 metres (78 feet) across its transepts. As the plan reproduced in Figure 4.3 shows, it is constructed to a cruciform layout and, like St Thomas' in New Winchelsea, incorporates substantial chantry chapels to the north and south of its exceptionally long chancel.[2] Extending westwards from the central tower and transepts is the nave, only marginally longer than the chancel and flanked to north and south by aisles of lean-to type. There are two south porches (one with an adjoining vaulted chamber) and a north porch.

No structural evidence within the building can be dated to before the middle years of the 12th century. The main eastern part — the chancel, crossing and transepts — are the earliest, with the nave and its attendant side aisles erected slightly later, towards the end of the 12th century: this section uses transitional Norman/Gothic detailing. Given that Rye had by then already been in existence for about a century, it seems likely that this sequence represents the progressive reconstruction of an earlier, less substantial church upon the same site. By local standards, the work was carried out to a high standard. A number of good, albeit in some instances restored, mid and late 12th-century architectural features remain, a selection of which are illustrated in Figures 4.4 to 4.12. They include a pair of reliquary cupboards in the east wall of the chancel

Figure 4.5
Parish Church of St Mary. Nave showing late 12th-century south arcade with clerestory above.

Figure 4.6
Parish Church of St Mary. Pair of 12th-century reliquary cupboards in the east wall of the chancel.

Figures 4.7 to 4.9 (above)
Parish Church of St Mary. 12th-century wall arcading in north transept (including details).

(Figure 4.6), the remains within the transepts of two tiers of blind wall arcading, the upper tier of which incorporates foliated corbels resting upon grotesque heads (Figures 4.7-4.9), the fragment of a fine canopied external doorway with chevron and nail-head ornamentation in the south wall of the south transept (Figure 4.12), pinnacles to some of the buttresses, and

Figures 4.10 and 4.11
Parish Church of St Mary. 12th-century capitals.

Figure 4.12
Parish Church of St Mary. Remains of 12th-century canopied doorway (blocked), located west of central in the south wall of the south transept.

the remains of high-level wall passages. Many other early features were swept away by later medieval improvements.

The northern chantry chapel (now dedicated to St Nicholas) was built onto the chancel about 1220 and its southern counterpart (now dedicated to St Clere) perhaps thirty years later. As with the main body of the church, these too incorporate the remains of wall passages associated with the high-level side windows — in this instance the cills are elevated 3.2 metres (10 feet 6inches) above the floor (Figures 4.13

Figure 4.13
Parish Church of St Mary. Paired lancets in north wall of the north chapel, viewed from within the north transept. The 15th-century screen is just visible at the bottom of the shot.

Figure 4.14
Parish Church of St Mary. Detail of passage in wall of north chapel.

Figure 4.15
Parish Church of St Mary. Detail of north arcade to chancel showing clustered columns.

Figure 4.16 (left)
Parish Church of St Mary. Detail of vaulting boss in south porch.

and 4.14). The north chapel includes clustered columns to its surviving arcade pier (Figure 4.15) and internal window hoods enriched with dog-tooth ornamentation, whilst the interior of the windows in the south chapel have stops ornamented with heads to the internal hoods and edge-roll shafts rising to moulded capitals with foliage ornamentation. Apart from the subsequent addition of porches, the chantry chapels represent the last enlargements made to the church.

In the 14th century new, presumably larger windows were inserted in the walls of the aisles and two-storeyed north and south porches were added into the re-entrant angles between the transepts and side aisles. That on the south incorporates a small ground-floor vaulted chamber which may have served as an additional chantry chapel. Alternatively, it may have formed accommodation for a chantry chaplain with associated space for teaching, which was frequently carried out by such chaplains, of whom there were many in Rye.[3] The room's vault has foliated capitals and a decorative central boss (Figure 4.16). A good doorway leads from the porch into the nave's south aisle (Figure 4.17) whilst a blocked doorway in the east wall of the northern porch chamber suggests that this was entered from the adjacent wall passage. Having been superseded by a new north doorway, protected by the

Figure 4.17 (left) Parish Church of St Mary. Doorway leading from south porch into south aisle of nave.

Figure 4.18 (left) Parish Church of St Mary. Detail of lower panels within 15th-century screen between north transept and north chapel.

new porch, the original late 12th-century north doorway leading into the nave's north aisle midway along the north wall was blocked: in contrast the opposing south door appears to have remained in use. Buttresses were added, including an angled flying buttress at the south-eastern corner of the southern chantry chapel.

Early in the 15th century the chancel's south arcade was either rebuilt or inserted, as too was the western arch within the north arcade (Figure 4.19). In order to counteract the thrust of the new southern arcade a flying buttress was built in line with it, beyond the eastern wall of the chancel (*see* Figure 4.2). Also from this period belong the arches between the transepts and chantry chapels and the nave's enlarged clerestory windows, as well as the south, east and west arches of the crossing — the northern arch had been rebuilt the previous century. Probably the present upper tier of the squat central tower also dates from this time, though this could be a little earlier. Perhaps a little later in the 15th century is the western of the two south porches, built to protect the replaced late 12th-century doorway in this location — the porch is visible in Figure 4.1. Re-set fifteenth-century timber screens divide the chantry chapels from the transepts (for a detail *see* Figure 4.18), and most likely other screens separated them from the chancel.

Corresponding to the dramatic upsurge in the town's fortunes during the opening years of the

Figure 4.19
Parish Church of St Mary. General view looking from crossing into chancel and north chapel.

Figure 4.20
Parish Church of St Mary. General view looking east.

16th century, the end walls of the transepts were remodelled to incorporate large and impressive late-perpendicular windows, flooding this part of the church with light (*see* Figures 4.21 and 4.22). In particular, the north-facing window formed an impressive focal point at the top of Lion Street, dominating the view of all who passed up this street from High Street.

The church suffered badly following the reformation, and this was particularly the case with

Figure 4.21
Parish Church of St Mary. General view looking from crossing into south transept.

Figure 4.22
Parish Church of St Mary. Northern gable of north transept showing early 16th-century window and re-fixed 12th-century doorway.

regards the two large east-end chantry chapels flanking the chancel. Both are lucky to have survived, and, indeed, were probably retained only because they were put to alternative secular use, walled off from the remainder of the church. As noted in Chapter 3, one of the two was utilized as a munitions store. The south chapel was later divided into two floors, the upper of which served as a school for poor pupils. The chapels were not re-opened to the church until the 1860s. All the medieval roofs have been rebuilt: some are post-medieval, others modern. Van Dyck's illustration of the south side of Church Square made in 1634 (*see* Figure 6.29) shows the nave with a very shallow roof pitch, in contrast to the present arrangement which replicates the pitch of the earlier roof. Access to the upper stage of the central tower is today via a 17th-century staircase intruded into the north porch. In the 1880s galleries, which had been erected around the nave, were removed, the clerestory windows rebuilt, the off-centre Norman doorway in the north wall of the north transept re-positioned centrally, and the late 12th-century west doorway was blocked.

FRIARY OF THE SACK[4]

The Friars of the Sack were a minor order who begged, heard confessions, preached and performed the burials of non-parishioners. Settled in Rye sometime before 1263, they were one of the orders discontinued by the Council of Lyons in 1274, though it was some decades before all the houses of Sack Friars disappeared, with some surviving until the end of the thirteenth century or just beyond. A tenement (house) which had formerly belonged to the friars is recorded in a Rye rental of Edward 1's reign (1272-1307). Since the rental is not precisely dated, this gives only an approximate *terminus ante quem* for their disbandment within the town. When the rental was made, John, son of Robert Paulin the bailiff, was occupying the former Sack Friars' house and paying a quit rent of 4d on it.

Old Stone House, 40 Church Square, has traditionally been identified as their house, though this appears to be solely based upon the fact that it is a stone structure and is known subsequently to have owed a 4d quitrent. However, the rental of Edward I recorded

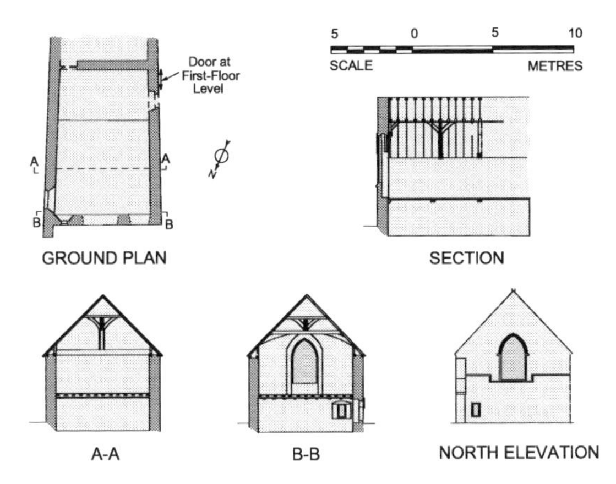

Figure 4.23
The Stone House, 40 Church Square.
Reconstruction as during the 15th century.

nineteen quit rents at this rate.

There are other problems in identifying 40 Church Square with the house of the Sack Friars, not least the fact that the surviving architecture is datable to *c.*1300 — at the very end of the order's existence. Furthermore, the building shows no similarities in layout to a conventional friary building, being aligned north-south with a large window (heavily restored) incorporated into the street elevation. The work is of good quality and is, perhaps, more likely to have been built by a wealthy Rye merchant. Even if this was the site of the friary, the weight of the evidence suggests the present structure was more likely to have been erected by John Paulin soon after he acquired it.

Little of the building of *c.*1300 survives. What remains is but the northern end of the range, the southern part having been demolished in antiquity. The east elevation was always an external wall, built against a narrow lane, but doorways in the west wall at both ground- and first-floor level indicate that a building to the west has been removed. Both the first-floor joisting and the crownpost roof represent reconstructions of the 15th century, and thus very little is known regarding the layout of the structure in *c.*1300. Even if built by a Rye merchant, it is difficult to reconcile either the original features or those of the 15th century with a normal dwelling. The nearest local comparison is with the (earlier) Marlipins in New Shoreham, West Sussex, which is thought to have been erected as a commercial building.[5]

THE AUSTIN FRIARS

In contrast to the Friars of the Sack, much more is known about the Austin Friars within the town, both in respect of their interaction with the townsfolk and their monastery. The history of the friary has been discussed elsewhere by Gill Draper and, except in the briefest of summary, will not be reiterated here.[6] It was a late foundation, established following the issue of a papal licence in 1364: as such it was the earliest of the four successful Austin foundations established after the Black Death, though preceded by an unsuccessful attempt at Coventry. Furthermore, whereas all the other late houses were founded by aristocratic patrons, that in Rye was established under the patronage of the town elite. The house remained closely linked to the townsfolk — especially the elite — throughout its existence. It was always small, and appears to have hit a particularly low point in the middle of the 15th century, perhaps reflecting the town's economy, when the Friary was described as almost without brethren.

Figure 4.24
The Stone House, 40 Church Square.
Northern (street) elevation.

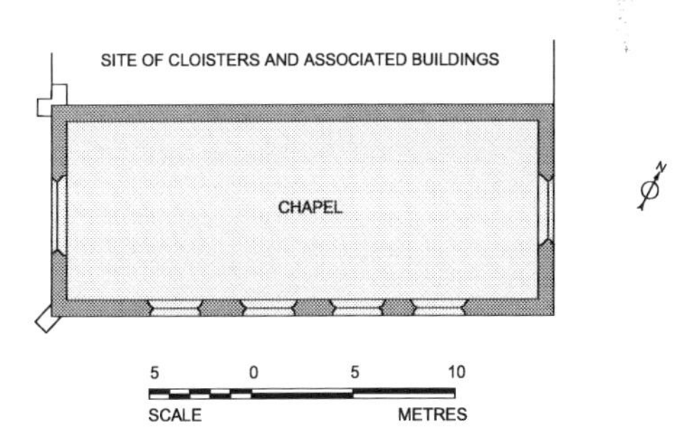

Figure 4.25
Chapel of the Austin Friary.
Reconstructed phase-1 plan of the chapel.
*[After a plan reproduced in VCH **9**]*

Initially the monastery was established upon a two-acre site which had became submerged by water and made worthless: the site had once been occupied by five houses. This site evidently became unsatisfactory for the friars and in 1378 (following the French raid on

Figure 4.26
Chapel of the Austin Friary from the south west as drawn by S. H. Grimm, c.1785.
[© The British Library Board. Add Ms 5670, f.17 [32]].

the town in 1377) they were granted a more favourable location on common ground called The Halton just inside the north-eastern corner of the town, within the defences (*see* Chapter 3). In this, the history parallels the re-location of the Dominican Friars at New Winchelsea which, having moved to a low-lying site in 1339, in 1357 re-located to higher ground, just within the defences in the north-eastern part of the town.[7]

In Rye, all that survives today of the friary buildings above ground is the chapel, constructed with its western end wall hard against Conduit Hill, leading down from High Street to the former postern gate in the town wall, which gate gave access to St Mary's Marsh and the drinking-water sources beyond. As Figures 4.25 and 4.26 illustrate, the chapel is a simple rectangular structure measuring about 23.2 metres by 8.40 metres (76 feet by 27 feet 6 inches) internally. The west wall incorporates buttresses at the corners and there are the remains of original windows with two-centred arched heads in the west, south and east walls. The west window has lost its tracery and only fragments of that to the east window survive, but the four openings in the south wall have fared much better (Figures 4.27 to 4.29). A new roof was erected over the chapel in 1524, but this has since been destroyed and the walls raised in height.[8]

The apparent absence of original windows in the north wall is probably explained by the fact that the cloisters stood on this side, as evidenced by the remains of a weathering course. Towards the western end of the north wall is a doorway, constructed using secondhand material, probably salvaged from the original friary site.[9] Although no upstanding remains now survive in this area, in 1847 Holloway recorded that 'running from the north east angle of the chapel in a northerly direction and in a straight line from the eastern gable, is still traceable the foundation of a building, to the extent of 30 feet (9.15 metres) in length from south to north and

Figures 4.27 to 4.29
Austin Friary: one of the chapel's four south windows. Top: Detail of tracery. Above left: Base to moulded jamb. Above right: Face on stop to hood moulding.

12 feet (3.65 metres) in width from east to west.'.[10] What may have been the cloistral buildings are shown on this side of the chapel in Van Dyck's 1633 drawing of the town viewed from the north (Figure 4.30), but there are problems of interpretation.[11]

The Austin Friars' Rye house was dissolved in 1538, at which time its precincts were described as having a garden, orchard and small close, containing one acre, valued at 8s 4d.[12] The boundaries of the friary precinct are uncertain, but do not seem to have occupied the entire block of land bounded by East Cliff, High Street, Conduit Hill and Turkey Cock Lane. In extent, this area comprises 1¾ acres, which does not equate well with the one acre mentioned at the dissolution. Some of this discrepancy (about three-eighths of an acre) is perhaps explained by the fact that the southern part of the precinct (to the south of the chapel) seems to have been sold off prior to the dissolution for the construction of new properties abutting the north side of High Street (*see* Chapter 2 and Chapter 7). The rest of

Figure 4.30
Detail from illustration of Rye from the north drawn by Van Dyck in 1633, showing the buildings on the site of the Austin Friary. The chapel is the substantial building shown with the dominant roof and two-centred window in its gable. Projecting forwards from the left-hand end is depicted a building which may have been the east range of the cloisters with, at right angles to it, running parallel to the chapel, a structure which may have been the friary's north range. No west range can be seen against Conduit Hill. The buildings to the west (right) of the chapel are houses (since demolished) extending down the western side of Conduit Hill.
[© The Pierpont Morgan Library, New York. III, 178. Not to be reproduced without the express permission of the Trustees of the Pierpont Morgan Library]

the difference could be explained by the approximate nature of the assessment given in 1538, though it is also worth bearing in mind that there appear to be the remains of a medieval domestic dwelling contained within Dormy House [104], whilst there are medieval references to properties on the eastern side of The Halton. There is more than one way to interpret this data, but it could indicate that the friary precinct never extended as far east as present-day East Cliff (the street which enters town through Land Gate) but was instead confined to the western two-thirds or three-quarters of this block of land.

After the dissolution the buildings were put to a number of short-term uses, including (apparently) as a place of residence for Huguenots during the second half of the 16th century, and as a warehouse or storehouse at one time during the 17th century.

HOSPITAL OF ST BARTHOLOMEW [13]

Founded by Fécamp Abbey and of early origin, the hospital stood beside the main landward link about half a mile to the north of the town and, as such, lay outside the borough boundaries. It is known that the bulk of the lands which supported it were on the western side of the road within that part of Rye parish retained by Fécamp when the King took back the town in 1247: it is here that the hospital's garden was sited and this is generally also considered to have been the location of its buildings. However, it may be relevant that a 1670 survey of the late hospital's 32½-acre residual demesne lands (the lands had been divided up in 1560) refers to a vacant one-acre plot on the opposite side of the road, in Playden parish, as 'a little piece whereon formerly the manor house stood'. In this respect, it might be relevant that although the hospital is usually referred to as 'the hospital of St Bartholomew of la Rye' or similar, it was on occasions referred to as St Bartholomew's, Playden. In truth, not only is the precise location of the hospital currently unknown, it is not known for certain upon which side of the road it lay.

The hospital was an establishment for lepers, though a notification of 1249 makes clear that it accommodated others besides, and these others were perhaps the great majority. It took both men and women, described as poor in 1380, 1420 and 1442. From 1337 the hospital was in the king's hands, being a property of an alien house, and following the final confiscation of the lands of Fécamp abbey it was granted first to Syon Abbey and subsequently to Westminister. However, gradually the hospital became a free chapel and increasingly the chaplain or warden/master was a non-local person appointed by the crown. As a result, as was so often the case, the buildings fell into an increasing state of dereliction. A visitation of 1442 found that the master of the hospital had been absent for six or seven years and had let the revenues to lay people, the chapel and the house (*mansio*) of the master and paupers were in complete ruin, and no paupers were maintained there.[14] There is no reason to envisage any subsequent revival. With the loss of an active hospital, the poor of Rye were deprived of an institution which had supported them. Evidence about the care of Rye's poor is lacking for this period. However, at the end of the 15th century and in the early 16th century, a period of sharp population increase (*see* Chapter 5), there were beggars in the town and the jurats of Rye set them to work on the town walls and on other tasks.

THE ALMSHOUSE

In the early 16th century the Landgate suburb stopped abruptly at the edge of the marshland of St Mary's Marsh, at the point where the narrow, slightly elevated spit of land linked to the upland to the north. Here, in the middle years of the century on the very edge of the marsh, a little to the north of Landgate Square, the corporation set up an almshouse. The site, given to them for that purpose by Alexander Welles in 1550, was described in the grant as 'one piece of waste land lying without the Gate, called Land Gate, to the king's highway there towards the east, containing on this part 32 feet (9.75 metres); on the south 60 feet (18.30 metres); on the west 21 feet (6.40 metres); bounded on the north by the common lands of the town'. The grant was on condition that the mayor, jurats and commonalty erect within a stated time 'a certain house and closes and make a garden adjoining to the said house ... to the use of the poor of the said town, viz., of the decaying, sick, diseased, feeble and infirm, to be constituted as a hospital for ever'.[15]

That the almshouse was built is confirmed by the chamberlain's accounts which in 1552 record the expenditure of £29. 15s. 2½d for the erection of the building itself. This included the purchase of an existing timber-framed building in the town for £3, a further £3 to a carpenter for taking it down and re-erecting it as the new almshouse, plus the purchase of an additional 7 tons of timber, 2 loads of laths, 130 bushels of lime for the plaster, tiles, and payment for 10,000 bricks made locally at Eston's Kiln at 9s. per thousand for the construction of the chimney in the new almshouse, together with 2,000 Flemish brick at 6s. per thousand 'to make the top of the chimney in the almshouse'.[16] Later, in 1581, the building was extended, a further chimney stack was erected, and the Corporation conveyed an additional piece of ground at the rear, stating that 'the donage and offall of the town shall be there laid [to make up the ground level] and then to be enclosed'. The plot of ground was intended to serve as a new garden.[17]

The only depictions of the building are in the Jeake map of 1667, the town map of 1771, and in two mid 17th-century sketches of Rye. Holloway, without giving his source, states that access to the upper level of this two-storeyed timber structure was by an external timber staircase. In the 18th century the building fell into increasing dereliction, and in 1784 the corporation pulled it down and replaced it by 'two small low dwellings' erected upon the same site. These were in turn pulled down in 1849 in order to make way for the road bridge over the railway: they were replaced at the railway company's expense by three new dwellings built on the southern side of the Royal Military Road on the edge of the marsh, close to the boundary between Rye, East Guldeford and Playden parishes.[18]

The almshouse at Landgate was not the only provision the corporation made for the care of the disadvantaged. In 1580 they purchased a dwelling in what is now Watchbell Street in order to house 'all the poor children kept of alms by the town ... under the government of an honest man and woman'. Here they would be 'brought up to serve God and to be kept to work'.[19]

THE GRAMMAR SCHOOL

The existence and importance of education is clearly indicated in medieval Rye, which had an early literate culture, underpinned by education provided by chaplains. Rye wills between 1497 and 1560 include bequests for the education of children (several boys and one girl), rather than for a school building. They name sixteen clerks, curates and chaplains, besides the vicars and the parish clerks. Earlier there may have been as many as six or seven chantry chaplains at Rye's one parish church, a strong indicator that some were teaching the town's youth.[20] What happened during the years immediately following the suppression of the chantries is unclear, but the corporation was certainly aware of the importance of education.

In April 1564 it was agreed that a schoolmaster be employed by the corporation, paid for by a levy of £25 12s. 4d on the wealthiest inhabitants, while the 1576 sesse (local tax) lists two schoolmasters.[21] Even so, it is not until the foundation of the grammar school under the terms of the will of Thomas Peacock, a freeman and jurat of the town, that the first specific reference to a school house is found. In his will, drawn up in 1638, he stated that he was 'minded and determined to found a free school in Rye for the better educating and breeding of youth in good literature' adding that he had 'erected and built a house in the Longer Street [High Street] which he intended should be employed and converted for the keeping of the said school'. The premises he vested in the mayor and jurats in trust, for the sole purpose of founding the school for the benefit of the poor of Rye. The schoolmaster was to be supported by endowments specified in the will. The formal conveyance to the corporation was by deed dated 16th October 1644.

Both the history of the school and the building itself have been fully described elsewhere.[22] Peacock had built his structure in 1636 and it remains one of the outstanding buildings of the town. As Figure 1.6 illustrates, it has a fine brick elevation of five bays divided by giant pilasters standing on high pedestals, with bases of stone and moulded capitals of brick, together with a brick entablature. The pilasters are carried up through both storeys. The attic storey is lit by three pedimented dormers which project forward, through the front slope of the steeply-pitched gabled roof. Originally there was a single room on each of the two main floors, that on the first floor being 11.45 metres x 6.65 metres (37 feet 6 inches x 21 feet 9 inches) reached by a steep internal stair. A narrow passage leads under the eastern end, giving access to the rear of the property. The rear wall is of stone rubble.

5 POPULATION, HOUSEHOLD DENSITY AND OCCUPATIONS

POPULATION TRENDS, *c*.1300 TO 1490

Population size and wealth-distribution during the medieval period are notoriously difficult to estimate in English towns generally, and this is made far worse in the case of the Cinque Ports on account of their exemption from the taxes normally used to assess size and wealth. Given that Rye and Winchelsea shared a common harbour and were subjected to the same general economic conditions, the likelihood is that during this period they experienced a broadly similar fluctuating pattern of growth and recession though — as far as can currently be judged — Rye was by far the smaller of the two. If this generalisation is true, then the populations of both towns grew throughout the early medieval period, reaching a high-point during the 13th century. It may be no coincidence that it was at that time that Rye's parish church attained its present dimensions (*see* Chapter 4).

Winchelsea was able to maintain its size well into the following century, after which the increasing effects on seaborne trade of the Hundred Years War, decimation caused by the Black Death, and, above all, a devastating raid on the town by the French in 1360, had a crippling overall effect upon the size of population.[1] As has already been indicated, a French raid had already caused problems at Rye somewhat earlier, in 1339, and in addition to this Rye had to contend with inundation of low-lying land to the east of the hill (*see* Chapter 2). Bearing these points in mind, it seems likely that population decline started a decade or so earlier than at Winchelsea. Even so, these problems still lay in the future when the town's earliest extant rental was drawn up during the years around 1300.[2] Although far less detailed than Winchelsea's well-known rental of 1292, the document does, nevertheless, contain some useful information and allows a size comparison — albeit *very* crude — to be made between the two towns.

Headed 'Rents of our lord king, of his town of Rye' the rental contains 225 entries. In all 141 properties are described as tenements (including three which are qualified as being half tenements and one blanket entry which reads 'from the heirs of John Bone for all their tenements'. Additionally, there are two entries for burgages (one expressed in the plural), one for a house, another for stone walls (*walle lapidee*, presumably indicating an abandoned stone-built structure), two for salt-houses, one for a tannery, one for a tavern (*taberna*), and five entries in which the wording implies a mill, or land associated with a mill. There are five entries for '*placea*' (meaning open space, site, plot, or square) including one for the farm of 'the Courton' — an area already discussed in Chapter 2, located between the church and market. A total of 31 entries relate to land, including a farm rent for pasturage from the field of the lord king. Rather disappointingly, a further 34 entries give ambiguous descriptions or state nothing more than the name of the tenant, and these include an entry for 2½ marks due from the 'mayor and community of the aforesaid town' — this entry alone could conceal a number of properties.

Occasional entries give information about the location of the tenements: for instance, three tenements are described as *in the market*, three as *outside the gate* and one is described as *under the cliff*. In all, 19 entries qualify the properties as being principal tenements. In fact, a not inconsiderable number of tenants held more than one holding within the town, indicating that some acted as rentiers — John Torel, for instance, is entered for seven properties and Pharon John for no fewer than ten. It is also worth bearing in mind that property would commonly have been leased out, and thus those listed in the rental were not necessarily Rye residents. One property was held by the Abbot of Robertsbridge.

Assessed at a very crude level — 225 entries in the Rye rental, compared to 802 in the Winchelsea equivalent — Rye was about a quarter the size of Winchelsea. Such a figure is not inconsistent with the situation as indicated from other sources (*see* Chapter 1) though by no means should the rental evidence be used as proof of this impression. Many variables and unknown factors must be taken into account: for instance, the Winchelsea rental relates to the built-up area of the town only, whilst the numerous entries for land contained within the Rye rental imply that in Rye the rural borough lands in the north of the liberty were included; all the Winchelsea entries relate to individual plots (although some probably had more than one dwelling upon them, whilst others had none) whilst an unknown number of entries within the Rye rental encompass more than one holding. Furthermore, unlike at Winchelsea, there is no guarantee that all the properties in Rye owed a rent to the crown. There is no way of overcoming these problems and inconsistencies.

An absence of known rentals for the town throughout the rest of the medieval and Tudor periods has removed the chance of reliably charting change over time, though the schedule of decayed rents made in 1351 confirms that twelve years after the 1339 French raid 52 tenements and a mill were still deserted, whilst another 18 had been lost to the ravages of the sea (*see* Chapter 2). This total of 71 decayed rents had risen to 88 by 1356-7, indicating that desertion was continuing. Based upon the data contained within the Edward I rental, it would seem that by 1356-7 approximately 40 per cent of the king's rents were claimed to be decayed. This figure is not too dissimilar from the 48 per cent recorded at Winchelsea a little under a decade later.[3]

Information from deeds seems to confirm that population within the town was falling during the 14th century and that no major improvement occurred until late in the following century. For instance, the density of housing in the Landgate suburb seems to have still been decreasing in the 15th century, whilst a considerable expanse of undeveloped open land is referred to at the eastern end of High Street in the 1490s (*see* below and Figure 2.6).[4] In the same general area at least ten properties are mentioned in deeds between 1334 and 1376 as being on the eastern side of The Halton, just inside the Land Gate. Some of these were at that time built upon, others were described as plots of land: most were abandoned soon afterwards, though whether this was due to erosion, devastation by the French, general depopulation, or a combination of all three is impossible to tell.[5] Many of these properties are likely to be included within the list of decayed rents.

The only town-wide assessments which survive from this period to give an indication of the minimum number of households within the town are a half-scot and a scot of the early 15th century — one is dated 1414, the other undated, but was probably compiled between 1415 and 1420.[6] These two documents are the first which indicate the ward structure of the town. Both list separately the mayor, jurats, and perhaps the bailiff (14 persons in all) at the head of the return, with the other residents grouped by ward below — 21 and 23 respectively in the ward *Extra Portam*; 28 and 31 in Nesse Ward; 45 and 55 in Watermill Ward; 20 and 16 respectively in Market Ward. Thus, in the 1414 half-scot a total of 128 householders paid, whilst the undated scot lists the slightly higher total of 140. How many households were exempt is impossible to tell. If the household totals implied by the early 14th-century rental and by the 1356-7 decayed rents are at all reliable, the number of persons assessed in the scot and the half-scot suggest that by the early 15th century there may have been a modest (though possibly temporary) recovery in the population total, as, indeed, was the case at Winchelsea.

The boundaries of the ward structure at this time are unknown, so the two returns can tell nothing about the distribution of population at this period. A further impediment is the fact that the mayor and jurats are not listed by ward. Despite these deficiencies, some useful information can be gleaned regarding the distribution of wealth. In the (fuller) undated return all fourteen members of the 'town corporation' were taxed at sums between 3s 4d. and 13s 4d. Only fifteen other residents were taxed at similar levels — two in *Extra Portam* Ward, five in Nesse Ward, two in Market Ward, and six in Watermill Ward. Thus, 21 per cent of taxpayers were assessed at 3s 4d. or above, increasing to 25 per cent at 3s 0d. or over. The figures therefore suggest that at Rye the corporation members were drawn from a small elite group. Even by extending the tax-base for the urban elite down to 2s 6d., the total increases by only six persons. Watermill appears to have been by far the most populous of the wards, with 44 per cent of taxpayers (excluding corporation members).

It seems safe to assume that all 29-35 members of this 'elite' class would have occupied houses of reasonable quality, yet very few houses within the town remain from this period — depending upon precise construction dates, the total lies between a minimum of four and a maximum of eleven. Compared with the houses which survive from a century later, all these 'early' houses are of good size and quality. At what point down the social scale residents lived in houses which, on account of their small size and/or inferior quality, were not capable of surviving to the present day is unknown.

The lowest tax assessments in the return were for one shilling. In all, 51 residents (36 per cent of all taxpayers) fell into this group. They accounted for 57 per cent of taxpayers in *Extra Portam* Ward, 42 per cent in Watermill, 39 per cent in Nesse, but only 18 per cent in Market. The implication of this is that *Extra Portam* was the poorest part of town and few poor persons lived in Market Ward — potentially the town's commercial centre. However, by including those who paid 1s 4d and 1s 8d the statistics become much more evenly balanced between the wards: 78 per cent,

83 per cent, 84 per cent and 88 per cent respectively. It would be dangerous to extrapolate further.

RYE IN 1490

As discussed in Chapter 1, during the years around 1490 cross-channel trade in the area continued to be dominated by Winchelsea, with Rye fulfilling an important, but secondary role. On account of its better overland routes, Rye already served as the principal local market centre. During these years Winchelsea's foreign trade accounted for a staggering 60 per cent of the total customs revenues collected from the eastern port towns of the south coast: Rye contributed only 17 per cent (*see* Figure 5.3).

As for previous periods, the surviving documents for the years around 1490, on the eve of Rye's meteoric rise in both prosperity and population, are too sparse to allow much to be said in detail about household density and distribution within the town, but there are a few important clues. For example, one group of deeds demonstrates that the eastern end of present-day High Street (former Longer Street otherwise Lower Street) was at this period undeveloped open ground — the entire area on the southern side of High Street, extending eastwards from East Street to the Cliff and southwards as far as present-day Ockmans Lane, was vacant land owned by the Corporation (*see* Figure 2.6). Today this same area is occupied by 105-114 High Street and 18-19 East Street. Furthermore, the wording of the boundary clauses makes it all but certain that no houses stood opposite this vacant land, between the friary and the northern side of High Street, extending eastwards from Conduit Hill to the cliff, where 1-8 High Street now stand. Apart from a cottage, the strip of land flanking the southern side of Ockmans Lane was likewise undeveloped.[7] Thus, the town included a large area of open ground just a hundred metres from the market and parish church. Perhaps more significant, this open land was passed through by all who entered town from the only overland approach. Such a picture suggests that in 1490 the town centre was neither populous nor crowded.

This impression of low population density and spaciousness is likewise suggested by the surviving houses of the period. The 55 metre (180 feet) length of High Street frontage between East Street and Lion Street — immediately to the west of the open ground mentioned above — was at this time occupied by just three large plots, each with a detached building standing upon it. Immediately to the west, on the opposite side of the junction with Lion Street, was a substantial detached medieval house on the site of the present George Hotel [24]. Opposite these, on the north side, is 11 High Street [2], a fully-hipped detached house rebuilt early in the 16th century, but retaining a vaulted cellar beneath it. On the western sides of both East Street and Lion Street (short streets linking High Street to the market and church) structural evidence within the surviving buildings indicates that at this period there were undeveloped sections of street frontage in these areas too, though the gaps were perhaps nothing more than access ways. Here too at least two houses on the western side of Lion Street were fully detached. Likewise, the southern side of Market Street, extending from Church Square to the cliff, was occupied by just two detached buildings. This general area of principally detached houses and open lands forms part of the town's trading mercantile core and, given its location close to the general market and church, must always have been regarded as part of the town's heart.

None of the above should be considered as exceptional within Rye at this period. The surviving buildings in both Church Square and Watchbell Street (in the southern part of town) reveal a similar picture of low-density housing with undeveloped gaps between a number of the buildings, and the same is true of the western side of West Street. Until as late as 1555 there was a 37 feet (11.3 metre) length of undeveloped street frontage in Watchbell Street, extending westwards from the corner tenement (now 1-2 Watchbell Street and St. Anthony's, 48, 50 Church Square [87, 90]) which stands immediately to the southwest of the churchyard. Most likely built during the decades either side of 1490 as a principal messuage with an attached secondary dwelling of good quality, there is evidence to suggest that this building too stood totally detached, not only having open land to its west (now occupied by 3-4 Watchbell Street [91]) but also to its north where 52 Church Square now stands.

The central section of High Street, extending westwards from The George Hotel on the corner of Lion Street to an extant (though heavily camouflaged) medieval house on the corner of West Street, has effectively been rebuilt on both sides since medieval times, and thus there are no clues as to household density at this period along this length of street. Further west and south, in the part of High Street now known as 'The Mint' and in Mermaid Street, late-medieval survival is good. Here too, there were undeveloped gaps in the street frontage, but the character of the streetscape is different — the gaps are not so numerous, the frontages of the individual plots tend to be smaller, and the number of houses built to an 'urban' plan is greater (*see* Chapter 7). It is this part of town which appears at this date to have been the most urban in character. It is probably no coincidence that this is the part of Rye's ancient core closest to the Strand quayside.

Although the extra-mural road extending

northwards from Landgate to the upland had formed part of the town's built-up area in the 14th century (*see* above) it subsequently became all but deserted and this seems to have remained the case in 1490 — the only houses likely to have stood in this area are 1 Landgate and, perhaps, a house set well back from the street, in what later became Landgate Square. The second suburb, occupying The Wishe, immediately to the north of the fishmarket area, may not have existed at this time — at this period only one reference has been found to a house in this area: it was in the process of being sold off from its land (*see* Chapter 2).

The picture of Rye's built-up area in 1490, as portrayed by the documents and surviving buildings, is that of a relatively small and un-crowded town. The few houses which remain from before this date are, as will be demonstrated in Chapter 6, mostly well built and of good size. The fact they were not rebuilt during the town's 16th-century regeneration phase suggests they represent the better houses of the preceding century. This impression is largely confirmed by occasional fragments and 'ghosts' of earlier houses incorporated within their successors — although apparently competently constructed, these buildings were much less lofty and considerably narrower and smaller than those which replaced them.

Whilst Rye in 1490 can be identified as 'small' and 'un-crowded' (both relative terms) the above account gives no definitive indication of the size of the town at this period, nor does it give specific data with regards to household density. Can anything more explicit be said as to *how* small and *how* un-crowded the town was at this time? Luckily, it is from this period that one of Rye's earliest and fullest surviving sesses (local tax assessments) dates, and furthermore, it is accompanied by a muster roll and a hundred return, all written within a year or two of each other.[8]

The sesse, which can be dated to 1491/2, is in two parts. A list gives individual valuations of wealth for each person represented. The data upon which the assessments were made is not stated — it was most likely the value of goods, wages and/or lands and rents. Without knowledge of the specific criteria used the data is of little or no value in making comparisons with other similar assessments for other periods, or with other towns. Nevertheless, it is of use in making comparative judgements regarding the distribution of wealth within the community at this date. The second list records the actual sum due to the corporation from each individual included in the valuation list. Ignoring one or two anomalies, the tax is calculated at a flat rate of 2d in the pound. The valuation does not list the taxpayers by ward, whereas, with the exception of the first three names — John Voxon, John Brigges and William Newbury — the tax return itself does. The three names not allocated to ward are persons of neither exceptional wealth nor rank, and it therefore seems likely that they lived beyond the boundaries of the ward structure, perhaps in the isolated upland part of the liberty to the north and north-west of the town, across St. Mary's Marsh and the Tillingham estuary.

Four wards are listed: Market Ward (called 'The Market Place' in the hundred return), Paternoster Ward (Called 'Paternoster Rowe' in the hundred return), Fisherstreet Ward (called 'Old Fisher Street' in the hundred return), and Bucklersbury Ward (called Bucklersbury' in the hundred return). The largest, with 55 entries, was Fisherstreet, followed in size by Paternoster (47 entries), and Bucklersbury (41 entries). Smallest of the four was Market with only 30 entries. In addition to these wards the hundred return includes a 'district' called Chepe, but most of the names listed under this head appear in the tax assessment under Bucklersbury Ward. Eight names appear in the tax list which do not appear in the valuation: all were taxed at the lowest rate of 4d. Four names appear in the valuation, but not in the tax list — three of these (with valuations of £50, £20 and £10) are deleted and therefore may have died or moved away prior to the tax being levied: the other is a clerk, valued at £10. In total the tax list includes 176 names.

To judge from the inclusion of foreign-sounding names, the return appears to include alien householders, and this impression appears to be confirmed by an alien subsidy raised by Parliament eight years earlier in 1483. At that date there were 20 aliens within the town of which one was a keeper of a beer house, five were resident householders and the remainder were specified as not being householders. Despite the time-lag between the two documents, the beer house keeper and two of the alien householders are included in the sesse.[9]

Conspicuous by his absence is the courtier, John Shurley, the King's Bailiff for Rye, who, in addition to holding an extensive urban estate within the town comprising 24 houses, 7 shops, 6 gardens and 3 acres of land, had a large mansion to the northwest of the parish church, next to the vicarage.[10] If he and the vicar (also unassessed) are added, the data indicates a minimum of 178 households within the town at that date. The assessment extends down the social scale to include householders valued at just £2 (taxed at 4d). This implies that the return is inclusive of poor households, though inevitably there would have been some below this level who were exempt through extreme poverty. Widows, for example, account for just 6 per cent of the total and, as a group, are therefore very poorly represented — poor widows are entirely absent. Some destitute males likewise appear to be missing. A deed made the same year as the return refers to a cottage on the south side of Ockmans Lane as being occupied by John Laby. A condition of the grant was that he be allowed to continue to hold one of the three parcels of land being conveyed, together with the cottage, for the remainder of his life.[11] John Laby does not appear in the return — he was probably too poor to pay.

The question which needs to be asked is, how many households headed by impoverished widows or destitute males were exempt? In discussing the sesses raised in 1576 and 1596 Mayhew used the parish registers (the burial registers in particular) to estimate the level of exemptions at those dates. He suggests that in 1576 33 per cent of households and in 1596 28 per cent of households were exempt on grounds of poverty.[12] If (and it is a big if) a similar number were exempt in 1491/2 the total number of households within the town would have been within the range 228 to 237. The impression is that the 1491/2 sesse penetrated considerably further down the social scale than did the 1576 and 1596 returns, though assuming this not to be the case, is a figure as high as 237 households supportable from other sources? If, for example, there were as many as 237 households within the town in 1491/2 could that number be fitted into the space available, given what is known about plot and house sizes during the late medieval period?

The answer to this appears to be yes, but only just. Assuming the Landgate suburb to be virtually deserted at this time and The Wishe not yet colonized (*see* above) and taking into account the known undeveloped lands at the eastern end of High Street, the absolute maximum street frontage available for development in 1491/2 was *c.*2,250 metres (7,380 feet). The street frontages of over 50 plots within the town are known from the structural evidence of the surviving early houses. Unlike later, these were not divided into multiple occupations, but were designed as dwellings occupied by a single household — for this period only three semi-detached pairs have been identified within the town and even these could post-date 1490.[13] Of course some other instances of multiple occupancy are likely, but the available evidence suggests such instances were exceptional.[14]

For this period the average frontage for the known plots within the town is 9.85 metres (32 feet 4 inches) which, ignoring the likelihood of some empty plots, would have given approximately 230 houses. Based upon these admittedly very approximate calculations, a total as high as 237 households in 1491/2 is just about possible. What seems safe to assume is that the actual number was somewhere between a minimum of 190 (allowing a minimal percentage for poor widows and destitute males) and a maximum of 250 — a figure of 200 to 240 households seems a fairly secure assessment.[15]

What, if anything, can the 1491/2 sesse tell about the distribution of wealth within the town at that time? Not surprisingly, the range of wealth is considerable. The total valuation for the town amounted to £6,303. The lowest valuations included within the return were £2, whilst the highest was Adam Oxenbridge (a previous mayor and brother of Sir Goddard Oxenbridge of Brede Place) with a valuation of £500.[16] If the king's bailiff, John Shurley, had been assessed it is possible he would have topped this sum.

In all, 53 households (30 per cent of the total) were valued at the lowest figure (£2): despite accounting for nearly a third of the assessed population they contributed only 1½ per cent towards the total valuation. At the opposite end of the scale were the seriously rich. Eight residents (4½ per cent) were assessed at £200 or above, with a further five (or possibly six) (3 or 3½ per cent) at £120 and £140 each.[17] These 13 (or possibly 14) men accounted for 57½ per cent of the town's total valuation. The range of assessments which signify townsfolk of the 'middling sort' (itself a relative term) is a matter for debate — if valuations of £40 to £100 are used the 'middling sort' amounted to just 15 households (8½ per cent): lowering the threshold to £30 (at which sum the mayor was assessed) increases the figure to 23 (13 per cent): whilst a £20 threshold produces a figure of 52 households (29½ per cent of the total).[18]

That a £40 low-end threshold for the middle classes is too high is suggested by the valuations placed upon the town's mayor and jurats. Not surprisingly, most of these fall into the 'seriously rich' category, but four had valuations of below £100 (one at £80, another at £40 and two — including the mayor — at only £30). Furthermore, a non-jurat, Richard Gervais, lived at St. Anthony's (48, 50 Church Square [87]). To judge from the quality of his house he must have ranked high in town society, yet was assessed in the return at only £40. Admittedly the typological date for the construction of St. Anthony's is *c.*1490, which means it could have been built as early as 1465 or — more significantly — up to 25 years after the assessment was made, during which time Gervais' wealth could have increased considerably. In the absence of other taxpayers who can be attributed to specific extant houses, the necessary corroborative data is missing. Even so, it seems safe to conclude that a low-end threshold of either £30 or £20 for the middle class is more realistic. By including the King's Bailiff and the vicar, 39 taxpayers (22 per cent of the total assessed) were valued at £30 or more: using the lower threshold increases the number to 68 (38 per cent of the total).

An indication of the geographical distribution of wealth within the town can be gained from the wards — Market, Paternoster, Fisherstreet and Bucklersbury

— within which the assessed lived. In 1574 the ward system was (rather belatedly) reorganised to take into account the town's growth over the previous half-century. At this time the number and names of the wards were changed. The boundaries in use in 1491/2 are not known for certain, but there are clues. For instance, deeds which survive from this period allow the locations of the homes of a few taxpayers to be identified, if only approximately. The first name in Paternoster Ward is that of Richard Gervais (or Jarvis) who resided at present-day St. Anthony's [87] in Church Square. Two rich widows listed next to each other in the sesse under Fisherstreet Ward lived adjacent to one another on the northern side of Longer Street (present-day High Street/The Mint). Furthermore, four of the first five persons named within Market Ward had been granted vacant plots of land at the eastern end of High Street in the years immediately preceding the sesse.[19]

Additional potentially relevant data can be gleaned from a sesse raised in April 1563, nine years prior to the known reorganisation of the boundaries. The document lists the wards — sadly, un-named — and gives a brief statement of properties included within four of them, as follows:

- '*The Middle Street, the west cliff and so to the Watchbell Corner*'.
- '*The Lower Strete and so to the Strande gate*'.
- '*The Butchery, Ockmans Lane, without Landgate, and so the Long Strete to Bushes Corner*'.
- '*The Watchebell Streate, Baddinges and from the Church Stile to Mr Whites Corner*'.

A fifth ward, 'The Wishe' is included at the end of the return and varies from the others in that no geographical boundaries are given.[20] This could be because, being extra-mural, the boundaries were obvious, or could indicate that this ward was a relatively new creation, added to take into account new housing development which is known to have occurred in this area in the middle of the 16th century.

It is known from the boundaries quoted in the subsequent re-ordering of the wards that 'Mr Whites corner' was located at the northern end of West Street.[21] Therefore, the phrase '*from the church stile to Mr Whites Corner*' given above refers to West Street, transferred to Middle Street Ward when the boundaries were reorganised.

Based upon the above data, the following ward boundaries prior to reorganisation can be suggested:

- *Bucklersbury*: Middle Street and West Cliff, including the entries described in the hundred return as 'Chepe', which entries appear to equate to the ward which, in 1563, was called 'The Wishe'.
- *Fisherstreet*: the built-up part of High Street (extending from the junctions of Conduit Hill and East Street in the east) through to Strand Gate.

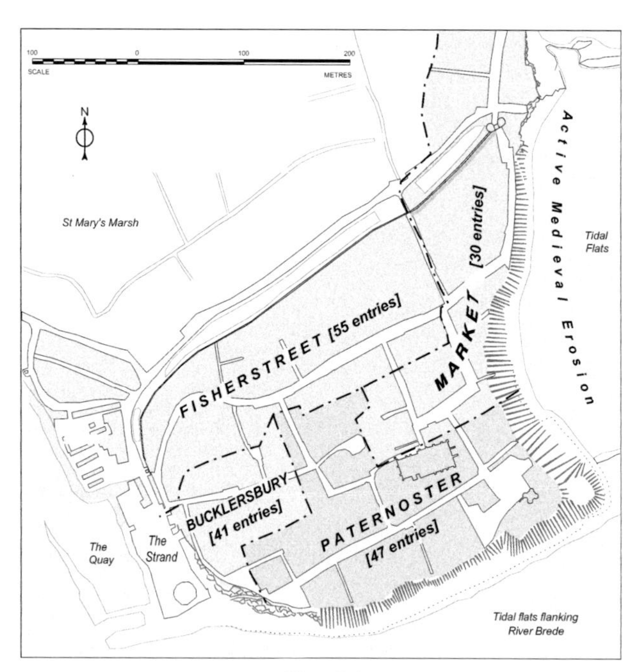

Fig. 5.1
Suggested approximate boundaries of the wards as in use in 1491/2

- *Market*: Market Street (The Butchery), East Street, Ockmans Lane, the undeveloped eastern end of High Street and the diminutive Landgate suburb.
- *Paternoster*: Watchbell Street, Church Square and West Street.

This suggested layout of the wards is summarized in Figure 5.1 and should be compared to the boundaries shown in Figure 5.8 following reorganisation.

How was the wealth within the four wards distributed? Analysis of the values reveals surprisingly little variation between the wards, the percentage of entries valued at £30 or over varying from a high of 26.6 per cent in Market Ward (Landgate, East Street, Lion Street and Market Street) to a low of 17 per cent in Paternoster Ward (Watchbell Street and West Street area). It was the smallest ward — Market — which had the highest proportion of seriously-rich residents: five in all, amounting to 16.6 per cent of the ward total. In contrast, the ward with the lowest density of rich residents was the largest of the four, Fisherstreet (High Street and The Mint area) with only two (3.6 per cent). Bucklersbury (Mermaid Street area) had three rich residents (7.3 per cent) as too did Paternoster Ward (6.4 per cent). In Paternoster all three were amongst the seriously rich — Adam Oxenbridge (£500), William Eston (£400) and William Stonacre (£400) — and it was in this ward too that the exempt John Shurley had his mansion. The similarly valued Robert Crouche (£400) lived in Fisherstreet Ward, whilst Sir John Sutton (£400)

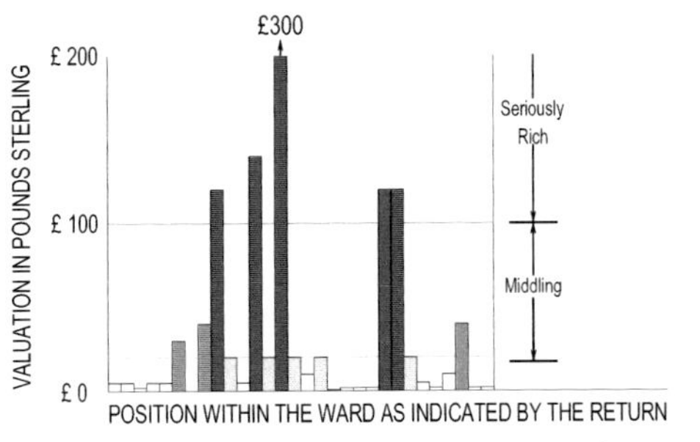

MARKET WARD (Market Street area)

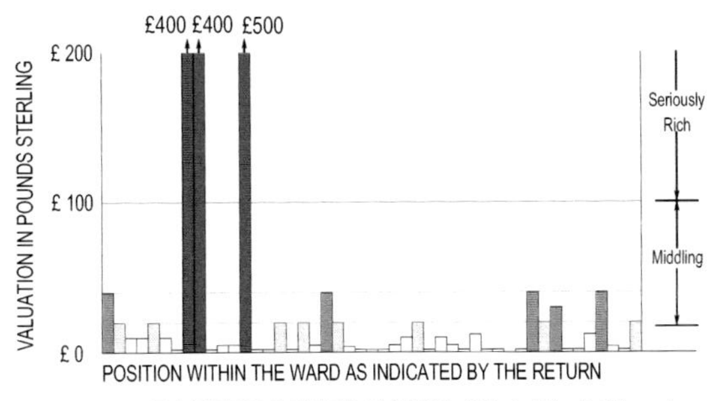

PATERNOSTER WARD (Watchbell Street area)

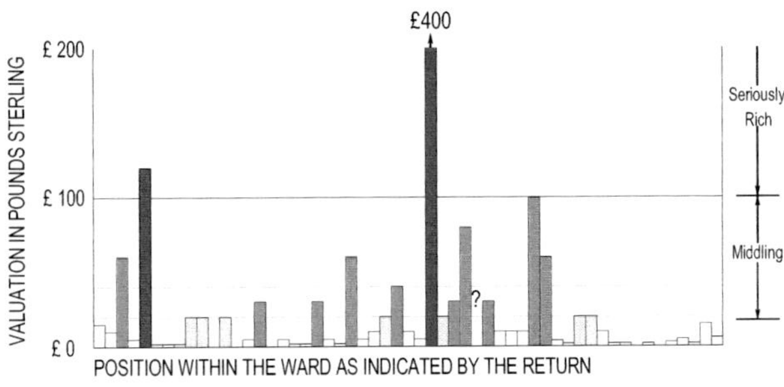

FISHERSTREET WARD (High Street and The Mint area)

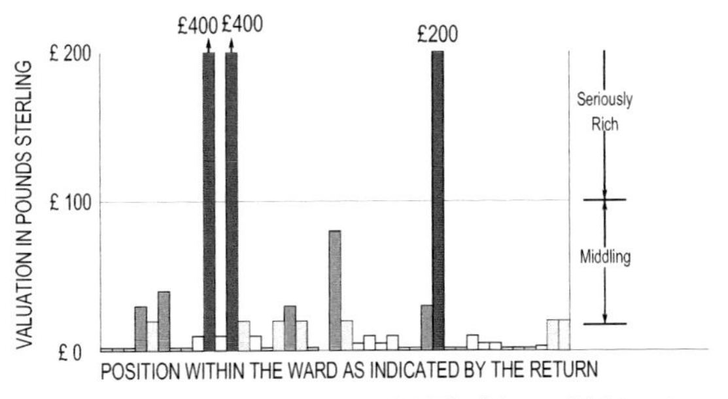

BUCKLERSBURY WARD (Mermaid Street area)

Fig. 5.2
Distribution of wealth by individual assessment, 1491/2

and William Parnell (£400) resided in Bucklersbury Ward.

Despite a relatively even distribution of wealth across all the wards, this does not necessarily mean that the wealth was evenly distributed geographically within each ward. It is possible, for example, that the middle classes and the urban elite congregated within discrete parts of individual wards, with 'slum' areas concentrated within other parts. Here too, the 1491/2 sesse appears to allow some tentative conclusions to be drawn in that the returns for each ward are not headed by the most wealthy/influential. Instead, the entries seem to be arranged in topographical order, either working progressively along one side of a street and returning up the other, or working along the streets zigzagging from side to side. The deeds known for this period are far too few to confirm this impression, but it is worth noting that the two rich widows known to have been living as neighbours in Longer Street are listed next to each other in the sesse, whilst Richard Gervais heads the list for Paternoster Ward — his corner-site house, St. Anthony's, is ideally located to have been the starting-point for this ward.[22]

The return can tell us nothing of potential concentrations by occupation, but, if the sesse is indeed arranged topographically, then it can be used to identify concentrations by wealth. Figure 5.2 shows the relative wealth of each taxpayer arranged by order of entry within the return. No clear-cut segregation by social class is recognizable. For example, if the locations of the entries valued at £40 and over are considered, rarely do two valuations in this range appear together — there are two instances in Market Ward, one in Paternoster Ward (in which instance both taxpayers were seriously rich) and one in Fisherstreet Ward. There are no others. If assessments within the range £30-£39 are included the pattern changes very little. By extending the range down to include all valuations of £20 and over the number of groupings rises considerably. There are seventeen such groupings; three each in Market and Paternoster Wards, five in Fisherstreet Ward, and six in Bucklersbury Ward. It should be no surprise that some of these groupings are made up of longer runs of three/four properties: even so, no runs are recognizable which exceed four properties and there are only two of these — one in Market Ward, the other in Fisherstreet Ward.

Turning to assessments of £5 and less, as Figure 5.2 shows, some concentrations of poor properties are recognizable, with sequences of both four and five neighbouring low-value assessments within both Market and Paternoster Wards, a group of six in Bucklersbury Ward, and groups of both four and eight in Fisherstreet Ward. Indeed, the third quarter of the return for Fisherstreet Ward is dominated by low-value assessments, as is the final third of the Bucklersbury Ward return. These latter two concentrations are the nearest the sesse comes to indicating what may have been predominantly poor districts. Excepting these, the low-value assessments either appear individually or in runs of two or three entries only. Of course, it should always be borne in mind that the sesse excludes exempt properties — the poorest of them all. If these were included it is likely that larger groupings of poor houses would be visible. Even so, the available figures suggest that at this period the wealthy and poor lived side by side.

POPULATION GROWTH, 1490-1565

The bulk of the medieval domestic buildings which survive in Rye incorporate features which date them with a high degree of confidence either to the last quarter of the 15th century or the early part of the 16th century. It therefore seems likely that a substantial number of the 'medieval' and 'transitional' houses which survive today had not been built when the 1491/2 sesse was raised. The reason for the upsurge in building activity within the town during the reigns of both Henry VII and Henry VIII is to be found in the history of the town itself, for the 1490s, and even more so the first forty years of the 16th century mark a transition between two very different phases in Rye's history. It was during this half-century that Rye was transformed from a relatively minor port town into the dominant sea port of the area.

Rye's economic flowering is well illustrated by the customs returns for the area, which likewise graphically illustrate the catalyst for the town's success — the collapse of Winchelsea. As late as 1489-91 Winchelsea still dominated local overseas trade, accounting for a massive 60 per cent of the total customs revenues raised from all the ports from Folkestone in the east to Chichester in the west. At that time Rye's revenues represented a mere 17 per cent of the total — a figure which should, nevertheless, not be belittled in view of the fact that the other nine local ports contributed only 23 per cent between them.[23] If, as seems likely, the customs returns for the period are a true reflection of economic activity within the local ports, it was during the half-century after 1490 that Winchelsea collapsed, allowing Rye to successfully fill the trade vacuum. By 1513/14 Winchelsea's contribution to the Port of Chichester's revenues had dropped to 41 per cent, by 1528/9 it was only 13 per cent, and by 1531/2 just 5 per cent. Between that date and the 1550s (when Winchelsea totally disappeared as

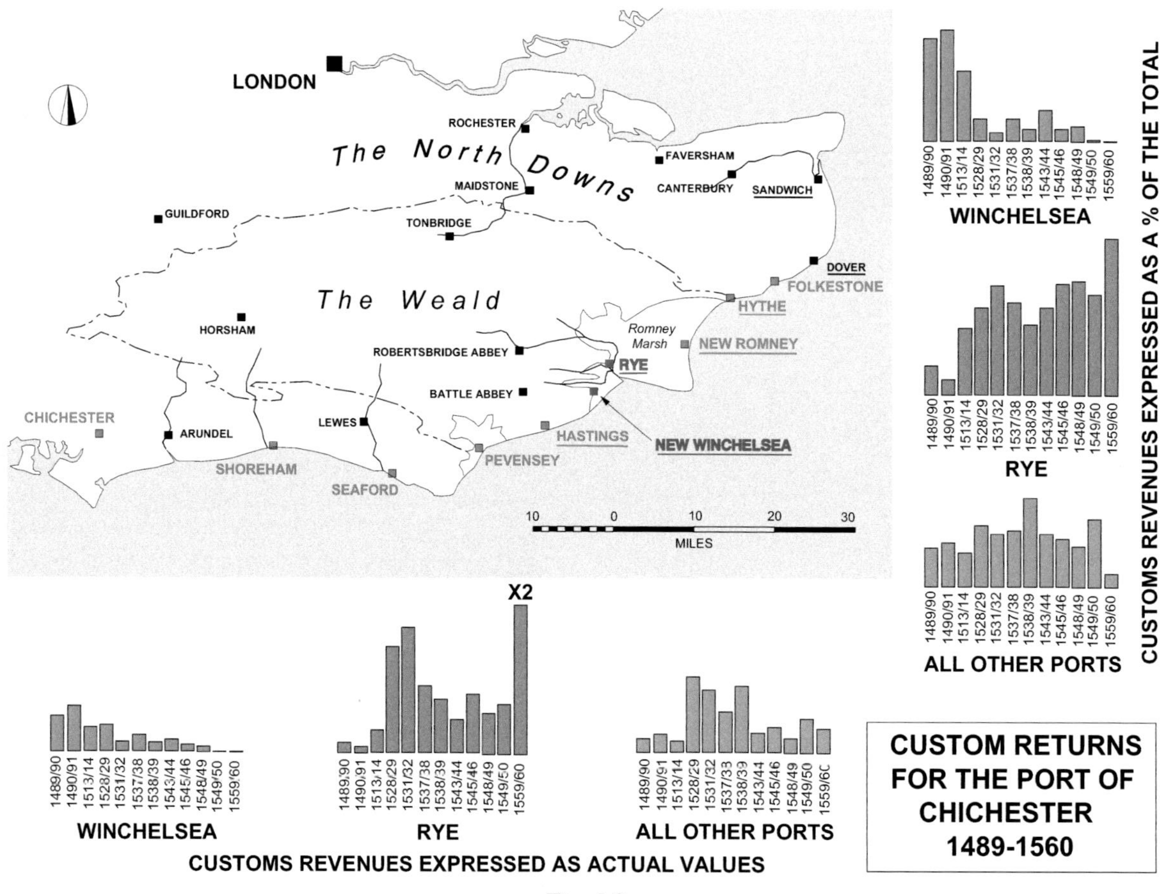

Fig. 5.3

Changes in the amounts of customs revenues paid by Rye, Winchelsea and the other ports under the jurisdiction of the customs officials of the Port of Chichester, 1489-1560 [After Mayhew, 1987, Table 36]

a port) its contribution oscillated between a peak of 18 per cent in 1543/4 to just 1 per cent in 1549/50. During this same period Rye's returns rose inversely, equalling Winchelsea's contribution in 1513/14, reaching four times that of Winchelsea by 1528/9 (*see* Figure 5.3). As Mayhew points out, throughout this period 'The combined share of trade of the two towns situated on the Camber (77.2 per cent of the revenues of the Port of Chichester in 1489/90, 76.5 per cent in 1549/50 [*recte* 1548/49]) remained remarkably constant during this period of transformation'.[24] The reason for Winchelsea's decline was the silting of its harbour, a progressive action which eventually left too little draught of water, even at high tide, to allow ships to reach the town. With the loss of its harbour, the merchants and fishermen of Winchelsea moved away, mostly, it would seem, to Rye which, being located further down the estuary, was at that time unaffected by the silting.

A further indication of this shift in the balance of economic activity is to be seen in the lay subsidy returns of 1524/5, which record no fewer than 55 foreigners taxed within Rye, but only 18 in Winchelsea. Even Hastings, a minor port, had 21 resident foreigners.[25]

If the hypothesis of a mass migration from Winchelsea to Rye is correct — and it is certain that Winchelsea suffered major desertion at this time — it explains why Rye's population soared. This population rise is well attested, though whether it is all accounted for by the influx of Winchelsea residents, or whether some of the increase represented immigration from other areas as Rye's economy boomed, is open to debate.

Despite the approximate nature of the estimated population for 1491/2 (*see* above) it seems likely that the number of households within the town more than doubled during the three-quarter century between 1491/2 and 1565, in which year an inquiry into the ports, creeks and landing places in the rapes of Hastings and Pevensey found the total number of households within the town to be 530, of which 225 were fishermen households and 60 were engaged in merchandise and passage.[26] A rise of this magnitude is consistent with the conclusions reached by Rye's historians. Hipkin, for example, opens his paper on the maritime economy of Rye with the statement that 'During the first half of the sixteenth century the town of Rye enjoyed an economic boom which led to a doubling of its population'.[27] Within his seminal book, *Tudor Rye*, Mayhew implies a similar if not larger increase for the same period, though nowhere does he make a definitive statement as to what he considered the actual increase to have been. Whilst accepting this major increase as fact, what needs to be considered is when after 1491/2 Rye's population explosion occurred. Was the bulk of the increase limited to a relatively short period between 1491/2 and say *c.*1530, following the rapid collapse of Winchelsea, or was it spread over a longer time frame? If the latter, how much increase occurred early and how much later in the century? These are vital questions if Rye's late-medieval/early-Tudor building stock is to be adequately understood.

As is so often the case with population studies, the available data is incomplete and difficult to interpret, incorporating many apparent contradictions. The sources have been thoroughly studied by Mayhew, and we can do no better here than to make use of his analysis, whilst, in some instances, reserving the right to draw slightly different conclusions from the same data. Where population trends are concerned the most obvious sources of data are the parish registers, especially where, as in the case of Rye, only one parish is involved. In simplistic terms a period during which the increase in population within the town is accelerating should be reflected in an increasing overall number of births, deaths and marriages. Furthermore, the greater the increase in population the more marked the acceleration should be. Rather unfortunately, the period of greatest interest from the point of view of the surviving late-medieval and early-Tudor houses is the period of Winchelsea's economic and demographic collapse, which occurred immediately before the start of the Rye registers in 1538. Nevertheless, the registers should indicate the population trends within the town for the period from 1538 onwards. These trends should have implications for the earlier period.

The relevant figures are summarized on an annual basis in Mayhew Appendix 1 (p.270), with the data depicted graphically in Mayhew Fig. 3A (nine-year moving averages) and Mayhew Fig. 4 (annual data). In his discussion of the data Mayhew notes that the 'overall high levels of burials throughout the period ... necessitated continual immigration on a considerable scale in order to maintain the town's population'.[28] High levels of epidemic mortality, resulting in marked spikes in the graph, render the burial record the least useful of the three sources. Unless the immigrant population needed to maintain/increase the town's population was made up principally of married couples of above child-bearing age, or juveniles who either died or moved away before setting up families (both of which seem highly unlikely) trends in marriages and christenings should have been unaffected by the town's reliance on immigration.

So what do the statistics show? Based upon a recalculated five-year (as opposed to a nine-year) moving average, between 1540 and 1557 the average number of marriages per annum remained very constant, fluctuating between a high of (average) 44.6 in 1543 to a low of (average) 33.2 in 1553. After this there is a rise in the five-year moving average to a peak of 61.4 in

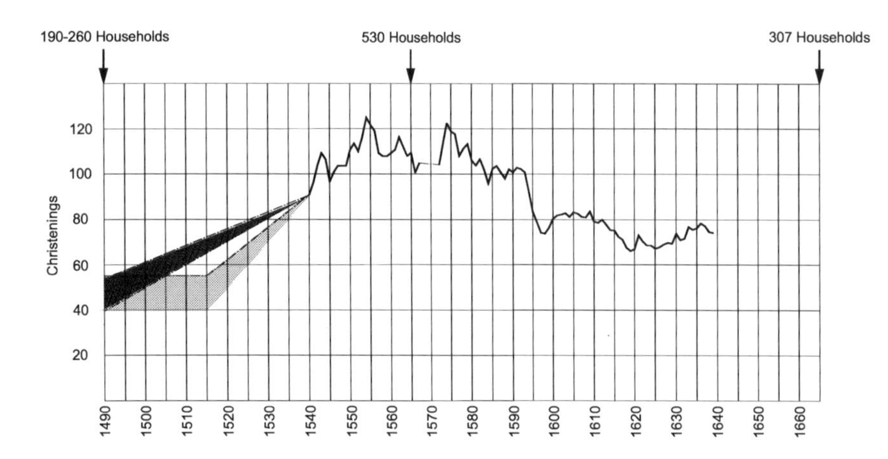

Fig. 5.4 (left)
Five-year moving average of christenings recorded in Rye. Alternative models are given for the period 1490-1540 for which period data is lacking.

1562. This rise, however, is caused by one-off high totals of 61 marriages in 1559, 73 in 1560, 56 in 1561 and 91 in 1564. These were triggered by specific epidemics which killed alarmingly high numbers of residents during the three years 1557-1559 and during the summer/autumn of 1563.[29] As a result, newly widowed townsfolk were remarrying to re-establish family units. If these false peaks are ignored, the number of marriages remained very level throughout the period.

Again based upon a recalculated five-year moving average, the numbers of christenings climb gradually from an average of 99.6 per annum in 1541 to (average) 109.0 in 1543, temporarily dropping back slightly to 97.0 in 1545 before rising gradually to 125.4 in 1554, after which they fall back again. They thereafter remained constant through the period 1557 to 1564 at about 110 christenings per annum (Figure 5.4).[30]

What is at first surprising is that the statistics indicate nothing more than slight variations in marriages throughout the period 1538/9 to 1565. The gradual rise in the number of christenings between 1540 and 1555, on the other hand, could suggest either an increase in the number of married couples of child-bearing age who were moving into the town, or alternatively that Rye men were marrying women from outside the town. Although the apparent consistency in the number of marriages within the town suggests that, at least with regards marriages, the *status quo* was being maintained, without knowing the population trend at the date when the registers start this adds nothing to knowledge — the figures could represent a stable population during this period or — far more likely given other known factors — a population which was growing at a consistent rate. This ignores any changing trends in the age at which people were marrying for the first time.

Given that the parish registers offer little real help in ascertaining the profile of Rye's population growth, it is only through a combination of sources that a likely model can be suggested. Winchelsea's collapse — so graphically illustrated by the customs returns and by the references to abandoned houses — has already been referred to. As Figure 5.3 has illustrated, Rye's maritime economy started to grow during the period between 1491/92 and 1513/14 and peaked in 1531/32. After an apparent slump, further growth occurred between 1545/46 and the end of the sequence of returns in 1559/60.

The chamberlains' receipts for the town show a similar pattern: gradual, but sustained growth from 1485 through to a peak in 1513/14, after which income levelled off somewhat until 1537/8, with subsequent further growth through to 1565 and beyond.[31]

The evidence from the standing buildings is subject to the vagaries of typological dating but, as will be indicated, shows an upsurge in building work during the early Tudor period with clear signs of infilling of gaps in the street frontage and subdivision of houses during the second and third quarters of the 16th century. Thus, the data is consistent with a major transference of population from Winchelsea to Rye during the period 1490 to 1530, but, in addition, suggests continued significant growth — though perhaps at a somewhat slower pace — through to 1565 and beyond. That this growth could be achieved despite recurring epidemics which caused major peaks in mortality is impressive and suggests that the town was acting as a magnet, drawing people in from other towns and from the rural hinterland.

CHANGES IN THE LATE 16th CENTURY

The household total of 530 given in the 1565 inquiry does not represent Rye's population peak — that still lay a decade in the future. As mentioned in Chapter 1, economically the late 1560s and 1570s were challenging times for the town. The fact that Rye's population continued to rise during this period had more to do with the town's religious allegiances than economic success. With the outbreak of religious strife on the Continent, French protestants, particularly Huguenots from northern France, sought sanctuary in Rye. Over 500 refugees fled to the town in 1562 with more following in

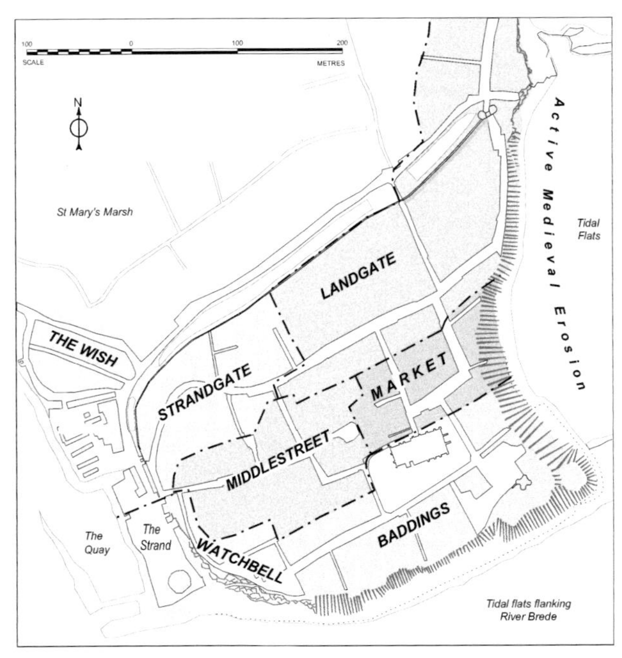

Fig. 5.5
Boundaries of the wards as reorganised in 1574. Note how Watchbell and Wishe ward and Strandgate Ward cross at the Strand Gate

July 1568. The largest influx followed the St. Bartholomew's Day massacre on 24th August 1572 and, unlike in earlier years when the refugees fleeing to the town tended to be wealthy, these included many poor and destitute families. A high proportion stayed until the end of the troubles in the early 1590s, with a reported 1,534 French refugees resident within the town in 1582.[32]

Throughout this period the immigrants were served by their own religious leaders who kept separate church registers. Because these have not survived, there is no way of knowing the number of births, deaths and marriages which occurred within the immigrant population. Even so, the level of christenings amongst the indigenous population maintained a high, albeit stable level through to the middle of the 1570s, with (average) 117.0 annual christenings around 1575. After this they tailed off gradually to (average) 102.6 in 1590, and then rapidly to 79.2 by 1605. (Figure 5.4). A peak in marriages during the late 1550s and 1560s was followed by a gradual decline in numbers to an average of 36.1 per annum in 1590. Thereafter, as with christenings, numbers reduce rapidly as Rye's population began to drift away, reaching an average of just 25.6 by 1605.

RYE IN 1576

With the indigenous population still rising through to the mid-1570s and a major influx of resident refugees during the 1560s and early 1570s it would seem safe to conclude that by the mid-1570s the number of households within the town stood considerably in excess of the 530 recorded in 1565. Yet, taken at face value, such an assumption does not appear to be supported by the corporation records for the period. In 1574 the town's ward boundaries were reorganised and the number increased to six (Figure 5.5). Two years later a particularly far-ranging sesse was raised. The documents relating to both give important information and have been extensively studied by Graham Mayhew within his seminal work, *Tudor Rye*.

Of immediate significance to the present study are the number of houses quoted within the topographical description for each ward: 70 houses in Landgate Ward, 63 in Market Ward, 70 in Strandgate Ward, 65 in Middlestreet Ward and 75 in Baddings Ward. Very disappointing, the total for the sixth ward — Watchbell, which included The Wishe suburb — is left blank, though (by comparison with the other wards) the number of entries suggests a likely total of about 80 houses. It is worth noting that the topographical description for the ward includes 'all the new buildings along the town dike', confirming that new construction was indeed taking place within the town at this period.[33] Excluding Watchbell Ward, 343 houses are accounted for within the five wards for which data is given, whilst the total including Watchbell is unlikely to have been much above 425. This is over 100 houses short of the number of households given in the 1565 return, even without allowance for the implied significant increase in households during the decade since that date.

The likely explanation for the above apparent contradiction is to be found in the terminology used — households in one instance, houses in the other. As is the case with terms such as dwelling, tenement (as used to indicate a building, rather than a holding) and messuage, these two terms have subtly different meanings: a house, for instance, can be divided into a number of separate tenements and can give shelter to a number of separate households — in both instances the internal divisions can be either formal or informal.

Other complications include the ways in which persons or groups of persons renting individual rooms within a house, or occupying rooms over a shop/workshop are enumerated. At a time when the town's population was growing rapidly and, as will be demonstrated in Chapter 7, houses were being divided into multiple occupancy, it would not be hard to account in this way for the apparent contradiction noted above. Even the sesse itself gives credence to this suggestion. For example, in no instance does the number of assessments agree with the number of houses stated in the head: some have more, others less. Furthermore,

CATEGORY	LANDGATE	MARKET	MIDDLESTREET	STRANDGATE	BADDINGS	WATCHBELL & WISHE	TOTAL
PERSONS OF RANK & PROFESSIONALS [1]	1	-	4	1	1	-	7
SEAFARERS & ALLIED OCCUPATIONS							
Mariners, Fishermen etc. [2]	19	7	19	20	44	38	147
Shipwrights and Chandlers	-	3	2	1	3	6	15
FISH WHOLESALERS etc. [3]	3	2	3	1	8	5	22
FOOD & DRINK/HOSPITALITY							
Butchers	-	4	1	-	6	-	11
Bakers	3	-	2	3	2	2	12
Innkeepers, Brewers etc. [4]	8	5	4	7	1	2	27
CLOTHING [5]	15	9	18	13	6	1	62
CRAFT & RETAIL							
Metalworkers [6]	3	4	-	3	-	3	13
Sundry Craft Workers [7]	4	-	-	1	1	-	6
Sundry Shopkeepers	1	-	3	3	1	-	8
BUILDING TRADES							
Carpenters and Joiners	4	2	-	1	3	-	10
Masons, Painters and Glaziers	1	1	-	-	1	-	3
SUNDRY							
Carriers (General)	1	-	-	-	-	-	1
Yeomen/Husbandmen	3	-	-	-	2	-	5
Labourers	-	1	-	-	1	1	3
Widows [8]	1	1	-	1	2	3	8
UNKNOWN OCCUPATIONS	6	3	7	9	13	18	56
Source: Mayhew 1987, Table 23	73	42	63	64	95	79	416

1. Gentlemen (2); Customer (1); Schoolmaster (1); Bailiffs (2); Surgeon (1)
2. Mariners (50); Fishermen (94); Lightermen (2); Cockboatmen (1)
3. Feter/Ost (21); Rippiers (1)
4. Innkeeper (6); Beer Tippler (7 without other primary occupation); Tapster (1) Brewers (10); Vintners (3)
5. Tailors and Drapers (15); Cordwainers, Shoemakers & Coblers (9); Mercers (37); Cappers (1)
6. Blacksmiths (6); Goldsmiths (3); Locksmiths (1); Cutlers (1); Hookmakers (1); Brasiers (1)
7. Coopers (3); Fletchers (1); Upholsterers (1); Basketmakers (1)
8. Only those widows for whom there is no evidence of occupation are included

Fig. 5.6
Occupational structure by ward, 1576

some of the assessments are for tenements (plural). Baddings Ward (75 houses, 100 entries) includes John Vincent for his tenements, Mr Haynes for his tenements, and Mr Tufton of Peasmarsh, gent. for his tenements. As a further guide, the return lists 416 separately-named residents plus 23 named non-residents: this total excludes impoverished exempt households.

What the above highlights is the danger in placing too great a significance upon statistical data derived from varied historical sources. Despite the above warnings, as with the 1491/2 sesse it is possible to use the 1576 return to gain an impression of the distribution of wealth within the town and — because of the extensive background research carried out by Mayhew — in this instance it is also possible to add some useful observations concerning the geographical distribution of occupations.

The occupations of people at this period are a difficult subject, for as Hipkin has pointed out, many derived their incomes from a number of sources. As an example, in 1602 "of seventeen persons presented at Rye ... for 'using the trade of a barber surgeon' two were butchers, three were brewers, two were victuallers, one an innkeeper and eight ran tippling houses".[34] Despite this complication, at a general level the information collated by Mayhew allows something to be said about the spectrum of occupations present within the town, identifying areas of the town within which specific types of occupations clustered, and to say something about the relative distribution of wealth. Full details are given in Mayhew 1987, Table 23: for a summary *see* Figure 5.6.

It is not hard to identify the bulk of the persons missing from the 1576 sesse. The 1565 government inquiry identified 285 of the 530 households as headed by either mariners or fishermen, yet in 1576 only 147 of the 360 ratepayers for which the occupations can be identified were mariners or fishermen, this at a time when the population should have been markedly higher than a decade earlier. No doubt part of the discrepancy is accounted for by the 56 entries for which the occupations are unknown, though this still leaves a substantial number of seafarers absent from the sesse: presumably they fell below the taxable threshold. For the same reason many households headed by labourers and poor widows are almost certainly missing from the sesse — such persons served as the heads of 7 per cent and 12 per cent of households in 1660, but less than 1 per cent and 2 per cent respectively are identifiable in the 1576 sesse (*compare* Figures 5.6 and 5.7). Equally lacking are identifiable foreigners — Mayhew was able to identify only 12 French and one Spaniard, and thus the religious refugees are all but, if not entirely absent from the return.[35]

The 1491/2 and 1576 documents allow an interesting wealth comparison to be made. Whereas in the 1491/2 sesse the 13 wealthiest of the town's 176 non-exempt residents — about 8 per cent — contributed 57½ per cent of Rye's taxable wealth, in 1576 a similar percentage of wealthy residents — 41 of the 416 persons assessed — contributed a somewhat smaller 43½ per cent of the taxable wealth. Not surprisingly, these 41 residents included the mayor and all but two of the jurats. The group was headed by eight men, including two butchers, a brewer, a wine merchant (vintner), a wholesale fishmonger (ost), and a fisherman — five of these served as jurats. Between them these eight men accounted for 13½ per cent of the assessed wealth, which compares unfavourably with the staggering 47½ per cent contributed by the richest 8 men assessed in 1491/2. The impression is that in 1576 there was a broader spectrum of wealth at the top of society, though in all probabilities there was also a greater degree of poverty at the base.[36]

Another change within the town which appears to have occurred since 1491/2 was greater polarization with regards the geographical distribution of wealth. The 1491/2 sesse seems to show little wealth variation between the wards (*see* above), whereas by 1576 most of the wealth seems to have been concentrated within Middlestreet and Market Wards, something which appears already to have developed by 1558. Nine of the 13 jurats lived in these two wards in 1576, as too did 19 of the 41 persons assessed at £20 and over: these included 9 of the 14 residents who were assessed at over £40. Of equal significance, only 3 of the 135 persons assessed at the lowest valuation (£1-£2) lived in Market Ward, and only 12 in Middlestreet Ward. Next in rank were Landgate and Strandgate Wards — 2 jurats lived in Strandgate Ward. By far the poorest areas of town were Baddings (4 assessed £20 and over) and Watchbell (2 assessed £20 and over): here lived 61½ per cent of the poorest ratepayers.[37]

The town's occupational structure as revealed by Mayhew's research into the 1576 sesse is very much what is to be expected (Figure 5.6). Even without any allowance for the high degree of exemptions amongst the seafaring population (*see* above) maritime-related occupations accounted for just over half the population for which the occupations are known. Included amongst them were 22 feters and osts (wholesale fishmongers, including those serving as agents for the London Company of Fishmongers). Most of the non-seafaring occupations were directed towards providing the townsfolk and the town's immediate hinterland with food, drink and hospitality (14 per cent), clothing (17 per cent), craft and retail (8 per cent), and building trades (4 per cent). There was a surgeon and a schoolmaster within the town, as well as a customs searcher, but only two men of rank are specifically identified as gentlemen — Rye was a working port, not a place of residence for the gentry. Apart from the usual craftsmen who were manufacturing for local retail, there were very few producers of goods, though three goldsmiths (two in Strandgate Ward and one in Watchbell and Wishe Ward) and a locksmith (in Landgate Ward) are worthy of special note.

Many of the residents who had maritime occupations lived nearest the Strand, whilst those who followed land-based occupations tended to gravitate towards Landgate and Market Wards. However, perhaps on account of the small geographical size of the town, the pattern was not as polarized as might be expected. Although many of the seafarers did indeed reside in Strandgate, Middlestreet and Watchbell/Wishe Wards, as Figure 5.6 illustrates, the highest number rather unexpectedly lived in Baddings Ward, whilst nineteen and seven seafarers respectively have been identified living in Landgate and Market Wards. In like vein, concentrations of persons engaged in the manufacture and supply of clothes and footwear can be identified living in Strandgate and Middlestreet Wards, though there is no way of telling whether these clustered towards the landward or seaward ends. Bearing in mind the town ordinances which forbade the opening of butchers' shops away from the town butchery, less unexpectedly all but one of the eleven butchers lived either in Market Ward or towards the eastern end of Baddings Ward, close to the Market Place and Butchery.[38]

It is surprising to note that wealth within the town varied enormously, not merely across different occupational groups but also within individual occupations. Most of the seafarers who chose to live in Landgate and Market Wards were of middling to high status. As already noted, one fishermen — the ship-owning Mr Davy, who lived in Market Ward and served as mayor in 1576 — was at that time one of the eight wealthiest residents in the town. People like Davy were the elite of their occupations. Most of the town's fishermen and sailors were, of course, ordinary crew members — many were the maritime equivalents of agricultural labourers.

A similar wealth divide is to be found amongst the non-maritime occupations too. In the food and drink trade, for instance, just three wine merchants (vintners) accounted for 60 per cent of the wealth of all the town's victuallers. Many drinking establishments within the town were run as secondary sources of income, some by relatively impoverished families. This diversity is well illustrated by the 36 keepers of licensed houses listed in 1575. The keepers of all but one are identifiable in the sesse: six were kept by merchants, four by feters, four by 'innholders/innkeepers', two each by cordwainers, vintners, and widows, and one each by a lighterman, fletcher, tailor, baker, shipwright, tapster, chandler, painter, rippier and a mariner. The primary occupations of the other six are not known. Some of the families were impoverished, others such as William Didsbury of the Mermaid [72] in Middle Street, ranked amongst the elite. Didsbury doubled as a ship-owner and substantial merchant.[39]

Such examples of dual, even multiple economies were common within the town. In 1575 John Mercer, brewer, described himself as a merchant, and the same year William Ratliff, tailor, obtained a vintner's licence. Shares in merchant ships were not only held by merchants, but by butchers, innholders, shipwrights and gentlemen. Men often infringed upon the crafts of others. Brewers baked, mercers made caps, whilst tailors were retailing goods pertaining to mercery.

Often an individual occupation was dominated by a small number of principal players. In 1576 just three tailors accounted for almost two-thirds of the wealth assessed on 15 tailors; three persons accounted for over half the assessments for the 21 osts/feters; nine men for over half the assessments on 37 merchants. Four brewers (each assessed at £30+) accounted for two-thirds the wealth of their trade, whereas only one of the ten brewers was assessed at £1, and he was an employee. Just seven men accounted for a little under a third the collective assessment on fishermen and two craftsmen accounted for over half the total valuation for the 12 shipwrights. There was an even greater wealth divide in the food and drink trades. Two butchers, assessed at £40, accounted for three-quarters the valuation on the 11 butchers within the town, whereas five others were assessed at as little as £2 10s. Similarly, five men (£10+) accounted for 85 per cent of the assessments on 12 bakers, whilst in comparison half were assessed at as little as £1-£2.[40]

A brief consideration should be given to whether, at this period, Rye townsfolk included agriculture amongst their secondary occupational activities. Certainly in other local towns a few residents ran smallholdings, as, for instance, at Battle in the mid-16th century where, in 1569, nine barns are listed.[41] Occasional references to yeomen and husbandmen in Rye suggest minor involvement occurred here too, though apart from references in the early 16th century to a barn near Ypres Tower and another at Montes outside the built-up area on the northern outskirts, and a third in 1557, just within the town wall, no references have been located to agricultural buildings within the town.[42] However, Rye men did invest in agricultural land in the area and a few seem to have involved themselves personally in farming, if only at a 'hobby' level involving small acreages only.

In this respect it is worth noting that in adjacent Playden parish in *c.*1568 22 Rye residents occupied a total of 216 acres — about 30 per cent of the lands listed within the parish. The 216 acres comprised 59 acres of meadow, 13 acres of arable, 11 acres of rough, and the rest pasture. The occupations of the 22 residents have not been ascertained: it would be interesting to know how many were butchers holding land for the accommodation of beasts prior to slaughter. There is no similar return for Rye Foreign (though most of The Foreign consisted of two large farms) or for Udimore, so it is possible that Rye residents likewise held small plots in these areas too. However, such involvement seems to have been very localized, restricted principally to the parishes immediately adjacent to the town. A return of the same year for Iden Parish, which abuts to the north of Playden, lists only 3 Rye residents occupying land within that parish — one farmed 24 acres, another occupied 6 acres of pasture and another 3 acres, amounting to just 2 per cent of the lands listed within the parish.[43]

CATEGORY	LANDGATE	MARKET	MIDDLESTREET	STRANDGATE	BADDINGS	WATCHBELL & WISHE	TOTAL
PERSONS OF RANK & PROFESSIONALS [1]	10	5	9	1	-	-	25
SEAFARERS & ALLIED OCCUPATIONS							
Mariners, Fishermen etc. [2]	7	4	8	21	47	20	107
Chandlers	2	-	-	-	-	-	2
FISH WHOLESALERS etc. [3]	-	-	-	1	-	-	1
FOOD & DRINK/HOSPITALITY							
Butchers	2	5	2	-	-	-	9
Bakers and Grocers	2	-	1	1	-	-	4
Innkeepers, Brewers etc. [4]	6	3	2	1	1	1	14
CLOTHING [5]	6	7	9	3	-	-	25
CRAFT & RETAIL							
Metalworkers [6]	4	-	-	-	-	1	5
Leatherworkers [7]	5	-	-	-	1	-	6
Sundry Craft Workers [8]	3	-	2	1	-	-	6
BUILDING TRADES							
Carpenters and Joiners	1	-	1	-	2	1	5
Bricklayers, Painters and Glaziers	1	3	2	1	1	-	8
SUNDRY							
Gardeners	1	1	-	1	1	1	5
Miscellaneous [8]	2	1	-	1	-	1	5
Yeomen/Husbandmen	1	1	-	2	-	1	5
Labourers	3	2	7	6	1	1	20
Widows and Spinsters	11	6	9	2	7	3	38
Source: East Sussex Record Office RYE 82/82.	67	38	52	42	61	30	290

1. Mayor & Jurats (7); Gentlemen (10); Merchants (2); Schoolmaster (1); Clerks (2); Surgeons (2); Apothecaries (1)
2. Mariners (35); Fishermen (16); Seamen (50); Lightermen (4); Ship Carpenters (2)
3. Feter (1)
4. Innkeeper (5); Brewers (2); Victuallers (6); Maltster (1)
5. Tailors and Drapers (10); Cordwainers (11); Haberdasher (2); Weavers (2)
6. Blacksmiths (4); Pewterer (1)
7. Tanners (2); Curriers (2); Fellmongers (2)
8. Coopers (2); Saddler (2); Salter (1); Pipemaker (1)
9. Musicians (1), Millers (2), Chapmen (1), Tinkers (1)

Fig. 5.7
Occupational structure by ward, 1660

THE YEARS OF DEPRESSION

As discussed in Chapter 1, the decade commencing 1575 witnessed the twilight of Rye's period of boom and prosperity. Initially change was slow, but over the forty years from *c.*1590 decline accelerated markedly. During this period the effects on Rye's economy — particularly its port-based activities — are revealed by a marked decrease in population, graphically illustrated by a major reduction in the number of baptisms, marriages and burials recorded in the parish registers (*see* Figure 5.4 for christenings).[44] This dip in population resulted in a gradual, but terminal abandonment of The Wishe — the poorest part of town — and a corresponding marked reduction in household density elsewhere in the urban centre. An upsurge in economic activity during the 1630s saw promise of revival but, in the event, it was extinguished by the outbreak of civil war. Despite lack of regeneration, a

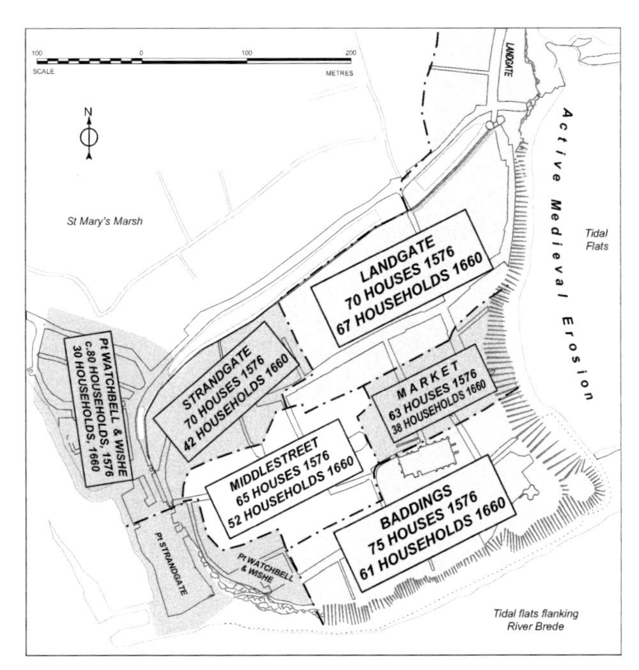

Fig. 5.8
Wards showing change in number of households/houses between 1576 and 1660

degree of stability gradually returned. From the 17th century onwards Rye's role was that of a local market centre augmented by a small, though viable estuarine quay.

With an increasing number of houses falling into gradual dereliction during the first half of the 17th century, others being demolished, and almost no new building work taking place, the end of Elizabeth's reign might seem a natural point at which to finish this architectural study. Yet there are good reasons for extending through to the Restoration of the Monarchy in 1660, albeit in abridged form. The very full national poll-tax taken that year survives for the town, allowing an accurate reconstruction to be made of the occupational structure at that time. These details and those reconstructed by Mayhew for 1576 allow a comparison to be made at two very different phases of development. In addition, hearth tax returns survive for 1662, 1663 and 1664, as too does a town plan made 1667, albeit as a copy of 1728.[45]

RYE IN THE 1660s

The early 17th-century depression years saw the number of households within the town virtually halved: in the 1570s the total stood in excess of 530, but by 1660 only 290 remained (*see* Figure 5.7). The hearth tax return for two years later confirms these figures — it lists 308 houses of which 291 were occupied and 17 were described as empty.[46] By the next year the number of occupied houses had dropped to 286. This slight reduction during the three years since 1660 could easily be a statistical hiccup, but there are other indications which suggest the low point in population had not yet been reached. For example, the 1667 town map shows the footprints of several rows of shops in the fishmarket noted as 'pulled down'. What is significant is that in 1619 some of these were referred to as '32 cottages called the Fish Shoppes', indicating that they were, in fact, at that date being used as dwellings. There is reference in 1671 to a piece of land in the Wishe 'on part of which late stood six tenements', and another the same year to a plot where a house had stood towards the western end of Longer Street, adjacent to the town wall.[47] All these could have been demolished prior to 1660, but it is known that desertion continued thereafter — a town plan of 1771 shows areas of abandoned street frontage where houses stood in 1667 (*see* below).

By comparing the number of houses in each ward in 1576 and 1660 it is possible to show which parts of the town were becoming depopulated. In considering these figures it should be borne in mind that the comparison is not like for like: as discussed earlier, the 1576 figures relate to houses, not households, and therefore represents an underestimate of the actual number of dwelling units within the town at that time. This makes the reductions which occurred in Strandgate and Watchbell/Wishe Wards all the more significant (Figure 5.8). The figures relating to Market Ward are harder to explain: they are probably partially due to the loss over the cliff of development in the Ockmans Lane area and partially due to an abandonment of the western part of the marketplace (*see* Chapter 2). The ward least effected was Landgate, least orientated towards the sea.

The fact that houses were still being lost from the town during the middle years of the 17th century might sound at odds with the earlier suggestion that gradually during the 17th century a degree of stability was returning to the town. However, the (apparent) continued loss of houses during the middle years of the century should be seen as part of the stabilization process during which both the population and the housing stock became rationalized. Although Rye still possessed a working quay, by this date the town should no longer be regarded as a significant port and had ceased to function as a fishing centre of any note. This change is well illustrated by comparing the number of maritime-based families present in 1565 and 1660. In 1565 there had been 275 households headed by mariners, sailors and fishermen, whereas by 1660 this figure had reduced to 107. The fishing fleet had been decimated: 225 households were directly supported by the industry in 1565 with a further 22 engaged in the wholesale distribution of fish: in 1660 the figures stood at 16 and 1 respectively (Figure 5.7).

WARDS	FLUES 1	2	3-4	5-6	7-8	9+	TOTAL
LANDGATE							
Charged	4	18	12	7	4	1	46
Exempt	7	11	3	-	-	-	21
Empty	-	2	4	-	-	-	6
TOTAL	**11**	**31**	**19**	**7**	**4**	**1**	**73**
MARKET							
Charged	5	9	11	4	2	-	31
Exempt	2	4	2	-	-	-	8
Empty	-	-	4	-	-	-	4
TOTAL	**7**	**13**	**17**	**4**	**2**	**-**	**43**
MIDDLESTREET							
Charged	-	11	10	4	2	2	29
Exempt	5	13	8	-	-	-	26
Empty	-	4	2	-	-	-	6
TOTAL	**5**	**28**	**20**	**4**	**2**	**2**	**61**
STRANDGATE							
Charged	-	4	2	1	1	-	8
Exempt	8	22	6	-	-	-	36
Empty	-	4	2	-	-	-	6
TOTAL	**8**	**30**	**10**	**1**	**1**	**-**	**50**
BADDINGS							
Charged	4	11	5	1	-	-	21
Exempt	11	21	6	-	-	-	38
Empty	-	1	-	1	-	-	2
TOTAL	**15**	**33**	**11**	**2**	**-**	**-**	**61**
WATCHBELL AND WISHE							
Charged	1	7	1	1	-	-	10
Exempt	3	7	2	-	-	-	12
Empty	-	2	-	-	-	-	2
TOTAL	**4**	**16**	**3**	**1**	**-**	**-**	**24**
	50	**150**	**80**	**19**	**9**	**3**	**312**

Source: Hearth Tax Return for the Town of Rye, 1663. [ESRO - RYE 83/2-4]

Fig. 5.9
Summary of Hearth Tax Return for Rye, 1663

Those mariners and fishermen who remained within the town during the 1660s were concentrated primarily within Strandgate, Baddings and Watchbell/Wishe Wards, where they accounted for half, three-quarters and two-thirds of the households respectively. These were precisely the wards where loss of houses was greatest during the first two thirds of the century. Most of the non-seafaring households which remained within Baddings and Watchbell/Wishe in 1660 were headed by labourers or widows and spinsters

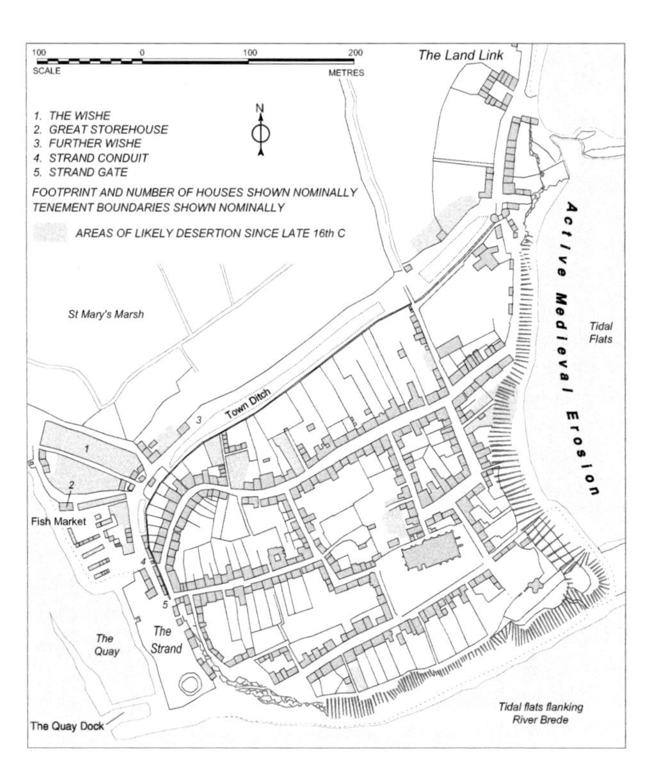

Fig. 5.10
Reconstructed plan of Rye in 1667 based upon ESRO RYE 132/15 and other sources showing extent of built-up street frontages

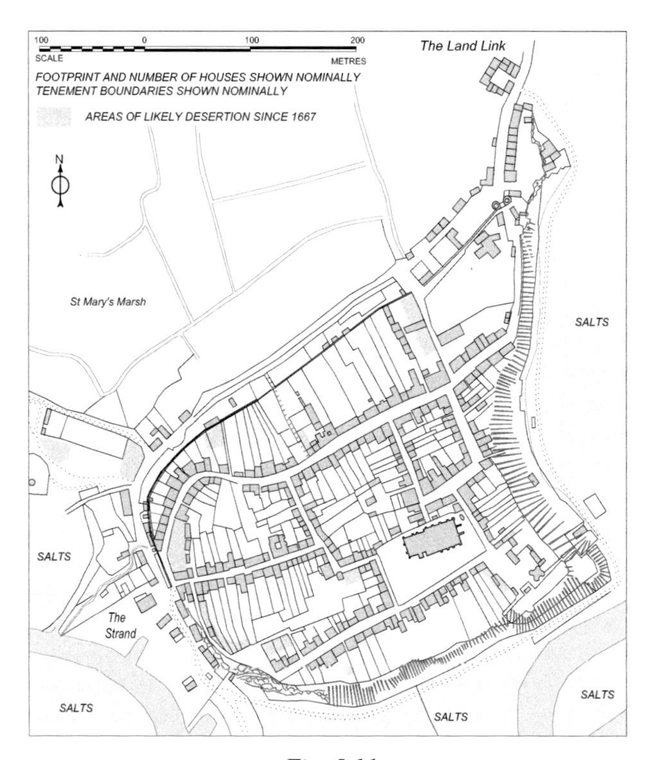

Fig. 5.11
Reconstructed plan of Rye in 1771, reproduced in Bagley 1982, showing extent of built-up street frontages

(Figure 5.7). It is not surprising to note that over 80 per cent of the occupants of Strandgate ward were exempt from hearth tax due to poverty. The proportion was somewhat less in Baddings and Watchbell/Wishe Wards — 64 per cent and 55 per cent respectively — though the latter ward was still continuing to lose houses. There were few wealthy families in this part of town: three each in Strandgate Ward (a yeoman, a tailor and a salter) and Baddings Ward (a jurat and two mariners) and one (a mariner) in Watchbell/Wishe.

Although by this date few seafaring families lived in Middlestreet, this ward had more than its share of resident labourers, widows and spinsters. It should therefore be no great surprise to find that here too a high proportion of the occupants — a little under half — were exempt from hearth tax. Even so, Middlestreet also included twelve of the wealthiest households in town, accounting for one in four of the urban elite. Six of these households were headed by gentlemen/jurats; the others were a baker, a fellmonger, a haberdasher, the widow of a wealthy cordwainer, a wealthy mariner who owned his own dock at the Strand, and two pipemaking brothers living in one household.

The wealthiest parts of town in the 1660s were the land-orientated wards of Landgate and Market. Here only one in three and one in five families respectively were exempt from hearth tax. Here too were concentrated the majority of the wealthy households. Of the 47 households assessed on wealth rather than paying headmoney in the poll tax, seven lived in Market Ward (which had 38 households in total) and 21 in Landgate Ward (67 households). Given that these were the wards in which the majority of the general retail and craft trades were concentrated, there can be no better indication that Rye was now predominantly a general-purpose market centre, rather than a town which earned the majority of its living from the sea. Here again, it would be wrong to overstate this fact. Its quay may have been far less busy than in the past, but goods of value were nonetheless imported through it and a limited number of merchants and mariners could still earn a good living. Reference in passing has already been made to mariners amongst the urban elite: in all, in 1660 seven of the 47 heads of wealthy households were described as mariners, another as the widow of a mariner and another as a merchant, who no doubt brought goods in through the port. This continued to be the case into the early 18th century and beyond.

Even though three hearth tax returns survive for the town, it would be misleading to use the number of flues recorded within individual houses to give information regarding mid 17th-century Rye. There are two reasons for this. Firstly, because there are returns for three consecutive years, direct comparisons are possible for individual houses: somewhat alarmingly the number of flues assessed for the same house in different returns varies (usually by only one either way) in a surprisingly high percentage of cases, bringing into question how much reliance should ever be put on individual assessments. The reasons for the variations are uncertain: perhaps fireplaces were being blocked and unblocked according to need, possibly there was doubt about whether some hearths were exempt under the tax on account of specialized use, or possibly the officials were exercising a degree of discretion in cases of hardship where full exemption on grounds of poverty was not applicable. Even if such variations did not exist, in the case of Rye rather than reflecting current relative wealth, the number of flues in individual houses indicates the distribution of wealth as it had existed within the town in the mid/late 16th century, when the houses were being built and/or upgraded. The parts of the town which, by the 1660s, were suffering from decay and neglect were nevertheless stocked with substantial houses built during the maritime boom of the previous century. This explains why in 1663 27 of the 141 exempt houses were assessed at three or four flues, and why half the 26 empty houses had within them between three and six hearths (Figure 5.9).

An invaluable source of information for this period is the 1667 map of the town prepared by Jeake, known from a copy of 1728. As with so many maps of this period, it should be used as a general indication of contemporary circumstances, not as a record of individual houses. Principal monuments, such as the church, town gates, town hall, Ypres Tower, school, *etc.* are accurately shown, but the ordinary houses are merely sketched-in so as to fill the built-up lengths of street. Time and again where the number of houses within a specific length of street can be reconstructed, the number shown does not equate. In some instances, such as the area of present-day Lamb House in West Street, the number shown is a serious overestimate: in other instances the reverse is the case. Even so, the general details depicted can be combined with the known architectural evidence to reconstruct a tolerable plan of the town as it is existed in the 1660s (Figure 5.10).

POSTSCRIPT — POPULATION CHANGE SINCE THE 1660s

By comparing the data derived from the 1667 town plan with that from a similar map drawn a hundred years later, in 1771, it is possible to highlight areas of change in household density which had occurred between these two dates (*compare* Figures 5.10 and 5.11). Some areas of street frontage (shown in yellow in Figure 5.11) had been abandoned during the intervening years, though there had also been limited development, most notably just outside Land Gate, along the street today known as Tower Street.

Detailed research into population change within the town during the 18th century has still to be carried out, but current indications are that by 1771 only minimal growth (if any) had occurred.

By the date of the first national census in 1801 the total population of the town stood at 2,035. There were then 368 inhabited houses occupied by 442 families: a further 8 houses stood empty.[48] Counting 'families' as equivalent to 'households', the number of households within the town in 1801 stood at approximately 150 above that in 1663, but was still more than 90 below the total recorded in 1565. To judge from the population trend over the next decade, it seems likely that already by 1801 the number of households within the town was increasing rapidly, for a staggering 96 houses were built between 1801 and 1811 and the number of families had increased by 105. Even if this was an accelerating total, the chances are that in 1771 there were fewer households within the town than in 1663.

As an indication of change since 1811, by 1831 the total of inhabited houses stood at 680, occupied by 751 families; and by 1841 there were 753 inhabited houses. Growth during the second half of the 19th century was minimal, the total population in 1901 being 4,337, compared to 4,031 in 1841: the number of families in 1901 stood at 940.[49] There has been considerable growth since that date.

6 RYE'S MEDIEVAL HOUSING

INTRODUCTION

In Chapter 5 some general observations were made regarding Rye's population at three specific dates during the medieval period. These were based upon the undated rental of *c*.1300, the scot and half-scot of the 1410s, and the sesse of 1491/2, the latter taken near the close of the medieval era, at the start of Rye's economic and demographic boom. No definition can be offered as to what exactly constitutes the end of the medieval period, nor can a precise date be given for its close: some historians use the battle of Bosworth Field (1485), others the dissolution of the monasteries half a century later. In terms of domestic architecture the end of the era is usually taken as the demise of the open hall, which in East Sussex occurred (with occasional exceptions before and after) during the first quarter of the 16th century. With these date-constraints in mind, what were Rye's houses like during this period?

With the exception of a stone wall running axially through 7-8 West Street [51], a more complete stone-built house to the south of the church (40 Church Square dated *c*.1300), and at least three of the vaulted cellars within the town, none of Rye's extant domestic buildings existed when the *c*.1300 rental was prepared. The only feature within the wall at 7-8 West Street is a continuously-chamfered doorway with a two-centred arched head, and although more detail exists at 40 Church Square, there are few clues to its original internal layout. By tradition this latter building formed part of the Friary of the Sack (*see* Chapter 4, in which the building is discussed). However, by the date of the rental the friary had been dissolved and its property was owned by one of the town's leading residents, Robert Paulyn. If the site identification is correct, 40 Church Square may not initially have been a secular structure, though it is so close in date to the dissolution of the order that it is perhaps more likely to have been erected by Paulyn after his acquisition of the site.

In addition to being of considerable interest in their own right (*see* below) the vaulted cellars serve as proof — if proof were needed — that at least some of the domestic buildings which existed within the town in *c*.1300 were both substantial and well built, and the same is true of the axial wall which exists within 7-8 West Street [51]. The fact that no other domestic buildings from this period are known to survive is of no significance: at this social level the same is true of rural and urban communities in England as a whole. The presence of early buildings within towns such as Southampton, Sandwich and, indeed, Winchelsea is very exceptional.

Houses of 'ordinary' people start to survive in both rural and urban contexts from the mid 14th century, around the date of the Black Death. It is to the late 14th and early 15th centuries that Rye's earliest timber-framed buildings belong, as too does 46 Church Square [86], a stone structure built over a probably contemporary vaulted cellar. Typological dates for houses are too imprecise to determine how many of the extant houses pre-date the half-scot and scot prepared in the 1410s. Three tolerably complete examples and one fragment certainly existed by that date, to which can be added four probable and two possible further examples, and perhaps a few other *very* fragmentary remains.

By the close of the medieval era the picture had changed markedly. Again, due to the inaccuracy of dating, it is impossible to say for certain how many of Rye's known extant houses existed when the detailed sesse of 1491/2 was taken, but with one possible exception (the tiny semi-detached pair at 26 Church Square [80]) all the town's 23 open-hall houses (some fragmentary) had been constructed by the 1520s. To these can be added a small number of early fully-floored houses, none of which have features to suggest a date before the last quarter of the 15th century, and most — probably all — post-date the 1490s. Even so, some are undoubtedly contemporaneous with late examples of open halls. For simplicity these will be considered in detail within the next phase — those houses erected within the town during Rye's rise to prosperity — though it would be very misleading to ignore them totally within the discussion of the medieval period. Primarily, however, what will be discussed here are the medieval vaulted cellars and the houses built with open halls.

THE VAULTED CELLARS

Many English towns have medieval vaulted cellars beneath the occasional building within their central areas, and in some larger places — such as Winchester — they cluster in specific areas. Generally, however, numbers are very few. For example, six are known in Oxford, all of quadripartite type and all associated with, or used as taverns during the medieval period. In East Sussex there are known to be either three or four vaulted cellars within the county town of Lewes and one each in Battle, Eastbourne, Seaford and Mayfield, but none have so far been found in either Hastings or Pevensey. The Lewes examples are barrel vaulted, while those in Battle, Eastbourne, Seaford and Mayfield are of more elaborate quadripartite type.[1]

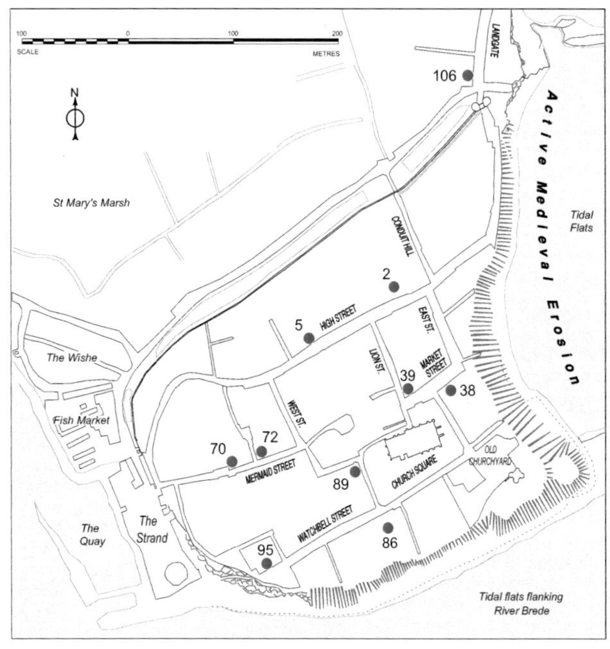

Fig. 6.1
Location of the known vaulted cellars in Rye
[For key to numbers see Fig. 6.2].

With ten identified examples (of which one has two linked chambers) Rye has a significantly greater number of vaulted cellars than most towns, though it is only fair to stress that all have simple barrel vaults. Despite their simple form, such a high number is worthy of specific note, though this total pales somewhat when compared with the 33 accessible examples — with others known — which exist within Rye's sister port of Winchelsea, just across the estuary.

Bearing in mind that Winchelsea's vaulted cellars have already been subjected to detailed study (*see* below) and that, in general terms, those which survive in Rye follow the same design features, there seems little point in pursuing a detailed study of Rye's examples. A more useful approach is to compare and contrast the cellars of the two towns. The location and details of the extant Rye cellars are illustrated in Figures 6.1 to 6.4.

At Winchelsea all but one cellar — a 15th-century addition at the rear of an earlier example — date from the years immediately following the foundation of the town upon its present site late in the 13th century. The known examples loosely cluster in the north of the town, closest to the harbour, and are all but absent from the market area further south. This is thought to be a true reflection of the original distribution. The few examples near Monday Market are notable in that they are either set back from the street or accessible from a secondary highway. Otherwise, all the accessible cellars in Winchelsea are reached direct from the street via a wide staircase. This implies that easy access from the highway was of prime importance, either allowing bulky goods to be easily transported in and out, or allowing public access to the spaces for commercial purposes, or both. In this respect it must be relevant that about two-thirds never had direct internal access to the house above and were therefore capable of being let out separately.

It has been concluded that most of Winchelsea's cellars were associated with the Gascon wine trade

Bldg. No.	Address	Suggested Date	Orientation to road			Main access from street			Width of main stair	Gradient of main stair	Secondary stair		Size of Cellar		Floor area (M^2) Excluding stair	Type of Vault			Bay ribs		Windows		
			Parallel	90°	Corner plot	Enclosed corner stair	Central stair	Others			Yes	No	Length	Width		Barrel	Quadri-partite	Mixed	Yes	No	Yes	No	Borrowed light only
2	11 High Street	15th C		●				●	1.35m	35°		●	8.45m	5.20m	39.0	●				●		●	
5	24 High Street	L13th/E14th C		●		●			1.55m	38.8°		?	2.80m	2.80m	7.90	●			●		●		
5	24 High Street	L13th/E14th C		●					1.55m			?	6.45m	5.00m	32.25	●			●			●	
38	4/5 Market Street	L13th/E14th C	●			●			1.55m	35.9°		?	6.50m	4.25m	25.50	●			●				●
39	8 Market Street	L13th/14th C			●	?	?	?	?	?	Added		5.00+m	4.15m	20.75+	●			●		?	?	?
70	32 Mermaid Street	L13th/14th C		●			●		1.35m	39.8°	●		8.65m	4.40m	38.0	●			●		?	?	?
72	The Mermaid, Mermaid St.	14th/E15th C		●			●		1.20m	41.7°	Added		4.80m	4.30m	20.6	●			●		?		
86	46 Church Square	L14th/E15thC		?	?		●		1.20m	35.8°		●	7.15m	4.90m	35.0	●			●			●	
89	58,60 Church Square	L15th C			●		●		1.35m	34.3°	?		9.40m	5.10m	47.95	●			●		●		
95	16 Watchbell Street	14th/15th C		●		●			1.25m	35.9°			5.90m	4.25m	21.7	●				●	?	?	?
106	Landgate	L13th/E14th C		●		●			1.45m	35°	Added		7.15m	4.60m	28.80	●			●		●		
			1	7	2	4	4	1			1	2				11	0	0	9	2	3	3	1

● = Proven ? = Unknown

Fig. 6.2
General details of accessible cellars.

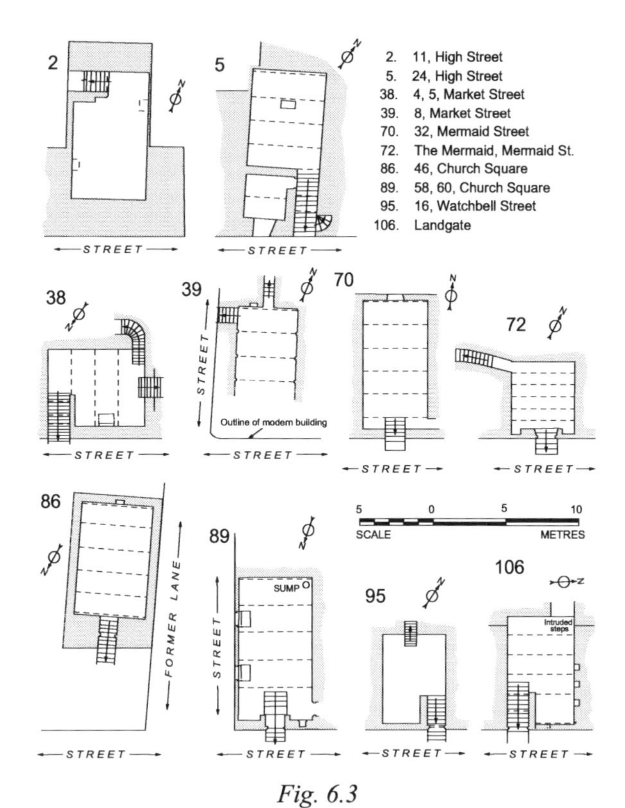

Fig. 6.3
Plans of Rye's vaulted cellars showing methods of access and variations in size. The entrance to cellar 39 represents a later insertion, as too, in all probability, do the secondary stairs to cellars 38, 39, 72, 95 and 106.

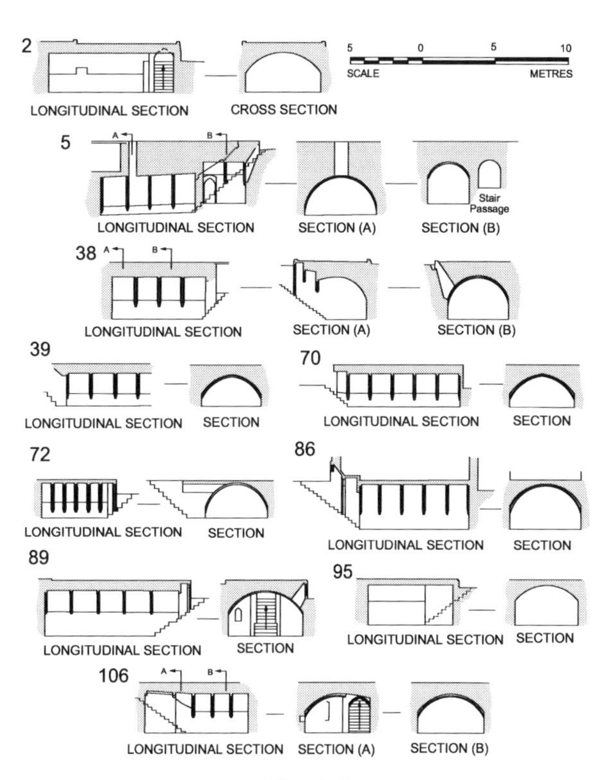

Fig. 6.4
Comparative sections through Rye's vaulted cellars. Ground levels are as existing today, as too are the floor levels of the buildings sited over the cellars. [For a key to the numbers, giving locations, see Figure 6.3]

— the town is known to have been a major English participant during the late 13th and early 14th centuries. To a much lesser extent, involvement in that trade continued through to the late 15th century. Individual cellars are likely to have fulfilled different functions within the wine trade, these functions being reflected in subtle differences in details of design. Some, plainly finished and totally unlit, are likely to have served solely as storage warehouses, whilst others are noticeably better finished and probably doubled as wine shops and tasting areas. A few are so well finished and well lit that they almost certainly functioned as taverns, despite their subterranean locations, and this was most likely the case with many of those which exist elsewhere — for example, that at The Lamb Inn, Eastbourne. Those cellars within Winchelsea which lack direct access from the street are likely to have served a domestic function but, as already noted, there are very few of these. For the full study of the Winchelsea cellars *see* Chapter 9 'The Winchelsea Cellars' in David and Barbara Martin, *New Winchelsea, Sussex, a medieval port town* (2004).

Although Rye imported small quantities of wine throughout the medieval and Tudor periods, unlike Winchelsea it never figured as a key player, which perhaps makes the existence of such a relatively large number of vaulted cellars all the more remarkable. A striking variation between the cellars of the two towns is to be noted in their distribution, for whereas those in Winchelsea are concentrated in one area, those in Rye are evenly, though sparsely distributed (Figure 6.1). This may, however, be of less significance than might at first be thought, for the comparative acreages of the two settlements needs to be taken into account. At only *c*.36 acres in extent, Rye covers less than a quarter the area of Winchelsea and thus no point within the town is located particularly far from the quayside. What is certainly true, however, is that on average the Rye cellars are noticeably smaller than those in Winchelsea — in area they average 31.8 m^2 (342 square feet) compared to 43.9 m^2 (472 square feet) for Winchelsea. Seven Winchelsea cellars exceed the largest example in Rye (*compare* Figure 6.2 with Figure 9.4 in Martin and Martin, 2004). Furthermore, those at Rye are noticeably less elaborate. Whereas five of Winchelsea's cellars have quadripartite vaults, all of those in Rye are barrel-vaulted and none have moulded corbels.

There are other major differences too. Whereas only one of Winchelsea's cellars appears to post-date the

Fig. 6.5
Cellar beneath 58, 60 Church Square [89] showing entrance steps with recess on left.

Fig. 6.6
Cellar beneath 58, 60 Church Square [89] showing very depressed arch over entrance doorway.

early 14th century, the Rye examples seem far more varied in their dates of origin. The largest in the group — that beneath 58, 60 Church Square [89], illustrated in Figure 6.5 — is almost certainly of late 15th-century date and incorporates quite large quantities of brickwork within the lower courses of its vault, as well as within the rear wall of a cupboard recess and within the jambs of its 'windows'. Not that brickwork is unknown in the Winchelsea cellars, but the bricks here are of a larger and later type. Similarly late in its design is the very depressed three-centred arched head of the entrance doorway (Figure 6.6). The cellar at 11 High Street [2] likewise incorporates features which could indicate an equally late date, as too is the case with the three-centred arched entrance to the cellar beneath The Mermaid [72], a cellar which is notable for the extreme shortness of its ribbed bays (Figure 6.7). Although not as late as the date suggested for the examples at 58, 60 Church Square [89] and 11 High Street [2], both in the style of its entrance doorway and that of the main doorway into the apparently contemporary superstructure, the cellar at 46 Church Square [86], shown in Figure 6.8, is likewise likely to be somewhat later in date than the Winchelsea examples, probably having been built *c.*1400. Some of the other Rye examples are so lacking in diagnostic features that they cannot be accurately dated. Even so, a date of *c.*1300 for the cellars beneath 4, 5 Market Street [38] and a house in Landgate [106], as well as for the two-chambered cellar beneath 24 High Street [5] seems more secure.

Despite being of smaller size and (apparently) having a greater range of construction dates, many of the comments made regarding the Winchelsea cellars hold true for those at Rye. As will be evident by consulting the plans reproduced in Figure 6.3, the principal means of access is either via enclosed corner stairs or by means

Fig. 6.7
Cellar at The Mermaid, Mermaid Street [72]. Note head to the entrance doorway and the closely-spaced ribs to the vault.

Fig. 6.8
Cellar beneath 46 Church Square [86]. Looking north towards entrance doorway in end wall.

Fig. 6.9
Plain cellar without ribs, 16 Watchbell Street [95]. Note the remains of the entrance steps on the left, descending from a blocked doorway leading to the street.

Fig. 6.10
58, 60 Church Square [89]. Window/light well incorporated into the eastern side of the barrel vault, rising to a metal grill in the front wall. Note the bricks used in the construction of the jambs.

Fig. 6.11
Window/light well incorporated into northern side of barrel vault, 4, 5 Market Street [38].

of a staircase placed centrally within an end wall. This replicates the arrangements found at Winchelsea. Roughly half the cellars in Rye have corner stairs and half central staircases: in this respect too the proportions of each type echo those at Winchelsea. The entrance stairs within both towns are of similar width, implying intended commercial (as opposed to domestic) use. As at Winchelsea, the majority of the vaults are divided into bays by chamfered ribs, though in both towns a few are entirely plain, one of the two Rye examples being that beneath 16 Watchbell Street [95] shown in Figure 6.9.

There is greater doubt at Rye regarding the original inclusion of windows, due mainly to the more altered state of the Rye examples. Even so, as at Winchelsea, some cellars can be shown to have been totally unlit. Cupboard recesses exist (as, for instance, shown in Figure 6.5) but are less common than in Winchelsea.

As at Winchelsea, some cellars in Rye incorporate secondary stairs leading to the houses above but, whereas at Winchelsea a number of these can be demonstrated to be contemporary with the cellar, at Rye there is more doubt. In fact, none of the five secondary stairs in Rye can be proven to be original and in most instances they can be shown to have been added. Only at 32 Mermaid Street [70] does a variation in bay size suggest the secondary access may be original. In a sixth cellar — beneath 58, 60 Church Square [89] — a blocked doorway probably leads to a stair giving access to the adjacent (and earlier) Lamb Cottage [53], though the possibility of it having led to a second, now inaccessible cellar cannot be ruled out.

One final observation concerning access is worth making. In two instances — 11 High Street [2] and 46 Church Square [86] — the cellars are set back from the street, with no direct access from the road. In this respect these examples seem to share features noted regarding some of the more peripheral, now inaccessible cellars in Winchelsea. The cellar at 11 High Street [2] has a standard enclosed corner stair, and here the possibility of access from a now lost lane extending back from High Street cannot be entirely ruled out, though it is more likely to have been reached from a rear yard. Whichever the case, the cellar was never accessible direct from the main street, a fact which must be of significance. There is known to have been a side lane at 46 Church Square [87] but, despite this, no access was provided from it. Instead, the stairs lead down from within what was probably a commercial space (now a yard) sited between the cellar and the main street.

In discussing the original use of Winchelsea's cellars a general connection was noted between existing cellars in English towns and taverns, and a more specific connection was made between a number of

Winchelsea's cellars and the town's inns and taverns, though it should be stressed that we cannot determine when these buildings first became inns. Similar observations are possible at Rye. The example [106] in the suburb outside The Land Gate is ideally situated to have served as an inn, being immediately outside the main town gate — a classic location. There are vaulted cellars beneath 24 High Street [5] (now The White Vine and certainly an inn during the 16th century), 4, 5 Market Street [38] (The Flushing Inn), and at 35-38 Mermaid Street [72] (The Mermaid Inn — again an inn from at least the early 16th century). However, despite these observations, it will be noted from the plans shown in Figure 6.3 that none of these cellars are well lit, a point which seems to rule out their use as below-ground taverns; if the connection between Rye's vaulted cellars and inns is a valid one, the cellars must have been utilized as stores serving drinking areas sited within ground-floor rooms above. Alternatively, they may have doubled as storehouses for retail distribution. The only Rye cellar where use as a subterranean tavern is worth considering is that beneath 58, 60 Church Square [89] (*see* Figure 6.5). As is clear from Figures 6.2 and 6.3, it is the largest in the group and, once served by two side 'windows', it was also the best lit. However, even here the windows (if that is what they can be termed) are plain and rather awkwardly contrived (*see* Figure 6.10). The same is true of the window/light-well which serves the cellar beneath The Flushing Inn [38] (*see* Figure 6.11). Indeed, it is true generally that the cellars in Rye are less well lit than those at Winchelsea.

So, as elsewhere, at Rye there are good reasons for suggesting tentative links between at least some of the vaulted cellars and houses used as inns, though not in this instance used as below-ground taverns. The connection between vaulted cellars and vintners extends beyond the period covered by this study. Beneath 8-10 High Street (rebuilt by the Rye brewer, vintner, and one-time mayor, James Lamb, in 1736) is an extensive network of vaulted brick-built cellars used by him in connection with his wine business.[2]

In concluding this section on medieval vaulted cellars it would be prudent to repeat the warning made by Patrick Faulkner in 1975 not to assume that all medieval urban cellars were of vaulted type.[3] This is a warning which is certainly relevant to Winchelsea where an un-vaulted cellar of *c.*1300 exists beneath the present Town Hall, and it is equally true of Rye. Although most un-vaulted cellars in Rye can be demonstrated to be of 16th-century and later date, the ages of some cannot be ascertained on account of the absence of datable architectural features and/or their relationship to the building above. Occasionally — as at Winchelsea Town Hall — an extant datable architectural feature demonstrates the medieval origin of an otherwise un-datable cellar. Just such an example is the un-vaulted cellar beneath 1, 2 Market Street [36], entirely un-datable except for a doorway with two-centred arched head incorporated in the western wall (Figure 6.12). Another example which, to judge from the nature of its main street entrance, could be of medieval date is the cellar beneath 20 Watchbell Street [97], and yet another is that beneath 29, 30 High Street [8], which incorporates the remains of a semi-circular spiral staircase and a street opening with dressed stone jambs.[4]

Fig. 6.12
Blocked doorway with two-centred arch head in western wall of un-vaulted cellar beneath 1, 2 Market Street [36].

No doubt, the list of both vaulted and early un-vaulted cellars mentioned above could be extended. Nevertheless, the evidence suggests that medieval vaulted cellars were always rare within the town and, until the 16th century, un-vaulted cellars were even more scarce.

THE MEDIEVAL HOUSES: REGIONAL CONTEXT

Although broad trends are discernible across England as a whole, vernacular buildings are by their very nature regional, with notable variations recognizable even within the length and breadth of a single county. This statement is equally valid for both design features and constructional detail. Therefore, to put Rye's surviving medieval houses into their local geographical context it will be advantageous to review the characteristics of the medieval rural houses which survive within the 'High Weald', the geographical area of Kent and East Sussex within which Rye is located.

Survival

It was not until the closing two or three decades of the 14th century that the 'peasantry' began to build houses which have survived through to the present day. These houses are by no means common, but from that date onwards the number increases markedly.

It has been estimated that in East Sussex as many as 10 per cent of the rural houses which existed at the close of the medieval period still survive to this day.[5] Although the survivors vary widely in size and quality, in comparison to later cottages they are well built and of reasonable size. There can be little doubt that, with very few exceptions, they represent the houses of a relatively wealthy middle class comprising successful merchants, farmers and craftsmen. Small medieval houses are virtually unheard of within the High Weald; there are no extant medieval rural cottages.

What proportion of the population the middle-class builders of the surviving houses represented varied from region to region, and indeed from parish to parish, but in overall terms, even at the end of the medieval era they probably accounted for no more than a quarter of the total population of the High Weald.[6]

The 'Standard' Medieval House

By the close of the 14th century, when 'ordinary' houses begin to survive, a surprisingly standard design had already been adopted: a building which was rectangular in plan and incorporated three units or 'cells' arranged in line (Figure 6.13). The layout chosen suggests that late-medieval middle-class households were very hierarchical and closely aped their social superiors.

Almost without exception, houses were dominated by one room, known as the hall: a large, usually centrally-placed communal space open from ground to roof. The house was entered at the *low* end of the hall by two opposing doorways — one in the front wall, the other in the rear. This created a *cross-entry* or *cross-passage* at the socially inferior end of the hall. The passage was often, but by no means always, partially screened from the remainder of the hall by short fixed draught screens or *speres*.

Beyond the hall's low end was a partitioned-off, storeyed area with either one or (more often) two ground-floor rooms and a further room — known either as a chamber or loft — on the floor above. At this

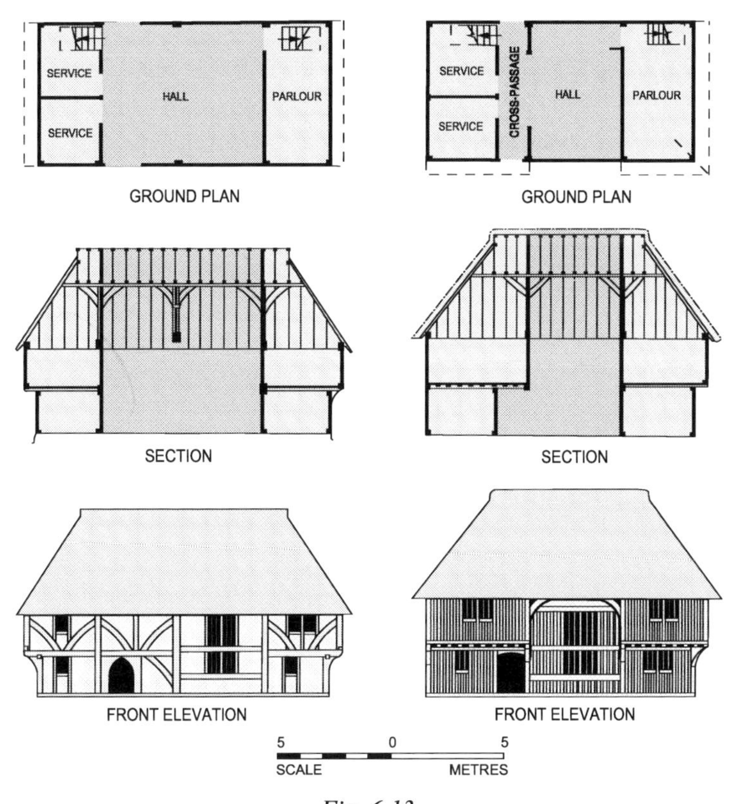

Fig. 6.13
Typical plans, front elevations and long sections through a house with a two-bay hall (left) and a house with a single-bay hall and overshot cross-passage (right).

Fig 6.14
Interior of a typical local rural two-bay hall.

period the first-floor area would have been open to the roof. This end of the house was primarily dedicating to processing: typically the production of various dairy products in the *milkhouse* and storage in the *buttery*. The minority of houses which possessed only one service room presumably combined these activities. The space on the first floor appears usually to have served either as a storage loft or as an additional private chamber, perhaps dower quarters. In modern literature these rooms are normally labelled as the services (ground floor) and service-chamber (first floor).

The open hall, including the cross-passage, was usually near-square in plan and was lit by large windows in the front and rear walls. These two windows normally extended from window-cill level up to the top of the wall and were arranged as a block of four openings (*see* Figure 6.13). Typically, all windows in the house would have been unglazed and closed, when necessary, with shutters. The hall windows usually incorporated sliding shutters to the lower lights, but hinged versions within the upper tier. These shutters could be used to regulate the draught, and so control the fire on the hearth — a defined area of about two metres square, usually biased towards the *high* end of the room.

The high end was located at the opposite end of the hall to the entrances and, as the term implies, was socially the more important part of the room. It was here, on a bench set against an often specially elaborated section of wall known as the *dais partition,* that the owner would have sat with his immediate family, looking down towards the service doorways and entrance area. In front of them stood a trestle table, and in front of that the open hearth. Thus, upon entering the house and turning into the hall the visitor would have been confronted by the head of the household, seated at the dais bench, bathed in light entering through the hall windows. In this way the 'middle-class' owner very deliberately aped his superiors.

In south-east England the open hall had two basic design variations. In one the entire hall was open, including the area over the entrance area; in the second variant the service chamber extended over the entrance area (*see* Figure 6.13). This latter form is described as having an *overshot cross-passage*. As indicated by Figure 6.14, fully-open halls required the strengthening element of an open truss which prevented the walls from spreading and added strength to the roof within the length of the room. A decorative element was often added here, as the truss was usually arch-braced with an elaborate crownpost rising into the roof space. Where an overshot cross-passage was used the open section of the hall was usually sufficiently small not to require the inclusion of an open truss. Although early overshot cross-passages are known, they tended to be more common in later houses and have been linked to a reduction in the importance of the open hall and an increase in the need for space at first-floor level.

Within the fully-developed standard-plan house it was normal for there to be a partitioned-off, storeyed area beyond the hall's high end. This served as the private quarters of the owner and his immediate family. Usually this took the form of a single ground-floor room with a chamber above, open to the roof, though a small number of late 15th- and early 16th-century houses had two high-end ground-floor rooms, one normally being of recognizably higher status than the other. At Great Worge, Brightling, the high-status room was referred to in a document as the *parlour*, whilst the lower-status room was called the *best buttery* — a room for the storage of quality drinks.[7] Unlike the low end, where each room was separately accessed from the hall, the high-end rooms usually acted as a self-contained suite: they were jointly accessed from the hall via a single doorway at one end of the dais partition, typically against the rear wall of the house. The staircase leading to the upper area was thus reached from the ground-floor room and not directly from the hall.

By the close of the medieval era the wealthiest yeomen had adopted the recent trend of the gentry in separating these high-end rooms into a ground-floor *parlour* (from the French word *parler* — to speak) and first-floor *solar*, a private withdrawing/sleeping chamber. However, the vast majority of middle-class vernacular households did not have specialized rooms which could be called parlour and solar. Instead, the ground- and first-floor high-end chambers served as multi-purpose bed/sitting rooms. Regardless of this, in modern literature the ground-floor room at this end of the house is usually termed the parlour, whilst the room above is normally referred to as the parlour chamber.

The typical size of a 'standard' medieval house

The above overview relates to what might be termed 'textbook' medieval houses as surviving in the High Weald. They vary considerably in size, a point well illustrated by the examples shown in Figure 6.15, but the majority of three-cell examples range from 11.5 metres to 13.5 metres (about 38 feet to 44 feet) in length and usually have an overall width of between 5.5 metres and 6.5 metres (roughly 18 feet to 21 feet). Throughout most of Kent and East Sussex the side walls are lofty, the upper chambers typically having walls which measure between 1.5 metres and 2.0 metres (5 feet to 6 feet 6 inches) from floor to top of wallplate. Occasionally medieval houses are found in which the upper chambers are located primarily within the roof space, but such buildings are extremely rare among the surviving houses of the High Weald. Roofs are usually hipped and steeply pitched at between 50 and 55 degrees.

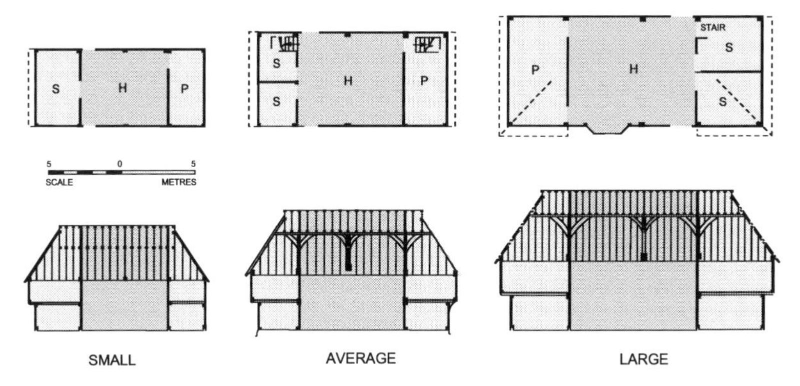

Fig. 6.15 — Variations in size.
Plans & long sections of three houses with two-bay halls.
Left - Old Thatch, Northiam (a small house);
Centre - Parkhill, Burwash (average size);
Right - Great Bucksteep, Warbleton (a large 'Wealden' house).

Variations in layout and design

Not all surviving local hall houses conform to the textbook pattern. For example, some houses have two cells only and never had accommodation beyond the high end, whilst in others high-end accommodation has been added to a house of service-and-hall plan at a later date so as to convert them to standard textbook plan. Based on these examples, it could be argued that two-cell houses without high-end accommodation were perhaps common in earlier times — they may even have been the norm.[8]

With regards to these small two-cell houses, it is worth considering whether some were intended for use by families of lower status. Furthermore, there must have been a social threshold below which the primary concern of the household was the provision of a place to live. For these people the perceived 'usual' hierarchical internal layout may have been inappropriate. Normally, it would seem, the houses occupied by such people were too small or inadequately built, (or, in many instances no doubt both) to have survived to the present day. However, there may be some survival of these buildings, and since one or two small medieval buildings do not show the rigid hierarchical layout so easily recognized in the rest, this could indicate that the threshold for the adoption of hierarchical layouts was only a little below that for most surviving houses from this period.[9]

At the other end of the social scale occasional examples in the area have more elaborate high-end accommodation than that found within the textbook model. This additional accommodation is usually set within its own range aligned at right-angles to the hall. Such ranges are known as *crosswings* (Figure 6.16). In some parts of England crosswings are common, but in the High Weald of East Sussex they have always been rare and are almost always at the high end.[10] In yet other houses, rooms and accommodation more usually found within a detached kitchen are incorporated into the low end of the house, normally — though not always — in a rear range.

Even 'textbook' three-cell houses incorporate some design variations. For instance, the first-floor chambers often project beyond the ground-floor rooms either at one or both ends to give end jetties, whilst others were entirely un-jettied. Either as an alternative to the end jetty, or in addition to it, the first-floor chambers could be jettied forward resulting in the upper part of the hall being recessed between the jettied-out floored ends, though still set under a single roof. Houses of this latter type are known as *Wealdens* (Figure 6.17). Contrary to popular belief, in most instances jetties do not increase the size of a building,

Fig. 6.16
Hall with high-end crosswing (right) and porch (left). Great Dixter, Northiam.

Fig. 6.17
A 'Wealden' house. Bayleaf, Chiddingstone, Kent (now at Weald and Downland Open Air Museum).

but rather the reverse, whilst at the same time they increase building costs (*see* 'Wealdens' in 'Rye's Medieval Houses' below). Thus, in rural and village houses, and in those towns where plot-size was not a concern, they were incorporated solely for aesthetic reasons and should be regarded as a social statement.

Variations to suit an Urban Context

The majority of medieval hall houses which have been studied within the High Weald are either rural or located within small villages. Many of their inhabitants derived their entire income from the land, though others were dual economists — craftsmen or traders who were also involved in agriculture. Thus, the low-end rooms in most rural houses had farming-based functions, such as milk processing and storage of sundry farm produce. In comparison, although a few townsfolk may have kept a stalled milk-cow or run a smallholding on land adjacent to the town, most would have purchased their grain, butter, cheese and other agricultural produce in fully processed form, as and when required.[11] Within rural or village environments plot-sizes would rarely have imposed constraints upon plan-form, whereas, within an urban context street frontages — and in some instances total plot-size — could be restrictive.

The urban environment imposed its own special trade- and service-related requirements. There would have been workshops/shops for the manufacture of goods and for the retail of these and other imported products. Warehousing and bulk storage for both raw materials and import and export goods would also have been needed. These functions could either be incorporated into the house or catered for separately. Such considerations are especially relevant within a port, as too are the employment specialisms of a town. For example, large concentrations of seamen (both mariners and fisherman) whose employment was principally on-board ship would potentially have required nothing more than living space for them and their families, without the need for additional space for storage, retail *etc*. Similarly, a port gave work to a large number of porters, carriers and the like, people best compared to rural landless labourers, but present in greater numbers. Given the very special circumstances of towns in general, and port towns in particular, did the standard medieval house-plan have any relevance within a town such as Rye, or were the town's requirements such that an entirely different housing solution was adopted?

Certainly in some large towns and cities such as Canterbury and Sandwich (both in East Kent) population pressures — particularly in the commercial districts — resulted in a concentration of confined plots. These required residents to build three-storeyed houses turned at right-angles to the street with their lofty open halls pushed back on the plot in order to maximize commercial activity along the street frontages.[12] From the time of its move to its present site in 1285, Rye's much larger neighbour, Winchelsea, occupied an exceptionally spacious site with many generous street frontages. Even here half the plots had frontages of 10 metres (32 feet 9 inches) or less, though only 5 per cent had frontages of less than 5.6 metres (*c*.18 feet 6 inches) and thus although houses with specialized plan-forms adapted to cramped plots must once have existed, they were relatively few in number.[13]

Because of Winchelsea's subsequent collapse, very few houses remain — too few to give a clear picture. At Rye, on the other hand, the number of surviving late-medieval houses is sufficient to indicate whether standard plan forms were commonly adopted or whether, as at Sandwich and Canterbury, the pressures on plot-sizes and the specific requirements of the occupants were such that special forms of non-standard house developed and, at least within the commercial areas, became the norm.

RYE'S MEDIEVAL HOUSES

Bearing in mind the comments made above, it is worth stressing immediately that most of Rye's medieval houses would be entirely at home within the four principal, albeit small nucleated villages in the area (Burwash, Robertsbridge, Sedlescombe and Ticehurst) and, indeed, most would not be out of place standing in isolation in the High Weald countryside. There are a few houses of non-standard layout (*see* below) but even in these the size and quality of the timber used, the method of framing, the range of wall designs, window details, roof types, and styles of mouldings are entirely typical of the area.

House Sizes

In chapter 5 it was emphasized how, prior to the town's demographic growth in the 16th century, many plots were spacious. If the surviving examples are a guide, this was also true of many of the medieval houses, at least with regards to those occupied by the more wealthy Rye residents (*see* Figures 6.21 to 6.22). The longest extant hall house for which the length is known is 99-100 High Street [25 in Figure 6.18] which measures 17.10 metres (56 feet) overall. The two shortest houses with open halls are the early 16th-century semi-detached pair of renters at 26 Church Square [80] which, at just 6.15 metres (20 feet 2 inches) each, are virtually a third the length of 99-100 High Street [25]. An even smaller house, this time of good quality and having an early floored-over hall (rather than

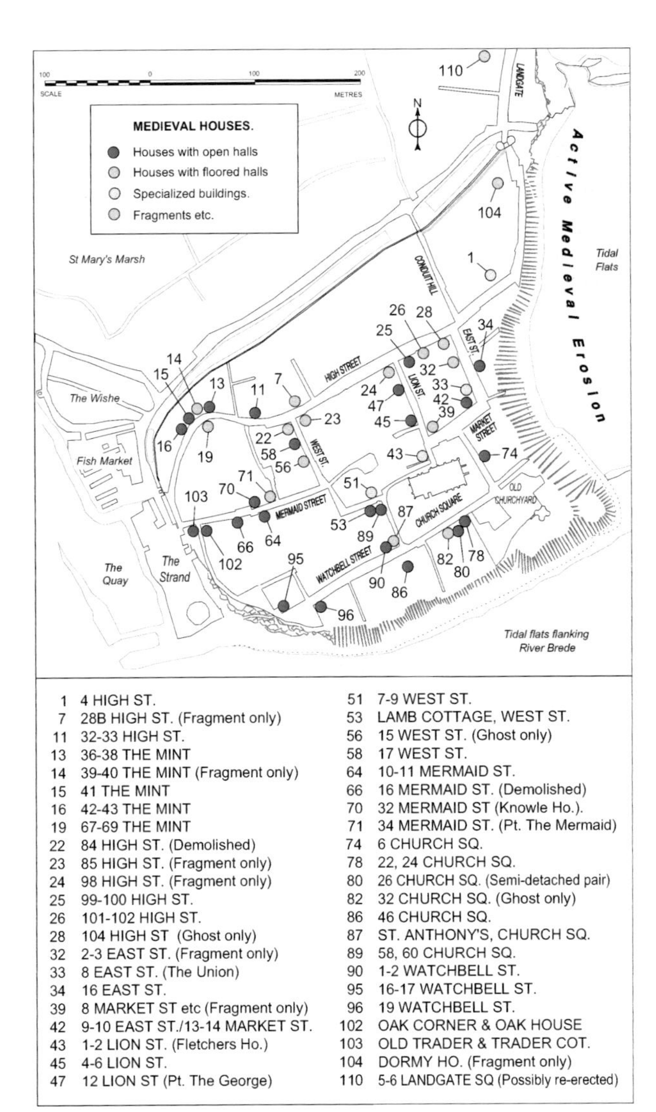

Fig. 6.18
Location of Rye's Known Medieval Houses

an open hall) is that built *c*.1500 at 34 Mermaid Street [71]. Its frontage is only 5.35 metres (17 feet 6 inches) and its hall and associated cross-passage take up the entire length of the street facade. However, for the surviving houses of medieval Rye these are exceptions. Even including those open-hall houses which incorporate only two cells, two-thirds of Rye's extant medieval houses exceed 9.15 metres (30 feet) in length and over a third exceed 11.45 metres (37 feet 6 inches) (Figure 6.19). It needs to be stressed, however, that these figures relate to *surviving* houses — houses which are likely to have ranked amongst the better built, occupied by the more wealthy of Rye's residents. Plots occupied by the less wealthy are likely to have been smaller and likewise their houses. In some instances where only fragments of medieval houses survive the frontage of the plot enables a maximum length for the medieval building to be established. Similarly, there are

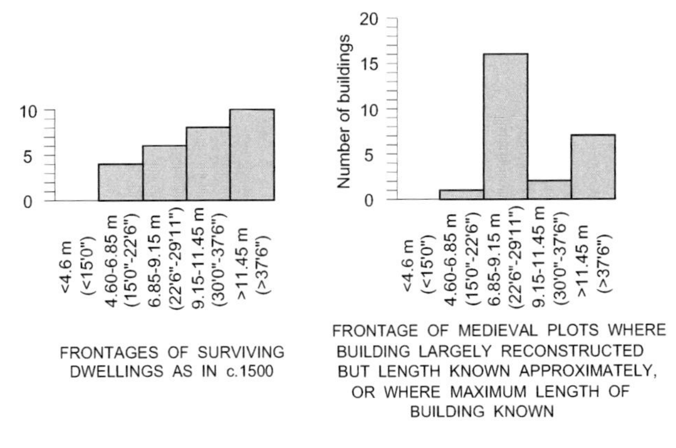

Fig. 6.19

other instances where the house upon the plot has been rebuilt in the early/mid 16th century but the frontage of the medieval plot can be reconstructed, giving a maximum length for the earlier house. The 26 examples where lengths can be established show a very different pattern to that for the surviving medieval houses (compare the two charts in Figure 6.19). Even so, the difference relates mainly to medium-sized frontages of 6.85 metres to 9.15 metres (22 feet 6 inches to 29 feet 11 inches). No plots are known for this period where the frontage was less than 4.60 metres (15 feet 0 inches) and frontages of between 4.60 metres to 6.85 metres (15 feet and 22 feet 6 inches) are, if anything, less well represented than amongst the surviving medieval buildings.

Roof spans, *excluding* rear aisles (for which *see* below) range from the exceptionally narrow 17 West Street [58] at only 4.10 metres (13 feet 6 inches) to a very respectable 8.00 metres (26 feet 3 inches) at 32-33 The Mint [11]. Half the buildings are within the range 5.50 to 6.50 metres (18 feet to 21 feet) with equal numbers above and below this. However, the widths of three of the houses with narrow roof-spans are augmented by rear aisles. Even including its aisle, the width of 17 West Street [58] was less than 5.50 metres (18 feet), whereas when the aisles are taken into account the widths of the other two [53, 103] exceeded 6.50 metres (21 feet).

As Figure 6.18 shows, the extant medieval houses are not concentrated within any one part of town, but are relatively evenly spread throughout. Furthermore, there is no clustering by age or size — the early and late buildings are scattered and, in the main, the small houses are interspersed with the large. This picture is consistent with the impression given by the 1491/2 sesse (for which *see* Chapter 5).

House Types

A common feature of successful, intensely built-up urban centres is the existence (or former existence) of buildings which rise through three full storeys, often jettied towards the street at each storey. Occasional buildings of this type occur in the most intensely built-up parts of some smaller towns also, as at the lower end of Tonbridge High Street, Kent. Other examples (now destroyed) are known near the seaward end of High Street, Hastings.[14] The fact that such buildings are all but absent in Rye reinforces the notion that the town was not pressured for space during the medieval period, even within its most commercial areas.

The only three-storeyed medieval buildings known within the town are 4 High Street [1] and 8 Market Street/23, 23a Lion Street [39]. Number 4 High Street [1] was built after 1490 upon part of the Austin Friars' garden. Apparently the westernmost in a terrace of four, it is of specialized plan with a single room on each of its three storeys. It was most likely built as a speculative venture at a time when the town's population was beginning to rise. Although of three full storeys, it appears to be built against the retaining section of the friary's precinct wall with the lower storey entirely below ground on the side against the street. Thus the public view of it was as a standard two-storeyed structure (*see* Figure 10.1).

In contrast, 8 Market Street/23, 23a Lion Street [39] seems to have been a three-storeyed building of more conventional design, but it is today known from a few residual fragments only. Occupying a prominent corner plot beside the market, it has totally lost its upper storey, but sufficient evidence remains to suggest it was jettied towards both streets (*see* Figure 11.16).

Other three-storeyed medieval buildings within the town could have been destroyed without trace, but it is all but certain that any such buildings were very few in number and were never clustered.

Occasionally the main range of a Rye house was augmented by a *rear range/wing* and there are at least three, possibly five instances of *crosswings*. Even so, the majority — at least 70 per cent — of the town's surviving medieval houses consisted of a single rectangular range. As noted in the overview of local medieval houses above, even within this configuration variations were possible. Two such variations encountered within the town are the use of *rear aisles* and the inclusion of Wealden facades.

Rear aisles

In total five single-aisled medieval houses are known in Rye and others are likely to have existed: a few may still await discovery within the extant building stock, the evidence now obscured by later alterations. Although not the largest of Rye's medieval houses, the late 14th-century Lamb Cottage, West Street [53] is a

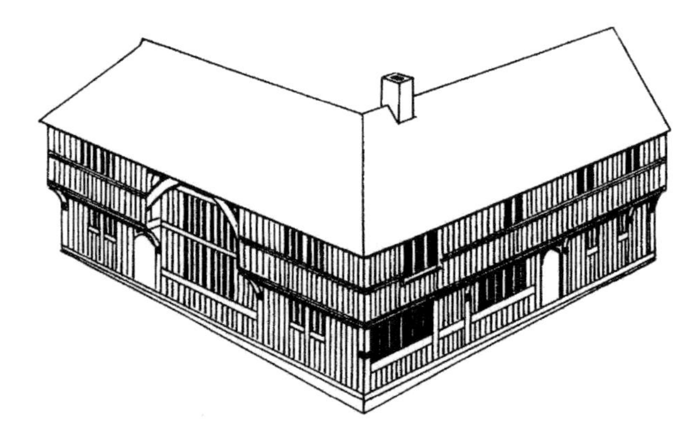

Fig. 6.20
Sketch reconstruction of the fully-floored, continuously-jettied house called St Anthony's, Church Square [87] (right) and the 'Single-Ended Wealden' known as 1-2 Watchbell Street [90] (left) projecting from the end wall of St Anthony's. The end wall of St Anthony's gives 1-2 Watchbell Street the impression of being a 'Full Wealden'.

very impressive 7.10 metres (23 feet 3 inches) in width, but this size was only achieved by incorporating a rear aisle — overall its main wallplates the house measures only 5.20 metres (17 feet 1 inches). Another late 14th-century example exists at 16 East Street [34], whilst Old Trader/Trader Cottage [103] is also likely to be one of the town's earlier houses. Aisles are not restricted to the larger houses. Even including its aisle, 17 West Street [58] is amongst the smallest medieval houses in the town (*see* above): the width excluding the aisle is only 4.10 metres (13 feet 6 inches). There is evidence for the former existence of another single-aisled hall at The George, High Street [24].

It must be admitted that for the High Weald such a high concentration of single-aisled buildings is somewhat unusual: locally two are known in Burwash village, one in Winchelsea, one in Bexhill and a few others are scattered across the rural areas. Outside the High Weald, an early urban example exists on Romney Marsh within the Cinque Port town of New Romney. However, single aisles are far more common a little further west along the coast, within Downland villages such as Alfriston.[15]

'Wealdens'

The definition of a Wealden as given in the Council for British Archaeology's illustrated glossary is a 'Type of medieval house ... with an open hall in the middle and a two-storeyed bay at each end, roofed in line. The upper floors of the end bays are jettied to the front and the eaves are continuous, so that the hall roof projects in front of its wall and is carried on a *Flying wallplate* (*see* Figure 6.17). These could be termed *Full Wealdens*, for a recognized variant is the *Single-ended Wealden* which, as the name implies, is a Wealden house with a jettied bay at one end only.[16] In Rye all extant or evidenced Wealdens comply to the above two definitions, so there is no need to discuss other variant forms which are occasionally encountered. Although often referred to as a special house-type, a Wealden is in reality an ordinary house which incorporates within its front elevation the specific configuration of features mentioned above. These features were deliberately planned in order to enhance appearance. As such a *Wealden facade* can be designed into houses encompassing a variety of different internal layouts, either of commonly-used type or of specialized or unusual design. This is an important point which is all too often overlooked.

The inclusion of jetties within a structure gives the impression of increasing the size of the upper floors, though in most instances this is a false notion. An un-jettied building capped by an identical-sized roof gives first-floor rooms of identical size to those in a jettied building, but with a larger ground-floor footprint. Furthermore, because of the extra work and timber involved in constructing a jetty, the cost of the un-jettied building is less. Therefore, unless built upon a site where the plot-size is restricted, the commonly-held belief that jetties were built to increase the size of a structure is false. In rural and village houses, and in those towns where plot-size was not a concern, they were used solely for aesthetic reasons. Thus the purpose of incorporating a Wealden facade was to impress by giving the building architectural distinction. Despite this, the feature was not reserved solely for use in houses built for owner-occupation. This point is convincingly illustrated by the terrace of nine well-finished Wealden houses (eight single-ended and one of full type) built for rent by Battle Abbey next to their precinct wall at Battle, and by the equally well-built, handed semi-detached pair of Single-ended Wealdens which stand next to the church lychgate in Bexhill. Nor were Wealdens always large buildings. An example in Hastings (perhaps one of a semi-detached pair) had on the ground floor nothing more than a small two-bay hall, one bay of which was open to the roof whilst the other included a first-floor chamber over it: the only other room in the house. What this surely indicates is that not all houses built for rent were of low quality: some were built with display features intended to attract good, reliable tenants.

An adequate understanding of the background to houses which incorporate Wealden facades is essential if their relevance is to be properly understood. In Rye this is important because ten Wealdens have been proven within the town and another two are all but certain. Therefore, Wealdens account for about half the open-hall houses for which there are adequate details. In both date and size they range across the entire spectrum. The earliest, 16 East Street [34], dates from the late 14th century, whilst the latest are amongst the last open halls built within the town. Sizes vary from the tiny example at 17 West Street [58] to the large (unproven) example at 99-100 High Street [25]. Only the unproven 99-100 High Street [25] had a hall of two open bays: the others had single-bay halls, most (if not all) served by overshot cross-passages.

A minimum of three and a maximum of five of the buildings are Full Wealdens, though 16 East Street [34] developed into this form only in the 15th century when its parlour bay was added to a Single-ended Wealden. The added bay was either built on the site of an earlier, lower, parlour or replaced a separate structure in different occupation. There are similar 'complications' with regards the other Single-ended Wealdens. That at 22, 24 Church Square [79] was almost certainly constructed as the second phase of a progressive rebuild, leaving an earlier 'non-Wealden' service-bay standing, whilst although 1-2 Watchbell Street [90] was always of two-cell layout and is therefore technically a single-ended example, the structure was given the appearance of being a Full Wealden by the jettied end-wall of the contemporary fully-floored neighbouring building, St Anthony's, Church Square [87] (Figure 6.20).

The fact that the front wall of a Wealden hall was recessed inevitably reduced the hall's width in comparison to the span of its roof. It may seem odd, therefore, that having reduced the width of the hall, in a few Wealdens a rear aisle was incorporated, effectively pushing the back of the room outwards. Single-aisled Wealdens are rare and thinly distributed: in the eastern High Weald of East Sussex examples are known at Bexhill (a semi-detached pair), Salehurst, Winchelsea and Uckfield, with two further examples within the Downland village of Alfriston.[17] Rye likewise has two known examples — the late-14th-century 16 East Street [34] and the tiny 17 West Street [58], probably built during the mid/late 15th century. Cross-sections through these buildings are reproduced in Figure 6.25.

The construction of a house of Wealden design posed the carpenter a series of structural and aesthetic problems to overcome — the principal of these relate to the way in which the flying wallplate is supported across the hall's recessed front and the way in which the framing of the hall's end-partitions is designed to overcome a phenomenon known as the *off-centred Wealden effect*. Both these aspects of design and construction have been discussed elsewhere and will not, therefore, be dealt with further.[18] However, a specific constructional feature within one Rye house — 16 East Street [34] — is worth mentioning because it indicates the carpenter's concerns in devising a method of supporting the end of the flying wallplate in this early Single-ended Wealden. For a discussion of this aspect *see* the entry for 16 East Street included in Chapter 11. His solution to the problem is most unusual, if not unique.

Rear ranges/wings

At 19 Watchbell Street [96] the accommodation within a standard three-cell rectangular main range was augmented from the outset by a rear wing (perhaps housing a kitchen) and there is also a rear range at 99-100 High Street [25]. In the latter instance the extra range flanks a side-street (Lion Street) and may represent an early addition rather than an original feature. Furthermore, the 99-100 High Street range need not have been part of the main house and may have been in separate occupation, as was certainly the case with the 'L-plan' structure at St Anthony's/1-2 Watchbell Street [87 and 90] shown in Figure 6.20, and perhaps also at 16-17 Watchbell Street [95].

Depending upon the original configuration, other potential rear wings to principal street-ranges exist at the stone-built 46 Church Square [86] and at 39-40 The Mint [14]. Both are quite early, No. 46 [86] probably being built over a vaulted cellar in about 1400, whilst the details of the doorway at 39-40 [14] suggest a date no later than about 1450. Number 46 [86] has totally lost its street range, whilst that at 39-40 [14] was rebuilt in the early/mid 16th century. From what survives, both buildings seem to have been truly 'urban' in their layout — *very* rare in Rye. A rear range must also have existed behind the hall at 67-69 The Mint [19] when it was rebuilt in fully-floored form in *c.*1500, whilst there are two fragmentary rear ranges at 7-9 West Street/ 62 Church Square [51] which almost certainly flanked a courtyard. This too is a house of truly 'urban' design in that it was built as the urban mansion of one of Rye's elite families. In this instance the street range appears to have consisted of a number of separate specialized units which fronted two storeys of cloister-like walkways overlooking the courtyard. The main body of this house — the hall — seems to have occupied a rear range closing the back of the courtyard (*see* Figure 6.24). Unfortunately the entire rear part of the house has been demolished and the remainder much altered: as a result, the details are tantalizingly vague.

Crosswings

Rather than making use of a rear range, at 36-38 The Mint [13] an additional room and chamber were incorporated at the rear of the high end, within a three-bay crosswing which had a two-bay principal room and chamber at the front and a single-bay room and chamber to the rear. To judge from the location of a later side chimney, the parlour at 99-100 High Street [25] was likewise sited within a crosswing, as was that within the now very fragmentary 98 High Street [24].

Other medieval crosswings exist at 32 Mermaid Street [70] and 41 The Mint [15] but, as Figure 6.23 indicates, these are somewhat different in that, once built, they dominated the tiny main ranges which housed the (subsequently rebuilt) open halls. At 41 The Mint [15] the crosswing seems to have been built on the site of an earlier in-line bay — probably a service bay — and was designed as a crosswing out of necessity in order to fit the large heated ground-floor room (perhaps a beer room) and unheated first-floor chamber onto the restricted space available. The crosswing at 32 Mermaid Street [70] likewise replaced part of an earlier building, but in this instance its predecessor must have been of the same size and footprint, for the replacement sits neatly over one of Rye's early vaulted cellars. Furthermore, the predecessor was replaced in two phases of progressive reconstruction; the front part first, followed by the rear bay. As with three of the examples mentioned under the heading *Rear Ranges/Wings* above, these two buildings are rare Rye examples of true urban designs.

Internal layouts and uses

Figures 6.21 to 6.24 illustrate in simplified form the ground-floor layouts of Rye's 28 medieval domestic buildings for which reasonable details survive. Shown beneath each plan is a longitudinal section, indicating the vertical configuration of the rooms and chambers and the overall proportions of each building. As with the other architectural drawings included within Part 1 of this study, all are drawn to a consistent small scale. The examples are arranged in broadly chronological order with the hall and any associated cross-passage (in some instances inferred only) shaded in dark grey and the floored ends in light grey. The buff shading emphasizes the point that all these houses are aligned along the town's streets. Thus, in each instance the hall took up a large part of the street frontage. Where there is known to have been an abutting building its approximate outline is shown in pink, whereas where the house is known to have stood against open ground the space is depicted in green.

Following the trends outlined above for local non-urban houses, the most common plan-form adopted in medieval Rye's surviving buildings was that which consisted of three cells arranged in line, with the open hall dominating the central part. These three-cell layouts (including three in which the street part is (or was) augmented by an additional element projecting to

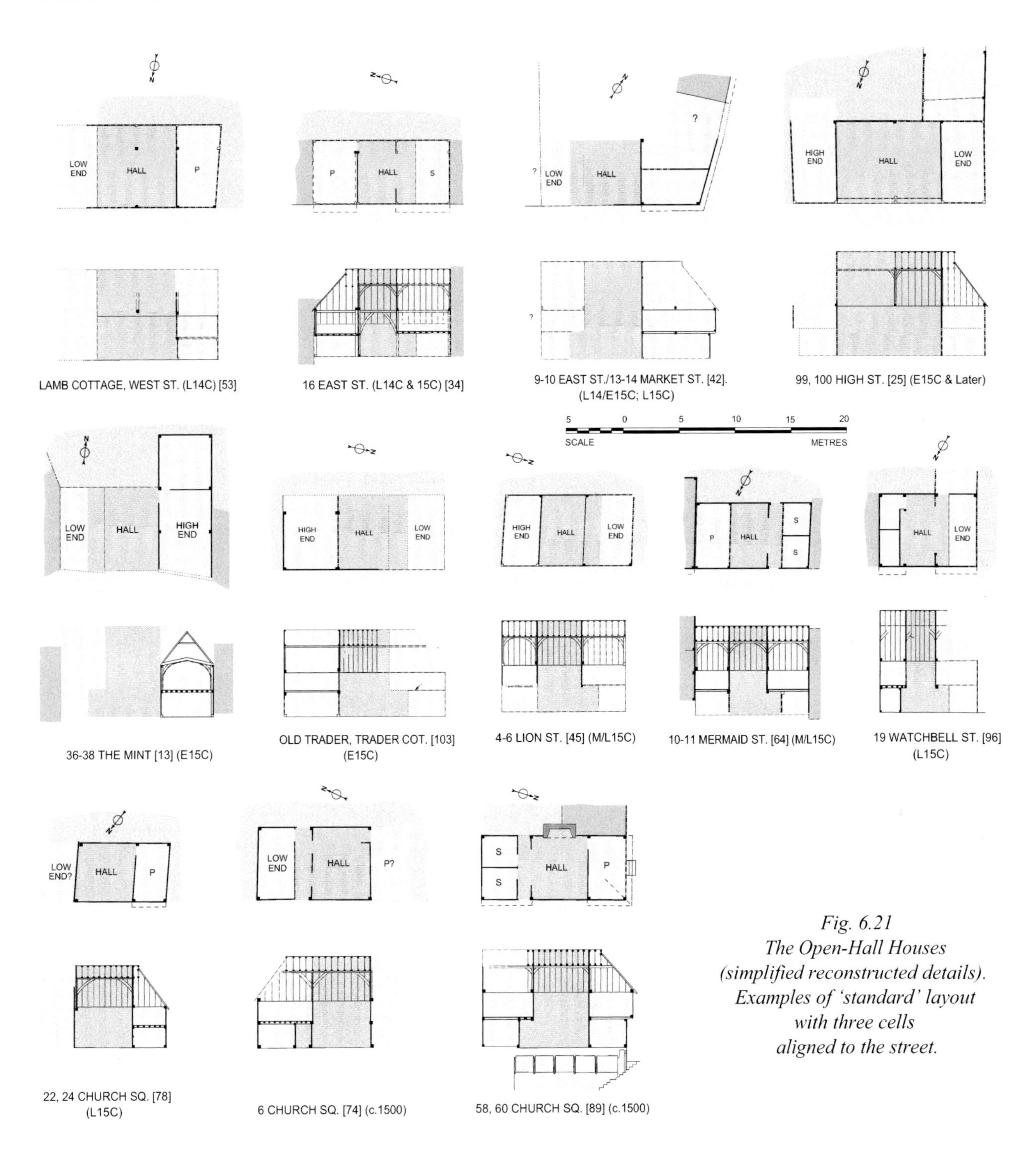

Fig. 6.21
The Open-Hall Houses (simplified reconstructed details). Examples of 'standard' layout with three cells aligned to the street.

the rear) are illustrated in Figure 6.21. A very obvious feature is the gradation in size — the earliest examples are noticeably larger than those built during the mid/late 15th century. All the widest buildings and largest halls fall into the early date-range. This may be due in part to the more restricted nature of the plots available during the later period, but the sub-division of plots is not thought to have started within the town until the 16th century and, in any case, by no means all the later buildings occupied the entire street frontage of their plots and therefore they could have been built larger if the owner had wished. More likely, the gradation reflects the fact that the earliest extant houses within the town represent the homes of the urban elite and, as such, were the first to be built using durable techniques capable of surviving for centuries and, indeed, thought worth adapting to changing needs subsequently. If this is so, it suggests that only towards the close of the medieval era were good-quality, good-sized timbers, up-to-date building techniques, and designs capable of

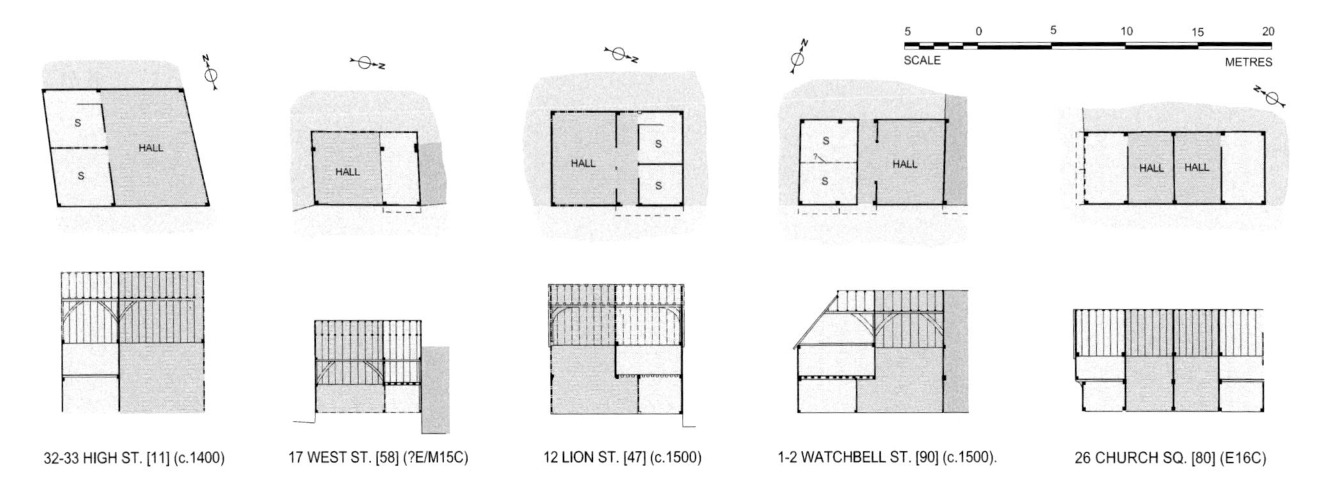

Fig. 6.22
The Open-Hall Houses (simplified reconstructed details).
Examples of layouts with two cells aligned to the street.

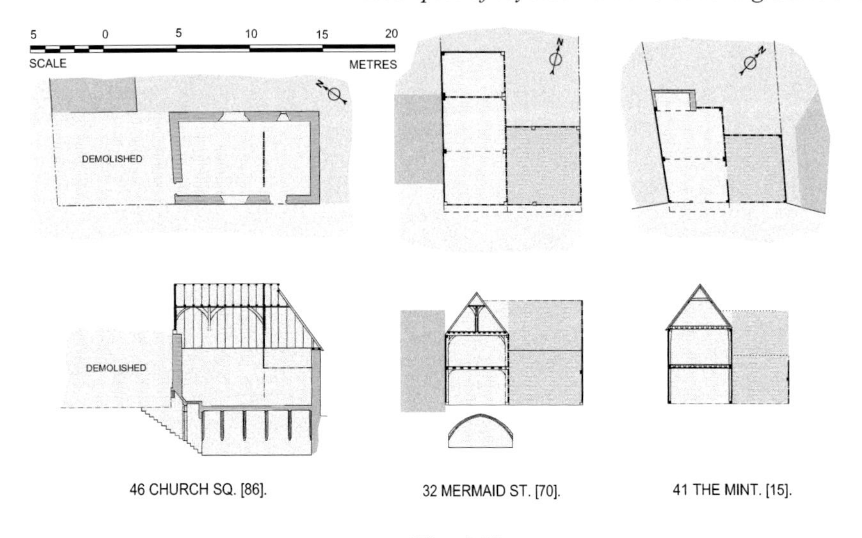

Fig. 6.23
Open-Hall Houses of non-standard type (simplified reconstructed details).

subsequent adaptation used by the less prosperous 'middle-class' residents of the town.

In the overview of local medieval houses given earlier it was noted how in a few instances extant rural and village houses were built without accommodation beyond the high end of their hall, and how in some instances high-end accommodation was added subsequently in order to convert them into textbook three-cell layouts. Further, it was suggested that at an earlier period two-cell arrangements may have been the norm for persons of ordinary status and that even by the end of the medieval period the majority of houses occupied by the lower classes — those not capable of surviving through to the present day — may have been of this type. In this respect, it is surely no coincidence that from the late 16th century, when they start to survive, almost all rural cottages in the eastern High Weald are of two cells only.

In common with the town's rural hinterland, Rye has a few surviving two-cell medieval houses and, as has already been demonstrated (*see* 'House Sizes' above) a number of small-frontage plots seem to indicate that medieval houses of this type were once far more common than the extant buildings suggest. The six known surviving examples (which include the semi-detached pair at 26 Church Square [80]) are illustrated in Figure 6.22. In addition, several houses known from extant fragments and weathering ghosts were probably also of this type. For instance, prior to the addition of its crosswing late in the 15th century the tiny hall at The Standard, 41 The Mint [15], could have had nothing more than an in-line end-bay to augment it, whilst the same is also true of 32 Church Square [82]. At widths of 4.50 metres (14 feet 9 inches) and 4.90 metres (16 feet 1 inches) respectively, these are amongst the narrowest known medieval buildings within the town. Even so, the indications are that they were adequately built. Although in relative terms they were low structures, in each case they were sufficiently tall to have been capable of incorporating two storeys beyond the hall.

In height and width both 41 The Mint [15] and 32 Church Square [82] were similar to the pair of dwellings incorporated within 26 Church Square [80]. Being sited upon the same plot as the small, but well-built and well-finished house known today as 22, 24 Church Square [78], the pair of cottages at

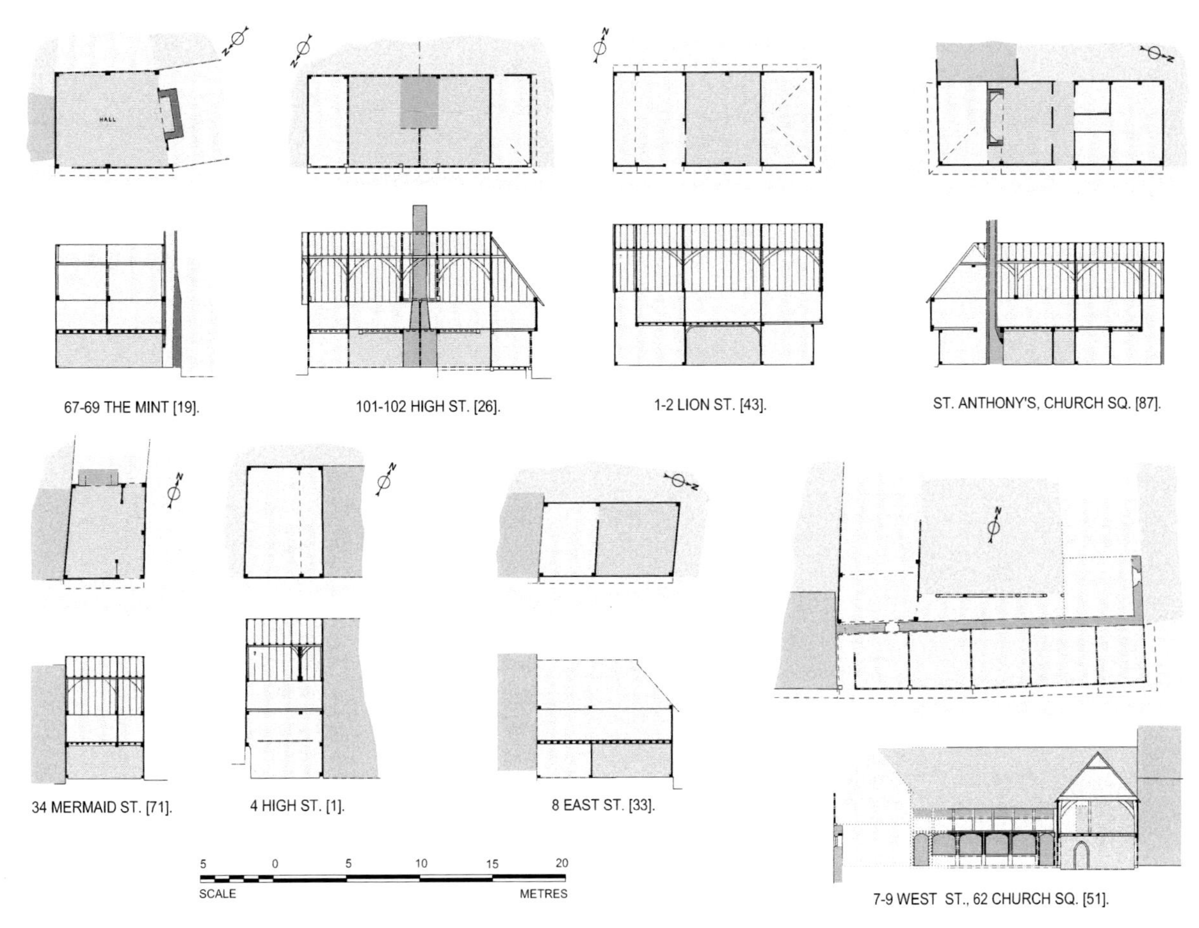

Fig. 6.24
Fully-floored buildings of c.1500 (simplified reconstructed details).

No. 26 [80] were almost certainly erected for rent by the owner of the main house.

An equally tiny though adequately built two-cell structure is the single-aisled house at 17 West Street [58]. Being so plain and basic in the detailing of its framing, it incorporates very little upon which to base a date, but it could be mid 15th century. Neither this hall nor the pair within 26 Church Square [80] incorporate clues as to which was the low end and which the high end of the hall. It is, of course, entirely possible that a hierarchical approach to the use of the hall was considered an irrelevance at this relatively low social level. However, it is worth pointing out that 17 West Street [58] was, none-the-less, built with a recessed Wealden front (*see* above), not a feature normally associated with the home of one of society's lower social groups: its inclusion would have added unnecessary expense to the construction costs.

Whether either 41 The Mint [15], 32 Church Square [82], or 17 West Street [58] were intended for owner occupation or were built for rental income is impossible to tell, but they must surely have been occupied by people who were recognizably further down the social scale than most who occupied Rye's extant medieval dwellings. Despite their two-cell design, the same cannot be said for the other three examples illustrated in Figure 6.22. Admittedly 1-2 Watchbell Street [90] must have been built either for rent or for occupation by a relative of the owner, for not only is it attached to St Anthony's, Church Square [87], it is contemporary with it, being part of the same structural frame. In comparison, St Anthony's is a large house which, for its date, incorporates advanced design features. Almost certainly it was built by John Jarvis as the capital messuage of the complex (*see* [87]). Yet the secondary dwelling is equally well built and very well finished, indicating that it too was intended for occupation by one of Rye's middle-class residents. The same is equally true of the exceptionally wide and lofty 32-33 High Street [11] (an early house of *c.*1400 date) and the very well finished Wealden of about a hundred years later at 12 Lion Street [47] (now part of The George Hotel [24]). Both were built to two-cell designs on account of the restricted frontages of their plots. Even so, neither owner felt sufficiently restricted in the number of rooms to consider incorporating a rear range to accommodate the 'missing' high-end elements.

The open halls

With two exceptions — the stone-built house at 46 Church Square [86] set back from the main street and accessed direct from a small side-lane, and the tiny semi-detached pair at 26 Church Square [80] — all Rye's extant open halls are built against and parallel to the main street. As with overall house size, the earliest halls tend to be the largest. Those built during the late 14th and early 15th centuries range in ground-floor area from 25 square metres (269 square feet) at 16 East Street [34] to more than double that size at 99-100 High Street [25], the hall of which had a ground floor area of approximately 59 square metres (635 square feet): the median of the group is 38 square metres (409 square feet) and the average size is 40 square metres (430 square feet). In contrast, the open halls built during the mid 15th century and later range from the pair of tiny 13 square metre (140 square feet) halls at 26 Church Square [80] to 37 square metres (398 square feet) at 6 Church Square [74], the median being 31 square metres (334 square feet) and the average 26 square metres (280 square feet). The sample of buildings is too small to draw any meaningful conclusions from these figures, though it is worth stressing that the three smallest known Rye halls are smaller than the smallest known rural open hall within the Rape of Hastings, though comparable with the smallest within the town of Hastings.[19]

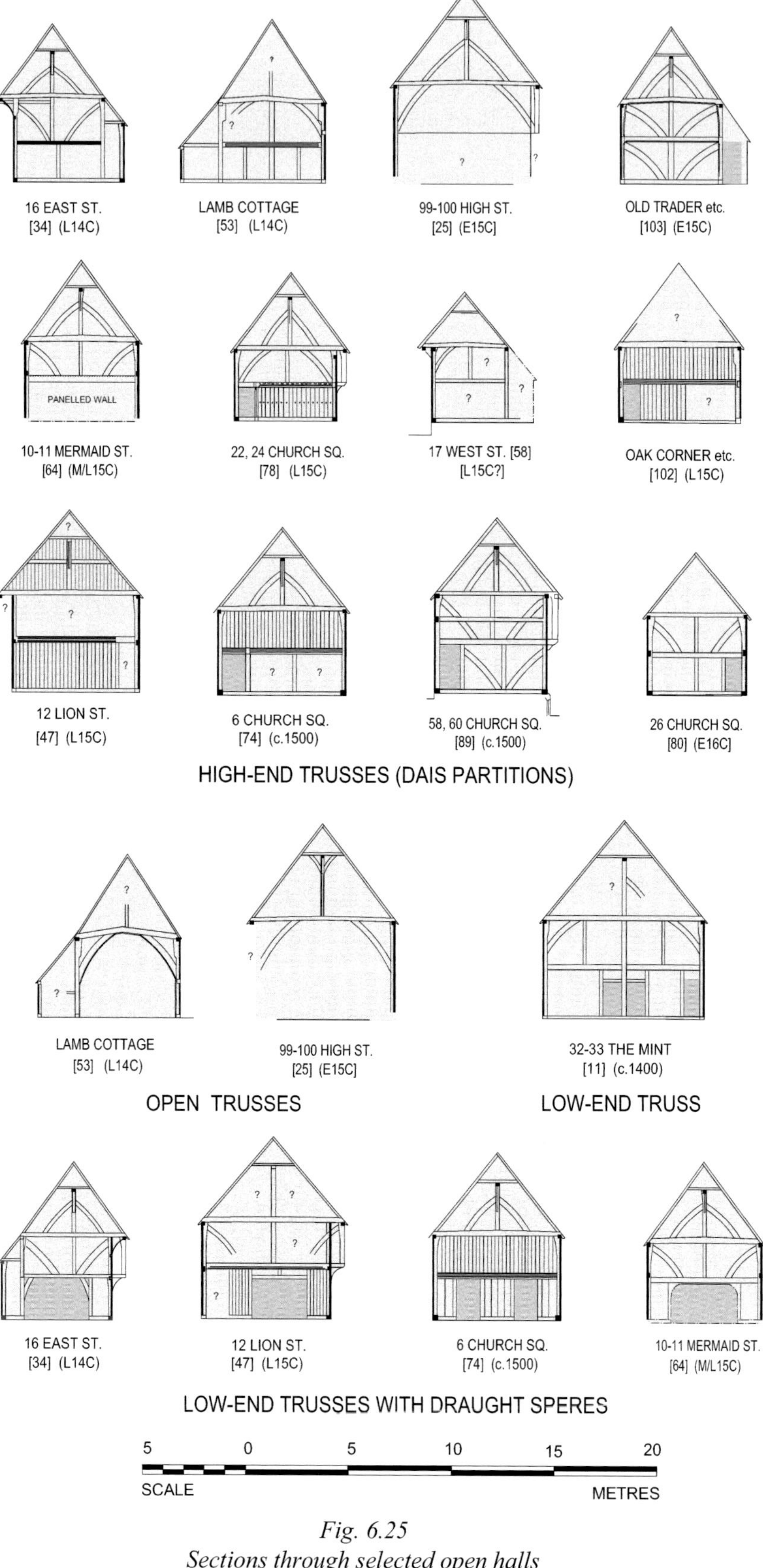

Fig. 6.25
Sections through selected open halls (simplified reconstructed details).

Most of the halls were designed to function in a standard hierarchical way, with low-end external doorways and a high-end dais partition. Moulded dais beams exist in 12 buildings (for details of eleven of these *see* Figure 6.27).[20] Three [34, 42, 53] are late 14th-century in date and are cut to a 'decorated-style' profile, whilst the others are 'perpendicular' in style. These later beams all incorporate *cavetto* moulds which are typical of the 15th century, though the form was first used late in the 14th century and continued through to the early 16th century. In four houses (three of which are Wealdens) the moulded dais beams are matched by a second moulded beam at the low end of the hall. At 19 Watchbell Street [96] the profile on both appears similar, but in the others the low-end moulding is less complex.

The Wealden at 58, 60 Church Square [89] breaks with convention in that it incorporates a simply-moulded crossbeam over the service doorways in the overshot cross-passage, whereas the crossbeams in the end-walls of the open hall bay (including the dais beam) are unmoulded. Neither does this late open hall incorporate panelling or elaborated wall framing below its dais beam, but is instead infilled with a simple footbraced large-panel design. The likelihood is that this hall was intended to have a cloth or tapestry hanging at this point, though it should be stressed that Rye contains more examples of simple wall designs beneath dais beams than is normal locally (for a selection *see* Figure 6.25). For example, none of the three late 14th-century halls incorporated dais panelling, and panelling can also be proven to have been absent in seven other examples of later date. Admittedly two of these are the low-status early 16th-century semi-detached pair, whilst in two *c*.1500 examples high-status close studding is used in this location in lieu of panelling. Even so, in only three Rye halls can a panelled dais partition be proven.

Although two-bay open halls are more common than single-bay examples in the rural hinterland, the reverse is the case in Rye itself where only three two-bay examples have so far been identified. Here the majority (16 halls) are of one-bay type and, to judge from circumstantial evidence, another four are likely to be. Eight of these single-bay halls (including the late 14th-century example at 16 East Street [34]) are known to have been served by overshot cross-passages. All but one of these incorporated draught screens between the passage and the main body of the hall. In the eighth example (4-6 Lion Street [45] — mid/late 15th C) the evidence is hidden or destroyed.

Most of the draught speres followed the normal local pattern of short projecting partitions shielding the external doorways, leaving the remainder of the area between passage and hall entirely open. However, in one late example an additional central draught screen was included, thereby more fully segregating the two elements by forming two narrower openings between the hall and passage (Figure 6.25). This 'developed' tripartite form of screen is also found in the fully-floored hall at St Anthony's, Church Square [87] (*c*.1500) and in several of Rye's slightly later (early 16th-century) fully-floored halls (for which *see* Chapter 7).

Despite the use of single-bay open halls, in only one instance (19 Watchbell Street. [96] — late 15th century) does the single-bay design seem to have been necessitated by a restricted street frontage, and even in this building it was instigated due to the owner's desire to incorporate a three-cell plan aligned parallel to the street (*see* Figure 6.21). Here the open bay of the hall is only 2.50 metres (8 feet 2 inches) long and not only was a low-end overshot cross-passage incorporated, but also a narrow high-end overshot area (sometimes called an *internal jetty*) which produced a canopy-like effect over the dais bench. This feature allowed a hall with a respectable *c*.4.25 metre (*c*.14 feet) length on the ground floor, but at the expense of a ridiculously small ground-floor high-end room. Another example where the dais bench may once have been recessed beneath an overshot chamber is 42-43 The Mint [16], though the building is so fragmentary the evidence in this instance may indicate an overshot cross-passage. Overshot high ends/internal jetties are rare in the High Weald, but are more common in Surrey.[21]

Usually in the High Weald the existence of a single-bay hall indicates the presence (or former presence) of an overshot cross-passage, though very occasional examples are encountered where this was not the case. Most such exceptions are at the extreme low end of the range of sizes for surviving medieval houses. Rye includes five single-bay halls where it can be proven no overshot cross-passage existed, and the same may be the case in a sixth example. In each case entry was direct into the hall and in four instances (including the semi-detached early 16th-century pair at 26 Church Square [80]) the halls are tiny — the pair are 3.10 metres x 4.70 metres (10 feet 2 inches x 15 feet 4 inches) each, another is 3.95 metres x 4.45 metres (12 feet 11 inches x 14 feet 7 inches) and the fourth (the single-aisled 17 West Street [58]) slightly larger at 4.70 metres x 4.80 metres (15 feet 5 inches x 15 feet 9 inches). The three smallest are smaller than normally survive and may truly represent the homes of lower-class residents who did not follow a hierarchical regime within their hall (*see* below). The hall in the sixth example, 22, 24 Church Square [78], is similar in size to 17 West Street [58], but is well built, well finished, and has a moulded dais beam and dais panelling (for a photograph of which *see* Figure 13.7). In this case the hall is built open-framed against a (since rebuilt) earlier low-end structure and it is therefore possible that the demolished part incorporated an overshot cross-passage.

Contrary to the norm, the town contains one example of a large direct-entered single-bay hall — 32-33 The Mint [11] (*c*.1400). In fact, this is the widest hall known within the town, having a roof which spans

8.00 metres (26 feet 3 inches). Due to the curve on the street at this point, the hall is built out of square, but somewhat unusually its length is less than its width. As the cross-section at its low-end truss (illustrated in Figure 6.25) shows, the house is also unusually lofty for its date. Despite its size, the structure is entirely plain.

Only three two-bay open halls have been identified within the town — all are early and one is 14th century. They include Rye's two largest halls. That at 99-100 High Street [25] is an impressive 9.20 metres (30 feet 2 inches) in length whilst the hall at Lamb Cottage, West Street [53] is somewhat shorter at *c.*7.00 metres (*c.*23 feet). The third hall (46 Church Square [86] — probably *c.*1400) is the only extant domestic stone-built structure and presents problems in that the entrance is located beyond the hall in what, to judge from the bay configuration, was the high-end room. This is one of the few Rye halls where the hierarchical system appears not to have been observed and, for a number of reasons, the possibility that it was not designed as a dwelling must be considered.

There is virtually no documentary evidence to indicate how the open halls in Rye were used, though, except for specific exceptions mentioned above, all the architectural evidence suggests that no concessions were made (or were indeed necessary) to suit their urban location. The only description yet identified which lists the contents of a Rye hall in the 15th century comes from the fragmentary probate inventory of the town's vicar, William Wykwyk, compiled in 1498. The house has been rebuilt, but to judge from reference to a heated parlour (*see* below) Wykwyk appears to have been amongst the most wealthy of Rye's residents, and therefore the contents of his hall may not have been typical. It was sparsely furnished, with a table and two trestles, a form, the luxury of two round tables, three cushions and a hanging of red saye, valued in all at 9s.4d. The entry contains no reference to fire goods.[22]

Early fully-floored halls

There is no guarantee that the hall of William Wykwyk mentioned above was of open type, for Rye has six houses (of which two are sited within a semi-detached pair at 101-102 High Street [26]) which have fully-floored halls, but are nevertheless datable on stylistic grounds to *c.*1500. Another may have a fully-floored domestic hall, but is more likely to have been built as a specialized commercial structure. These buildings are illustrated in Figure 6.24. Their precise dates are not known, but all were almost certainly built during the half-century 1475-1525.

Despite the relatively long date-range, there can be little doubt that some — perhaps all — of these examples were built prior to the erection of some of the town's late open halls, and the same could be true of some of the earliest houses of similar type discussed in the next chapter. That both open and fully-floored houses of similar status were being erected during the decades around 1500 (particularly during the opening decades of the 16th century) has been known for some time, and is entirely logical: no new innovation instantly displaces its precursors. Even without the benefit of dates derived from dendrochronology, in Rye this fact is well illustrated at St Anthony's, Church Square and 1-2 Watchbell Street [87/90]. This single-build, 'L-plan', high-quality structure occupies a corner plot and incorporates a fully-floored, continuously-jettied capital messuage in its principal range, facing onto Church Square. A smaller, though equally well-built Wealden open-hall house occupies the other part, facing onto Watchbell Street (*see* Figure 6.20).

The examples illustrated in Figure 6.24 are so similar in design, form and function to some of the buildings discussed in Chapter 7 that it would be pointless to describe them in any detail here. Even so, it would be negligent to ignore their existence in this account of Rye's late medieval buildings — to do so would be to give a misleading picture.[23]

Other rooms and chambers

With very few exceptions, throughout the medieval and immediate post-medieval periods the hall served as the principal room of a house: all other areas were in a sense secondary to that space, serving as adjuncts intended to fulfil what could be termed ancillary functions. As discussed in the general overview, in the textbook examples these other functions were in effect segregated into two, sometimes three discrete groups. Beyond the low end of the hall were what could be classed as the support functions (both domestic and occupational), whilst beyond the high end were the living areas (perhaps best described as private family space). Additionally, some houses were equipped with dedicated areas at the hall's low end for cooking, washing, brewing *etc.* Others, of two cells only, used the first-floor chamber over the low-end rooms as the only private space. Whereas the high-end rooms tended to be interlinked with each other and accessed from the hall by a single door, the functional rooms beyond the low end were normally accessed independently from the hall. The extant remains are often too damaged to allow full details to be recovered, but as Figures 6.21 and 6.22 indicate, the typical low-end arrangement in Rye followed the textbook standard with usually two, but occasionally only one service room on the ground floor, capped by a first-floor chamber and, in at least some instances, augmented by a kitchen, either attached or detached.

There is today little surviving architectural evidence for kitchens within the town. The only confirmed attached kitchen is that at St Anthony's, Church Square [87], but another may exist at 1-2 Lion Street [44] and a former kitchen-like room once occupied a rear range at 19 Watchbell Street [96]. Although largely rebuilt and attached to the main house since the late 16th century, the very fragmentary remains of a medieval detached kitchen survive embedded within the rear range of The Mermaid, Mermaid Street [72] (*see* Figure 12.49). Despite this being the only physical evidence noted for such a structure, detached kitchens seem once to have been more common and continued in use through the 16th century and beyond. A casual search of Rye deeds has revealed nine references to messuages/tenements with separate kitchen structures described with them.[24]

In a rural/village context the service rooms were normally used principally for the processing and storage of food and drink, with one of the two rooms — the milkhouse — dedicated to dairying activities. In a town such as Rye there would normally be no call for a dairy/milkhouse and perhaps less need for storage of drinks and foodstuffs, which could be readily purchased within the town. Even so, rooms called butteries certainly existed and the contents of one such room is described in the probate inventory of the town's vicar, William Wykwyk, in 1498. Despite its name, it seems that his buttery was used primarily as a general store. Listed are his table cloths, napkins and towels, as well as basins, ewers, 8 candlesticks and other similar items.[25]

An obvious urban use for the second service-room (that at the front of the house) would have been as a shop/workshop, a use confirmed in some towns in the south of England — particularly in East Anglia — by the shop fronts which survive in this location. Similar evidence exists in East Sussex, but it is rare on account of the extensive reconstruction of local ground-floor walls.[26] On account of this, only two shop fronts serving front service-rooms of textbook layout are known in Rye and both are post-medieval, dating from the early/mid 16th century (*see* Chapter 7). It has to be accepted that many front service-rooms in Rye's medieval houses could have been used in this way, but without the evidence of the shop fronts it is impossible to tell. Just as the first-floor service-chambers in local High Weald farmhouses seem commonly to have been used (at least in part) for the storage of farm produce such as fruit, threshed crops, *etc*., so the service chambers of some of Rye's houses are likely to have served as storage for commercial goods, and perhaps even as workshops. Equally, some high-status occupations may have made use of ground-floor high-end rooms as 'commercial/office' space. There is some evidence for this, for instance, at St Anthony's, Church Square [87] and such a use could explain the existence of the former front room within the fragmentary axially-divided high-end at 9-10 East Street/13-14 Market Street [42] (*see* Figure 6.21), but this is pure speculation.

What is certain is that in a port town such as Rye there must have been a reasonable amount of space dedicated to commerce during the medieval period, some located within the houses, some in detached workshops built in rear gardens, some (perhaps) in detached non-domestic buildings occupying what might appear today to have been gaps in the medieval street frontage, and some within terraces of units dedicated to this use and thus separate from the occupant's house.

Two buildings which seem to reflect the latter two arrangements are 7-9 West Street/62 Church Square [51] and 8 East Street [33] (*see* Figure 6.24). In the former what appear to have been five separate units along the street facade of this urban mansion most likely served as shops. The westernmost of these appears to have been occupied with the mansion itself, but the others seem to have been self-contained rentable units. How the first-floor areas above the units were used is now impossible to tell, but at least one was linked by a stair to the ground-floor unit below it. The second building, 8 East Street [33], may in truth be a house and certainly has the appearance of having a floored-over hall (albeit unheated) with an adjacent service area on the ground floor, but the stair leading to the first floor is unusually wide and the entire first floor seems to have been a single, large, plain, store-like chamber. This building could easily have been used as a shop and workshop on the ground floor with storehouse above, and was perhaps owned with adjacent 9-10 East Street/13-14 Market Street [42]. Buildings of the type described above are known within Rye from documentary evidence, with examples at The Strand (from at least the late 15th century) and others in the general market place up by the church (*see* Chapter 2).

Despite the lack of good structural evidence relating to commercial activities within the town, both during the medieval period and the 16th century, the layout of some buildings constructed in the 16th century is such that, coupled with documentary sources, much more is known about shops and workshops during the post-medieval period than for era discussed here. These later arrangements, addressed in Chapter 7, help to shed extra light on the likely arrangements during the 15th century.

In addition to supporting life and, in some instances, providing space for work-related activities, the buildings also provided private space (for both living and sleeping) for the occupier and his family. Within the houses of the poorer residents such accommodation is likely to have been minimal, and, as already mentioned, in houses of two-cell type it must have been restricted to the first-floor chamber over the services at the low end of the hall. In the three-cell examples, however, there was the potential for two private spaces beyond the high end of the hall and, even at a relatively early date, the large ground- and first-floor high-end rooms at 36-38 The Mint [13] were augmented by single-bay ante-chambers at the rear. Such a degree of (potential) private accommodation, however, must always have been rare at this period and even at 36-38 [13] the additional rooms could have been used in other ways — for instance, the house could have functioned as an inn. The only surviving medieval building which is likely to have incorporated a heated sitting parlour is the urban mansion at 7-9 West Street/62 Church Square [51], though even here the surviving fabric is too fragmentary for certainty.

That heated sitting parlours used for entertaining did indeed exist within the town by the close of the 15th century is indicated by William Wykwyk's 1498 inventory. At that date such rooms must have been restricted to the premier inns and the houses of the top tier of the urban elite, as identified in the 1491/2 sesse discussed in Chapter 5. At his death the contents of Wykwyk's parlour included a group of firegoods associated with his hearth — a pair of andirons, a fire fork and a pair of tongs, as well as a brass chafer. The furniture within the room was listed as a table, three turned stools, a cupboard, and six leather cushions. As was the case in his hall, one wall was ornamented with a saye hanging. The importance of this room is well illustrated by the value of its furnishings: 20s.2d. compared to 9s.4d. for the contents of the hall.[27] Although well-appointed parlours of comparable quality became more common during the 16th century, they were nevertheless always restricted to the middle and upper classes, as will be demonstrated in Chapter 7.

Construction Techniques

Except for the stone-built 46 Church Square [86 in Figures 6.18 and 6.23] all the medieval houses are of standard local timber-framed construction and are weathered by steeply pitched roofs (*see* below).

Wall design [28]

Where the design of the external walls can be determined, in all houses which pre-date the middle years of the 15th century they are of large-panel type. In contrast, virtually all houses datable to the second half of the century or to the opening decades of the 16th century use close studding within their principal facades. Because of the extra expense involved — use of additional timber and extra jointing — close studding was a show technique intended to demonstrate wealth and quality.

Methods used in constructing close-studded walls vary from region to region, but in Kent and Sussex the close studs were nothing more than planks and were not structural. As such they were used solely as a decorative conceit and, in consequence, were not normally incorporated within elevations not easily visible to the public. The medieval houses of Rye are no exception. All adopt cheaper large-panel framing within their rear elevations, and in some (for example, at 22, 24 Church Square [78] and in the demolished 16 Mermaid Street [66]) this cheaper form was also used within at least one end-wall, despite being easily visible from the street.

In south-east England the fashion for close studding is known to have been introduced over a period of time. This makes its widespread use within the late-medieval buildings of the town all the more noteworthy. The only proven examples where it was not used are in the small, low-status semi-detached pair at 26 Church Square [80], built for rent in the early 16th century within the garden of 22, 24 Church Square [78] and at 6 Church Square [74]. Its absence in the latter example is particularly surprising because close studding is incorporated into both end-walls of its open hall: usually the reverse is true, with close studding used externally, but rarely internally. The front elevation at 10-11 Mermaid Street [64] is likewise of large-panel design and therefore (depending upon its date) this could be another late example — its features suggest a long mid/late-15th-century date-range. The same is true of the similarly dated 4-6 Lion Street [45]. Apart from these, at present no other medieval houses within the town are known which are datable to the late 15th or early 16th century and which did not have close studding within their street facade. At 9-10 East Street/ 13-14 Market Street [42] (late 14th-century) close studding was notched and pegged into the facade at a later date in order to update the building to the new design.

In all probability this widespread use of close studding within the town indicates both the speed at which the new wall-design was adopted and the late date of most of the buildings. It reinforces the suggestion based upon the town's known economic and demographic rise that many of Rye's open-hall houses were built at the very end of the medieval period.

Regardless of whether the external walls were designed with large panels or infilled with close studding, braces were included in order to triangulate the frame and prevent racking. At this period the only difference between the two wall-types is the way in which the braces are fixed into the frame. In the former the braces are positioned so as to be exposed to view externally but masked by daub internally, whilst in the latter the braces are inset so as to pass behind the plank-like close studding and thus be masked from view externally.

Braces can rise to triangulate the head of a panel (*headbracing*, also known as *up-bracing*) or descend from the posts so as to brace the foot (*footbracing*, also known as *down-bracing*). Both types were used throughout the medieval period though it has been noted that within the eastern High Weald there was a tendency to use headbracing more commonly in early buildings and in those of early 16th-century (transitional) date, whereas footbracing predominated between these two extremes.[29] This same tendency is detectable in Rye in that most walls are footbraced, though mixed headbracing and footbracing occurs at 16 East Street [34], 9-10 East Street/13-14 Market Street [42], and Lamb Cottage, West Street [53] — all late 14th century.

Headbracing has been recorded at 32-33 High Street [11] (*c*.1400) and 99-100 High Street [25] (early 15th century) as well as in a few of the early 16th-century transitional buildings described in the next chapter. In the early buildings the wall-braces tend to be quite long and spindly, whilst arch braces (to open trusses, arcades and crownposts) are of thick, almost square cross-section. In comparison, later arch-braces are much thinner and 'plank-like' in section.

Doorways [30]

Because of the large amount of reconstruction which has occurred within the ground-floor external walls, very little is known about the external doorways of Rye's medieval houses. Luckily, much better evidence survives internally. Regardless of whether external or internal, the doorways of the poorer houses were plain and square-headed. In Rye this was likewise the case with doorways which led out of the high end of the hall, even in otherwise well finished houses: this appears to have been due to the generous depths of the dais beams, which meant there was inadequate height beneath the beam to incorporate an arched head.[31] For practical reasons, stair doors at the service end of all medieval houses were square-headed, partly due to the need to maintain adequate headroom at the foot of the stair and partly because the door needed to open outwards in order to avoid the rise of the stair.

Very little evidence survives to indicate the form of the doorways within Rye's early open-hall houses. Ignoring a continuously-chamfered, two-centred stone doorway incorporated within the internal axial wall at 7-9 West Street [51] the only known examples of early internal openings are at 32-33 High Street [11]. Here two blocked service-doors remain. Both appear to be plain and have un-arched heads. A simply-moulded external stone doorway with early four-centred arched head and hood-mould survives within 46 Church Square [86] (probably *c*.1400, *see* Figure 13.25) but otherwise the only other early (assumed external) doorway known within the town is a plain two-centred timber opening of *durn* type in the very fragmentary rear range at 39-40 The Mint [14] (*see* Figure 10.24). Too little survives to make sense of its context, but the design is typical of the type one would expect to have existed in the town's other early buildings.

All other evidenced or remaining arch-headed doorways are located within houses built after the middle years of the 15th century. In each case the arch is cut into a horizontal plank which is housed into the opening, immediately beneath the head. Simple mouldings of two orders extend up the jambs, with the inner order continued around the leading edge of the arch and the outer around the square-headed outer surround. Potentially the earliest example of this type is that at 41 The Mint [15] (late 15th century): the others, at 67-69 The Mint [19]; 1-2 Lion Street [43]; 7-9 West Street [51], St Anthony's, Church Square [87] and 58, 60 Church Square [89] all date from *c*.1500. At 58, 60 Church Square [89] and 67-69 The Mint [19] the spandrels are of simple pyramidal sunk type (*see* Figures 10.37, 10.38 and 13.34) whilst those at 7-9 West Street [51] have plain sunk spandrels (*see* Figure 12.4). At 41 The Mint [15] and 1-2 Lion Street [43] the spandrels are elaborated with foliage (*see* Figures 10.28 and 11.22). Doorways survive in two locations at St Anthony's [87]. One leads to a kitchen passage whilst the other leads out of the high end of the hall. The designs are graded to reflect the relative importance of the two openings with simple pyramidal sunk spandrels to that leading into the kitchen passage, whilst that at the socially superior high end of the hall is elaborated with a simple foliage decoration.

Windows [32]

In those relatively few instances where windows are evidenced, most comply with the normal medieval un-glazed form with diamond-section mullions, sometimes closed by sliding shutters, sometimes not. The only known departures from this norm are to be found in buildings erected at the very end of the period. For instance, in the high-status St Anthony's, Church Square [87], which was built from the outset with a fully-floored hall, the windows in the close-studded front elevation are moulded and designed to be glazed, whereas those located within the less ornate rear wall but serving the same rooms were of normal un-glazed type. This should be no surprise. It maintains the same philosophy adopted within the designs of the late-medieval walls in general whereby greater attention to detail was given to those external parts easily visible to the public. Likewise, in the heart of the former market area immediately to the north of the church, high-quality windows were used at 1-2 Lion Street [43] (*c.*1500) — another early fully-floored building — and here at least one of the first-floor windows appears to have incorporated arched heads, a moulded surround, and a moulded central mullion. The double-width window lighting the floored hall was likewise fitted with moulded mullions, and, in similar vein, at least two, probably three of the windows within the front wall of St Anthony's [87] were larger than the norm and of more elaborate type.[33] Also of late date, the tiny but well-appointed fully-floored house at 34 Mermaid Street [71] had windows which were larger and better designed than was the norm. To judge from the former overhanging front gable, the first-floor chamber in the late 15th-century crosswing at 41 The Mint [15] was almost certainly lit by a projecting first-floor oriel. A 19th-century drawing shows a projecting oriel window in the front elevation of the demolished 16 Mermaid Street [66] (*see* Figure 12.33). Whether this was original to the build or added subsequently is impossible to tell.

These occasional examples of better-designed windows in some of Rye's very late medieval houses should not be regarded as exceptional. By 1500 similar occasional examples are found in houses in the town's rural hinterland.[34]

Floors and jetties [35]

The distinctive appearance of the joists which support the upper floors is an important feature of the town's medieval houses. In keeping with the region as a whole, the joists are of large scantling and are formed either out of whole trunks (a technique known as *boxed heart*) or from *halved* trunks. Depending upon the size and quality of the timber and the requirements of the client, in most instances the joists are neatly squared with very little inclusion of either waney edges or sapwood, but in a few instances (such as 32-33 High Street [11] and 10-11 Mermaid Street [64]) they are less neat in their finish and 'wobble' along their length. Care needs to be taken in assessing the original quality. Today the late 14th-century joists within the service bay at 16 East Street [34] appear rough, but this is due to subsequent loss of sapwood: when the house was first built they were neatly squared. In contrast, those within the added/rebuilt 15th-century parlour in the same house were waney from the outset.

Joist sizes within the town at this period are surprisingly consistent. All are of rectangular cross-

Fig. 6.26
Late 14th-century joists in service bay, 16 East Street [34]

section laid flat and in only four out of the 21 buildings for which the joist sizes are known are the average widths less than 170 mm (6¾ inches). Averaging 200-210 mm (8 inches to 8¼ inches), the widest are at 32-33 High Street [11], 32 Mermaid Street [70], 67-69 The Mint [19] and 58, 60 Church Square [89]. Neither the size nor age of the house appears to have had a bearing on the size of joists used. Some of the smallest are at 16 East Street [34] where those within the late 14th-century part measure 160 mm x 110 mm (6¼ inches by 4¼ inches) and those in the 15th-century addition/rebuild 150 mm x 100 mm (6 inches by 4 inches). The small late-medieval fragment at 42-43 The Mint [16] has joists of only 130 mm x 110 mm (5 inches by 4¼ inches). In width these are even smaller than those within the diminutive semi-detached pair of early 16th-century cottages at 26 Church Square [80] where they average 140 mm (5½ inches) wide, though only 90 mm (3½ inches) deep.

The distinctive 'heavy' appearance of medieval ceilings is not solely due to the use of large joists, but also to joist spacing: where joists are spaced more widely apart the effect is 'lighter' and far less dramatic. Despite this, no pattern of change is discernible, though it should be stressed that details are recoverable from only 17 buildings within the sample. The centres of the joists vary from as little as 380 mm (1 foot 3 inches) in one fully-floored house of *c.*1500 to 560 mm (1 foot 10 inches) in two open-hall houses, one datable to the late 14th century and the other built *c.*1500. In each case the houses are of good quality and well built.

Recording the spacing of joists does not take into account the width of the joists in question — two floors with joists set at identical centres, one with 140 mm wide (5½ inches) joists and the other 210 mm (8¼ inches) would look very different in appearance. However, even with this additional factor taken into account no chronological or status pattern emerges. The buildings in which the ratio of joist width to joist centres is the greatest (five examples) range in date from the late 14th century through to the early 16th century and in size from small to quite large. The same is equally true at the other end of the scale where the gaps between the joists are the smallest. At 8 East Street [33] the joists in the front half of the building are more closely spaced than those within the rear half, resulting in more joist-ends exposed within the front jetty than would otherwise have been the case. This desire for robust external appearance may explain in part the relatively close centres of the joists in some other jettied buildings of the period. As with the use of close studding, the feature should be regarded as an example of 'conspicuous consumption' (i.e. showing off). In Chapter 7 this pattern of joist size and spacing will be compared with that recorded in buildings of later date.

Medieval joists are usually un-chamfered and un-moulded. In Rye, the only known exceptions to this are at 17 West Street [58] (probably late 15th century), 8 East Street [33] (*c.*1500) and within 34 Mermaid Street [71] (also *c.*1500).[36] In each of these the joists are neatly chamfered, a feature which became common during the 16th century (*see* Chapter 7).

The way in which a floor was framed usually depended upon the length of the individual bays and the width of the building. If a bay was equal to or shorter than half the width of the building the joists were usually aligned along the structure: otherwise they would span across the building and be jointed at the centre into a principal axial beam or *central girder*. An important exception to this 'rule' is where the house incorporates a jetty, for in such circumstances the overhanging upper storey relied upon the projecting joist ends for support, and thus the joists needed to run at right-angles to the overhanging wall. Where a jetty returns around an external corner the direction of the joists is turned through 90 degrees at an angled girder-like timber called a *dragon beam*, of which there are five known medieval examples in Rye, and others of later date.

Rye is particularly rich in jettied buildings — jetties are evidenced within 21 of the 31 medieval houses for which good floor details survive, and they may have been present in two others. It is therefore not surprising that most of Rye's medieval floors are of central-girder type. In three crosswings the joists are aligned axially to the wing and support jetties at the front, whilst at the diminutive 26 Church Square [80] the joists are likewise aligned longitudinally and support an end-jetty onto the main street. Otherwise, in only four houses are the joists aligned longitudinally. Two of these are early un-jettied buildings — the late 14th-century Lamb Cottage, West Street [53] and 32-33 High Street [11]. In another 14th-century example, 16 East Street [34], the joists had to span across the building in order to support the front jetty incorporated into this early Wealden house. Even so, the joists are not supported at centre span by a girder but by a trimming joist which, at 165 mm x 135 mm, is only marginally larger in section than the 160 mm x 110 mm common joists (Figure 6.26). Furthermore, to the rear of the trimming joist the common joists are aligned along the axis of the building, not across it. This arrangement is not uncommon in early jettied buildings.

Although early central girders and dragon beams are only slightly larger in section than the common joists they support, by the early/mid 15th century they had developed to become principal timbers, considerably wider and deeper than the common joists. All the medieval central girders in Rye are of this 'developed' type and are neatly chamfered along their lower leading edges. That within the floored hall at 1-2 Lion Street [43] is enriched with hollow-chamfered leading edges and a roll-moulded nib down the centre of its soffit, continued around brackets at each end and down the face of the supporting posts (*see* Figure 6.27). In like manner, the leading edges of a crossbeam at 41 The Mint [15] (which in many ways fulfils the same function as a central girder) has a chamfer-and-cyma moulding to its lower leading edges. Although not elaborate, this level of decoration is unusual for Rye at this period, though more common later (*see* Chapter 7). It likewise became more common later for the ends of the joists at the jetties to be masked by a moulded fascia beam, but such elaboration is rare during the medieval period and where it occurs is always late. Moulded fascia beams are used at 1-2 Lion Street [43], 101-102 High Street [26], St Anthony's, Church Square [87], and 34 Mermaid Street [71], but generally the joist-ends were left exposed at the jetties, though rounded off.

Roofs [37]

Unlike some parts of England, there is a predictability about the type of roof used in the medieval houses of Kent and East Sussex. Invariably they are of paired-rafter-and-collar construction, usually fitted with crownposts carrying a collar purlin. Except for differences in proportions, the crownposts themselves vary only in that those located within closed partitions have two-way footbracing triangulating to the tiebeam with headbracing to the collar purlin, whilst those located over open trusses have four-way headbraces and usually incorporate some form of decoration. Other variations are found, but they are rare.

Rye is no exception to this generalisation. The sample of medieval buildings contains 24 extant roofs or part-roofs. They vary in pitch from 47 to 55 degrees, but three-quarters fall within the range 49-53 degrees. There is a recognizable trend towards shallower pitches towards the end of the period in that half the late 14th- and early 15th-century roofs (three out of six examples) are of 53-55 degree pitch and none fall below 50 degrees, whilst nine of the 11 houses of *c.*1500 date have roofs pitched at 50 degrees or below. This may reflect a change in fashion rather than a switch from thatched coverings to other materials (but *see* below).

All but four of the 24 roofs are of standard crownpost construction. Two of those which are not — that at 17 West Street [58] and that over the crosswing at 36-38 The Mint [13] — are of related type in that they comprise paired rafters linked by collars but, on account of their small span, crownposts and collar purlins were not fitted.[38] For a similar reason, the roof over 26 Church Square [80] likewise lacks crownposts and collar purlin, but in this instance it also lacks collars — it comprises paired rafters only. This is the most basic form of roof it is possible to construct.

The roofs mentioned above have rafters of common scantling throughout. The final example — that over the late 15th-century crosswing at 41 The Mint [15] — is the only one which is of 'non-local' type in that it is a trussed roof and incorporates windbraced interrupted-side-purlins. For extra details, including other similar examples from elsewhere in Kent and East Sussex, *see* the entry for this building in Chapter 10. The adoption of this form of roof in this instance seems to have been in response to the roof having been used as an attic, and thus the need to keep the area free of obstructions. All other medieval houses in Rye had first-floor chambers which were open to the roof.

As Figures 6.21-6.24 illustrate, Rye's medieval roofs used a mixture of hipped and gabled terminals, despite the fact that during medieval times hips were a virtually ubiquitous feature of the area. Gables were sometimes utilized because the house abutted against a neighbour, but this was by no means always the case, as is shown by the roofs at 1/2 Lion Street [43], 12 Lion Street [47] and 26 Church Square [80].

By the close of the medieval period the predominant roof-covering within the town was probably tile rather than thatch, though thatched roofs were certainly present — the renewal of thatch within the town or within 200 feet (61 metres) of its walls was banned in 1561.[39] It could be argued that reducing roof pitches reflects a switch from thatch to tile, but this change in pitch is thought more likely to have been dictated primarily by fashion rather than by the type of roof-covering, though the latter may have had an influence.[40]

Chimneys

Nationally, from an early date fireplaces are found in the homes of the elite, both secular and ecclesiastical. Prior to the demise of the open hall and the open 'kitchen', heating in vernacular buildings was by means of open hearths only. Other rooms and chambers were almost always unheated.

When other forms of heating begin to be introduced they tend to be found earlier in towns than in villages and the countryside. Indeed, evidence of their early use has been recorded in a number of English towns, including neighbouring Winchelsea.[41] Unless the evidence has been destroyed, this was not the case in Rye. True, two relatively early fireplaces exist at Ypres Tower, and there is another in the Land Gate (*see* Chapter 3) but these are non-domestic buildings. It is not until the late 15th century that the first evidence is found of chimneys within the town's houses. Even so, this is still relatively early in comparison with the vernacular houses of the surrounding rural area, where chimneys were very rarely built before the beginning of the 16th century and became common only during the middle years of that century.

Potentially the earliest of Rye's 'chimneys' is that which served the late 15th-century crosswing within the house of specialized plan at 41 The Mint [15]. Constructed using small 'Flemish' brick, the feature is fragmentary. From what remains it appears to have been more akin to a brick-built restricted smoke-bay than a conventional chimney in that its flue appears to have risen within a vertical-walled external enclosure, without any tumbling. It incorporated one fireplace which served the large high-quality specialized ground-floor room. It is possible that the upper part was timber framed, rather than of brick. The example at 41 The Mint [15] is exceptional in that, unlike the other late medieval examples, it served neither a hall nor kitchen.

Conventional timber-framed smoke-bays exist within end-rooms at 1-2 Lion Street [43] and St Anthony's, Church Square [87] (*see* Figure 6.24), all datable to *c.*1500. That at St Anthony's [87] served an attached kitchen located beyond the low-end service rooms and augmented a fireplace of conventional design (built of 'Flemish' brick) within the fully-floored hall. The smoke-bay at 1-2 Lion Street [43] probably also served an end kitchen, but the room in question has its own external doorway and it is unclear whether there was internal communication between it and the adjacent hall, so it could have been in separate occupation. A further complication relating to this building is the fact that the hall was initially unheated. This is a point noted in one or two other houses of slightly later date and is discussed further in Chapter 7.

Rye's other early chimneys are at 67-69 The Mint [19], 101-102 High Street [26], St Anthony's, Church Square [87] and 58, 60 Church Square [89]. The latter may have been added when the open hall was floored over, perhaps in 1504, and has a stone surround with

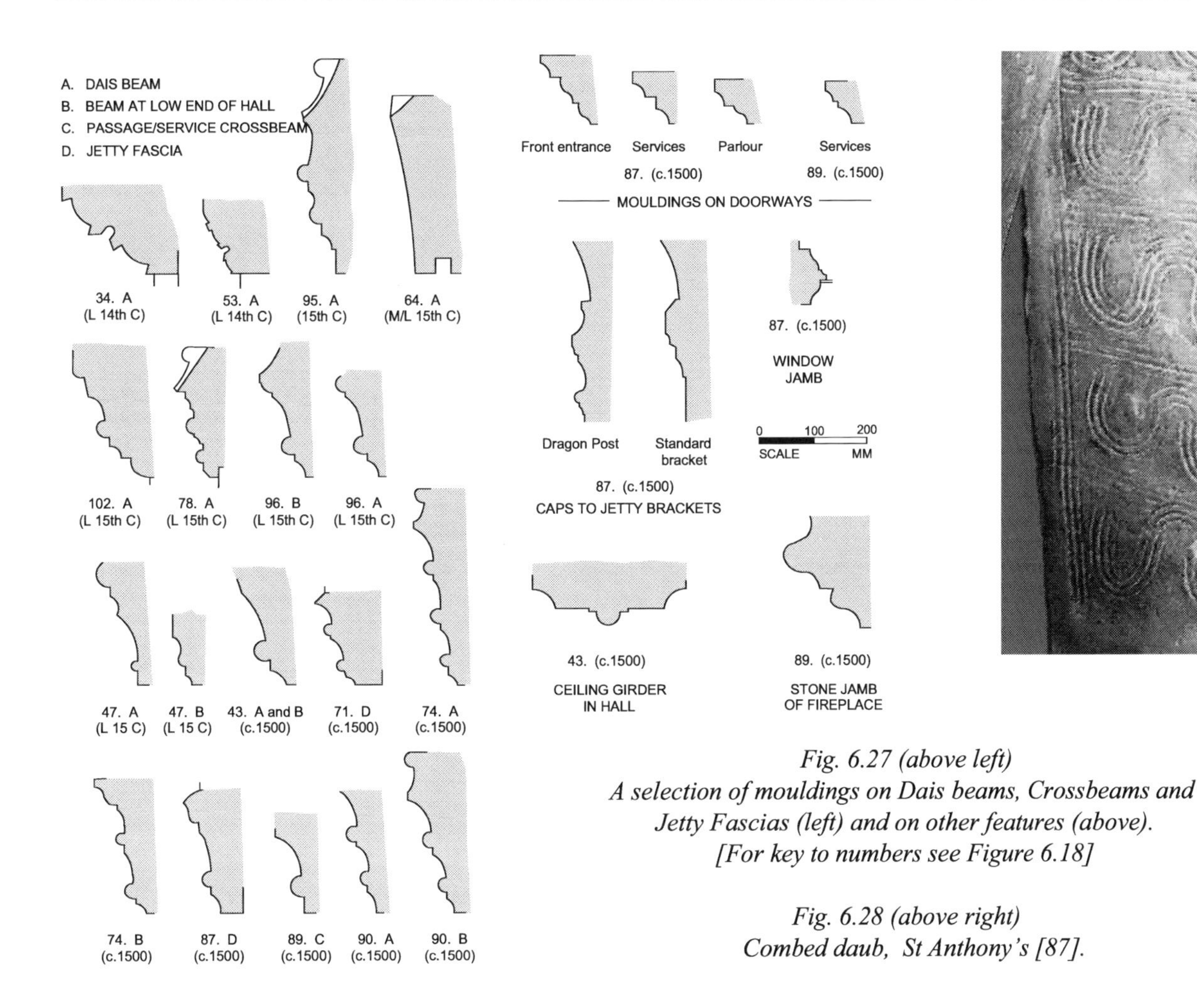

Fig. 6.27 (above left)
A selection of mouldings on Dais beams, Crossbeams and Jetty Fascias (left) and on other features (above).
[For key to numbers see Figure 6.18]

Fig. 6.28 (above right)
Combed daub, St Anthony's [87].

moulded four-centred arched head (*see* Figure 13.33 — for a detail of the moulding see Figure 6.27). The other three, all of *c*.1500 date, heat fully-floored halls and occupy the space usually reserved for the high-end bench. Thus, although these halls have very traditional layouts in terms of access and their relationship to the other ground-floor rooms, they were used in a new way (for which *see* above).

As mentioned, the chimney at 58, 60 Church Square [89] could be original to the build or could represent an early insertion. Unlike the early examples mentioned above, it is positioned against the rear wall of the hall and thus the room could continue to function in the traditional hierarchical way. The same was also true of the fully-floored hall of *c*.1500 at 34 Mermaid Street [71], where the chimney has been destroyed but its location is known (*see* Figure 6.24).

A number of other chimneys of early date were inserted into open halls when they were floored over, perhaps *c*.1500, but perhaps during the early 16th century (*see* Chapter 7). All these chimneys represent early examples of types which became standard during the transitional period. As with those mentioned here, initially they served floored-over halls and kitchens only, but subsequently chimneys with more flues were built in order that they could heat other rooms and chambers also.

Decoration

Moulded and carved timberwork is as rare in Rye as in the surrounding countryside. In the early houses it is entirely limited to mouldings on dais beams, although by *c*.1500 mouldings also occur on a few low-end crossbeams, jetty brackets, jetty fascia beams, principal ceiling beams, and on applied string courses located at window-cill level, as for instance at 1-2 Lion Street [43] and formerly at St Anthony's, Church Square [87]. Simple mouldings are found on some late windows, as well as on doorways and fireplace lintels, and it is in these locations that the only examples of medieval carving survive. A selection of Rye mouldings are illustrated in Figure 6.27. Except for moulded dais beams, all these features became more common during the 16th century (*see* Chapter 7).

There are no known examples of medieval wall paintings in Rye, though the use of hangings — particularly painted cloths — seems likely.[42] What do survive are panels of comb-decorated daub infill (Figure 6.28). Decoration of this type is a speciality of the region and in Rye examples are known in internal partitions in seven houses ranging in date from the early 15th century through to the early 16th century, as well as externally within the rear aisle of the added/rebuilt 15th-century parlour chamber at 16 East Street [34].[43] The patterns in all known examples are typical of the region. In the most modern example, The Mermaid [72] (early 16th century) an interlaced figure-of-eight design was used; all others are alternating straight and wavy bands, arranged vertically in some buildings, horizontally in others. All are incised into the surface using a multi-pronged comb whilst the daub was still green.[44]

Fig. 6.29
Rear walls of the properties on the southern side of Church Square as illustrated by Van Dyck in 1634. By this time the street was densely built up, but the situation in c.1500 was very different.
[© Gabinetto Disegni e Stampe delgi Uffizi, Florence, Italy]

7 POST-MEDIEVAL HOUSING

INTRODUCTION

The period 1500-1570 saw Rye at its most prosperous and most populous. During the first forty years of the century the town's population was rising rapidly, but growth in the indigenous population seems to have stalled somewhat around the middle of the century. However, during the years following 1562 the town faced new pressures as it struggled to cope with waves of religious refugees fleeing France. At a conservative estimate the period as a whole saw a doubling in the number of households in Rye and perhaps a near trebling would be no great exaggeration. By Elizabeth's death in 1603 most of the refugees had gone and the boom in both wealth and population had faded. Indeed, from the 1580s onwards Rye was increasingly forced to face up to very different circumstances: a silting harbour, crises in the fishing industry, a reduced resident merchant fleet, dwindling trade, increasing poverty, and a reducing population (*see* Chapter 5). It is against this economic and demographic background that the town's 16th-century buildings need to be assessed.

The surviving buildings confirm that the boom

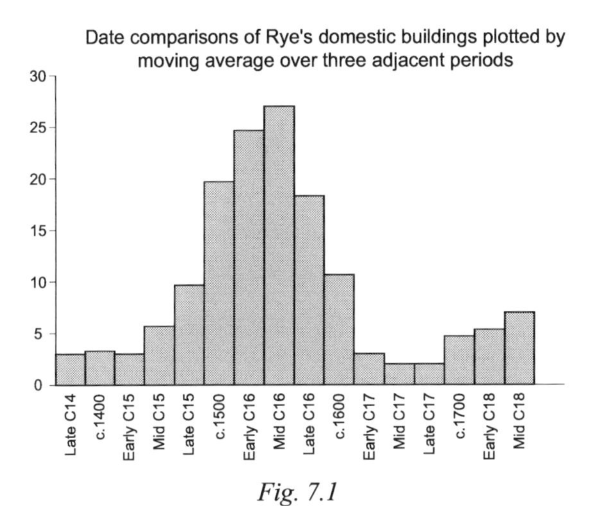

Fig. 7.1
The construction dates of new buildings and major phases of alterations.

years between 1500 and the 1570s resulted in a marked surge in building activity (Figure 7.1) Houses were still being built and rebuilt through the final decades of the century and into the opening years of the following century, but the numbers were far fewer. Furthermore, these late buildings are noticeably concentrated in the northeastern corner of the town, close to the land link to the adjacent uplands and away from the harbour. Thereafter, except for minor extensions and internal modifications, new building work all but ceased until the final decades of the 17th century when a slow revival in construction commenced.

As has been demonstrated (Chapter 2), the need for extra housing during the 16th century caused the construction of a new suburb at The Wishe to the northwest of the town, revived the modest Landgate suburb to the northeast, and prompted re-colonisation of the eastern end of High Street. Otherwise, apart from the infilling of gaps in the built-up street frontage, most of the extra dwellings seem to have been achieved by the reconstruction, sub-division and enlargement of existing buildings. In fact, the economic upsurge and increase in population appears to have had surprisingly little effect upon the general streetscape of the town. A few gables facing the road began to appear and there was a modest increase in the height of the buildings, though full three-storeyed structures started to be built only late in the century, and then in *very* small numbers. External details of construction such as the design of the wall framing and the details of windows, doorways and jetties changed only very slowly. As with the introduction of three-storeyed buildings, display fenestration was adopted in a few late 16th-century and early 17th-century houses. Had the town not experienced a dramatic downturn in its economy, projecting oriels and bay windows flanked by clerestory openings and capped by overhanging gables may have become a common sight in Rye, as they did in nearby Hastings. As it was, this was not to be, and as a result the external appearance of the town remained traditional throughout.

Whilst Rye's external appearance remained in

many ways unaltered, the same cannot be said of the internal spaces. The 16th century was, in any case, one in which the layouts of houses were changing nationwide, as firstly open halls were abandoned in favour of fully-floored houses, and subsequently increased levels of privacy were introduced (*see* below). But whereas previously the houses in Rye had tended to adopt the same layouts used in the surrounding rural hinterland (*see* Chapter 6) the same cannot be said for a substantial number of those built during the 16th-century The first signs of this change were noted at the very end of the period discussed in Chapter 6.

Figure 7.1 clearly illustrates the major period of redevelopment and regeneration brought about by the town's 16th-century economic success, particularly during the period *c.*1500 to the 1570s. With a rapidly increasing population and resultant pressure on space new forms of internal layout were perhaps inevitable. As will be shown, some internal layouts within the town's new houses — particularly within the smaller dwellings — continued to follow configurations similar to those used earlier within the town and in use in the surrounding countryside during the 16th century. But the same cannot be said for the majority of the average-sized and larger houses. Despite their very traditional external appearances, internally most of the middle-sized and larger buildings were decidedly urban in their configuration of rooms.

To appreciate just how different many of Rye's new buildings were it will be necessary to review, albeit briefly, the normal arrangement for this period in the surrounding countryside. This review will be followed by a discussion addressing the ways in which the additional numbers of households were accommodated within the existing streets, for this in turn both influenced and dictated some of the internal layouts which were adopted. Only after these two aspects have been considered will the town's 16th-century housing stock be reviewed and discussed.

SIXTEENTH-CENTURY HOUSES IN THEIR REGIONAL CONTEXT

The 'Transitional' House

The passing of the medieval era is marked in terms of domestic vernacular architecture by the demise of the open hall. In the area around Rye it was during the first part of the 16th century, extending through to the 1540s that houses with first-floor chambers above all rooms began to be built as the norm. Such houses still incorporated a hall, but no longer was it an impressive-looking lofty room served by an open hearth. Instead the hall had a chamber over it and was usually heated by an enclosed fireplace. In the surviving rural and village

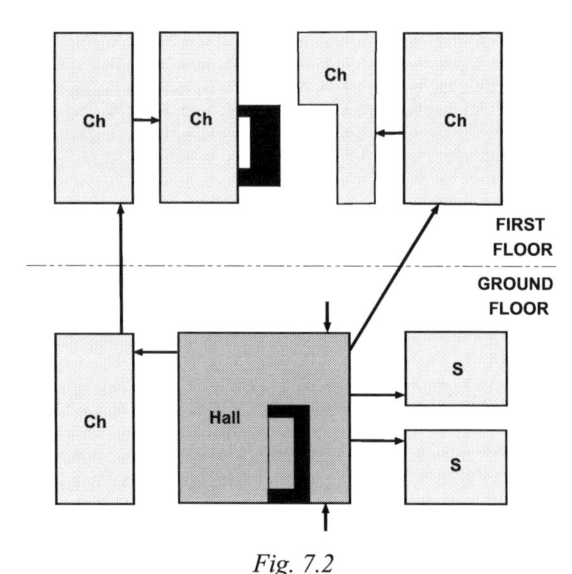

Fig. 7.2
Diagram indicating the means of access between rooms in a 'textbook' transitional house, in this instance with no access between the entry chamber and the hall chamber.

examples this new hall chamber could be reached from either the parlour chamber or, less often, the service chamber, but very rarely from both. Thus, as indicated in Figures 7.2 and 7.3, despite the building being floored throughout its length, the two ends were usually reached by separate staircases. This surely indicates that the service chamber continued to be used either for storage or as a separate self-contained unit. Most upper chambers remained open to the roof at this period: where an attic was incorporated, this was confined to a small area, usually over the hall chamber.

Although visually very different, the change from the old-style open hall to the new fully-floored form was simply achieved. Structurally, the only difference between those houses built with open halls and those with a floored-over hall was the inclusion of an additional area of first-floor joisting and the construction of a smoke-dispersal system. The introduction of fully-storeyed houses was therefore not driven either by technological advances or by a major increase in personal wealth: only a few houses at this time had more than one hearth and such luxury items as glazed windows were as rare as they had been in houses with open halls. Instead, the new style of house was brought about by a change in the mental attitudes of 'peasant' society; a willingness, even an eagerness, to abandon the traditional open hall. What has come to be known as the *transitional* house (bridging the transition between the medieval and post-medieval periods) is but one of a series of indicators which illustrate the cultural revolution which was spreading rapidly through England at this time. The medieval era was dead — at least in

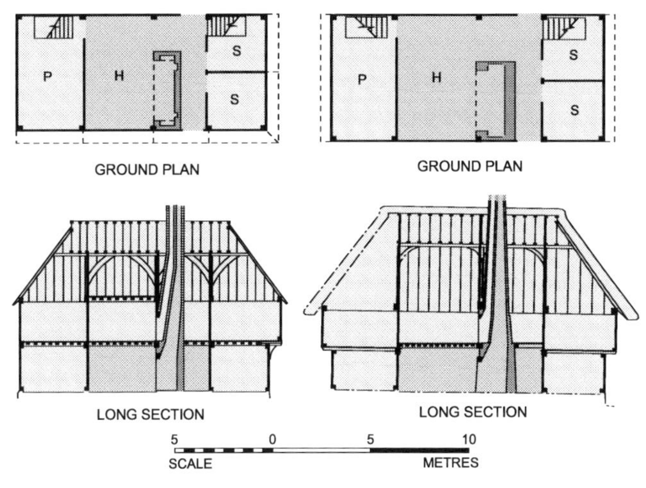

Fig. 7.3
Typical Transitional Houses.
Left:- A newly-built house, c.1530.
Right:- A medieval hall house as updated c.1540

terms of housing — but the early-modern era had not yet fully arrived.

As with the construction of those late-medieval hall houses which have survived to the present day, the surviving 'transitional' houses represent households which could now afford to replace their earlier 'substandard' houses with what might loosely be termed 'permanent' buildings. Despite their lack of an open hall, the new-style houses continued to be used in a wholly traditional manner. Both types had 'low end' service rooms with a chamber over, a hall entered at the 'low end' with a bench set against the 'high end' wall (looking down the hall) and, in most instances, a 'high end' inner room with a chamber over it. The only difference was that the previously open hall now incorporated an enclosed hearth and was not open to the roof, but had a chamber over it.

Even though middle-class householders very quickly ceased building houses with open halls, the old-style houses themselves were not destroyed: they were tailor-made for easy conversion to the new form, and that is precisely what most people did (*see* Figure 7.3). Thus, in the High Weald, the introduction of new-style 'transitional' houses rarely caused the destruction of late-medieval houses of the calibre of those which still survive. In those instances where earlier houses were replaced, a number of factors may have contributed to the decision to rebuild rather than upgrade — the existing house may have been too small or too inconvenient to be worth converting, it may have been of great age, subjected to neglect, built of inferior materials, or used poor construction techniques, or a combination of these.

In comparison to the number of hall-houses which survive, the number of transitional houses is not large. This is mainly because the time-frame during which they were built is far shorter than is the case with hall houses. In addition, the statistics are muddied by the fact that for a while old-style houses with open halls continued to be built alongside their newer cousins. What the surviving houses of the area appear to indicate is that the new-style transitional houses were built to serve the same class as were the open halls before them: certainly they were very much the same size and shape and were built to similar standards of finish. Small houses dating from the first half of the 16th century are now virtually nonexistent in the rural High Weald. As was the case during the medieval period, there are no extant cottages.

It used to be thought that existing hall houses were not upgraded to comply with the new standards until *c.*1600. The main reason for this assumption was the common inclusion within the converted houses of true early-modern architectural features (for which *see* below). Although a few middle-class householders were slow to convert their open halls, it is now clear that, unlike in some other parts of the country, in the High Weald most conversions were carried out at about the same time as the construction of their newly-built transitional counterparts. The early-modern features represent a second phase of conversion during which transitional layouts were transformed into true early-modern forms.

Early-Modern Houses

During the transitional period described above the hall remained a very public, central space with most other rooms and chambers within the house accessed directly from it. This type of configuration has been termed by Matthew Johnson as 'open'.[1] Furthermore, although during the 16th century the floor joists very quickly changed from rectangular-scantling laid flat, to much narrower, neater, joists of near-square section, other essentially medieval constructional details were slow to change. Except for those windows in the front wall of the hall and hall chamber, small unglazed windows remained the norm through the middle years of the century, and, in some instances, beyond. Likewise, during the half-century from *c.*1490-*c.*1540 medieval-style crownpost roofs were only slowly superseded by post-medieval roofs of windbraced, clasped-side-purlin construction. Furthermore, prior to the post-medieval period, heating was usually reserved for the hall and, occasionally, the hall chamber, even in houses of the middle classes. High-end rooms were still usually unheated and, as already noted, first-floor chambers usually remained open to the roof.

The points raised in the above paragraph hint at the changes which occurred within the houses of the

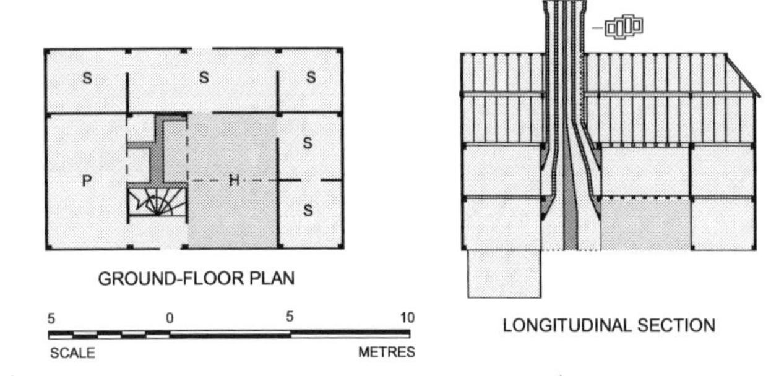

Fig. 7.4
A typical rural house of c.1600 with a lobby entry and a centralized staircase giving access to the first floor.

area during the final part of the 16th century, extending into the early years of the following century. It was during this period that the early-modern house can be said to have finally arrived. Features such as multi-flue chimneys, lime-plastered walls, plastered ceilings (either sited between the joists or masking them from view) started to be incorporated as the norm in all but the poorest of houses. Midrails (horizontal timbers located halfway up a storey height) had been introduced into a few walls as early as the late 15th century, but it was only during the second half of the 16th century that their use became firmly established, with the result that large panels of infill were increasingly supplanted by small-panel framing, and at the same time wall braces were either omitted altogether or concealed from view externally. Where close studding was used, the studs were increasingly interrupted by midrails. A particularly important feature of this period was the introduction of glazed windows into the living rooms and bed chambers of middle-class houses. Often the schemes incorporated within the principal elevations were quite elaborate, comprising oriel and/or bay windows flanked by high-level clerestory openings and capped by overhanging gables. By the early 17th century all these features had become the norm in houses of any quality.

The internal layouts of the houses were likewise evolving. These improvements derived principally from the abandonment of the old-style 'open' layout in which the functions of the house revolved around the centralized hall, to a much more 'closed' or private arrangement in which the house was commonly entered via a separate lobby and the hall (later re-named 'kitchen') became smaller and served as just another, albeit an important living/working room within the house. Many middle-class houses now incorporated a heated parlour which, where present, served as the principal private living room. At this social level cellars beneath the parlours were not uncommon. Most average-sized houses of the period incorporated a number of specialized service rooms. Sometimes the additional rooms were located within two-storeyed rear ranges, but often in lean-to outshuts built against the rear wall.

Increasingly the entire first-floor area was reached by a single centralized staircase and functioned as a sequence of bed chambers. By this date most houses of average size incorporated storage attics within the roof, lit by windows within gabled or half-hipped terminals. Probate inventories indicate that even in the early 18th century it was here, in the roof, that the valuable processed farm crops were stored.

Documentary sources show that during the 16th century small rural houses and landless or near-landless cottages existed in considerable numbers, but for one reason or another these were incapable of surviving through to the present day. From *c.*1600 onwards they begin to survive, though before the 18th century the numbers are small. Those which remain are perhaps not typical of their class and are likely to represent the better-built examples. Typically they follow the constructional details found in larger houses, but use timbers of smaller scantling. Most of the cottages have two first-floor chambers (usually open to the roof) and have on the ground floor a heated hall and a service room, very occasionally augmented by additional service space within a rear outshut. The chimney is usually built against a gabled end-wall, with the opposing end hipped. Small houses (as opposed to cottages) are more likely to have three rather than two cells arranged in line, and these are normally served by an axial rather than an end-stack, but usually the stack is of one or two flues only. As with cottages, at this period the chambers usually remain open to the roof.

ACCOMMODATING RYE'S ADDITIONAL POPULATION

As pointed out in Chapter 6, during the 15th century Rye seems to have been a spacious town in terms of household density. Just how un-congested parts were is indicated by Figure 7.7, a reconstruction of the area immediately to the south of the church as in about 1500. The undeveloped plots and the gaps between houses are very obvious. Although at this time the plot on the corner of Church Square and Watchbell Street had two houses upon it, the building which contained them was then very new, and even this had open land to its west, and probably to the north also. Being close to the market, the area north of the church, illustrated in Figure 7.8, was perhaps not surprisingly more densely built up, but in the northern part of this area — towards the eastern end of High Street — stood quite large detached buildings on spacious plots. And,

Fig. 7.5
Section of Mermaid Street, showing what are, for Rye, narrow plots. Most of the houses in the picture date from the early 16th century, but occupy earlier plots which retain their medieval boundaries.

Fig. 7.6
The Standard, 41 The Mint, showing the double-gabled frontage and congested streetscape following late 15th- and early 16th-century modifications (for further explanation see text).

despite being so close to the market, the extreme eastern end of High Street, extending partially up the eastern side of East Street, was open wasteland during the 15th century, at least until the 1490s. Even in the most densely built-up part of this area to the north of the church there were gaps in the built-up street frontage, albeit mostly small, serving as access-points to the rear of the plots. The north side of Market Street was perhaps the most densely packed part (probably four, perhaps five houses with no gaps) but on the south side of the street, between Church Square and East Street, there are no signs of pressure on space.

The above two areas are not exceptional within the town, though it should be stressed that, as Figures 7.5 and 7.6 show, nearer The Strand (in Mermaid Street and along the western end of The Mint) the street frontages do seem to have been more continuously built up. For a detailed plan of Mermaid Street *see* Figure 7.10. Furthermore, in these areas the plots tended to be narrower. The view of 41 The Mint (Figure 7.6) shows a rare use of front gables, but even here the righthand gable is later (early 16th century), replacing a low hall built parallel to the street, whilst the house on the extreme left is a much disguised 'Wealden' hall house which blocks a window in the side-wall of the late 15th-century gabled crosswing. So even here there was previously a gap in the built-up street frontage.

Given what has been said in Chapter 6, the picture of spaciousness painted above should be no great surprise. It should be remembered that in *c.*1490 Rye was a town of 190-260 households — by 1565 there were 530, more than double the earlier total, and this was still not the peak.

The problem caused by this major population increase was very much a question of where to put the extra houses. Rye was effectively a tiny 'island' site and had nowhere to expand. As was stressed in Chapter 2, the land above high-tide level amounted to about 36 acres only. The area to the north was marsh (St Mary's Marsh) and not suitable for colonisation. When the sea walls to the north of the town were breached in 1572 this marsh was submerged at high tides, threatening 15 new houses constructed on its fringe since 1555 by Robert Sheppard of Peasmarsh.[2] These were probably the houses shown in Prowze's map of 1572 in the area known as Further Wishe, immediately to the northeast of present-day Ferry Road and to the northwest of Cinque Port Street, just outside the town walls (*see* Figures 2.11 and 2.19). The marsh had been inundated on several occasions earlier and, following the 1572 breach, remained un-reclaimed until the 1590s. Excepting vulnerable Further Wishe, there were only two small areas outside the town walls available for expansion. One of these was the finger of slightly raised land called Wishe, between Ferry Road and the Strand, where a suburb did indeed develop (*see* Chapter 2). The second was immediately outside the Land Gate, extending along the road to Playden. Here a suburb of no more than 15 houses (probably fewer) was built during the middle and latter years of the 16th century, re-colonizing an area abandoned during the 14th century. With these exceptions, all the extra households had to be accommodated within the walls.

Some of the first land to be developed was that at the extreme eastern end of High Street which had been abandoned in the late 14th century, probably as a combined result of French raids, a reduction in population and collapse of the cliff. Here, as has been discussed (Chapter 2), plots of wasteland on the southern side of High Street were granted out by the corporation between 1489 and 1490. Construction also occurred at around the same time immediately opposite, apparently within the grounds of the Austin Friary. The area of wasteland granted out by the corporation was bounded on the south by Ockmans Lane, a minor thoroughfare which extended eastwards from East Street. Here, on the southern side, John Ockman erected seven houses between 1542 and his death in 1569. It would seem that by 1589 the northern side of this street was flanked by a similar number. Other areas of what could be classed backland development may have occurred in the northwest of the town in Ponde-garden and Coggles Lane and in the southwest at Fawtleyes Lane, Watchbell Lane and Rucks Lane (*see* Figure 2.5). In total these new extra-mural and intra-mural areas of development probably accounted for no more than a hundred or so houses: the remainder of the population increase had to be accommodated in other ways.

The method by which this was achieved within the already built-up part of town is probably best illustrated by looking in a little more detail at the two areas described earlier — one to the south of the church, the other to the north.

The rears of the properties to the south of the church are illustrated in a sketch made by Van Dyck in 1634 in which the street is shown as a continuously built-up sequence of buildings (*see* Figure 6.29). These include the area shown in the reconstruction plans presented in Figure 7.7, the first as in *c.*1500, the second around 1560. The appearance in 1634 is very much as it would have been in *c.*1570, but the contrast between these and the picture in *c.*1500 is very marked. In this section of street there had been between six and nine dwellings in *c.*1500, depending upon whether houses stood in the white areas marked '?'. Two-thirds of a century later there were at least 16, perhaps 19 dwellings packed into the same area.

In *c.*1500 the easternmost plot in Figure 7.7 [Plot 1] was, as far as can be told, occupied by a single house — the 'Wealden' hall-house known today as 20, 22, 24 Church Square [78]. In the early 16th century a pair of semi-detached houses (26 Church Square [80]) was built along the western boundary of the plot, accessed from one of a series of cul-de-sacs which led back from Church Square to the cliff top. At this date there was a gap between these and the earlier Wealden, but the gap was very rapidly infilled, blocking windows in both buildings. The infill structure [79] is a simple building with one room on each of its two storeys. How it functioned is arguable. It could have been a one-up, one-down cottage, or perhaps a shop with a storage chamber over, but if it was either of these options there is today no indication of an internal staircase. Alternatively, it may have been a self-contained shop with (as is the case today) the chamber above forming part of the front house within the adjacent semi-detached pair. The final phase in the plot's development seems to have been the separation of the Wealden's service bay to form an additional dwelling, augmented by a large rear addition, the chimney within which also heated the hall of the Wealden. Until this date the main house had been served by a smoke-bay inserted when its hall was floored over. Thus, by the middle years of the 16th century a plot which had originally been occupied by a single house had either five houses or four houses and a shop located upon it.

Crossing the lane which ran down the western side of the semi-detached pair, a similar situation is found on the neighbouring plot [Plot 2]. Here, a property which had accommodated one house eventually had three dwellings on it. Only the weathering shadow of the original medieval house (28, 32 Church Square [82]) now remains, but the evidence suggests a modest two-cell house with a service bay to the east and a hall to the west. Early in the 16th century the hall was rebuilt larger (heated and floored) and a heated parlour was incorporated to its rear. The earlier services were retained. At this date the structure was almost certainly still in single occupancy. It stood in isolation, with the lane to its east and open ground to the west — there is a window in the western end-gable of the attic room over the early 16th-century fully-floored hall. A lean-to outshut added to the rear of the parlour in the mid-16th century probably indicates the date at which the retained medieval service bay was divided off to form a separate, tiny cottage. It can be argued that the outshut was built to compensate for the loss of the original service bay. Around this time too — perhaps at the same date — an extra house (30 Church Square [81]) was built in the rear garden, accessed off the lane. Although the new house is small, it is of good quality with an end-jetty, a two-flue chimney, and transomed windows (one of which is an oriel) serving the principal room and chamber. The house is clearly visible in the Van Dyck drawing reproduced in Figure 6.29, as is the lean-to outshut to its left and the semi-detached pair of early 16th-century houses on the

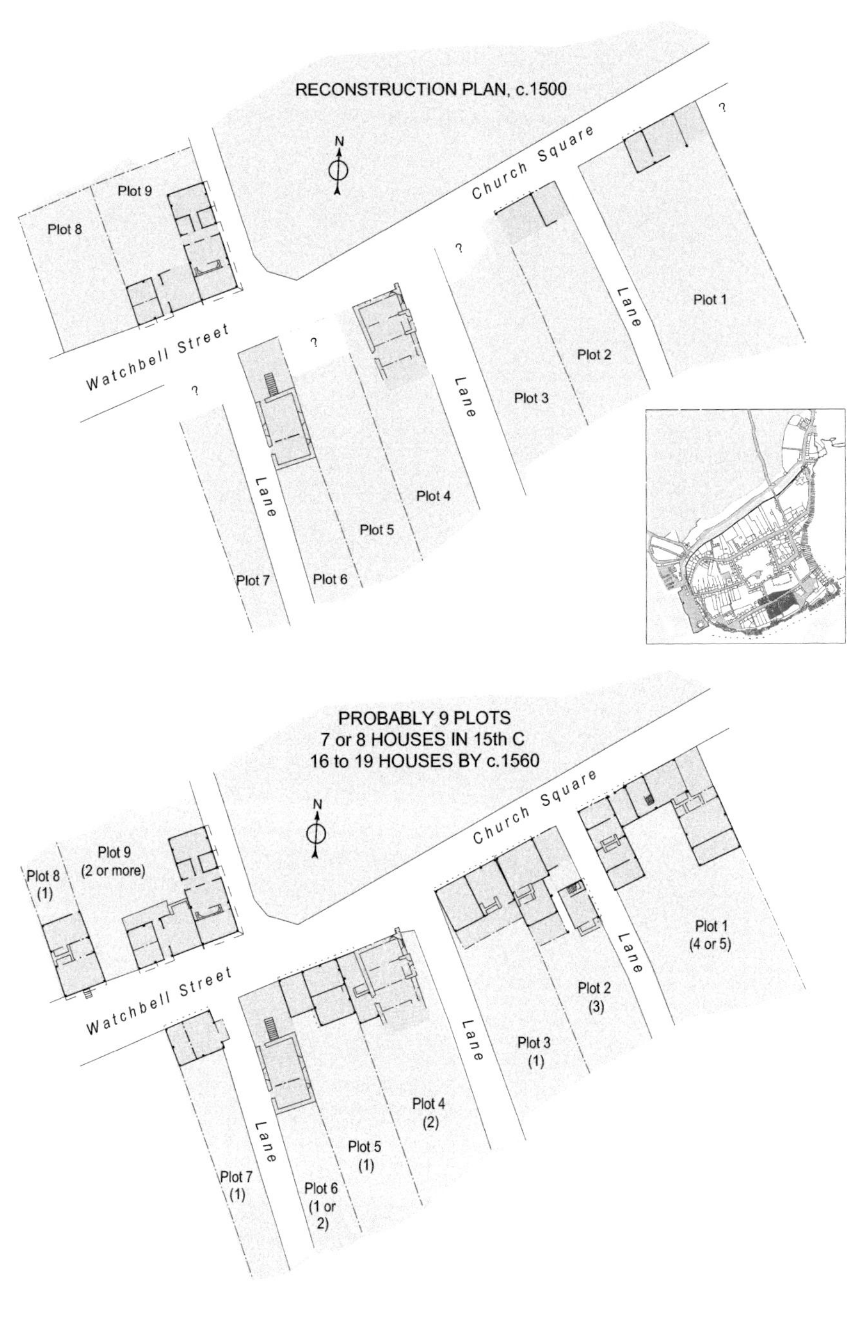

Fig. 7.7
Reconstructed development of the south side of Church Square

plot 4 upon which stands 40 Church Square, a stone-built structure of *c.*1300 alleged to be the site of the Friary of the Sack (*see* Chapter 4). Between this and the early 16th-century 44 Church Square [85] on plot 5 is number 42, built about 1540. It is squeezed into a tiny gap, widening from only 2.70 metres (8 feet 10 inches) at the street to 3.10 metres (10 feet 1 inch) at the rear. Despite the narrowness, the house extends 10.30 metres (33 feet 9 inches) back down the plot. It has two rooms on each level and on the first floor incorporates a small terracotta peep window looking eastwards down Church Square.

Further to the west, on the other side of the road, was an empty garden plot [Plot 8] sold to John Shurley, king's bailiff of Rye in 1500. He probably purchased it for building, but, if so, he did not follow through on his intention. It was sold again in 1519, this time to the eastern neighbour [Plot 9] at St Anthony's, 1-2 Watchbell Street [87, 90] who laid it into his garden. And so it remained until 1555 when the western half of plot 8 was sold off. This time within five years a house had been built, taking up the full width of the sized-down plot and — perhaps significantly — with no windows overlooking the enlarged plot 9. Was this a condition of sale, to prevent the new house overlooking St Anthony's and 1-2 Watchbell Street, or did the vendor have designs on building upon the retained half of the original plot? That is what eventually happened, but not until after 1777.

The story of the area to the north of the church, in Market Street and Lion Street, is more fragmented, but no less interesting. A reconstruction as in the early 16th century is given in Figure 7.8 (the date is somewhat nominal on account of the approximate dates for the buildings). On the south side of Market Street, on the corner of Church Square, is 4-5 Market Street, 2, 4 Church Square [38]. The house was probably built in

adjacent plot to the right.

To the west of this complex is 34, 36 Church Square [83], built very soon after the hall of 28, 32 Church Square [82] was rebuilt, blocking the window in the latter's end-gable. It is assumed that this represents the reconstruction of an earlier, smaller building, but it should be stressed that there is now no proof of a medieval house upon this site — the plot could have been vacant.

Next west was another of the lanes (Balls Lane) extending back to the cliff top, and, to the west of that,

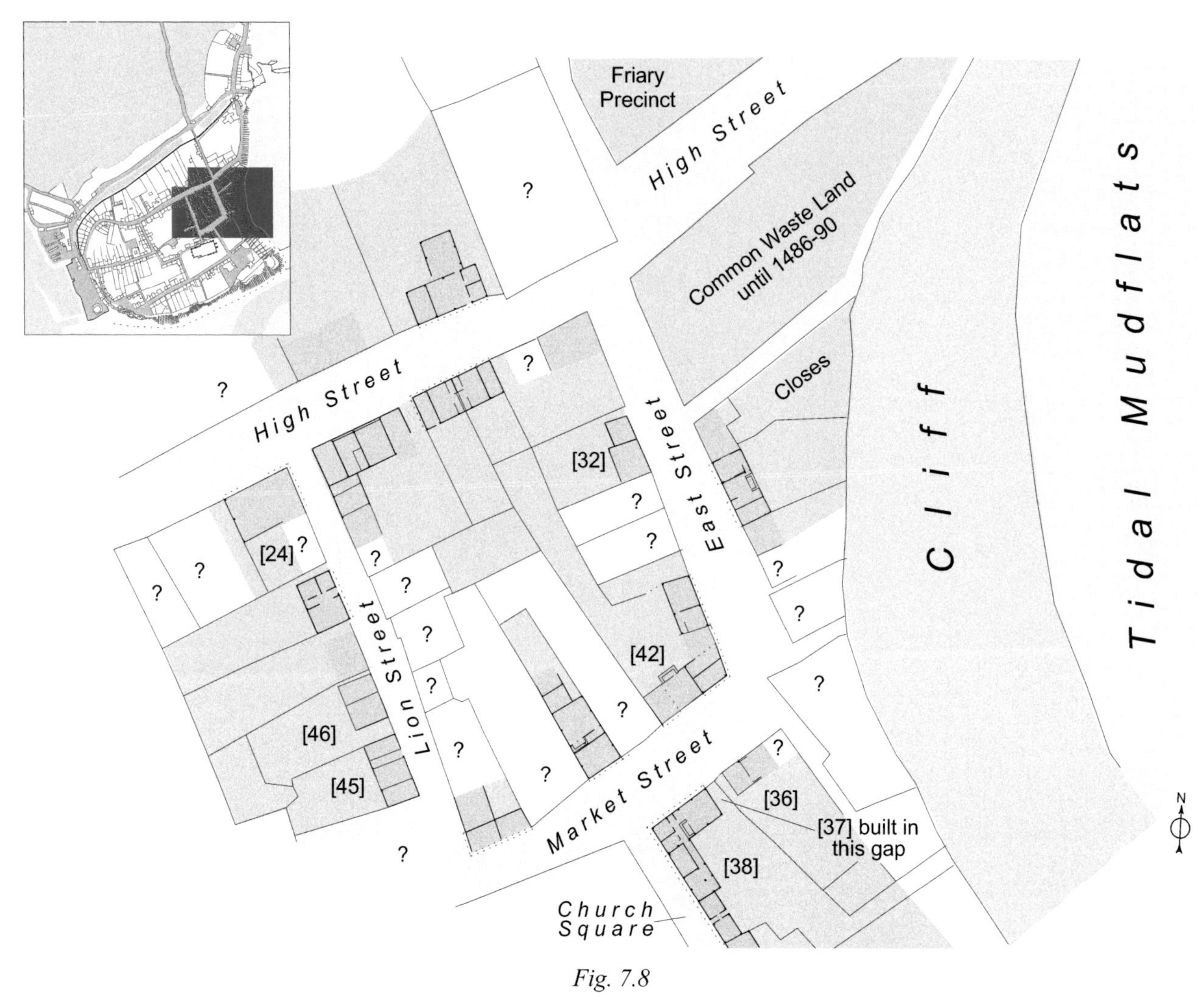

Fig. 7.8
Reconstruction of the area between Market Street and High Street, north of the church, as in the early 16th century, prior to the infilling of gaps.

the 1520s or 30s by Richard Inglett who was elected a jurat in 1525, served as mayor on three occasions in the 1530s and was one of the town's two MPs in 1537. Initially, as Figure 7.8 shows, there was open space to the east. The long rear range facing Church Square may also represent a slightly later addition — certainly it blocks an un-glazed window in the end-wall of adjacent 6 Church Square. Very soon after Inglett built the house the gap to the east was infilled to give an additional dwelling, 3 Market Street [37], but this could be achieved only by adjusting the property boundaries and demolishing the western part of what is now Durrant House, 1-2 Market Street [36]. Numbers 4-5 Market Street, 2, 4 Church Square [38] were built as a single dwelling. It was clearly a high-status building, as shown by the wall painting — an imitation of tapestry — which still adorns the dais partition (*see* Figure 11.11). Already by the middle years of the century the interior was being redesigned — the chimney was moved and the hall sub-divided. More important, major extensions were added at the rear. But by 1544 Richard Inglett had already moved to High Street, where later his son and grandson were to live. These alterations seem not to represent Inglett's enlargement of the house: instead it was being divided up and let out (*see* Figure 7.9). What happened to the narrow southern part of the rear range fronting onto Church Square is unclear, but by the 17th century (after the town's population crash) this too was in use as two cottages and the internal boundaries between the two main parts had (apparently) also been altered. The likelihood is that this was already the situation by the late 16th century.

Many of the infills and additions which occurred in Rye not only resulted in increased density of occupation, but also produced houses of far more 'urban' appearance. Such a house is 7-9 Lion Street [46], just around the corner, halfway down the western side of Lion Street (Figure 7.8). From what little evidence remains it would seem that it was originally a standard two-cell hall-house built parallel to the street

Fig. 7.9
A selection of plots divided up so as to accommodate additional dwellings.

— it was certainly freestanding, with at its southern end what was probably a vehicular access-way between it and the neighbouring hall-house now known as 4-6 Lion Street [45]. The hall was retained, but the rest of 7-9 Lion Street [46] was rebuilt during the middle years of the 16th century (more likely before 1550 than after) wrapped around the retained hall. Furthermore, it was rebuilt not as one, but as two dwellings, both incorporating shops within the front part (Figure 7.9). As with a large number of the Rye houses of this period, it is very 'urban' in its layout and in the ingenuity of its design.

Further down the same street, on the corner of Lion Street and High Street, stood a large medieval house [24] aligned parallel to High Street. It is now incorporated into the George Hotel. The medieval house was first divided up into two parts and subsequently demolished piecemeal (leaving one wall only standing) to make way for three dwellings, one accessed from High Street (98 High Street [24]) and the other two reached from Lion Street (Figure 7.9). One of these — 13 Lion Street [48] — is a small two-storeyed, two-cell house built on open ground between the former service end of the medieval house and the close-studded end wall of a medieval Wealden known as 12 Lion Street [47]. As the outline plan illustrated in Figure 7.9 shows, the two dwellings which replaced the old medieval house were quite substantial. That occupying the service end and part of the hall (14 Lion Street [49]) is the same date as 13 Lion Street [48]. Aligned parallel to Lion Street, it is of three-and-a-half storeys and in its original form had three cells arranged in line. The other part (98 High Street [24]) occupies the site of the old parlour crosswing and the high end of the open hall and is a wide two-and-a-half storeyed building of *c.*1600, erected with its gable towards the street. Another example of subdivision is 2-3 East Street [32] shown in Figures 7.8 and 7.9. It was probably during this period too that 9-10 East Street/13-14 Market Street [42] was subdivided. To detail other examples of infill and subdivision would become tedious. Suffice it to say that the above are not atypical: a selection of examples are shown in Figure 7.9.

It is both interesting and instructive to note that in the majority of instances the fact that individual buildings had been divided into tenements prior to the 19th century was not identified from the architectural evidence at the time of survey: it was the documentary sources, not the architecture which demonstrated this point. In most instances the division was initially assumed to have occurred within the last two centuries. There is a further point which needs to be borne in mind. Where a medieval house was totally rebuilt in the process of division it is now usually impossible from the

Fig. 7.10
Reconstruction of Middlestreet Ward showing identified houses.

architectural evidence to prove that the two replacement buildings stand upon the site of what had been one dwelling.

Because of the above factors, the number of extant buildings identified from their architectural evidence alone as having been divided into multiple occupancy before the 19th century are few. Despite this, the deeds of the town reveal that during the 16th century the procedure was commonplace.[3] This is an important point to bear in mind for, given this observation, it would be naive to assume that the majority of subdivisions which occurred within the extant building stock during the 16th century have been identified. Indeed, the fact that many mid 16th-century subdivisions must still await recognition is demonstrated by an analysis of Middlestreet Ward. A reconstruction of the ward is given in Figure 7.10. Counting the Shurley Mansion at 7-9 West Street, 62 Church Square as one dwelling (i.e. ignoring the assumed 5 shop units fronting the street) the number of houses identified within the ward based upon a combination of architectural and documentary evidence is 49. There are three small areas (shown white in Figure 7.10) for which there is no information. These areas could have accommodated up to eight further houses, giving a likely maximum total of 57. There were 65 houses in the ward in the 1570s when its boundaries were described: the number of dwellings/households (as opposed to houses) is likely to have been higher than this (*see* Chapter 5). These statistics suggest that a number of dwellings are today invisible. Some are likely to have been multiple units sited within what are today considered to have been undivided buildings. Despite the few access points available, other dwellings may have been located within since-demolished backland developments. Whatever the case, Middlestreet Ward serves to highlight the problems involved in identifying individual housing units. By 1660 the number of dwellings within the ward had dropped to about 52, a number which is far easier to reconcile with the existing building stock.

The combined evidence from the documentary sources and standing buildings shows that the more than doubling and perhaps trebling which occurred in the number of households during the 16th century was achieved in a combination of ways. There was a little expansion of the former occupied area and some infilling of open spaces between (and occasionally behind) existing houses, but principally the extra housing was achieved by the division of existing buildings. Division of a plot sometimes entailed retaining the original medieval house intact, sometimes one part was rebuilt whilst the other part was adapted, and sometimes the original house was totally reconstructed, either during a single building campaign or over a period of time.

None of the above should be surprising. Similar developments took place in many other towns, but at different times according to the economic fortunes of the individual settlements. At Great Yarmouth, Norfolk, it started early with the development of the Rows, with continued intensification thereafter. The East Sussex port town of Hastings witnessed the same process as Rye, but during the 17th century. And, of course, across the nation as a whole extra dwellings were packed into many, indeed most nucleated settlements during the 19th century as population expanded dramatically. For a time most growth in all but the largest towns was primarily contained within the boundaries of the existing built-up areas, with little expansion occurring beyond. A local example is the nucleated village of Robertsbridge which contained 48 houses in 1567, but more than five times that number by the late 19th century, yet within its original bounds.

What makes Rye interesting is the exceptional survival — over 100 structures (containing perhaps close on 200 dwellings) dating from the 15th and 16th centuries. This is more than a third of the original total. This level of survival allows the procedure by which household density intensified to be seen in greater detail than in many other towns at a comparable period. What this detail demonstrates — and again it should be no great surprise — is that this intensification was an oscillating rather than a gradual progression.

The variable pattern of occupation which could occur within a single building is clearly demonstrated by 24 Landgate [107] just outside the town's principal gate. It was built during the first half of the 16th century to a reasonably standard two-unit plan, though with extra upper chambers and, rather unusually for the time, with an attic (*see* Figures 14.12, 14.14). By the 1630s, when drawn by Van Dyck, it had been extended at the rear, the original chimney had been modified or rebuilt, and a second chimney added (*see* Figure 14.13). In its extended form it fits its 1662 hearth tax entry perfectly — Benjamin Martin, six flues. Thus, at this date the house remained in single occupancy. But this apparent continuity since the early 16th century (when it was built) is misleading. A deed of 1658 describes the building as 'a messuage', purchased by the owner's father by deed dated 1612 'by the name of 2 messuages'. This qualification was given in order to explain the difference between the wording in the 1612 deed and the situation as current in 1658. Although it was one house in the early 16th century and in both 1658 and 1662, in 1612 it had been in two occupations. As in other instances mentioned above, the additions at the rear (shown in outline in Figure 7.9) were not in response to any requirement for improved accommodation on the part of the occupant, but were aimed at adequately accommodating an additional dwelling.

By the early 17th century Rye's boom was over. During the first half of the 17th century the number of households in Rye virtually halved (Chapter 5). The pressure on space was off. Houses were being abandoned and demolished, particularly in The Wishe suburb, and it is therefore not surprising to find that many houses which had been divided into tenements were once again being merged back into single dwellings. It was not until the 19th century, extending into the early 20th century that pressure on space reasserted itself and once more houses were sub-divided. This latter phenomenon explains many of the complex modern postal addresses given for buildings included within this present study. Even though 24 Landgate [107] now has only one postal number, by *c.*1900 it too had once more been divided into two occupancies: it is shown as such in the 1909 edition of the Ordnance Survey plan and in photographs of the period. As had occasionally happened in the 16th century, at this period too houses were built in back gardens. By 1860, for instance, a terrace of four cottages had been erected in the garden behind adjacent 23 Landgate, accessed through the yard behind 24, with a further terrace of five behind 20 Landgate. Both terraces have since been demolished and 24 is now once more in single occupancy.

What Rye reminds us is that there is a danger in adopting a simplistic model of gradual, progressive intensification of household numbers over time. Excepting the catastrophic impact of the Black Death, or examples where settlements have been virtually or totally deserted, all too often too little attention is given to the fluctuations in household numbers — both upwards and downwards — which must commonly have occurred in urban centres. Given the difficulties in identifying these fluctuation this is perhaps inevitable.

RYE: NEW HOUSES FOR A NEW AGE

House Sizes and Types

An inevitable consequence of the points discussed above is that during the 16th century many of the houses within the town had much reduced street frontages compared to those of the previous century. As Figure 7.11 demonstrates, the lengths of the houses being built seems to have reduced rapidly in response to plot-size reduction during the first part of the 16th century. Based upon surviving examples, the chart implies that short-frontage houses were rare prior to this date, but a certain amount of caution is necessary in accepting this impression at face value. Whilst it is inevitable that frontages would have reduced dramatically once plots began to be subdivided, it should also be remembered that as population pressures within the town increased the class of resident willing to acquire plots with medium-length frontages of 6.85 metre to 9.15 metre (22 feet 6 inches to 29 feet 11 inches) would have increased. Due to pressure on space, middle-class residents are far more likely to have sought out smaller plots during the 16th century than during the 15th century when larger plots were more numerous. In many instances smaller plots acquired by the more wealthy residents were not chosen for the two-cell houses which stood upon them, but as potential redevelopment sites.

Whilst most of the new 16th-century houses built upon plots with frontages of less than about 6.85 metres (22 feet 6 inches) can be demonstrated to have been erected upon divided medieval tenements, many of those within the medium-sized category almost certainly replace two-cell medieval houses of similar length. As demonstrated by Figure 7.13, the large number of 16th-century two-cell houses of 'standard' layout which exist within the town seems to indicate that in part these reconstructions were aimed at providing up-to-date 'modern' floored-over halls with (in most instances) chimneys and improved storey heights. Even so, unless the existing houses were exceptionally low, of inferior construction, or in need of reconstruction due to their age/poor condition, this in itself was probably not the main impetus for total reconstruction. This point can be illustrated by 15 West Street [56] where the owner chose not to totally rebuild an adequate, albeit low two-cell hall-house. Instead he replaced the floored bay by a very up-to-date two-and-a-half storeyed crosswing of identical footprint, incorporating two rooms on each of its three floors. The crosswing was heated by a multi-flue chimney inserted into the retained, but floored-over hall. Only subsequently was the medieval hall rebuilt taller. In this instance too the earlier footprint was retained (*see* Figures 12.14 to 12.16).

In the case of 15 West Street the owner was content with the existing footprint of the building, but for many of middling wealth, especially those who traded from their premises, the medieval two-cell houses upon these medium-sized plots seem to have been regarded as too small to provide sufficient space for an

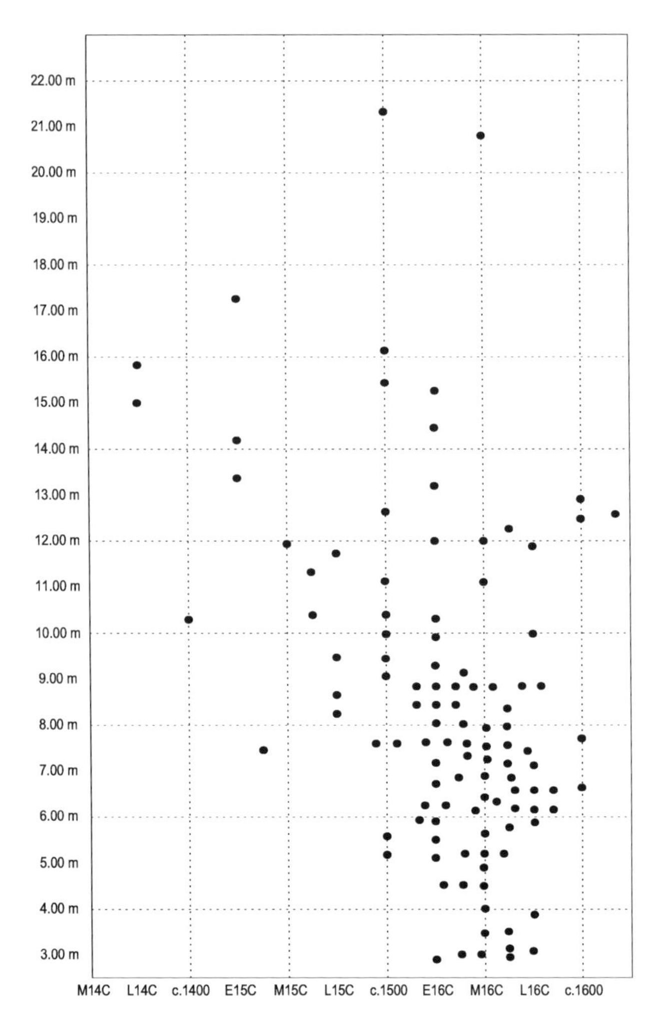

Fig. 7.11
Length of street frontages of houses plotted by approximate construction date.

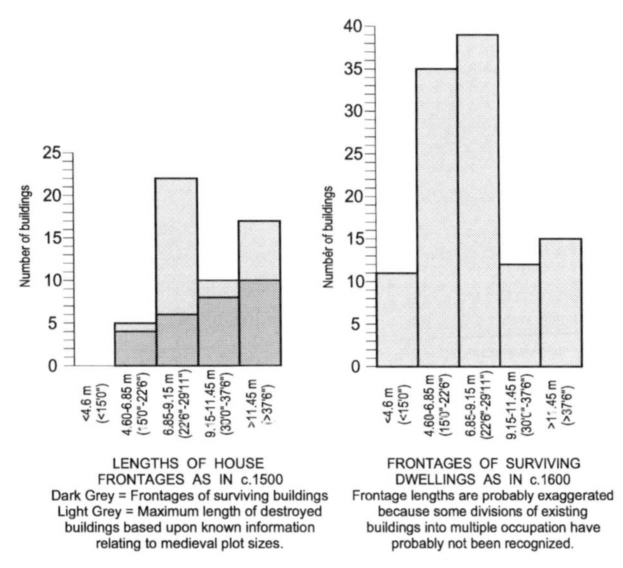

Fig. 7.12
Length of house frontages showing overall change during the century c.1500 to c.1600.

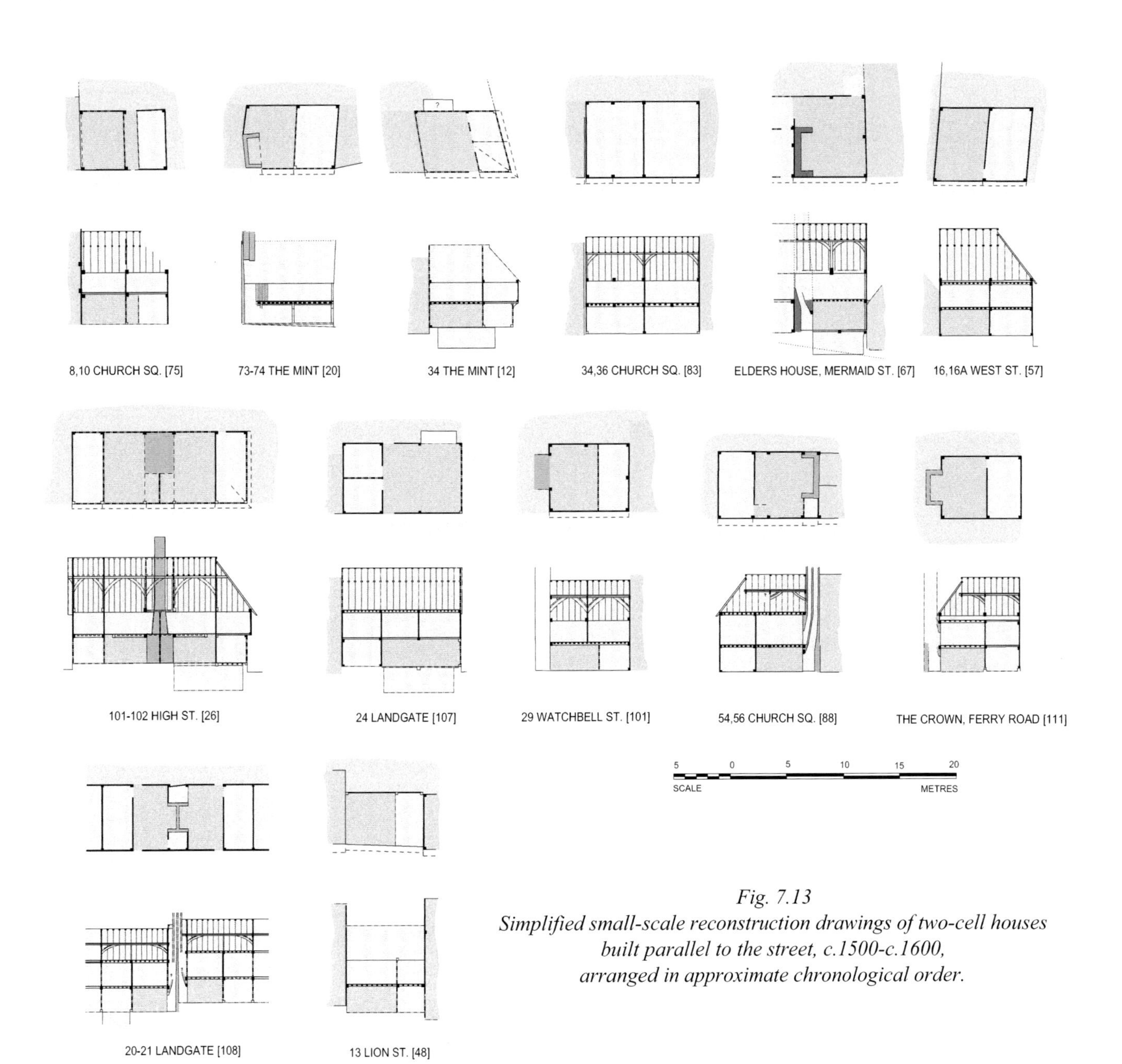

Fig. 7.13
Simplified small-scale reconstruction drawings of two-cell houses built parallel to the street, c.1500-c.1600, arranged in approximate chronological order.

acceptable home and work area. It was the need for extra space, obtained without accepting major compromises caused by adapting and enlarging an existing structure, which seems to have been a primary reason for middle-class traders replacing the earlier modest-size buildings. As a result, it seems likely that a disproportionately high number of two-cell medieval houses were swept away during the town's 16th-century regeneration.

Even allowing for this likely disproportionate loss of small medieval two-cell houses, it can be certain that by the end of the century a much higher percentage of Rye's houses had short street-frontages than had been the case a century earlier. In addition, as Figures 7.11 and 7.12 show, a number of these new dwellings were significantly shorter than any known from the 15th century. This in itself does not necessarily mean that most of the less prosperous amongst Rye's residents were being forced to make do with smaller houses than previously. Whereas during the medieval period the houses had been built parallel to the street with the open hall occupying the full depth of the building, and very few houses had rear ranges (*see* Chapter 6) it now became far more common for buildings to extend further back from the street frontage, often being two rooms deep.

In this way, in spite of its tiny 2.70 metre (8 feet 10 inches) street frontage, the smallest newly-built house which survives from the period — 42 Church Square [84] — was able to provide a surprising amount of internal space. Viewed from the street it is minute, yet its floor area is equal to that within each of the houses in the semi-detached pair at 26 Church Square [80] as updated, and more than a third larger in terms of total floor area than when the halls at 26 were still open to their roofs. Thus 42 was considerably larger than 26 had been in its early 16th-century medieval configuration. As already mentioned, at 7-9 Lion Street [46] extensions and modifications were made in the mid 16th century in order to divide the building into two dwellings. After conversion, number 7 had a street frontage very similar in length to that at 42 Church Square — 2.90 metres (9 feet 6 inches). Here too the tiny frontage is misleading. As the plan of the building included in Figure 7.9 shows, in this case the floor area was increased by wrapping the hall around that of 8-9 Lion Street. The result was a house with a ground-floor area one-and-a-half times the size of that at 42 Church Square.

By adopting designs of this type many of Rye's 16th-century houses were no smaller than their 15th-century equivalents, in spite of their narrower frontages. This ignores the fact that from the middle years of the 16th century onwards most of Rye's houses incorporated attic rooms, still further augmenting the space available.

At 42 Church Square the required floor area was achieved by turning the axis at right-angles to the street, with one room placed behind the other. Although this never became a popular solution within the town, 11 examples are known spread throughout the period here under discussion. Examples of this type are shown in Figure 7.14, including one — 34 Mermaid Street [71] — which was built as early as *c.*1500 (*see* Chapter 6). As at 7 Lion Street mentioned above, the same effect, but more piecemeal in layout, was achieved in some of the examples illustrated in Figure 7.9 in which existing buildings were divided into multiple occupancy.

All these dwellings had exceptionally short facades. In two mid/late 16th-century houses with moderate-length two-cell street frontages additional ground-floor rooms were gained by including a rear lean-to outshut (Figure 7.15) whilst in a few others extra space was achieved by incorporating rear ranges behind part of the street range, giving an 'L-plan' layout (Figure 7.16). Other

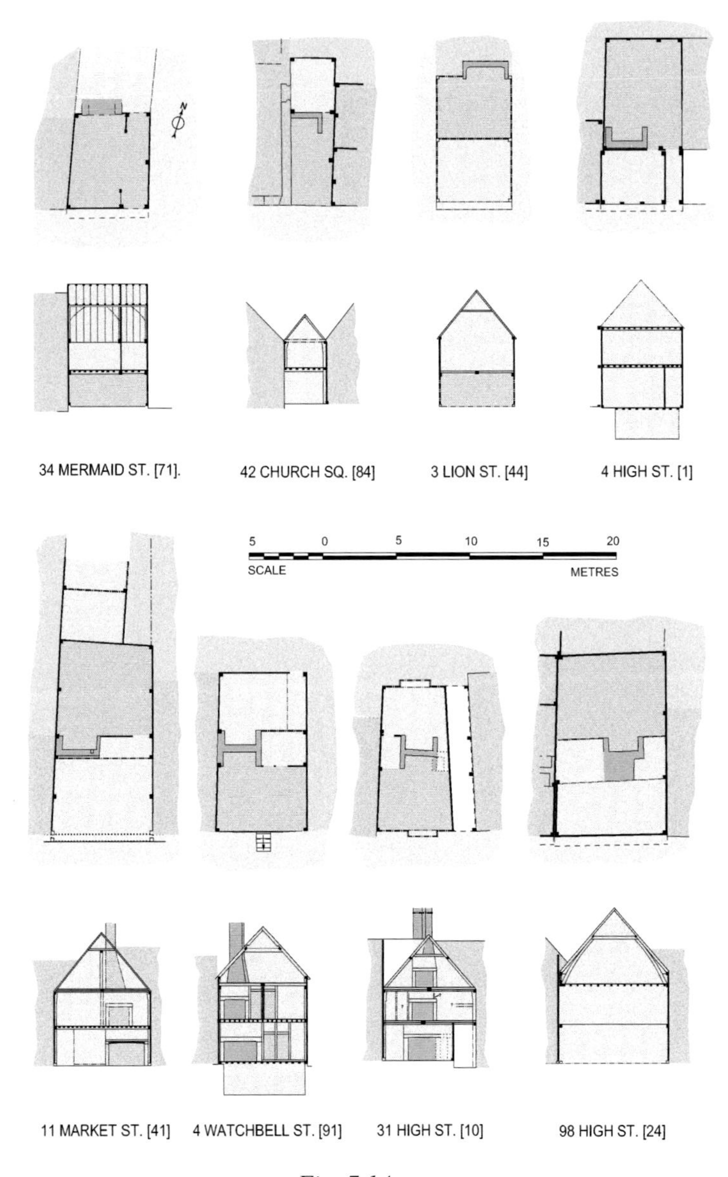

Fig. 7.14
Two-cell houses built at right angles to the street, c.1500-c.1600, arranged in approximate chronological order. (Simplified reconstruction details).

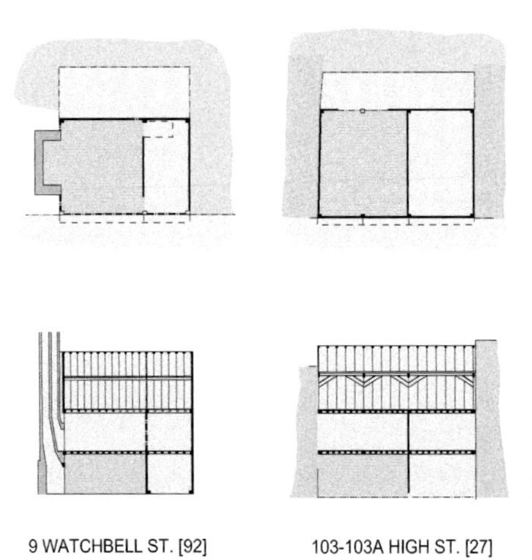

Fig. 7.15 (left)
Two-cell houses built parallel to the street, and incorporating rear lean-to outshuts. (Simplified reconstruction details).

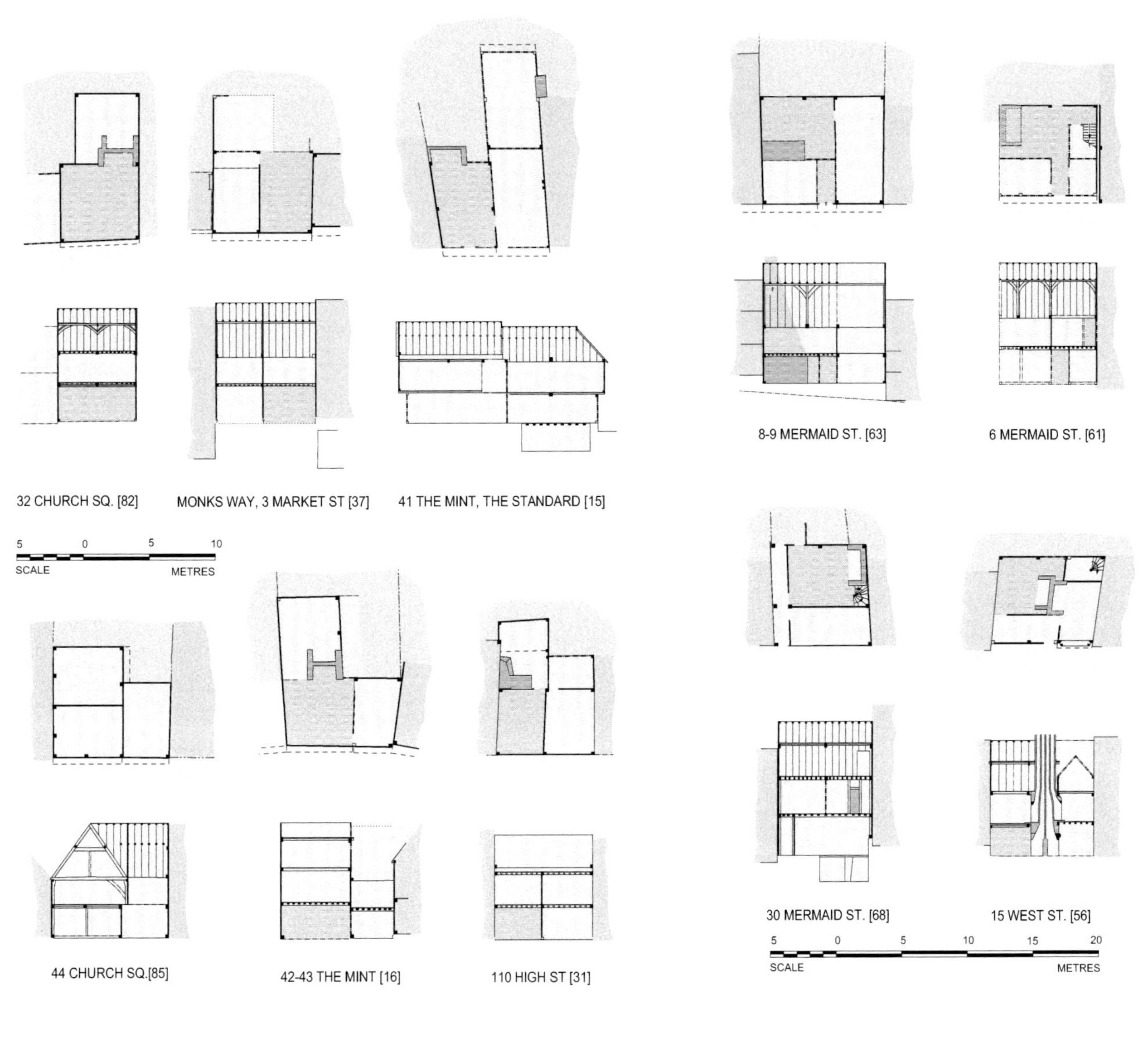

Fig. 7.16
Two-cell houses built parallel to the street, incorporating a rear range behind part. (Simplified reconstruction details).

Fig. 7.17
Two-cell double-pile houses built parallel to the street. (Simplified reconstruction details).

buildings with similar moderate-length street frontages, dating from the early 16th century onwards, were two-rooms deep throughout their entire length and on all storeys. These are an interesting group — they are early examples of a phenomenon known as 'double-pile' design: they mark the emergence of a new type of building for Rye. The required configuration was achieved in a variety of ways. In the four examples illustrated in Figure 7.17 all rooms were contained within a single exceptionally wide range capped by a massive roof aligned parallel to the street, whilst at 14-15 Mermaid Street [65] (*see* Figure 7.19) the same arrangement is augmented by a long rear range — an exceptionally rare feature for Rye. In two further examples (39-40 The Mint [14] and 20a-21 Watchbell Street [98] shown in Figure 7.18) a pair of rear ranges were placed behind the street range, whilst at 15 High Street [4] (Figure 7.18) two three-and-a-half storeyed ranges were set side-by-side, framed at right-angles to the street. Each configuration produced a different profile of roofs, but internally the layouts were similar. In one hybrid building (7 Mermaid Street — [62] in Figure 7.18) the entire building was accommodated within a single range turned and roofed at right-angles to the street with a very standard two-cell layout to the front, but with a single large heated room (function unknown) occupying the entire rear half. The layout was repeated on the upper floor.

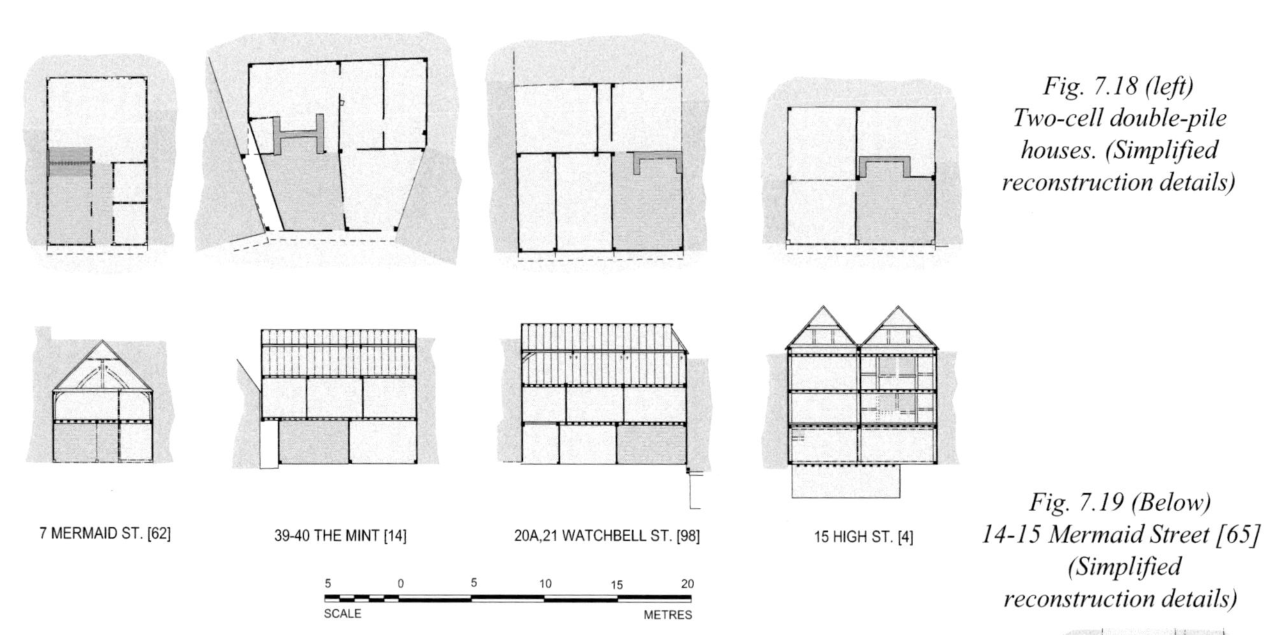

Fig. 7.18 (left) Two-cell double-pile houses. (Simplified reconstruction details)

Fig. 7.19 (Below) 14-15 Mermaid Street [65] (Simplified reconstruction details)

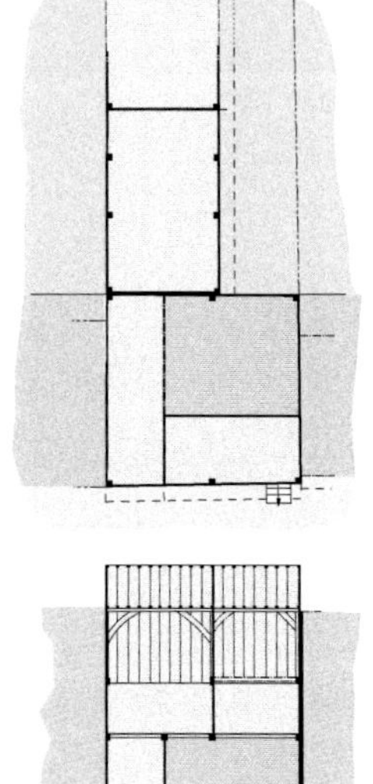

Houses of the urban elite.

Despite constraints on plot size during the 16th century, there remained a reasonable number of long-frontage buildings within the town (*see* Figures 7.20 and 7.21). and some of these occupied spacious plots. Sometimes (as at The Mermaid Inn [72]) the nature of the business carried on within the premises demanded space. The proprietor was invariably wealthy. In other instances wealth in itself was sufficient to maintain a large house upon a large plot. Some of these large plots persisted throughout the 16th century, despite population pressures. This was the case, for example, at 11 High Street [2], 13-14 High Street [3], 5-6 West Street [50], 31 Mermaid Street [69], The Mermaid, Mermaid Street [72], and Dormy House, East Cliff [104]. In fact, both The Mermaid and Dormy House continued to expand in size throughout the period. The late-medieval mansion at 7-9 West Street, 62 Church Square [51] is another example which (ignoring the shop units which fronted the street) was kept in single occupation throughout the 16th-century period of population pressure, despite being leased out to a tenant (albeit a leading resident of the town) during the latter part of the century.[4]

Some houses which started out large succumbed to the pressure for sub-division as the 16th century progressed. As has already been noted, this is what seems to have happened at 4-5 Market Street/ 2, 4 Church Square [38]. At 67-69 The Mint (itself probably built upon a late 14th- or 15th-century amalgamation of two tenements) the house of *c.*1500 was still in single occupancy when its western end was rebuilt as a spacious heated parlour in the early 16th century, but soon afterwards the two parts were divided into separate tenements. Another example is 24-25 High Street [5], built in the mid 16th century as a courtyard inn, apparently with a series of rooms and chambers to one side of the public rooms for the use of the proprietor and his family. The house was subsequently divided to give two totally independent dwellings.

As yet no documentary-based tenement analysis has been carried out for Rye. For this reason, in the absence of any detailed town surveys, only rarely is it known precisely where named prosperous merchants and other members of the ruling elite lived. In the absence of such data, the hearth tax returns of the early 1660s are the best guide to the size of the houses these elite families occupied. The 1663 return lists 31 houses with more than four flues, of which nine houses had either seven or eight flues each and three had nine or more. The mid 17th-century 'urban elite' of the town certainly numbered more than 12 families (*see* Chapter 5) so somc must have lived in houses assessed at fewer than seven flues.

In the 1660s at least two of the three largest houses within the town were in use as inns. The Jurat innholder, Michael Cadman, occupied the Mermaid Inn [72] (11 flues), and William Marson (assessed 10 flues in 1662, but 11 flues in 1664) was the proprietor of 'The Queens Arms' in West Street, an inn formed within the

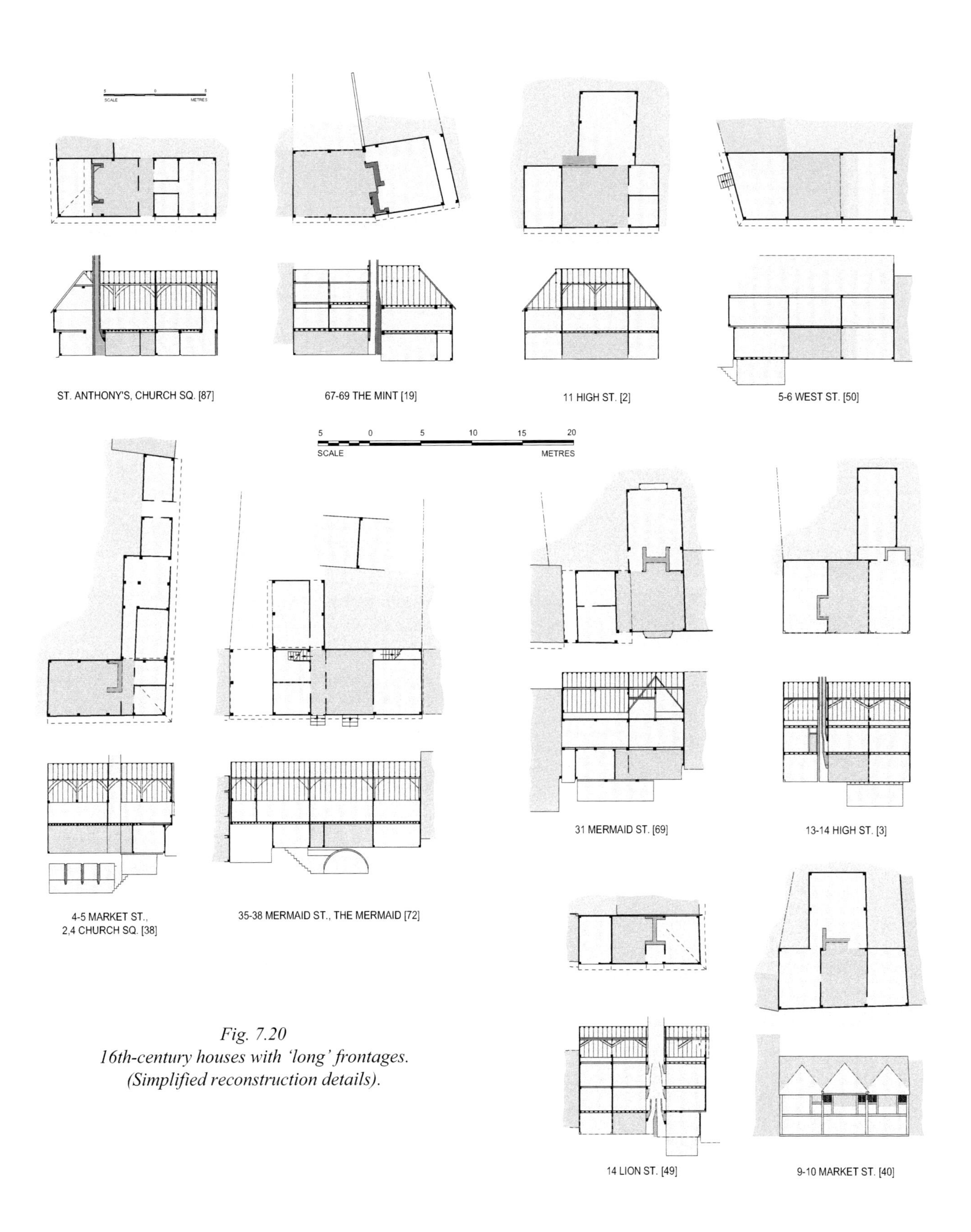

Fig. 7.20
16th-century houses with 'long' frontages.
(Simplified reconstruction details).

Fig. 7.21
Rye's principal 16th-century houses (simplified reconstruction details).

principal part of the divided-up former town house [51] of Sir John Shurley. In 1660 this house had been in the proprietorship of the alien innholder Lewes Pascall.[5] The third house (nine flues — site not identified, but in the present High Street, in Landgate Ward) was the home of Mary Thomas, widow of the late Mayor, the occupation of whom is uncertain.

Excepting these three 'mansions', one of the larger assessments within the return is that relating to Thomas Greenfield, jurat, 'his majesties searcher for the port of Chichester and members thereof'. His seven-flue house in Middlestreet Ward is 54, 56, 58, 60 Church Square and Lamb Cottage. Once called 'Grene Hall' the seven-flue assessment for this house is interesting in that it indicates the house to be an amalgamation of three earlier houses (for details of which *see* entry for [89]).[6] The most likely time for this to have occurred was during the period of low population following the late-16th century slump. Nevertheless, in 1576 it was the home of one of Rye's leading residents, Henry Gaymer, the royal purveyor of fish who was mayor at the time of Elizabeth I's visit to the town in 1573, so at least part of the amalgamation could have occurred earlier.[7] Another is The Dormy House [104] just inside the town walls, adjacent to Land Gate. Here too there is documentary evidence which suggests that the northern range, fronting Turkey Cock Lane, had once formed a separate house and was merged into the mansion only during the 17th century.[8] Like the Shurley mansion, Dormy House survives in fragmentary form only. In this instance, however, this is not due to its loss of gentry status but to dramatic remodelling as its 18th-century gentry owners strove to modernise their aging mansion. It had already had substantial extensions to front and rear in the late 16th and/or early 17th century. The earliest of these may have been carried out by Robert Farley, a wealthy Rye merchant who not only dealt in the export and import of glass but also acted as agent for London clothiers and, in 1575, was listed as a beer tippler. So in this instance too the house may at that time have doubled as an inn.[9] By 1646 the house had been acquired by Anthony Norton and in 1660 it was occupied by his son, Richard Norton, gentleman. By 1663 it was tenanted by John Martin, who was assessed for it at eight flues. The building narrowly escaped demolition during the 19th century.[10]

As has already been pointed out, not all of Rye's principal residents could have occupied houses with numerous hearths, a reminder that the number of fireplaces a house possessed is only a crude indicator of the wealth of its occupier. Several of the middle-sized extant houses were occupied by leading residents of the town, and although some of these incorporate seven or more hearths, others, such as 13-14 High Street [3],

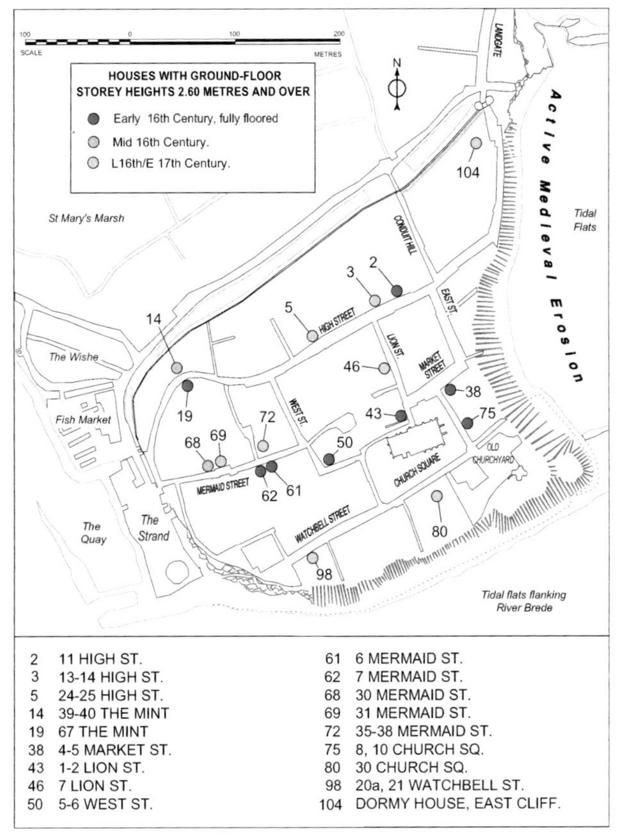

Fig. 7.22
The age and distribution of buildings with lofty ground-floor storey heights.

appear to have had only five fireplaces within them. Indeed, the best preserved of the town's 16th-century merchant houses — 31 Mermaid Street [69], built 1576 — was one such building.[11] Writing in 1680, Samuel Jeake II considered the house 'one of the best in the town': he was later able to acquire it through marriage and make it his home.[12] Like Dormy House, it subsequently fell derelict and narrowly escaped demolition.

Storey heights

In assessing house size the focus up to this point has been on floor area. Another consideration is storey height: two houses of identical ground-floor area can contain rooms of quite different height, giving very different impressions of space and wealth. This is particularly important in Rye where some storey heights are surprisingly lofty, even in houses built during the opening years of the 16th century at a period when ceilings were usually low.

Including the town's medieval hall-houses, the ground-floor storey heights are known with reasonable accuracy in 79 buildings. In 53 of these (about two-thirds) the storey height exceeds 2.30 metres (7 feet 6 inches). Perhaps surprisingly, these lofty buildings include five medieval hall-houses, though none of these are amongst the 18 buildings in which the storey height exceeds 2.60 metres (8 feet 6 inches). Even so, eight of the 18 loftiest buildings date from the early 16th century (Figure 7.22). In 10 houses the ground-floor rooms exceed 2.75 metres (9 feet). The tallest rooms are in the courtyard inn at 24-25 High Street [5] with a storey height of 3.40 metres (11 feet 2 inches). Here the generous proportions are understandable — a need to impress guests — as was also the case at the other courtyard inn, The Mermaid [72]. A similar motive applies at 4-5 Market Street [38], 5-6 West Street [50], 31 Mermaid Street [69] and Dormy House [104]: all were houses occupied by members of Rye's elite. At 39-40 The Mint [14] and 67 The Mint [19] too the storey heights are also in keeping with the high status of the buildings, as indicated by the use of moulded joists within the ceilings of the rooms in question. However, the significance/purpose of the tall rooms in other buildings, such as, for example, the early 16th-century houses at 6 and 7 Mermaid Street [61, 62] and the later, but similarly sized, 30 Mermaid Street [68] is unclear.

Bearing in mind that only 12 buildings have chambers which exceed 2.30 metres (7 feet 6 inches) from floor to ceiling, it could be argued that generous storey heights on the first floor were considered less important than at ground-floor level. However, in appraising these figures it must be borne in mind that until the middle years of the 16th century most first-floor chambers were open to the roof, and therefore tended to be lofty in appearance. Even so, in only five instances do the first-floor heights exceed 2.60 metres (8 feet 6 inches), the most generous being 2.70 metres (8 feet 10 inches) at 39-40 The Mint [14], 2.75 metres (9 feet) at 31 Mermaid Street [69] and 2.80 metres (9 feet 2 inches) within the lounge chamber at The Mermaid [72].

Once garret areas were introduced, these too could be surprisingly spacious and in a number of instances the height was deliberately augmented by positioning the attic floors below the level of the wallplates. This latter feature reflects the likely use to which the garrets were put, a point which will be discussed in greater detail later in this chapter.

Adapting existing buildings

All the surviving medieval buildings discussed in the previous chapter share one thing in common — they were able to adapt. They had to: if not they would have become outmoded and unwanted and would have been replaced. Already by *c.*1540 a number of Rye's hall-houses had been subjected to progressive reconstruction and others had experienced other forms of metamorphosis. For example, the late 14th-century single-aisled Lamb Cottage [53] in West Street seems to have been sized down in *c.*1500 to make way for an additional, more up-to-date house turned through right angles to it. This first alteration at Lamb Cottage illustrates in part a phase of modification which virtually all hall houses in England had to undergo if they were to survive — the conversion of their medieval-style open hall to a more suitable form with a chamber above and an improved mode of heating. The partial flooring over at Lamb Cottage meant that a crossbeam had to be inserted into its arch-braced open truss and the upper parts of the truss infilled with a daub partition. The same feature is recognizable at 99-100 High Street [25], another of Rye's early houses which likewise had a large two-bay hall.

Excepting these and the insertion of a smoke bay at 22, 24 Church Square [78], Rye's surviving medieval hall-houses were converted to fully-floored form in one operation, and in this the town follows the general trend found in the region as a whole. Even so, whereas the vast majority of local rural and village hall houses which survive had their floors inserted during the middle decades of the 16th century (and in some instances, later still) in Rye some of the floors appear to be early and use joists of medieval scantling (*see* 'Floors and Jetties' below). The medieval-style joists at Oak Corner, Trader Passage [102] are shown in Figure 13.55. Other examples are 16 East Street [34], 58, 60 Church Square [89], 1-2 Watchbell Street [90], Hope Anchor/16-17 Watchbell Street [95] and 19 Watchbell Street [96].

There would inevitably have been an overlap in date between the introduction of joists of post-medieval scantling and the abandonment of those of medieval type (*see* 'Construction Techniques' below): what is significant is that early-style joists of the type used within the Rye buildings listed above are not found in floors inserted into hall-houses in the rural areas of East Sussex, whereas, in that same area (as well as within Rye itself) post-medieval joists were used within fully-floored transitional houses built with crownpost roofs. Of the 17 hall-houses in Rye where the date at which the floor was inserted can be ascertained within reasonable parameters, it seems likely that well over half were inserted prior to *c.*1540 and none are obviously of late date. That many of the open halls in Rye were converted to floored type at a relatively early date should not be surprising given the early adoption of fully-floored houses within the town, and, indeed, this trend is consistent with houses such as 67-69 The Mint [19] and 28, 32 Church Square [82] where houses with open halls must have been rebuilt with an upper floor at an early date as an alternative to inserting a floor within the existing halls. Despite the surviving architectural evidence, some open halls no doubt persisted well into the second half of the century. One such example may have been the house of John Clarke which, at his death in 1558, is listed as having a hall, buttery and shop, but only one chamber, which is described simply as 'the chamber'.[13]

A noticeable feature of Rye's converted hall-houses is the fact that most which survive had a brick chimney inserted as part of the upgrade, rather than having undergone an intermediate phase during which either a smoke bay or timber-framed chimney was used. Of course, this may be statistical chance, or, more likely, it could be due to the fact that the surviving houses represent the homes of the more wealthy inhabitants of the town. Only two converted hall-houses (24, 26 Church Square [5] and 17 West Street [58]) incorporate evidence which suggests that a more basic type of heating was inserted — a smoke-bay at the former and a timber-framed chimney at the latter. This is despite good documentary evidence which demonstrates that a considerable number of timber chimneys remained in use within the town well into the second half of the 16th century (*see* below). In a further four hall-houses the initial form of heating used when the floor was added is unknown due to the nature of subsequent alterations, but all others have early-looking stacks built of small, buff or pink 'Flemish' bricks (sometimes incorporating stone dressings to the jambs) with timber lintels, most of which are moulded and have carved spandrels.

In the villages and rural areas of the district most chimneys inserted into converted open halls are located towards the low end of the hall, backing onto a cross-passage, and this design was also adopted in early fully-floored houses. This arrangement is found in some Rye houses, but is not common. Out of the 14 converted hall-houses for which details are known only three are of this type. Of these, those at 6 Church Square [74] and Old Trader/Trader Cottage [103] follow the usual pattern in that the fireplace is built with one jamb against the front wall, forcing people entering the house to walk around the chimney in order to enter the hall. In the third example, at 99-100 High Street [25] the fireplace is set to the rear, a somewhat uncommon location which was also used within the new-built, fully-floored 'Flushing Inn' [38] at 4-5 Market Street.

By far the most common location for an inserted stack in Rye is against the hall's rear wall. At 16 East Street [34], 1-2 Watchbell Street [90] and Oak Corner, Trader Passage [102], the chimney was sited within the building itself, but an alternative was to built it projecting externally, as with the early chimney at 58, 60 Church Square [89]. Rear chimneys account for eight of the inserted brick stacks — over half the total —

yet in the surrounding countryside this position is rare. It may be relevant that where chimneys were built in this location within rural and village houses they tend to be early. However, more likely the adoption of this position in Rye was due to the short length of the halls, necessitated by the relatively constricted street frontages. In these circumstances the insertion of a more typical axial chimney would have resulted in a very short, cramped hall.

All the inserted stacks considered thus far heat only the hall on the ground floor, with about half incorporating an additional fireplace serving the hall chamber above. The mutilated chimney inserted into 36-38 The Mint [13], on the other hand, is located at the high end of the hall. Other high-end stacks are known in the town, serving the early fully-floored halls at St Anthony's, Church Square [87] and 67-69 The Mint [19]. Even so, as elsewhere in the Weald, prior to 1600 high-end stacks were not common.

When floors were inserted into the pair of handed semi-detached hall-houses at 26 Church Square [80] the most economic means of heating them was to add a back-to-back axial chimney built astride the party wall, thereby giving a fireplace within each cottage. A similar arrangement, but with four flues, was incorporated at 19 Watchbell Street [96] when in *c.*1530 this tiny Wealden hall-house was divided into two dwellings.

Houses as homes and work-places

When considering the physical form of Rye's houses it is essential not to lose sight of the very obvious point that these buildings served as people's homes. It was the occupier's wealth, needs, expectations and aspirations which influenced both the design and form adopted at time of construction and equally dictated the nature of any subsequent alterations and adaptations. Although some owned their homes, many — as Mayhew has demonstrated — rented, with some landlords owning small urban estates of five or more dwellings.[14] As discussed earlier, some of these estates resulted from the sub-division of existing houses and the construction of extra dwellings on vacant parts of the tenements, but in some cases they were dispersed across the town, having been accumulated opportunely. The urban estate of the early 16th-century courtier, John Shurley, included no fewer than 24 houses, together with a number of shops and other buildings. By no means all the rented accommodation was occupied by the poor and middle classes: Shurley's estate included the impressive Grene Hall (58, 60 Church Square [89]), whilst in 1582 the ex-Shurley mansion [51] in West Street was itself rented out to a leading Rye merchant, James Milles.[15]

In considering the physical form of the houses, of equal importance to the pattern of occupation/ownership is the fact that the town itself served as home to two very different groups of people — those who gained their livelihood by manufacturing, trading and/or providing professional services, and those who earned their living in other ways. The latter group were mainly seafarers — fishermen and sailors — employed as the crew of ships owned by others, but also included general labourers, porters and the like. The importance of this when considering the buildings is that whereas both groups would have required housing for themselves and their families, the former would, in addition, have required rooms used in relation to their occupation. In some instances it is known that these occupational spaces were accommodated in buildings which were entirely separate from the houses, being located in the area near the general market by the church or down on The Strand (*see* Chapter 2 and below) but most used rooms and chambers within their houses. As a result, even where people within the two groups were of similar wealth, the houses they occupied would, potentially, have been very different.

In addition to commercial space, some of the merchants and the more wealthy amongst the tradesmen would have employed live-in apprentices and journeymen, all of whom would have required accommodation. However, the picture is not quite as simple as this: there are strong reasons for suspecting that the households of some, perhaps many seafaring families likewise included non-family members. It should, for instance, be remembered that in 1565 over half the town's seafarers were not heads of households, and although many of these were probably sons and relations of seafaring householders, others were probably lodgers. Many seafarers, especially those who were unmarried, seem to have lodged in other people's houses rather than run their own households.

The number of people occupying individual dwelling units — regardless of whether members of the family, apprentices/employees or lodgers — would have had a potential, and perhaps marked effect upon the way individual buildings were used. As part of his researches, Mayhew attempted to reconstruct household sizes within the late Elizabethan town based upon the sesse of 1596, covering 355 households.[16] He divided the households into three wealth groups — poorer, middle and wealthier. The poorest of all — those exempt from the sesse — are, of course, absent. He analysed household size from two points of view: family size, including children but excluding servants, and total household size including servants. As he pointed out, for a number of reasons his totals are likely to be underestimates.

Excluding servants (?and lodgers), he found little difference in household size between the three groups: the households of the poorer sort averaged 3.8 persons, the middling sort 3.6 persons, and the wealthier households 4.0 persons. Only a few households (about 7 per cent) comprised one person, though this total is likely to have been much higher amongst those who were exempt from the sesse. Most family households (61.4 per cent) comprised between two and four members, with a further 15.8 per cent, 7.6 per cent and 5.9 per cent comprising five, six and seven persons respectively. Above this size, numbers reduced rapidly: only eight households had either eight or nine persons, none had 10, and only one — a wealthy family — had 11. Not surprising, the household sizes of the poorer families increase only slightly when live-in servants are taken into account: the total persons rises by only 21, from 539 to 560, representing an increase of about 3.9 per cent. Equally un-surprising, the increase amongst the middling sort is more marked — an increase of 50 persons, or 9.7 per cent — and amongst the wealthier group the increase is the highest, with 51 persons added to a family total of 329 (a 15.5 per cent increase). Whereas only two poorer, four middling and three wealthier households were identified with more than seven family members, by including servants the totals rise to four, seven, and eight respectively.

Although household size would have had a profound effect upon life within individual dwellings, only at the higher social levels is it likely to have had much influence upon the design of the buildings. Regardless of household size, the provision of accommodation depended upon the availability not just of space, but of money for construction. If a poor family could not afford to build or rent space, they had no choice but to make do with what they had, despite serious overcrowding. If they earned their living through a trade which needed workspace within the house, this would, by necessity, have taken priority over accommodation: the workspace would have been essential for the family's survival.

Shops, workshops and storage

Regardless of the period, the need to accommodate commercial space had the potential to alter a town's streetscape. The upper walls and roofs may be no different than in a purely residential street, but — depending upon the density — shop fronts and their associated signage (in whatever form) could have a significant impact at eye level, the level most dominant to users. And this is not all: their presence in any quantity would have influenced the way a street was used — the types and numbers of people in the street at given times of the day, and the way in which those people moved along the street.

Commerce is what towns are all about. Today we tend to think of town centres as comprising streets packed with retail shops, with domestic space (if present at all) relegated to the rear parts of the properties or to upper floors. Is this what Tudor towns were like, or are such arrangements a relatively modern phenomenon? Were Tudor shops purely retail outlets or were they something more complex than this? Regardless of specific use, were the central cores of Tudor towns packed with shops, or did they resemble the village streets shown in early 20th-century photographs, in which individual shop fronts were interspersed with domestic frontages? To a large extent the configuration is likely to have varied from town to town depending upon the individual economies: more research is needed before this question can be adequately answered at either a local or national level.[17] Statistics are occasionally quoted: for instance, Derek Keene considered that in the city of Winchester in 1417 a little over half of 839 houses within the town are likely to have contained what could loosely be termed 'shops' (for a definition of 'shop' *see* below). Leigh Alston suggests a similar high proportion within the Suffolk cloth town of Lavenham where perhaps 40 per cent of houses incorporated 'shops'.[18]

Bearing the above points in mind, and the influence commercial space had not just on the streetscape, but also on the internal layouts of the buildings in question, shops and associated commercial storage seem a good point to start this assessment of the way in which Rye's 16th-century buildings were used. Lack of data meant that for Rye's medieval buildings there was little opportunity to do justice to this aspect in Chapter 6, but for the 16th century there is better detail, both architectural and documentary.

Today almost all shops are devoted entirely to retail, selling goods manufactured away from site. In a medieval/Tudor town 'shop' often meant something very different than it does today. As Alston has pointed out, 'The term "shop" is used very loosely in early documents as a place of work or business, and does not imply retail activity.' and adds, 'Specialist retail outlets were few...'.[19] Admittedly, because of the quantity of goods passing through a port, the number of pure retail outlets is likely to have been higher in a place like Rye — the largest trading port in the area — than in an inland town of comparable size. Most of this trade was in the hands of merchants who would have needed safe storage for their goods, a proportion of which was destined for re-shipment or redistribution across the hinterland. In addition to storage, these merchants would have needed dedicated space to transact business and show off their wares. Even so, as Alston explains, most 'shops' mentioned in documentary references were in effect small workshops — places of manufacture and/or processing.

Alston's discussion relates to an area of East

Anglia which specialized in cloth manufacture. As a result, a high proportion of the 'shops' to which he refers were workshops which specialized in the cloth trade. In this his 'shops' varied markedly from those of Rye, which had no specialized manufacturing industry (*see* Chapter 5). Instead, in Rye a wide range of goods were offered by the town's varied craftsmen traders. Whereas much of East Anglia's cloth was manufactured for export, much of the goods produced within Rye's workshops would have been sold direct to the public. Most of Rye's 'shops' are therefore likely to have been combined workshops and sales outlets. The businesses carried on within them were essentially family concerns, in some instances augmented by apprentices and journeymen, who may or may not have lived in. Goods would have been made both to order and on speculation, based upon perceived demand. In some instances the stock was, no doubt, augmented by specialized items bought in from elsewhere for retail.

It has already been pointed out (Chapter 5) that a high proportion of Rye's residents were employed at sea, so it would be wrong to expect an exceptionally high number of 'shops' within the town. But how common were they, and how were they distributed? Luckily, the town records allow this to be answered, at least in part, though only from 1573 onwards.[20] The chief source of corporate revenue at this period was through taxation of the town's economy. Conveniently, this was divided into two parts: sea-based and land-based occupations. The former, administered through the lesser box, is of little concern here: the latter was administered through the great box. Dues were paid by the victualling trades — innkeepers, beer tipplers, butchers, bakers, brewers and fishmongers (or 'feters') — and by other 'shopkeepers'. Until 1602, when the tax-net was increased, 'artificers of divers sorts' were not liable. Until this date tanners, fellmongers, carpenters, shipwrights, masons, pumpmakers, ropemakers and millers were exempt.

A number of persons who are known to have pursued non-exempt occupations are included in the 1576 sesse but are not mentioned in the 1575 list of those running 'shops'. In part this may have been due to specific exemption for one reason or another, but it is likely that in most instances the people concerned did not carry out taxable activities from their premises, either because they worked in the 'shops' of others or, perhaps, because they manufactured solely to order. This point needs to be borne in mind as it means the number of 'shops' recorded in the returns may be understated. Even so, the 91 'shops' listed in 1575 is a surprisingly high number, and this excludes those run by the 29 bakers, butchers and fishmongers taxed separately. It therefore seems safe to assume that in the 1570s there were at least 120 'shops' in the town, suggesting that between one in four and one in five houses had 'shops' associated with them — the actual proportion depends upon the precise number of households in the town at this date. There is an important point which needs to be remembered when considering these ratios. Virtually no houses survive in the former built-up peripheral areas such as Ockman's Lane, Conduit Hill, Ponde Garden and Coggles Lane, away from the main streets (*see* Figure 2.5). If, as seems likely, these areas were primarily residential, making allowance for them is likely to increase the shop to house ratio along the principal streets.

The 1570s was, it must be remembered, the period when Rye was at its height. Subsequently, as the population fell so too did the number of 'shops'. By 1600 only 12 bakers and brewers, 10 fishmongers and butchers and 64 other shopkeepers were returned (*ie* 86 'shops'), and by 1630 the totals had fallen still further to six bakers and brewers, four fishmongers and butchers and 50 other shopkeepers (total 60, half that in 1575). This excludes the 'artificers of divers sorts' added in 1602.

The returns enrolled in the great box are not simply anonymous lists: the 'shops' are entered by 'street' and many of the names of the proprietors are identifiable on the 1576 sesse. The 'streets' are arranged as follows:- 'Landgate to Strandgate', 'Strandgate to the church stile', and 'from John Douce's to the Watchbell Street', the latter being described elsewhere in the return as 'in the Butchery and the Watchbell Street'. These headings give a tolerable indication of the distribution of the 'shops' within the town. By cross-referencing the names to those in the 1576 sesse it is possible to allocate about 70 per cent of the shopkeepers to their ward of residence, allowing further refinement of the topographical locations.[21]

In general the pattern of 'shops' which emerges reflects the occupational structure discussed in Chapter 5. There were virtually no 'shops' in Baddings Ward (dominated by seafaring occupations) and very few — if any — in the residential part of the Wishe suburb. Excluding the victualling trades, 54 'shops' were returned 'from Landgate to Strandgate' of which 26 were in the eastern part of High Street (Landgate Ward) and 23 in the western part (Standgate Ward). A further two were occupied by residents of Middlestreet Ward: these were located either in the northern part of West Street, or perhaps they were rented premises in High Street, and thus located away from the occupiers' places of residence. Three of the occupiers lived in Watchbell Ward, but these 'shops' were probably sited in that part of Watchbell Ward which spilled over onto The Strand, just outside Strandgate.

All 21 'shops' listed as being between Strandgate and the church stile would have been located either in

Mermaid Street or in the southern part of West Street: all were in Middlestreet Ward. Today, apart from The Mermaid Inn, both Mermaid Street and West Street are exclusively residential, indicating a marked change since the 16th century. Sixteen of the proprietors listed in this area have been identified in the 1576 sesse, and although 12 of these lived in Middlestreet Ward, the other four did not. A mercer lived in Watchbell Ward, a draper in Strandgate Ward, a cooper in Landgate Ward and a person of uncertain occupation in Baddings Ward. Presumably these people leased shops which were separate from their houses, perhaps in the (assumed) lettable shop units within the street range of the former Shurley mansion [51] just to the west of the church (*see* below).

The 16 non-victualling 'shops' entered under the head 'from John Douce's to the Watchbell Street' were dispersed across present day East Street, Lion Street, Market Street, Church Square and Watchbell Street, and therefore covered both Market and Baddings Wards. Of the nine names identified in the 1576 sesse all but one (a Baddings Ward resident) lived in Market Ward.

It should be remembered that the above totals need to be enhanced to take into account the 'shops' operated by bakers, butchers and fishmongers (regarding which *see* below). Obviously, the brewers and tipplers (who were included within the victualling trades) would have needed work premises, but it seems unlikely that their brewhouses and taprooms would have been described as 'shops' within contemporary documents. Even so, as discussed below, there are reasons for suspecting that at least one taproom incorporated what looks to have been a standard shop front. Although bakehouses are unlikely to have been termed 'shops', the premises from which the cooked products were sold most likely were. In this regard too it is difficult to make definitive rulings, for a kitchen-like area at 4-5 Market Street [38] incorporates Rye's best-preserved shop front, suggesting that here the product may have been baked and sold from the same room (*see* below).

Although most 'shops' were located in the houses of their proprietors, as hinted earlier, this was not always the case. Two important groups whose 'shops' seem usually (if not always) to have been separate from their houses are those of the butchers and fishmongers. By statute the butchers of the town were compelled to keep no shop other than within the town butchery, located in the marketplace in Market Ward.[22] At this time the butchery was most likely sited in the subsequently abandoned western part of the marketplace, near the church, to the west of Lion Street (*see* Chapter 2). Although it is possible that some butchers lived over their shops, the butchery was more likely a row of quite minor single-storied structures — Mayhew refers to it as a 'row of butchers' shops'.[23] Even so, most of the butchers lived nearby (*see* Figure 5.6). In 1576 shops (plural) in the butchery were occupied by Robert Marshe, butcher, who lived in Middlestreet Ward, whilst another, also in the butchery, was occupied by Edward Harry, butcher, who lived in Baddings Ward.[24] The 1575 return to the great box lists eight butchers, all but one of whom — Thomas Harry, perhaps a close relation of Edward Harry — are identifiable in the 1576 sesse. Both Robert Marshe of Middlestreet Ward and Edward Harrye of Baddings Ward are included. Of the others, three lived in Market Ward and two in Baddings Ward.

The fishmongers (feters) seem to have kept shop exclusively in or near the fishmarket, down on The Strand, though most lived elsewhere in town.[25] Even in 1668 several rows of shops and stalls still remained in this area, and others were at that time annotated as having been taken down (*see* Chapter 2). In 1575 two of these rows were in corporation ownership. In a rental of that year six of the 11 shops in the two rows were occupied by feters who lived in Baddings and Market Wards. All these men are listed amongst the 13 feters included in the return to the great box: of these two lived in Landgate Ward, one each in Strandgate, Market and Middlestreet Wards and six in Baddings Ward, south of the church, but only two in Watchbell Ward, in which ward the fishmarket was located. Two other men who leased town 'shops' in the rows were merchants who lived in Baddings and Strandgate Wards, and two were tailors who lived in Strandgate and Middlestreet Wards.

The presence of tailors down on The Strand is a surprise, though the likelihood that they were dual economists involved in a second occupation which benefitted from a 'shop' located on the Strand has to be borne in mind. No doubt John Clarke, cloth merchant (whose house and draper's/mercer's shop was located in the High Street) would have benefitted from the use of a Strand-side shop, for at his death in 1558 he shared his only bedchamber with '3,000 dried herrings, 20 seams of 'dorsers' (fish baskets), 200 (ft.) of new nets and a small barrel of vinegar'. It is interesting to note that the lofts above the town's shops were mostly occupied by fishermen and mariners who lived away from the Strand and were either masters or owners of vessels: it is assumed they used their lofts as safe storage for equipment.[26]

It was evidently not only the butchers and fishmongers who occupied 'shops' away from their homes. If the interpretation of the row of units associated with the former Shurley mansion [51] as shops is correct, these too must have been used by people who lived elsewhere. As already noted, in this respect it is perhaps no coincidence that a number of people recorded in the 1575 return to the great box as having 'shops' in this part of town lived in other wards.

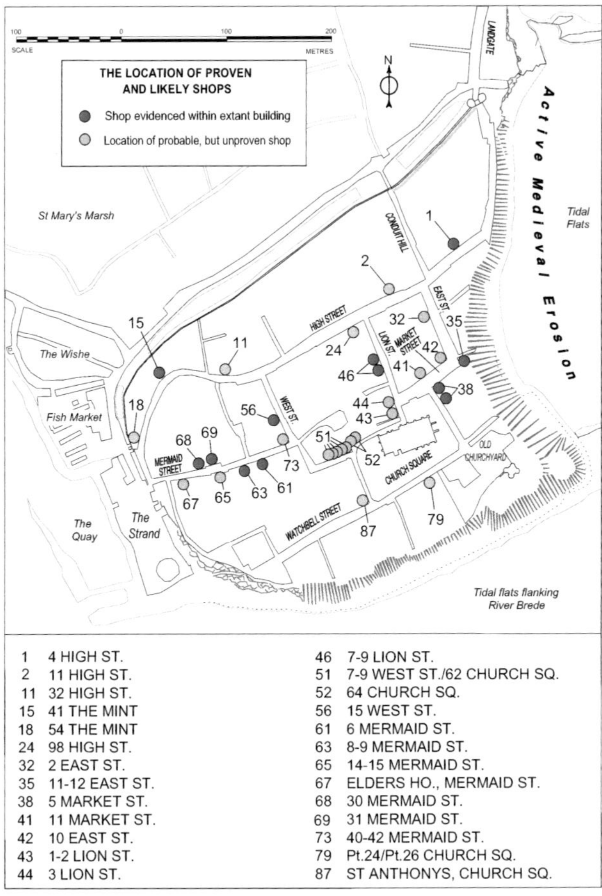

Fig. 7.23
The location of known and probable shops as suggested from architectural evidence.

Documentary reference to just such a 'shop' is found in a deed of partition dated 1589 relating to a messuage on the east side of a street. By that date it was already divided into three separate occupancies: a messuage occupied by John Bannister, a shop and garden occupied by Martin Hayward, and a third part occupied by [blank] Gillam, cooper.[27] Examples of 'shops' of this type which were separated from the occupiers' houses are known throughout England. However, as Alston notes, they were always in a minority.[28]

In summary, whether incorporated within the proprietor's house or not, the 1575 return indicates that at that date there was a 'shop' to every three or four houses in each of Landgate, Strandgate, Market and Middlestreet Wards. There were also large numbers of 'shops' and 'lofts' down on the Strand. Away from the Strand and its associated fishmarket there seem to have been very few 'shops' within the residential part of Wishe Ward, and similarly few in the largely seafaring district which made up Baddings Ward, in the area known today as Church Square and Watchbell Street.

Knowing that large numbers of 'shops' existed in Rye is one thing, identifying them on the ground is an entirely different matter. The same problem was encountered when considering commercial space within the town during the medieval period. Because almost all evidence at ground-floor level in the front walls of Rye's buildings has been destroyed, rarely are there any indications of shop fronts. Without such evidence it is usually impossible to tell whether or not a front service room was used as a 'shop', and the same applies to rooms built against the street beyond the high end of a hall — this is as true of the 16th century as it had been during the medieval period. Luckily, increased pressure on street frontages during the 16th century meant that in new-built houses of the period more creative internal layouts needed to be adopted. In some of these it is possible to detect rooms which were, apparently, designed for use as 'shops'.

Rarely where an existing building was adapted without reconstruction is it possible to detect a newly-formed 'shop', though there must have been many such examples. One of these seems to have been 32 The Mint [11] where an existing hall was divided axially so as to insert what is assumed to have been a 'shop' between the sized-down room and the street, and the same can be seen at 15 West Street [56]. That other instances occurred is indicated by a deed of partition dated 1582 relating to a house at Whites Corner, on the junction of West Street and High Street, occupied today by the Natwest Bank (85 High Street [23]). The deed relates to a lease by a feter of specified rooms, including a hall, parlour, kitchen and chambers, to a tailor. Permission was included for the tenant to 'translate the foresaid parlour into a shop' and 'erect a new pen[t]house over the said shop, to keep away the weather from it'.[29] Without the survival of the shop front and its pentice roof it is highly unlikely that such a conversion would be recognizable from the architectural evidence — there would be nothing to distinguish the parlour's new 'shop' use from its original function.

This combination of purpose-designed 'shops' contained within areas which are otherwise indistinguishable from domestic rooms, and buildings incorporating domestic rooms which were converted into 'shops' is likely to mean that a substantial number of 'shops' have escaped detection. Even so, the number missed may be less than imagined, for the sample of houses included within the present study contains 29 instances in which 'shops' are either proven or are suspected. This equates to approximately a quarter of surviving houses, a figure not dissimilar to that suggested by the documents (*see* above).

The locations of the known and suspected 'shops' are plotted in Figure 7.23, whilst simplified plans of the buildings in question are presented in Figure 7.24 in which the likely 'shop' areas are depicted in pink,

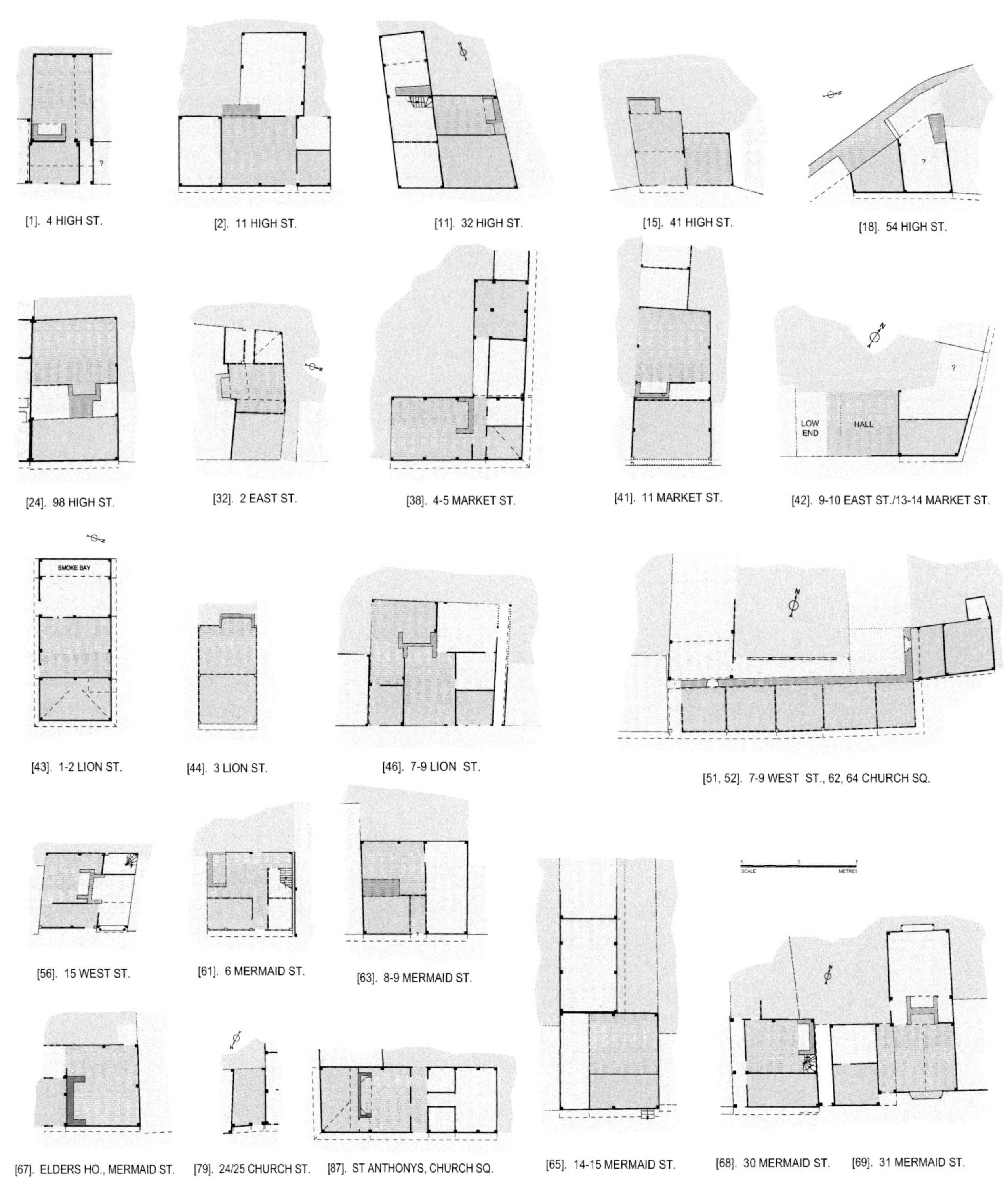

Fig. 7.24
Simplified small-scale plans showing locations of likely 'shops' [shown in pink].

contrasting with dark grey for the halls. It could be misleading that all the examples illustrated in Figure 7.24 are located against the street: Alston has noted many workshop-type 'shops' in East Anglia, located at the rear of houses, and even on first floors. In the absence of shop windows, such 'shops' (used as workshops) would not be detectable. One example, within a fragmentary rear range of *c.*1600, may exist at 4-6 Lion Street [45].

As is indicated by Figure 7.24, in common with

other parts of England the identified 'shops' tend to be small. They range in floor area from about 9 square metres or *c.*100 square feet (usually about 3 metres by 3 metres or roughly 10 feet square) in the case of those which occupy what otherwise appear to be standard service rooms, to about three times that area in the largest examples. These have floor areas of between 25 and 33 square metres (*c.*270-*c.*355 square feet): equal in size to some halls. Examples of the former are 11 High Street [11], 4-5 Market Street [38] and 7-9 Lion Street [46], whilst the largest in the group are 32 High Street [11] 41 The Mint [15] and 11 Market Street [41].[30] If shops of larger size existed within the town, they have not been detected. It should be noted that many of the shops illustrated in Figure 7.24 are recognizable only because they have been squeezed into the front of the house, relegating the hall to the rear. The wide variety of sizes should not be surprising given the multiplicity of uses to which the 'shops' were put (*see* above and Chapter 5).

Of significance is the fact that in only 15 examples does the 'shop' take up the entire frontage (excluding entrance passages), and seven of these are located within a single building — the street range of the former Shurley mansion at 7-9 West Street/ 62, 64 Church Square [51, 52]. In the other 14 examples a substantial part of the frontage was in domestic use and thus, even if adjacent buildings incorporated 'shops', the shop fronts would have been interspersed with facades of non-commercial appearance.

In only nine instances is anything known of the layout of the shop-front itself, and in four of these the data is restricted to the location of one window or a doorway only. A number of doorways are evidenced connecting the 'shop' to other parts of the house — for instance, at 4 High Street [1], 11 High Street [2] 41 High Street [15], 4-5 Market Street [38], and 6 Mermaid Street [61] — whilst in others, such as 7 Lion Street [46] and 15 West Street, the house itself could be entered only by passing through the 'shop'. At 30 Mermaid Street [68] both the shop and house were entered via doorways off a through-passage leading to the rear garden. In other instances it is uncertain whether the 'shop' could be reached from other parts of the house, and in at least one instance — 8-9 Lion Street [46] — it can be shown that there was no interconnecting internal doorway.

It is from this latter building that the best evidence for the form of the shop-front comes. One of the smallest 'shops' known within the town, it was lit by a pair of adjacent equal-width openings with a narrow entrance doorway at the southern end, sited adjacent to the doorway leading into the hall. All jambs have been removed, and thus the cill-level of the two openings is not known: nor is there any evidence to tell whether the openings were square headed or incorporated arches. The 'shop' of similar size within the second dwelling in this building — 7 Lion Street [46] — seems to have had a shop front of similar design, but in this instance access to the remainder of the house was through the shop, via the shared entrance door, whereas at 8-9 there was no interconnection, and thus, if needed, the shop could have been leased out separate from the house.

At 4 High Street [1] the mid 16th-century 'shop' had three equal-width openings in its front wall, to the side of which was an entrance giving access to a passage leading to the house behind. The two outer openings were certainly shop fronts, fitted with external shutters which closed into rebates. If there was public access into the shop it must have been via a central doorway, but, given the equal *c.*1.20 metre (4 feet) internal widths of the three openings, it seems far more likely there were three shop windows and that the only means of access into the 'shop' was via the doorway leading forwards from the hall. Similar evidence exists within the late 15th-century crosswing at The Standard, 41 The Mint [41], though in this instance the central opening is narrower than those which flank it — *c.*0.85 metres (2 feet 9 inches) compared to *c.*1.40 metres (4 feet 7 inches) for the outer openings — and thus the likelihood must be that there was a central doorway flanked by openings. This would be an unusual arrangement for a shop front — neither Alston nor Stenning show examples of this design in their published works, though more recent work by Stenning indicates that a few shop fronts of this type exist in England and he has also noted continental parallels.[31]

The shop-front is not the only unusual feature of the 'shop' at 41 The Mint [15]: it is also the only proven instance where the room was heated from the outset. This, together with the large size of the room and the layout of the early 16th-century additions suggests that the building probably functioned as an inn from an early date. If this were so, there is the distinct possibility that the 'shop' was designed as a high-quality taproom.

A likely inn of *c.*1525 which incorporated not one, but two 'shops' is 4-5 Market Street [38], later known as the Flushing Inn. Furthermore, in this instance neither 'shop' appears to have served as the taproom and neither seems to have been separately leased out — both were part of the main house. The shop-front in the Church Square elevation is the only one in Rye which is today easily visible from the streets: it retains its arched-headed doorway with the remains of one arched-headed opening beside it. The room they served is quite large and was entered from the cross-passage of the main range via a passage which extended down the side of an un-heated parlour of very similar layout to that at The Mermaid [72], of similar date. In its location, the Church Square 'shop' equates to the

Fig. 7.25
The specialized shop front at 31 Mermaid Street [69] showing the large windows (left) and doorway (right) boarded up, prior to restoration.

kitchen range at The Mermaid and would have been ideally placed to serve the main part of the house. It must remain speculation, but could this 'shop' have doubled as the (assumed) inn's kitchen and a cook shop? Of course, this does not explain the second shop within the building, located within the front service room, the evidence for the windows of which is still visible from the interior, occupying the corner and looking out towards both Church Square and Market Street. Assuming the building was indeed an inn at this period (and it should be stressed that the point remains unproven) the presence of this second shop is not as unusual as it might seem. The leading inn-keepers of the town were amongst the most wealthy of the residents at this time and several were, in addition, important merchants and factors for London businessmen: others combined their inn-keeping with a second, less important occupation (*see* 'Inns and tippling houses' below).

Another non-standard 'shop' arrangement is that at 31 Mermaid Street [69], a high-quality merchant's house built in 1576. Here the 'shop' projects from the main part of the facade and was entered from the street via a doorway located in the return wall next to the front door, within an unenclosed 'porch'. The adjacent windows, partially visible in Figure 7.25 — a photograph taken when the house was semi-ruinous — are in the form of two large four-pane glazed openings separated from one another by a moulded king mullion. Today, most likely this 'shop' would be termed an 'office' in that it probably served as the nerve centre for the owner's mercantile activities. In 1689 the then merchant owner, Samuel Jeake, built a separate storehouse (warehouse) further down the street on the opposite side, but in the late 16th century it seems more likely that goods were stored in the spacious garret area of the house itself.

Despite Rye's need for copious storage space, the town's deeds contain no references to purpose-built private store houses until the second half of the 17th century, though there was a corporation-owned storehouse on the Strand. This apparent lack of private storehouses probably explains the numerous spacious garrets which still survive within the town, the capacities of many of which were deliberately increased by elevating the wallplates above the level of the garret floor. The earliest recognized example of this use of elevated wallplates is in the early 16th century at 41 The Mint [15], though in this instance the garret was probably intended as low-quality accommodation. Most belong to the second half of the century — for examples *see* Chapters 9-14.

Until the second quarter of the 16th century most first-floor chambers within the town were open to the roof. One of the earliest garrets which seems to have been designed specifically for storage is that at 24 Landgate [107], built *c.*1525 and shown with a loading hatch in its front roof-slope in Van Dyck's illustration of the building made in the 1630s (*see* Figure 14.13). Earlier examples exist elsewhere. For instance, storage lofts dating from the 14th and/or 15th centuries have been recorded within the port town of Sandwich, Kent,[32] but in Rye medieval storage appears to have been confined to first-floor chambers. As noted earlier with regards to John Clarke, for some this continued to be the case until at least the middle years of the 16th century. One building which may have been purposely designed for commercial use in which the entire first floor was perhaps given over to storage is 8 East Street [33], built *c.*1500, though it must be accepted that there could be other explanations for the building's unusual design.

Whereas storage within chambers and garrets would have been ideal for many kinds of goods, perishables which needed to be kept cool would have been better housed within subterranean or semi-subterranean cellars. Ignoring the early vaulted cellars, a number survive from the 16th century[33] and some, especially along the northern side of High Street and in Mermaid Street, are substantial. Furthermore, a number have good access direct from the street. Some of these cellars could have belonged to inns, others may have been used by the town's merchants. Indeed, as will become obvious from the section which follows, the principal inns were mostly in the hands of substantial merchants, and thus the distinction between the two is in any case likely to be blurred, if not invisible.

Inns and tippling houses

Two buildings within the town — 24-25 High Street [5] (now The White Vine) and 35-38 Mermaid Street [72] (The Mermaid) — can be identified from their architecture and layout as having been designed and used as inns during the 16th century. To these can be added a number of others which, for one reason or another, are considered likely to have been designed or adapted to function as such during the same period. In this respect, both 41 The Mint [15] and 4-5 Market Street [38] have already been mentioned. Operating today as The Standard, its early 16th-century layout makes it almost certain that 41 The Mint was already an inn by that date, though its operating sign at that time remains unknown. Likewise, the present name of the eastern part of 4-5 Market Street came into being only in 1739 when the then tenant, John Igglesden, obtained a licence for it as the 'Flushing Inn'.[34] Assuming, as its layout suggests, that it was already an inn by the 16th century, this name may reflect its earlier sign, but this is improbable. One of the problems in identifying the locations of the inns and tippling houses is the speed at which both the proprietors and signs moved from one building to another. This is not a peculiarity of Rye, but a feature of many towns and villages. Inns and victualling houses continually opened and closed and often changed names as landlords moved from one establishment to another.[35] To illustrate this point, one of Rye's present-day leading hotels, The George (which occupies 12-14 Lion Street and 98 High Street [24, 47, 48, 49]) came into being in its present form and under its present name only in the 17th century. Even so, part of the complex (14 Lion Street [49]) seems already to have been an inn by the latter part of the 16th century. It traded under the sign of 'The Red Lion', which itself should not be confused with the later inn of that name which stood at the opposite end of the same street.[36] Although The George took its present name only in the 17th century, there was already a substantial inn of that name in the town during the 16th century, but it was located at 9-10 Market Street [40].[37]

Another problem regarding inns is the high number of licensed establishments which existed within the town, ranging in size from leading inns such as 24-25 High Street [5] and 35-38 Mermaid Street [72] to minor drinking establishments. In 1575 no fewer than 37 people were licensed either as beer tipplers or vintners (or in three instances both) to which should be added four unlicensed premises. Most were run by dual economists. For example, eight of the principal establishments were operated by merchants or by the widows of merchants: most had seafaring interests and several were members of the town elite. In addition, there were three feters (one of whom was also Town Sergeant), two tailors, a cordwainer, a painter, a rippier, a chandler, a shipwright, a lighterman and three 'poor' widows. Only three of the 37 persons were regarded primarily as innholders.[38]

Of the premises licensed in 1575, 21 were located either in the High Street/The Mint or on The Strand. Of these, between eight and ten were in Landgate Ward, between six and eight in Strandgate Ward, and four on or near The Strand. Six were in Middlestreet Ward (in Mermaid Street and West Street) and ten 'in the Butchery and Watchbell Street', of which three were in Market Ward, six in Baddings Ward and one in Watchbell Ward.[39]

Whereas the high number of tippling houses in the town is no doubt largely explained by the size of its population and the number of visiting seafarers requiring liquid refreshment and 'entertainment' whilst in port, the number of inns offering accommodation was most likely primarily influenced by the port's role as a trading centre and as an important passenger route to the continent. There would have been a continual trickle of travellers requiring accommodation whilst trading, or whilst awaiting ship. In 1574 the town's licensed premises had within them 94 beds for the use of strangers.[40] On occasions travellers awaiting passage would have been marooned in town for days due to bad weather or lack of appropriate vessels in port. For them such delays would have been annoying. For us they were fortuitous: they were doubtless the reason for Van Dyck's sketches of the town made in the 1630s.

The total for licensed premises in 1575 appears to represent a high: the typical number during the 16th century was usually between 26 and 30.[41] In their general external appearance and internal layout the lesser drinking establishments would no doubt have been indistinguishable from their neighbours, and the same is likely to have been true also of the minor inns. However, the principal inns had well-equipped kitchens, areas for dining/feasting and entertaining, and suites of well-appointed letting chambers. It was in these establishments, for example, that the corporation provided hospitality to visiting dignitaries.[42] In some towns the courtyards of principal inns were used for holding plays and other organized entertainments, and this may on occasions have been the case here, but such entertainments seem mainly to have been held in 'The pageant house at Landgate'.[43]

On account of the more select nature of the letting chambers, perhaps the number of beds for the use of strangers would have been fewer within the principal inns than within some middle-sized inns. These latter buildings are more likely to have had chambers set aside as common dormitories. Such a dormitory may survive at 14-15 Mermaid Street [65], though the possibility of the chamber having been a public meeting room or even a storeroom/workshop cannot be ruled out. To judge from its internal layout, this building is likely to have been purpose-designed as an inn early in the 16th century and was, apparently, trading as 'The Swan Inn' in 1658 — if it was an inn earlier, its 16th-century sign is unknown.[44] Use as a dormitory could be argued for the large chamber which occupied the entire first floor at 8 East Street [33] (now 'The Union'), though in this instance the space is, perhaps, more likely to have been a storehouse serving the rooms below.

There are other buildings which, on account of their layout, could have been designed as licensed premises, either with or without letting chambers. In this respect reference has already been made to 41 The Mint [15] which it is thought may have been designed in the late 15th century with a large beer shop/taproom, accessed both direct from the street and from the adjacent hall. There are three other buildings where a similar function is possible, including the neighbouring building (39-40 The Mint [14]) which has two very lofty front rooms of similar size to each other, linked by a high-quality doorway sited part-way along the dividing wall, and fitted with moulded joists. Both rooms were apparently accessible direct from the street. This configuration has many similarities to its neighbour, and also to the arrangement within the western two bays of 9-10 Market Street [40], known to have traded as 'The George' in the late 16th century. A somewhat similar arrangement of two equal-size rooms located against the street exists at 16-16a West Street [57] where again both rooms have moulded ceiling joists, and in this case the second of the two rooms is embellished with an impressive wall painting (*see* Figure 12.17). The plan at 34-36 Church Square [83] is similar. It is the inclusion of what might be termed good-quality 'public rooms' which make these examples stand out. At 15 High Street [4] it is the inclusion of multiple chambers, arranged on the building's two upper storeys, which suggests a possible inn use: in this it is not dissimilar to the three-storeyed building — 14 Lion Street [49] — which stands almost opposite and almost certainly traded as 'The Red Lion'. Today 15 High Street is known as 'The Mariners', but the origin of this name is unclear — could this be 'The Three Mariners' mentioned in 16th-century documents, reinstated as the present name based upon deed evidence?

Without detailed documentary research the identification of the above buildings as licensed premises must remain speculative. Because of their size, the premier inns are easier to identify, though even here care is needed in not mistaking an urban mansion for an inn. With its central courtyard and gallery, such a misinterpretation could easily be made regarding the former Shurley mansion at 7-9 West Street [51]. That the layouts should be similar is hardly surprising: a common function of urban mansions owned by courtiers or aristocrats was that of a private inn catering to the needs of the owner's friends, associates and officials.[45]

Given the size and layout of 7-9 West Street, it is no surprise to find that by the 1650s the principal part of the mansion had been converted into a sizable inn known as 'The Queens Arms'. Indeed, bearing in mind that other principal inns, such as 'The Mermaid' [72] were run by successful merchants, it is possible that the building's new use as a public inn dated back to the late 16th century, during its tenancy by the Rye merchant, James Milles. By 1658 the mansion had already been divided into three occupancies: in 1660 that part in use as 'The Queens Arms' was in the proprietorship of the alien innholder Lewes Pascall, and by 1662 the tenancy had passed to William Marson, assessed for it in hearth tax at ten flues.[46]

Two principal inns

The Mermaid [72] is one of the inns Van Dyck is likely to have used during his stays in Rye. One of the town's most important and best-known establishments, it has experienced greater continuity than most: it still trades under its early name and still occupies its purpose-designed 16th-century building, though it should be stressed it has not been in continual use as an inn: by 1860 the building was divided into cottages and at one time it served as a poor house![47]

Ignoring an earlier vaulted cellar, the present building was erected in the early 16th century, most likely by the jurat innkeeper Richard Pedyll (died 1536). The plan of this initial phase is illustrated in Figure 7.20. It is a large, continuously-jettied building with a long street frontage. Internally it is designed to a 'textbook' three-cell layout, but with a covered wagon-way beyond its services, giving access to a rear yard. To the rear of the inn's main range, behind the service rooms, is a contemporary rear range housing a well-appointed parlour for the use of guests, with a corridor divided off at the side to provide independent access to a rear detached kitchen/service range. The building's use as an inn is further indicated by the serving hatch incorporated within the cross-passage wall of the buttery — the rear of the two service rooms. The buttery itself is linked directly to the early barrel-vaulted wine cellar. On the first floor were five chambers, plus perhaps others in the detached service block. Beyond the wagon entrance is a slightly earlier house — 34 Mermaid Street [71] which could represent the proprietor's private residence. It is small but well finished.

It was not until the third or fourth quarter of the 16th century that the building was further enlarged, integrating the main structure to the until now detached kitchen/service block. The enlargements — carried out over two phases — improved the catering facilities and considerably increased the number of good-quality letting chambers. By the time of its completion, The Mermaid had grown to incorporate no fewer than ten chambers plus a series of lesser-status garret areas. As the plan illustrated in Figure 7.21 shows, it had by now developed a courtyard layout with enclosed passages, allowing independent access to all six of its principal letting rooms. The proprietor during this period was the innkeeper and merchant William Didsbury (died 1593), a jurat who, in addition to running The Mermaid, was an importer of goods (principally wine) and a factor for London Merchants. Didsbury was described as 'a man of good credit' who kept the Mermaid for merchants and the wealthier sort of visitor, the names all being registered in his book.[48] By the early 1660s the proprietor was Michael Cadman, jurat innholder, who was assessed 11 flues for this property: the assessment seems to have included adjacent 34 Mermaid Street [71], suggesting it was still in use as private quarters for the proprietor.

A second purpose-designed inn of considerable architectural note is 24-25 High Street [5], the eastern half of which is today known as The White Vine, but formerly as Holloway House. An inn called The Vine traded on the northern side of High Street during the 16th century, though it should be stressed that to date no firm link has been established between this and the present building. Bearing in mind that the upstanding buildings at 24-25 High Street are of one period, it is perhaps no surprise that the method of accessing the six first-floor letting chambers is more sophisticated than the somewhat contrived arrangement found at The Mermaid. Comparison of the plans of the two properties included in Figure 7.21 makes clear that, despite the common feature of an enclosed court, this is a somewhat different inn from The Mermaid. It is not only more compact in its design, but provides a greater variety of chamber sizes — three good heated chambers of quality and three of considerably smaller size, only one of which was heated. In addition to these, as at The Mermaid there is a collection of garrets, presumably used to provide lower-class accommodation. In this instance the garret spaces are interconnected and their main walls are stilted in order to give improved usable space. The proprietor's quarters appear to have been spacious and to have been kept entirely separate from the public rooms, being located within what was, in effect, a separate house occupying the western end of the complex. As has already been noted, the same seems also to have been the case at The Mermaid, but there the private quarters appear to have been less spacious.

The inn of James Pearsall

Both The Mermaid [72] and 24-25 High Street [5] give a good impression of the size and architectural splendour of Rye's leading late 16th-century inns, but can portray them only as empty shells. This shortcoming can, to some extent, be redressed by a probate inventory of 1593 which lists the contents of the inn run by James Pearsall, gentleman innholder and merchant of London and Rye.[49] In 1576 his inn had been located in Market Ward (either in East Street, Market Street or Lion Street) and Mayhew has identified him as living in the same area, in Market Street, at his death, though whether in the same inn is at present unclear. Another inventory, that of Francis Daniell, butcher and innholder, taken less than a year earlier contains a remarkably similar configuration of rooms. Indeed, the configuration is so similar as to suggest the two documents may relate to the same building. If so, at his death Pearsall had only recently taken over and upgraded the furnishings of the inn.[50]

Given that the location is unknown, it is possible that Pearsall's inn not only survives, but is included within these pages — one candidate must be the principal part of 4-5 Market Street/2, 4 Church Square (Flushing Inn) [35]. Although the building was not huge, the inventory nonetheless indicates that it was sizable. On the ground floor it had seven rooms (Hall, Little Parlour, Great Parlour, Kitchen, two Butteries and Entry) with a further six chambers above (Hall Chamber, Old Chamber, Middle Chamber, Lyon Chamber, Star Chamber and Green Chamber). Bearing in mind the number of ground-floor rooms, it seems likely that all six chambers were located on the first floor and were either open to the roof or the roof spaces were unused. There is reference to a cellar and to a backside (rear yard), as well as a stable, 'ostry' (tack room), wheat loft and hay loft. Some items, such as linen and plate, are listed at the end of the inventory and thus their locations within the house are unknown.

The entry — the point at which the house was entered from the street — was evidently more extensive than a medieval-style cross-passage, for it had space within it for a table, dresser and a second, 'little table', but nevertheless the contents do not suggest a room of any great size. Perhaps it was a cross-passage enlarged slightly to one side of a chimney, for the rooms listed next to it are 'the two butteries'. This wording is consistent with a pair of medieval-style service rooms.

They contained the sort of goods which are to be expected within service rooms of this type — two basins, two chargers, ten platters, two little basins, five pewter dishes, nine saucers and two porringers, one 'pottle pot', two quart pots, two pint pots, one half-pint pot, a firkin of butter, an old table and a pair of trestles, in one of the two rooms: a great brass pot, a 'lymback' (an alembic, or still), three old flower pots, a broken ewer, a brine tub, four shelves, one table and a pair of trestles in the other room. Given that the two rooms were called butteries, the surprise, perhaps, is that no barrels of drink are mentioned (but *see* below).

If the house conformed to the usual plan, even loosely, the hall would have been located on the opposite side of the entry to the butteries. It served as the heart of the house and, to judge from the mention of a long table with a form and a long settle, it was used for dining. In addition to the table and its associated seating the room contained another form, a great cupboard, a joined chest and additional seating — a chair, a little chair and a little stool. The room was decorated with a 'curtain painted' (ie. a decorative painted wall hanging) and there was a 'curtain for a window' — an unusual item at this time. Extra comfort was given by a wrought carpet, two needlework cushions and a leather cushion. A sword and dagger were presumably displayed for show, hopefully out of reach of any revellers! There was a fireplace, indicated by the mention of two andirons.

Although the inventory refers to two parlours, the Little Parlour was evidently in use as a bedroom at the time of Pearsall's death, for it contained a bedstead with a featherbed, two bolsters and two blankets (one white and one red). Additionally, the room was furnished with a joined table, a form, and a joined settle and had painted cloths on the walls. Here also the presence of two andirons indicates that the room was heated.

In contrast to the Little Parlour, the Great Parlour functioned in the way one would expect at this period: that is, as a room to relax in. It was clearly a comfortable, well-furnished apartment which contained two joined tables with their frames, a form, three stools, two chairs and a cupboard with a cushion upon it and a cupboard cloth. There is reference to 'two table pictures' and to 'two little curtains of buckram' as well as three nutcrackers. In deference to this room's high status, here the two andirons in the fireplace were of brass.

The final ground-floor room was the kitchen, which was exceptionally well appointed. No fewer than 44 brass vessels are mentioned (all listed) plus two pewter candlesticks, a cistern of lead, a gridiron, a slice, a flesh hook, two stone mortars, crocks, *etc*, together with eight spits and other listed fire goods (including a bread grate). The furniture is itemized as a chopping board, a dresser, two shelves, a table with frame, a form and a little cupboard. The room also contained a pair of boots!

The contents of the cellar make clear why the butteries had no drink barrels within them — it contained a tun-and-a-half of ale and beer, with the stallages. Bearing in mind that in 1583 Pearsall was one of the few people within the town licensed to sell wine, surprisingly, there is no reference to wine in the inventory.[51]

Only five of the first-floor chambers were evidently in use as bed chambers though the sixth — the chamber over the hall — did contain a pair of curtains for a bed, but these were listed with other sundry items of cloth and linen. The furniture in this chamber was restricted to a table with its carpet and frame, two forms (one described as green), two small stools of needlework, a small 'cipers' box and a 'picture in oil of a knot of roses'.

The five bedchambers give no indication of their locations within the house beyond the fact that, presumably, the Middle Chamber was sandwiched between two others. The remaining four are referred to as Old, Lyon, Star, and Green, the latter three perhaps referring to their mode of decoration. The first of the bedchambers to be listed is the Old Chamber. This contained two joined bedsteads and a truckle bedstead, the former two with featherbeds and the latter having a flock bed. They are listed with their bolsters, coverlet, blankets and quilt. The room was heated by 'a joined garth to burn coles' but tantalizingly there are no further hints as to what was meant by this phrase. Ten old chests contained a collection of linen valued at 33s.4d., but no other furniture.

Although the contents of the Middle Chamber were valued at a lesser sum than those in the Old Chamber, this room was clearly of higher status, especially when allowance is made for the fact that almost half the value within the Old Chamber related to the chests and their contents. Furthermore, whereas the Old Chamber contained three bedsteads (admittedly one a truckle) within this chamber there was only one, and (in addition to its featherbed and bed cloths) in this instance it was fitted with buckram curtains. As in the Middle Chamber, this room too contained chests — one great and one small — but, in addition, it was furnished with a table and form and here there were painted cloths on the walls.

To judge from its contents, the largest letting chamber in the house was the Lyon Chamber. In this instance there were two beds in use, one a great joined bedstead and the other a small bedstead. Both were supplied with featherbeds, bolsters, coverlets, blankets and pillows, but only one of the two (possibly the great bedstead) was fitted with a pair of curtains, in this instance of saye and described as old. A truckle bedstead was evidently in store under one of the other beds, for there is no reference to it having a bed or linen. Other furnishings within the room were a square table, a joined chair, two old quilts, a straw chair and painted cloths on the walls.

Although valued at half that of the Lyon Chamber, the Star Chamber was, perhaps, more select in that it contained only one bed; a joined bedstead with mattress, featherbed, bolster, coverlet and two old blankets, but no curtains. The other furnishings were sparse, being a joined table and a chest containing linen. The lack of any reference to painted cloths need not means the walls were bare, as the room could have been panelled or may have been decorated with wall paintings.

The best chamber within the house was without doubt the Green Chamber, but, given that it contained a caliver complete with flask and touchbox, a sword, and two head pieces, this surely served as James Pearsall's own bed chamber. It was equipped with a great joined bedstead, a featherbed, blankets and coverlet, and around the bed hung a pair of curtains of white and red. In addition to the bed, the room was furnished with a joined table, three stools, two little stools of needlework, and a chair with a cushion. There were two chests containing linen and clothes, including a doublet and a pair of leather breaches. The walls were decorated with painted cloths and there was also a painted picture. Ignoring the reference in the Old Chamber to the 'joined garth to burn coles', this is the only chamber which can be demonstrated as having a fireplace; it contained a pair of andirons. It would seem that James Pearsall, gentleman innholder and merchant of London and Rye, kept within his house a very comfortable bed-sitting chamber reserved for his own use.

Taken together, the two surviving inns and Pearsall's inventory give a tolerable picture of what the town's principal inns were like during the Elizabethan era. In comparison to the many lesser inns, taverns, alehouses and taphouses which existed within the town at this period, establishments of this calibre and size would always have been few in number, but, as the documentary record shows, these three examples by no means stood alone.[52]

Domestic Areas in Rye's Houses

As in many other towns, amongst the poor there were those who could afford to live in nothing more than a single room, within which all activities had to take place. In 1565, for example, John Ripley, a poor man, was excused his rent on the garret within which he was living, and in 1594 four poor widows were each renting lofts in the fishmarket.[53] However, excepting poor persons who were living alone, most — even amongst the poor families — seem to have had a living room (hall) and a bed chamber, and usually at least one service area. An example, apparently without service space, is Thomas Roben, a poor fisherman who, at his death in 1594, occupied a house which contained a hall, chamber and garret only. The contents of his house will be discussed later: what is important here is that in terms of the number of rooms, Roben's house was smaller than any of the surviving examples recorded for this period.

Halls and parlours (see Figures 7.14 to 7.22)

In terms of living space, the primary room in all dwellings which incorporated more than a single area was the hall. In addition, some houses had a withdrawing room (or parlour) and the largest houses sometimes had more than one. However, within Rye parlours seem always to have been the reserve of the better-off residents. Excluding the known inns (for which *see* above) few of the 16th-century houses which survive (between 16 and 21 within a sample of 57) had a room recognizable as a parlour. Of these, only 11 (or at best 13) show evidence of having been heated.[54]

In contrast to parlours, all 57 houses in the sample had a room identifiable as a hall. In houses with parlours the furnishings within the hall were most likely quite basic and minimal (regardless of the status of the owner) with the better furniture, not surprisingly, reserved for the parlour. A further variable which would have affected the type of furnishing present within the hall was whether the house incorporated a separate kitchen, either attached or detached. In those houses which included a kitchen the hall would usually have been dedicated totally to living space, whereas in the other houses it would have needed to double as a cooking area.

Comparison of the examples shown in Figures 7.10 and 7.14 to 7.22 reveals that the halls were of relatively consistent floor area: this is especially so when the wide range of house-sizes is borne in mind. None were obviously entered via a lobby, but given the absence of 17th-century houses within the town, this is perhaps not too surprising — lobbies tend to be a relatively late feature in East Sussex. Something approaching a lobby could be argued to have existed at four buildings (4 High St [1], 6 Mermaid Street [61], 8-9 Mermaid Street [63] and 14-15 Mermaid Street [65]) where, because of a shop, a passage penetrated through the front rooms in order to reach the hall. But such a suggestion would be misleading — these were nothing more than a function of the specialized urban layouts of these buildings. Even where a lobby would have been easy to form, as, for instance, beside the chimney at

14 Lion Street [49], the opportunity was not taken. Indeed, although they were floored over, in plan most of Rye's post-medieval halls continued to closely resemble those of their medieval precursors. Where space permitted, cross-passages continued in use well into the 16th century. Most of Rye's 16th-century halls were entirely capable of being used in a medieval hierarchical way, and were entered at their still recognizable low end. One obvious development, however, was the introduction in some houses of a high-end chimney, which precluded the use of a high-end bench. This is a feature already noted in Chapter 6 regarding 67-69 High Street [19] and St Anthony's, Church Square [87], both built at the very end of the medieval period. Other probable early high-end fireplaces were those within the semi-detached pair at 101-102 High Street [26]. Early/mid 16th-century examples of the same feature exist at,15 West Street [56], 6 Mermaid Street [61] and 30 Mermaid Street [68]. In all these instances the hall had to be used in a new, post-medieval way, as must also have been the case with the halls within the houses shown in Figure 7.15, turned at right-angles to the street. Even so, in many other buildings the hall was capable of being used in a totally traditional way. Indeed, the configuration of the hall in the imposing merchant's house at 31 Mermaid Street [69], built in 1576, was wholly medieval in its concept, complete with what seems to have been a cross-passage.

It is true to say that by the second half of the 16th century all the houses contained within this present study had halls heated by fireplaces. Further, it would be fair to expect that this had been the case since the demise of the open hall, though perhaps at that early date a greater proportion of the enclosed hearths (particularly within the poorer houses which have not survived) would have been served by smoke bays or timber-framed flues, rather than by brick stacks. Although in most of the early 16th-century buildings the hall was indeed heated by a fireplace, there are 15 houses where, despite the hall being floored over, it can be shown that the present chimney is later than the floor. Perhaps significantly, most belong to the early years of the century and only one is obviously late.[55] In about half the cases it is likely that the phenomenon can be explained by the fact that the original heating system was considered primitive and was replaced by a larger, more substantially-built stack, in most instances upon the same site, thereby overwriting the structural evidence of its predecessor. At 8 East Street [33] the explanation could be that the building was not initially in domestic use and although the same is possible in one or two of the other buildings, most were certainly domestic. In five buildings the evidence for an unheated hall is compelling.

The same lack of heating has been noted in a few houses in other towns, and some researchers have given as a possible explanation the use of cookshops for the supply of all heated food. One of the Rye buildings in the group (The Mermaid [72]) is known to have been served by a detached kitchen, which in itself may explain the lack of a heated hall — after all, most rooms in medieval and transitional houses were unheated, so why not the hall also? A similar explanation could apply to 1-2 Lion Street [43] which has a kitchen-like room (served by a smoke bay) adjacent to its hall, but both rooms have their own external doorways and there is no proof of inter-communication, and thus no guarantee that the rooms were initially in common occupation. Even so, the former existence of detached kitchens may well explain the other unheated Rye halls. Whatever the answer, this apparent lack of heating seems rapidly to have been regarded as an unacceptable inconvenience, for in most cases a chimney was added with little delay.

Service-rooms and kitchens

A noticeable feature of rural buildings during the post-medieval period is an increase in the number of rooms dedicated to service use — butteries, pantries, milkhouses, brewhouses, bakehouses, kitchens and the like. Many houses possessed three or more such rooms and some had as many as six. As the room-names imply, these were primarily dedicated to the storage, processing and cooking of food. Not surprisingly, therefore, when the acreages of rural holdings are factored into the equation it becomes apparent that the number of service-rooms present within individual houses was influenced by the size of the holding, with landless and near-landless properties usually having only one service-room.[56] With this in mind, it should not be surprising to find that in Rye, where provisions were doubtless bought on a relatively regular basis and did not need to be stored or processed, service rooms were few in number.

Due to the incompleteness of the record and doubts regarding the use of some rooms, it is usually not possible to assess with certainty the number of service-rooms present in Rye's houses. Even so, it is worth noting that out of a sample of 36 small- and medium-sized houses for which reasonable data survives, three show no indications of having had any service rooms whatsoever, 22 had a single service room, ten had two, and only one had three such rooms. These figures include cellars, but exclude kitchens. The number of service-rooms within the large houses and principal inns was clearly somewhat greater, but probably not significantly.

It would be reasonable to expect kitchens to have been common, but only seven or eight kitchens have been recognized integrated within the surviving 16th-/early 17th-century buildings.[57] To these must be added kitchens which were either totally detached or built against the main house (*see* Chapter 6). The number of these ancillary structures is now impossible to assess as most have been destroyed. Surviving examples of what appear to be low attached kitchen ranges have been noted at 13-14 High Street [3] (probably 17th century), 33 The Mint [11] (mid 16th century), and 11 Market Street [41] (early/mid 16th century). Even when allowance has been made for kitchens housed within ancillary ranges/buildings and also for integrated kitchens which have escaped recognition, there seems little doubt that a large number of Rye's post-medieval population used their hall fireplace for cooking.

The documentary sources tend to confirm the picture of few service rooms and provide some indications of what they were called. Out of a total of ten 16th-century inventories which list rooms, two make no reference to service rooms, two mention only a buttery, three mention a kitchen and buttery, and one refers to a kitchen only. Even the substantial inn of James Pearsall mentions only four service areas — his kitchen, two butteries and a cellar. One incomplete inventory — relating to a substantial house — mentions other rooms: in addition to a buttery it refers to a 'backhouse' (perhaps an alternative name for a kitchen) and a bolting house.

Upper chambers

Excluding those in converted open-hall houses, 55 upper chambers can be ascertained with reasonable confidence. With two exceptions, which include full-height second-floor chambers, all are located on the first floor. For the purposes of this present study, roof garrets have not been counted as chambers, though at 31 High Street [10] (*c*.1610) the front garret was heated by a fireplace, as was originally the case in the large rear garret room at 98 High Street [24]: both must have served as accommodation of reasonable quality.

Despite the respectable size of the sample, the details it gives with regards to the number of chambers per house are unlikely to be particularly reliable since in a number of instances the sub-division of properties into more than one dwelling is likely to have been overlooked (*see* earlier in this chapter). This suspicion tends to be confirmed by the presence in the sample of only one single-chambered building. The most common number was two chambers, with 25 identified buildings. Above this the numbers reduce progressively: 13 had three chambers, six had four, three had five, four had six chambers, and a further three buildings had seven, eight and ten chambers respectively. Two of the latter group were principal inns, as may also be the case with some of the others in the five- and six-chamber category.

As will be evident from the case studies included within Part 2 of this analysis, most chambers within the houses built during the opening years of the 16th century were open to the roof, but by the middle years of the century it was usual to incorporate ceilings with garret areas in the roof spaces above, and by the end of the century most of the early open chambers had had ceilings inserted, at least amongst those houses which survive. Given the low number of hearths per house assessed in the 1660s hearth tax returns (for which *see* Figure 5.9) it is hardly surprising that most chambers were unheated, particularly during the first two-thirds of the 16th century. Within the present sample of buildings at least 16 houses had no heated chambers whatsoever, whilst a further 33 are identifiable which had only one heated chamber. A further eight had two first-floor fireplaces. Only five houses have been identified which had three or more fireplaces heating their chambers and in two of these some of the chambers were on the second floor. The highest totals were at 24-25 High Street [5] and The Mermaid [72] — both large inns.

Without a good inventory record it is impossible to give any reliable impression of what proportion of the chambers were used exclusively as bed-chambers or exclusively for trade storage, or, indeed, how many were used for a mixture of both, though the amount of trade storage within chambers is likely to have reduced once roof garrets became the norm. At least some roof garrets are likely to have doubled as dormitories for menial members of the larger households, but, as already noted, in only two late buildings — 31 High Street [10] and 98 High Street [24] — is there a heated garret.

As is the case with the other rooms in the houses, the best, indeed the only guides to the way the chambers were furnished and used are the extant inventories, though those which are of use are disappointingly few in number. It is these which will be addressed next.

Inventories of 16th-century houses

Mayhew has analysed 40 inventories listing the goods and chattels of Rye residents, dating from 1498 to 1599, and has published a detailed overview.[58] Unfortunately, only seven list rooms and appear to be complete. In some instances the lack of room-names is likely to be explained by the tiny size of the dwelling in question — the poor commonly occupied tiny spaces and, as has already been pointed out, some single persons (particularly the elderly) rented nothing more than a room, loft or garret.[59] Widows in particular were often impoverished. Widow Prophette seems to have been typical. At her death in 1567 she had within her lodgings in the house of Widow Fyndall goods valued at 55s.4d. They are listed as a flock bed, a blanket, coverlet, pillowcoat, four pairs of sheets, a carpet, some clothing, three candlesticks, nine pieces of crockery, a brass pot, a little pan, a little kettle, a cauldron and a chest. Equally minimal were the goods of a fisherman found hanged in his garret home in present-day High Street in 1584: he had an old bedstead with its old bed, an old table, a little cupboard, two old basins, and two 'manfare of nets' unmade. All Thomas Swayne, fisherman, had in his dwelling area when his goods escheated for felony in the same year were two chests, a little table with its trestles, a bad featherbed and bolster, an old covering, two straw beds, three bad bolsters, four painted cloths, two pieces of fishermen's lines, a meal sieve, an old settle of wood and an old (clothes) press. Perhaps the dwelling area occupied by Richard Goodwins, fisherman, at his death in 1583 consisted of more than one room, but to judge from his goods the size is likely to have been minimal. He had two bedsteads (furnished), two cupboards, an old table and form, three chairs and five chests. On the walls were five old painted cloths. Despite the apparent small size of the house, he was evidently better off than many, for he had 21 assorted pewter dishes, a dozen (probably wooden) trenchers, and a little tankard, together with a pair of bellows, a gridiron, spit, two kettles and an iron pot for cooking, a small amount of clothing and 'half an old trammel net' with an old net rope.[60]

Although the four inventories mentioned above are of interest in that they give an indication of how the poorest members of society lived, it is the seven apparently complete inventories which are more informative. They are too few in number to be considered a reliable representation of the contents of houses within Rye, but are nonetheless the best indication we have of how the town's individual houses were used and furnished during the second half of the 16th century. Those of Francis Daniel (1592) and James Pearsall (1593) both relate to substantial inns and that of James Pearsall, gentleman, merchant and innholder, has already been discussed in some detail earlier under inns and taverns (*qv*): it gives a particularly good impression of the types of furnishings and equipment to be found within a substantial Rye house.

The smallest house in the sample of inventories is that of the impoverished fisherman, Thomas Roben, 1594, which consisted of a hall, chamber and garret.[61] His goods were valued at only £1.15s.4d. Curiously, no cooking vessels/utensils are listed and there is a lack of other small items, so the completeness of the list of goods is questionable. Accepting this possible shortcoming, in his hall was a table and a form, two trestles and a cupboard, whilst his chamber contained three chests and two bedsteads with their furnishings, including featherbeds, bolster, coverlet and quilt. In addition to lumber, the garret was used for storing his fishing gear — a net and net ropes, and two trammels.

Another inventory of a single-chambered house is that of John Clarke, cloth-merchant, made nearly 40 years earlier in 1558.[62] Located in present-day High Street, this was a larger and better furnished house, perhaps with an old-fashioned hall still open to its roof. If so, it may have been of standard two-cell medieval type, similar in layout to those discussed in Chapter 6. It contained a hall, buttery and shop on the ground floor with just one chamber (described as *the* chamber) above. The shop could have occupied the front service room of a typical pair, with the buttery occupying that at the rear. The hall was the only living room and doubled as the cooking area. It contained the usual table and form, together with an old cupboard (with cupboard cloth) and two chairs. Also listed are a carpet (use unspecified), seven cushions, four candlesticks, a painted cloth on one of the walls, and a full set of fire goods (chaffer, andirons, pair of tongs, fire rake, fire shovel, gridiron and a pair of bellows).

Utensils and equipment stored within the hall included various pots and pans for cooking, a brass mortar, four quart pots, three pint pots, a drinking glass, two salts, two silver tasters, 22 silver spoons and a collection of pewter (including 15 platters, five dishes, eight saucers and six pottingers). Other vessels (including two kettles, two brass pots, two dripping pans, 12 trenchers, a chafing-dish, skillets, frying pan and the spit) were stored in the only service room, which was called the buttery. This room also housed the more usual goods for such a room — two crocks, a kneading trough, a water pot and a sieve. The shop contained Clarke's extensive stock of cloth, together with an old cupboard, a table, chest, playing table, balance and weights, and two painted cloths on the walls. His trade stock was not restricted to cloth, the shop also contained a barrel of salt, a half of wheat, and a firkin of soap, whilst he shared his one chamber with his extensive stock of dried herrings, fish baskets and new nets (*see* above). The furniture in the chamber was minimal — two beds, a basket, and three chests, one of which housed the linen and another his woollen items. Additionally there were a pair of bellows, his gown and cloak, and his bow, arrows and jack. The inventory finishes in his stable, which housed his gelding and its hay. At £63.5s.9d, the total valuation was a very respectable figure, though just over £40 of this was accounted for by his trade stock, with the horse and hay accounting for a further £1.10s.0d. Even so, at £21.5s.1d, the value of his household goods indicates Clarke's relative wealth, despite his minimal number of rooms. The impression given is that this was a house which was still awaiting upgrade to post-medieval standards.

The other three houses in the sample were considerably larger, at least in terms of the number of chambers: three in each case. In 1575 John Hammon's house in Baddings Ward (either in Church Square or Watchbell Street) contained a hall, parlour (described as little), kitchen, buttery and shop on the ground floor, with chambers over the hall, parlour and shop.[63] The absence of chambers over the kitchen and buttery (both of which were assessed at the end of the inventory) suggests that these may have been within a single-storeyed range at the rear, either attached or detached from the main part of the house. Hammon, a carpenter, was one of nine persons in Baddings Ward taxed at 2s.6d. — 39 people in the ward were taxed less, 52 more. The contents of his shop are not listed, so perhaps it had been leased out due to his ill health or old age! Despite the existence of a parlour, the hall was comparatively well furnished and contained ample seating. It contained a long table with a frame, a long form, a joined cupboard, a joined chair, another chair and two old hangings. No fire-goods are listed, nor any utensils. This was evidently the principal living room of the house, for the name 'little parlour' was in this instance apparently not intended to differentiate the room from a second, larger parlour, but to signify the room's small size — it housed nothing more than a table, its frame and a form. The lack of vessels in the hall is explained by a well-equipped kitchen. Within it were two iron pots, two kettles, a dripping pan, six platters, various pewter dishes and other vessels, divers old tubs, two spits and other fire goods. The buttery contained very little — six candlesticks, a chafing-dish and a frying pan. As is usual, no furniture is listed within this room, no doubt because it took the form of fitted benches and shelves. The inventory is not valued and therefore it is impossible to assess for certain which of the first-floor chambers was the principal of the three. In all probability it was the parlour chamber which, in addition to a joined bedstead and its furnishings, contained a table and frame, a form, a joined stool and wall hangings. The hall chamber seems to have been a larger room, but was evidently more communal in the way it was used. Here were three plain joined bedsteads with painted testers and their furnishings, a great joined chest and the hangings to the chamber. The third chamber — the 'chamber over the shop' — was the poorest equipped of the three. It contained a small bedstead, two truckle beds (all three with their furnishings) and three old chests. The small bedstead had a featherbed, but those on the truckle beds were straw. There are no references to hangings within the chamber.

Two years later, in 1577, an inventory was taken on the death of Peter Adrian.[64] He too occupied what appears to have been a three-cell house, having within it a hall, parlour and shop (not listed, so either empty or, more likely, leased out) with chambers over all three. Also listed is a kitchen, but this is included at the end of the inventory, after the chambers, and therefore appears to have been a single-storeyed structure, most likely detached. In this instance too the hall was well furnished — indeed, better so than that within Hammon's house. It contained the ubiquitous table and frame, together with two forms, two highly-valued long joined settles of wainscot, a chair of needlework, a joined cupboard, an iron rod with an old green canvas curtain, painted cloths on the walls, a book of holy psalms, a pair of pot hangers in the fireplace, and a small collection of weaponry which included two hand guns. As is commonly portrayed in 16th-century inventories, the parlour doubled as a bedchamber, having within it the second most valuable bedstead in the house, described as 'a joined bedstead of wainscot'. It may be of significance that no mattress or bed furnishings are listed in association with it. In addition to the bed, the room contained a valuable long settle of wainscot, a little 'snare' table with a cupboard, a straw chair, painted cloths on the walls, and an iron pot hanger in the fireplace. Despite being called a parlour, the small quantity of seating does not suggest it was used as a room for entertaining guests. The contents give more the impression of a private withdrawing room. Apart from the kitchen, there is a total lack of service rooms and even the equipment listed in the kitchen is minimal in the extreme — an old kettle, an old coop, a kneading trough, an old chest, and a 'trindle'.

All three chambers were in use as bedchambers, of which that over the hall was assessed at the greatest value. Here was a joined bedstead with its furnishings, a settle chest with a lock, a chair, and painted cloths (the latter described as old). In contrast, the parlour chamber seems to have been virtually unused — a joined bedstead (no furnishing listed), two vanes (counterpanes?) with two chamb[ers], a stallage, and an old form. Could this suggest that in his infirmity/old age Adrian had moved downstairs into the parlour? The third chamber — the shop chamber — seems to have remained at least partially in use, having within it two old, but furnished bedsteads (one joined, one boarded), a little 'danske' chest, a joined press of wainscot, and old painted cloths. Also within this chamber were sundry items, including an old quiver with arrows, iron in a basket, an old harness, a capbox, and an old distaff.

The final inventory which will be discussed here comes from the very end of the 16th century, being that of David Hewett, taken 1599.[65] He was a pewterer who had within his shop a considerable stock of pewter vessels, both old and new. Unlike the other two, his three-chambered house did not incorporate a parlour but, in addition to his shop, had a hall, kitchen and buttery, with chambers over the shop, hall and kitchen. It is impossible to say whether the shop and buttery occupied a pair of standard service rooms with the shop chamber extending over both, or whether the buttery was located elsewhere, for instance, in a single-storeyed range/outshut at the rear. For a house equipped with a kitchen, but no parlour, the contents of the hall are very much as is to be expected. The furniture consisted of a table and its frame together with associated form, a press table, a little round table with its frame, two joined cupboards, one joined chair, one joined stool and four old chairs. There were the usual fire goods (fire shovel, andiron, and a pair of tongs). In addition, there was a mortar and pestle, a pewter, a salt, and a beaker of pewter, as well as a small collection of weaponry. Listed within the kitchen is a little iron pot, a caldron two little spits, a great pan, a little kettle a [?] of iron, a candlestick, chamber pot and some old lumber. The contents of the buttery are typical of the other houses — two brass pots, a collection of platters, dishes, saucers, porringers, pots (half pint and pint), cups, a warming pan, colander, grate and dripping pan: in this instance too no furniture or barrels are listed. Only two of the three chambers were in use as bedchambers. That over the shop contained a joined bedstead (with furnishings). three chests, and a box. The chamber over the hall contained a joined bedstead (furnished), a truckle bed, a chest and a straw chair. To judge from its furniture, the kitchen chamber seems to have been used as a sitting room, having within it a joined table and form, two joined stools, two other forms and two chests. In the stable were two geldings.

Construction Techniques

Throughout the 16th and early 17th centuries timber framing remain the sole form of construction used within the town, the only exception being the non-domestic Peacock School (1636) in High Street which has external walls of mass construction — decorative brickwork at the front and rubble sandstone masonry at the rear (*see* Chapter 4). Likewise, Jeake's Storehouse in Mermaid Street, built after the close of the study period in 1689, uses rubble masonry external walls.[66] It was not until the early 18th century that occasional brick-built houses began to appear.

Due to lack of space, only a brief overview will be given here of the principal techniques of construction used during the 16th and early 17th centuries. Detailed analyses relating to some aspects of construction in Rye and the surrounding region have already appeared in print: others are intended to form the subject of future studies.[67] Despite the general correlation with the local norm, it is worth noting that two features found within the town at this period are non-local in character, though, given the town's foreign trade links and the influx of refugees from overseas between 1562 and 1590, it is significant that these non-local features are not only exceedingly rare, but are English rather than Continental in character. The features in question are the occasional use of thick, structural close studding (as opposed to the thin plank-like close studding used locally) and the adoption of roofs, which, measured against the local norm, are shallow in pitch.[68]

Wall design

Despite the continued use of timber framing throughout the 16th century, subtle changes can be recognized in the external appearance and internal character of the houses: these variations increased as the century progressed. Close studding, introduced into the town during the second half of the 15th century (*see* Chapter 6) was the norm for external walls during the first part of the 16th century and continued in use within the principal facades of the better-built houses throughout the entire period. As noted in Chapter 6, local close studding was almost always of thin plank type, exposed as a decorative feature in the principal wall-face only. However, two 16th-century Rye buildings — 4-5 Market Street [38] and 54, 56 Church Square [88] — seem to employ non-local thick close studding and at the former the wall bracing is trenched across the face of the studs. Although thick in depth, at 54, 56 Church Square the close studs are quite slender in their width and are more widely spaced than usual, and the same is true of the studding within the western end wall of the street range at 7-9 West Street [51]. In all three of these buildings the studs seem to be considered structural elements of the frame rather than a decorative conceit.

Given the almost ubiquitous use of external close studding within the early/mid 16th-century houses, it is hardly surprising that externally-visible bracing occurs hardly at all during the post-medieval period. Notable exceptions are at 24-25 High Street [5], 15 West Street [56] and 42-43 The Mint [16] where braces were used to enhance decorative panels — multiple ogee bracing at the former (*see* Figures 10.13 and 10.14), quadrant bracing at 15 West Street (*see* Figure 12.15) and cusped straight bracing forming diamonds at 42-43 The Mint (*see* Figure 10.30). Bracing continued to be employed within internal partitions throughout much of the century, though here too its use appears to have all but died out by 1600.

Horizontal rails (midrails) at mid-storey height

are first identified within the town in the end-wall of the open hall at 58-60 Church Square [89] (*c.*1500) and in the front wall of the fully-floored 45-46 The Mint [17] at about the same date, but the feature is mostly a late 16th-century phenomenon, a good dated example being 31 Mermaid Street [69] (1576). The rear external walls at 31 Mermaid Street are infilled with daub to produce small plain square plaster panels, but within the street facade the panels were probably (as now) always infilled with close studding, as was certainly the case at 45-46 The Mint [17] and in the late 16th-century kitchen range a little further up the street at The Mermaid [72]. Because of the major slump in building activity experienced within the town from about 1590 onwards, small-panel framing never became common in Rye. In addition to those already mentioned, examples are known at 13-14 High Street [3] (*c.*1600), 15 High Street [4] (late 16th century), 24-25 High Street [5] (*c.*1560), 31 High Street [9] (*c.*1610); 9-10 Market Street [40] (*c.*1600), 14 Lion Street [49] (*c.*1560), 1-3 Landgate Square [109] (late 16th century), and at the rebuilt late 16th-century main range at 15 West Street [56]. Rather than small-panel framing, the internal walls and partitions in the earlier examples make use of large-panels (*ie.* without midrails), indicating that the midrails were intended as a display feature. In contrast, the late examples incorporate midrails in both the internal partitions and external walls.

Doorways

Little good detail survives with regards to post-medieval doorways within the town, but that which does suggests that the pattern conformed to the regional norm, with arched-headed doorways (used for the principal openings of the better-built houses only) giving way to more simple (though sometimes moulded) square-headed openings during the second quarter of the 16th century.[69] Thus, during the opening decades of the century the principal internal and external doorways of the better-quality houses within the town were enriched with depressed four-centred arched heads of the type found in the late-medieval houses described in Chapter 6. The latest recorded examples of arched heads within the town are those within the shop addition of *c.*1550 at 4 High Street [1] and within the front range of *c.*1535 at 39-40 The Mint [14]. Slightly earlier examples of *c.*1525 survive within the main ranges at The Flushing Inn [38] and The Mermaid [72] (*see* Figure 12.47).

Windows [70]

Most (but not all) early 16th-century houses within the town were fitted with medieval-style unglazed windows. However, from the middle years of the century window glass became much more widely used: even so, windows in some lower-status houses continued to be unglazed throughout the century. Glazing was initially reserved for the principal rooms of houses, a particularly good example being 30 Church Square [81] (*c.*1565) where the hall and hall chamber were fitted with good-quality glazed windows, whereas the ground-floor storage area and the landing-like lesser first-floor chamber had unglazed openings with diamond-section mullions. The same was true of the narrow, tall, high-end crosswing of *c.*1550 at 15 West Street [56] where the parlour and parlour chamber are served by large high-quality glazed windows whilst the ground-floor rear service room had a standard unglazed opening. At The Mermaid [71] (*c.*1525) the kitchen passage leading down the side of the rear range was lit by unglazed windows, whereas the adjacent high-quality ground-floor room was served by a long, shallow, eight-pane glazed projecting window fitted beneath the jetty (*see* Figure 12.52, West Elevation). There are other examples.

The widespread adoption of glazing during the second half of the 16th century is well attested in the town's documentary record. For example, Mayhew notes how during this period deeds, wills and other documents not uncommonly specify that glazing was in some cases to be retained *in situ* or in others was allowed to be removed. In his will of 1577, for instance, George Raynoldes, jurat, specified that the fittings inside his principal messuage, including the glass windows, were not to be altered or removed by his executor. To quote Mayhew, "A standard clause in leases related to the maintenance of the glass windows for the term of the lease by the lessee after they had been first put into a state of good repair by the lessor. Four leases of properties within the range of £4 to £6 annual rent dated between 1579 and 1585 include this clause, whilst a civil action brought in the court of record in 1572 by Robert Wymond for the recovery of goods left in the house of Francis Harris, specified 'the glass in the windows which the said plaintiff brought and set up when he dwelt there' …".[71]

As elsewhere in the east of Sussex, the schemes of fenestration became increasingly elaborate as the century progressed, incorporating large central openings flanked by high-level clerestory windows. This was particularly the case within the street facades, where the schemes were on rare occasions combined with the use of multiple display windows capped by gables, as, for instance, at 31 Mermaid Street [69] (dated 1576 — *see* Figures 12.36 to 12.39) and, a little later, at 13-14 High Street [3] (*c.*1600) and probably at 9-10 Market Street [40] (*c.*1600). All these trends are to be expected during this period, though, probably due to the relative dearth of building work carried out at the close of the century and its virtual absence during the 17th century, display facades never became anything like as common in Rye as in some south-eastern towns. At nearby Hastings such features dominated during that town's early 17th-century building boom.

Floors and jetties

Methods adopted for floor construction in Rye during the 16th and early 17th centuries are of more than average interest, particularly because of the large number of examples which survive from the first half of the 16th century — a time of rapid change in the area. In contrast, relatively few buildings survive from this period within the rural hinterland, though the same general developments are detectable.

As discussed in Chapter 6, the floor joists in the medieval houses are very uniform in their design, being wider (usually 170 mm to 210 mm — 6¾ inches to 8¼ inches) than they are deep, each cut from either a single timber or halved to give two joists from one timber: they are undecorated. All joists within the town's surviving open-hall houses are of this type, as too are those of *c*.1500 in the four early fully-floored houses and four fully-floored early buildings of specialized layout discussed in Chapter 6. Another seven fully-floored houses of probably only very slightly later date are included in the sample of 'post-medieval' houses discussed here and one or two further examples may lie hidden behind later plaster ceilings. As already discussed under the heading 'Adapting existing buildings', joists of this type were used to support a number of floors inserted into open halls, suggesting early conversion to fully-floored type. As with the 'medieval' examples, all joists of this form are plain. In four of the newly-built houses the joists measure less than 170 mm (6¾ inches) wide, but are none-the-less laid flat — those at 34 The Mint [12] and 24/26 Church Square [79] are 155 mm x 110 mm (6 inches x 4¼ inches) and 150 mm x 80 mm (6 inches x 3¼ inches) in section respectively.

The great change which occurred during the opening decades of the 16th century was a switch from whole-tree and halved-tree joists laid flat to narrower timbers formed by cutting a number of joists from a single length of timber — a technique known as 'multiple conversion'. These new-style joists are either square in section or are slightly deeper than they are wide. During this early phase the joists were commonly positioned close together: those at Elders House, Mermaid Street [67] are typical, being at 340 mm (1 foot 1¼ inches) centres with a gap of 225 mm (9 inches) between them. The closest recorded spacing is at 11 Market Street [41] where the joists are at 315 mm (12½ inches) centres, leaving only 175 mm (7 inches) between them. Spacing increased markedly during the second half of the century. Whether the early close spacing was due to uncertainty regarding the strength of these smaller joists, or is an instance of 'conspicuous consumption', used to indicate status, is debatable.

Because of their very different proportions when compared with their medieval predecessors, the new-style joists give a ceiling of very different appearance, a point still further emphasised by the common use of stopped chamfers and, less often, mouldings to the lower leading edges of the joists forming the ceilings over many halls and parlours (*see* below).

There must have been a period of transition during which some houses were built with old-style joists, whilst others employed the new type Because the new style was so different in appearance, giving a far less 'heavy-looking' ceiling, achieved at little or no additional cost, the transition is likely to have been rapid — this is certainly the impression given by the surviving buildings. Houses dated on typological grounds (based upon other features) suggest that new-style joists were commonplace by the 1520s and 1530s, if not before. Eleven of Rye's houses built with new-style joists have crownpost roofs, a roof type which in East Sussex was superseded by clasped side purlins during the first part of the 16th century (*see* 'Roofs' below). Despite these observations, it should be emphasized that without an extensive programme of tree-ring dating, this hypothesis cannot be confirmed. Good early examples in high-quality houses are The Flushing Inn, 4-5 Market Street [38] (*c*.1525) where the joists measure 100-120 mm (4 inches to 4¾ inches) wide, 8-9 Mermaid Street [63] (*c*.1525) with joists 115 mm (4½ inches) wide, 14-15 Mermaid Street [65] (*c*.1520) with joists 120 mm (4¾ inches) wide, and The Mermaid, 35-38 Mermaid Street [72] (*c*.1525) with joists 100 mm (4 inches) wide. At 6 Mermaid Street [61] (*c*.1525) most of the joists are un-chamfered and measure 100 mm (4 inches), but those over the hall (located to the rear of a shop) are 130 mm (5 inches) wide and are stop-chamfered.

The latter example emphasizes another marked difference between the way in which the medieval and post-medieval joists were employed. Whereas medieval-style joists are consistent in their appearance throughout the building, the lower leading edges of the post-medieval examples are commonly treated differently in order to reflect the relative importance of the room within which they were visible. In most buildings the elaboration was restricted to simple stopped chamfering within the ceilings of the hall and/or parlour, but in a number of the better-quality houses the schemes were more elaborate. In fact, a little over 40 per cent of the houses which are considered to date from the first half of the 16th century incorporate some form of moulding within the ceilings of their principal ground-floor rooms.

At 16, 16a West Street [57] (*c.*1530) only the principal ceiling beams are moulded, the common joists being merely stop-chamfered, whereas in three other houses both the girders and the joists in the principal room are moulded. In a further two instances the arrangement is varied to suit the specific location. At 8-9 Mermaid Street [63] (*c.*1525) hollow-chamfered joists are used over the shop, but moulded joists over the hall, whilst at The Mermaid, 35-38 Mermaid Street [72] (*c.*1525) moulded joists and a moulded girder are used within the hall, but chamfered joists supported by a moulded girder within the rear parlour. The same combination seems to be repeated at The Flushing Inn, 4-5 Market Street [38] (*c.*1525) though here the joists within the rear parlour are currently masked, leaving only the moulded girder visible. Likewise, the joists are currently masked by plastered ceilings in another five buildings which have moulded principal ceiling timbers, making it impossible to know whether the joists are chamfered or moulded. Despite the use of moulded joists over the hall, at both The Mermaid and The Flushing Inn the joists within the ceiling over the cross-passage are merely stop-chamfered.

In the main the mouldings used in Rye's early 16th-century ceilings are relatively simple in profile and are typical of the period — a selection is illustrated in Figure 7.26. One building — 39-40 The Mint [14] (*c.*1535) — is worthy of specific note in that not only are the ceilings in both of its similar-sized ground-floor street rooms moulded, but in addition the stops are elaborated with foliage decoration (*see* Figure 10.25). Similar moulded joists with foliage stops are reused in two other Rye houses. The ceilings at 16, 16a West Street [57] (*c.*1530) share the arrangement found at 39-40 The Mint in that both of its two street rooms have moulded girders, but here, rather than moulded, the joists are merely chamfered.

The second half of the 16th century saw a number of changes in design and technique: most were subtle. One of these — spacing the joists more widely apart — has already been referred to. Another was the gradual introduction of plastered ceilings. It seems likely that until the third quarter of the century the undersides of the floor boards were in most instances left exposed to view, without any plasterwork. Admittedly, already by *c.*1490 at St Anthony's, Church Square [87] boards were deliberately incorporated, aligned along the axis of the joists, so as to leave no joints visible from beneath, and boarded ceiling panels were likewise used between the joists at Flushing Inn, 4-5 Market Street [38] (*c.*1525). Furthermore, the occasional use during this period of daub coverings applied to laths nailed direct to the undersides of floor boards cannot be ruled out.

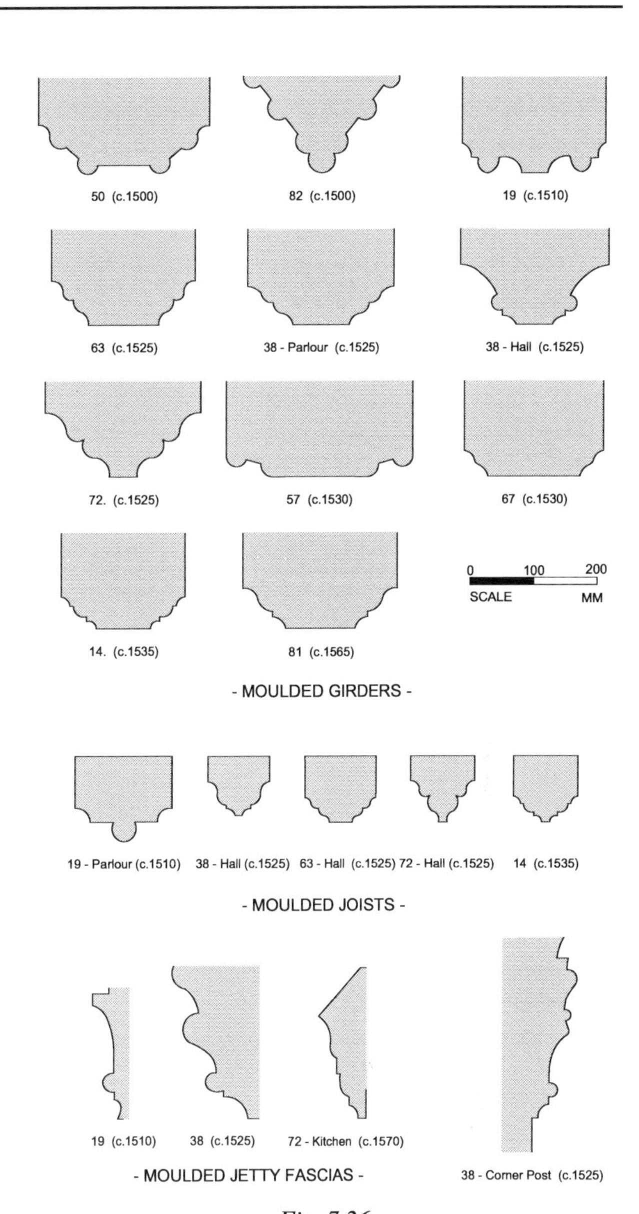

Fig. 7.26
A selection of mouldings on 16th-century ceiling beams
[For key to numbers see Figs. 9.1 and 9.2]

However, available evidence suggests that the widespread use of plaster applied between joists became common only during the second half of the 16th century, and it was during the same period that plaster ceilings which masked the joists from view were adopted in the better built houses. The ceilings within the merchants' mansion at 31 Mermaid Street [69] (dated 1576) are of this type, with the leading edges of the exposed principal ceiling timbers simply moulded using combinations of ovolo and cyma profiles. Similarly, the under-plastered ceiling of *c.*1600 within the kitchen at Dormy House [104] (*c.*1600) has ovolo-moulded principal timbers giving a coffered effect (*see* Figure 14.3). The ceilings within the town's other principal houses of similar date seem likewise to have been under-plastered, hiding the joists from view, though in these instances the girders were not moulded, but merely stop-chamfered. Indeed, during the middle years of the 16th century the use of moulded ceiling timbers appears to have rapidly gone out of fashion. Only four examples have been recorded within the houses and extensions attributed to the late 16th and early 17th centuries — this accounts for around 10 per cent of the town's buildings which date from this period. The moulded beams at 31 Mermaid Street and Dormy House have already been mentioned: the other two — the crosswing at 15 West Street [56] and 30 Church Square [81] — date from *c.*1550 and *c.*1565 respectively.

This move away from moulded structural timbers and the widespread adoption of stopped chamfers on girders and crossbeams seems to reflect a general desire for less ornate interiors, perhaps in response to the more general use of well designed, good-quality furnishings. Increasingly, display seems to have relied upon items put into a building, rather than upon the structural details of the building itself. Understanding this is essential in order to put into context another major innovation in floor construction which was introduced into the highest quality buildings of the town at this time.

The feature in question is the adoption of plastered ceilings (either plain or decorated) which are entirely unencumbered by structural timbers projecting below the line of the plaster. In addition to Rye, examples have been recognized in the largest of the rural gentry mansions. Until recently, early local examples of this type of floor existed in the tower at Laughton Place, built by Sir William Pelham around 1534, and within the parlour at Brede Place, remodelled by the Oxenbridge family *c.*1540. Both have been destroyed, but there are slightly later examples in other large gentry mansions in West Kent and East Sussex, though (because hidden from view by plaster) they are usually recognized only during structural repairs.[72] Despite the unencumbered nature of such ceilings, large structural timbers were necessary in order to provide adequate support to the floor above. Therefore, in order to achieve this objective it was essential to either incorporate two sets of joists — an upper tier carrying the floor and a lower tier positioned flush with the soffits of the main structural timbers — or to use joists equal in depth to the structural timbers which support them. Where joists of this type were employed they were commonly over 200 mm (8 inches) in depth but, significantly, normally only about 80 mm (3¼ inches) wide, giving them a very modern appearance. Often they are jointed to the principal structural timbers using double tenons, normally haunched.

Ceilings of this type are known to exist in five of Rye's late 16th-century buildings. Three are in the town's premier buildings of the period; 24-25 High Street [5] (*c.*1560), The Flushing Inn, 4-5 Market Street [38] (Rear addition of *c.*1565) and The Mermaid, 34-38 Mermaid Street [72] (addition of *c.*1580). The other two examples are more surprising in that they are in much smaller houses. That at 7 Lion Street [46] (*c.*1550) is restricted to the hall only and, because the joists are merely lodged into position, there is the possibility that they represent a later repair. However, at 4 Watchbell Street [91] they form an integral part of the structure. Furthermore, this house can be dated from documentary sources to between 1556 and 1560 and is therefore perhaps the earliest example in the town. Only at 24-25 High Street (viewed during building works) do the plaster ceilings now survive: they are entirely plain, as is likely to have been the case in the other examples also.

A final point which needs to be made regarding the floors of this period is the use of jetties, particularly towards the street. Their common inclusion during the medieval period was discussed in Chapter 6, reflected in the town's high number of hall houses of Wealden design. With the adoption of fully-floored houses as standard during the first half of the 16th century, street jetties became the norm. All but three of the 27 houses attributed to the first half of the 16th century for which the street details are known incorporated a jetty. Only towards the end of the 16th century did their popularity begin to wane. The merchants' mansion at 31 Mermaid Street [69] (date 1576) is un-jettied at first-floor level, as too is the courtyard inn at 24-25 High Street [5] (*c.*1560), the modest row of six houses at 18-23 Landgate [108] (*c.*1575) and the rebuilt main range at 15 West Street [56] (*c.*1575). The quite substantial houses at 13-14 High Street [3], 31 High Street [10], 105 High Street [29] and 9-10 Market Street [40] all date from around 1600 and are likewise un-jettied.

During the medieval period the joist ends were almost always exposed to view externally, but already by the close of that period jetty fascias began to be adopted (*see* Chapter 6). This trend continued through the 16th century and, indeed, became the norm, though by the late 16th century the mouldings had become simple, usually being restricted to the lower leading edges only (*see* Figure 7.26).

Roofs[73]

In East Sussex it was not until the first half of the 16th century that the ubiquitous paired-rafter-and-collar roof (usually incorporating crownposts) was superseded by a totally different construction technique. Whereas in the earlier form every rafter couple was linked by a collar, in these later roofs the common collars were omitted and instead the common rafters were strengthened from beneath by clasped side purlins, supported at wide intervals by framed roof trusses, as shown in Figures 10.11 and 10.49. Such roofs were not new: in Hampshire, less than 100 miles to the west, they had already become the norm by the early 15th century.[74] Despite the time-lag of a century between their use in Hampshire and their adoption in the Rye area the switch, when it came, was rapid. Only one of Rye's known medieval roofs is of the 'new' trussed form (*see* Chapter 6), yet by *c.*1550 the earlier style of roof had ceased to be built.

Despite the apparent correlation between this change, the abandonment of medieval-style open halls, and the switch from floor joists of 'medieval' to 'post-medieval' scantling (*see* above), these developments did not precisely coincide. In fact, the town has an exceptionally high number of fully-floored transitional/post-medieval houses which date from the early decades of the 16th century, yet have roofs of paired-rafter-and-collar type, mostly with crownposts. Examples are depicted in Figures 12.26 and 12.32. Excluding the small number of fully-floored late-medieval houses discussed in Chapter 6, a total of 22 early 16th-century houses with roofs of this type have been recorded within the town. The first floors in the vast majority of these houses are supported by joists of 'post-medieval', as opposed to 'medieval', scantling.[75] The significance of the high number of early-style roofs which persisted into the first part of the 16th century should not be overemphasized, for it must be remembered that this was a pivotal period in Rye's history, during which an exceptionally large number of new buildings were erected in order to house the town's rapidly rising population.

Of those 16th-century early-style roofs which do not incorporate crownposts, 42 Church Square [84] omitted the crownposts simply because its minimal roof span did not justify their inclusion, whilst at 14 West Street [54] and 24/26 Church Square [79] economic constraints are more likely to have been the incentive. These reasons for excluding crownposts are not new. However, some houses built during this period present a third possible reason for dispensing with the crownposts — the inclusion of a storage garret within the roof. Examples are 67 The Mint [19], 16, 16a West Street [57] and 24 Landgate [107], all three of which are well built and have a respectable roof span. To have incorporated crownposts and associated braces in these buildings would to some extent have restricted the use of the roof void. Despite the presence of a roof garret, crownposts were used at 11 Market Street [41] but here the posts incorporate minimal bracing. Indeed, the plain freestanding crownposts midway along the length of each of the two storage garrets are totally un-braced, whilst those at the partitions were braced up to the collar purlin only.

The early widespread adoption in some parts of England of trussed roofs with clasped side purlins proves that this alternative side-purlin form of construction was not developed to free floored roof spaces of obstructions — in these non-local early buildings the open halls and first-floor chambers were built open to the roof.[76] Even so, it seems likely that this advantage over the crownpost roof was an additional factor in promoting the rapid adoption of side-purlin construction once introduced into Kent and East Sussex. Indeed, in Chapter 6 it was argued that this was likely to have been the reason why a trussed roof (in this instance with interrupted side purlins) was used over the crosswing at 41 The Mint [15] late in the 15th century. Likewise, it is perhaps no coincidence that the town's earliest known clasped-side-purlin roof — over the fully-floored hall at 32 Church Square [82] — is associated with an early roof garret. The early date of this roof is demonstrated by the fact that a window in its western gable is blocked by the construction of the neighbouring house — 34, 36 Church Square [83] — which has first-floor chambers built open to a crownpost roof of traditional design. The neighbouring house uses 'medieval-scantling' joists to support its first floor.

Whilst an extensive programme of tree-ring dating would be needed before offering a precise date at which the new form of clasped-side-purlin roof finally superseded older-style crownpost construction, typological dating suggests it occurred during the 1530s or early 1540s, though it has to be admitted occasional early-style roofs may have been built as late as the 1550s, or perhaps even the early 1560s. The town's most recent crownposts are thought to be those at 3 Market Street [37] and 11 Market Street [41], and similar late dates seem likely for the paired-rafter-and-collar roofs (lacking crownposts) at 16, 16a West Street [57] and 42 Church Square [84]. All of these buildings are of average size and quality.

Once established, the town's clasped-side-purlin roofs became as ubiquitous as had the earlier form. Only one house built during the century 1550-1650 is known which does not have a roof of this type. This is 31 High Street [10] (*c.*1610) which makes use of staggered-butt-purlin construction, a form also found in some of Rye's houses erected during the late 17th and early 18th centuries, beyond the period covered by the present study.

The majority of Rye's 27 recorded 16th- and early 17th-century clasped-side-purlin roofs are windbraced and, as is usual, most have their trusses located over the tiebeams of the main frame. The standard form of truss uses collars to carry the purlins, 'supported' from beneath by a pair of queen studs. An alternative method (raking struts rising from tiebeam to purlin without the inclusion of a collar) is all but absent from the town, despite its not uncommon use in local rural houses and barns.[77] In a substantial minority of Rye's roofs the trusses do not coincide with the tiebeams and in these — as in a few other roofs where the roof trusses and tiebeams do coincide — the side purlins are supported by collars only. This is a feature not found in the rural hinterland at this early date.[78]

Most principal rafters in Rye's roof trusses are of diminished type — that is, they reduce in depth above the level of the purlins — though there are a few instances, spread throughout the period, in which the principal rafters are notched to accommodate the purlins.[79] In the town's earliest clasped-side-purlin roofs, such as that at 32 Church Square [82], the diminished principal rafters incorporate jowls at the apex.

In 16 houses built with roof garrets the usable floor space is increased by raising the wallplates above the level of the attic floor.[80] This has the effect of providing increased head-room at the eaves. The earliest known examples in the town are over the rebuilt main range at 41 The Mint [15] (*c.*1525) and at 16, 16a West Street [57], of similar date. Both have roofs of paired-rafter-and-collar construction — all the others are of clasped-side-purlin type.

At 16, 16a West Street the amount by which the wallplates were raised is so slight that the tiebeam crossing the garret was stepped over and, although the wallplates at The Crown, Ferry Road [111] (*c.*1560) are elevated to a greater degree, the same was true of the tiebeam here too. As Figures 12.36 to 12.41 illustrate, at 31 Mermaid Street [69] (1576) a combination of methods were adopted to trim the tiebeams at the trusses. Surprisingly, however, in most of Rye's buildings of this type no tie was included at wallplate level, relying instead on the crossbeam of the attic floor and the projecting upper parts of the main wall posts for strength. This is an acceptable method where the upstand is not very great, but where the upstanding walls were of any height it resulted in a weakness which was prone to failure. For instance, at 98 High Street [24] it became necessary to add 'sling braces' into the open roof truss in order to arrest structural movement (*see* Figure 10.48), whilst at 107 High Street [30] the design was so weak it resulted in partial structural failure.

Continuing the trend noted in the medieval roofs (*see* Chapter 6) there was a gradual tendency through the 16th century towards shallow-pitched roofs, though no roofs are known during the period which reduce below 45 degrees and most fall within the range 48 to 50 degrees. Undoubtedly, by this period most roofs were tiled, though it was not until 1561 that thatch was finally banned from the town, and even then the regulation applied only when existing thatch needed to be replaced. The ruling was reiterated in 1564, but existing thatched roofs evidently persisted for some time thereafter. For instance, when in 1578 a tenement in Watchbell Lane was presented as being very dangerous, it was specifically noted that its roof was thatched. In 1587, a quarter of a century after the ban, a lease made of church properties was conditional on the thatched coverings being taken off and replaced with tile.[81] With owners of some thatched buildings being so slow to repair and renew their roof coverings, the possibility of a few thatched buildings persisting into the early 17th century cannot be ruled out.

Chimneys

As discussed in Chapter 6, houses served by brick-built chimneys were already appearing within the town by *c.*1500, and many other brick-built chimneys were constructed during the early part of the 16th century, including those added into open halls when they were floored over (for which *see* 'Adapting existing buildings' above). This is not the place to analyse these chimneys in detail: suffice it to say that most are of standard construction and are competently built. Although the early examples occur in far greater numbers than they do in the surrounding rural districts, their only variations in construction are Rye's common use of exceptionally small, presumably imported 'Flemish-style' bricks and in the fact that the timber lintels over the main fireplaces usually have depressed four-centred arches, moulded over-mantles, and carved spandrels, whereas those in most rural buildings are plain. Good examples of these elaborated lintels are those at 9 Watchbell Street [92] and Old Trader/Trader Cottage [103] depicted in Figures 13.43 and 13.58. All the early post-medieval houses (including those of good size and quality) incorporate one or two fireplaces only: it was only after the middle of the 16th century that houses with multiple fireplaces began to be built within the town, and even then more than four flues were not common (*see* Figure 5.9). Despite this, individual chimneys at 31 High Street [10] (*c.*1610) and 14 Lion Street [49] (*c.*1560) have five and six flues respectively, located over three storeys.

In common with the use of shaped door-heads, ornamented timber fireplace lintels went out of fashion as the 16th century progressed and were superseded in most buildings by plain timber lintels, simply chamfered and identical to those used in the surrounding rural hinterland. Decorative fireplaces of high quality were still used, but were restricted to principal rooms in the highest-status buildings only. In these the fireplace surrounds were of stone. In fact, Rye's late 16th-century stone surrounds are very distinctive, with moulded 'shouldered' arches capped by a deep panel, in most cases enriched by a horizontal row of alternating circular and diamond-shaped 'medallions' (*see* Figure 12.54), but in one or two examples (as in Figure 13.30) with a more elaborate design. Stone surrounds are known at 24-25 High Street [5] (*c*.1560), 31 Mermaid Street [69] (dated 1576), The Mermaid [72] (additions of *c*.1570 and *c*.1580), 54-56 Church Square [88] (*c*.1565) and 58, 60 Church Square [89] (*c*.1565). The chimney at 58, 60 Church Square is built against an end wall, serving a parlour, and is particularly impressive, incorporating as it does an arched external doorway leading under the fireplace in order to gain access to the cellar beneath (*see* Figures 13.37 and 13.38).

Based upon the surviving buildings, it would seem fair to assume that in Rye the medieval-style open hearths were replaced by brick-built chimneys without any intermediate phase during which more primitive smoke dispersal systems were adopted. True, evidence of smoke bays and timber-framed chimneys are known within one or two of Rye's fully-floored houses of the period, proving that they were, at least occasionally, used within the town, but such evidence is very rare. Mention was made in Chapter 6 of the smoke bays of *c*.1500 at 1-2 Lion Street [43] and St Anthony's, Church Square [87], and there was another, of slightly later date, inserted when the hall at 22, 24 Church Square [78] was floored over. At 7 Mermaid Street [62] (*c*.1510) there is good evidence for a back-to-back timber-framed flue, and there seems to have been another timber-framed flue associated with the floor inserted into the single-aisled 'Wealden' at 17 West Street [58]. Slight circumstantial evidence exists for one or two others, especially in Mermaid Street.

Proof that primitive-style flues were once more common within the town than the surviving buildings suggest is to be found in the corporation archives. Such heating systems were deemed a fire risk and therefore, in the 1570s they were banned within the town. After the ban, lists were compiled of persons presented for having them within their houses.[82] In 1579/80, for example, 12 named individuals (including the King's Bailiff) were presented for the offence of having 'wooden chimneys' in their tenements, 'whereof divers are very dangerous', and to these persons should be added the corporation itself. Twenty-two such chimneys are listed, spread throughout the town. Two were in 'the rents' by the southern side of the church gate, three in houses 'in the lane in the middle of Watchbell Street', one in a tenement in Watchbell Street, 'which is very dangerous as the house is thatched', three more were in houses owned by the corporation (of which one was 'outside the gate'), one in a 'house on the shop at Strand', four were in tenements at Strand, one in a tenement 'by the friars', two in tenements in the Landgate suburb, two in the bailiff's tenements in Longer Street (High Street), one in a tenement 'in Pond Garden' (off The Mint), another was in a house in the Butchery, and yet another was in a house for which the location is unspecified. Those properties owned by the corporation or by wealthy residents were let to tenants. The following year there were presentments for 40 wooden chimneys, suggesting that more had come to the notice of the authorities. This particular return included a Frenchman who occupied Mr Spilstead's house in High Street and was presented for '... making a fire against a wall joining to [the house of] the skinner, endangering the house thereby...'. By the 1580s the number of presentments for wooden chimneys had dropped to less than a dozen, probably indicating that such chimneys had by then mostly been replaced in brick, though it is also possible that the legislation was by that time not being so rigorously enforced.[83]

As Mayhew points out, 'Brick chimneys were not cheap. In December 1552 the chamberlains' accounts record payment for 10,000 bricks at 9s. per thousand for the construction of the chimney in the new almshouse together with 2,000 Flemish brick at 6s. per thousand "to make the top of the chimney in the Almshouse", a total expenditure of £5.2s.' He further notes that 'In 1577 the will of George Raynoldes, jurat provided £6.13s.4d. towards erecting a further chimney at the almshouse with two fireplaces along the north gable head ...'.[84] Given the high cost of non-flammable brick chimneys, it is assumed that wooden chimneys were banned only once bricks became affordable by ordinary townsfolk, implying that previous to the 1570s timber flues were more numerous than the records suggest. What precisely the authorities meant by a 'wooden chimney' is open to debate, but presumably smoke bays would have been included.

The impression the evidence gives is that by the middle years of the 16th century 'primitive', potentially-flammable heating systems were primarily a feature associated with Rye's lower-class houses, a view which is consistent with the fact (mentioned above) that very little evidence for either smoke bays or timber chimneys has been found for the post-medieval period within the town. Even so, it should be emphasised that this sparsity of surviving examples is likely to give the wrong impression regarding the situation earlier, during the late 15th and early 16th centuries. The likelihood is that in those houses which abandoned the use of open halls and open cooking areas prior to *c*.1540 timber chimneys and their antecedent forms were probably the norm at all social levels — it was the houses with brick chimneys which were exceptional. It was probably only over time that the balance and ratio of timber chimneys to brick chimneys shifted in favour of houses occupied by the lower classes. That some of the early known 'primitive heating systems' in Rye occur in good-quality houses built during the medieval/post-medieval transition suggests that initially these seemingly 'primitive' methods of smoke control were not limited to the homes of the poorer members of society. The high number of timber chimneys which survived into the 1570s in houses which are known to have been occupied by the disadvantaged merely shows that it was at this social level that they persisted longest.

Decoration

Although moulded and carved timberwork was never common in Rye, the construction of chimneys and first floors in halls during the first half of the 16th century gave the opportunity for some work of this type to be incorporated (*see* 'Floors and Jetties' and 'Chimneys' above). In addition, a few mouldings occur on jetty fascias and on principal doorways and windows. But generally such work remained rare and the houses of the period were very plain. Indeed, during the second half of the 16th century interiors became even less ornamented and more austere in appearance. As already noted, wall framing became repetitive and in the best houses ceilings within principal rooms were flush under-plastered, hiding the timberwork from view.

Increasingly, it would seem, householders relied upon furniture and applied furnishings to make their houses seem more homely and to display their wealth. The late 16th-century inventories discussed earlier in this chapter portray this well. Painted cloths — cheap, affordable versions of tapestry hangings — were normal in the living rooms and chambers of most, if not all classes of Rye's residents.

Such decorative schemes leave no architectural evidence and thus their visual impact cannot easily be assessed. An alternative in which the decorative scheme was painted directly onto the walls, on the other hand, goes some way towards indicating what other interiors may have been like. The best example in Rye is the imitation tapestry on the high-end wall of the hall at The Flushing Inn, 4-5 Market Street [38] painted in 1537 or very soon afterwards (Figure 11.11), followed closely by another of similar date at 16-16a West Street [57]. Whereas that at Flushing Inn includes the *Magnificat* in English (close to the version in Tynedale's Bible of 1525) and royal coats of arms on its frieze, that at 16-16a West Street has a topographical scene showing Rye and Winchelsea (see Figure 12.17). There are painted texts on ceiling beams in the latter building and traces of other painted schemes in the hall at The Flushing too, so in each case the paintings were not restricted to one wall only. Other similar paintings, now exceedingly fragmentary, have been noted in the crosswing at 98 High Street [24] and in the hall chamber at 4-6 Lion Street [45].

Given its religious text in English, the painting at Flushing Inn must surely have been hidden from view during the reign of Mary, and survived only because it was covered by a new scheme of decoration — applied timber panelling (or 'wainscoting'). Similar panelled wall linings were introduced into other high-class houses of the town during the second half of the century. Always restricted to the best rooms of the upper classes, as for instance in the parlour at Grene Hall, 58, 60 Church Square [89], panelling seems to have been particularly popular within the town's principal inns, with schemes surviving at 24-25 High Street [5] and The Mermaid, 35-38 Mermaid Street [72]. Likewise, to judge from the poor finish on the timberwork, 9-10 Market Street (once The George) [40] seems to have been designed from the outset to have panelled walls within its principal rooms, though only a fragment of the scheme now remains.

Panelling is very liable to be moved and refixed, and thus there is no guarantee that any of the Rye schemes are *in situ*. Indeed, even at the time there was doubt as to whether it should be regarded as a fixture — part of the house — or as a furnishing. In 1577 the town paid the outgoing sergeant 46s.8d. for the 'wainscot work' *etc* which he had set up in the Court House, whilst in the same year George Reynolds specified in his will that certain items, including the 'long settle of wainscot fixed to the walls or the timberwork of the same' in his principal messuage should not be altered or removed by his executor. In 1603 William Ratcliff, jurat, left 'all my wainscot stuff, viz. portal (internal porch between rooms), study, settles and other wainscot' in his principal messuage in the Butchery to his Bristol cousin.[85]

Just as with tapestries, for those who could not afford to line their walls with wainscoting, there was always the option of imitating such schemes in paint. In the chamber at 4 High Street [1] (Figure 10.3) the paintwork seems to be based upon panelling which was either inlaid or decoratively painted, a reminder that not all wainscoting was left as untreated timber. Hidden by later plasterwork at 13-14 High Street [3] is an even more elaborate scheme (Figure 10.8) which gives a vivid indication of just how rich, indeed gaudy, some interiors of the period could be. These rare survivals remind us not to judge the interiors of buildings based solely upon what we see today.

8 CONCLUSIONS

It would be a cliché to say that Rye is unique — all places are unique — but it is certainly true that the town has a character which is hard to parallel elsewhere in England. As Pevsner notes in his introduction to Rye,

> *'Hill towns are rare in England. In Sussex Lewes is one, Winchelsea another, but Rye, its sandstone rock rising out of the total flat of the fen, makes its statement yet more unmistakably. The houses building up to the low tower of the church are reminiscent of the north of France'.*[1]

His comments relate to the town's physical appearance: add to this its historical background and Rye becomes a place of more than average interest.

The present study has deliberately concentrated upon the town's built environment and has largely ignored Rye's early developments: for these and an account of the people who populated the town the reader is directed to Gill Draper's 'Rye History' (*see* Bibliography). Only those early aspects which had a marked influence upon later structural developments within the town have been discussed here. As in many urban centres in southern England, domestic architecture in Rye survives only from the late 14th century, presenting an obvious starting point for this volume. Similarly, the town's economic slump of the 17th century (during which hardly any new building work took place) provides a natural terminus. Thus, the tenor of this present work has been the quarter millennium from 1350 to 1600. These were, as far as the surviving fabric is concerned, the town's formative years.

As has been shown, in terms of domestic architecture the late 14th and 15th centuries contain few real surprises. Rye is a typical example of an average, relatively successful local coastal port. Given that it was served by the only good sheltered harbour along this part of the south coast, one might have expected more, but at this date it stood in the shadow of its more dominant and successful neighbour, Winchelsea, which at this time dominated foreign sea trade and maritime activity along this section of the coast. Indeed, it is surprising that Rye prospered to the extent it did. The extant domestic buildings portray it as successful and un-crowded, with an above-average number of well-built timber-framed open-hall houses, all aligned parallel to the street and many standing detached.

All this changed during the 16th century. The catalyst is well known — the collapse of Winchelsea due to silting of the River Tillingham. Rye not only usurped Winchelsea's role, but developed it. Given the town's importance during the 16th century, it is hardly surprising that Hipkin and Mayhew concentrated upon this period. But those and other studies concentrated mainly upon people, economics, politics and religion, not upon the physical fabric of the town. This is not a criticism of their work. For them, such a focus was a necessity, for at the time most of the buildings had yet to be studied. Thanks to their work, this present study has been able to combine the two disciplines. It is this blend which has, hopefully, allowed so much which is new to be said about the town.

Reading Mayhew's *Tudor Rye* and, in particular, his view that the town was of national importance during the 16th century, it seems at first sight hard to reconcile this with the Rye we know today. Remove the many tourists and Rye is a quaint backwater. Furthermore, it is so small that it is hard to imagine it as ever having been anything else. True, its streets are packed with old and interesting-looking houses, but they do not give the impression of having served a packed and bustling, economically vibrant community. Certainly it does not give the impression of having once been home to the greatest concentration of houses in south-east England, excepting only London and (perhaps) Canterbury. Rather, Rye has a distinctly 'small-town' feel about it. Yet, what has come out of this study is that Mayhew and Hipkin were indeed correct. Their view is totally in keeping with statistics given in a series of returns on port towns made to Parliament in 1565.[2] These show Rye as having 530 households — the largest number of any port in Kent and Sussex. At that date the next largest was Sandwich (420 households), followed closely by Faversham (380 households) and Dover (358 households). The inland town of Maidstone was included in the Kent returns because it doubled as a river port: it was recorded as having 294 households. The only inland town in either Kent or Sussex which is likely to have rivalled Rye with regards to its number of households is Canterbury, for which statistics are not available. Within the Rape of Hastings — the eastern sixth of Sussex — it is estimated that in the mid 16th century one in five of all houses within the rape were located in Rye, yet the Rape of Hastings covered a total area of 250 square miles, compared to 36 acres for Rye! The next largest concentrations of population in the area were Hastings (280 households) and Battle (124 households).[3]

So how can these two apparently contradictory views be reconciled? The answer appears to be the town's specific pattern of growth and decline. In this it is a good example of how the past influences the future.

As already noted, the study has shown that by the late 15th century Rye was a small but prosperous and spacious town, with large plots and good-sized houses built to a standard, predictable design. It has further demonstrated that initially during the 16th century the additional population was principally accommodated by infilling gaps in the street facade, with only *very* limited expansion of the built-up area. Subsequently, as the population continued to rise during the middle years of the century, the footprint of the medieval town could not be enlarged to accommodate the increase due to the topography of the site. This forced existing houses to be sub-divided into multiple units. Because much of the existing housing stock was at that time still new and well built, there was no large-scale redevelopment — the increase in population was mostly accommodated by adapting the existing houses. Unlike the earlier buildings, these modifications produced houses with internal layouts of distinctly 'urban' character.

Although the town had two physically quite separate focal points (the church/market and the Strand/fishmarket) it was so small and compact there was no need to concentrate commercial activity in one confined area — everywhere was close to everywhere else. This point is clearly indicated in the distribution of shops — they were spread evenly across most of the town. Thus, as the town filled up, no one part was put under extreme pressure for space. Had Rye occupied a larger site, or been able to expand, it may have developed a discrete commercial district within which demand for space may have become intense. Under such circumstances, regardless of the recent age of the buildings, economic pressures would have caused wholesale redevelopment within the commercial core as buildings rose ever higher in an attempt to maximize floor space. The result would have been a very different streetscape, far more akin to that found within the principal streets of places such as Canterbury and Sandwich.

Significantly, by the end of the century such high-rise developments were beginning to appear. If the population had continued to increase at its 16th-century rate it is quite possible that lofty, narrow-fronted houses would have become far more numerous in specific areas, utterly transforming the townscape within the commercial heart, giving us today a very different impression of the town's past. As it was, the reverse happened. Population levels dropped and many of the houses which had been divided up were returned to single occupancy. Port activities shrank to a fraction of their 16th-century levels, leaving the areas closest to the quay seriously impoverished and in places deserted.

Despite the downturn, because there was no local rival community, the town's land-based market activities survived, concentrating commercial enterprises towards the eastern end of High Street — the present trading centre. But even here, despite an increase in the pace of redevelopment during the late 18th, 19th and early 20th centuries, the pressures never became such that wholesale redevelopment occurred. Thus, the town we see today came into being, its unique character a product of its varied and colourful past.

PART 2

THE HOUSES TO c.1660 SUMMARIZED

9 INTRODUCTION TO PART 2

This second section in the study of Rye's Medieval, Tudor and Stuart built heritage gives summarized details of the individual historic houses within the town. The entries, which are presented as illustrated 'stand alone' descriptions arranged by street, aim to give an impression of the total sample within the study, underpinning and augmenting the overviews given in Chapters 6 and 7. It is divided into five chapters. Chapter 10 covers the High Street and The Mint (effectively Landgate and Strandgate Wards); Chapter 11 deals with East Street, Market Street and Lion Street (Market Ward); Chapter 12 covers West Street and Mermaid Street (Middlestreet Ward); and Chapter 13 encompasses Church Square, Watchbell Street and Trader Passage (Baddings and Watchbell Wards). The final chapter, 14, takes in East Cliff and the Landgate suburb (both part of Landgate Ward) and also includes the one surviving building of the period in the Wishe suburb.

To avoid overburdening the gazetteer with detail, much simplification has been necessary within both the text and the accompanying illustrations. For detailed interpretation of individual features/buildings (including further clarification and discussion of controversial aspects) the reader is directed towards the archive of individual surveys held at East Sussex Record Office (ESRO) where they form part of a much larger body of historic buildings reports. The reference to each report is quoted at the end of each entry in the gazetteer. An explanation of the method of stylistic dating adopted is given in the preface to this volume, and there too the conventions used in the architectural drawings are explained.

Part 2 contains entries for 111 houses — a full list (including generalized construction dates) is given in Figure 9.1, with the locations shown in Figure 9.2. Only nine of the houses (plus two relatively uninformative fragments) can be confidently dated to before the preparation of the town's earliest extant sesse (local tax) made in 1491/2. Another 32 houses and seven fragments have either insufficient datable evidence or are too close in date to 1491/2 to say whether they existed when the sesse was prepared, but there seems little doubt that all had been built by 1515-1520. Bearing in mind Rye's known economic and demographic background (*see* Part 1) it is tempting to suggest that most of these 39 houses and fragments post-date 1491/2, but this cannot be proven.

By extending the time frame up to *c.*1540 — what might be termed the very end of the medieval era — the number of houses in the sample rises considerably. Including the medieval examples already mentioned, Rye has 53 known houses which can be confidently dated to before c.1540, to which can be added a further 19 which are likely to predate 1540 and (even if later) were built soon afterwards. By any standards this is a good size sample.

In many ways the houses built after *c.*1540 form a natural progression from those of late medieval and transitional date. In appearance these were much the same as in the preceding period, though sometimes of greater height, with an increased tendency to incorporate modest schemes of glazed display fenestration and gabled facades. One obvious change was the increasing division of houses into multiple occupancy, though this largely affected internal layout rather than external appearance.

No	Address	Principal Dates
1	4 High St.	*c.*1500; M16C
2	11 High St.	E16C
3	13-14 High St.	*c.*1600
4	15 High St.	L16C
5	24-25 High St.	M16C
6	26 High St.	16C?
7	28b High St.	15C or E16C
8	29b High St.	16C
9	30 High St.	[Cellar only]
10	31 High St.	L16C/E17C
11	32-33 High St.	L14/E15C; M16C
12	34 The Mint	E16C
13	36-38 The Mint	E15C; M16C
14	39-40 The Mint	Medieval; M16C
15	41 The Mint (The Standard)	Medieval; L15C; E/M16C
16	42-43 The Mint	L15/E16C
17	45-46 The Mint	*c.*1500; M16C
18	54 The Mint	M16C
19	67-69 The Mint	*c.*1500; E16C
20	73-74 The Mint	*c.*1500
21	79 High St.	?
22	84 High St.	*c.*1500
23	85 High St.	*c.*1500
24	98 High St. (Pt. The George)	Medieval; *c.*1600
25	99-100 High St.	E15C; M16C
26	101-102 High St.	L15/E16C; M16C
27	103-103a High St.	L16C
28	104 High St.	[Fragment]
29	105 High St.	E17C
30	106-107 High St.	Undatable
31	110 High St.	M/L16C; *c.*1600
32	2-3 East St.	L15/E16C
33	8 East St. (The Union)	*c.*1500
34	16 East St.	L14C; L15C; E16C
35	11-12 East St.	16C
36	1-2 Market St. (Durrant Ho)	[Cellar]
37	3 Market St. (Monks Way)	E/M16C
38	4-5 Market St., 2, 4 Church Sq.	Medieval; E16C, M/L16C
39	8 Market St/23, 23a Lion St.	14C; *c.*1500
40	9-10 Market St.	*c.*1600
41	11 Market St.	E/M16C
42	9-10 East St./13-14 Market St.	*c.*1400; *c.*1500; L16C
43	1-2 Lion St. (Fletchers Ho.)	*c.*1500; M16C
44	3 Lion St.	E16C
45	4-6 Lion St.	M/L15C; E/M16C; *c.*1600
46	7-9 Lion St.	L15C; M16C
47	12 Lion St. (Pt. The George)	L15C
48	13 Lion St. (Pt. The George)	M/L16C
49	14 Lion St. (Pt. The George)	M/L16C
50	5-6 West St (Temple Ho.)	*c.*1500
51	7-9 West St./62 Church Sq.	13/14C; *c.*1500: E16C; *c.*1600
52	64 Church Sq.	E/M16C
53	Lamb Cottage, West St	L14C; *c.*1500; E/M16C
54	Pt.14 West St.	E16C; *c.*1600
55	Pt.14 West St.	E/M16C; *c.*1600
56	15 West St.	M16C; L16C
57	16, 16a West St.	E/M16C
58	17 West St.	L15C?
59	18-19 West St.	E16C
60	5 Mermaid St.	16C
61	6 Mermaid St.	E16C
62	7 Mermaid St.	E16C
63	8-9 Mermaid St.	E16C
64	10-11 Mermaid St.	M/L15C; M16C
65	14-15 Mermaid St.	E16C
66	16 Mermaid St (Demolished)	L15C
67	Elders Ho., Mermaid St.	E16C
68	30 Mermaid St.	M16C
69	31 Mermaid St. (Hartshorn Ho)	L16C
70	32 Mermaid St. (Knowle Ho.)	14C; L15C; E16C
71	34 Mermaid St. (Pt. The Mermaid)	*c.*1500
72	35-38 Mermaid St. (The Mermaid)	E16C; M/L 16C
73	40-41 Mermaid Street/13 West Street	[16C?]
74	6 Church Sq.	*c.*1500; E/M16C
75	8,10 Church Sq.	E16C; M16C
76	12 Church Sq	16C
77	20 Church Sq.	M/L16C
78	22, 24 Church Sq	L15C; M16C
79	Pt.24, Pt.26 Church Sq.	E16C
80	26 Church Sq.	E16C; M16C
81	30 Church Sq.	M/L16C
82	28, 32 Church Sq.	E16C
83	34,36 Church Sq.	E16C; M/L16C
84	42 Church Sq.	E/M16C
85	44 Church Sq.	E16C
86	46 Church Sq	L14/E15C
87	St Anthony's, Church Sq.	*c.*1500
88	54, 56 Church Sq.	M16C
89	58, 60 Church Sq.	*c.*1500; M16C
90	1-2 Watchbell St.	*c.*1500; M16C
91	4 Watchbell St.	M16C
92	9 Watchbell St.	M16C
93	10 Watchbell St.	L16C
94	11-13 Watchbell St.	M16C
95	16-17 Watchbell St.	15C
96	19 Watchbell St.	L15C; M16C
97	20 Watchbell St.	[Cellar only]
98	20a, 21 Watchbell St	M16C
99	26 Watchbell St.	?
100	27-28 Watchbell St.	?
101	29 Watchbell St.	M16C; *c.*1600
102	Oak Corner & Ho., Trader Pass.	L15C; E16C; *c.*1600
103	Old Trader, Trader Cot.	E15C; E16C
104	Dormy House, East Cliff	L15/E16C; L16C; *c.*1600
105	1-4 East Cliff	M16C
106	1 Landgate	[Cellar Only]
107	24 Landgate	E16C; L16C
108	18-23 Landgate	L16C
109	1-3 Landgate Sq.	L16C; *c.*1600
110	5-6 Landgate Sq.	15C or later
111	The Crown, Ferry Rd.	M/L16C

Figure 9.1
Table of buildings included within Part 2.
[For location of the buildings see Figure 9.2]

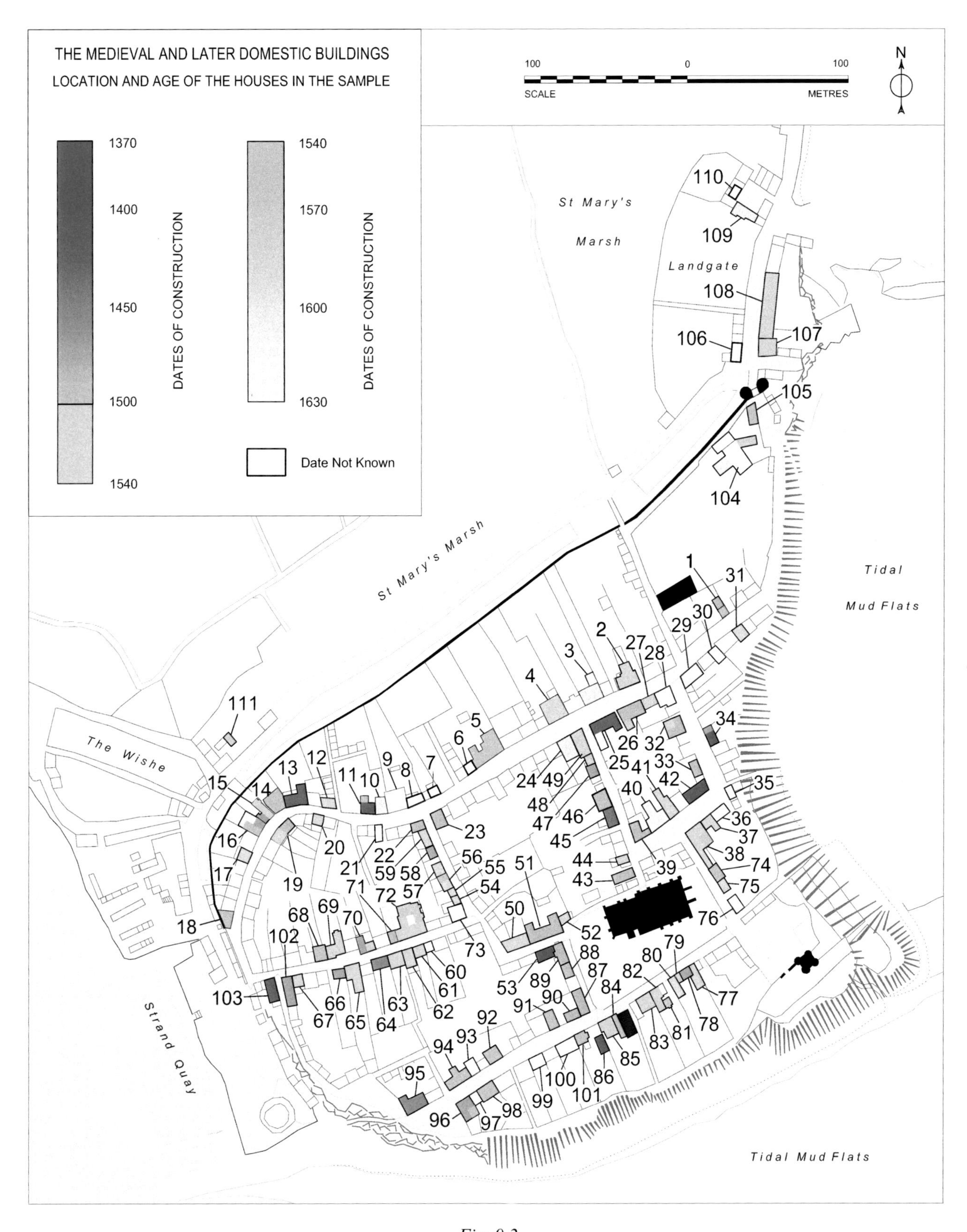

Fig. 9.2
Plan showing the location and age of the buildings described in Part 2.
[For key to numbers see Fig. 9.1]

10 THE HOUSES TO *c.*1660 SUMMARIZED: HIGH STREET AND THE MINT

1. 4 High Street — *1500 +/-25; 1550 +/-25*
(Figures 10.1 - 10.4)

4 High Street is the western end of a terrace which, to judge from a depiction of it by Van Dyck made in 1634 (*see* Figure 2.3) once extended eastwards to included numbers 1 to 3. It backs onto the Austin Friary, occupying a site which was almost certainly still open ground in 1490 (*see* Chapter 2).

Phase 1 (c.1500). It seems likely that the medieval part of the building is within the original precinct of the friary and possibly represents a speculative development undertaken by the friars upon what was referred to as their garden in 1490. The site has been cut into the hill slope, and as a result the building shows two storeys towards the street, despite being a three-storeyed structure (Figure 10.1). It is possible that it was divided into multiple occupancy at a subsequent date, though rows of multiple units are a well known feature of speculative developments undertaken on the fringes of churchyards and monastic precincts. The surviving part is very odd, being of two unequal bays with, apparently, a single room on each floor. The truss dividing the two bays is arch braced at the upper level, shows no evidence of having been daub infilled, and supports a moulded freestanding crownpost (now refixed) but also incorporates two studs (section A-A in Figure 10.1). The studs, together with the extreme narrowness of the eastern bay, suggest that the bay was intended to incorporate some form of freestanding flue, but there is insufficient evidence to confirm this hypothesis. The arrangement of the windows within the street facade shows that at this period the building did not incorporate a shop.

Phase 2 (c.1550). An addition to the front which, on the ground floor, contains a shop. It represents the only known extant example within the town of highway encroachment, apparently regularizing the street alignment at a point where the street frontage formerly stepped back. This step seems to have been caused by the construction of houses on formerly undeveloped land to the west, these new houses having been built with their facades further forward than that of the medieval terrace. Today there is a regular alignment along this entire section of street, but the properties to the east appear to represent later reconstructions. What is not known is whether similar additions were built in front of these also, or whether only this property was enlarged, thereby effectively 'moving'

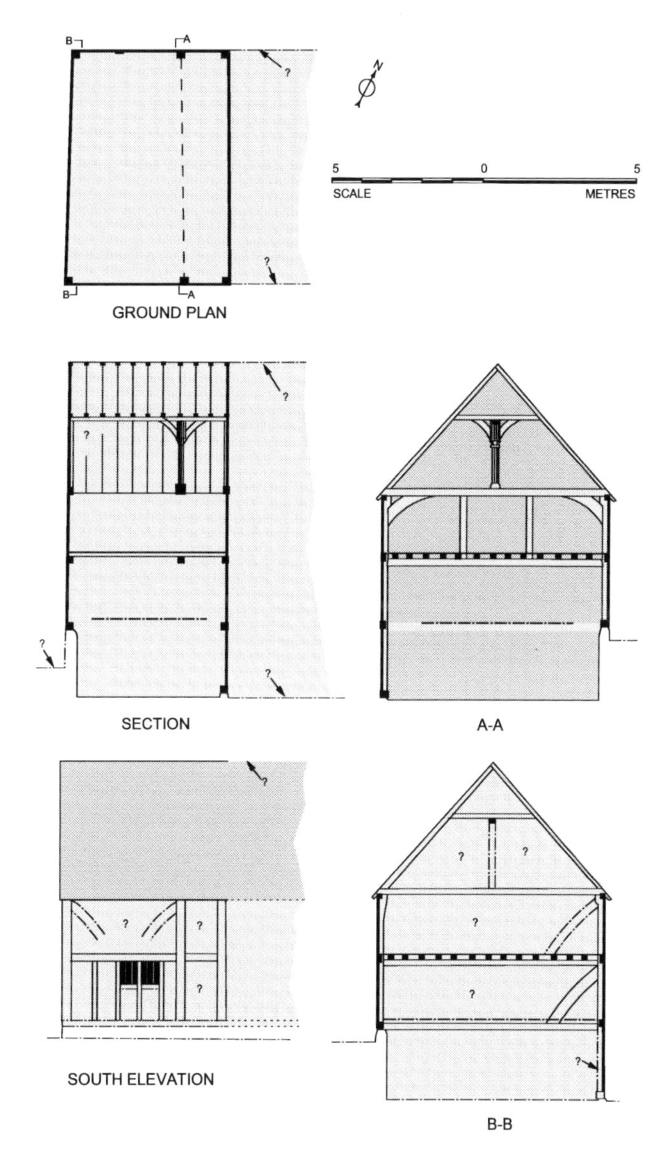

Fig. 10.1
Reconstruction of 4 High Street, phase 1.

Fig. 10.2
Refixed phase-1 crownpost at 4 High Street.

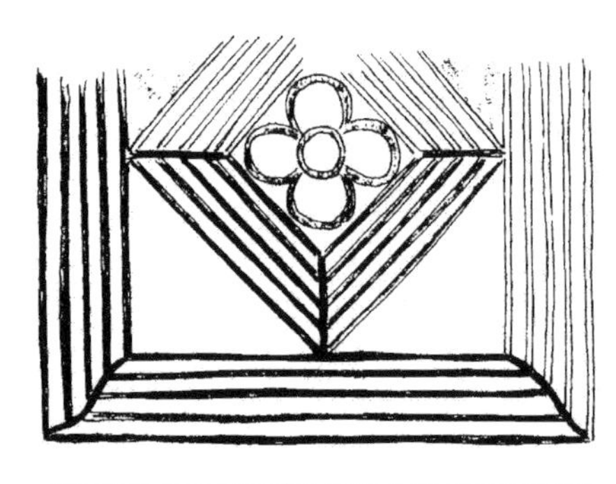

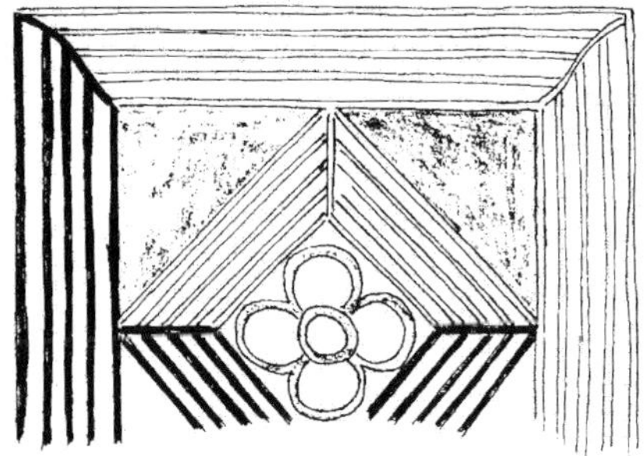

Fig. 10.3
4 High Street. Phase 2 wall painting on east wall of front first-floor room.

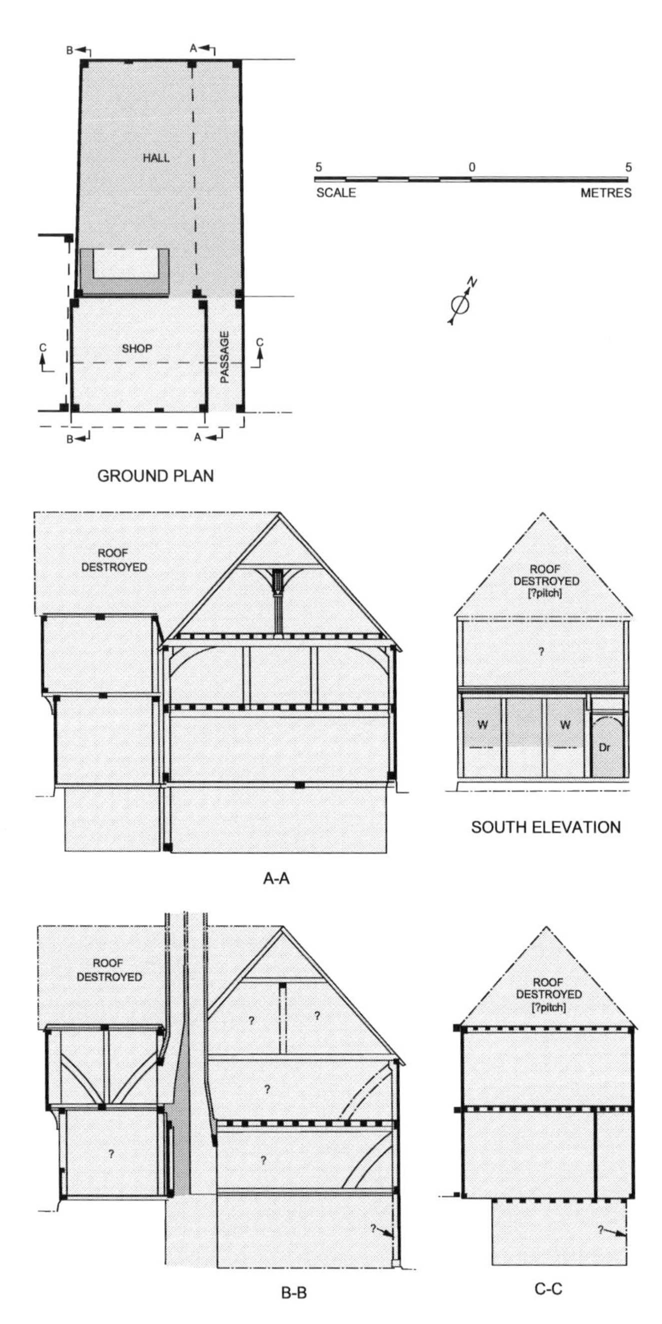

Fig. 10.4
Reconstruction of 4 High Street, phase 2.

the step in the frontage eastwards.

The new addition was built open framed against the front wall of the earlier structure and incorporated a first-floor jetty with a moulded combined soleplate and fascia formed out of a single timber: it is wrapped over the ends of the joists so as to mask them from view. At the eastern end of the facade a doorway with moulded surround and arched head led into a passage which gave access to the house at the rear. There was no access to the shop from the passageway. The shop front itself consisted of three relatively wide openings of which the two outer openings were windows, closed by externally hinged shutters which extend down to 840 mm (2'9") above the level of the present ground floor. It is possible that the central opening served as a doorway, though it is equally possible that there was no public access into the shop.

Internal access to the shop was from the hall within the rear range, which was by this date served by a chimney built against the old southern wall. There was no fireplace heating the chamber above: instead the first-floor fireplace faced south towards the shop chamber. The heated shop chamber was evidently the principal of the two first-floor apartments and incorporated wall paintings in imitation of panelling (Figure 10.3). By this date a ceiling had been inserted into the medieval range in order to allow its roof area to be utilized. Because the storey heights within the added front part are higher, the upper floor within this front section is positioned some distance above that of the rear range. The roof of this part has been destroyed and therefore it is not known whether the attic area was positioned entirely within the roof or whether it incorporated side walls, though the former seems the most likely. What does seem safe to conclude is that the roof was aligned at right-angles to the street and almost certainly incorporated a gable within the facade. At basement level the lower storey of the medieval range extends under the shop addition as a cellar. [*ESRO HBR/1/0944*]

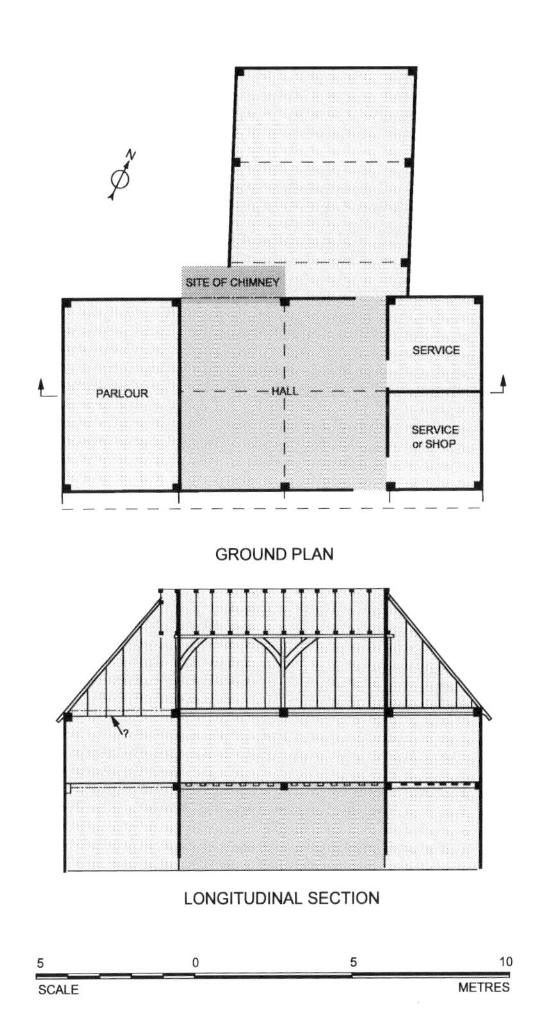

Fig. 10.5
Reconstruction of 11 High Street, phase 2.

2. 11 High Street — *1510 +/-25; 1525 +/-25*
(Figure 10.5)

Phase 1 (c.1510). A detached four-bay transitional' building with a floored-over hall and a continuous front jetty. It has a standard high-end bay to the west of the hall and a low-end bay which, on the ground floor, was divided into the usual two 'service' rooms. However, rather than the pair of 'service' doorways being adjacent to one another, in this instance the door giving access to the front 'service' room is sited hard against the front door. To judge from other examples of this phenomenon, this suggests that the front 'service' room functioned as a shop.

Phase 2 (c.1525). A two-storeyed rear range added to the rear of the hall and slightly overlapping the service bay, blocking a window in the rear wall of the hall chamber. This appears to replace a very squat single-storeyed rear range upon the same site, for it is built over an earlier barrel-vaulted cellar which extends forward, encroaching beneath the main range. The cellar appears always to have stood partially proud of the adjacent garden/yard.[1] *[ESRO HBR/1/0732]*

3. 13-14 High Street — *1600 +/-25*
(Figures 10.6 - 10.8)

A three-cell house, aligned parallel to the street, of very similar late date to 9-10 Market Street [40] and in the same general part of town. With a good street frontage of 12.50 metres (41'0"), and lofty storey heights, this was an imposing building. It once sported an elaborate facade incorporating projecting windows flanked by clerestory openings capped by a continuous row of three projecting gables (all removed — *compare* Figures 10.6 and 10.7). All three front gables were supported off the main slope by means of layboards, but large trimmed openings through the rafters allowed access into the gables. There is a spacious cellar

Fig. 10.6
13-14 High Street (centre), now stripped of its impressive multi-gabled facade. The white tiled house on the right is infill, whilst the brick building on the left was built in 1636 to replace a lower building with a gap between it and 13-14.

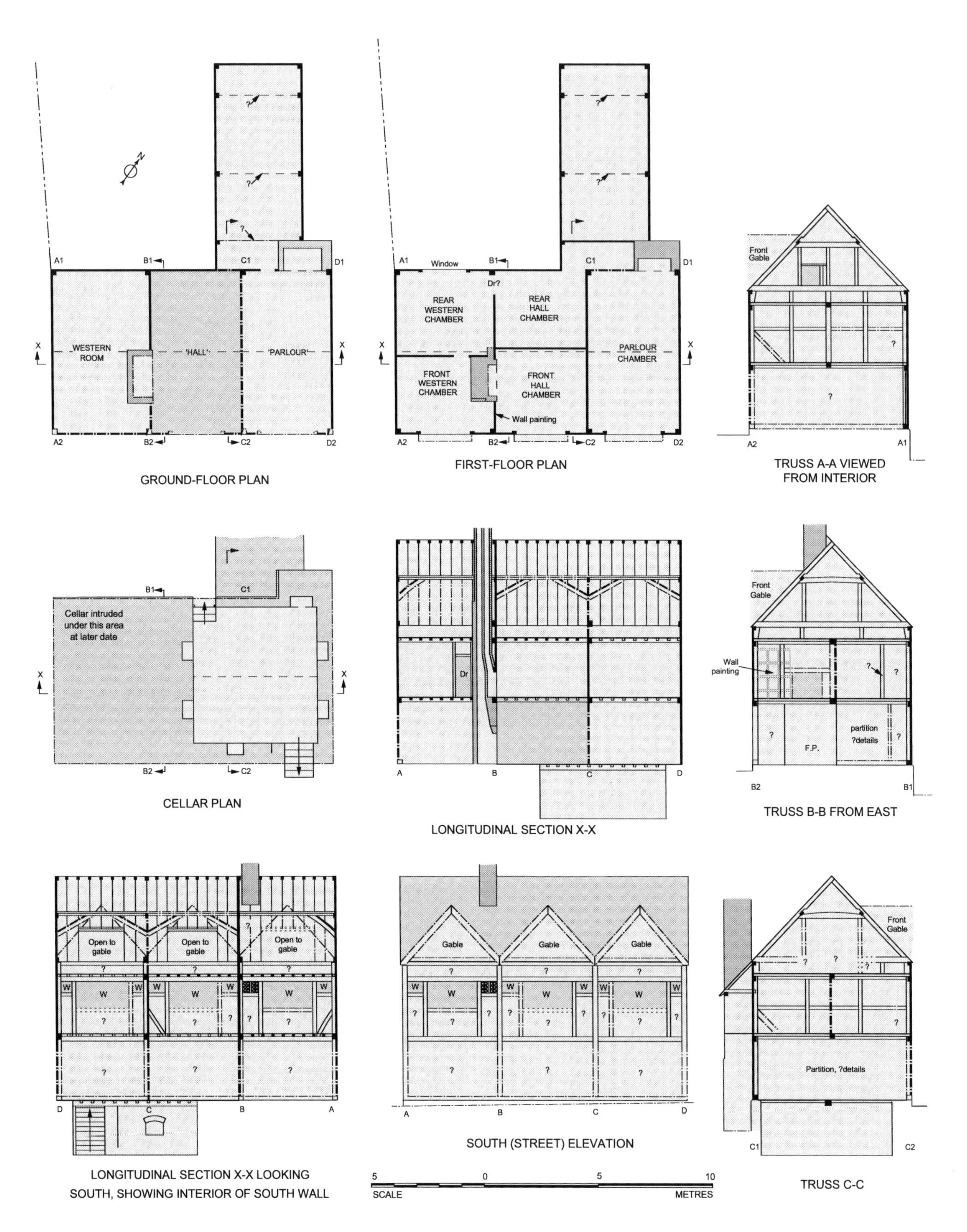

Fig. 10.7
Reconstruction of 13-14 High Street.

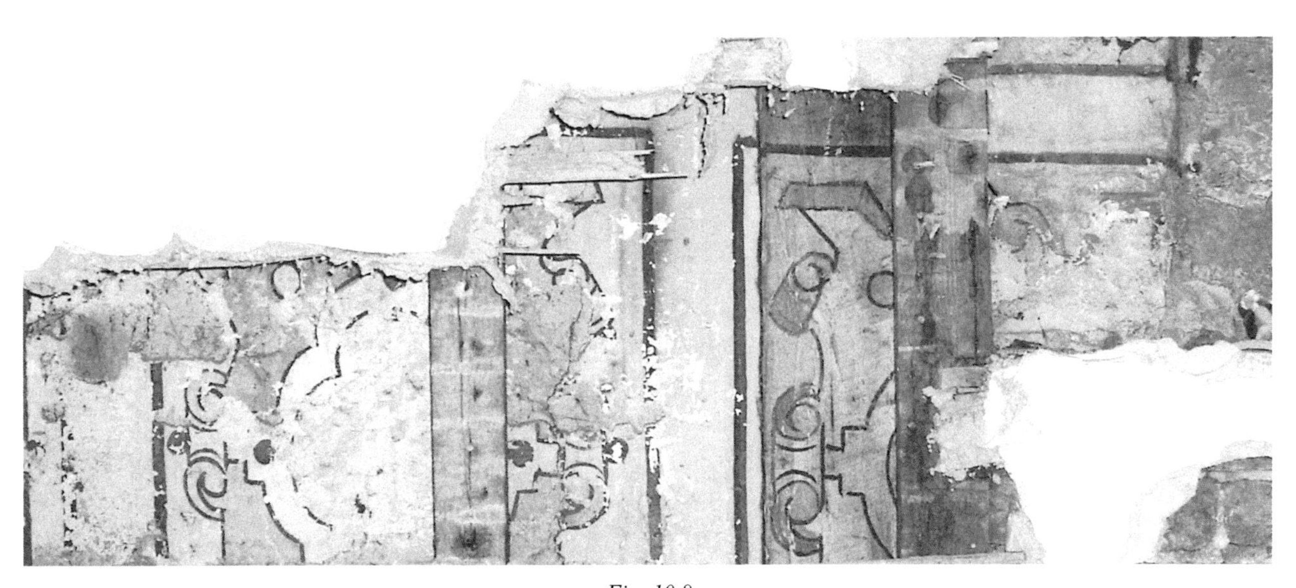

Fig. 10.8
Wall painting discovered beneath later plaster on the west wall of the Front Hall Chamber, 13-14 High Street.

which extends under a large part of the building and was entered direct from the street by a wide flight of steps. Because of the natural slope, this cellar is largely above ground at the rear and here there is a second opening leading to the garden/rear yard. Although now adjoined by buildings on either side (of which one is the Grammar School, built in 1636), the available evidence strongly suggests that the building was originally freestanding.

The original form of the building is illustrated in Figure 10.7. Its street range comprises three equal-length bays and incorporates a tall outshut (capped by a lean-to roof) running part way along its rear wall, abutting against a projecting chimney. This chimney heated the eastern of the three bays, which served as a parlour and parlour chamber. The central ground-floor room — the hall — was also heated, in this instance by an axial chimney built within the western bay. The use to which the western room was put is uncertain. Whereas the eastern chamber extended the full 7.00 metres (23'0") width of the building, the other two bays were from the outset divided by axial partitions in order to give two chambers within each. The rear chambers were lit by large windows in the back wall. The front chamber over the hall retains the remains of elaborate, geometric wall paintings (Figure 10.8), but these cannot be original to the build as they cover the blocking to an intruded doorway which led into the adjacent chamber. At attic level the two eastern bays appear to have formed a large inter-linked spacious room, the low-level tiebeam apparently being trimmed by queen posts in order to allow through access. In contrast, there has never been a doorway linking this space to the western attic area, and thus this latter area must always have been separately accessed. A shuttered external hatch incorporated into the western gable (now blocked by the Grammar School) suggests that this area may have been used for storage.

The infill framing of the main house is of small-panel type with some footbracing. The roof is of clasped-side-purlin construction triangulated by means of straight windbraces.

A low, perhaps single storeyed but possibly lofted three-bay range extends back from the eastern end of the house. The narrow northern bay implies the former existence of a chimney, suggesting a service use (?wash house, brewhouse, kitchen). Although of antiquity, the range has been much altered and its date remains uncertain, though it appears to represent a 17th-century addition. Even so, its general constructional details are similar to those of the main house. *[ESRO HBR/1/1541]*

4. 15 High Street — *1590 +/-25*
(Figures 10.9 - 10.11)

Today the original form of this house is much disguised by 19th-century reconstruction work within the part adjacent to the street, but in its initial form it comprised a tall, near-square block measuring on the ground floor 10.00 metres (32'10") along the street by 9.05 metres (29'8") deep. In its constructional detail it shows a number of similarities with 14 Lion Street [49] immediately opposite. It is a lofty three-and-a-half storeyed building. The rear wall is jettied at first-floor level, but there are no jetties higher up the elevation: another characteristic which it shares with No. 14 [49]. The arrangement of the street facade cannot be recovered, though in all probabilities this too incorporated a first-floor jetty. Bearing in mind the fact that the structure is framed as two adjacent and parallel ranges turned at right-angles to the highway, it is likely that these presented twin gables towards the street.

Beneath the western part of the building and extending partially under the rear eastern room is a cellar which, because of the downward slope on the site, is largely above ground at the rear but fully subterranean at the front. Thus the house rises through a full four-and-a-half storeys at the rear — unprecedented within the town.

Despite the front rooms having been rebuilt, there is sufficient evidence retained within the frame to indicate that on the ground floor the layout comprised a block of four rooms, the heated eastern front room being divided from the unheated room to the rear by a large chimney. Either a staircase area or a (since removed) chimney — or perhaps both — separated the western front room from that at the rear.

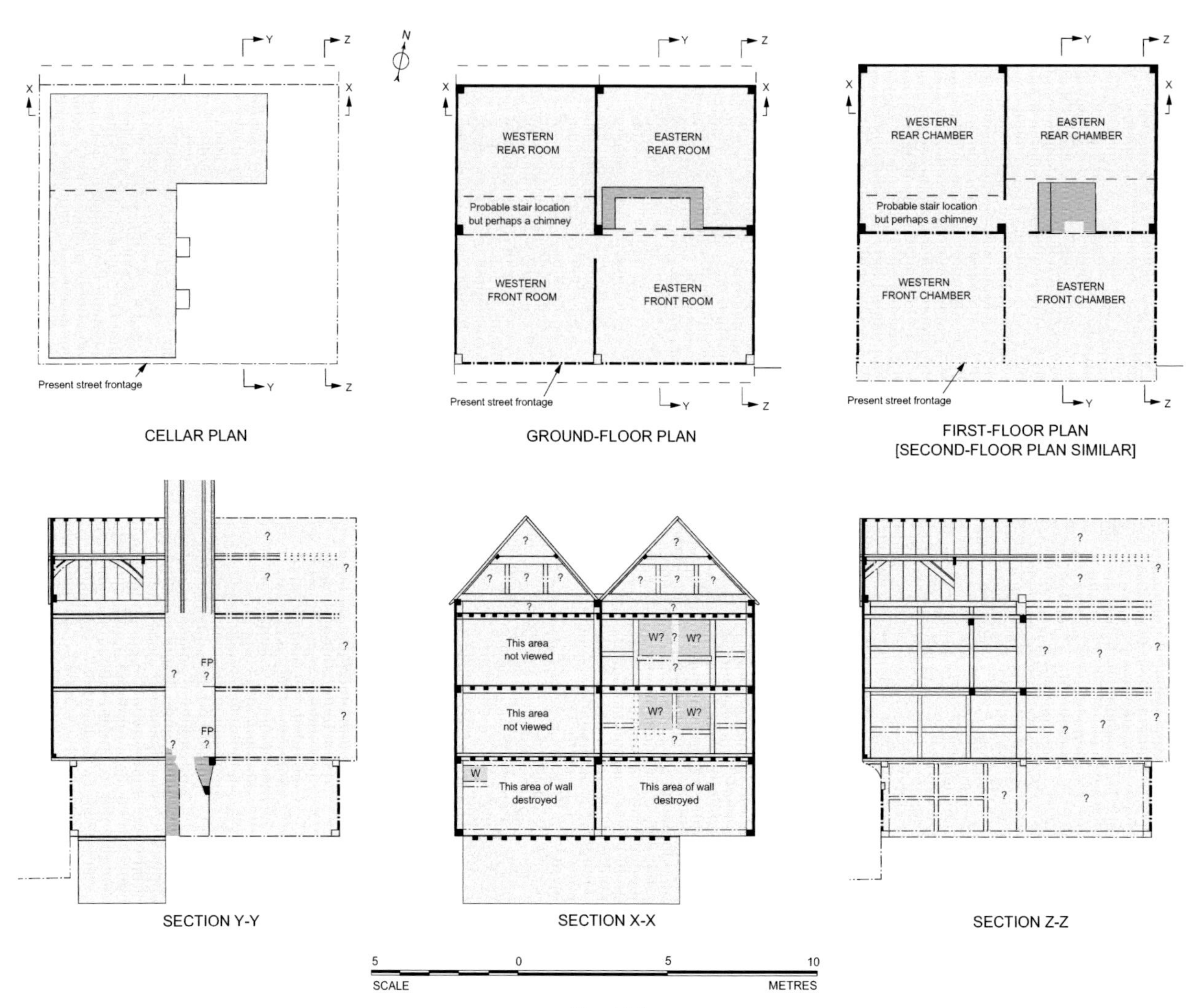

Fig. 10.9
Reconstruction of 15 High Street.

Fig. 10.10
15 High Street. Heated front room showing mortices for joists of former first floor. The area was formerly divided into two rooms by a partition in line with the principal post. A mortice for a door head is visible in the front face of the post.

At attic level the wallplates are elevated 450 mm (1'6") above the floor in order to improve headroom. The underside of the rafters show no evidence of having been masked by plaster, and thus this spacious roof area appears to have been utilized for storage or, at most, low-grade accommodation.

All visible walls within the building are of small-panel design, similar in appearance to the design utilized at 31 Mermaid Street [69], built in 1576. Evidence within the rear wall on both the first and second floors suggest that both levels incorporated large central windows. Their cills were jointed to the jambs by means of mortices with haunched shoulders: a type of joint which normally indicates the former existence of projecting oriels. At these two levels the windows do not appear to have been flanked by high-level clerestory lights, though in the same wall at ground-floor level, beneath the jetty, evidence survives of at least one clerestory opening with a chamfered external surround. Unfortunately the remainder of the detail at this level is lost.

The roof of the building is of clasped-side-purlin type incorporating straight windbraces. As at 39-40 The Mint [14] and a number of other Rye houses of this period, some roof trusses do not coincide with the bay divisions beneath. *[ESRO HBR/1/1541]*

Fig. 10.11
15 High Street. Straight windbrace in eastern slope of eastern roof.

5. 24/25 High Street [2] — *1560 +/-25*
(Figures 10.12 - 10.15)

This property was purpose built as an inn during a single (though perhaps phased) building campaign, most likely during the third quarter of the 16th century. However, the site was not totally cleared of earlier structures: a late 13th- or 14th-century vaulted cellar was incorporated deep beneath the new structure and, in part, runs under the 16th century basements. There is no connection between the basement and cellar. Instead the vaulted cellar was reached via a flight of steps leading down from its own street entrance, with a short curving flight of side steps leading to the hall.

The proprietor's quarters appear to have been kept entirely separate from the public rooms, being located within what was, in effect, a separate house occupying the western end of the complex. As far as can be told, the only link between the two parts was a single ground-floor doorway. Subsequently they became separated with regards both tenancy and ownership and it is entirely possible that this split occurred at an early date — the hearth tax returns indicate that it had certainly occurred by 1662. The house part (now 25 High Street) is of 'T' plan and appears to have incorporated three rooms on each floor. However, it should be stressed that all features on the ground floor within this part were either destroyed or masked when it was converted to modern retail use.

Even within that part occupied by the inn (No. 24) the ground-floor plan is not totally clear. In the street range were two rooms: an eastern hall which is now featureless but which was formerly heated by an axial fireplace (now removed), and a western 'parlour' heated by a shouldered stone fireplace of typical 'Rye' type, moulded and carved. This latter room is panelled and incorporates the linking doorway to the 'house-part' to the west. Between the hall and parlour runs a passage which gives access to both these rooms and to a small, now roofed-over central courtyard beyond.

Each of the east and west ranges housed a single unheated room. Neither the layout nor the means of access to the eastern room is clear: it may have extended into the eastern

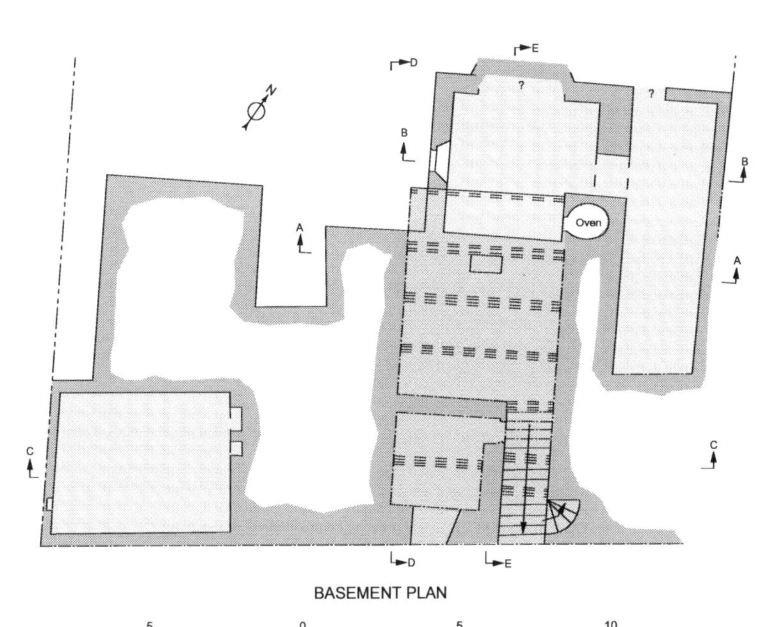

Fig. 10.12
24-25 High Street. Reconstructed plan showing basements and medieval vaulted cellar

Fig. 10.13
24-25 High Street. Multiple bracing to north wall of former courtyard viewed from top of stairs. The western gallery is visible on the left. The ceiling visible at the top of the picture was added when the courtyard was roofed over.

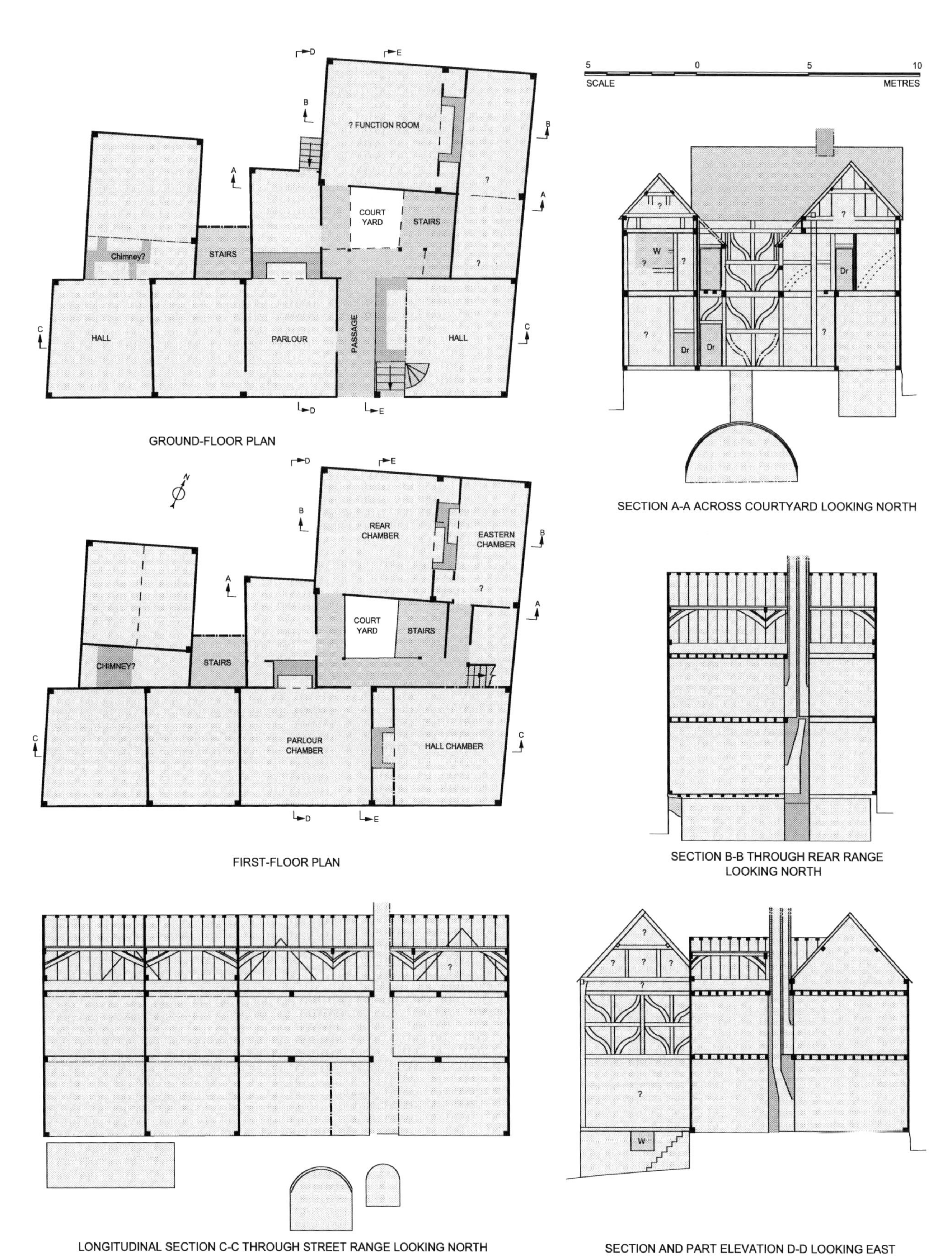

5 0 5 10
SCALE
METRES
? FUNCTION ROOM
COURT YARD
STAIRS
Chimney?
STAIRS
HALL
PARLOUR
PASSAGE
HALL
GROUND-FLOOR PLAN
REAR CHAMBER
EASTERN CHAMBER
COURT YARD
STAIRS
CHIMNEY?
STAIRS
PARLOUR CHAMBER
HALL CHAMBER
FIRST-FLOOR PLAN
SECTION A-A ACROSS COURTYARD LOOKING NORTH
SECTION B-B THROUGH REAR RANGE LOOKING NORTH
LONGITUDINAL SECTION C-C THROUGH STREET RANGE LOOKING NORTH
SECTION AND PART ELEVATION D-D LOOKING EAST

Fig. 10.14
Reconstruction of 24-25 High Street.

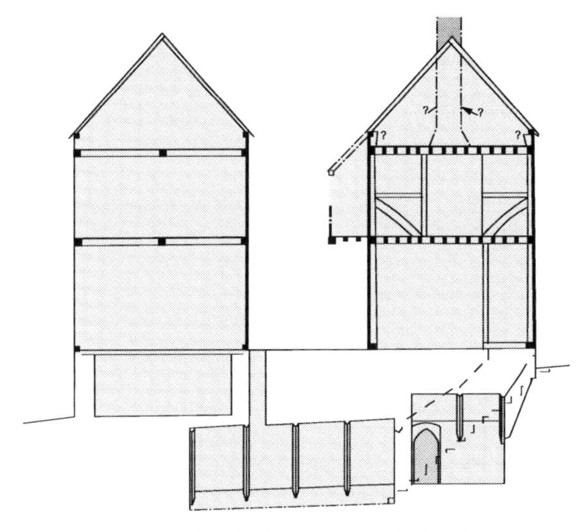

SECTION E-E THROUGH COURTYARD AND BASEMENTS/CELLARS LOOKING EAST

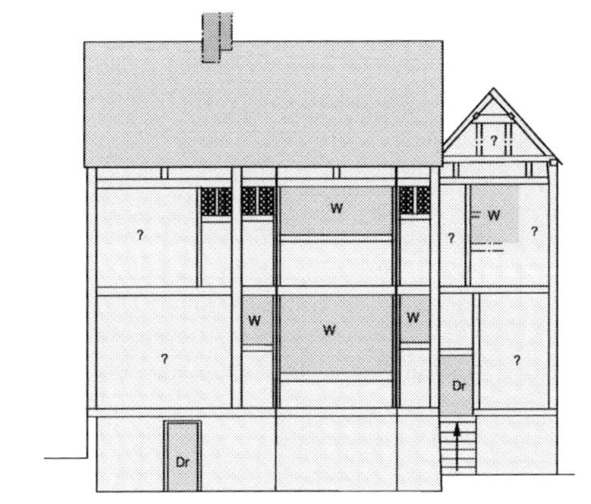

NORTH ELEVATION OF REAR RANGE, VIEWED FROM REAR YARD

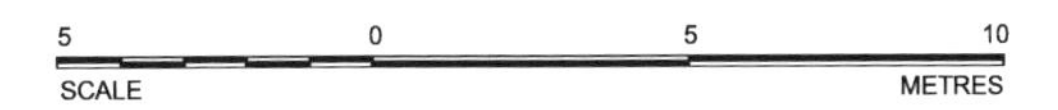

Fig. 10.15
24-25 High Street. Reconstructed details.

bay of the rear range. Certainly the two areas must have been linked by a doorway at the very least. The small western room had no internal access, but was instead reached via a doorway leading off the courtyard. There was also an external doorway in the rear wall, reached via steps from the back yard. The main section of the rear range housed the largest room in the complex and was of high quality. It was accessed solely from the courtyard and was most likely intended as the inn's function room. As with the parlour, it is heated by a 'Rye-style' decorative stone fireplace. It was lit solely from the north by some form of large bay window flanked by deep clerestory openings. The room is panelled throughout. Assuming that this area did serve as a function room, members of the public entering the building from the street would have approached it via the street range's through-passage. Upon entering the courtyard the visitor would have been confronted by a wall incorporating an array of decorative ogee bracing (*see* Figure 10.13) a feature also incorporated into the western end wall of the range. The use of display bracing within this latter wall begs the question as to the intended use of the small unheated room in the west range — did it serve as an entrance foyer for patrons entering the inn (and thus the function room) via the rear stable yard? The stable complex was probably reached via the lane known as Pongarden (now Market Road); certainly this was the means of access to the yard in the 19th century.[3]

Within the central courtyard an external stair rose to an open-sided gallery which ran around all but the northern side. Doorways led off the gallery to give access to the six first-floor letting chambers. In the interests of privacy the doorways were spaced widely apart and there were no first-floor windows overlooking the gallery. A doorway in the south-eastern corner gave access to a stair leading up to the inter-connected garret rooms in the roof.

Beneath the rear and eastern ranges is a two-roomed basement area which, due to the slope of the ground, was largely above yard level at the rear (*see* Figures 10.12 and 10.15). A doorway in the northern wall of the eastern basement room connects to the yard and this was probably the principal (if not the only) means of access to these lesser rooms. A clue to the use of these rooms is to be found in the remains of a bread oven. It should also be noted that the complex lacks a kitchen. Given the absence of a cooking hearth in the basement complex, there must surely have been a detached structure within the rear yard. *[ESRO HBR/1/1025]*

6. 26 High Street — *1525 +/-50*
(Not Illustrated)

Though the front section has been rebuilt, fragmentary remains survive of a two-bay rear range built at right angles to the street. The design suggests a 16th century date with a large principal rear room served by a smoke-bay against the rear wall. This was subsequently closed down and a new chimney built between the front and rear ranges, but this too has since been removed and is only visible at cellar level. *[ESRO HBR/1/1616]*

7. 28b High Street — *1500 +/-50*
(Not Illustrated)

The visible medieval remains at this property are restricted to one roof truss, a length of wallplate, and a reused moulded fascia beam. The roof truss, which has racked badly, is of paired-rafter-and-collar type and is heavily sooted on its western face. It is located 4.70 metres (15'5") from the western boundary of the site, whilst extending eastwards from it for a distance of 2.80 metres (9'2") is a length of wallplate containing the groove for a sliding window shutter. All this could indicate a building approximately 7.60 metres (24'11") long x 5.40 metres (17'8") wide with either an open hall or alternatively a hall served by a smoke bay to the west and a floored bay to the east. *[ESRO HBR/1/0968]*

8. 29b High Street — *16th C*
(Not Illustrated)

Timbers visible within the present banking hall of Barclays Bank indicates that an early timber-framed building survives within the present structure. The visible work is consistent with a 16th century date. *[Not surveyed]*

9. 30 High Street
(Not Illustrated)

The superstructure here has been rebuilt, but pre-dated adjacent 31 High Street, which was built open-framed against it. A probably 16th-century cellar survives under the front range, though truncated in height by the lowering of the ground floor within the present shop. The cellar incorporates a semi-circular stone wall for a spiral staircase with neatly-dressed door jambs. The opening onto the street likewise has neatly-dressed stone jambs. *[Not surveyed]*

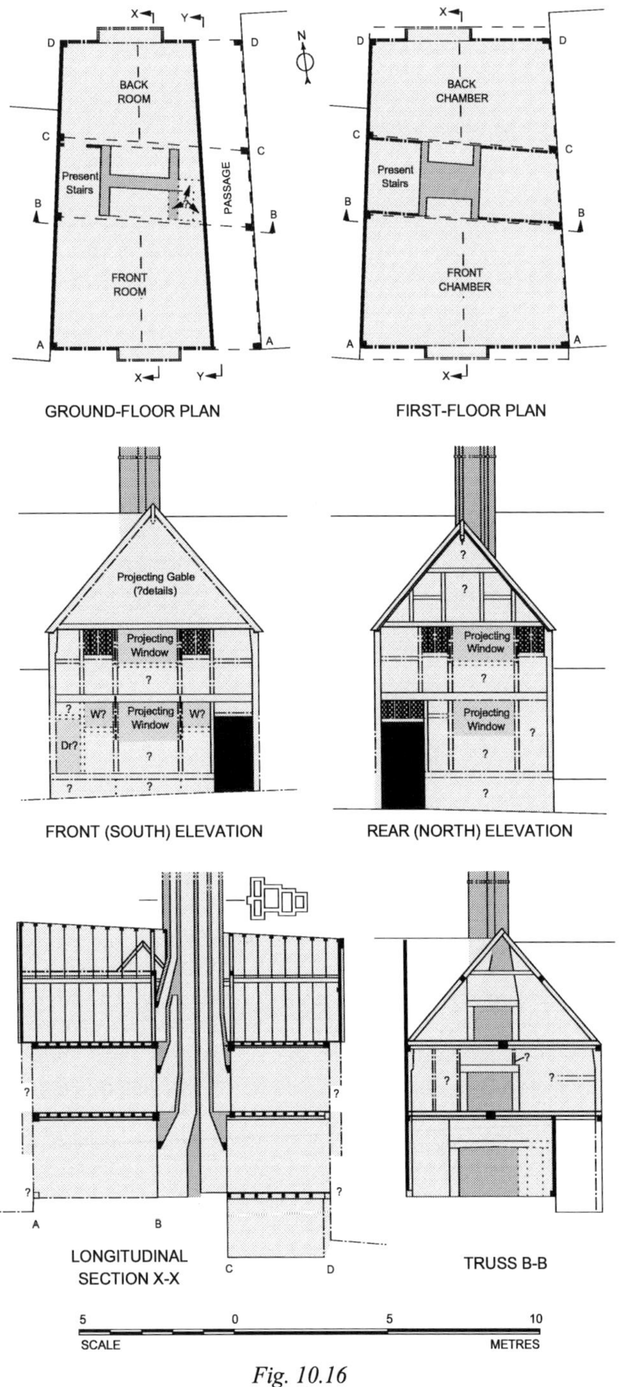

Fig. 10.16
Reconstruction of 31 High Street.

10. 31 High Street — *1610 +/-25*
(Figures 10.16 & 10.17)

This may be one of Rye's rare 17th century houses. It is dated on typological evidence to *c.*1610, but since the construction sequences established within some Rye buildings indicate dates earlier than would normally be given for similar buildings located in a rural or village context, this typological date could be a little too late. Even so, it post-dates the buildings which flank it and must have been built at the very end of Rye's 'Tudor' building boom.

The site is wedge shaped: the gable facing the street measures 6.75 metres (22'2") wide, whereas, the rear gable measures only 5.80 metres (19'0"). In consequence, because a consistent roof pitch is maintained throughout, the butt-purlin roof is less tall at the rear than at the front, which looks bizarre when the building is drawn in longitudinal section (Figure 10.16). Despite this, because of the adjacent buildings in reality the difference in height is hardly discernible. As indicated by the ground-floor plan illustrated in Figure 10.16, a wide passage is divided off down the eastern side, whereas on the first floor the chambers extend the full width of the building. Both ground-floor rooms and both first-floor chambers are heated by the axial chimney, as too is the front garret room: thus the chimney incorporates five flues. Because of the adjacent buildings, all rooms and chambers are lit via the front and rear walls, both of which formerly incorporated projecting bay windows flanked by clerestory lights and capped by overhanging gables elaborated with bargeboards and pendants. Such attention to detail is clear indication of the relative high status of the building, though it should be borne in mind that the rear elevation would have been more easily visible than one might at first imagine, for houses and a street once filled at least part of the space between the property's back garden and the town wall (*see* Chapter 2).

The location of the front door is not known for certain, though it is likely to have been at the opposite end of the facade to the side passage. Most likely the front room served as the hall, with the back room fulfilling the function of

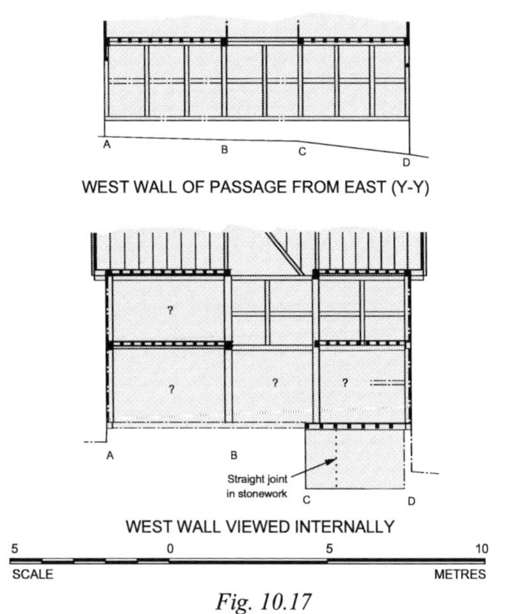

Fig. 10.17
Reconstructed details of wall framing, 31 High Street.

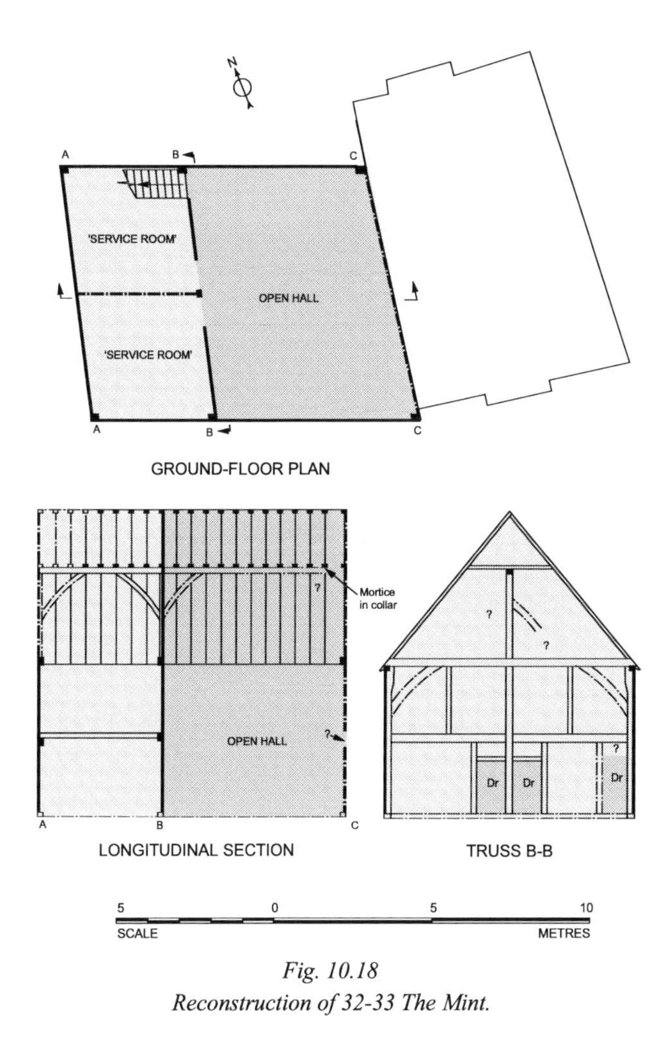

Fig. 10.18
Reconstruction of 32-33 The Mint.

parlour, an interpretation borne out by the location of the cellar beneath this room. *[ESRO HBR/1/1579]*

11. 32-33 High Street — *1410 +/-33; 1545 +/-25*
(Figures 10.18 & 10.19)

Phase 1 (c.1410). An exceptionally wide, substantial two-cell hall house comprising on the ground floor a hall and services (Figure 10.18). Though the present structure is a complete frame, it is not certain that this represents the complete building: there could have been a separately-framed parlour crosswing at the high end. The house which now occupies the space beyond the hall is aligned at right angles to the street in crosswing-like fashion (*see* 31 High Street [10]).

Phase 2 (c.1545). The addition of a small range to the rear of the medieval services and the subdivision of the hall into two rooms during this phase probably coincided with the splitting of the house into two properties (Figure 10.19). It is thought that it was divided in the 16th century and then returned to single occupancy when population pressures decreased in the 17th century: on the first floor there is an intruded doorway between the two parts which is very obviously of later date (now blocked), indicating that at one time the two parts were once more amalgamated. The house was divided again as a result of the national population explosion which occurred in the 19th century. *[ESRO HBR/1/1618]*

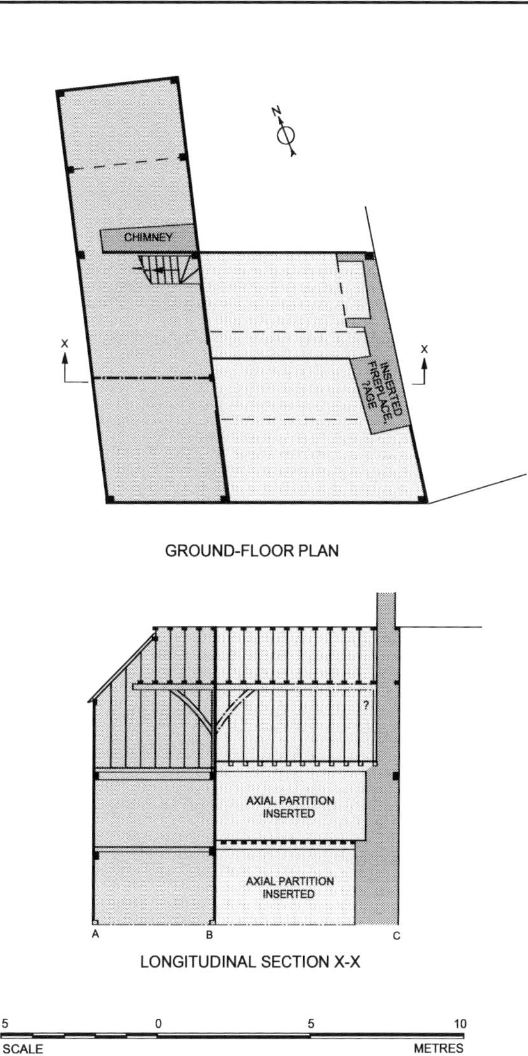

Fig. 10.19
Reconstructed details of 32-33 The Mint showing alterations apparently associated with division of the building into two occupations (depicted by light and darker grey shading).

12. 34 The Mint — *1500 +/-25*
(Figure 10.20)

A fully-floored continuously-jettied house built upon a very out-of-square plot. The hall bay is much longer than the service bay and in consequence the entry is direct into the low end of the hall and the two upper chambers are of different sizes, with a large hall chamber and a considerably smaller service chamber. Evidence for twin service doors indicate that the service area was divided into two rooms by an axial partition, though the form the partition took is unclear. The hall is today heated by a very unconvincing late-looking rear fireplace which could hide earlier work. Alternatively it could replace a chimney upon the same site or the hall could have been unheated. *[ESRO HBR/1/1621]*

13. 36-38 The Mint — *1425 +/-33; 1550 +/-50*
(Figures 10.21 - 10.23)

Phase 1 (c.1425). A large and impressive house of 'developed' form. Despite its fragmentary nature (only one

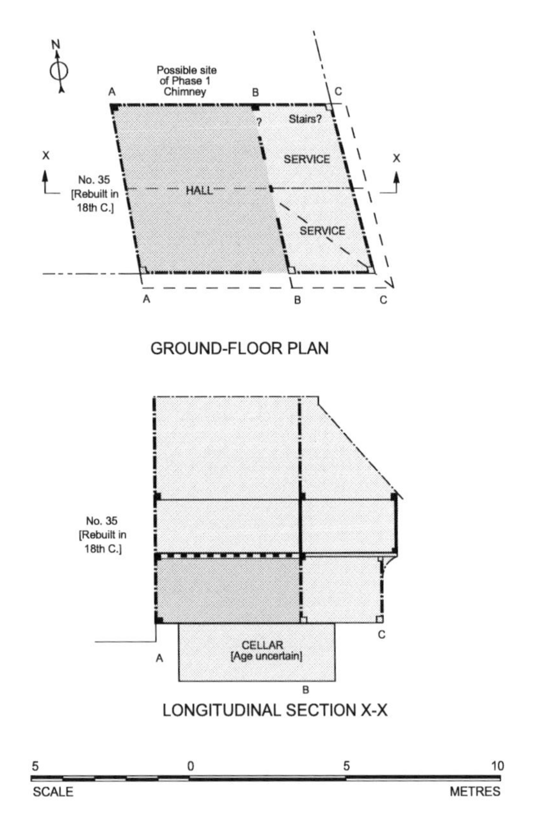

Fig. 10.20
Reconstruction of 34 The Mint.

Fig. 10.21
36-38 The Mint. Heavy-section medieval joists within front room of crosswing.

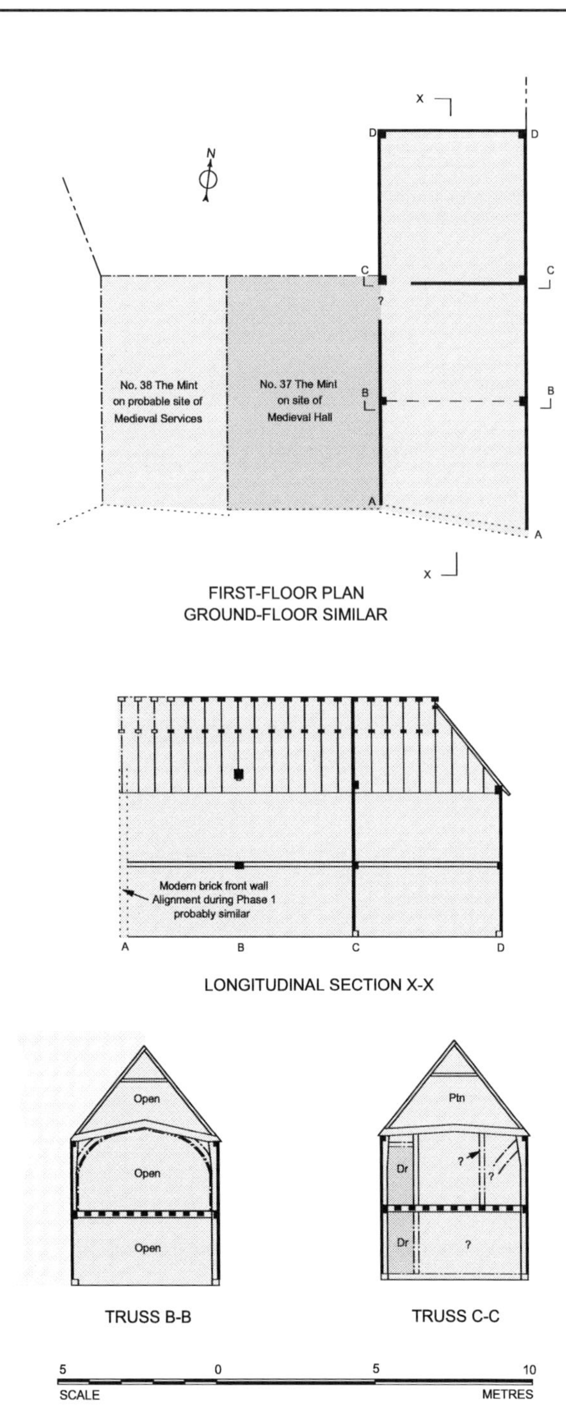

Fig. 10.22
Reconstruction of 36-38 The Mint.

third of the street frontage survives) the basic layout of the missing parts is reflected within their replacements. The house had a *c.*13.50 metre (*c.*44'3") street frontage and a main range which measured at least 7.25 metres (23'9") wide. Built upon a gently sloping site, the services were at the down-hill end to the west, with the high-end accommodation to the east of the open hall. As Figure 10.22 indicates, the high-end accommodation is located within a substantial three-bay crosswing built with its canted gable towards the street and extending 11.80 metres (38'8") back down the plot. The main high-end room was large — *c.*7.15 metres x 4.50 metres (*c.*23'5" x 14'9") internally — and had an equally large two-bay chamber above it, crossed by an open truss with cranked tiebeam (Figure 10.23). To the rear, projecting back beyond the rear wall of the main range, is the third bay, housing a further ground-floor room with chamber above. Such an arrangement is equal to that found within the largest rural houses of the area. Whether, as seems to have been the case in the rural examples, the main ground-floor room served as a parlour, or was put to some other specialized 'urban' use is unclear.

Fig. 10.23
36-38 The Mint. Cranked tiebeam to Truss B-B. The braces have been removed, but are indicated by mortices.

Phase 2 (c.1550). When the house was upgraded, a chimney (now mutilated) was inserted at the high end of the hall. It had two ground-floor fireplaces, one serving the (since rebuilt) hall and the other the exceptionally large front room within the high-end crosswing. Prior to 1600, high-end stacks were not common within the town, though examples do exist at St Anthony's, Church Square [87] and 67-69 The Mint [19]. *[ESRO HBR/1/1626]*

14. 39-40 The Mint — *Medieval; 1535 +/-25 (Figures 10.24 - 10.26)*

Phase 1 (Medieval). All that is clearly visible of the earliest phase of this structure is a former external doorway of durn type trapped in a wall which separates two adjoining rear ranges (Figure 10.24). It served the western of the two ranges, the eastern range having been added against it at a later date. The doorway seems to belong to the first half of the 15th century (or perhaps even the late 14th century) and could represent the entrance to an open hall aligned at right angles to the street, behind a since rebuilt street range. Unfortunately, so little of the early structure is visible this possibility remains pure speculation.

Fig. 10.24
Former external face of doorway of durn type incorporated within the eastern side wall of the western rear range at 39-40 The Mint.

Phase 2 (c.1535). A continuously-jettied street range with excessive storey heights, in this instance 2.95 metres (9'8") on the ground floor and 2.70 metres (8'10") on the first floor. Here the room requirements for each floor mean that the ground-floor and first-floor partitions of the range are not placed one over the other, and thus the method of construction had to be modified from the norm: the problems caused by the variation in layout (*see* Figure 10.26) were further exacerbated by the wedge-shaped footprint of the plot.

The 'square' block of accommodation required by the owner was achieved by the use of a street range backed by a pair of adjacent and adjoining rear ranges roofed at right angles and of much lower height. In part this design must have been influenced by the decision to retain and incorporate the medieval western rear range, and it is possible that the eastern rear range likewise incorporates earlier work.

Access to the rear yard is via a passage divided off on the ground floor. The line of this compromised the side wall of the retained or part retained medieval western rear range, which in consequence was canted over, leaving the southern section of the range's wallplate flying. Today this passage is a public right of way leading through to Cinque Ports Street; this may have been the case from a relatively early date. Such a passage would have been very convenient: it would have allowed pedestrian access to the town from the Wishe Ward suburb and from the Udimore ferry. Regardless of the date at which it became public, this has not always been the case, a point which is shown by the fact that at its street end the passage was initially closed by a door with a moulded surround and arched head (now removed).

Next to the passage is a heated hall accessed direct from the street by another high-quality arched-headed doorway and lit by a large window which took up virtually all the space between the two external doorways. The finish within the room is of a high standard: moulded ceiling beams (elaborated with foliage stops) and close-studded partitions. To the east is a room of similar size which also has moulded ceiling beams (*see* Figure 10.25). This was originally entered direct from the

Fig. 10.25
Moulded joists and girder with foliage stops, 39-40 The Mint.

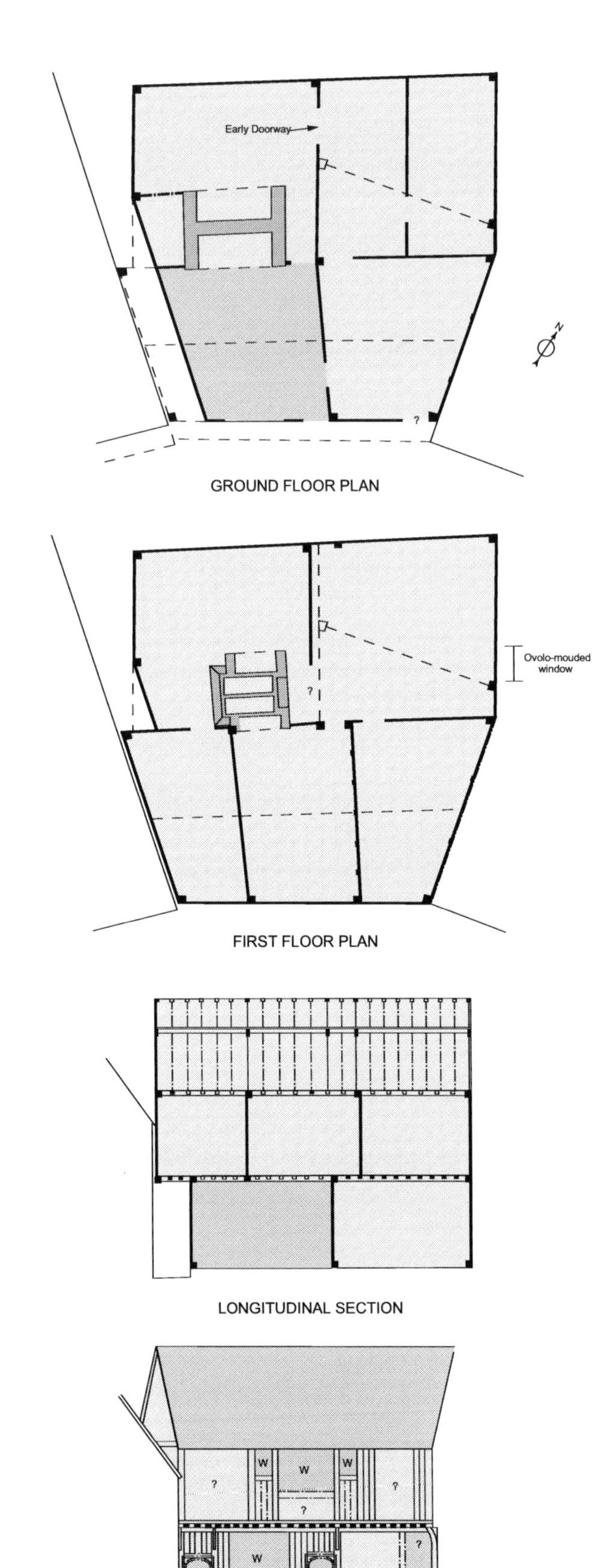

Fig. 10.26 (Right)
Reconstruction of 39-40 The Mint.

hall by a good quality, arch-headed doorway and may also have incorporated an external entrance at the eastern end of its street elevation.

The ground-floor rooms within the two adjacent rear ranges (of which the western incorporates medieval fragments and the eastern may also predate the street range) are far more modest in both storey height and finish, and to some extent the same applies to the upper storey throughout the entire building. Here there are no moulded timbers. Within the street range at this upper level the layout departs entirely from that on the ground floor. Whereas the ground floor has two rooms of virtually identical size, the first floor has three chambers, and whereas the two ground-floor rooms are interlinked, neither of the first-floor partitions incorporate doorways. Instead, access to all three chambers was from the rear via doorways in the rear wall of the range: in this respect, as in others, the house shares similarities with 20A, 21 Watchbell Street [98].

Of the three front chambers the central chamber seems to have been regarded as the principal apartment. This is the one which is heated and this too is the chamber which was served by a large central window flanked by clerestory lights: perhaps the earliest example of this type of fenestration evidenced within the town. All three chambers had ceilings from the outset and, following the common arrangement found in Rye at this period, the roof area above seems to have been a single large room, most likely used for storage.

Very little of the roof construction is visible, though this is sufficient to indicate that it is of clasped-side-purlin type incorporating collar trusses absent of queen studs. In contrast to the roof over the street range, 'medieval-style' paired-rafter-and-collar construction was used over both of the low rear ranges and here simulated crownposts form the rear gables. Within this rear part of the house the first-floor loft-like areas were open to the roof. Indeed the wallplates of the retained medieval western range are so low they are only slightly above the level of the lofty street range's first floor. The wall heights within the eastern range are only slightly better. *[ESRO HBR/1/0791]*

15. 41 The Mint (The Standard) —
1400 +/-100; 1475 +/-25; 1525 +/-25
(Figures 10.27 - 10.29)

Phase 1 (15th C). A timber-framed hall house with neatly-cut timbers. These were of good scantling considering the tiny size of the building: the overall roof span of the hall was only 4.50 metres (14'9"). The height of the hall is not currently known, as the upper part of its one surviving truss is hidden from view, but the level of the crossbeam suggests the eaves must have been located only slightly above the first-floor jetty of the later crosswing. Only the end truss of the hall survives, trapped against neighbouring 39-40 The Mint [14].

Phase 2 (c.1475). What is assumed to have been the low-end bay of the hall house was demolished to make room for a new, lofty two-bay crosswing of very up-to-date design (Figure 10.27).[4] The Standard shares the same sequence of reconstruction as 32 Mermaid Street [70] in that the hall was initially retained when the remainder of the house was rebuilt.

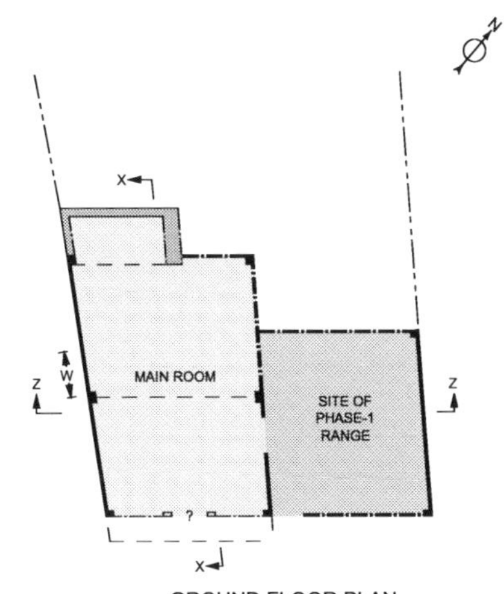

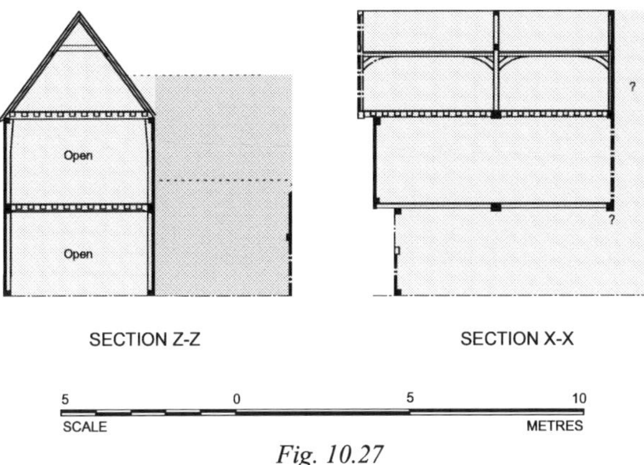

Fig. 10.27
Reconstruction of The Standard, 41 The Mint, phase 1.

Fig. 10.28
The Standard, 41 The Mint.
Doorway leading from hall into possible beer shop.

It is probably no coincidence that both of these rebuilds occurred early (during the second half of the 15th century) and involved the construction of a crosswing: the same almost certainly happened at The George, 98 High Street [24].

Within the new crosswing not only are the storey heights impressively tall, but an attic room was included from the outset, with its street gable jettied forward. The half-height walls in this attic make The Standard another of Rye's two-and-a-half storeyed buildings. Probably because of the attic room and the small size of the roof, the roof itself is not of crownpost construction, but has interrupted side purlins, windbraces, principal rafters and collar trusses. Although such a roof is unusual at this period within this part of England, it is not without precedent: rural examples are known at Rocks, East Malling and Larkfield in Kent (1507/8) and over a hall house at Pepperingeye Farm, Battle (undated). In a village context, the roof at 75, 77, 79 High Street, Edenbridge, Kent (1476/7) is of this type, whilst an urban example, built *c.*1477, exists at Glebe, Quarter 13, in Rye's sister port town of Winchelsea.[5]

Justification for an early date at The Standard comes from the adjacent 'Wealden' hall house at 42-43 The Mint [16], which not only makes use of the crosswing's side wall as its end wall, but also blocks at least one window. The new crosswing incorporates two large, good quality rooms, one on each storey. That on the ground floor has moulded principal ceiling beams and was heated from the outset by a fireplace within what appears to have been a rear brick-built smoke bay. The pattern of blocked mortices in the underside of the jetty plate and within the one exposed front principal post suggest that the crosswing's street frontage had a central doorway flanked by shop-like windows with shaped heads. A second street doorway led into the hall and there was internal access to the crosswing's room via a doorway (with four-centred head) sited centrally within the low-end wall of the open hall. The wall, which is part of the crosswing's frame (rather than that of the hall) shows close studding towards the hall and, furthermore, it is the hall face of the doorway's arched head which is carved (*see* Figure 10.28). Thus, the wall's principal face was meant to be seen from within the hall, not from within the large heated room. The building is currently an inn and its layout suggests that it may have been so since early times. If it was already an inn when the crosswing was built it is possible that the large heated room within the crosswing served as a beer shop, accessed direct from the street through the 'shop front'.

Phase 3 (c.1525). The earlier open hall was rebuilt, replaced by an exceptionally large wing built parallel to the late 15th-century crosswing, extending back down the plot at right angles to the street (*see* Figure 10.29). Although the point cannot be proven, the front room probably continued to serve as a hall, but larger in floor area and having a chamber above it. To its rear, above a cellar, was another large heated ground-floor room with moulded principal ceiling beams, above which was a good first-floor chamber, also heated and evidently fitted with a projecting window above a jettied end. This chamber was open to its roof, which was set at a slightly lower level than that over the front part, giving a stepped external appearance (visible only from the rear of the property). This configuration not only allowed an attic room to be incorporated within the front part of the range, but also elevated the roof at this point to the same height as that of the late 15th-century crosswing, giving the building a symmetrical, jettied, double-gabled street frontage (*see* Figure 7.6). Unlike within the 15th-century crosswing, these roofs are far more traditional in design — paired rafters linked by collars. Although the 16th-century layout, with three large ground-

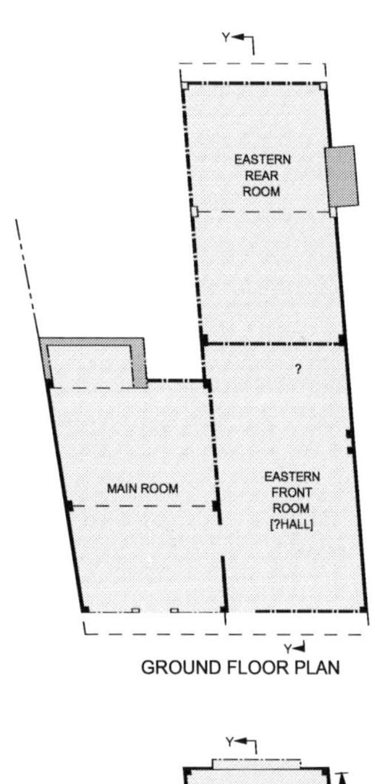

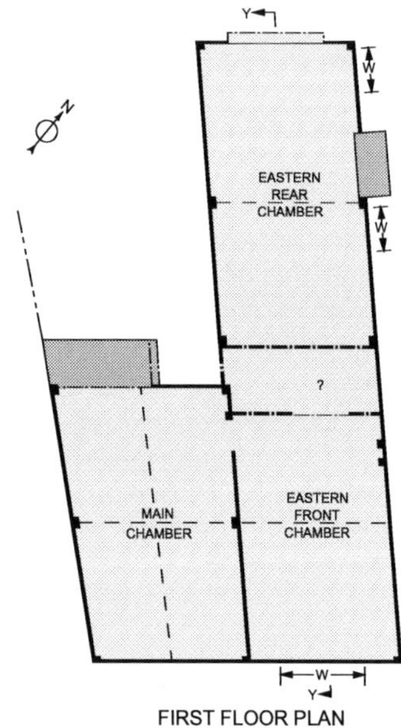

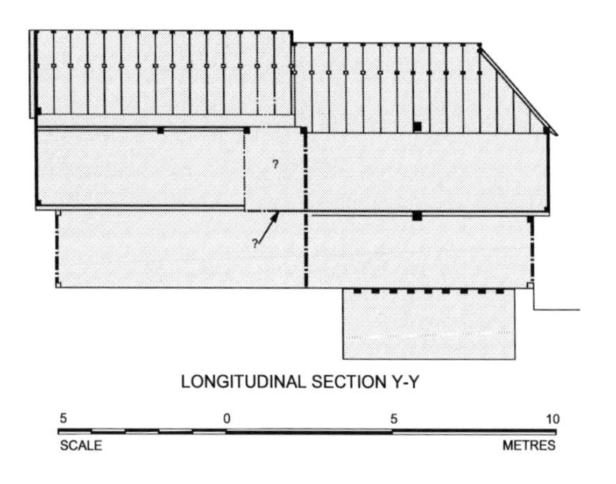

Fig. 10.29
The Standard, 41 The Mint as extended, phase 3.

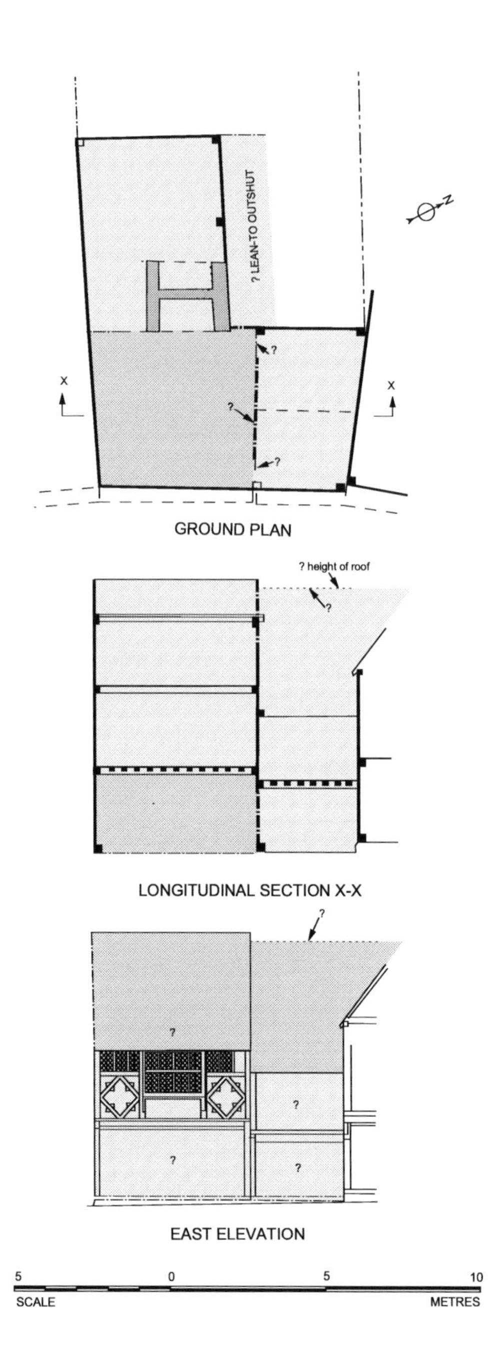

Fig. 10.30.
Reconstruction of 42-43 The Mint, phase 2, prior to addition of mid 17th-century rear range.

floor rooms and a suite of similar sized chambers above, is consistent with an inn use, there is currently no documentary evidence to substantiate this. The lack of a kitchen, or, indeed, other service rooms within such a large building must favour the former existence of a detached kitchen. *[ESRO HBR/1/1610]*

16. 42-43 The Mint — *1485 +/-25; 1570 +/-25*
(Figures 10.30 - 10.32)

Phase 1 (c.1485). A very fragmentary, late 'Wealden' hall-house built subsequent to the erection of the crosswing of *c.*1475 at The Standard, 41 The Mint [15] (*see* above). The

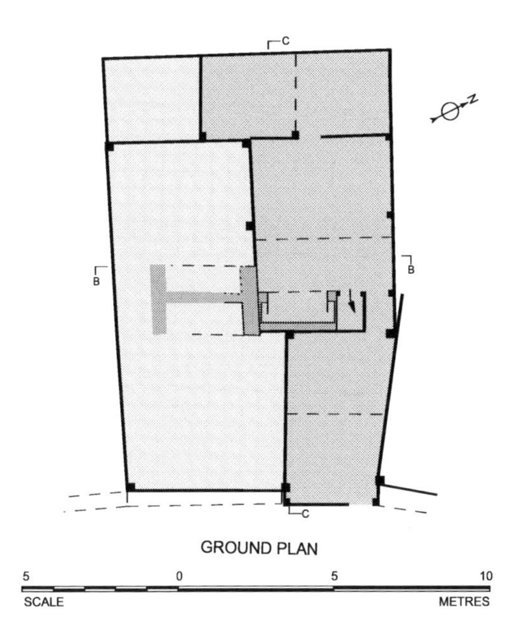

Fig. 10.31
Reconstructed plan of 42-43 The Mint
as in the mid 17th century showing division
into two occupations

partition beneath the crossbeam between hall and floored bay could have been added later. If so, this implies either that the house had an overshot cross passage or, as at 19 Watchbell Street [96], that it had a high-end jetty.[6]

Phase 2 (c.1570). The hall of this 'Wealden' was rebuilt continuously-jettied towards the street in c.1570. Its facade is somewhat noteworthy on account of the decorative design used within the front elevation — the panels beneath the clerestory openings which flank the oriel window are elaborated with cusped diamond panels, the only example known in the area. Although the medieval floored end was never rebuilt, it was radically altered at a subsequent date in order to raise both walls and roof to the same level as the rebuilt hall. Without documentary evidence it is impossible to tell whether the retained medieval bay continued to serve as part of the main dwelling or whether it was let separately. It was in two occupations by the mid 17th century, though even then it remained in single ownership (Figure 10.31). At that time the width of the rear range was doubled and capped by a massive, steeply-pitched roof with an unbelievable *c.*9.00 metre (*c.*29'6") span (Figure 10.31). It is possible that these major alterations indicate the date at which the building was finally divided into two occupations, though it seems more likely it reflects the date at which the second, smaller dwelling was upgraded and enlarged. *[ESRO HBR/1/0894]*

17. 45-46 The Mint — *1500 +/-25; 1560 +/-25*
(Figure 10.33)

Phase 1 (c.1500) A continuously jettied, fully floored early house, the hall of which is entered by a cross passage sited within part of the service bay. There was a wide spered opening between passage and hall, and the service area was divided into the usual arrangement of two service rooms. If

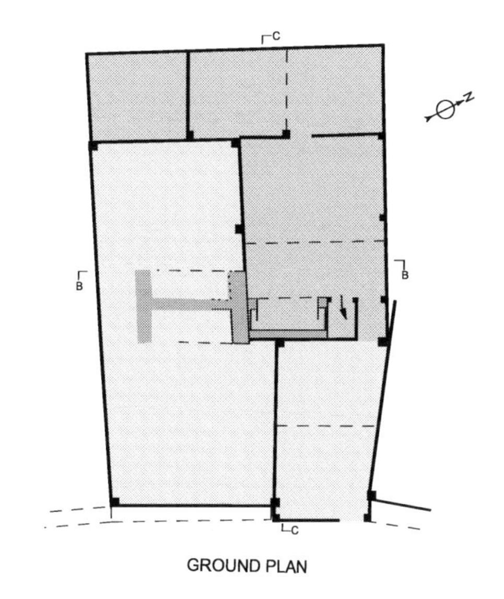

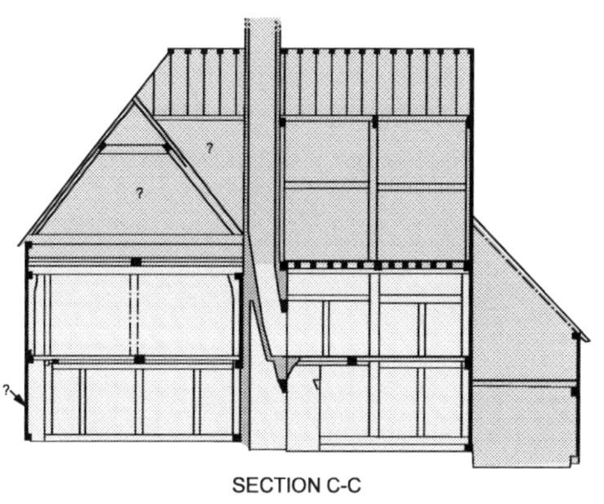

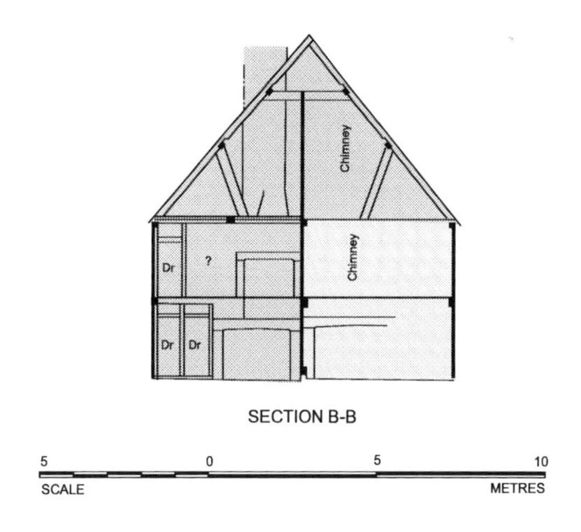

Fig. 10.32
Reconstructions of 42-43 The Mint
as in the mid 17th century showing retained earlier work in
light grey and new work in darker grey.

the space beyond the high end of the building's hall was part of the same property (which is very doubtful) the hall could have been heated by some form of ?external high-end stack, but otherwise it was unheated. There are two near-equal chambers on the first floor, both open to the roof.

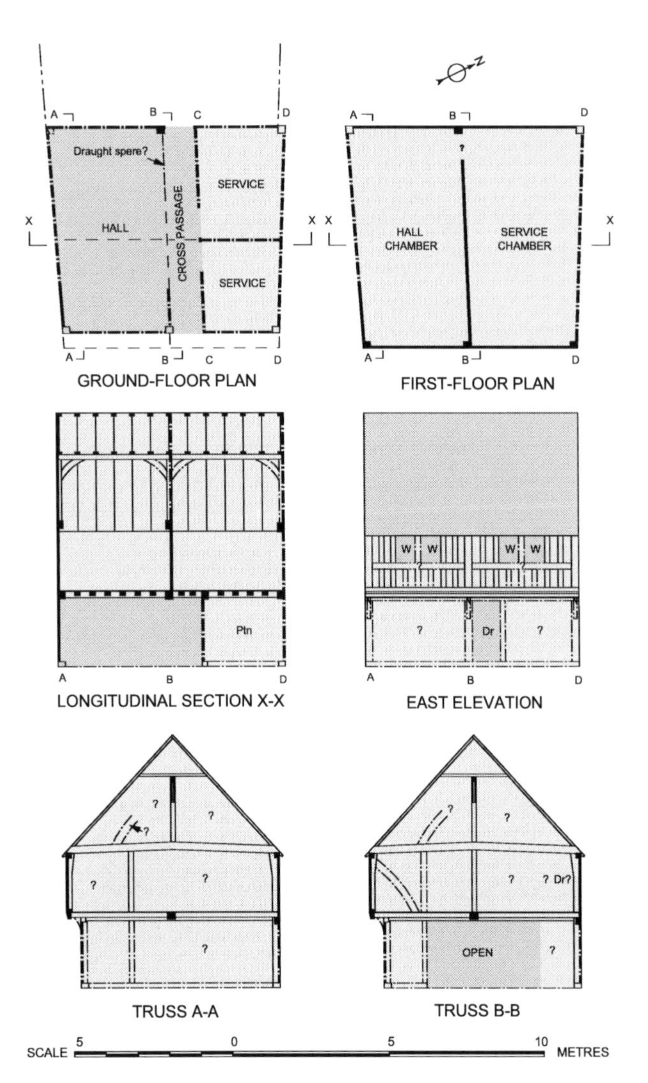

Fig. 10.33
Reconstruction of 45-46 The Mint.

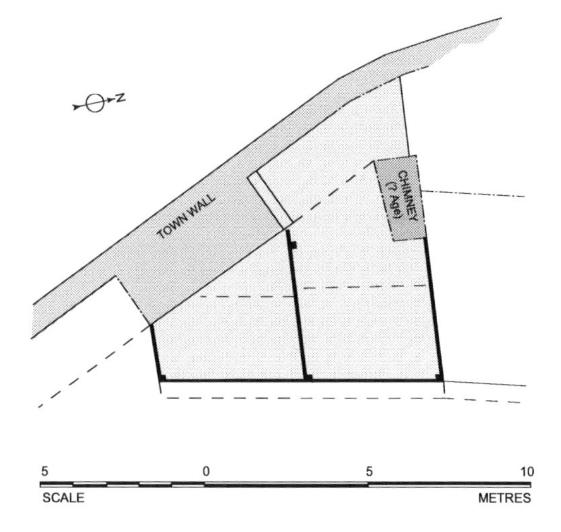

Fig. 10.34
Reconstructed plan of 54 The Mint.

Phase 2 (c.1560) A small single-bay range was constructed to the rear of the hall and a first-floor ceiling inserted into the hall chamber. *[ESRO HBR/1/1625]*

18. 54 The Mint — *1550 +/- 25*
(Figures 10.34 & 10.35)

A two-cell building significant for its plan. It is wedge-shaped, having been built upon a confined, irregular plot at the point where 'The Mint' converges upon the town wall. The rear wall of the house is formed by the masonry of the town wall, the wall walk of which was at this point carried upon an arched arcade. The structure appears to have utilized one of the recesses formed by this arcade in order to enlarge thc internal floor area of the eastern bay. Unfortunately, much of the detail within the building is hidden and in consequence many of the design features are uncertain.

Due to the plot's shape the western wall measures only *c.*1.70 metres (*c.*7'6") on the ground floor, whereas the eastern wall is in excess of 7 metres (23'0") excluding the wall recess. Because the two side walls of the building converge the builder very wisely chose the practical solution of roofing the structure in two parts, aligned at right angles to the street. This resulted in a twin-gabled facade similar in appearance to that at The Standard [15] further up the street (*compare* Figures 10.35 and 7.6). The method of construction adopted is clasped side purlins with windbracing to the front gables. As in a number

Fig. 10.35
Exterior of 54 The Mint showing rebuilt section of town wall in background with a later addition to No. 54 filling the gap.

of other Rye buildings of this period, in this building too the attic rooms have been fitted with low walls to give a structure two-and-a-half storeys in height. In order to gain still more space the front gables are jettied forward above eaves level. This resulted in what might (to modern eyes) be considered a curious internal feature: a shelf-like projection located part way up each gable. Such a feature may indeed be considered curious, but is not without parallel, even in Rye. The same arrangement exists at 31 Mermaid Street [69] and is likely to have been present at 13-14 High Street [3], and in other houses also. The external visual effect of the projecting gables can still be appreciated both here and at 31 Mermaid Street [69]. Here the effect was still further emphasized by an overhanging jetty which formerly extended along the facade at first-floor level. This jetty was underbuilt when the lower part of the building was re-fronted in 1728, an act commemorated by a plaque bearing the date and initials N F I built into the front wall. J. W. Bloe writing in the Victoria County History of Sussex attributes a date of *c.*1540 to the initial build, though perhaps a slightly later date would be more applicable.[7]

There is no linking doorway through the dividing partition on the ground floor and thus both rooms must have functioned as separate units. There is a chimney against the eastern wall within the eastern room, but all details are hidden and its age is unknown. If the stack represents a later insertion it seems likely that both parts of the ground floor were shops. The situation on the first floor and at garret level is unknown. *[ESRO HBR/1/1649]*

19. 67-69 The Mint — *1500 +/-25; 1510 +/-25*
(Figures 10.36 - 10.39)

An unusual house built upon a curved plot and having been subjected to alternate rebuilding. The alternate reconstruction took place about the high-end partition of the hall and occurred not once, but at least twice. As it has been totally rebuilt, the date of the Phase 1 structure is unknown.

Phase 2 (c.1500). The first detectable phase of reconstruction is the hall at the up-hill end of the building. It was rebuilt as a two-bay fully-floored, jettied structure with a canted wall towards the retained high-end (down hill) bay, and two chambers on its first floor (Figure 10.36). This was probably an alternative to inserting a first floor into the earlier open hall, which was probably quite a low structure. Despite the new hall block being roofed parallel to the street, it can be certain that there was a range to its rear, for the two first-floor chambers over the hall were not directly interconnected, but were both accessed via doorways in the rear wall. A length of extant brick wall built in small buff 'Flemish' brick (now incorporated into the replacement rear range) may respect part of the original rear range's side wall. The hall itself is of good size and was entered from the street by a moulded doorway adjacent to the end wall: there were no services beyond the low end of the hall. If services existed they must have been within the since-rebuilt rear range. From the outset this hall was heated by a high-end stack built within the earlier high-end bay. Flanking the fireplace are moulded doorways with arched heads simply but effectively elaborated on the hall face (*see* Figures 10.37 and 10.38). The inclusion of two doorways presumably indicates that the earlier high-end bay was divided into two on the ground floor, unless the rear door lead direct to a stair giving access to the upper chamber within this earlier

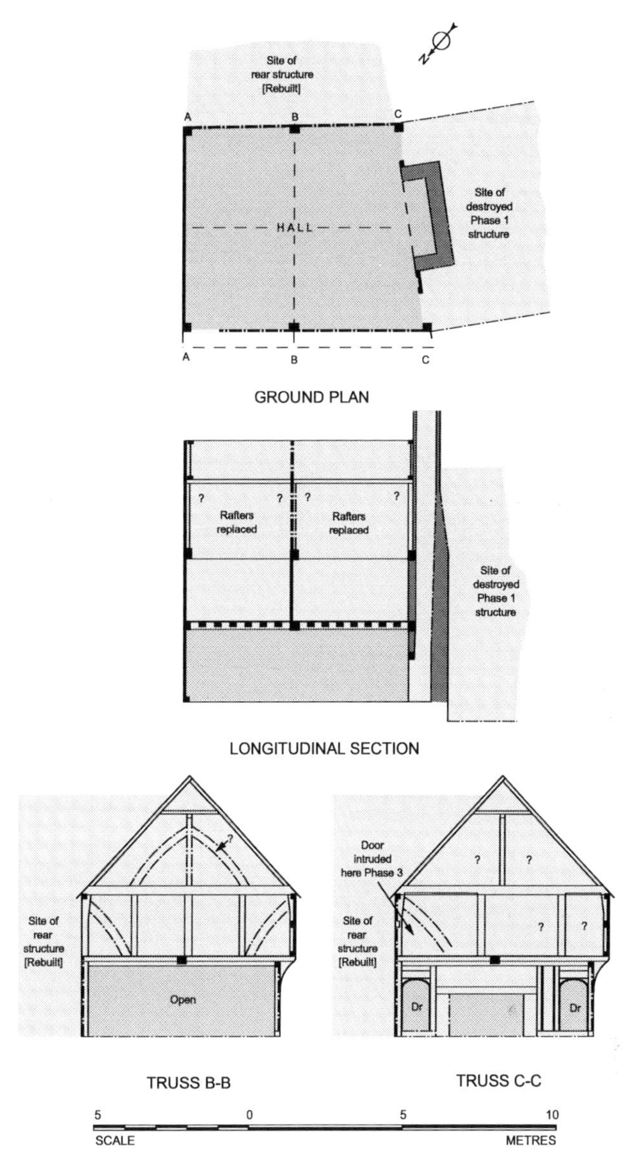

Fig. 10.36
Reconstruction of 67-69 The Mint showing rebuilt hall (left) with retained bay on site of 67 The Mint (right), phase 2.

part, which is possible. What is certain is that the retained bay had its own staircase, for no first-floor interconnecting doorways were included between the two parts. This is not surprising — the rebuilt hall has a lofty storey height and it is therefore likely that the first floor within the earlier part was much lower.

Phase 3 (c.1510). The retained earlier part was demolished and replaced by a new section even more lofty than the rebuilt hall (Figure 10.39). A first-floor doorway cut through the end wall of the hall chamber, together with the squeezed-in nature of the stairs which now blocks this first-floor doorway, indicates that the new section continued to form part of the same dwelling at this time, though it was soon afterwards divided off to form a separate house (67 The Mint), at which date a rear lean-to was added. Initially the rebuilt part was intended as a large and lofty parlour heated by its own

Fig. 10.37
67-69 The Mint. One of the two ground-floor doorways leading out of the hall into the retained (but since rebuilt) bay beyond. Note the contemporary fireplace just visible on the left.

Fig. 10.38
67-69 The Mint. The rear ground-floor doorway leading into 67 The Mint.

fireplace, which blocks one of the two doorways in the end wall of the hall. Because the rebuilt section extends up to the boundary of the plot, an alleyway was included, leading to the back yard. On the first floor, however, the entire phase-3 section housed a single room, fitted with a ceiling and having a spacious, apparently unlit storage garret within the roof, which has a hip at the end. *[ESRO HBR/1/0600 (67 The Mint); HBR/1/1630 (68-69 The Mint)]*

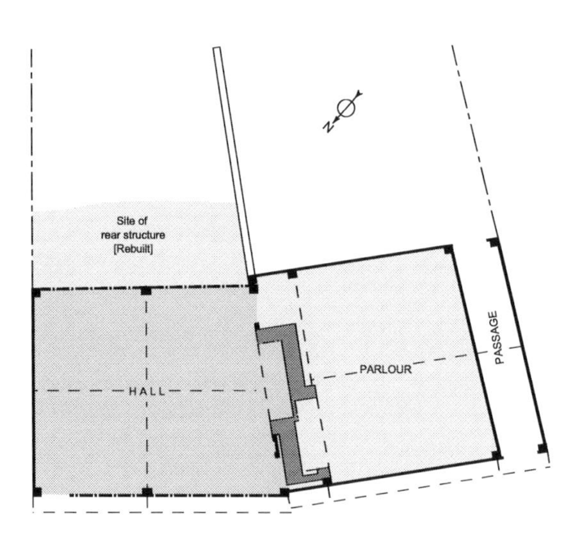

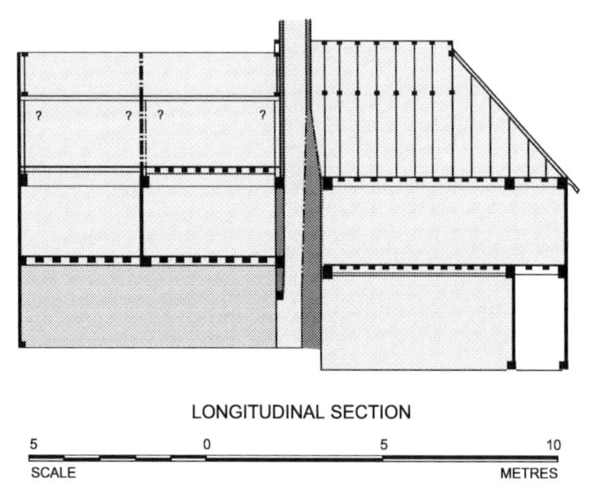

Fig. 10.39
Reconstruction of 67-69 The Mint, phase 3, showing rebuilt parlour end (now 67 The Mint) on the right.

20. 73-74 The Mint — *1500 +/-25*
(Figure 10.40)

A fragmentary continuously-jettied two-cell house with a brick chimney built into one end of the hall. There is a shorter bay beyond the opposite (western) end. The position of the chimney, hard against the front wall, surely means that the front entrance either led direct into the western end of the hall or — less likely — direct into the smaller western bay. Bearing this in mind, the western ground-floor room is unlikely to have served as a high-end room: it is more likely to have functioned either as a service area or shop. The hall fireplace's mutilated timber lintel is moulded and incorporates a four-centred arch with spandrels carved with rose-and-foliage decoration. Above is a stack constructed of small buff-coloured 'Flemish' bricks. *[ESRO HBR/1/0940]*

21. 79 High Street — *Date unknown*
(Not Illustrated)

A two-cell timber-framed house built at right angles to the street with the front and rear parts separated by an axial chimney built of 'Flemish' bricks. Only fragments of the

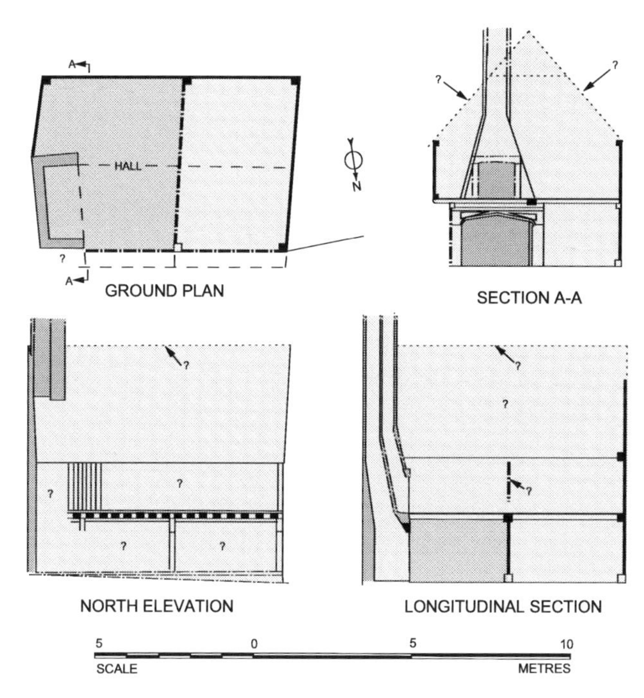

Fig. 10.40
Reconstruction of 73-74 The Mint.

Fig. 10.41
18-19 West Street (left) and 84 High Street (right) prior to reconstruction.

frame are visible, with the rear part at a different level to the front section. Rebuilt roof incorporates some reused sooted medieval rafters. There is insufficient fabric visible to be certain of the building's date, but it is 16th century or earlier. *[ESRO HBR/1/1609]*

22. 84 High Street — *1500 +/-25*
(Figure 10.41)

One of two buildings demolished *c.*1900 to make way for what is now Lloyds Bank — a large brick building.[8] Joist ends visible in early photographs indicate that the building was jettied to both streets, but by this time the jetties had been underbuilt. The long jettied house shown adjoining it in Figure 10.41 was 18-19 West Street [59]. *[ESRO HBR/1/0899]*

Fig. 10.42
85 High Street. The remains of the timber-framed part is hidden behind the West Street elevation on the right.

Fig. 10.43
85 High Street. First-floor framing within truss A-A with crownpost above.

23. 85 High Street — *1500 +/-50*
(Figures 10.42 - 10.44)

Despite its modern external appearance this was a substantial 7.00 metre (22'10") wide timber-framed building with trusses 3.55 metres (11'8") apart, indicated by the parts of two (one of which is illustrated in Figure 10.43) which remain embedded within the present brick-built Natwest Bank. The house 10.44 was not aligned to the High Street, but to West Street. Traces of soot suggest that the trusses may have formed the end walls of an open hall, but, if so, this does not explain why the braced stud within the northern truss is positioned off centre. *[ESRO HBR/1/0853]*

24. 98 High Street (George Hotel) — *Medieval; 1600 +/-25*
(Figures 10.45 - 10.49)

Now part of the George Hotel, this large house was

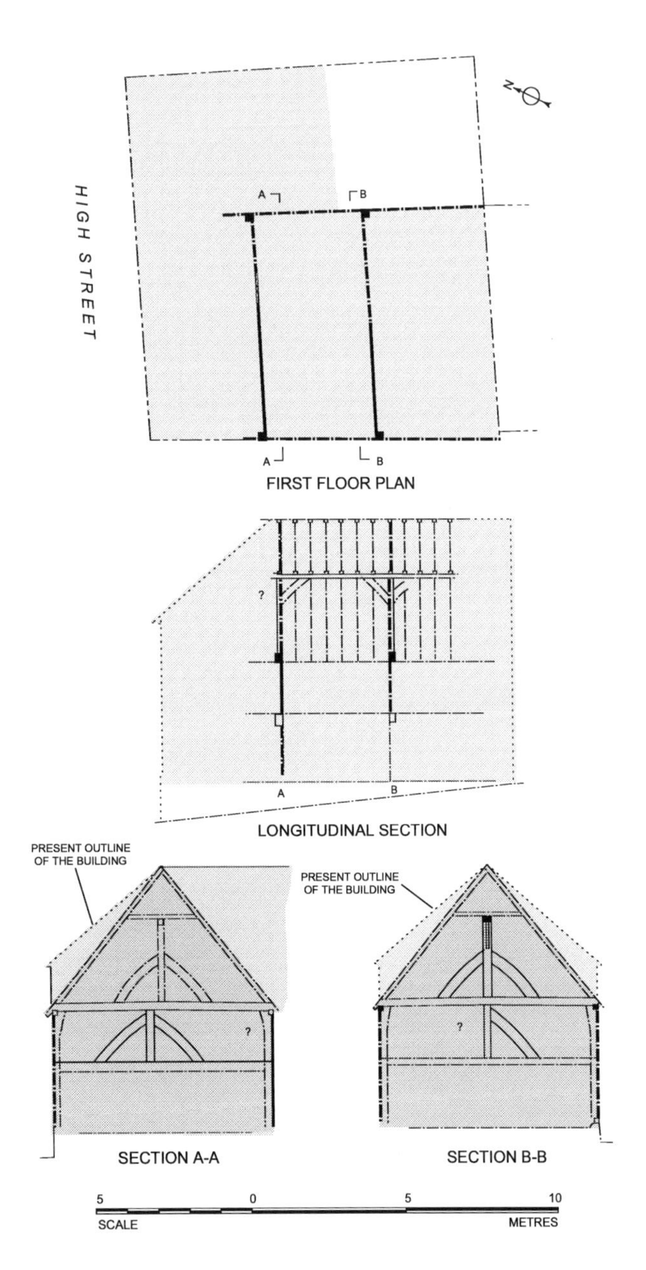

Fig. 10.44
Reconstruction of 85 High Street.

Fig. 10.45
The George Hotel, 98 High Street.
Weathered face of crosswing's western external wall showing close studding.

subdivided during the 16th century so as to form more than one tenement, comprising 14 Lion Street [49] and 98 High Street [24]. The two unequal parts were subsequently rebuilt.

Phase 1 (Medieval). A well built, good quality late 15th-century house which fell victim to subsequent redevelopment (Figure 10.45). In the late 15th century the house was a substantial, fully detached structure extending 12.30 metres (40'4") along High Street and perhaps returning part way along Lion Street, but not extending as far south as 12 Lion Street [47]. As Rye's population grew the building was divided into two houses, and both parts were subsequently rebuilt.

Although the closely-studded side wall of the house's late 15th-century western crosswing had initially been an external wall with an area of un-built-up street frontage beyond, by 1600 the house on the neighbouring plot had either been rebuilt or extended so as to abut against the crosswing. In consequence, the wall had become a shared party wall and therefore had to be retained when the crosswing was demolished as part of the *c.*1600 redevelopment. By the early 19th century not only had the two halves of the original property been reunited and re-fronted to form the present core of the George Hotel, but, as the hotel expanded, its owners acquired the neighbouring plot to the west, which in 1818 they redeveloped as the Hotel's new assembly room. The trapped side wall of the crosswing was once more retained *in situ,* even though nothing else of the medieval house survived the progressive reconstruction.

Despite its destruction, the width and some details about the height of the medieval main range can be recovered through the presence of 'weathering ghosts' observed during building works undertaken in 2006. These weathering ghosts indicate where the retained part of the medieval main range once abutted against the rebuilt eastern house (14 Lion Street [49]). Above the roof line and beyond the rear wall of the medieval hall the frame of 14 Lion Street was exposed to the prevailing south-westerly winds, causing heavy weathering. There is a particularly rotten zone at the point water became trapped where the roof coverings met the building Figure 10.47. Beyond this, where protected by the medieval building, the timbers remain in pristine condition and not only show crisp saw marks, but also faint setting-out lines indicating the positions of the joints in the pre-fabricated frame. When the western part of the medieval house was rebuilt in *c.*1600 the entire wall was internalized, and as a result all further weathering ceased.

The story the weathering ghost tells is in marked contrast to that indicated by the same building's surviving crosswing wall. As Figure 10.46 shows, both the hall and crosswing extended back 8.15 metres (26'9") from the road, with the upper storey of the crosswing jettied forward into the street in the usual manner. Unlike that of the crosswing, the rear wall of the hall was exceptionally low (*see* section X-X in Figure 10.46). The only logical explanation for this is that the medieval hall incorporated a rear aisle.

This should not be too surprising: Rye houses with rear

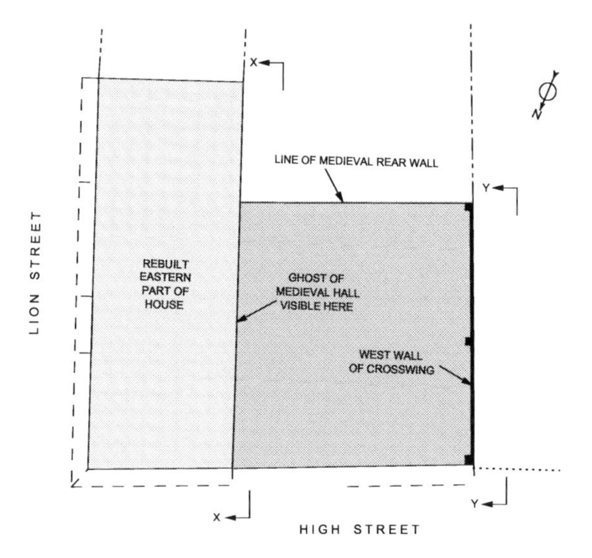

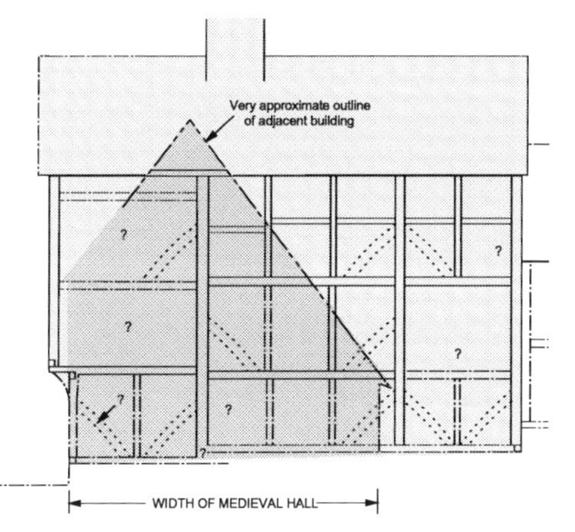

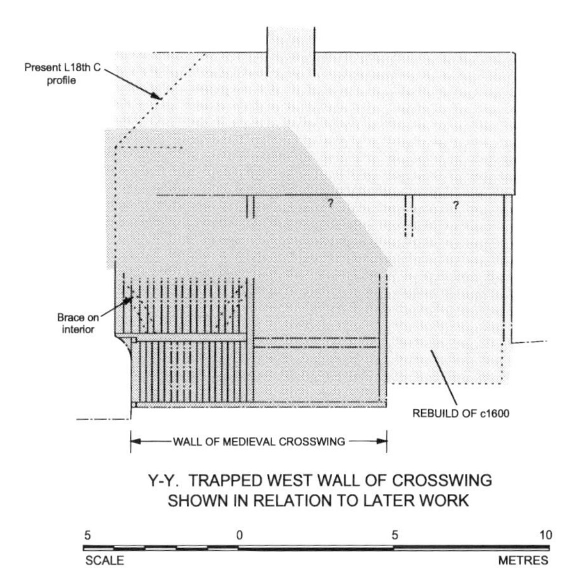

Fig. 10.46
The George Hotel, 98 High Street.
Reconstruction drawings showing medieval work, phase 1 as indicated by weathering lines on adjacent building.

aisles survive at 16 East Street [34], 17 West Street [58], Lamb Cottage [53] and Trader Cottage/Old Trader [103], but none of these incorporated a crosswing. Despite the fact that the rear walls of the hall and crosswing were built in line with each other, when viewed from the back the two parts of the building would have looked very different, with the crosswing towering over the low, sloping roof of the aisle. Viewed from the street the eaves of the hall would have been at a similar level to those of the crosswing and thus the town's residents and visitors would have perceived the house as being of average height. Only when the eastern end (14 Lion Street [49]) was replaced by a three-and-a-half storeyed house later in the 16th century would the retained medieval western part have been dwarfed by its neighbour.

By the late 16th century the retained fragment of the medieval open hall is likely to have looked decidedly old fashioned, for almost certainly the late 15th-century crosswing had replaced an earlier in-line floored end upon the same site, retaining the earlier hall. A similar sequence occurred at Plantagenet House, West Street, New Romney, Kent, where the service end of an early 14th-century single-aisled hall was replaced by a crosswing in *c.*1400.[9]

Phase 2 (c.1590). In *c.*1560 the dwelling formed within the divided-off eastern part was rebuilt as a lofty, three-and-a-half storeyed house fronting onto Lion Street (*see* 14 Lion Street [49]). Subsequently, in *c*1600, the western dwelling (*ie.* the remainder of the main range and the entire crosswing) was demolished and replaced by a substantial two-and-a-half/three-storeyed house built at right angles to the street and of similar height to its lofty eastern neighbour.

The surviving truss of the medieval house indicates that by then the building had suffered severe subsidence and this must have been a prime motivation for reconstruction rather than enlargement when additional floor space was needed. Even so, with a 7.75 metre (25'5") frontage, the owner's requirements could easily have been achieved by designing a street range with an additional wing of narrower width to the rear. Instead, it was designed as a wide three-bay range extending 12.25 metres (40'2") back from the street. The front half was again rebuilt in the 18th century when this and adjacent 14 Lion Street [49] were once more merged to form the present George Hotel.

Sufficient survives to show that the new structure had a front and back room on each storey, both served by a centrally-placed axial chimney (Figure 10.48). The building is of two-and-a-half storeys in height with relatively generous 710 mm

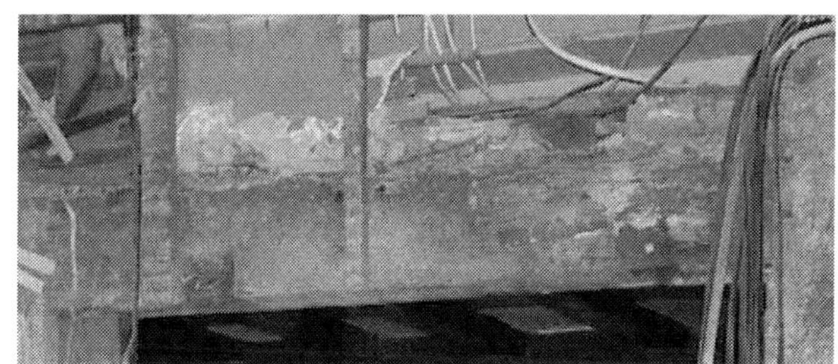

Fig. 10.47
The George Hotel, 98 High Street.
Detail of side girt showing weathering line (right) with un-weathered section of timber on left.

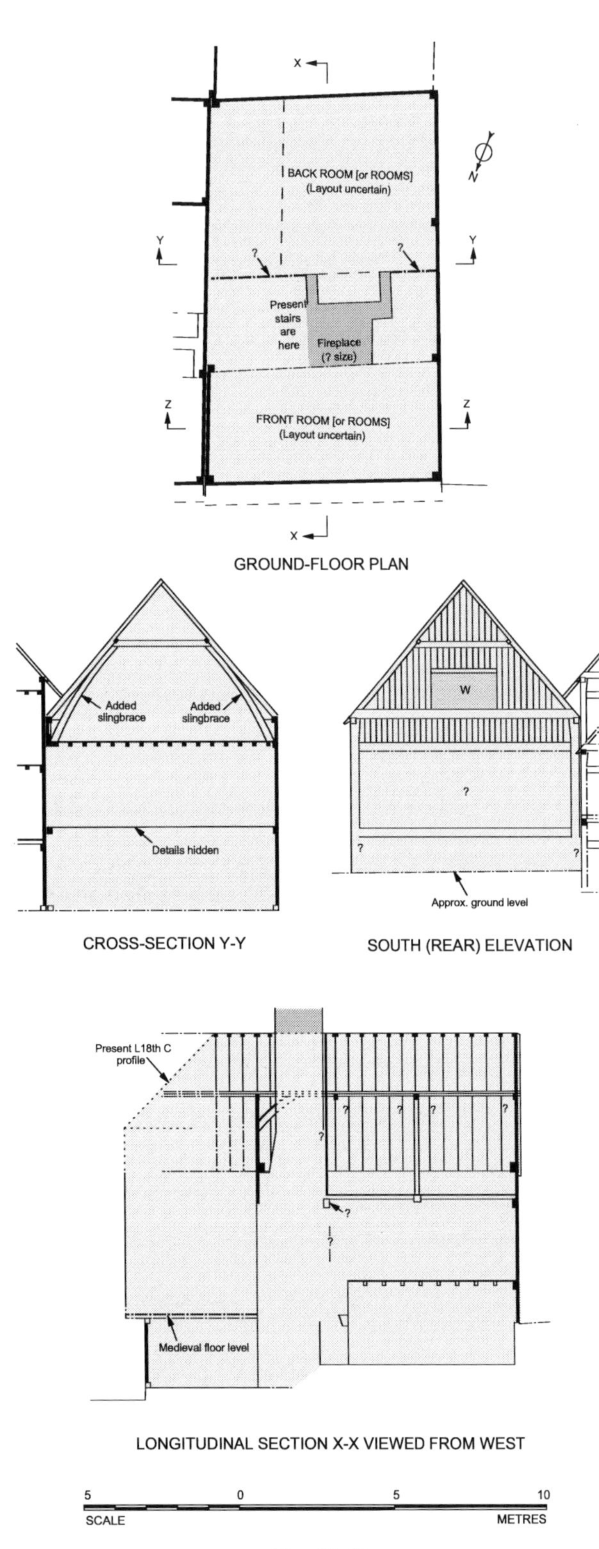

Fig. 10.48
Reconstruction of 98 High Street, phase 2.

(2'4") side walls within the rear attic room. A tiebeam is incorporated into the truss immediately to the north of the chimney but, despite the height of the walls, the roof over the rear two-thirds of the building is framed in three bays without

Fig. 10.49
98 High Street.
Close studding within apex of gable, above the large rear window lighting the attic room.

tiebeams. As at 107 High Street [30], the weakness of the design resulted in structural failure, though in this instance movement was arrested by the timely insertion of sling-braces. An indication of the building's impressive appearance can still be gained from the design of the massive rear gable, which was close studded and incorporated a large window sitting on the tiebeam so as to light the spacious attic room (Figure 10.49: *see also* Figure 10.48). This arrangement would originally have been repeated within the street elevation, with a jetty no doubt at first-floor level and possibly the gable projecting forward over the pavement. *[ESRO HBR/1/1576]*

25. 99-100 High Street — *1420 +/-33; 1550 +/-50 (Figures 10.50 - 10.52)*

Phase 1 (c.1420). The largest of the surviving hall houses, probably representing the home of a man of considerable importance within the town. Though much altered and partially rebuilt, it is evident that in its original form it incorporated an exceptionally long two-bay open hall which measured 9.20 metres (30'2") and was either 6.65 metres or 7.05 metres (21'10" or 23'2") wide, depending upon whether or not it was built with a recessed 'Wealden' front. An (implied) high-end crosswing could have been added later in the medieval period. There is a rear range behind the service bay, returning up Lion Street, but this survives in part only and shows no closely datable fabric — it is 16th-century or earlier and could, at least in part, have been separately let.

Phase 2 (c.1550). The formerly open-hall was floored over, necessitating the insertion of a crossbeam into its arch-braced open truss. The upper parts of this truss were infilled with a daub partition. The inserted comb-decorated partition still survives (it is visible in Figure 10.51) and it is clear that from the outset there was a chimney built against it, rising within the chamber formed over the hall's low-end bay. There has never been a doorway through the inserted partition at first-floor level, but what cannot be told is whether this was because

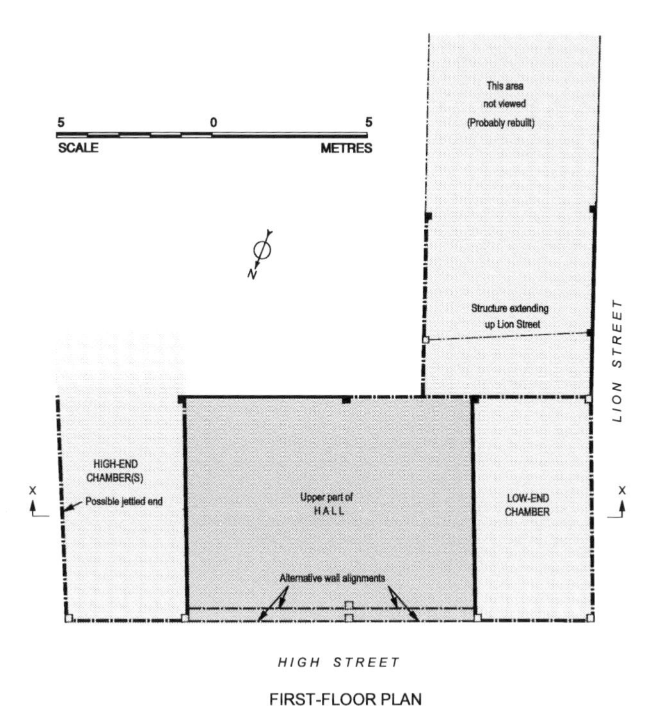

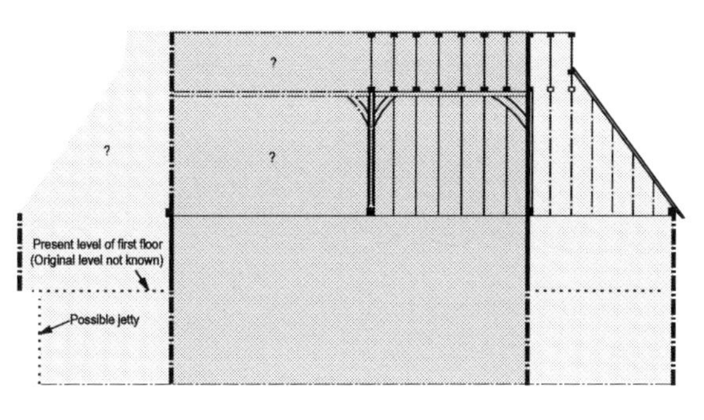

Fig. 10.50
Reconstruction of 99-100 High Street prior to phase 2.

Fig. 10.51
99-100 High Street. Crownpost over hall's former open truss. The daub partition was inserted in 16th C.

Fig. 10.52
99-100 High Street. Crownpost at 'low' end of hall showing heavily sooted comb-decorated daub infill.

only one of the two open bays was initially floored, or whether the door was omitted simply because there was no need for direct communication between the chambers on either side of the partition. Lack of through first-floor communication was a feature common in rural houses at this period, but a possible alternative explanation is that the partition was inserted in order to divide the house into two dwellings.[10] *[ESRO HBR/1/1573]*

26. 101-102 High Street — *1490 +/-25; 1565 +/-25 (Figure 10.53)*

Phase 1 (c.1490) An intriguing semi-detached pair of fully-floored, continuously-jettied houses. As Figure 10.53 illustrates, both halls were served by a contemporary back-to-back brick-built chimney constructed astride the party wall, pushed towards the back of the house. The part of each hall to the front of the chimney could have served as an entrance area, and, if so, the smaller end bays could, as at 16-16A West Street [57] have served as high-end, as opposed to low-end rooms. More likely, however, the fireplaces were sited at what was considered to be the high end of the hall, for at the opposite end the ceiling within each hall incorporates a crossbeam which trims the triple girders of the main part of the ceiling. These intermediate crossbeams serve no purpose, unless they delineate narrow cross passages located at the low end of each hall. In neither instance is it known whether the ground floor of the end bay formed a single room or was subdivided by an axial partition.

Phase 2 (c.1565) Although the eastern house remained unaltered, the western house was upgraded by the addition of a two-bay rear range, jettied along its western wall and heated by a projecting end chimney. A central-newel staircase was inserted in order to provided improved access. *[ESRO HBR/1/1275]*

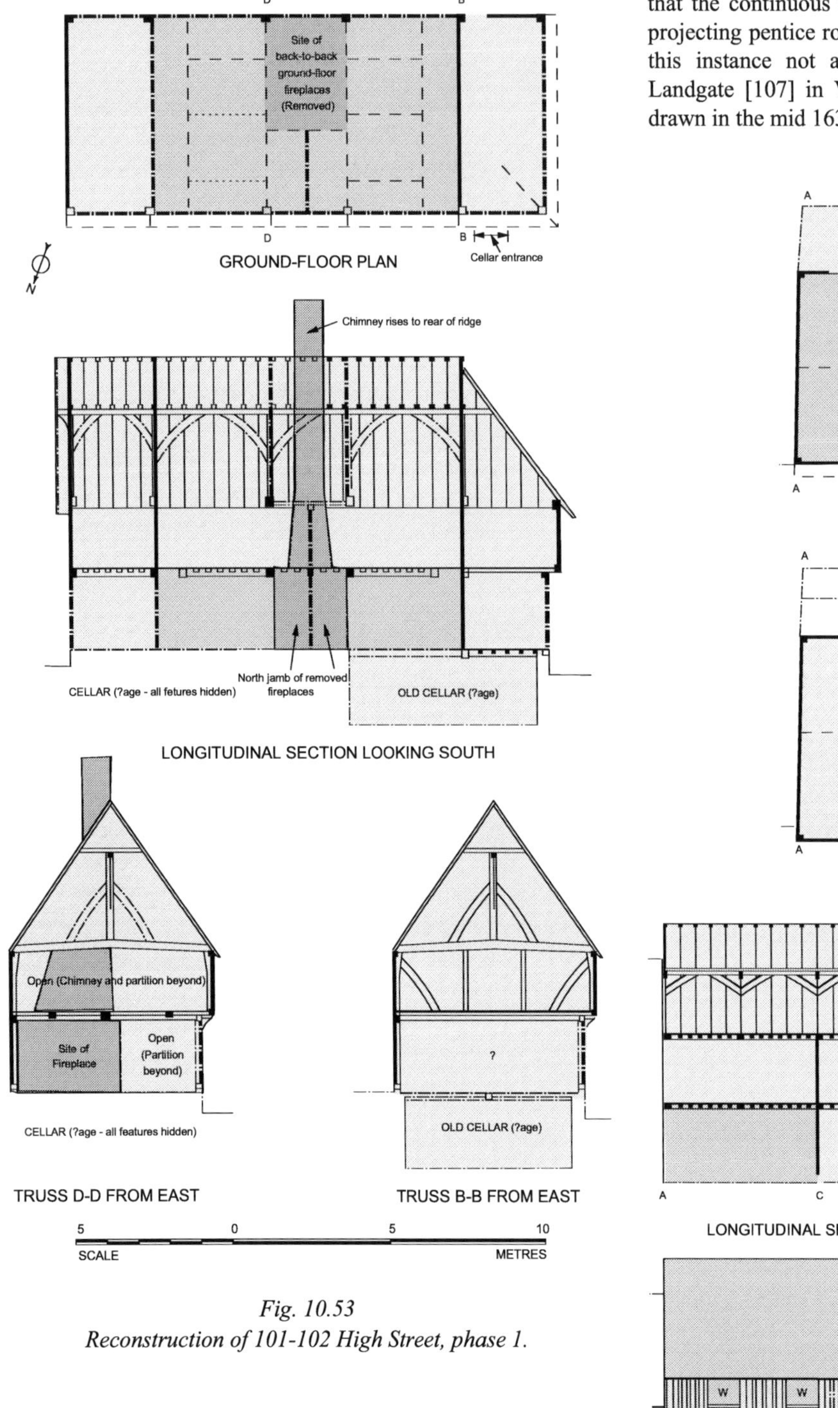

Fig. 10.53
Reconstruction of 101-102 High Street, phase 1.

27. 103-103A High Street — *1575 +/-25*
(Figure 10.54)

A two-cell house, with a two-bay hall and hall chamber and an attic room which extended the full length of the house. There is no axial chimney, but perhaps both hall and hall chamber were served by a rear stack. As at the earlier 9 Watchbell Street [92], there is evidence for a (since rebuilt) rear outshut. The three-bay roof is of clasped-side-purlin type, fully windbraced, with open collar trusses dividing the bays. Most walls are of footbraced large-panel design, but the street facade is close studded. There are some indications to suggest that the continuous front jetty may have incorporated a small projecting pentice roof. A similar-style pentice roof (though in this instance not associated with a jetty) is shown at 24 Landgate [107] in Van Dyck's illustration of the Land Gate drawn in the mid 1630s. *[ESRO HBR/1/0659]*

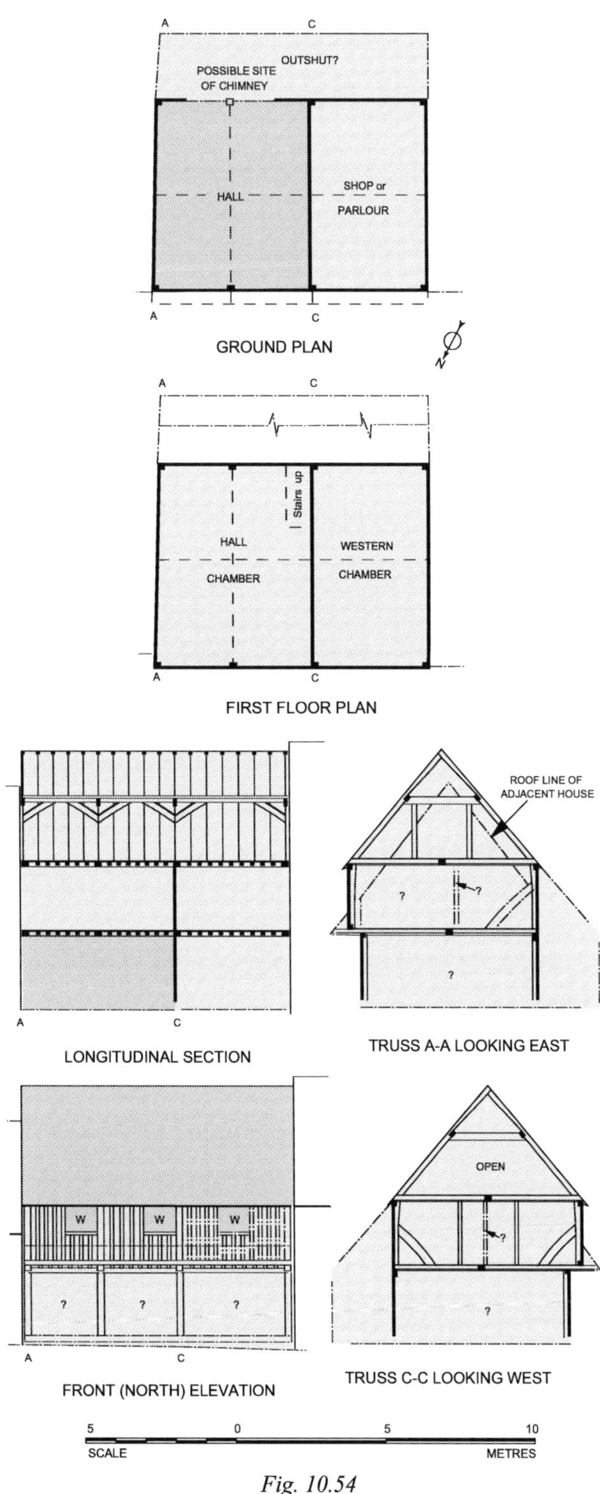

Fig. 10.54
Reconstruction details of 103-103A High Street, phase 1.

28. 104 High Street — *Date unknown*
(Not Illustrated)

Part of the end wall of this house remains embedded within the eastern wall of 103, 103a High Street [27]. When 103, 103a was erected late in the 16th century it utilized the end wall of the adjacent house, which therefore had to be retained when 104 was rebuilt three storeyed in *c.*1800. The building was squat, for the walls of the original 104 were *c.*3.50 metres (*c.*11'6") from floor to top of wallplate, but there is no way of knowing the span. The size of its neighbours suggests that it ought not to have been a poor building, as does the fact that it escaped reconstruction until *c.*1800, despite its location in what had by the early 18th century become the commercial heart of the town. But these facts are no guarantee that the house was of quality. *[see ESRO HBR/1/0659]*

29. 105 High Street — *1600 +/-25*
(Not Illustrated)

For Rye, this is a rare early 17th century building. Sadly, today it is very fragmentary, but evidently had a long facade to the High Street and probably returned up East Street. The visible framing has relatively slight timbers and is of typical 17th-century small-panel design. The front wall retains a large opening for a display window flanked by at least one two-pane ovolo-moulded clerestory light. There is extensive stone-walled cellarage beneath the entire High Street section. No old roofs survive. *[ESRO HBR/1/1611]*

30. 107 High Street — *Date unknown*
(Not Illustrated)

A building which is so altered at the front and so covered internally by later plasterwork that it is now impossible to date — it could belong to the late 16th-century but could equally represent one of Rye's rare 17th-century buildings. It has an axial chimney and is of two-and-a-half storeys, with 1.10 metre (3'8") high walls at attic level. Despite this, it has no tiebeams to the internal trusses. This building was of poor design and it shows in the major structural problems which have ensued. Although probably built as a separate dwelling, the structure became merged into adjacent 106 High Street [30] to the west, and became an inn — The Oak. It has now been returned to separate occupancy. *[ESRO HBR/1/1627]*

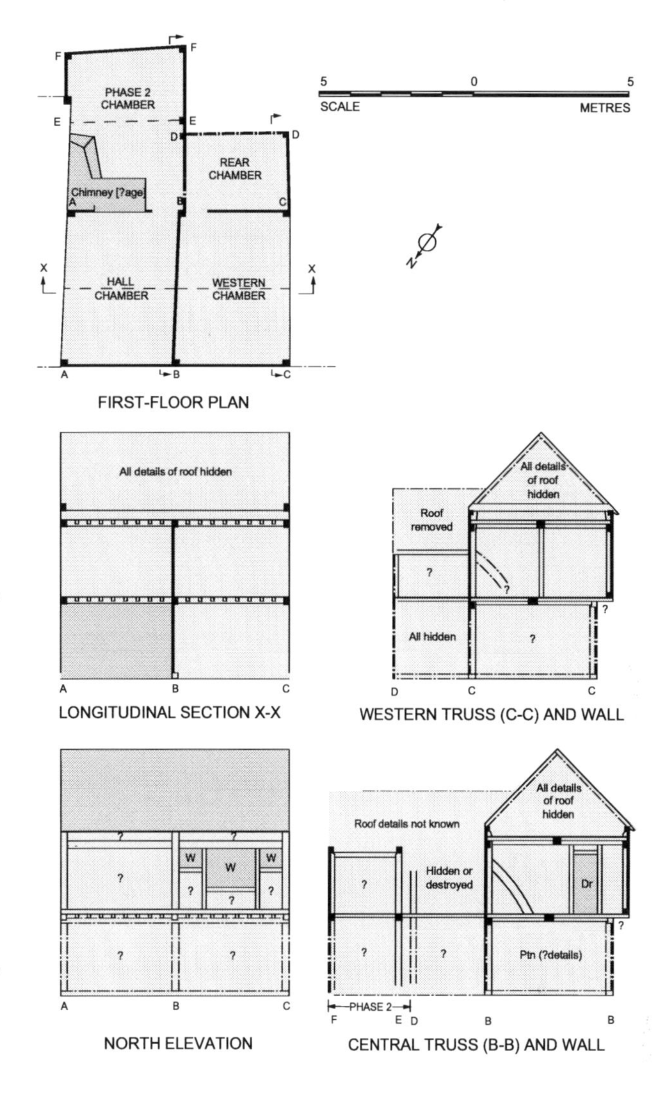

Fig. 10.55
Reconstruction of 110 High Street, phase 2.

31. 110 High Street — *1565 +/-25; 1600 +/-25*
(Figure 10.55)

Phase 1 (c.1565). A two-and-a-half storey, two-cell house aligned parallel to the street, with the two ground-floor and the two first-floor rooms of identical size. Being heated by a rear stack, it is assumed that the easternmost of the two rooms was the one utilized as the hall. Perhaps the western room had to be the size it was in order to be utilized as a shop, but this is pure supposition. To the rear of the bay are the scant remains of a low, two-storeyed single-bay rear range, but too little of this survives to allow any meaningful comments to be made.

The street range is very narrow — only 4.15 metres (13'8") on the ground floor — and it is therefore no surprise that a continuous first-floor jetty was originally incorporated into the street facade. Even so, despite the small size, the building should not be regarded as being of mean status, a point well illustrated by its former display fenestration. This is today only evident within the street facade of the western bay at first-floor level, and then only from the interior. Here there is evidence for a large central window (perhaps of projecting type) flanked by high-level glazed clerestory windows. It would be surprising if the design within the similar-length eastern bay of the facade was not similar. Houses which incorporated this form of fenestration commonly incorporated projecting front roof gables, and although some gables of this type survive within the town, others have been destroyed. Whether front gables existed at 110 High Street [31] is at present impossible to tell.

The roof above the two first-floor chambers was always intended to be utilized. It served as a two-bay attic, presumably designed for storage. Given the modest 4.65 metres (13'3") overall roof span, it is not surprising that low side walls were incorporated in order to increase usable space. In this instance the wallplates are elevated 300 mm

(1'0") above the attic floor and no tiebeam was incorporated within the central truss, the crossbeam supporting the attic floor presumably being considered an adequate structural tie.

Phase 2 (c.1600). A second, two-bay rear range was added adjacent to the original structure. In more recent times the original rear range has been all but rebuilt. *[ESRO HBR/1/1619]*

11 THE HOUSES TO *c.*1660 SUMMARIZED: EAST STREET, MARKET STREET AND LION STREET

32. 2-3 East Street — *1475 +/-33; 1530 +/-25*
(Figure 11.1 - 11.3)

Phase 1 (c.1475). Of all the fragmentary buildings in Rye, this is the most difficult to interpret, but is nevertheless of considerable significance in that it illustrates the kind of piecemeal, complex development which can occur within an urban context, especially within a town which is experiencing population growth upon a restricted site. The three earliest identifiable phases within the building cannot now be sequenced with any confidence on account of their fragmentary nature. The remains of the northern truss to the southern range (now within the party wall between Nos. 2 and 3) are sufficient to indicate that the southern part of the *c.*11.80 metres (*c.*38'9") street range (now occupied by 3 East Street) had a roof span of approximately 5.20 metres (*c.*19'9") and measured *c.*6.20 metres (*c.*20'4") long; it was therefore probably framed in two bays. It was of average height and was two storeyed, though the possibility of an open hall within one of its (assumed) two bays cannot be ruled out. The infill framing of the northern end truss was set flush with the northern face: it was footbraced and supported a partition crownpost. This southern part was rebuilt as a brick structure in the 19th century. On the northern face of the truss is visible a distinct weathering ghost indicating the outline of the street range's northern part, (currently 2 East Street) which was rebuilt in the early/mid 18th century, roofed at right angles to the street. The weathering ghost shows that the northern part of the street range was of lesser width (about 5.35 metres, or *c.*17'6") or was perhaps rear aisled and was lower, thus mimicking the sequence of progressive reconstruction known to have existed at 28, 32 Church Square [82] and elsewhere within the town. However, in this instance, there is no way of telling whether this northern part represents the northern bay of an earlier house retained when the southern part was rebuilt larger or whether it represents an addition. The former of the two seems the most logical scenario.

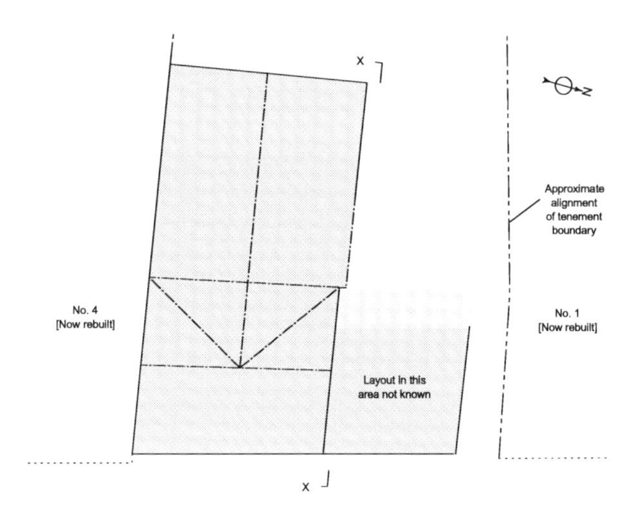

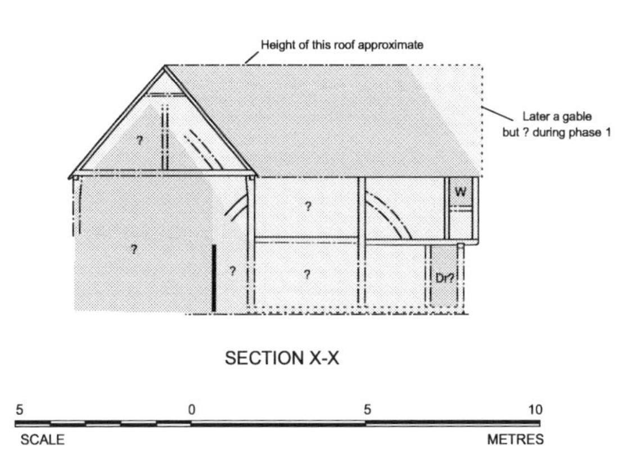

Fig. 11.1
Outline reconstruction drawings of 2-3 East Street, phase 1.

Built at right angles behind the wider southern part of the street range are the fragmentary remains of a wide timber-framed rear wing incorporating a jetty towards the rear yard/garden. As Figure 11.1 illustrates, this wing's northern side wall slightly overlaps the alignment of the surviving truss in the street range, a configuration which implies that it either post dates both phases of the street range or is contemporary with one of the two parts. Even so, those features which remain indicate that this rear wing is no later in date than the early 16th century.

Phase 2 (c.1530). This is the most important historical work to survive within this complex, and the most complete. It

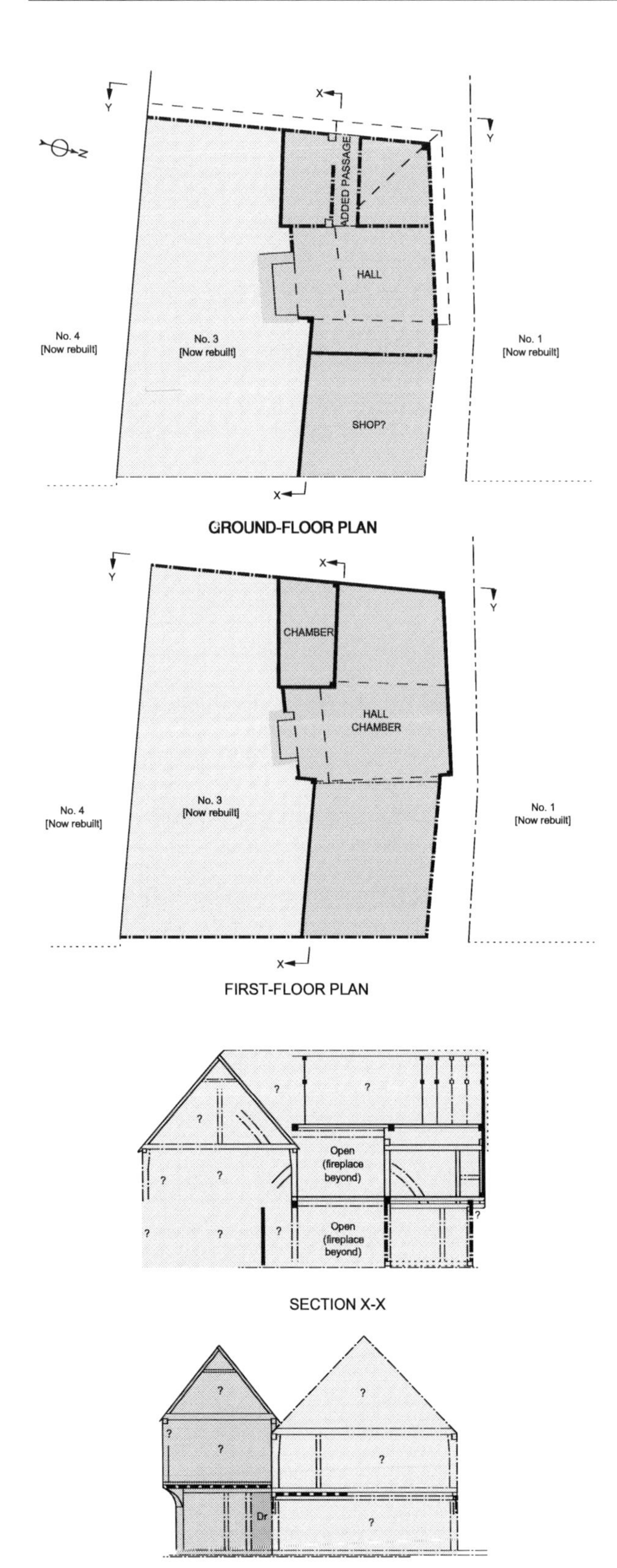

Fig. 11.2
2-3 East Street, phase 2.

is a narrow, but tall range which occupies the re-entrant angle between the street range and the rear wing. Its construction converted this complex 'L-plan' house into a square block (Figure 11.2). Its sequence within the development of the building is in no doubt — it makes use of the rear wing's northern wall as its side wall and, at roof level, cradles partially over that wing's roof. Like its southern neighbour, it has a rear jetty towards the yard/garden, but in this instance the jetty is at a higher level and returns at a dragon beam (Figure 11.3) to continue along the northern side wall, with the upper storey overhanging the alley leading to the rear of the plot. The joists supporting the jetty are of 'transitional' medieval/post-medieval scantling and the fragmentary roof is of paired-rafter-and-collar type, both features which suggest that the addition predates 1540.

What makes this range significant is the internal detailing which shows that its main room (and almost certainly the main chamber too) extended southwards to include part of the adjacent southern rear wing. An area within the southern rear wing's rear bay is likewise occupied as part of the structure, although this division may have occurred a little later in the building's sequence of development. The main room and chamber are heated by a chimney built in a curious location within the southern rear range. Although it should be emphasized that this chimney could date from the 17th century, the layout of the building suggests that, even if rebuilt, it occupies the site of its predecessor. What the evidence suggests is that the new range was built at the same date as the plot was divided into two occupations and that the party wall between the two dwellings was shifted southwards into the existing southern rear wing in order to form two houses of near equal size. The internal layout of the northern dwelling, with its centrally-placed hall set back from the street, strongly suggests that by this date the northern part of the street range was in use on the ground floor as a shop — indeed, this could have been the case ever since it was first built. In many ways, despite its present day appearance, this is the most urban of the historic houses which survive within the town and certainly echoes most closely the chaotic *ad hoc* internal layouts depicted by Ralph Treswell in his surveys of London houses prepared in the early 17th century.[1] *[ESRO HBR/1/1566]*

Fig. 11.3
2-3 East Street. Joists and dragon beam within ceiling, phase 2.

33. The Union Inn, 8 East Street — *1500 +/-25*
(Figure 11.4)

A continuously-jettied, two-cell range, built parallel to the street, which at this point slopes gently downwards towards the north. The two bays are unequal, with the larger 'hall' bay at the downhill northern end. Beyond this end was open space, presumably giving access through to the rear yard. The other end was built against an existing building. Although chimneys have been added, the structure appears initially to have been unheated. A single doorway leads southwards out of the 'hall' into an area against the rear wall which incorporated a large opening through the first floor, the joists at this point being trimmed by a principal ceiling girder. Presumably this area allowed access to the smaller southern ground-floor room, but it must also have led to a substantial staircase rising to the first floor. Unless some form of lightly built internal partition has been removed which did not coincide with the first-floor truss, the entire first-floor space was a large chamber crossed by a plain, utilitarian, arch-braced open truss — not a layout typical of a house! Was 8 East Street designed as a commercial building, housing a shop/workshop with warehouse above, or was it (as it is today) used as an inn, perhaps with a meeting room above? Regardless of which was the case, a further question needs to be posed — was it let to a person who lived elsewhere in the town, or did it form part of the large 'Wealden' complex [42] occupying the corner of East Street and Market Street, and with which it shared a wall? Once chimneys were added the building seems to have functioned as an independent property, but this could have been the result of pressures caused by Rye's 16th-century population boom. *[ESRO HBR/1/0808]*

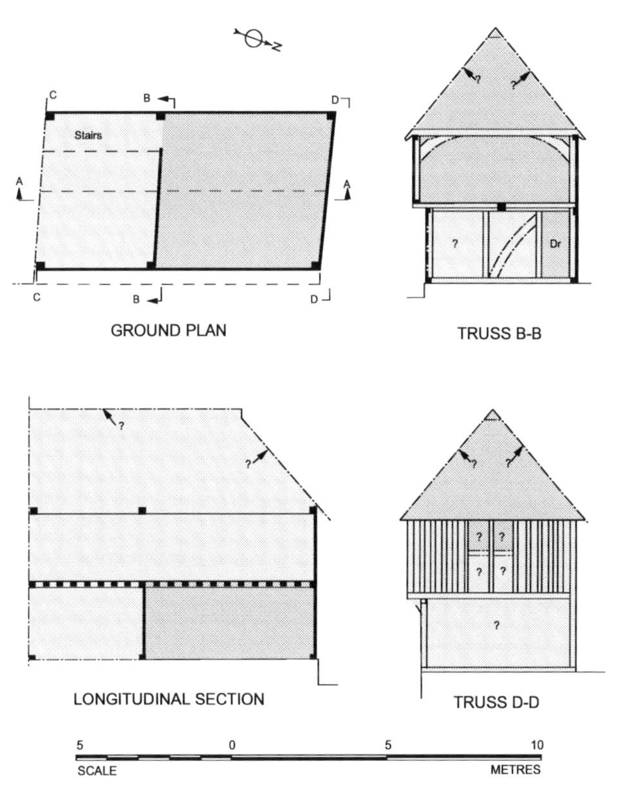

Fig. 11.4
Reconstruction of Union Inn, 8 East Street.

34. 16 East Street — *1375 +/-25; 1465 +/-25; 1530 +/-25*
(Figures 11.5-11.8)

Phase 1 (c.1375). One of the earliest houses in the town. Despite having a recessed 'Wealden' front, 16 East Street incorporates a rear aisle. Such a combination of aisle and recessed front is rare, but is by no means unique, even in Rye. Neither the rear aisle nor the recessed front affected the internal layout, or the way the house functioned. Rather than having the usual arrangement of two service rooms, the service area was always a single room. There is a good moulded dais beam and an early spered opening between hall and overshot cross passage.

The unusual method of supporting the flying wallplate at the high end of the hall (Truss A-A) indicates the

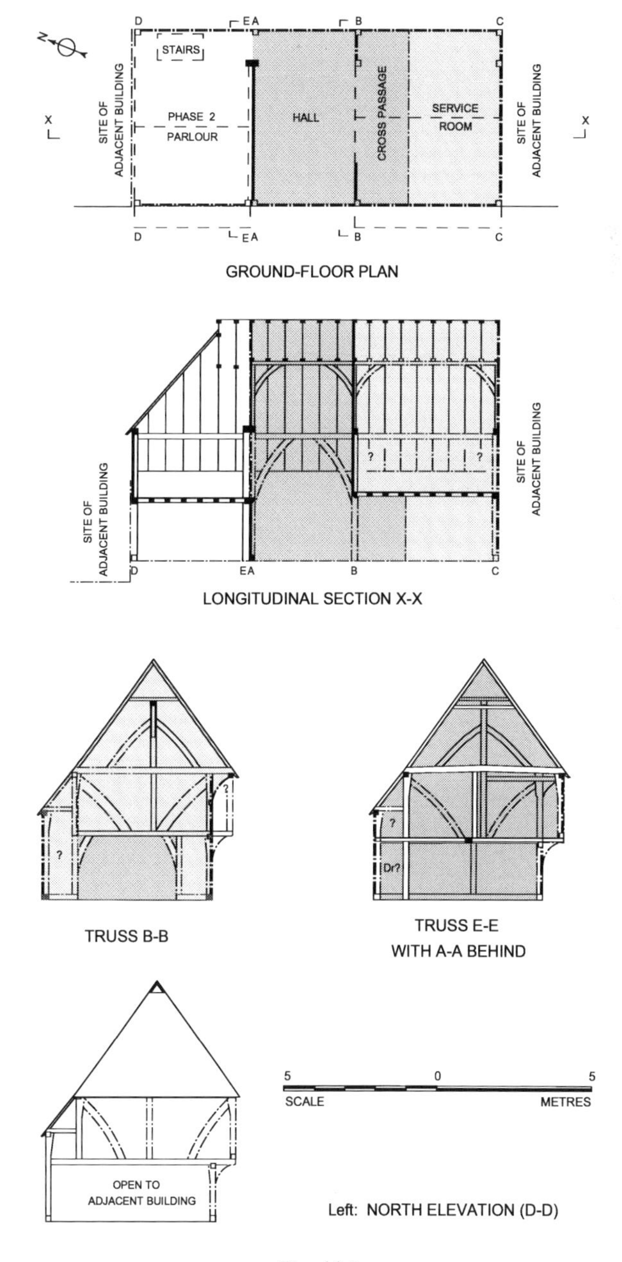

Fig. 11.5
16 East Street, phase 2.

Fig. 11.6
16 East Street showing high-end wall of late 14th-century open hall. The recessed front wall used to be inset in line with the main post with the bracket and spur beam to the left of the post supporting the flying wallplate. Note how the spur beam (a little below the main tiebeam) continues to the right of the post. See also Figure 11.7.

Fig. 11.7
16 East Street showing high-end wall of late 14th-century open hall viewed through later truss built against it on the north. Note how on this face the spur beam above the bracket is housed past the main post.

carpenter's concerns in devising a method of supporting the end of the flying wallplate in this early single-ended 'Wealden'. Because when first built there was no jetty beyond the high end of the hall to support the wallplate, the carpenter chose to support it from beneath by a spur beam and bracket. This in itself is not an unusual method. What is unusual is that the carpenter was unconvinced about the strength of this method and, in order to make sure it would not fail, he chose to halve the spur beam past the rear face of the principal post and

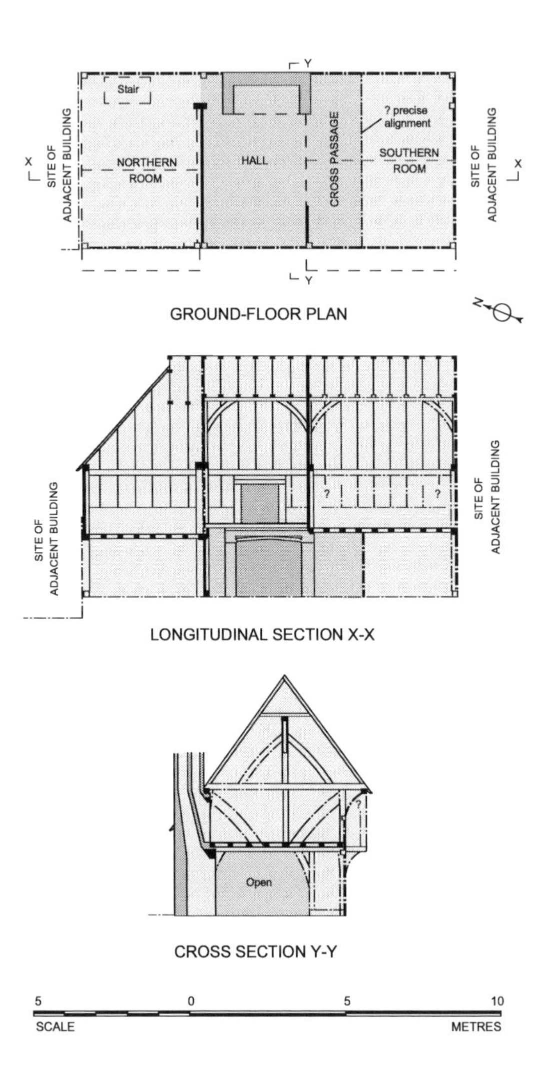

Fig. 11.8
Phase-3 reconstruction of 16 East Street showing inserted floor and chimney.

extend it halfway across the hall, jointing it into the central stud (*see* Figure 11.5, Truss E-E with A-A behind; and Figures 11.6 and 11.7).

Phase 2 (c.1465). A parlour bay was added, separately framed from the rest of the structure. The pattern of weathering on the old high-end wall of the 14th-century part indicates that the hall always stood against a structure on the site of the later high-end bay. What cannot be told is whether this earlier structure was a predecessor to the present high-end bay, indicating that the house has been subjected to progressive reconstruction (or '*alternate rebuilding*') during the medieval period or whether the present high end was built upon the site of a demolished separately occupied house or building. What is certain is that even after the present high-end bay had been erected there was still a building standing to its north, for the ground-floor section of the new bay is open framed, having made use of the end wall of the adjacent structure. Thus, the house may not always have had a textbook three-cells layout, but could be an example of a two-cell house upgraded to three-cell type.

Fig. 11.9
11-12 East Street, sketched in 1813. [© Rye Castle Museum]

Phase 3 (c.1530). Insertion of floor and chimney into the hall (Figure 11.8). Incorporating two flues, the chimney was inserted into the rear aisle: an obvious location to choose. The timber lintel over the fireplace serving the hall incorporates a four-centred arch with sunk spandrels, whilst that serving the hall chamber is plain, save for simple chamfering. Plain 140 mm x 120 mm joists are used for the floor inserted into the hall: these are simply lodged into position.

Phase 4 (17th C). A small rear range added behind the service bay, intruding partly into the phase-1 range. Little of the range now survives. *[ESRO HBR/1/1537]*

35. 11-12 East Street — *16th C*
(Figure 11.9)

The present house upon this site is of 19th-century date, but its predecessor is shown in a sketch of 1813. At that time there was no building to the north, upon the site of the present Checker (13 East Street): instead steps are shown descending the cliff and a boat is visible in the distance. As Figure 11.9 shows, the house was continuously jettied and incorporated a shop front. Beyond was a porch-like two-storeyed projection and beyond that is visible a roof set at right angles. The house just visible on the right is Durrant House, prior to reconstruction. *[Demolished]*

36. Durrant House, 1-2 Market Street
(see Figure 6.12)

Beneath the present three-storeyed replacement street range are the fragmentary remains of a medieval un-vaulted cellar incorporating a two-centred doorway in its west wall (*see* Chapter 6). The arrangement indicates that the original house extended further west than now, across part of the site of Monks Way [37]. Against the rear wall of the rebuilt street range is a chimney of earlier, but uncertain date. To the rear of the eastern part survives a substantial range of *c.*1700 with a good staircase. *[ESRO HBR/1/1614]*

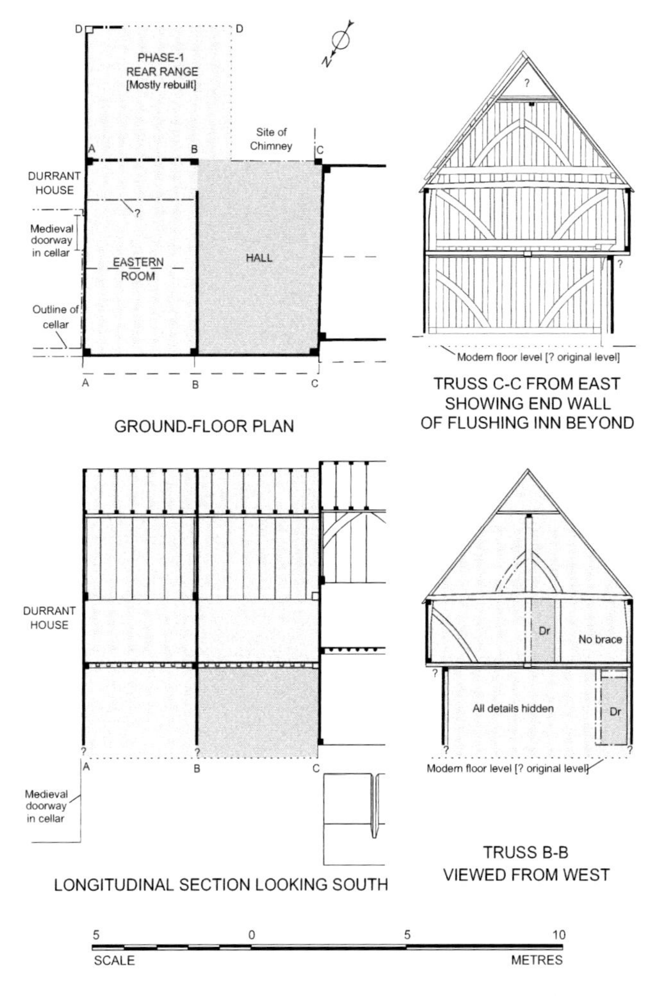

Fig. 11.10
Reconstruction of Monks Way, 3 Market Street.

37. Monks Way, 3 Market Street — *1540 +/-25*
(Figure 11.10)

A fully-floored, continuously-jettied house which indicates well the growing population pressures being experienced within the town during the first half of the 16th century. It was squeezed into a gap between 1-2 Market Street [36] and 4-5 Market Street (Flushing Inn) [38], though not without demolishing part of the former and taking over part of 4-5 Market Street's [38] plot. The house which was built as a result of these boundary adjustments has a 7.25 metres (23'9") two-cell street frontage but, as Figure 11.10 indicates, also incorporated a contemporary rear range, of which precious little now survives. The hall is within the larger western bay and was probably heated by an original chimney built against the rear wall — the chimney has since been demolished. The shorter bay to the east housed a single ground-floor room accessed from the hall by a rear doorway. This means of access is unusual for a service room and thus the space could have functioned as high-end accommodation, or perhaps even a shop. Unfortunately the original location of the front door is not known — the present door is at the western end of the frontage, but this need not reflect the original arrangement. Today only fragments of the eastern wall of the original rear range survive. This range was located principally behind the narrower eastern bay, but seems to have been accessed direct from the hall. It could have functioned as a kitchen or as services, or perhaps both. Whether it had an upper chamber is doubtful. If not, the house had two interconnected first-floor chambers, both open to the crownpost roof. *[ESRO HBR/1/1613]*

.

38. The Flushing Inn, 4-5 Market Street —
Medieval; 1525 +/-20; 1565 +/-15 (Figures 11.11 - 11.15)

Phase 1 (Medieval). Beneath the house is an early barrel-vaulted cellar, for which *see* Chapter 6.

Phase 2 (c.1525). An early 16th-century house with a two-cell main range facing Market Street and a long rear range extending along Church Square. This multi-phase structure is one of the most significant houses within the town. Its 12.25 metres (40'3") long four-bay street range has a return jetty at its western end and sits over the earlier cellar. It was almost certainly constructed by Richard Inglett, who was elected a jurat of Rye in 1525, served as mayor 1530, 1534 and 1537 and in 1537 was also one of the town's Members of Parliament. The house is rightly famous for its (?added) wall painting shown in Figure 11.11, which graces its dais partition. It may be no coincidence that the painting contains the arms in mourning of Jane Seymour, who died the same year as Richard was MP. Whether Richard ever occupied the house in person is in doubt: at his death in 1544 he was living in Longer Street (now High Street) and this house in Market Street was willed to his son, John I, in fee simple. John I had been appointed Town Chamberlain in 1540 and was probably already living at 4-5 Market Street at the time of his father's death. What is not clear is whether the house was rebuilt by Richard for John's use, or whether (as he aged) Richard moved out, leaving the use of the family home to his son. In turn, John I was succeeded by his son John II (a Rye shipwright). His will, proved March 1578, refers to his two houses in The Butchery.[2]

Despite the building's two-cell main range, the house is substantial (Figures 11.12 and 11.13). It occupies a corner plot with a 25 metre (82'0") secondary (western) frontage onto Church Square (at this point alternatively known as Pump Street). The length of secondary street frontage which extends beyond the end wall of the main range is occupied by a six-bay structure jettied towards the street. It is separately framed and need not be contemporary with the main range, though if added it is only slightly later. The storey heights here are lower, though this need not reflect a difference in date. At the opposite (eastern) end the main range was initially free standing, with a *c.*3 metre (*c.*10'0") gap between it and Durrant House [36] — the gap was soon afterwards built over by Monks Way, 3 Market Street [37]. Ignoring for a moment the rear range fronting onto Church Square, the two-cell main range was initially of classic 'textbook' layout, despite its large size. Entry was into a cross passage with a pair of service rooms to the west and an exceptionally long hall to the east. As is usual, the cross passage was partially screened from the hall by a draught spere adjacent to the front door, though in this instance instead of a rear screen (allowing a wide central opening) there was a low-end fireplace backing onto the passage, heating the hall. This left only a 1.10 metre (3'7") wide opening between the passage and hall, though significantly, despite its small size, this opening extended up to ceiling level and was not intended to be closed by a door. Including the cross passage, the hall was 8.40 metres (27'6") long and occupied three of the four bays. Such a large hall was clearly meant for entertaining and is reminiscent in its size of the halls found in principal inns. As the building's present name — The Flushing Inn — suggests, and documents confirm, it certainly functioned as an inn later in its life (*see* below) but was it built as such? Certainly there are similarities of layout between this building and The Mermaid [72], including the existence of a parlour-like room immediately

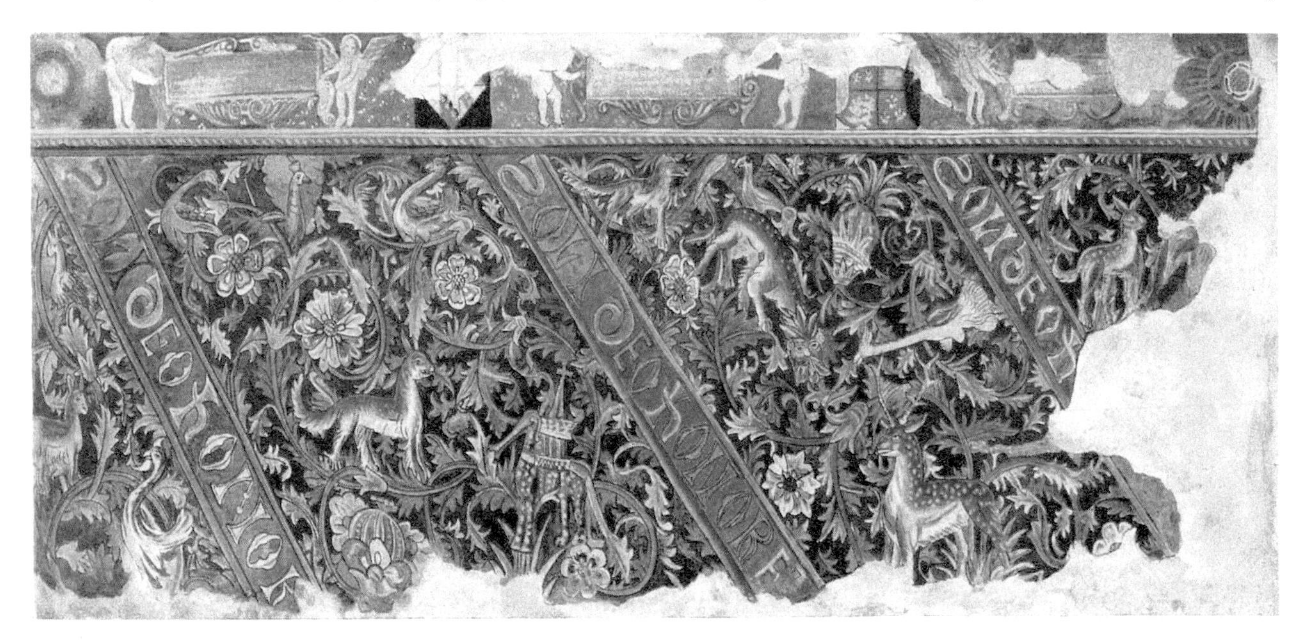

Fig. 11.11
Phase 2 wall painting on dais partition of the hall at The Flushing Inn, 4-5 Market Street.
(From a drawing by Francis W. Reader)

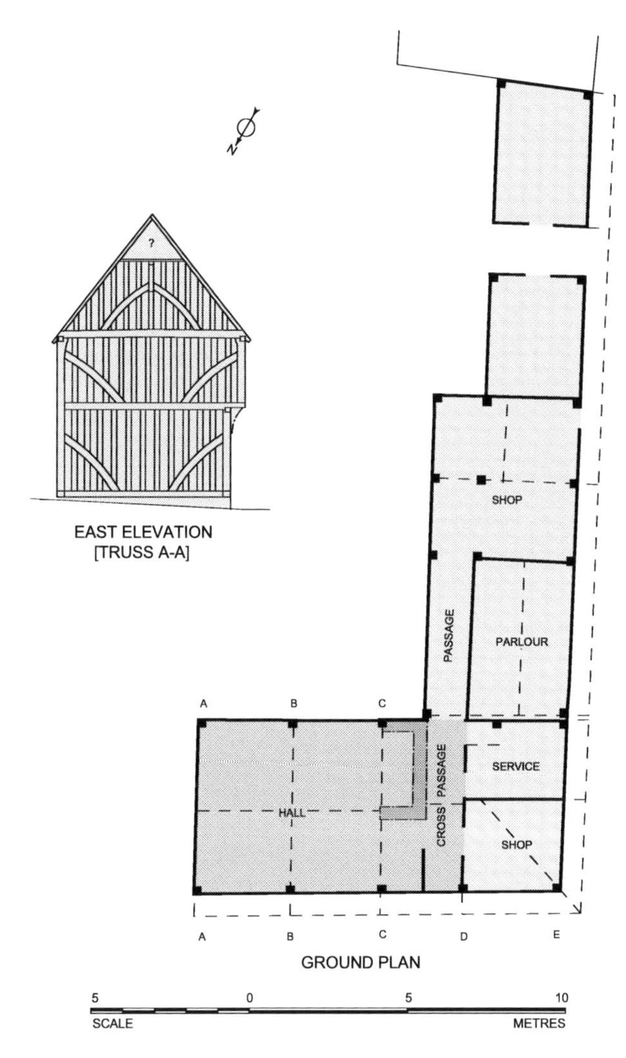

Fig. 11.12
Phase 2 reconstruction plan and end elevation of The Flushing Inn, 4-5 Market Street.

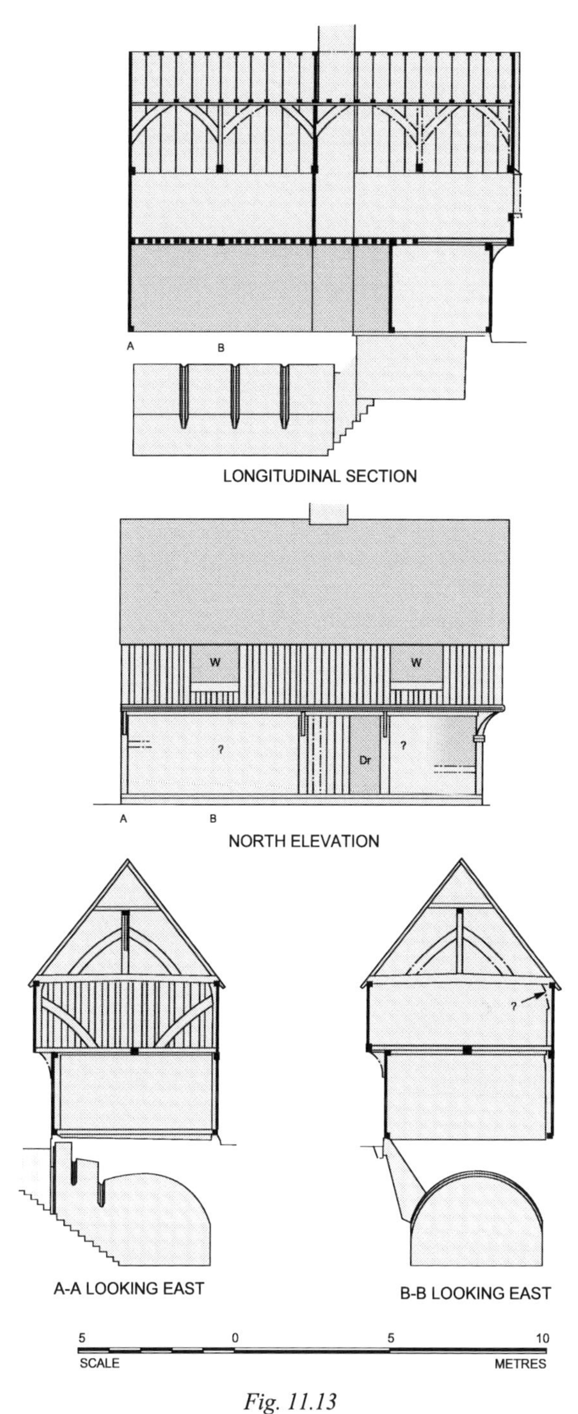

Fig. 11.13
Phase 2 reconstruction sections and front elevation of The Flushing Inn, 4-5 Market Street.

behind the services, within the rear range. As at The Mermaid, the rear range incorporated a corridor extending back from the cross passage, down the side of the 'parlour', accessing a room beyond. In this instance the two-bay room beyond incorporates a shop front with external doorway — not a feature which immediately comes to mind in relation to an inn, though it should be born in mind that Rye innkeepers are known to have involved themselves in more than one occupation (*see* Chapter 5). This was evidently not the only shop within the building, the 'front service room' also incorporates evidence of large shop fronts looking out towards both Market Street and Church Square. If the rear range is later in date than the main range, these shop fronts could have fallen out of use quite rapidly. However, in this regard too the multiple occupations of some Rye residents needs to be kept in mind: different commercial activities could have been segregated within different parts of the building. Upstairs the main range had two chambers of near equal size, with a further two chambers within the rear range. Despite being of reasonable width on the ground floor, that part of the rear range abutting the main range has an aisle at the rear, and in consequence the first-floor chambers are very narrow. Beyond these, the southern three bays have no aisle: the central one is occupied on the ground floor by a covered entrance-way leading through to the rear yard. The ground-floor rooms which flank this are accessed from the covered way and appear not to have had internal doorways interconnecting with the main part of the house. To what use these rooms were put is not known, nor is it known how the first-floor chambers at this end of the range were arranged, let alone used.

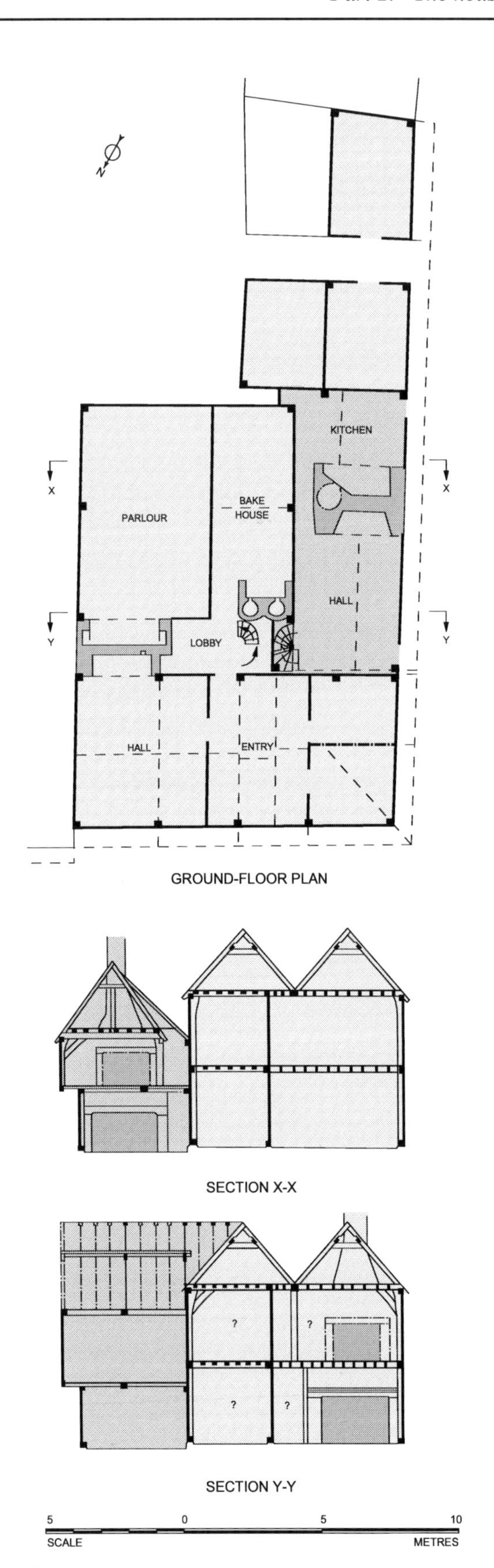

Fig. 11.14
4-5 Market Street (Phase 3). Suggested division of the building into two indicated by light and darker grey shading.

Fig. 11.15
Front elevation of 4 Market Street (left) and 5 Market Street (right). Note the inserted clerestory windows just below the eaves of No. 4

Phase 3 (c.1565). It appears to have been the division of the house into two occupations which prompted a phase of major alteration and enlargement (Figure 11.14). The extension — a substantial range built into the angle between the main part and the Church Square range — was necessary in order to give each of the two units adequate floor space. In similar vein, the alterations were essential to make the existing spaces usable for their new role. The method of division is not entirely clear. By the mid 17th century the two service doorways and the rear doorway within the original cross passage had been blocked, allowing the hall, cross passage and new rear addition to become one unit (4 Market Street) whilst the services, together with the Church Square range became the other (5 Market Street). However, initially the entire main range seems to have been kept together, with only the Church Square range separated off to form the extra dwelling.

Whatever the initial division, the eastern of the two dwellings was by far the larger. On the ground floor the original chimney backing onto the cross passage was removed and a new partition inserted so as to convert the large hall into two smaller rooms, one of which was unheated. To compensate for the loss of the chimney a new stack was built against the rear wall of the hall, with a second ground-floor fireplace serving a large rear parlour. Beside the parlour was contrived a bakehouse served by its own chimney incorporating a pair of small ovens. Access to the various rooms was from a central lobby buried deep in the heart of the house, and it was from this too that stairs rose to the first floor, with a flight of steps beneath descending to the cellar. The result was a dwelling of double-pile plan arranged as a block of rooms, not unlike the design adopted at 15 High Street [4].

The work is of good quality: moulded overmantels to the fireplaces in the four-flue stack; flush plaster ceilings within the rear parlour and parlour chamber; close-studded walls; and a frieze of ovolo-moulded windows inserted into the hall chamber (Figure 11.15). Because of the exceptional

7.75 metre (25'5") width of the rear range, it is capped by two parallel clasped-side-purlin roofs divided by a central valley (Figure 11.14). Although the southern terminals are hipped and are of antiquity, they replace gables. Because of the roof design, there were no attic rooms within the extension, though the roof space over the early 16th-century main range was utilized.

The second of the two dwellings within the complex is, by necessity, a long sliver of a house and likewise required considerable modification to make it usable (*see* Figure 11.14). The principal alterations involved demolishing the first-floor walls of the northern bay within the Church Square range (ie. the part located against the rear wall of the main range) and rebuilding it to a greater height in order to give a larger, more lofty first-floor chamber fitted with a flush under-plastered ceiling. Above it was framed a new roof at right angles to the street. This incorporated a front gable (since removed). It is possible that the gable projected forward in order to weather a projecting oriel window lighting the new chamber: certainly there are signs of such an arrangement having been inserted on the ground floor, flanked by two-pane clerestory windows with moulded mullions. In order to heat this house a new four-flue chimney was inserted, filling an entire bay of the original range.

What use was put to the two early 16th-century rooms and chambers within the southern end of the range, flanking the covered way into the rear yard, is not known. They may have acted as outhouses serving one or both of the two dwellings, or perhaps they were separately let (as was certainly the case later). The Inglett's did not keep the property for long after its subdivision. Following John II's death his heirs sold it to the Spilsteads. It remained with them until the 1650s when it was disposed of piecemeal.[3] *[ESRO HBR/1/0857]*

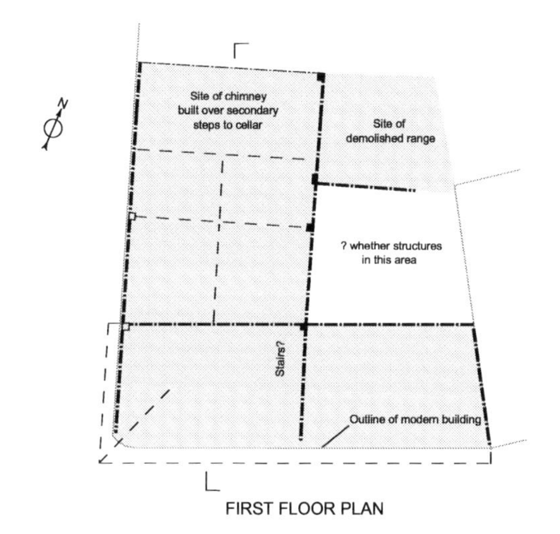

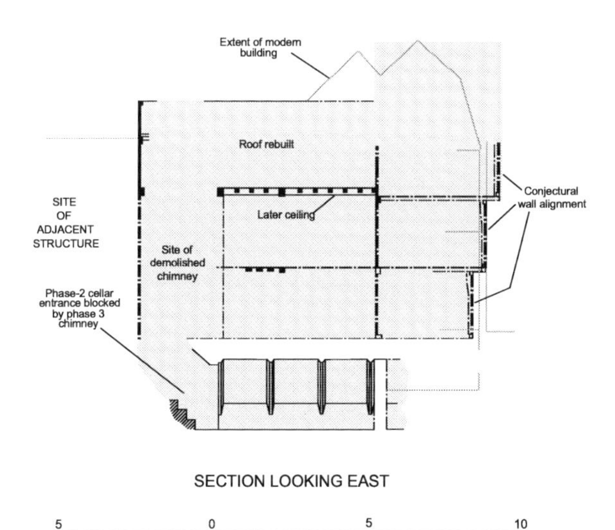

Fig. 11.16
Tentative reconstruction of 8 Market Street/ 23, 23a Lion Street, phase 2. The roof of the rear range appears to represent an alteration.

39. 8 Market Street/23, 23a Lion Street — *1350 +/-100; 1500 +/-25 (Figure 11.16)*

Phase 1 (14th C). Early barrel-vaulted cellar (*see* Chapter 6).

Phase 2 (c.1500). Despite its present two-storeyed appearance, this building was originally at least partly three storeyed, with jetties facing Lion Street and almost certainly returning along Market Street. The house could only be recognized for what it was when stripped out during extensive building works undertaken in 1984.[4] Even then, the surviving timbers were too few and too rotten to allow anything more than the basic outline to be recovered. The evidence suggested that perhaps only the front section, facing towards Market Street, was three storeyed with a two-storeyed range extending down Lion Street. There were other ranges filling the area to the rear, giving a 'square' block, possibly with a central courtyard/light well. *[ESRO HBR/1/0632]*

40. 9-10 Market Street — *1600 +/-25 (Figure 11.17)*

A straightforward three-cell house aligned parallel with the street. It is a 12.80 metres (42'0") long three-bay structure which incorporates a contemporary two-bay central rear range. The building is quite late, being dated by typological evidence to *c.*1600. It utilises small-panel framing (with interrupted midrails) as opposed to braced large-panel framing. Particularly noticeable is the relatively poor quality of both the timberwork and the craftsmanship. Yet this is by no means a poor building: the available evidence suggests that it originally incorporated a carefully designed symmetrical street facade with large display windows (probably of projecting bay type) each flanked by two-pane, ovolo-moulded clerestory lights. The central bay of the facade can be proven to have incorporated a projecting gable and it seems likely that this formed the central one in a continuous row of three gables.

Unlike most of the earlier houses of any quality within the core part of the town, at 9-10 there was no jetty at first-floor level. The general appearance of the building is reminiscent of the early 17th-century houses which survive in considerable numbers in nearby Hastings, a type which is generally absent from Rye. The relative crude nature of the carpentry may reflect the fact that the walls of the principal rooms were designed from the outset to be panelled, and thus the timber frame would not have been visible. Part of the panelling still survives within the hall.

In considering the plan form of 9-10 Market Street it must be borne in mind that the building may not have been built as a standard domestic house but as an inn called The George. By 1662 it had already ceased to serve that function.[5] It was described in 1671 as the 'tenement, now four tenements, of John Crouch and his sisters, sometime of John Prowze [a late 16th-century Rye innholder] called The George, with the stables thereto belonging'. From the abutments given it is clear that the plot was of 'L' plan and incorporated a secondary street frontage facing onto Lion Street, part way down that street: it was there that the stables *etc* were located. By 1671 the stabling had apparently been converted into tenements.[6]

The house itself takes up the entire length of its Market Street frontage and is built with its facade set askew in order to suit the alignment of the street: it thus narrows slightly in its length. In addition, the eastern end wall cants so as to suit the property boundary (*see* Figure 11.17). There are three rooms on the ground floor of the street range, the central of which is the heated hall. The unheated eastern room was entered by a doorway located against the front wall, whilst a centrally-placed doorway leads westwards out of the hall into the western bay. If built as an inn, this western room may have served as the beershop. From it a doorway leads northwards towards the two-bay kitchen within the rear range. This general layout is repeated on the first floor and above was a garret area which would originally have been well lit via the front gable(s). *[ESRO HBR/1/0634]*

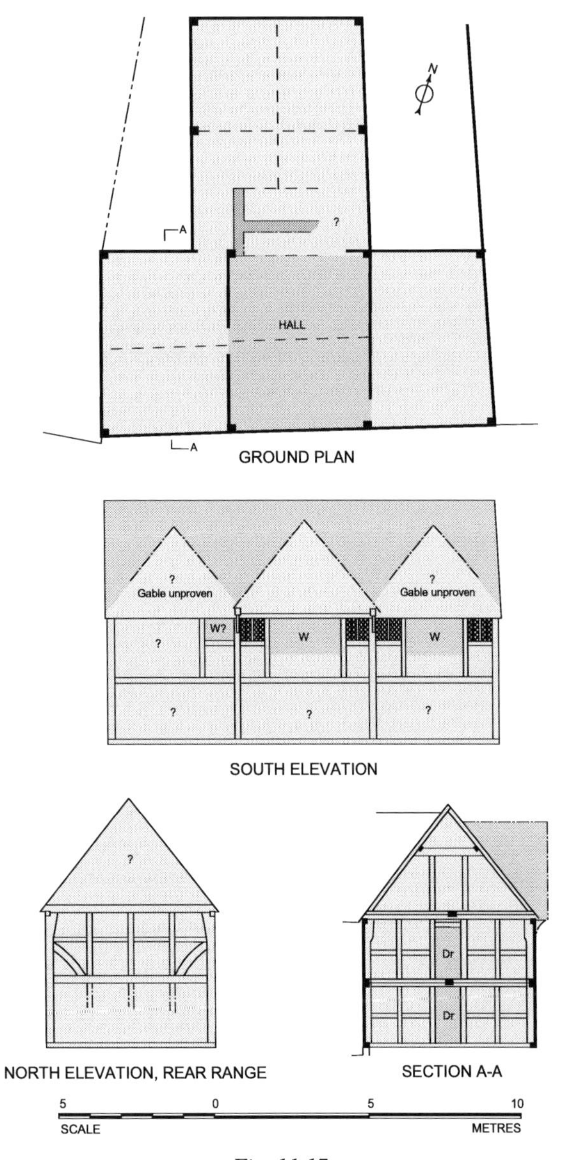

Fig. 11.17
Reconstruction of 9-10 Market Street.

41. 11 Market Street — *1530 +/-25*
(Figures 11.18 & 11.19)

Despite being turned at right angles to the street, this is a house with a generous 7.00 metres (23'0") frontage equal to many plots with 'standard' two-cell houses built parallel to the street. This and the adjacent 12 Market Street may have been one property during the medieval period, having become divided into two during Rye's early 16th-century population boom. It is a building in which the entire spacious two-bay front room appears to be designed as commercial space, with the two-bay hall (heated by an axial chimney within its own purpose-built bay) pushed back from the street, to the rear (Figures 11.18 and 11.19). Beyond the hall is a kitchen and further room(s) within a now fragmentary narrow, low, secondary range. The kitchen was open to its roof, which is sooted. On the first floor in the main part are three chambers — one (heated) at the rear and two (unheated) at the front, divided from one another by an axial cross partition. All chambers had ceilings, with garrets in the roof. The roof is of crownpost construction, but with minimal bracing so as not to

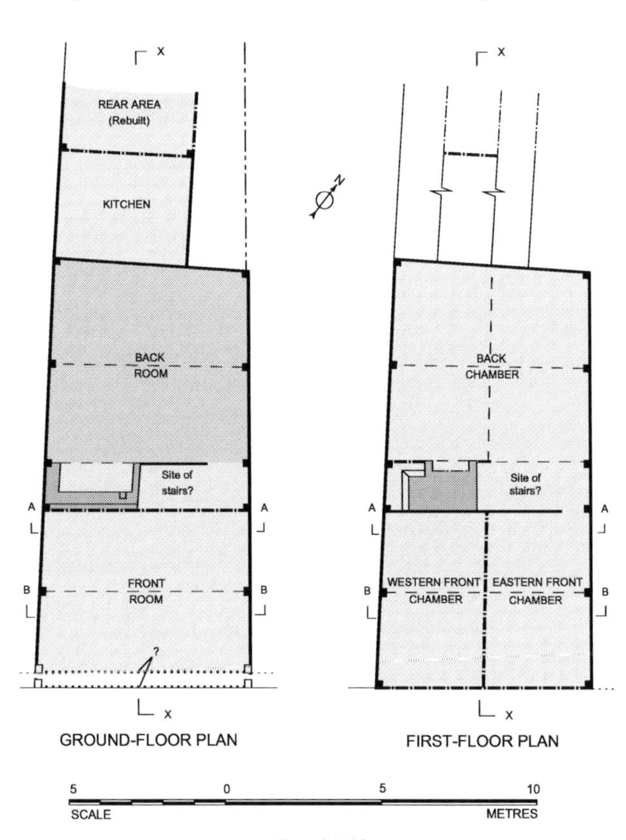

Fig. 11.18
Reconstruction of 11 Market Street.

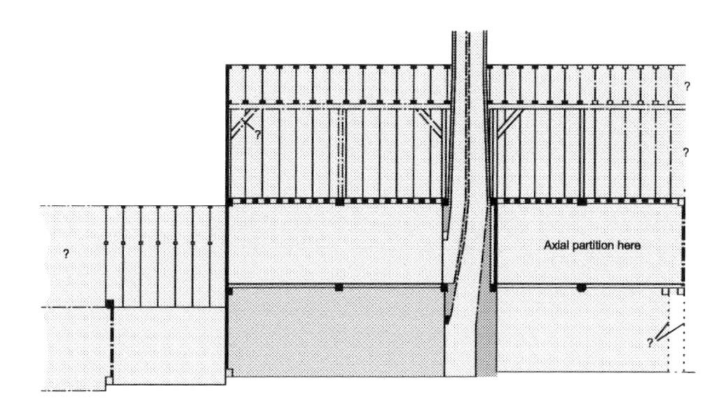

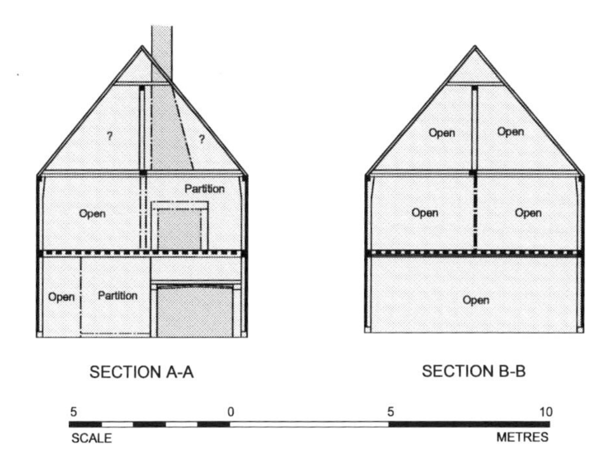

Fig. 11.19
Reconstruction of 11 Market Street.

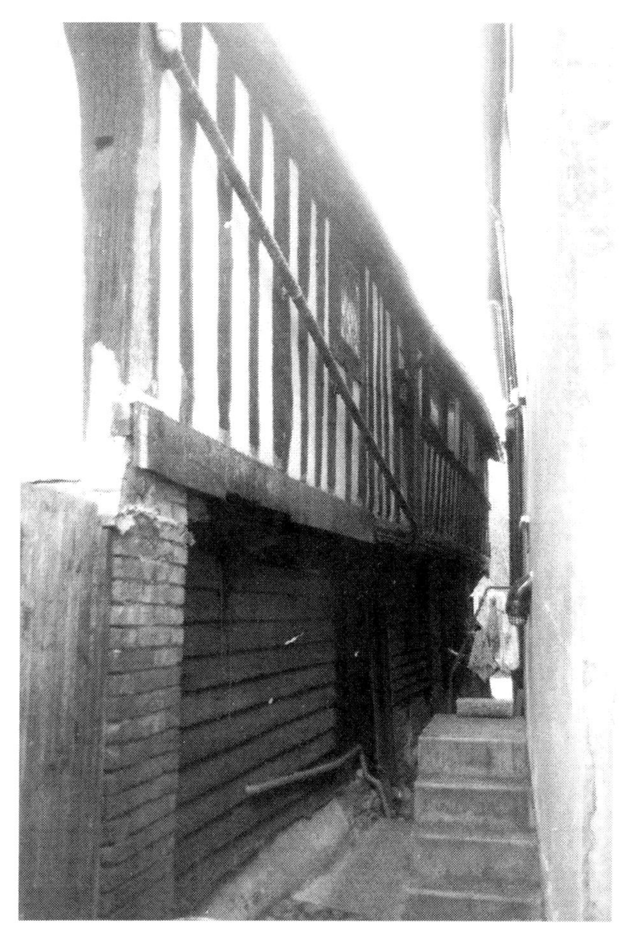

Fig. 11.20
'Vicarage Lane' showing old front of 1-2 Lion Street.

restrict the usable attic space. The adoption of a crownpost roof ought to indicate a pre-*c.*1540 date, but a date slightly later is not impossible. Certainly the crownposts look late, but the 140-mm-wide floor joists are set at exceedingly close (315 mm) centres and would be entirely consistent with a date between *c.*1510 and *c.*1540. *[ESRO HBR/1/1536]*

42. 9-10 East Street/13-14 Market Street —
1400 +/-25;1500 +/-33; 1570 +/-33 (see Figure 6.21)

Phase 1 (c.1400). At one time this property was divided into two and subsequently into four separate occupancies, but it was built as one house. It is a large, early 'Wealden' hall house, now very fragmentary, but originally incorporating a return jetty at its eastern end, fronting onto East Street. As at 99-100 High Street [25], the house occupies a corner plot and may have incorporated a return range fronting East Street from the outset. There is a heavily mutilated 'decorated-style' moulded crossbeam at the eastern end of the hall: this is the most complete of the trusses. The two-bay area at this end of the main range, beyond what appears to have been the high end of the hall, was divided longitudinally in order to give two ground-floor rooms, of which the long thin front room could have been designed as a shop facing Market Street.

Phase 2 (c.1500). Repairs carried out to the eastern end of the front elevation in the late 20th century revealed that close studding had been added into the first-floor framing in the late 15th or early 16th century in order to update the building's external appearance. The studs had been neatly housed into the face of the wallplate and pegged.

Phase 3 (c.1570). A floor was inserted into the hall at this period and a chimney added against the hall's rear wall. These are now the only features which survive in the area of the original open hall. The rest of the hall, together with the service bay, were totally rebuilt, taller, in the early 18th century. *[ESRO HBR/1/0729]*

43. Fletchers House, 1-2 Lion Street —
1500 +/-25; 1550 +/-25 (Figure 11.20 - 11.23)

Phase 1 (c.1500). The southern of two adjacent buildings standing at right angles to Lion Street, representing permanent development upon what are thought to have been market rows, probably incorporating commercial functions from the outset. It is substantial, being of four bays, 13.65 metres (44'9") long, 6.25 metres (20'6") wide on the ground floor and continuously jettied towards the north, east and south. All three of these walls are close studded for display and overlooked the street to the east and market lanes on north and south. Whether a street also passed to the west, or whether this wall abutted either open land or another tenement is unknown — there is a smoke bay at this end so the lack of a jetty tells nothing. It may be significant that an 8 feet

(2.40 metre) wide plot of land at the opposite end of the property was conveyed to the owner, Thomas Fletcher, fisherman, in 1500 — this could have been acquired as a prelude to him rebuilding his 'house' larger. Such a date is certainly consistent with the architectural evidence.[7]

Despite Lion Street being a principal route up to the church, and therefore presumably of some importance, the building appears originally not to have incorporated ground-floor windows facing onto that street. There were, however, windows within the north wall, facing towards the narrow northern market lane, and this wall could also have incorporated doorways. The principal external doorways — two in number, of which the eastern is shown in Figure 11.22 — faced south onto the narrow market lane later known as 'Vicarage Lane'.[8] This wall (and perhaps originally the others too) is embellished with a moulded and embattled jetty fascia and a first-floor moulded cornice. Today the elevation is largely hidden from view by 68, 70, 72 Church Square, a tall, narrow row of late buildings occupying the site between it and the churchyard, leaving only a narrow passage between the two (*see* Figure 11.20). This terrace occupies an earlier market row of what were doubtless narrow, low, market stalls when Fletchers House was first built. In a sense this house could be considered to be built at right angles to the street, but such an interpretation ignores the fact that it is also aligned to market lanes and occupies what historically was almost certainly a number of market plots consolidated to form a larger property.

How the interior of the building functioned is a mystery. One of the two main doors led into the eastern end of the large central room which, to judge from its moulded and bracketed ceiling beam, was a room of status, despite being unheated at this period. Lit by a pair of large windows, the whole arrangement looks hall-like. Presumably a door led out of this room into the eastern end room, which has two dragon-beams within its ceiling. The design of this eastern room's south wall is unknown, so it could have incorporated a shop front. A stair in the north-western corner of the room gave access to the first floor, where there were chambers (open to the crownpost roof) above the hall and eastern room, as well as another over the room to the west of the hall. Here there is another problem of interpretation — it cannot be told whether there was internal access between either the hall and western room, or the hall chamber and western chamber. Thus, given the existence of a second doorway in the south elevation, the entire western end of the building could initially have functioned as an independently let unit, or, even if there was a first-floor doorway, the ground-floor part could have been separately let. This ground-floor section is a single room, served by an end smoke bay.

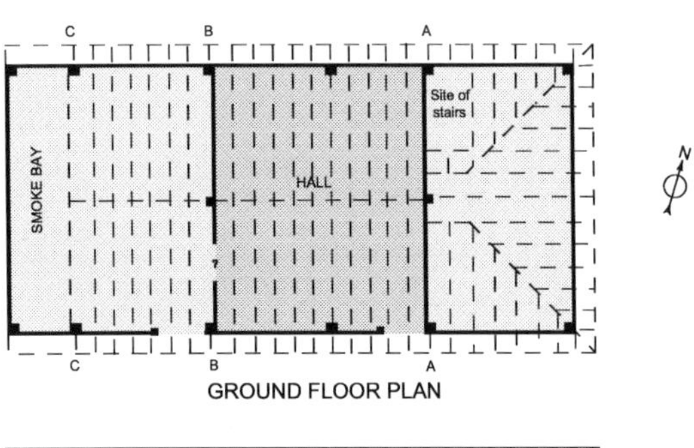

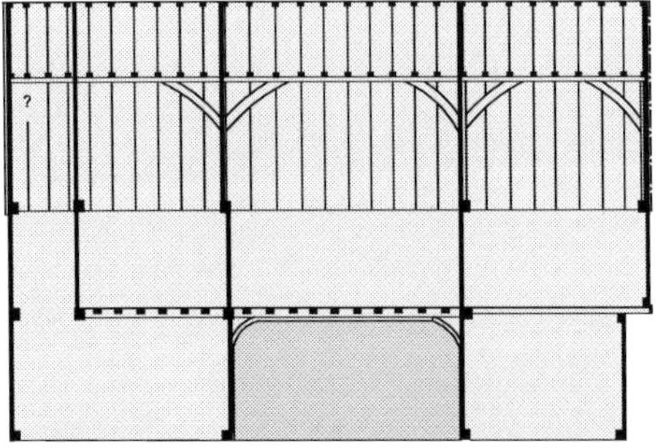

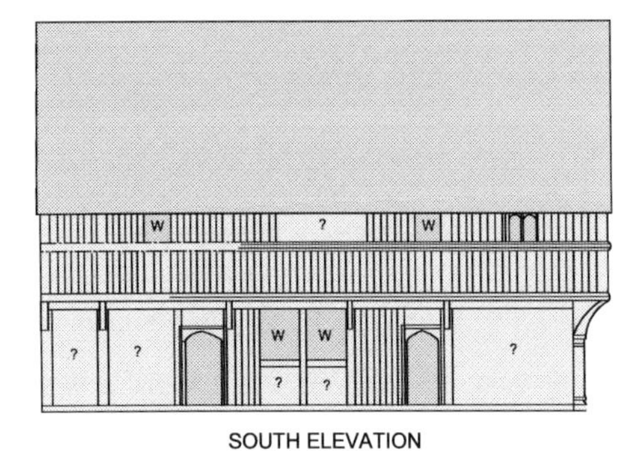

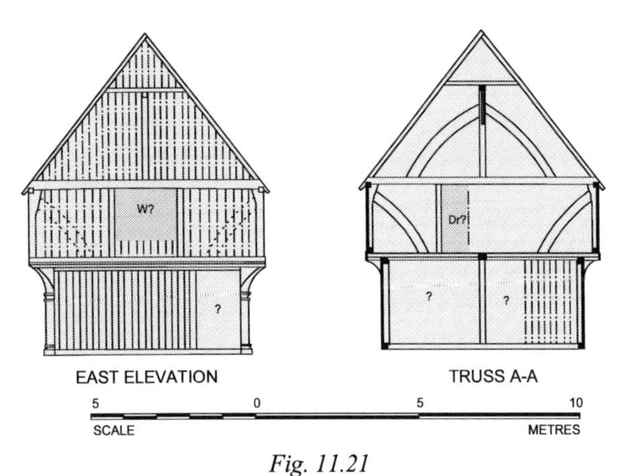

Fig. 11.21
Phase 1 reconstruction of Fletchers House, 1-2 Lion Street.

Fig. 11.22
Doorway leading off 'Vicarage Lane' into the 'hall' at Fletchers House, 1-2 Lion Street.

Fig. 11.23
Hall chimney added into western chamber against partition crownpost, phase 2, Fletchers House, 1-2 Lion St.

Phase 2 (c.1550). A good quality single-flue chimney was added into the western room, heating the hall. As part of this alteration the smoke bay was floored over and its first-floor partition removed (Figure 11.23). The present western roof terminal is hipped. *[ESRO HBR/1/0725]*

44. 3 Lion Street — *1525 +/-25*
(Figure 11.24)

A small building (8.85 metres x 5.10 metres or 29'0" x 16'9"), probably jettied towards Lion Street and initially totally detached, with lanes to north and south. Similar to the arrangement at Fletcher's House [43], this property is now aligned at right angles to the main street, but originally was aligned with a market lane, and was almost certainly built upon market stall plots. Now it is attached to Fletchers House by a 17th-century addition. However, not only was the house subsequently extended southwards over the lane so as to abut Fletchers House [43], but the next house northwards — later The Red Lion — had two ranges built extending southwards over the northern lane, enclosing a courtyard against the north wall of Number 3. These encroachments are associated with the final abandonment of this part of the market and with the stopping up of two of the east-west market lanes. The effect of this was to re-orientate the buildings to face Lion Street.

The property still extends a considerable distance westwards down its plot, but the western parts are much later, though perhaps occupying the sites of earlier buildings. Because of the extent of modern coverings, the internal layout of the house is very difficult to interpret, but, as Figure 11.24 indicates, it appears to have incorporated two ground-floor rooms and two first-floor chambers, probably with the western half of the western room open to the roof. If so, the present western chimney is a later addition, built when the open part was floored over. *[ESRO HBR/1/1624]*

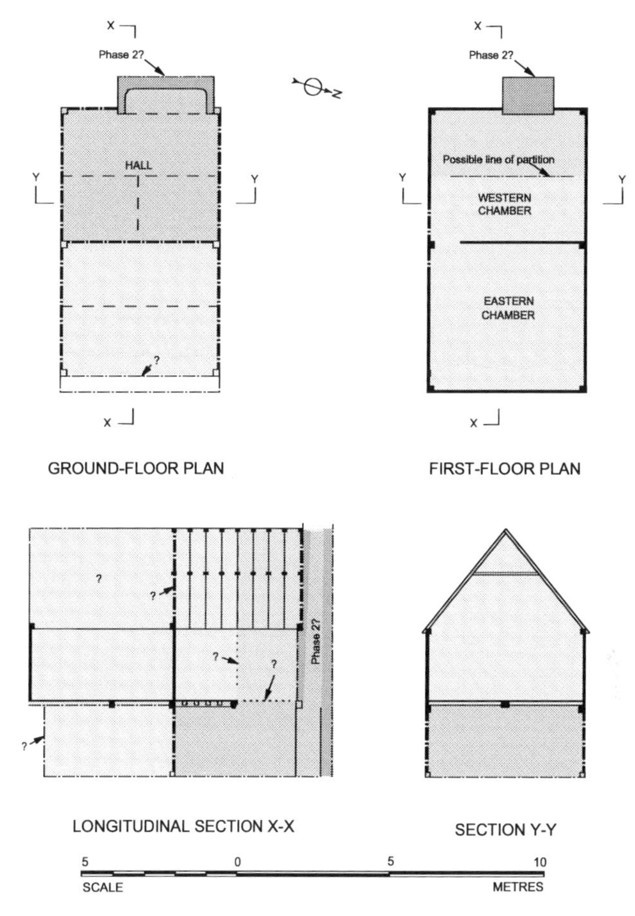

Fig. 11.24
Reconstruction of 3 Lion Street.

Fig. 11.25
4-6 Lion Street.
Upper part of Truss C-C. Some of the daub infill is comb decorated.

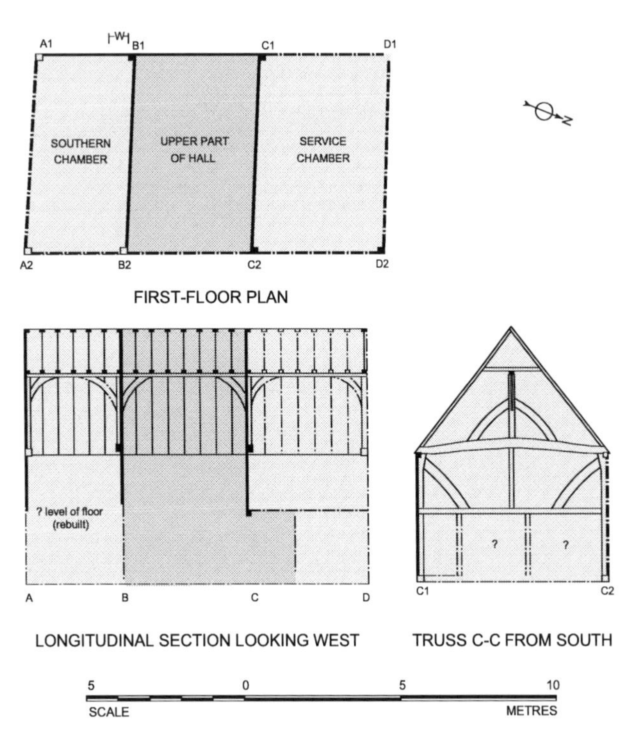

Fig. 11.26
Reconstruction of 4-6 Lion Street.

45. 4-6 Lion Street — *1470 +/-33; 1530 +/-25; 1600 +/-25 (Figures 11.25 & 11.26)*

A standard three-cell house with a single-bay open hall and no jetties. The internal layout of the service area has been lost due to later alterations, but evidence of a standard mullioned unglazed window shows there was not a shop at this end of the house.

Phase 2 (c.1530). The insertion of a floor into the open hall allowed the formation of an additional first-floor chamber, accessed from the south. There was no intercommunication northwards towards the service chamber. No doubt some form of chimney was added against the hall's rear wall, though the present stack on this site is a rebuild of *c.*1800. The hall ceiling is of good quality with moulded girders and closely-spaced stop-chamfered joists. Above, the walls were re-infilled using comb-decorated daub.

Phase 3 (c.1600). At this period a wide rear range was added behind the hall and southern bay, blocking at least one medieval window. On the ground floor the range is divided by an off-centred axial partition to give a large heated northern room and a long, narrow southern room facing towards an access lane. The configuration could indicate the existence of a shop facing the lane. There are faint traces of decorative wall paintings within the hall chamber. *[ESRO HBR/1/1540]*

46. 7-9 Lion Street — *1475 +/-50; 1550 +/-25 (Figure 11.27 & 11.28)*

Phase 1 (c.1475). A *c.*6.20 metres (*c.*20'4") wide hall house stood on the site of Peacock Tea Rooms, indicated by the pattern of weathering on the wall of the adjacent building. The building had low walls, but nevertheless the hall was thought to be of sufficient quality to be kept when the service

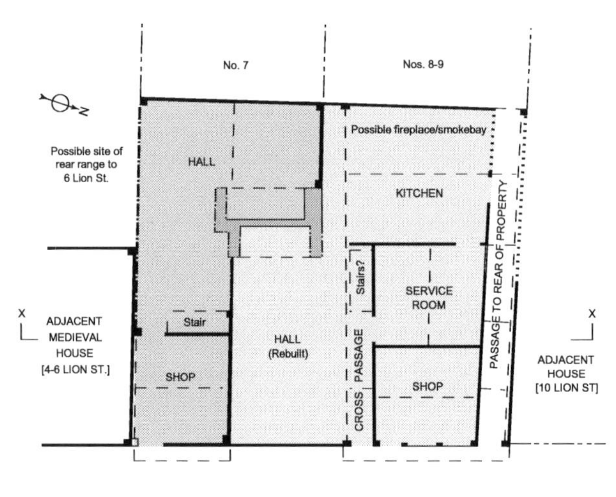

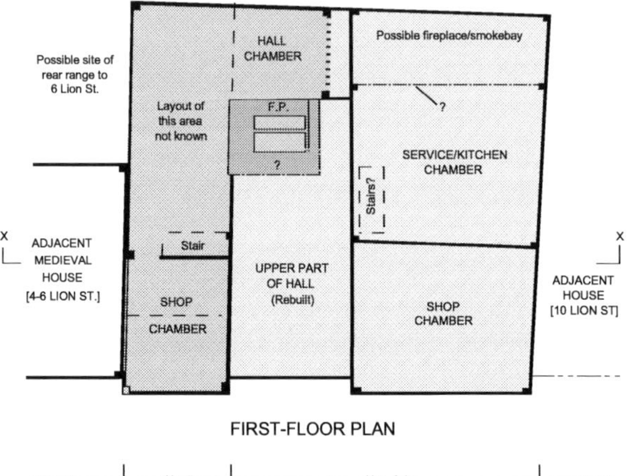

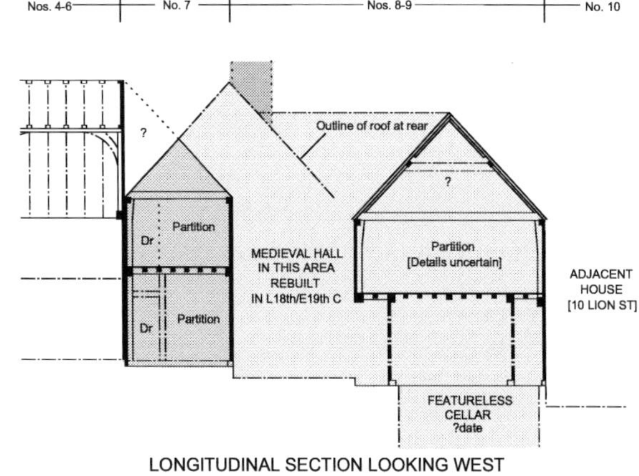

Fig 11.27
Phase 2 reconstruction of 7-9 Lion Street. The two dwellings are depicted by different shades of grey.

area to the north was rebuilt. It is all but certain that this house was entirely detached, with a narrow alleyway between it and the next house north and a wider space — sufficient for carts — between it and the medieval house to the south.

Phase 2 (c.1550). New work encapsulated the retained

hall of the building's medieval predecessor, though this part too was rebuilt subsequently. The mid 16th-century reconstruction did not merely involve replacing part of an earlier building with a more up-to-date and sophisticated structure, it also gave two dwellings where only one had existed previously. The substantial double-piled building occupies the entire 12.05 metres (39'6") street frontage of the plot and extends back *c.*10.60 metres (34'9") from the street (Figure 11.27). Viewed from Lion Street it probably had the appearance of two jettied crosswings (one wide and one narrow) flanking the un-jettied hall. In contrast, towards its rear yard it presented two wide adjoining gables.

Two dwellings are incorporated within the scheme — a principal northern dwelling and a much smaller southern one. At 9.00 metres (29'6") long, the main house took up three-quarters of the street frontage and on the ground floor incorporated a heated hall, shop, service room, and a rear 'kitchen', together with a narrow through passage giving pedestrian access to the rear yard. The service room was buried deep within the house, and, in consequence, had to rely upon an unglazed borrowed light incorporated into the side wall of the passage (Figure 11.28).

In contrast to the main house, at only 3.05 metres (10'0") wide the southern dwelling appears tiny, though this impression is misleading in that it wraps around its neighbour's hall and thus, at the rear, is double the size. In fact, the hall of this house has a reasonable floor area and is heated by a good quality fireplace, backing onto that which served the hall of its larger neighbour. The jambs of the fireplace are of Caen stone and the timber lintel is of good quality and is moulded.

The joists within the principal areas of both dwellings are neatly chamfered. In particular, the joist arrangement within the crosswing of the northern house is complex, being designed to suit the complicated room layout.

A peculiarity of the building is the use of exceptionally long side girts which support stilted principal posts restricted to first-floor level only. All the side girts are long, but two in particular seem to extend the full 10.60 metres (34'9") depth of the building with hardly any support beneath. The reason appears to have been an attempt to maximize available ground-floor space. One of the over-length side girts occurs at the side of the narrow through passage where the building utilized the wall of the adjacent house. The other spans the hall and kitchen and crosses both rooms continuously. This use of continuous side girts is not unique to 7-9 Lion Street: it has also been noted within the side walls of the (assumed) slightly earlier 7 Mermaid Street [62] and within the narrow crosswing at 15 West Street [56], a building which is likely to be contemporary with 7-9 Lion Street. *[ESRO HBR/1/1607 (7Lion Street); ESRO HBR/1/1622 (8-9 Lion Street)]*

Fig. 11.28
7-9 Lion Street. Mortices for unglazed borrowed light between service room (left) and former through passage (right)

47. 12 Lion Street — *1475 +/-25*
(Figures 11.29)

A 'Wealden' hall house with an almost textbook two-cell layout. Despite measuring only 9.05 metres (29'8"), it appears to have taken up the entire frontage of its plot. Even so, and despite the use of gabled ends to its roof, it was an entirely detached house with no other buildings against it. Because its end walls were fully visible from the street, the close studding used for display within the front elevation was returned around the end walls, though cheaper large-panel framing was used within the rear elevation. It is built with a single-bay open hall entered via an overshot cross passage, with a pair of service rooms beyond. In this it could not be more standard, though as Figure 11.29 indicates, this

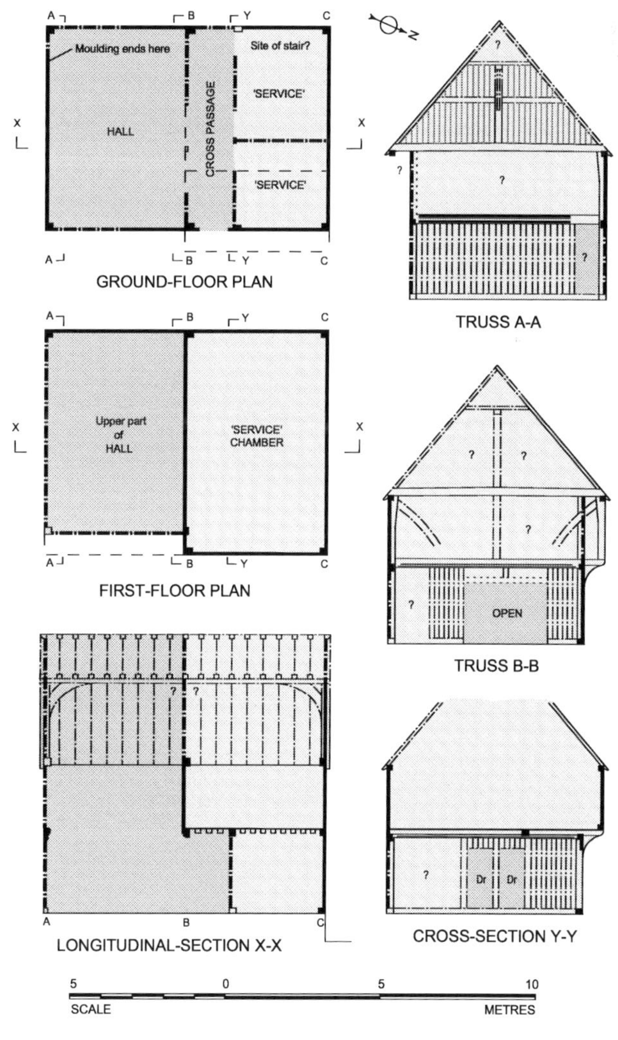

Fig. 11.29
Reconstruction of 12 Lion Street.

description masks one peculiarity — the axial partition and service doors are biased towards the front of the building. The off-centred positioning of the service partition could be explained by the likely site of a staircase against the rear wall and a desire to keep both service rooms of near equal size. But this is not the only design anomaly. The wide opening between the cross passage and main body of the hall is likewise placed off centre to the hall with the rear draught spere much longer than that at the front, whilst the moulding on the dais partition at the opposite end of the hall terminates 1.05 metres (3'6") short of the rear wall. This latter feature is not uncommon within houses of three-cell layout where the area at the rear end of the dais partition was taken up by a doorway leading out of the hall into the high-end accommodation, but in this instance no high-end accommodation existed. It is unlikely that an external doorway would have been sited in this location, unless, perhaps, the owner had designs on acquiring the adjacent plot and building the missing high-end accommodation at a subsequent date. Another, though even less likely explanation could be that the owner wished to mimic the design found in houses of 'fully developed' three-cell type by incorporating a 'false door' in this location in order to maintain appearances. But such theories do not explain the unequal-length draught speres at the opposite end of the hall, a feature which could be said to 'balance' the eccentric arrangement within the dais partition. Could it be that the real reason was the presence of an in-built chimney of some kind against the rear wall of the hall? The answer will never be known, for the hall's rear wall has been totally rebuilt, as too has all but the end gables of the roof. *[ESRO HBR/1/1575]*

48. 13 Lion Street — *1560 +/-25*
(see Figures 11.31)

A small, straightforward two-cell, continuously-jettied house 6.80 metres (22'4") long, tapering slightly in width on the ground floor from 4.45 metres to 4.75 metres (14'7" to 15'7"). It was a tiny building, towered over on the south by 12 Lion Street [47] and on the north by the three-and-a-half storeyed 14 Lion Street [49] (Figure 11.31). All are now part of The George complex. Despite the difference in size, Nos. 13 [48] and 14 [49] are of identical date to one another and form part of the same scheme of redevelopment. The scant remains which survive suggest that 13 Lion Street [48] had a standard two-cell plan with a small northern bay and a larger southern bay which housed the hall. The method of heating is not known. Incorporated into the rear (western) wall are the remains of a glazed first-floor window with a chamfered surround, indicating that the building did not incorporate either a rear lean-to outshut or any other form of rear range. *[ESRO HBR/1/1576]*

49. 14 Lion Street — *1560 +/-25*
(Figures 11.30 - 11.33)

The plot upon which this was built is very restricted — in fact the building occupies the entire space available and thus there was no rear yard or garden. Nevertheless, it does have the advantage of occupying a corner site, with the High Street to the north and Lion Street to the east. The plot was formed sometime in the early/mid 16th century by the subdivision of 98 High Street [24]. At a much later date (probably in the 18th century, but perhaps in the late 17th century) it was amalgamated back into 98 High Street to form the core of the present George Hotel. Late in the 18th century the exterior of both parts were altered so that, from the street, they give the impression of being of one date.

Despite the present exterior, 14 Lion Street is a long, narrow, tall, three-and-a-half storeyed three-cell house, which, as the dragon beam in Figure 11.30 indicates, was originally continuously jettied on the first floor against both streets, though un-jettied above. The walls are of small-panel design with externally-concealed bracing, though it is possible that the two street facades were additionally elaborated with close studding. All the indications are that the building dates from the third quarter of the 16th century. On the ground floor it measures 12.25 metres x 4.65 metres (40'3" x 15'3") though these dimensions are increased slightly on the upper storeys by the first-floor jetty.

The building is thought to have served as an inn called The Red Lion (not to be confused with an inn of the same name which later occupied a site at the opposite end of the street on the same side — *see* Chapter 7). As Figure 11.31 shows, it is framed in three bays, giving three rooms in line on each of the three main floors. The two northern rooms on each floor were heated by a six-flue chimney built into the northern end of the long central bay. The chimney is towards the rear of the range, with the space against the street housing an inter-linking passage and tight stair (now mostly removed) rising from ground floor to attic. Steps descend beneath the lower flight to give access to a stone-walled cellar beneath the parlour (northern room) whilst a further flight of steps set centrally within the north wall allowed direct access to the cellar from the High Street.

Sufficient detail of the western (rear) wall remains to prove that it incorporated neither doorways nor windows, whilst the available details at second-floor level suggest an absence of windows below attic level within the north wall too. The presence of adjacent 13 Lion Street [48] (of identical date) to the south excludes the possibility of windows below garret level within the southern end wall. Therefore, except at roof level, all windows lighting the house appear to have been located within the Lion Street facade. Here no effort was

Fig. 11.30
Dragon beam carrying former first-floor jetty around northeastern corner of 14 Lion Street.

spared. The arrangement can be reconstructed at both first-floor and second-floor levels: it was an alternating pattern of large projecting oriel windows and high-level clerestory lights extending the full length of the facade. All the oriels were of similar size, but the clerestory openings vary from two to four panes in width in order to suit the bay lengths. From the exterior the overall effect must have been impressive, though internally the windows were not symmetrical to the rooms. Instead, in each case the oriel was positioned against a partition (*see* Figures 11.32 and 11.33).

Although great care was taken to achieve external symmetry on the upper floors, on the ground floor the pattern was broken. Perhaps this was due to the need to incorporate the external doorway. It would have been logical to have placed this so as to lead into a lobby beside the chimney and stairs, but this was not the case — instead there was a passage here lit by a continuous clerestory window. Presumably, therefore, the doorway was located so as to lead directly into the southern end of the hall.

Unlike the three main floors of the house, the garret floor was divided into two rooms only. At this level the floor is positioned 450 mm (1'6") below the top of the wallplate in order to improve headroom. The two-bay southern garret room was lit by a window in the southern gable, positioned above the level of the roof of the much lower 13 Lion Street [48]. No doubt a similar gable window lit the northern garret, though this gable has been destroyed, having been removed as part of the 18th-century makeover. *[ESRO HBR/1/1576]*

Fig. 11.31
Reconstruction of 13 Lion Street (left) and 14 Lion Street (right). Both are now part of The George.

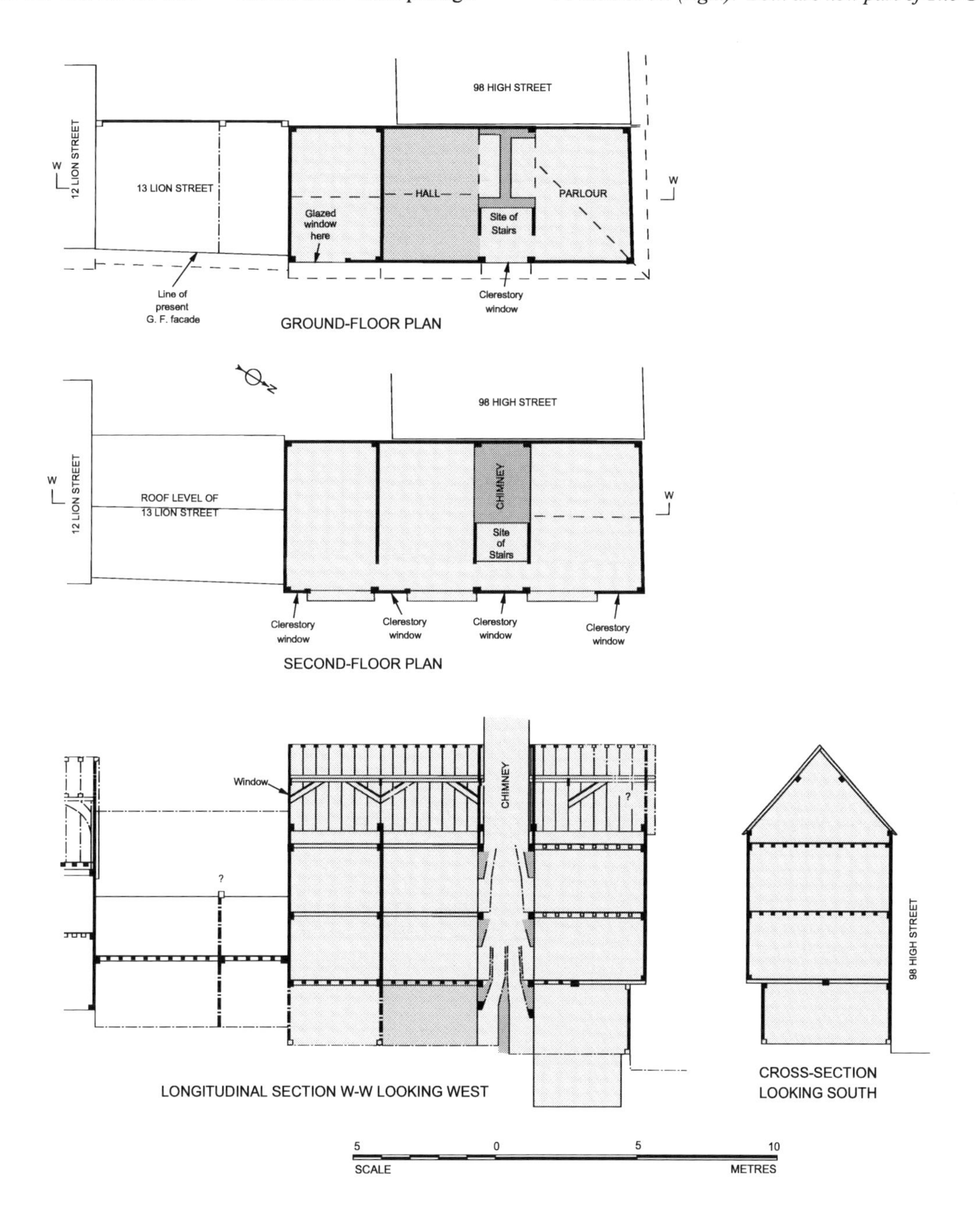

Fig. 11.32
14 Lion Street.
The street wall of second-floor hall chamber showing inset brace with three-pane clerestory window above and narrower modern window on the site of former projecting window.

Fig. 11.33
14 Lion Street.
Street wall of second-floor southern chamber showing two-pane clerestory window and modern window on site of former projecting window which extended up to the northern wall of the chamber.

12 THE HOUSES TO *c*.1660 SUMMARIZED: WEST STREET AND MERMAID STREET

50. 5-6 West Street — *1500 +/-50*
(Figure 12.1)

A large jettied house occupying a prominent corner plot with a 15.30 metres (50'2") facade measured overall its former western end return jetty. Because the street corner is out-of-square, the rear wall is even longer, at 17.30 metres (56'9"). It was extensively remodelled by Thomas Lamb in 1794, at which time he rebuilt the two street facades in brick and totally rebuilt the roof. Whether the former front jetty was continuous or interrupted to give a 'Wealden' facade depends upon whether the centrally-placed hall was initially open or floored over. The visible crossbeam and ceiling girder in this area have mouldings of typical early 16th-century date, which is consistent with the likely date of the other visible features, but so little of the structure is now exposed it is impossible to prove that the floor has not been inserted. The layout is of standard three-cell type with the high-end bay to the west and the service bay to the east. Nothing is known regarding the layout of the services, nor is it known whether the service bay included a cross passage — the likelihood is that it did. Beneath the high-end is a cellar (un-vaulted) accessed from the exterior through the end wall. The visible walls are of widely-spaced, slender close studding, infilled within the rear wall using buff 'Flemish' brick nogging. *[ESRO HBR/1/0914]*

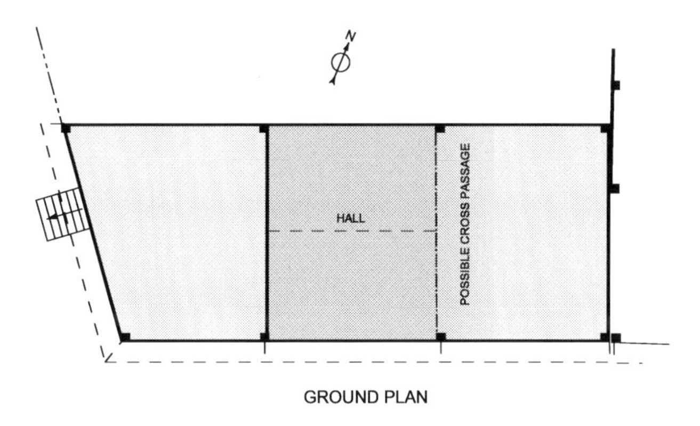

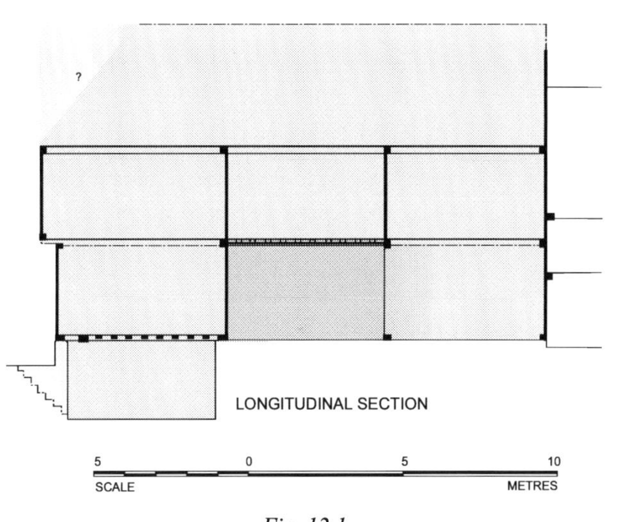

Fig. 12.1
Reconstruction of 5-6 West Street.

51. 7-9 West Street/62 Church Square —
1300 +/-100; 1490 +/-25; 1535 +/- 25; 1600 +/-25
(Figures 12.2 - 12.10)

Phase 1 (14th C). It would appear that there had been a structure of some status upon the site since early times, for running longitudinally through the building, parallel to and set back 4.40 metres (14'5") from West Street, is a substantial stone wall incorporating an undatable medieval doorway with a chamfered two-centred arched head, and the remains of a first-floor chimney 'corbelled' out slightly from the northern face of the wall. At the eastern end another stone wall returns northwards, and this incorporates an equally undatable square-headed stone window (*see* Figure 12.2). All this suggests a substantial stone building to the north of the main wall and implies that the present timber-framed building has encroached southwards onto the street. This, however, cannot have been the whole story, for the doorway is facing the wrong way, with its principal arch on the north and its rear arch towards the south. Therefore, something (presumably timber framed) must always have stood to the south of the wall. The most likely explanation is that a substantial stone house was set back from the street, fronted by a range of lesser, perhaps commercial properties acting as a baffle between the two, maximizing the commercial frontage of the tenement. A number of examples of this type are known from various towns. For example, there are the fragments of two such houses at St Anthony and Old Castle House in Castle Street, Winchelsea, Rye's sister town.[1]

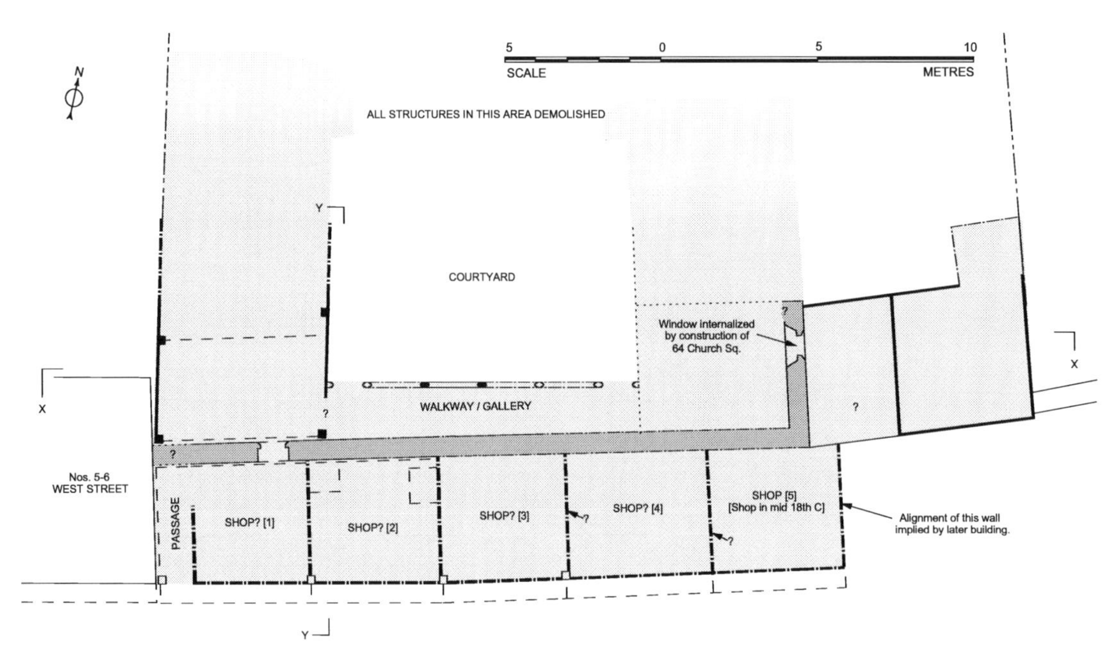

Fig. 12.2
Reconstruction ground-floor plan of 7-9 West Street and 62, 64 Church Square, as in phase 3

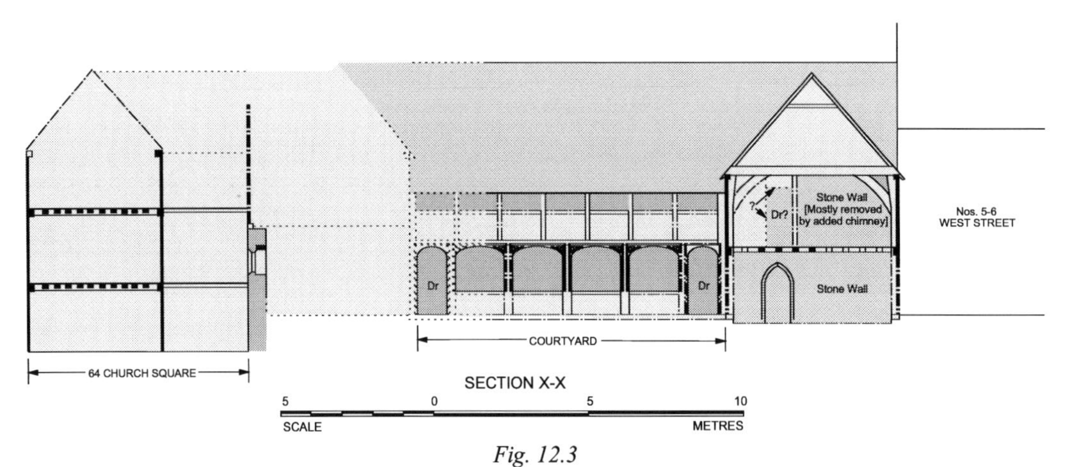

Fig. 12.3
Reconstructed part section and part elevation showing openings serving the southern gallery of the former courtyard, as in phase 3.

Phase 2 (c.1490). As is the case at Old Castle House, Winchelsea, the timber-framed structures which now stand upon the site are later in date than the stone wall. The best preserved work in the street range is the medieval joisting supporting the first floor, together with fragments of wall framing and (perhaps) parts of the roof above. What these remains indicate is a 22.20 metre (72'9") long two-storeyed, continuously-jettied street range housing five units (numbered 1-5 in Figure 12.2). At the extreme western end was a passage which was interlinked to the westernmost unit (Unit 1) and may also have led through to the building beyond. It is this western unit which incorporates the stone doorway, but whether this was open and in use or was blocked at this time is unknown — it is open today, but this could be the result of alteration/restoration. Above each unit was a chamber (Chambers 1-5). One of these (Chamber 2) was linked to the space beneath by not one staircase/hatch, but two. Curiously, the stair hatches flank the first-floor chimney, but it is impossible to know whether the stack was in use at this time. Perhaps significantly, westernmost Unit 1 (the one thought to have been interlinked to the mansion beyond) can be shown not to have had a stair through its floor. Despite the building having been split up and occupied by three named tenants by 1658, and having been still further divided subsequently, it may be relevant that as late as the mid 18th century the easternmost unit (Shop 5) — by that date separately owned — was in use as a shop with a small chamber over it, adjoined on the west and north by other properties. This arrangement is consistent with the impression given by the architectural evidence, namely that the units fronting West Street were intended as commercial space with chambers above. If so, the westernmost unit (Unit 1) must originally have been in the same occupation as the main mansion.

Incorporated within the rear parts of the present houses are sufficient remains to indicate that the mansion itself

Fig. 12.4
7-9 West Street and 62, 64 Church Square.
Detail of arched head to one of the openings separating the ground-floor gallery (foreground) from the former courtyard (background). The top of the opening was blocked when an addition was built within the courtyard after the mansion was divided up into individual dwellings.

Fig. 12.5
7-9 West Street and 62, 64 Church Square.
Detail of moulded jamb separating two of the openings between the courtyard (foreground) and the ground-floor gallery (background). The cill of the right hand opening is just visible at the bottom of the photograph at the point where the mouldings terminate.

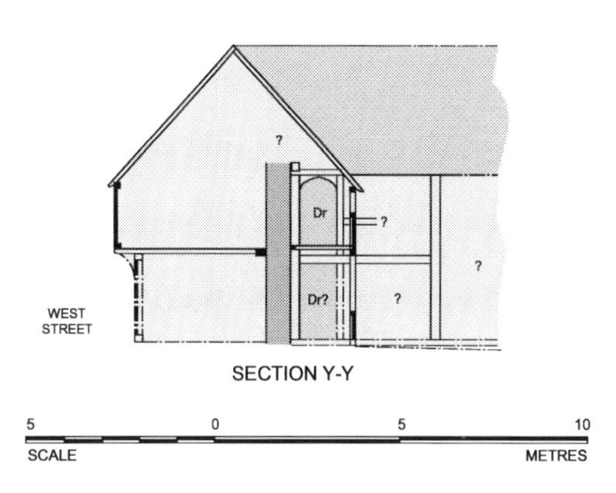

Fig. 12.6
Reconstructed section through street range, 8 West Street.

included a courtyard with substantial timber-framed ranges to east and west, linked at the southern end, against the stone wall, by a 1.60 metre (5'3") wide open gallery on two storeys. Sufficient survives in this area to give a good impression of the appearance of the gallery when viewed from the courtyard. As Figure 12.3 shows, on the ground floor were four wide window-like openings with elaborately moulded surrounds and semi-elliptical arched heads decorated with pyramidal sunk spandrels, all typical of a late 15th or very early 16th-century date. One of these openings is illustrated in Figures 12.4 and 12.5. The spacing of the arches suggests a doorway at either end, linking the ground-floor walkway to the courtyard, though other doorways probably linked the walkway to the east and west ranges. There are openings in this area through the surviving sections of the stone wall, which at this point formed the southern side of the walkway, but these have all been roughly cut through and must be of later date. The first-floor gallery likewise overlooked the courtyard, but at this level there were seven openings, all plain and square headed under a low eaves. Glazed windows were inserted into some of these opening later and others were blocked. At the western end of the gallery survives a doorway (with semi-elliptical arched head) giving access to the west range, and there must have been a similar doorway leading into the eastern range too, otherwise this upper gallery would have led nowhere. All the surviving openings through the stone wall at this level represent later insertions: the earliest (leading into Chamber 2) is of late 16th or 17th-century date and probably relates to the period when the mansion was in use as The Queens Arms. As indicated by Figure 12.6, a single roof spans the front chambers and gallery, cradling the axial stone wall, but whether this roof is of late-medieval date or was built subsequently is in doubt. Little of the roof is visible, though the rafters are certainly of sufficiently heavy scantling to belong to this period. However, at one point what appears to be the low pitch of a roof and partition is just visible within the roof void. Most likely this is explained as a canted ceiling inserted into one of the first-floor chambers, but this cannot be proven.

None of the spaces within the surviving part of the mansion are either large enough or of sufficient quality to be the principal rooms of the complex, and indeed the 13+ flue assessment for the building in 1662-4 proves that the majority of the building has been destroyed. Both the existence of the

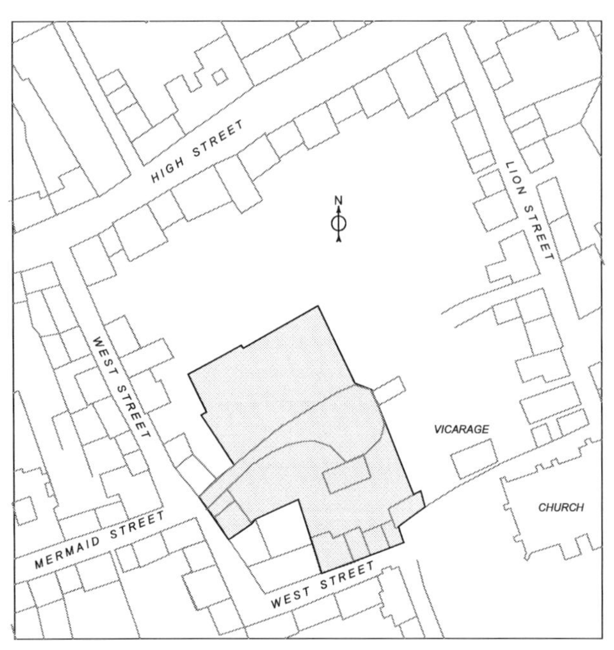

Fig. 12.7
The site of the Shurley mansion (later The Queen's Arms) showing a reconstruction of the property boundaries as they existed in the mid 17th century. [sources - ESRO RYE 33/20; ESRO PAB 4]

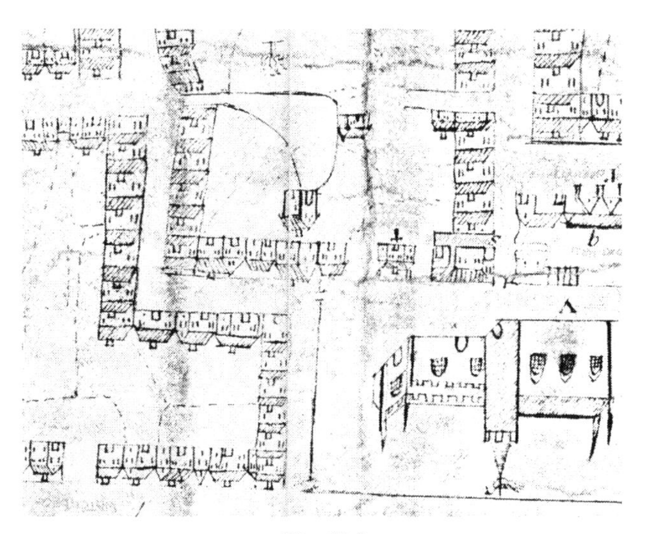

Fig. 12.8
Detail (rotated) from Jeake's map of Rye, 1667, [ESRO RYE 132/15] showing the mansion standing behind the houses in West Street, together with the access road leading in from the top of Mermaid Street

Fig. 12.9
The Shurley Mansion complex viewed from the churchyard.

gatehouse leading off West Street at the top of Mermaid Street (giving access to the core of the property) and the stylized sketch shown in the Jeake map indicate that the principal rooms were in the demolished ranges which stood in what are today back gardens.

In his book 'A New History of Rye' Leopold Vidler writes 'John Shurley, the King's bailiff, had bought much property in the town and appears to have resided in a large house to the west of the vicarage at the north-west corner of the churchyard [ie. this building]. He also owned the large house opposite called the "Grene Hall" [58, 60 Church Square [89]] . . . . At one time he owned in the town 24 houses, 7 shops, 6 gardens and 3 acres of land'.[2] During the years around 1500 Shurley was arguably Rye's most important resident. The son of Roger Shurley of Presteign in Herefordshire, he was not only a Rye jurat (1499-1502) and the King's bailiff of the town (before 1501 to 1524) but was also a courtier, serving as Chief Clerk of the Kitchen to Henry VII and subsequently Cofferer under Henry VIII. His Rye connections arose from his marriage to Parnell, daughter and heir of fellow courtier, John Grandford, Yeoman of the Crown and King's bailiff of Rye from 1474 to his death in 1481. How much time Shurley spent in Rye is debatable — he must have been resident at Court for most of the year. Furthermore, from 1507 when he purchased the manor of Isfield near Lewes, Isfield became the family's principal seat, and it was there that he was buried in 1527. Despite this, his will reveals that even at his death his main interests lay in Rye and Winchelsea.[3] The Rye mansion probably served primarily as a 'private inn' with a resident household serving the needs of both Shurley and his retinue when they visited, as well as acting as a staging post for Royal Officials and messengers passing through Rye en route to the Continent.

Phase 3 (c.1535 and later). Projecting eastwards from the main complex, fronting onto the churchyard, is the building known today as 64 Church Square [52]. This is of 'crosswinged' construction built *c.*1535, originally unheated, and used in part or in whole as a shop (or shops) with associated store rooms/workrooms. The shop front within the crosswing is evidenced by mortices for two wide windows occupying virtually the entire length of the churchyard facade. The two parts — single-bay crosswing and single-bay main range — have no obvious original doorways linking between them and thus could have been separately occupied. In fact, the so called crosswing could initially have been built as a totally detached structure, with the main range added soon afterwards, infilling the gap between it and the main part of the mansion. Although it and the remainder of the mansion continued to be in single ownership, either late in the 16th century or during the first half of the 17th century this part became a house in its own right, heated by an end chimney built upon adjacent glebeland. It is almost certainly the 'messuage adjacent to the said capital messuage' which was occupied in 1658 by John Jacob.

At what date the Shurley family disposed of their Rye mansion is not known — the next record of it is in 1582 when Robert Wyman of Midhurst, yeoman, leased it, together with his shops at The Strand, to James Milles, merchant, for 21 years at £6.6s.9d. per annum. It was then described as Wymond's principal messuage in the lane leading from the west side of the churchyard to Middle Street.[4] As is so often the case with unwanted urban mansions of this size and type, it was eventually converted into a public inn, and is described in a deed of 1657 as a 'capital messuage, ... gardens, closes or parcels of land called The Queens Arms in the occupation of Andrew Faith and John Porter, together with another messuage adjoining the said capital messuage in the occupation of John Jacob'. The abutments indicate a sizable plot extending westwards from the Vicarage, with frontages onto the churchyard and West Street to the south and partly onto West Street on the west, with the back gardens of other West Street properties to south and west and the gardens of High Street properties on the north (Figure 12.7).[5]

Andrew Faith, gentleman, was still occupying one part in 1660, at which date another part was occupied by an alien innholder named Lewes Pascall.[6] By 1662 the principal part was in use as the home of Mr William Mason, who was assessed for it at 10 flues, exceeded only by the Mermaid Inn [72].[7] This 10-flue assessment was for part of the property only, John Porter was assessed 3 flues for another part, to which must be added the assessment for the adjoining messuage occupied in 1658 by John Jacob, who had by 1660 either moved away or died. Later deeds, made when the property was in the process of being broken up, shows that the section fronting westwards onto West Street included a gatehouse, slaughterhouse and stables situated opposite the top end of Mermaid Street.[8] This configuration is consistent with Jeake's map of the town made in 1667 which shows a lane leading into the property at this point and depicts a house standing to the rear of the buildings fronting onto West Street (Figure 12.8).[9]

Analysis of the abutments given in 1658 and subsequent deeds show that the principal part of the tenement (ignoring a close behind the High Street properties) is represented today by 7-9 West Street [51] and 62, 64 Church Square [52], wrapping around Temple House [50] (on the right-angled corner in West Street) to include the gatehouse, slaughterhouse, stables *etc* upon the present site of Norman House, West Street. Although of antiquity, the group of houses which make up 7-9 West Street [51] and 62, 64 Church Square [52] do not have the appearance of being part of a substantial and important urban mansion, rather they look to be separate houses of disparate dates (Figure 12.9). This is partly due to the subsequent development of the site which, during the 18th century, was divided up into separate dwellings, two of which have been rebuilt. But this is not the entire story, for the range of buildings fronting the street never formed the principal part of the mansion — that lay behind, built around a courtyard and accessed via the gatehouse at the top end of Mermaid Street. This is the house shown in Figure 12.8, in very stylized form, standing behind the houses fronting the street. It had evidently already been demolished by 1771, for it is not depicted on the town map of that year.[10] *[ESRO HBR/1/0741]*

52. 64 Church Square — *1535 +/-25*
(see also 7-9 West Street/62 Church Square [51])

A fragmentary house occupying a site close to the northwestern corner of the churchyard, terraced into the slope. Thus it gives two storeys towards the churchyard, but three to the rear. Here the jettied crosswing is of one bay only,

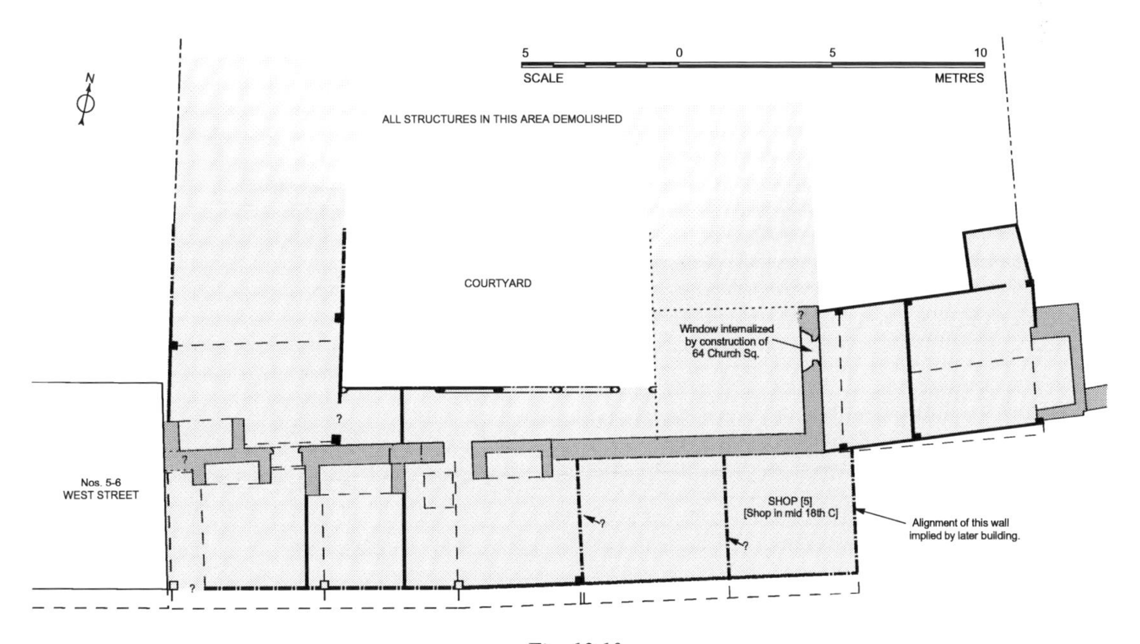

Fig. 12.10
Reconstructed ground-floor plan of 7-9 West Street and 62, 64 Church Square as altered in the 16th and/or 17th century.

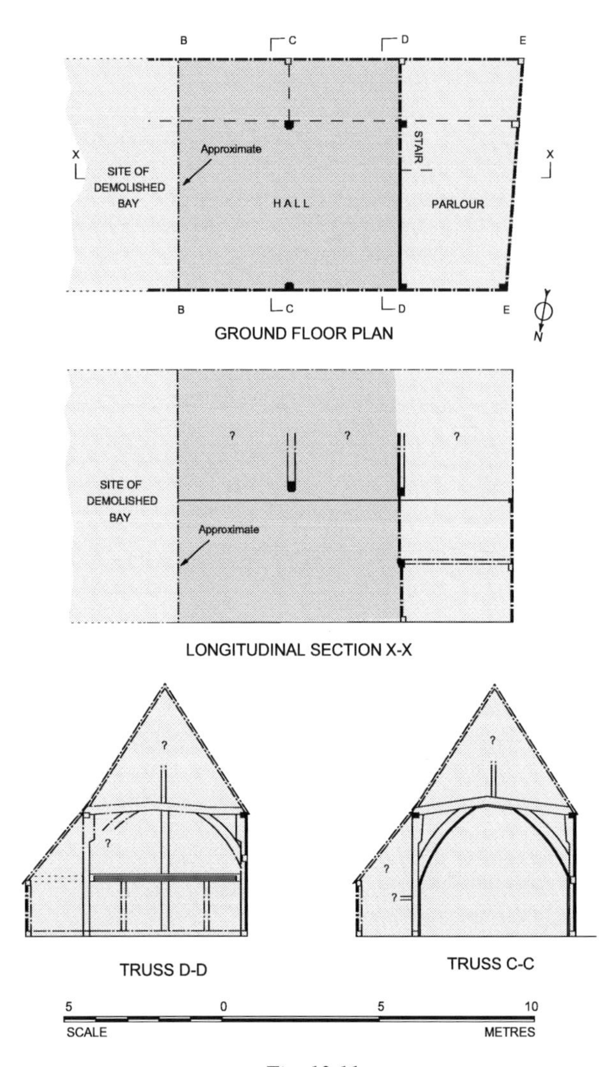

Fig. 12.11
Phase 1 reconstruction of Lamb Cottage, West Street

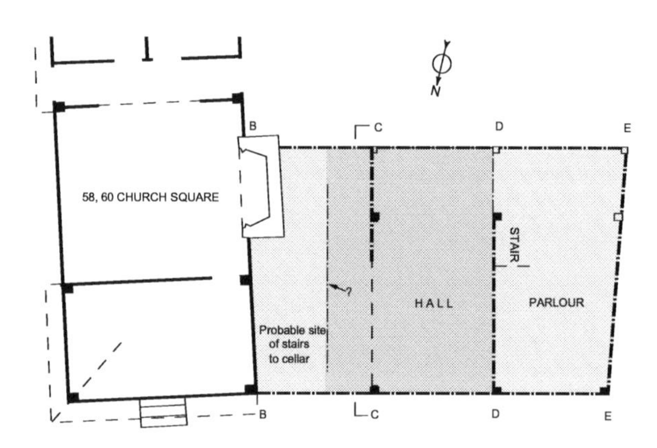

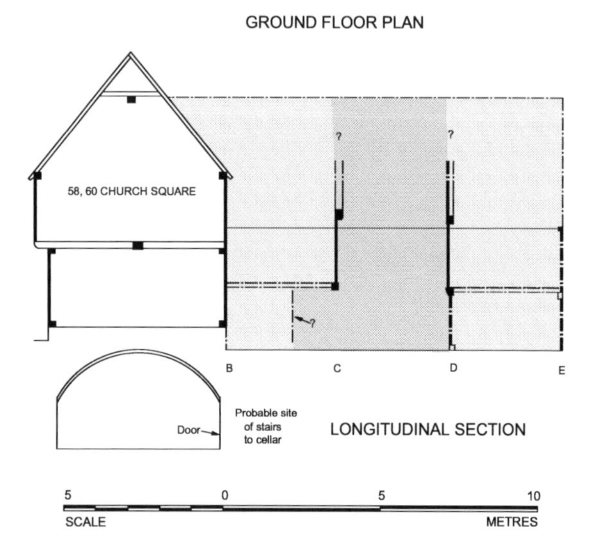

Fig. 12.12
Phase 2 reconstruction of Lamb Cottage, West Street

originally unheated and with a stair turret to the rear. The ground floor appears to have been intended as a shop. By the mid 17th century it formed part of the complex known as The Queens Arms — originally the mansion of the Shurley family (*see* [51]). Bearing in mind that the Shurley mansion shows evidence for shop units and chambers (assumed let to tenants) built against the street, perhaps 64 was built for wholly specialized use and, from the outset, formed part of the mansion complex. *[ESRO HBR/1/1100]*

53. Lamb Cottage, West Street —
1375 +/-25; 1500 +/-25; 1530 +/-25 (Figures 12.11 & 12.12)

Phase 1 (c.1375). A two-cell house which was probably originally of textbook three-cell type. What survives today is the large two-bay hall and high-end bay of a single-aisled house. Much of the hall's open truss survives, as too does its high-end wall, complete with 'decorated-style' moulded crossbeam (*see* Figure 6.27). It is possible that the part of Lamb Cottage at the low end of the hall (demolished, phase 2) always functioned as a separate building, turned at right angles to it (as is the case with St Anthony's, Church Square [87]/1-2 Watchbell Street [90] on the southwestern corner of Church Square) but it is far more likely that the service bay of Lamb Cottage was demolished to make way for the new house.

Phase 2 (c.1500). Part of the building at the low end of the hall was demolished *c.*1500 in order to give sufficient room for another three-cell hall house — 58, 60 Church Square [89]. It is probably no coincidence that around the same time as the bay was demolished part of the spacious two-bay open hall was floored over (Figure 12.12), which meant that a crossbeam had to be inserted into its arch-braced open truss and the upper parts of the truss were infilled with a daub partition. It seems likely that these rooms were newly-formed in mitigation for a lost service bay and represent the formation of new services and service chamber within the low end of the spacious open hall. Certainly, to judge from the Rye buildings which survive, it would have been unusual to construct a house of this type and size absent of a service bay.

Phase 3 (c.1530). The partial flooring over of the two-bay hall at Lamb Cottage was, for this house, only the first stage in this process: the hall continued to function in its shrunken form with one bay open to the rafters and, presumably, an old-style hearth on its floor for probably another generation before that bay too was finally floored over and a fireplace (with moulded and decorated timber lintel) constructed within the rear aisle. *[ESRO HBR/1/1390]*

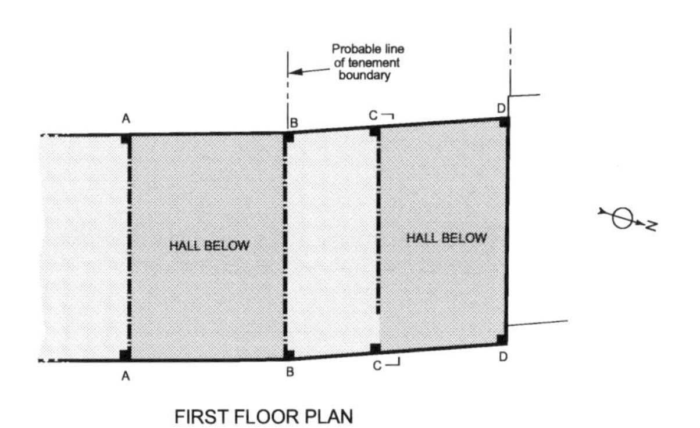

FIRST FLOOR PLAN

LONGITUDINAL SECTION

SECTION C-C

5 0 5 10
SCALE METRES

Fig. 12.13
Phase 1 reconstruction of 14 West Street

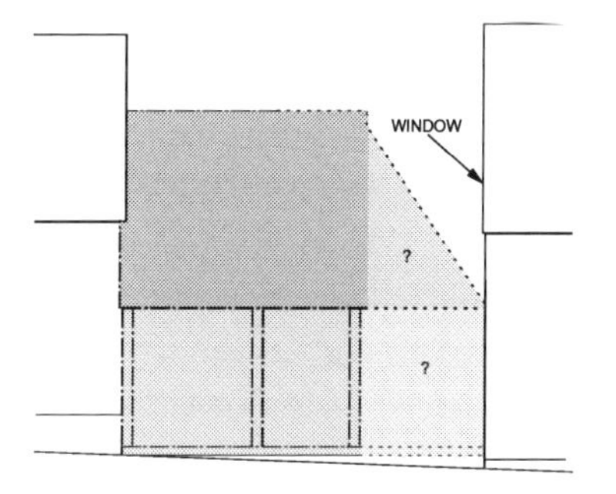

PHASE 1 - OUTLINE MEDIEVAL EAST ELEVATION

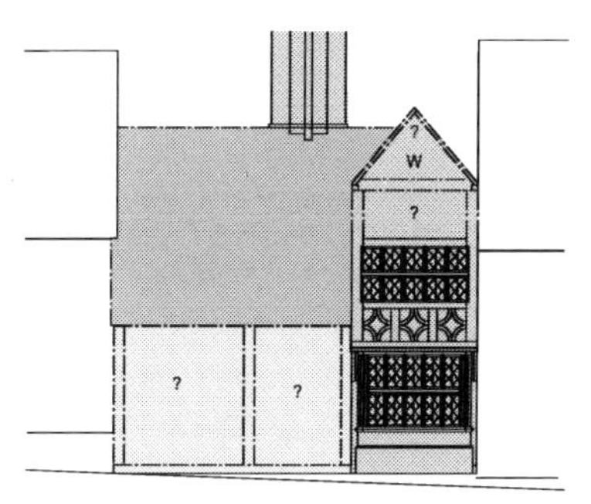

PHASE 2 - EAST ELEVATION, c.1550

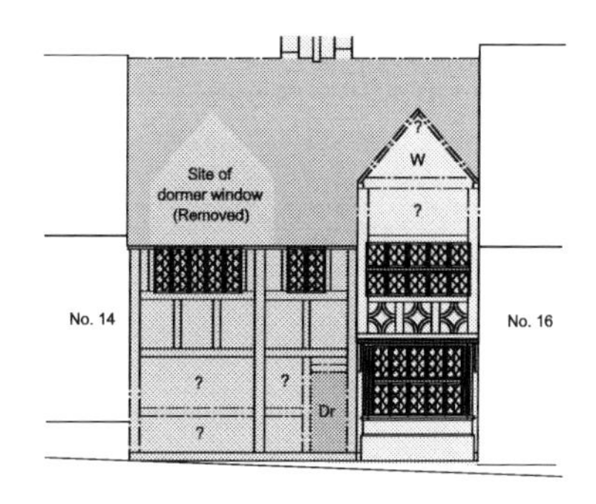

PHASE 3 - EAST ELEVATION, c.1575

Fig. 12.14
15 West Street. Front elevations showing the development of the building.

54, 55. 14 West Street — *1525 +/-25; 1600 +/-50 (Figure 12.13)*

Phase 1 (c.1525). Now one house, this was originally two separate dwellings. The northern part was built as a two-cell house with direct entry into the hall and a short service bay beyond. Impossible to date closely, this was an exceptionally short house — only 5.90 metres (19'4") long — almost square and un-jettied with no indications as to how the hall was initially heated. The southern part of No.14 was a separate two-cell house of apparently similar type: here too the original method of heating is unknown.

Phase 2 (c.1600). An axial chimney was inserted and the two houses were converted into one. *[ESRO HBR/1/0742; ESRO HBR/1/0743]*

56. 15 West Street (Thomas House) — *1475 +/-50; 1550 +/-25; 1575 +/-25 (Figures 12.14 - 12.16)*

Phase 1 (c.1475). A low, now totally rebuilt hall house, probably of three-bays, two-cells, with a hall to the south and a floored bay with hipped roof to the north (*see* below*)*. A good indication of the form of the phase-1 structure can be obtained from its replacement, which was rebuilt in phases (*see* Phases 2 and 3 below). A particularly important feature is the set of redundant weathering courses on the phase-2 axial chimney. These are now trapped within the present phase-3 roof. As the phase-1 and phase-2 reconstructions in Figure 12.14 make clear, the weathering courses are so far down the chimney that the medieval house must have been exceptionally squat, incorporating walls which, at best, can have been no more than 3 metres (*c.*9'9") high — less than this if the roof was thatched. Yet this was evidently not a poor building; it measured approximately 6.40 metres (21'0") wide — slightly above average for the area — and its hall was thought worth retaining when the present four-flue chimney and high-quality parlour were built during phase 2. Assuming (as seems likely) that the medieval house encompassed the entire street frontage of the plot, it would have measured 7.65 metres (25'0") long. To judge from the subsequent layout of the house and the size and position of the chimney, the phase-1 building was of standard two-cell type, with a two-bay hall and either a room or pair of rooms beyond it, to the north. Given the low eaves, and (assumed) hipped northern end to the roof (evidenced by a now blocked window in the neighbouring house) if there was a chamber over the end room/rooms during the medieval period it can have been nothing more than a storage loft. It would seem that in size and ground-floor layout the house was not dissimilar to its neighbours to north and south — just lower. In its height it is perhaps best compared to the early stone-built 46 Church Square [86], though as Figure 13.23 shows, even 46 appears to have been of sufficient loftiness to have incorporated a reasonable first-floor chamber.

Phase 2 (c.1550). The floored bay of the medieval house was rebuilt as a two-and-a-half storeyed crosswing which, incredibly, measured only 2.65 metres (8'8") wide but, nevertheless, towered over the retained adjacent medieval building. It was undoubtedly due to lack of floor space that the two-bay crosswing made use of continuous side girts supporting stilted principal posts and utilized the wall of the adjacent building. On the ground floor the wing housed a heated parlour with a small room to the rear. Above was a long, narrow, tunnel-like heated parlour chamber with a further chamber in the roof. This latter incorporated *c.*1.05 metre (*c.*3'6") side walls. Despite its small size, the crosswing should not be regarded as being of low status. High-quality, elaborately moulded glazed windows fill the entire width of the facade at both ground- and first-floor levels, whilst the wall panel between the two windows is elaborated with a rare example of quadrant bracing (Figure 12.15). This diminutive, but high-quality tower-like crosswing was not alone within the town, another 'pair' (probably of similar date) is illustrated at 5 Mermaid Street [60]. The 16th-century internal layout of the retained medieval hall at 15 West Street is unknown, though the chimney details make clear that a floor had by this time been inserted.

Fig. 12.15
15 West Street showing large glazed windows and quadrant bracing in front wall of crosswing. An upper storey and gable has been removed from over the window (see Fig. 12.16)

Fig. 12.16
Phase 3 reconstruction of 15 West Street

Phase 3 (c.1575). The set-back location of the hall fireplace suggests that during phase 2 an area may have been divided off against the street so as to serve as a shop. This was certainly the case from *c.*1575 onwards when the hall range was rebuilt taller, incorporating a dormer matching the roof of the crosswing (Figure 12.16). The arrangement of a shop divided off at the front of the hall in which both shop and hall are located within a range roofed parallel to the street is reminiscent of the early 16th-century 'double-pile' two-cell houses which exist around the corner in Mermaid Street. Indeed, this building is perhaps best regarded as representing a later example of the same type, though in this instance achieved through a scheme of progressive reconstruction. *[ESRO HBR/1/1132]*

57. 16-16A West Street — *1530 +/-25*
(Figures 12.17 & 12.18)

A fully-floored, continuously-jettied house. Built upon a sloping site, the hall is at the southern (uphill) end with the doorway which leads from it into the smaller second cell located hard against the front wall of the house. In this instance the use of the smaller room within the street range is in no doubt — both it and the hall have moulded ceiling beams and both have traces of painted decoration, that on the end wall of the smaller room being in imitation of a tapestry with a topographical scene of Rye and Winchelsea on its frieze (Figure 12.17). This must have served as a high-end inner room, and thus the house has no services, unless these were within a rear range of which no evidence survives. It is not known how the hall was heated, if indeed it was. Above are two interconnected chambers, which always had ceilings, with a large garret room within the roof. This garret area is not without interest in that the wallplates are positioned just above the garret floor, resulting in tiny low side walls and a tiebeam which had to be stepped over (*see* Figure 12.18). Furthermore, the space was lit by a three-light unglazed window set exceptionally low in the southern gable and — despite the assumed utilitarian use to which the space was put — it had

Fig. 12.17
16-16A West Street. Wall painting on northern wall of northern ground-floor room (Truss A-A). General view of painting (top) with details from frieze shown below. That on the left shows Rye and that on the right shows Winchelsea. The painting has been restored and retouched.

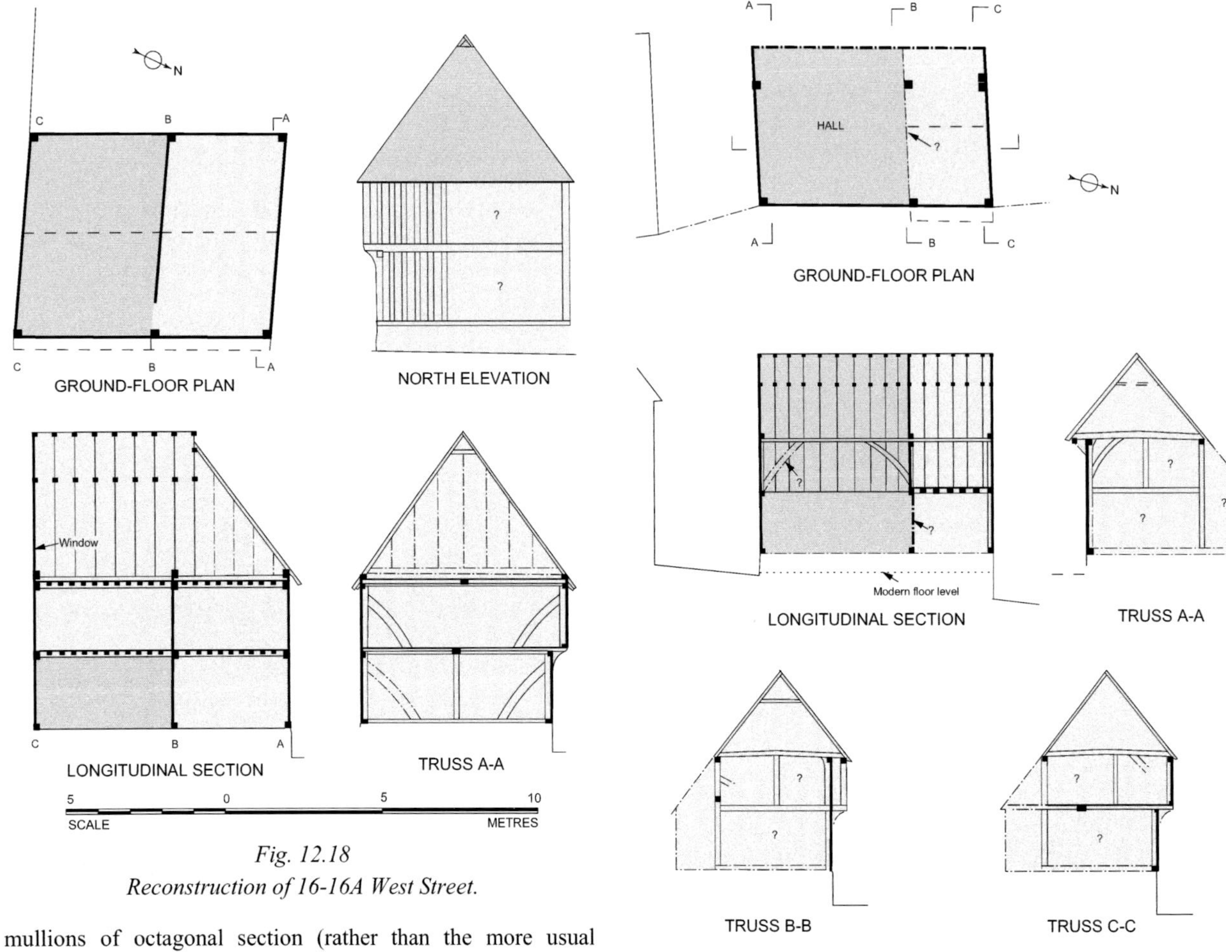

Fig. 12.18
Reconstruction of 16-16A West Street.

Fig. 12.19
Reconstruction of 17 West Street [58]

mullions of octagonal section (rather than the more usual diamond type). The northern end of the roof is hipped, robbing the garret area of usable space at this end. Despite its small size, this is in no way a poor house. The level of finish throughout is good, including moulded capitals to the jetty brackets. *[ESRO HBR/1/0744]*

58. 17 West Street — *1450 +/-50*
(Figure 12.19 & 12.20)

An exceptionally small single-aisled, single-ended 'Wealden' hall house. It has a short floored-over northern bay and (in comparison) a long single-bay open hall, beyond which was an un-developed gap in the street frontage, allowing access between this and the next house southwards. Entry to this property must have been direct into the hall, rather than by means of an overshot cross passage. This entrance was probably at the northern end of the hall, with the floored-over section beyond serving as the services, but there is currently no way of confirming this: it is possible that the reverse was the case and that the house lacked services. *[ESRO HBR/1/0816]*

59. 18-19 West Street — *1525 +/-25*
(Figure 12.21)

One of two adjoining pre-1540 buildings of average quality occupying the western corner plot between High Street and West Street; the second was 84 High Street [22]. In particular, note in Figure 12.21 the shaped door head and the moulded jetty fascia to the West Street properties, which are built level despite the slope on the street. As a result, at the

Fig. 12.20
17 West Street. Southern end wall of hall showing inset post (on left) indicating the original alignment of the recessed front wall.

Fig. 12.21
Detail of 18-19 West Street showing shaped and carved door head and moulded jetty fascia.

Fig. 12.22
Exterior of 5 Mermaid Street (Demolished)
Drawing by Henry Bourne
[© Rye Castle Museum. INV 8/79]

northern end the first floor was level with the wallplate of adjacent 84 High Street [22]. *[ESRO HBR/1/0898]*

60. 5 Mermaid Street — *16th C*
(Figure 12.22)

Although destroyed in the early 19th century in order to enlarge the garden of adjacent 4 Mermaid Street, the design of the facade is known from a drawing made by Henry Bourne prior to its demolition. Having a frontage of just over 5 metres (about 16'6"), the likelihood is that it represented infill between two existing structures. Jettied on the ground floor, with an arched-headed doorway at its eastern end, the superstructure rose through three storeys and incorporated oriel windows capped by a pair of small projecting gables. The eastern oriel was of standard type, but that adjacent to it was unusual in that it served both the first and second floors.

61. 6 Mermaid Street — *1525 +/-25*
(Figure 12.23)

An early 16th-century, fully-floored house with a continuous jetty and a crownpost roof. It is of above average width, despite quite a short street frontage of 7.10 metres (23'3"). In fact, it is almost square in plan, having an overall roof span of 7.15 metres (23'5"). It should be regarded as a modified form of the standard fully-floored two-cell layout, in this instance built wide so as to incorporate a 'shop' in front of the hall. Because of the excessive width of this building the opportunity was taken to incorporate axial partitions at first-floor level, so as to give additional chambers.

The hall occupies the eastern (up hill) two-thirds of the building and is entered by a low-end (western) door reached from the street via a short internal passage running between the front rooms (*see* Figure 12.23). That squeezed between street and hall almost certainly functioned as a shop. The area to the west of both the hall and passage was subdivided into two small service-like rooms, with the first of the two accessed direct from the passage. Whether this functioned as a standard service room is impossible to tell: it is, perhaps, more likely to have been a workshop or store room associated with the main shop. The rear service room was reached by means of a southern vestibule — effectively an extension of the hall — and this vestibule also led directly to the stairs which took up a large part of the service area. In reality the rear service area was little more than an unlit cupboard.

The first-floor plan is fully recoverable (*see* Figure 12.23). At this level the smaller western part of the house was subdivided by an axial partition so as to form two interlinked chambers. The third chamber (within the eastern part) spanned the full width of the building, though it should be stressed that its south-eastern corner was taken up by the

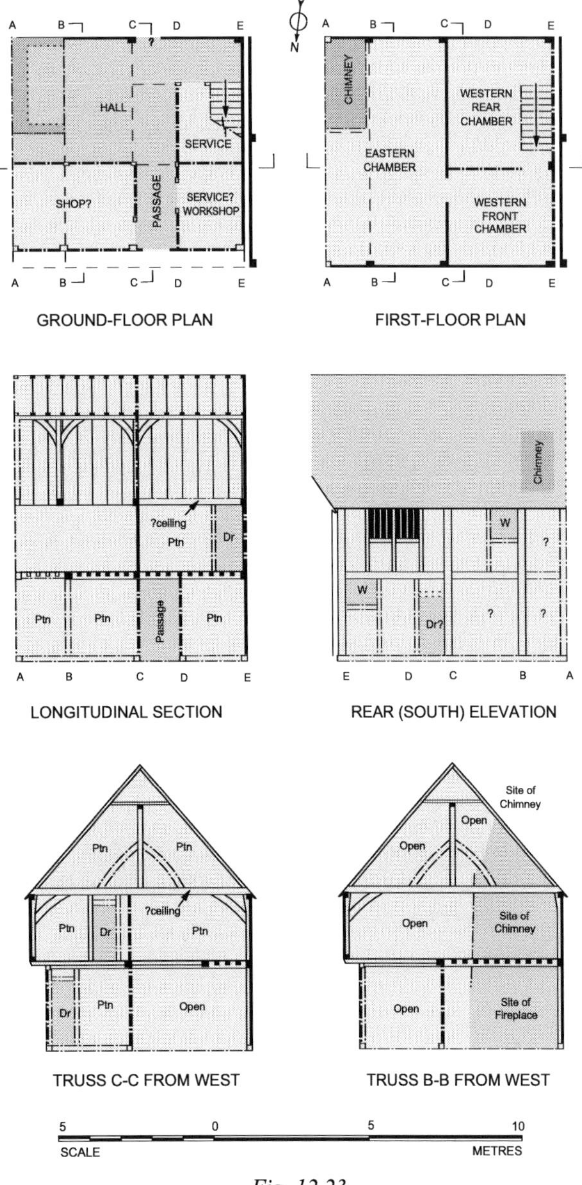

Fig. 12.23
Reconstruction of 6 Mermaid Street.

upper part of the chimney, since destroyed. The western chambers may have had ceilings, with a storage area in the roof above, but the eastern chamber was open to the roof. *[ESRO HBR/1/1623]*

62. 7 Mermaid Street — *1510 +/-25*
(Figures 12.24 & 12.25)

A building in which the logic of the carpenter is difficult to comprehend. Located on the southern side of the street, it is framed at right angles to the road and extends 11.60 metres (38'0") back up the plot. The street frontage is only 6.70 metres (22'1"), too narrow to conveniently achieve an 'L' plan with a rear wing sited behind the street range, which is perhaps why the builder chose to construct a single wide range taking up the entire front part of the plot. Despite this, either he or his client considered the width sufficient to align the front rooms along the street, in effect adopting a

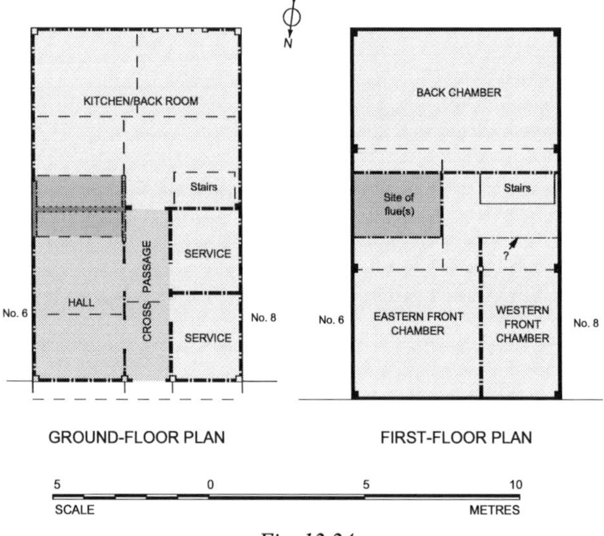

Fig. 12.24
Reconstructions of 7 Mermaid Street.

'standard' two cell plan, with a 'single-bay' hall, a cross passage, and a service area, the latter divided so as to give the usual pair of service rooms (Figures 12.24 and 12.25). The adoption of this arrangement within a frame of this type resulted in a very idiosyncratic design. Apart from the cramped nature of the hall, the only inconvenience in using this form of layout was that the rear service room was totally unlit, being in the core of the house against the neighbouring property. The cross passage was 'divided off' from the hall by a pair of draught speres and by a central screen, giving two openings rather than the more usual single wide opening between passage and hall. This development is found in a number of local houses dating from the years around 1500. There are Rye examples at St. Anthony's [87], The Mermaid [72] and 6 Church Square [74]. Another feature typical of the higher-status houses of Rye at this period is the lofty ground-floor storey height which within the hall, cross passage and service area is a very generous 2.75 metres (9'0") measured from floor to floor. Because of the upward slope on the ground, the storey height reduces to 2.35 metres (7'8") floor to floor within the rear part of the house, which incorporates a single large heated ground-floor room of uncertain use. This was perhaps a kitchen, though evidence of windows apparently fitted with shaped heads could imply a higher status function. Perhaps, given its small size, the hall fulfilled more the function of a parlour, with the much larger back room combining kitchen use with some of the more mundane functions of a hall.

The chimney heating the hall and rear room has been removed, but its site is indicated by a trimmed opening in the first-floor joisting. Occupying a similar position on the western side of the cross passage was the stair. This appears to have led to a landing, allowing independent access to each of the first-floor chambers. To the east of the stair and (assumed) landing rose the flue serving the two ground-floor hearths — this appears to have taken the form of a smoke cavity divided off from the remainder of the first-floor parts by lath-and-daub partitions. The first floor continued the same idiosyncratic design features as found on the ground floor in that the northern half of the building was subdivided along the street

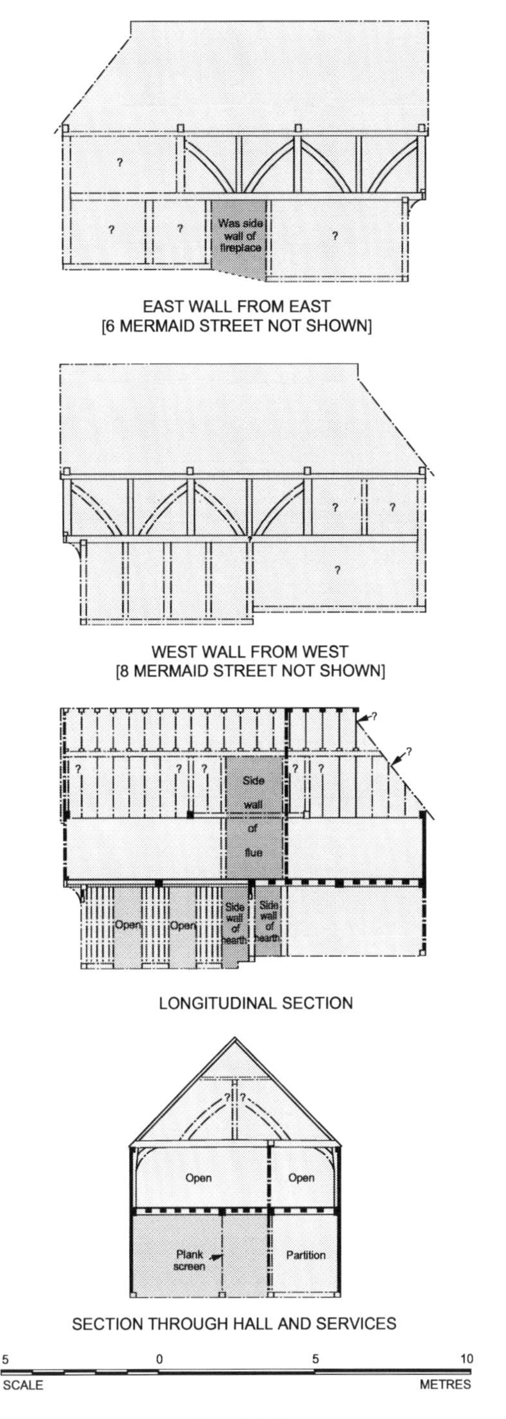

Fig. 12.25
Reconstructions of 7 Mermaid Street.

frontage by an off-centred axial partition so as to give a relatively large hall chamber (which oversailed the cross passage) with a smaller service chamber to the west. Despite this layout, it should be remembered that the frame is built at right angles to the street. Because at this level the building is framed in three (rather than two) bays, and these are of approximately equal length, the result is an open truss which crosses the building toward the southern end of the northern chambers, with parts of the open truss located within both the

Fig. 12.26
8-9 Mermaid Street. Roof space showing crownpost and later chimney.

hall chamber and the service chamber — visually a very curious feature! Despite the 1.85 metre (6'1") height of the side walls, both chambers were open to the roof. Whether the axial partition which divided them terminated at the axial headplate which spans between the tiebeams, or continued up into the roof area, is unknown. Whichever was the case, the design had an adverse effect upon the aesthetics of both chambers. The back chamber is more conventional in its design, though, unlike almost all other timber-framed houses of the period, its northern wall was not located at a truss, and thus the chamber was of one-and-a-part bays in length. Why the carpenter chose to design the house in this way remains a mystery. *[ESRO HBR/1/1632]*

63. 8-9 Mermaid Street — *1525 +/-25*
(Figure 12.26 & 12.27)

An early 16th-century, fully-floored house with continuous jetties and a crownpost roof. The hall occupies the eastern (up hill) two-thirds of the building and is entered by a low-end (western) door reached from the street via a short internal passage running between the front rooms (*see* Figure 12.27). The room squeezed between street and hall is likely to have functioned as a shop.

It is not at present possible to recover the ground-floor layout of the area beyond the hall and entrance passage, though

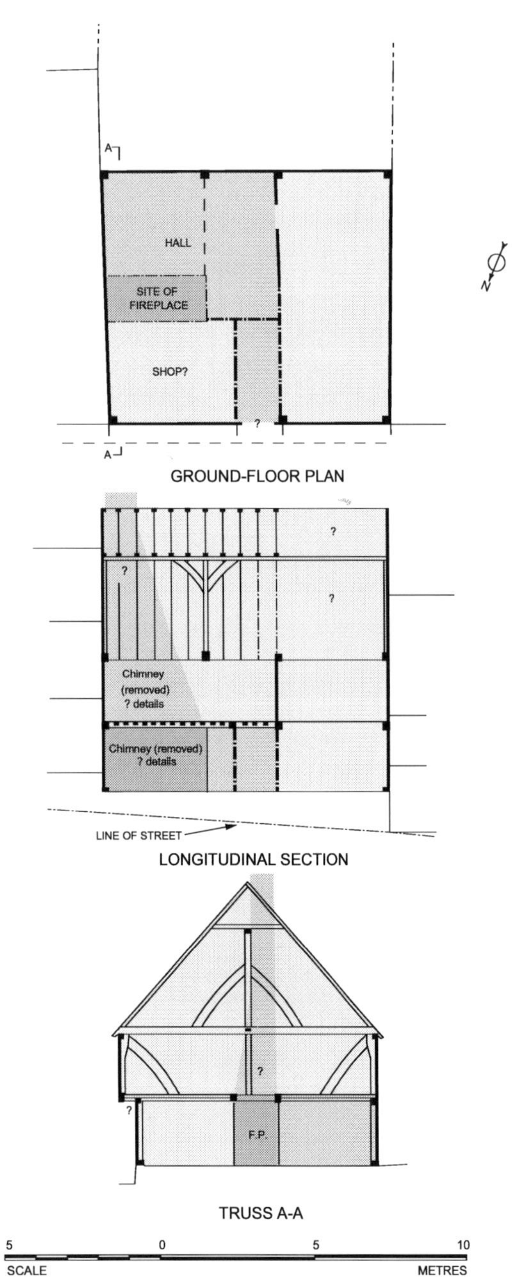

Fig. 12.27
Reconstruction of 8-9 Mermaid Street [63].

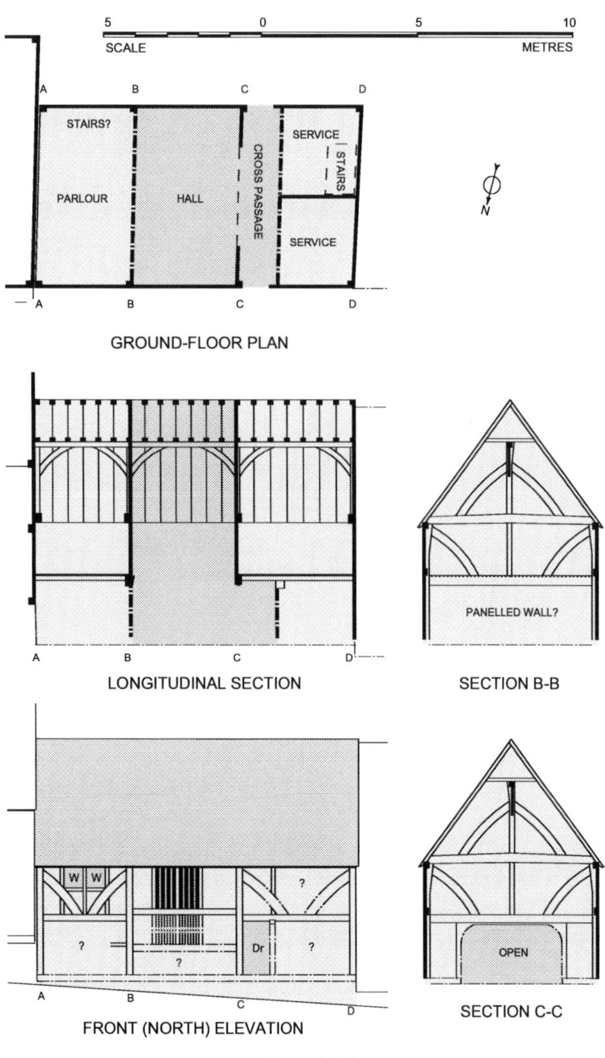

Fig. 12.28
Phase 1 reconstruction of 10-11 Mermaid Street.

it was probably subdivided into two rooms by an axial partition (similar to 6 Mermaid Street [61]) and must, in addition, have housed the stairs. All that is certain is that the rear part of this area was accessed direct from the hall via a doorway in the hall's low-end partition (Figure 12.27). The upper floor was likewise divided into two by a cross partition and the larger eastern part was crossed by an open truss with crownpost above. Because of the position of the chimney (almost certainly at the side of the hall) this area too must surely have been subdivided by an axial partition, probably giving a block of four upper chambers — two at the front and two at the rear.

A notable feature of this building is its above average width, despite a quite short street frontage of 9.15 metres (30'0"). In fact, it is almost square in plan, with an overall roof span of 8.45 metres (27'9"). It should be regarded as a modified form of the standard fully-floored two-cell layout, in this instance built wide so as to incorporate a 'shop' in front of the hall. Because of the excessive width of this building the opportunity was taken of incorporating axial partitions at first-floor level, so as to give additional chambers (*see* also 6 Mermaid Street [61]). *[ESRO HBR/1/0815]*

64. 10-11 Mermaid Street — *1470 +/-50; 1550 +/- 25 (Figures 12.28 & 12.29)*

Phase 1 (c.1470). A three-cell hall house of 'textbook' design, having on the ground floor the usual pair of service rooms, an overshot cross passage, hall, and high-end room.[11] It was constructed against an earlier building to the east and has no jettied upper storeys. There is a very simple moulded dais beam (*see* Figure 6.27) and good evidence for the hall's double-high street window.

Phase 2 (c.1550). The usual floor and chimney were inserted into the hall, the two flue stack being built against the

Fig. 12.29
Exterior of 10-11 Mermaid Street.

rear wall. Apart from the insertion of a ceiling into the hall chamber and modifications to the medieval hall window, no other obvious alterations were made. *[ESRO HBR/1/1260]*

65. 14-15 Mermaid Street — *1520 +/-25*
(Figure 12.30 - 12.32)

An exceptionally wide building, having a street frontage of 8.55 metres (28'1") and an overall span of 8.70 metres (28'7"). Here, as Figure 12.30 shows, the hall is tucked behind a room which is likely to have functioned as a shop. In this instance the hall and 'shop' occupy the down-hill end of the house and have a cellar beneath them. Furthermore, the hall was not reached from the street by means of a short passage tucked between the two front rooms. Instead, at ground-floor level the entire eastern end of the range appears to have been occupied by an exceptionally wide through passage giving access not only to the hall, but also to a substantial rear range.

The hall was floored over from the outset. Though the chimney has been destroyed, it may be assumed that it was always heated, and therefore the chimney must have been at the low end, backing onto the wide through passage — there is no possible alternative location.

In addition to the street range, three full bays and part of a fourth survive of a substantial rear range, and this could have extended some distance further back than it now does — maps of 1860 and 1871 show it extended back *c.*13 metres (*c.*42'8") from the street range. Jettied along its side wall towards a yard, it incorporated a large three-bay room with a

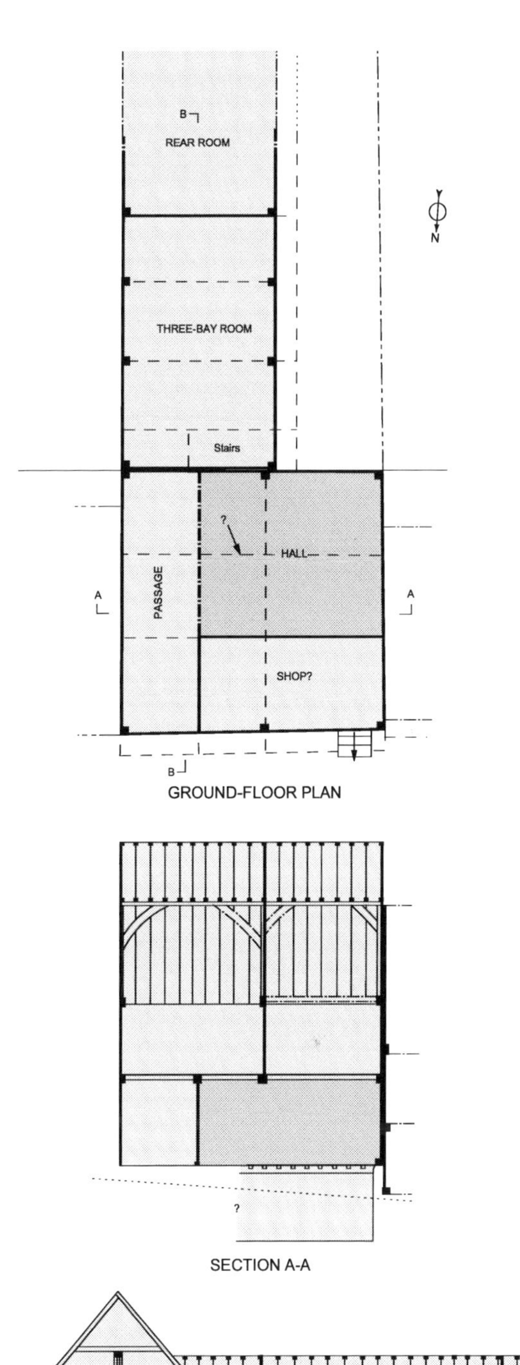

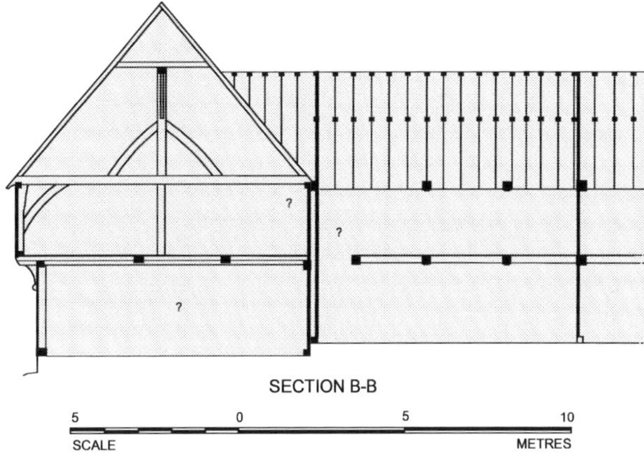

Fig. 12.30
Reconstruction of 14-15 Mermaid Street.

Fig. 12.31
14-15 Mermaid Street. Open trusses in rear range with fireplace added into present end wall.

Fig. 12.32
14-15 Mermaid Street. Crownpost roof over main range.

Fig. 12.33
Drawing of 16 Mermaid Street prior to demolition. Note the rear range just visible to right of chimney. [W H Brooke, 1772-1860 - Hastings Museum and Art Gallery. Ref L757]

single-bay area beyond on the ground floor, with three-bay and one-bay chambers above, both open to the roof. The three-bay chamber has arch-braced trusses (Figure 12.31). The ground-floor rooms and first-floor chambers were interlinked by a staircase against the back wall of the main range, and this may also have served as the means of access to the chambers within the street range. The purpose of the large room and chamber within the rear range is unclear — they could have been dormitories, public meeting rooms, or even warehouses/work areas. By 1658 this or an adjacent building on the south side of Mermaid Street was The Swan Inn, but this does not mean that the structure was built for that purpose.[12] *[ESRO HBR/1/0264]*

66. 16 Mermaid Street — *1475 +/-25*
(Figure 12.33)

A single-ended 'Wealden' absent of services, demolished in the late 19th century. Three drawings of the house were made before it was destroyed. From the configuration of the eaves detailing it seems safe to conclude that this is not a 'Wealden' which has lost its third bay, unless, of course, as at 16 East Street [34], the third bay was of a different date and was separately framed. If this was so, the down-hill roof terminal must have been adjusted subsequently, for all three drawings show this end hipped. The door leading

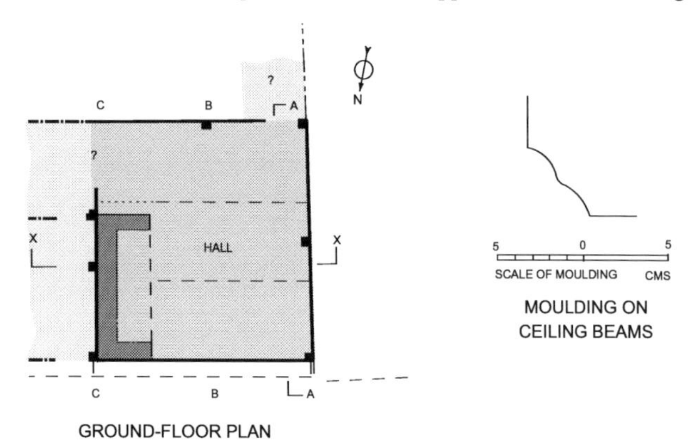

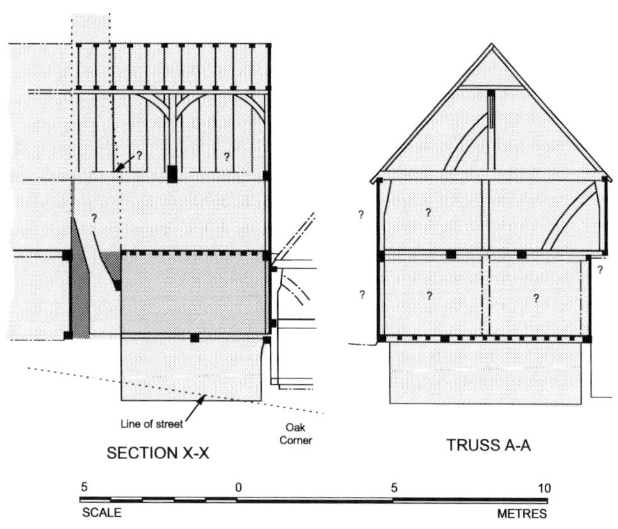

Fig. 12.34
Reconstruction of Elders House, Mermaid Street.

into the hall was at this down-hill end, so presumably the floored-over bay at the eastern (up-hill) end served as high-end accommodation. This interpretation is consistent with the projecting oriel windows shown lighting the floored bay. All this is strong evidence that the house lacked the usual services, though it should be stressed that the drawings do indicate a rear range. What is impossible to tell from the drawings is the date of the rear range, nor is there any clue as to the use to which the rear range's ground-floor area was put. *[ESRO HBR/1/0679]*

67. Elders House, Mermaid Street — *1530 +/-25*
(Figure 12.34)

A fully-floored, jettied two-cell house of the early 16th century, now fragmentary. It represents the hall bay and a small fragment of the low-end bay of a building which originally extended eastwards, up the hill: the other part was destroyed when the Quaker Meeting House (later converted into a Baptist Chapel, and now called Quaker House) was built in the mid 18th century. The floored-over hall is at the down-hill end of the building, against the rear wall of the hall house known as Oak Corner [102], which it towers over. In fact, because of the slope, the first floor of Elders House is above the eaves of Oak Corner [102] and there is a contemporary un-vaulted cellar beneath it. Entry was not direct into the hall but to the rear of the chimney, leading either into a passage or into a low-end room — perhaps a shop. This passage/room did not extend the full width of the house, for there is the moulded jamb of a doorway incorporated part way across the truss dividing the two bays, evidently with a second room or a small part of the hall beyond it. The hall fireplace is a mix of stone and buff 'Flemish' bricks and has a four-centred arched timber lintel with rose-and-foliage spandrels. The leading edges of the principal ceiling beams are wave moulded. In the rear wall, at the high end, is an original doorway with another above it on the first floor, indicating the site of a rear stair turret. This was replaced in the second half of the 16th century by a small rear jettied range which housed a heated parlour.[13] The design of the crownpost roof suggests that the first-floor chamber within the street range may have been fitted with ceilings from the outset, but this point cannot be confirmed. *[ESRO HBR/1/1157]*

68. 30 Mermaid Street — *1550+/-25*
(Figure 12.35)

A mid 16th-century house which has a footbraced, close-studded eastern end wall incorporating a loading hatch and windows, blocked by the construction of 31 Mermaid Street [69] in 1576. Continuously jettied and roofed parallel to the street, 30 Mermaid Street has a street frontage of only 7.25 metres (23'10"), yet the overall roof span is 8.00 metres (26'4"). As in the slightly earlier double-pile houses on the opposite side of the street, the excessive span of the house was necessary in order to squeeze a shop into the space between the street and hall. Nothing is known regarding the form of the shop front, though it had to be designed to take into account the slope on the street and a flight of external cellar steps located halfway along the facade, descending to the cellar which extends under the eastern half of the building. A further obstacle was a cellar window to the east of the steps. The steps were not the only means of access to the cellar: a brick-built central-newel stair rose to give direct access to the hall.

It is doubtful whether the shop front incorporated a doorway. If it did, it was not the only means of access — a doorway led into the shop from the through passage at the extreme western end of the house. Next to this door is the entrance to the hall which occupied the remainder of the ground floor and lacked direct access to the shop. The hall is heated by a chimney of soft, buff, 'Flemish' bricks built into

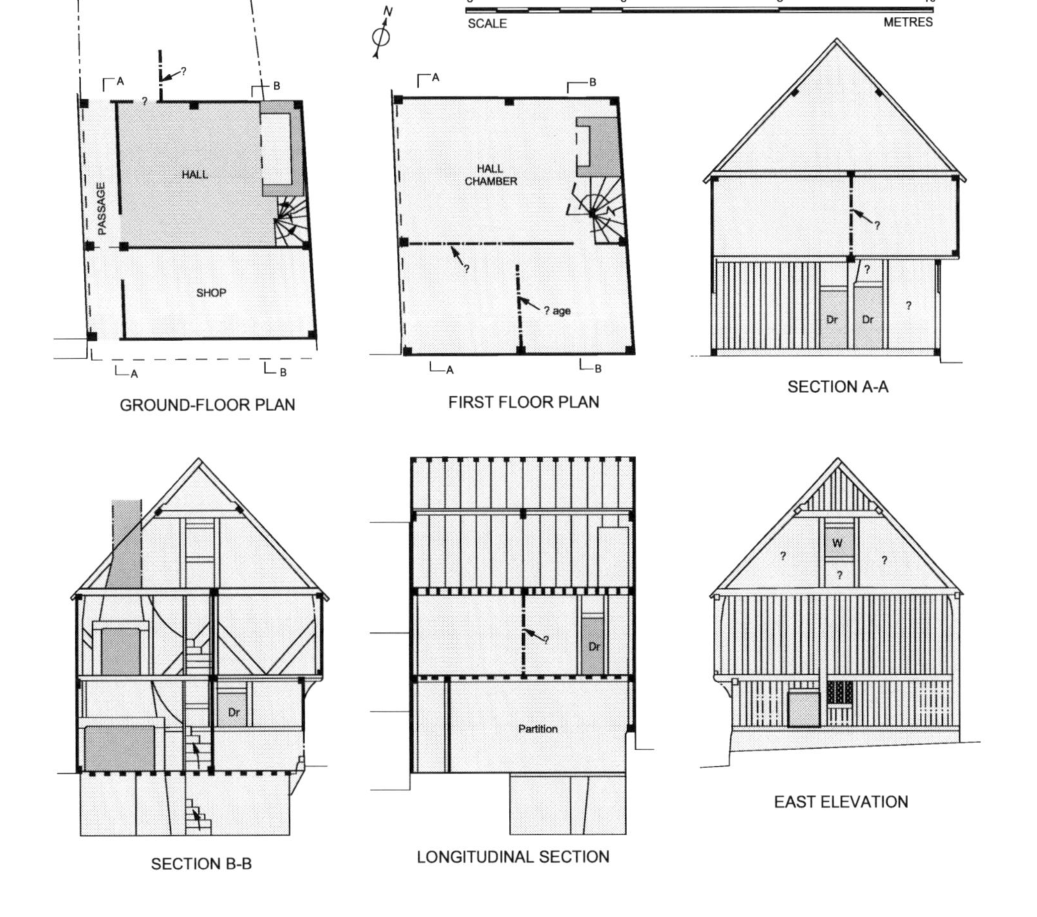

Fig. 12.35 (Left). Reconstruction of 30 Mermaid Street [68].

the northeastern corner, beside which is the tight stair giving access to the cellar and upper rooms. Evidence within the rear wall indicates that the present narrow single-storeyed rear range replaces an earlier structure upon the same site — perhaps a service room or possibly a pentice leading to an outhouse beyond. Whichever it was, adjustments to the wall in order to incorporate a door suggests that it may have represented a subsequent addition.

The ground-floor layout is repeated on the first floor, except at this level the rooms extend over the through passage and the front part was perhaps divided into two by a partition located beneath the central tiebeam. There is a featureless partition in this location today. The door frame is nailed into position and therefore the partition may represent a later insertion. The roof is of clasped-side-purlin construction — apparently un-windbraced — with a central collar truss.[14] The entire area formed a single, relatively large attic room. *[ESRO HBR/1/0873]*

69. 31 Mermaid Street — *dated 1576*
(Figures 12.36 - 12.42)

Also known as The Old Hospital or Hartshorne House, this is the best preserved of the town's 16th-century merchant houses. In the late 17th century it was the home of one of Rye's best known residents, the merchant diarist Samuel Jeake II and author of Rye's earliest known detailed plan. Samuel acquired the property from his mother-in-law, Barbara, widow of Richard Hartshorne (late master of Rye grammar school and a jurat of the town) as part of his marriage portion. Writing in 1680 he considered it 'one of the best in the town'.[15] Jeake was in the vanguard of Rye's modest late 17th/early 18th-century economic revival: it was he who, in 1689-90, built a new storehouse (now appropriately known as Jeakes House) further down Mermaid Street on the opposite side of the road.[16]

The house subsequently fell derelict and narrowly escaped demolition (*see* Figure 12.36). Constructed in the year 1576, it is not an overly large building, yet what it lacks in size it makes up for in quality — the facade is, by Rye's standards, packed with opulent display features. The street frontage is 12.10 metres (39'8") occupied by a range aligned parallel to the highway. This is augmented by a substantial rear range against the eastern boundary. In addition there is a twin-gabled forward projection at the western end of the street facade. The result, as Figure 12.38 shows, is a modified 'L' plan.

On the ground floor the street range is occupied by a large hall with 'service' rooms beyond the low end and a parlour to the rear. Thus, there is a sense in which 31 Mermaid Street could be regarded as being a standard (though large) two-cell house aligned parallel to the street, augmented by a rear parlour range. However, to classify it as 'standard' is to ignore its many design peculiarities.

Technically the building is constructed in four bays (two in the street range and two in the rear range) though each of the two bays in the street range, together with the northern bay in the rear range, is divided into two by intermediate crossbeams and roof trusses. The eastern bay of the street range is 5.85 metres (19'2") wide, whereas the somewhat longer western bay is wider, the street facade at this point

Fig 12.36 (Above)
31 Mermaid Street soon after restoration. Photograph taken whilst the adjacent plot was vacant, showing the large-panel design of the main range's framing where it abutted the former building, with small-panel framing to the side wall of the rear range (right).

Fig. 12.37 (Right)
31 Mermaid Street showing the building in the mid 19th century when in a derelict state.

being stepped 1.05 metres (3'6") forward of that within the neighbouring part. The narrower eastern bay houses the spacious hall, which is accessible by means of a cross passage within the eastern part of the adjacent west bay. There are today no obvious signs of an original partition between the hall and cross passage, but the former existence of a partial screen cannot be ruled out.

Despite being located within the wider western bay, the front door which leads into the cross passage is nevertheless positioned in-line with the front wall of the hall, the storey above being cantilevered forward in order to form an 'unenclosed porch'. To the west of the cross passage there were originally two 'service' rooms, beyond which is a contemporary through passage giving independent access to the garden. The passage incorporates a doorway in its street facade, but is entirely open to the garden at the rear.

The rear (northern) of the two 'service' rooms was entered by a doorway leading off the cross passage, whilst that to the south was served by its own external doorway located within the unenclosed porch, adjacent to the main entrance. A further doorway (marked '?' in Figure 12.38) may have connecting the two rooms. Being separately accessed from the exterior and having large continuous windows facing the street, the front room has all the superficial signs of having been a 'shop', but is more likely to have served as the owners 'office'. If this and the rear room were inter-connected by a doorway, the northern room probably also served a similar function: if not, it is likely to have been a standard service room. This northern room (or at least that part adjacent the cross passage) probably also housed the stairs leading up to the first floor and down to the extensive cellar which extends under most of the main range.

The rear range houses the parlour. This was accessible direct from the hall and, additionally, from the garden via its own external doorway. There is only one chimney, which is constructed of relatively small 'Flemish' bricks. It incorporates fireplaces heating the hall, parlour, hall chamber and parlour chamber. The fireplaces serving the parlour and parlour chamber have been blocked, but those heating the hall and hall chamber have stone surrounds. That serving the hall has a hollow-chamfered four-centred arched head set beneath an ovolo-moulded square surround: the spandrels are plain. In contrast, the fireplace within the hall chamber incorporates a typical 'Rye-style' shouldered-arched head beneath a square surround, both the arch and surround being ovolo moulded. The jambs terminate in moulded bases with foliage

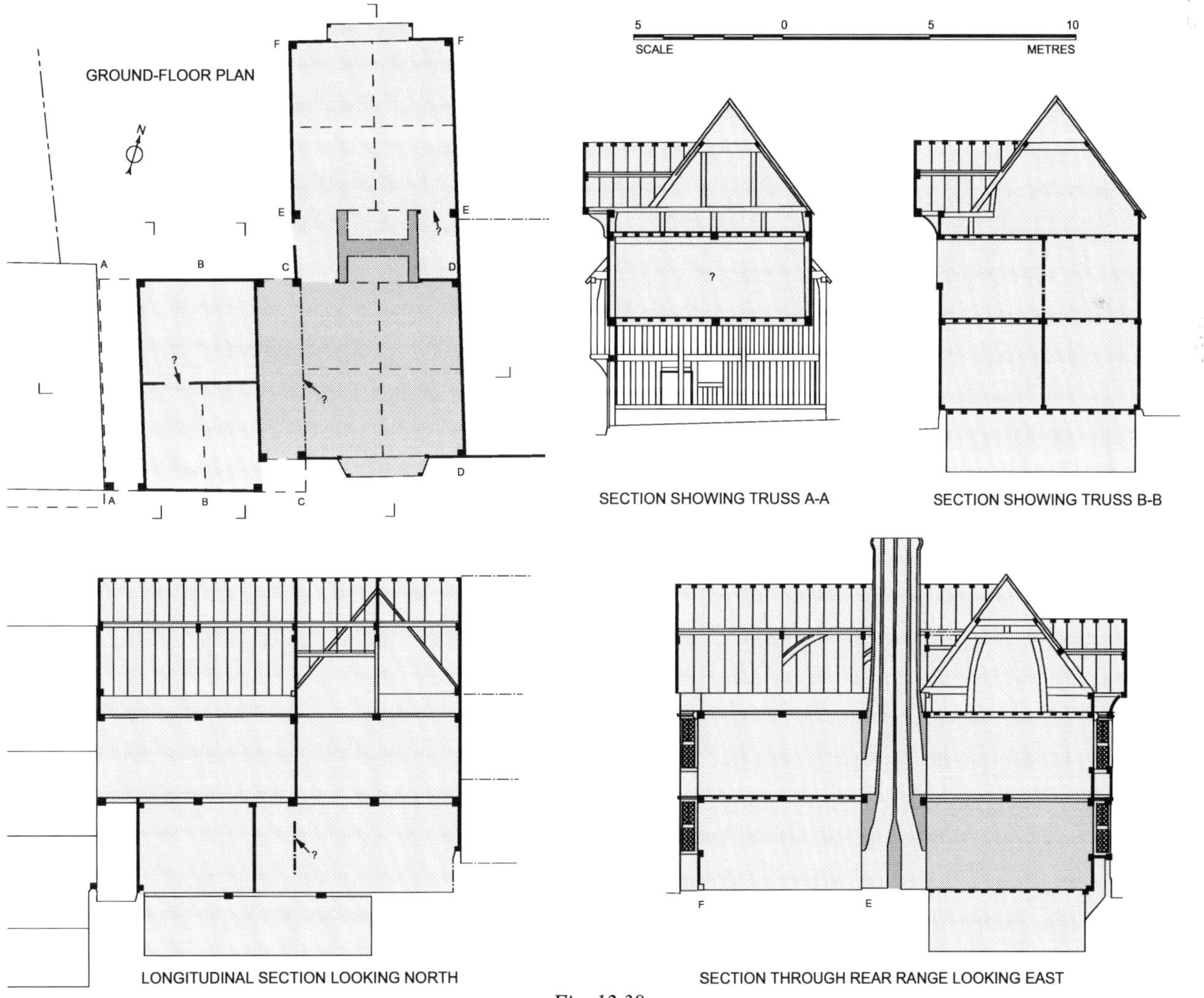

Fig. 12.38
Reconstruction of 31 Mermaid Street [69].

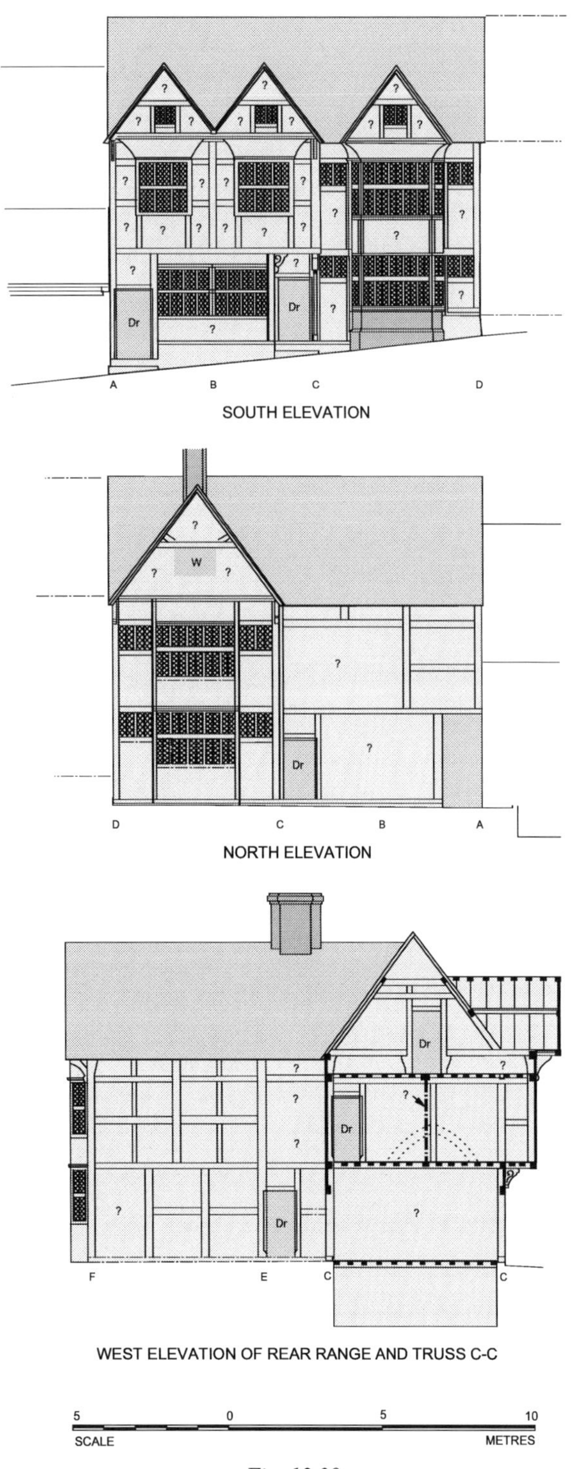

Fig. 12.39
Reconstruction of 31 Mermaid Street.

ornamented panels above, whilst the spandrels are carved with shields and tendril foliage. The overmantel is plain, save for a limited number of relatively small geometric carved designs. Conspicuous by its absence is a cooking hearth: it therefore seems likely that the kitchen was located within a separate building standing in the rear garden (*see* Chapter 7).

The ground-floor layout was repeated at first-floor level, though it is not clear whether at this level there was a partition beneath the central girder within the western bay, and thus this bay may have been occupied by a single chamber — perhaps a 'great chamber'. There are three garret rooms: two in the main range and one over the parlour. All have side walls which measure 600 mm (2'0") high, thereby increasing the usable floor space. Measuring 6.80 metres x 6.90 metres (22'5" x 22'8") the western garret is large, but no more so than in some other Rye houses.

Fig. 12.40
31 Mermaid Street. North (Garden) front of rear range showing projecting window lighting parlour and parlour chamber.

Whereas the visible internal partitions and the end walls of the main range (which abut adjacent buildings) are of large-panel design with at least some inset footbracing, all external walls are of small-panel type and incorporate heavy midrails (*see* Figure 12.37). The ceiling girders and crossbeams within the hall, cross passage, parlour and parlour chamber are ovolo moulded. Within the parlour the mouldings are more elaborate, the crossbeam being enriched by a cyma and double-ovolo moulding and the girders by a cyma and single ovolo. Elsewhere the principal timbers are stop-chamfered. The joists within the hall, parlour and north-western room are masked by plaster, and this may originally have been the case in the other rooms too. Except at attic level, the door frames are ovolo moulded and have shaped stops, whilst the front door is additionally enriched by a second order of cyma moulding.

Fig. 12.41
31 Mermaid Street. Cantilevered end of wallplate (truss B-B) supporting central valley of projecting gables within front elevation.

Most of the principal timbers in the street facade have been much repaired, whilst the majority of the secondary timbers are of entirely modern date. Today this wall incorporates close studding and this probably reflects the original design, though the point cannot at present be confirmed. For this reason, the design of these panels is indicated by '?' in Figure 12.36. Most of the original windows survive, despite some having been heavily restored: all are ovolo moulded.

As Figures 12.36, 12.37 and 12.39 make clear, the scheme of fenestration within the street elevation is particularly elaborate. The hall and its chamber are lit by a cant-sided bay window enriched with moulded string courses, capped by an overhanging gable carried by coving and supported by a chamfered brick base (now rebuilt). It was flanked on each storey by two-pane clerestory openings, though these now only survive at first-floor level. On the ground floor the whole of the western bay (between the two passage areas) is taken up by one large window, shown in the mid 19th-century photograph reproduced in Figure 12.37 capped by a moulded string course and incorporating a heavy moulded central king-mullion. It was this window which lit the owners 'office'. Above, at first-floor level, are a pair of 'planted-on' oriels. Although the design was changed when the house was restored, the original windows here were transomed and of three panes in width. As is the case today, each was capped by a moulded string course from which sprang plastered coving with overhanging gables above. All the gables within the facade have been re-timbered and the

Fig. 12.42
31 Mermaid Street. Trimmed rafters allowing access into the front gable over the hall.

associated windows enlarged slightly; the originals were of two panes each.

No original windows now survive in the rear wall of the main range and even those in the northern end wall of the rear range have been much adjusted. Despite being located within a rear elevation, this latter wall incorporates a full-height square-sided bay window, originally flanked by smaller clerestory openings (*see* Figure 12.40). Above the first-floor part of the bay window survives a cyma-moulded string course.

The roof over the main range is divided into two garret rooms, is framed in four bays, and is of un-windbraced clasped-side-purlin construction. Because the garrets incorporate low side walls, the internal trusses have been designed so as to maintain the building's strength, a requirement made more complex both by the presence of the overhanging gables incorporated within the front facade and by the fact that the two western roof bays are of greater span than those to the east. The additional 1.05 metre span is roofed by two overhanging gables which are extended back until they abut the main roof (*see* Figure 12.38, Sections A-A and B-B). The valley between the two gables is set in-line with the main roof truss crossing the garret room and is carried by a wallplate which extends back into the room some distance in order to support the southern principal rafter of the main truss (Figure 12.41). The main truss itself is of collar type. The eastern and western wallplates of the pair of over-hanging gables are formed by the tiebeams to trusses A-A and C-C which simply extend inwards beyond the southern wall. Beneath their projecting ends are shaped and moulded brackets, one of which bears the inscribed date 1576.

In order to allow free access into the gable heads and (more importantly) to carry the feet of the rafters, a trimmer resembling a butt purlin is framed into the southern slope of each bay in like fashion to those used at 13-14 High Street. Truss C-C (shown in Figure 12.39) incorporates the partition which separates the garret area into two rooms, inter-linked by a doorway which trims the tiebeam. Above the door are a pair of collars, a feature also found in the open roof truss to the east, in which curved 'queenposts' have been utilized in order to trim the intermediate tiebeam. It is at this point that the over-hanging gable above the hall's bay window projects. This is supported upon stub 'joists' morticed into the wallplate and, presumably, strengthened by some form of bracketing concealed by the plastered coving. Even so, the supports proved inadequate and the gable head has sagged. As with the two western over-hanging gables, the rafters are trimmed in order to allow access to the gable-head (*see* Figure 12.42).

The roof over the rear range is framed in three bays and is likewise of clasped-side-purlin construction, in this instance incorporating one way windbracing so as prevent racking towards the overhanging northern gable. As in the front elevation, the gable is supported off the projecting ends of the wallplates, the end of which are supported from beneath by shaped and moulded brackets. The two intermediate trusses within this range lack tiebeams. Instead, short hanging knees are included in the angles between the floor and the posts. This feature is unusual for a house, but is, reminiscent of the knees used in ship construction. *[ESRO HBR/1/0904]*

70. 32 Mermaid Street —
1350 +/-100; 1475 +/-25; 1520 +/-25
(Figures 12.43 & 12.44)

Phase 1 (14th C). Early barrel-vaulted cellar (*see* Chapter 6)

Fig. 12.43
Crownpost in crosswing, 32 Mermaid Street.

Phases 2 and 3 (c.1475). The present three-bay crosswing, seems to replace a predecessor of similar dimensions (but lower) for it fits precisely over the earlier barrel-vaulted cellar turned at right angles to the street. However, the rebuild is not of one date, but two (Figure 12.44). The likely scenario is that the front two-bay section of the crosswing was the first to be rebuilt more lofty, jettied towards the street, and the retained rear part was then rapidly rebuilt to the same height. The surviving medieval features are fragmentary. The vaulted cellar and large room within the crosswing could indicate that 32 Mermaid Street was once an inn, though this is pure speculation. Indeed, the

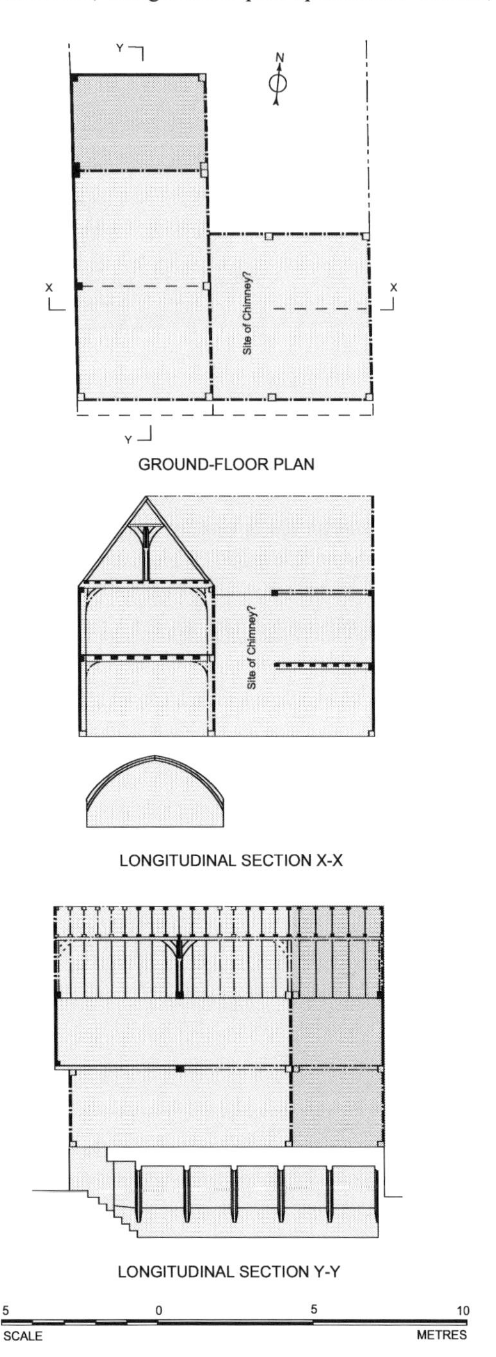

Fig. 12.44
Reconstruction of 32 Mermaid Street, as at phase 3

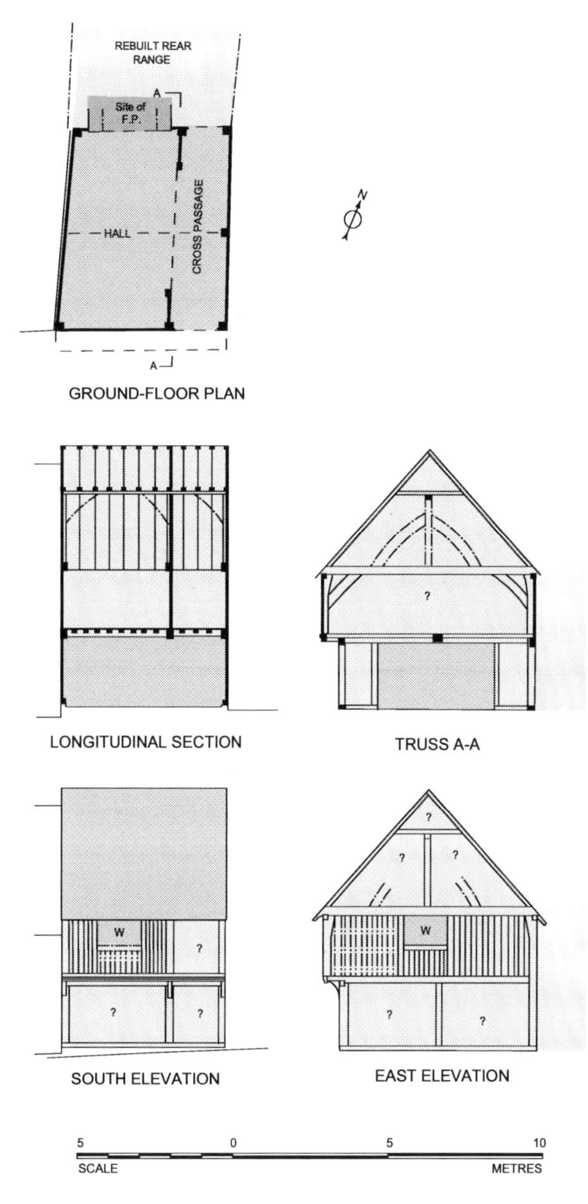

Fig. 12.45
Reconstruction of 34 Mermaid Street.

principal ground-floor and first-floor rooms within the crosswing appear to have been very plain and the freestanding crownpost is utilitarian in appearance (Figure 12.43). Thus it is equally plausible that either one or both front rooms within the crosswing functioned as warehousing attached to a merchant's house.

Phase 4 (c.1520). The present main range to the east is later than the crosswing: it is a two-bay, continuously-jettied range, replacing a no doubt lower main range upon the same site. The smaller bay, against the crosswing, probably housed an axial chimney, but this and much else within the range was rebuilt during the first half of the 18th century when the house was again upgraded. In its present form the house is square in plan, with a structure occupying the re-entrant angle between the main range and crosswing. This probably represents an addition, though, if so, the house lacked service rooms. *[ESRO HBR/1/1608]*

71. 34 Mermaid Street — *1500 +/-25*
(Figure 12.45)

This exceptionally well-finished building illustrates what can be achieved upon a very narrow plot. The street frontage is only 5.35 metres (17'6") overall, yet onto this space has been squeezed a two-bay continuously-jettied range having an overall roof span of 6.85 metres (22'5"). The roof is aligned parallel to the street and was of crownpost type: the rafters and collars survive, though the crownposts and collar purlin have been removed and are today evidenced by mortices only. Squeezed into this space on the ground floor is a floored-over hall entered via a cross passage located within its own tiny eastern end bay. Between the two was a wide spered opening of traditional type. Within the hall's rear wall is evidence for a former fireplace, but the chimney itself has been removed.

The eastern wall of the passage bay is close studded externally and incorporates a window, now blocked by the chamber over the wagon entrance of The Mermaid Inn [72], built *c.*1525. It can therefore be certain that the range is not the fragment of a once longer house which has lost its in-line service bay. The absence of a staircase leading to the first floor must indicate that there was a rear range (the present rear range is of 19th-century date) and it is likely that this rear part included at least one room and, probably, an additional first-floor chamber too.[17] Despite the short frontage, the street range has two upper chambers, that over the passage measuring only 1.80 metres (5'11") along the street — it was presumably intended for little more than storage. Despite the building's tiny size, it should certainly not be regarded as low quality — the timbers are good, the external walls are infilled with close studding, there is evidence to suggest some form of projecting window lighting the hall chamber, and a high quality moulded fascia beam masks the ends of the joists at the jetty.

Today the property forms part of the Mermaid Inn and the alignment of the property boundaries suggests that the plot had, in fact, been part of the Mermaid complex from early times. It was certainly part of that property in 1860, whilst the 11-flue assessment for The Mermaid in the 1662-1664 hearth tax returns exceeds the number of fireplaces at The Mermaid, implying that the assessment probably includes the chimney within this property (*see* Chapter 7). Bearing this in mind, and given the high quality of finish and general lack of service space, it seems likely that 34 Mermaid Street was built as the proprietor of the Mermaid Inn's private quarters, in like manner to the arrangement at 24-25 High Street [5] *[ESRO HBR/1/0507]*

72. The Mermaid, 35-38 Mermaid Street —
1350 +/-100; 1525 +/-25; 1570 +/-25; 1580 +/-25
(Figures 12.46 - 12.61)

Phase 1 (14th C). Early barrel-vaulted cellar (*see* Chapter 6).

Phase 2 (c.1525). This early 16th-century structure was built as an inn, most likely by the jurat innkeeper Richard Pedyll (died 1536).[18] It remained one of the town's principal inns throughout Rye's period of wealth. It is a large building with a street frontage which totals 18.75 metres (61'6") overall. On the ground floor the basic layout of the street range is of 'textbook' three-cell type, but the range extends beyond the twin service rooms, the 'extra' part serving as a covered wagon

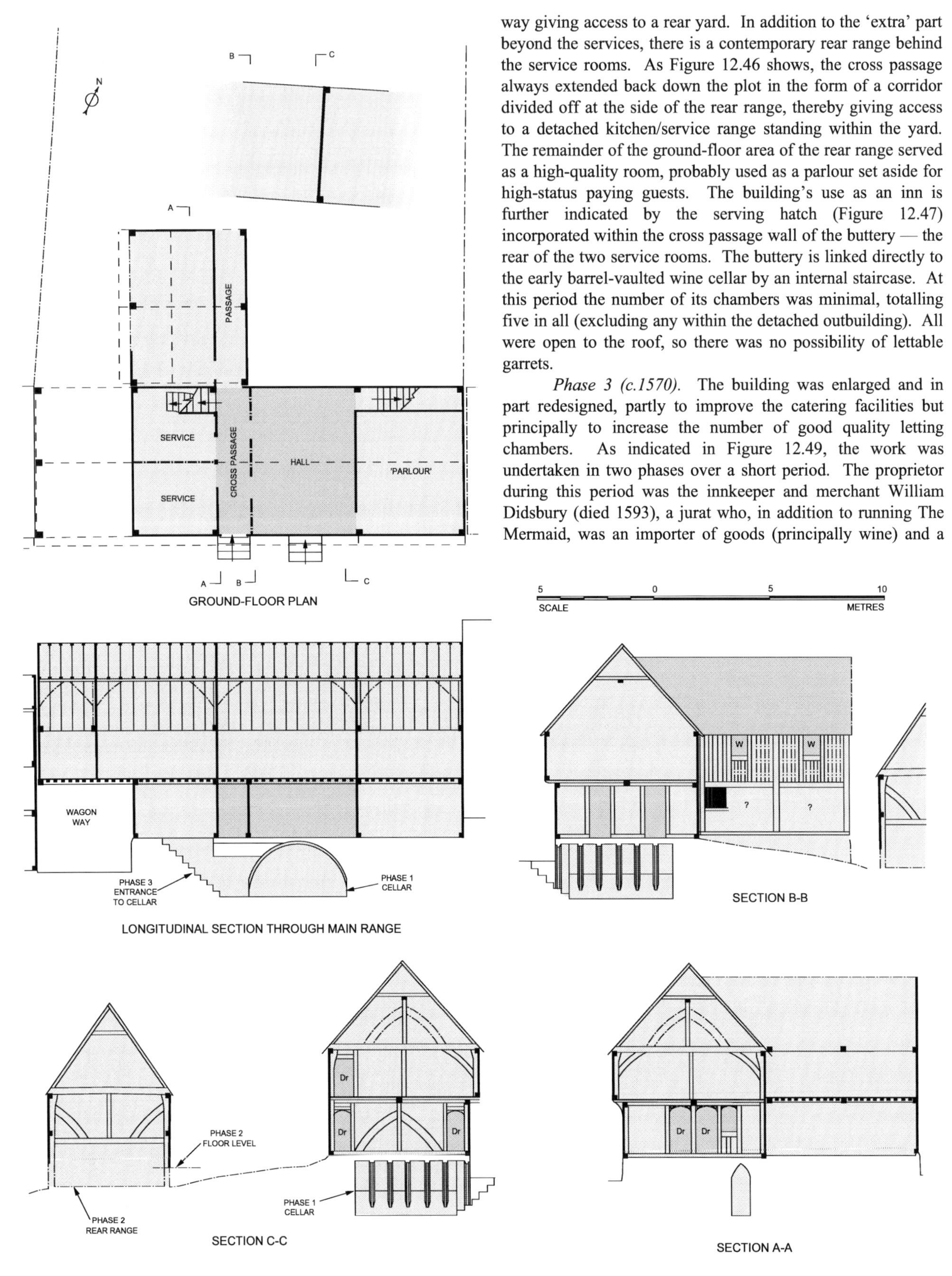

way giving access to a rear yard. In addition to the 'extra' part beyond the services, there is a contemporary rear range behind the service rooms. As Figure 12.46 shows, the cross passage always extended back down the plot in the form of a corridor divided off at the side of the rear range, thereby giving access to a detached kitchen/service range standing within the yard. The remainder of the ground-floor area of the rear range served as a high-quality room, probably used as a parlour set aside for high-status paying guests. The building's use as an inn is further indicated by the serving hatch (Figure 12.47) incorporated within the cross passage wall of the buttery — the rear of the two service rooms. The buttery is linked directly to the early barrel-vaulted wine cellar by an internal staircase. At this period the number of its chambers was minimal, totalling five in all (excluding any within the detached outbuilding). All were open to the roof, so there was no possibility of lettable garrets.

Phase 3 (c.1570). The building was enlarged and in part redesigned, partly to improve the catering facilities but principally to increase the number of good quality letting chambers. As indicated in Figure 12.49, the work was undertaken in two phases over a short period. The proprietor during this period was the innkeeper and merchant William Didsbury (died 1593), a jurat who, in addition to running The Mermaid, was an importer of goods (principally wine) and a

Fig. 12.46
The Mermaid Inn. Phase 2 reconstruction drawings.

factor for London Merchants. His preferred clientele were fellow merchants and the wealthier class of visitor. It was here that, during this period, the Corporation often provided hospitality to visiting dignitaries.[19] The Mermaid was of importance even before its expansion: upon completion of the work it was one of the largest buildings within the town. In this respect the valuation put on Didsbury for the 1576 sesse is perhaps more modest than might be expected — with six other entries he was joint 19th out of a total of 439 entries in the return. Given the typological date of the two periods of expansion, this could indicate that in 1576 the establishment remained in its unexpanded form, or at least had not been enlarged to its greatest extent.[20]

The primary focus for the initial (phase 3) modernization appears to have been improvements to the kitchen facilities and the provision of two high-quality lettable chambers serviced by shared facilities. This entailed some increase in accommodation space — including two lesser chambers at garret level — but in this respect the expansion was modest. The work involved rebuilding the kitchen end of the formerly detached outhouse, retaining the original site (set at an angle to the main house) but now linked to the rear range

Fig. 12.47
The Mermaid Inn. Service doorway leading into buttery with adjacent serving hatch.

Fig. 12.48
The Mermaid. Kitchen range from rear yard.

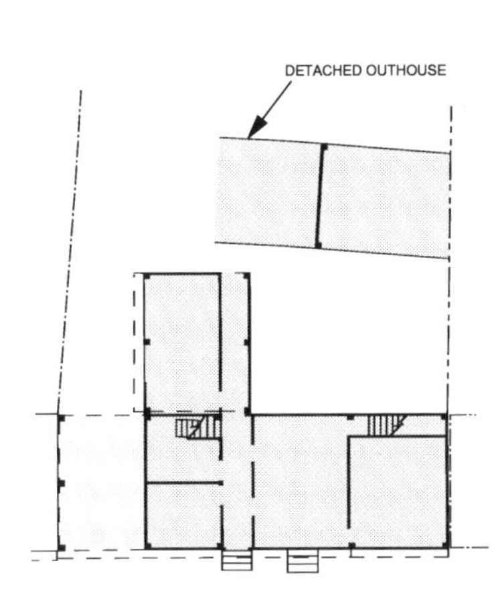

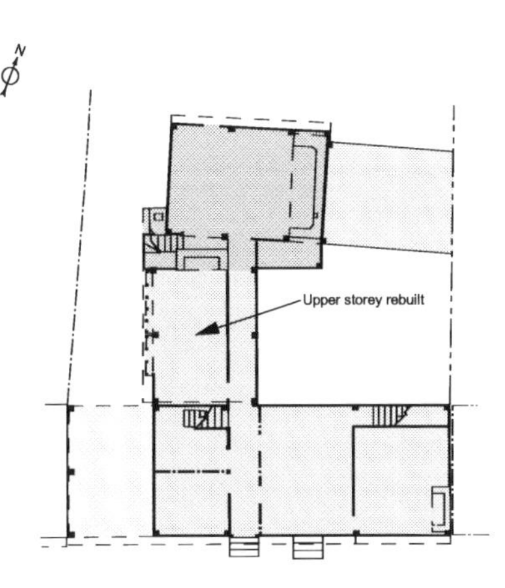

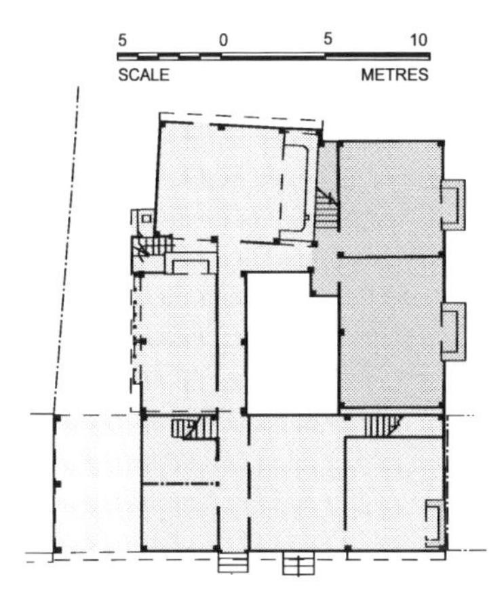

Fig. 12.49
The Mermaid. Ground-floor plans showing development during the 16th century.
Left: Phase 2. Centre: Phase 3. Right: Phase 4.

Fig. 12.50 (Left)
The Mermaid [72]. Letting chamber over Lounge showing close studwork in retained lower part of east wall.

Fig. 12.51 (Above)
The Mermaid [72]. Letting chamber over Lounge showing rebuilt west wall with clerestory windows.

of the early 16th-century building (*see* central plan in Figure 12.49). The new two-storeyed kitchen block is much taller than its predecessor, is continuously jettied along its north elevation, and has external walls which are infilled with close studding.

It is possible that the single-flue chimney serving the kitchen was retained from the earlier kitchen. Its fireplace, built of small 'Flemish' style bricks with Caen stone jambs and timber lintel is low but excessively wide, being 3.90 metres (12'9") internally (Figure 12.53). The large two-bay kitchen is lit on the north by a deep six-pane window (with moulded mullions) which occupies the entire length of the eastern bay and there was probably another large window in the western end wall (details currently hidden). An ovolo-moulded doorway in the western bay of the north wall gives external access to the room, whilst a similar opening in the southern wall connects the kitchen to the passage in the early 16th-century rear range via the new link. To the east of the link is a small contemporary lean-to outshut, the purpose of which is unclear — it seems to have been accessed from the exterior only. Within the existing house the upper storey of the rear range was all but demolished and rebuilt much taller than formerly, retaining the earlier first-floor joisting and eastern rear wall, but entirely rebuilding the western wall (Figures 12.50 and 12.51).

The western part of the link between the existing building and kitchen is taken up by a three-flue chimney, built of small 'Flemish' bricks and incorporating a high-quality stone fireplace serving the early 16th-century 'lounge' (Figure 12.54). The remainder of this wall is clad with heavily moulded

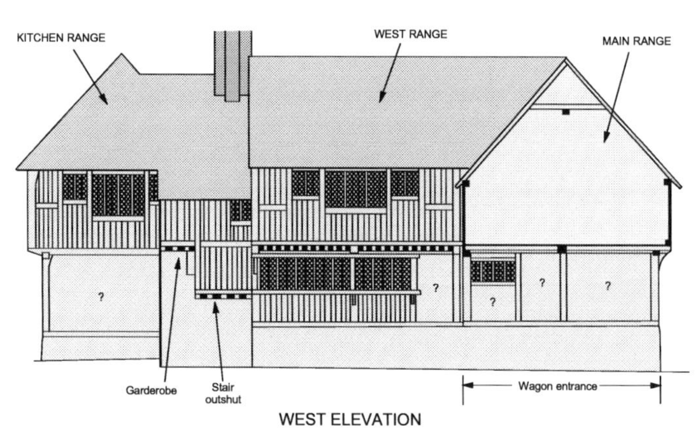

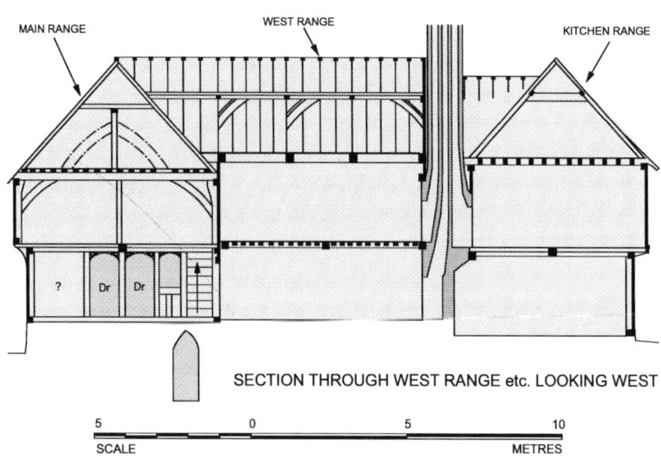

Fig. 12.52
The Mermaid. Reconstructed detail.

Fig. 12.53
The Mermaid. Kitchen fireplace.

Fig. 12.54
The Mermaid. Lounge fireplace.

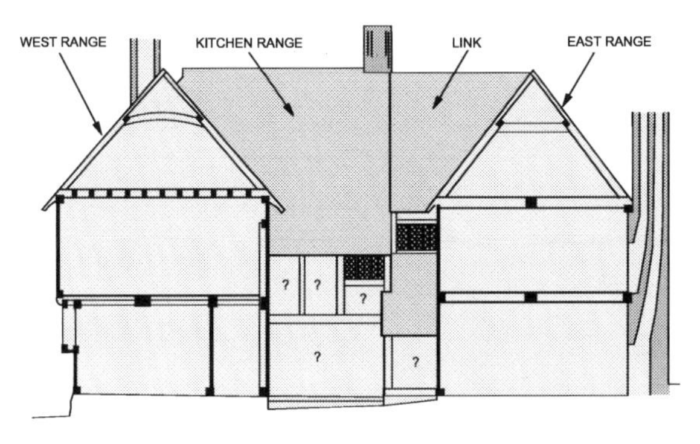

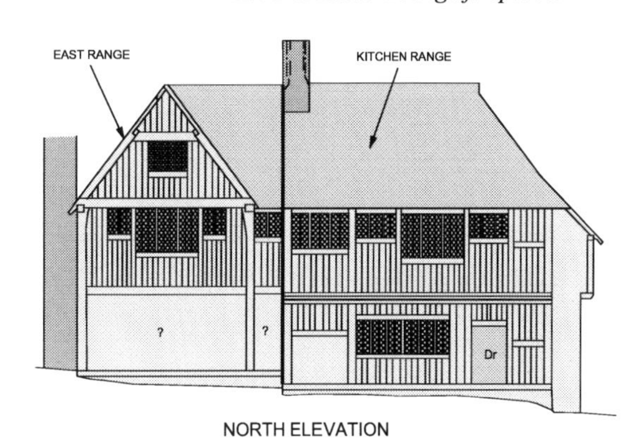

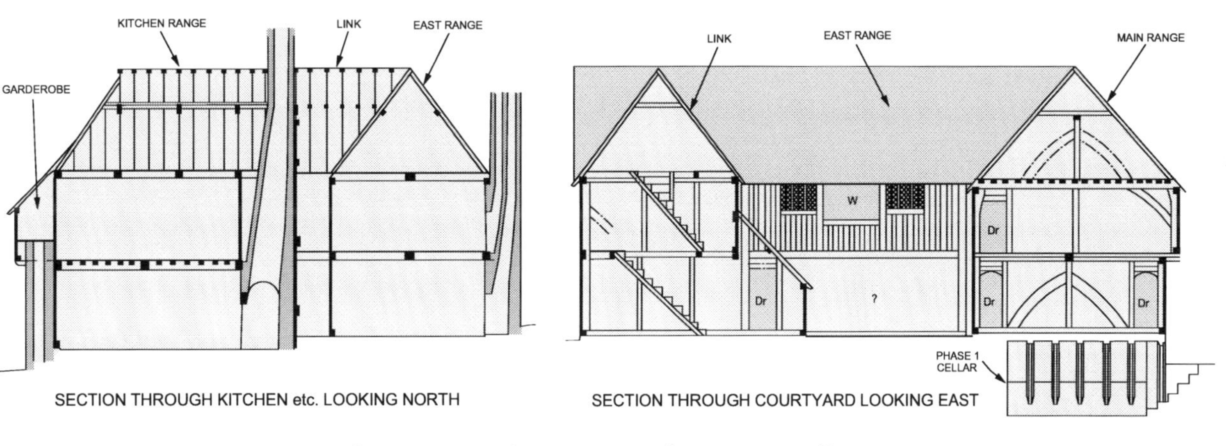

Fig. 12.55
The Mermaid. Reconstructed sections and elevations.

contemporary panelling. A doorway at the western end leads into a closet beside the fireplace, contrived beneath the stair which rises from the kitchen to the chambers over the lounge and kitchen and continues up to the garret rooms above. The lower part of the stair area's western wall is constructed of small 'Flemish' brick, but, as Figure 12.56 indicates, about halfway up the ground-floor storey the wall is jettied out and from this level it continues up in timber framing. A first-floor landing gives access to both letting chambers via neatly formed chamfered doorways. Accessed off this landing from the bottom steps leading to the garret is the shared garderobe which appears to be a contemporary feature despite the fact that it blocks one pane of the clerestory window lighting the kitchen chamber — the clash appears to result from a lack of forethought at the design stage. The support to the toilet seat survives (*see* Figure 12.57) but the timber seat itself has long gone. Descending from it is the 380 mm x 260 mm (1'3" x 10") brick-built chute which remains open to a depth of 3.60 metres (11'10").

Both the kitchen chamber and lounge chamber are of good quality. They have lofty storey heights, carved-and-moulded stone fireplaces similar to that on the ground floor,

Fig. 12.56
The Mermaid. West wall of west range viewed from wagon entrance with stair outshut and garderobe visible on right.

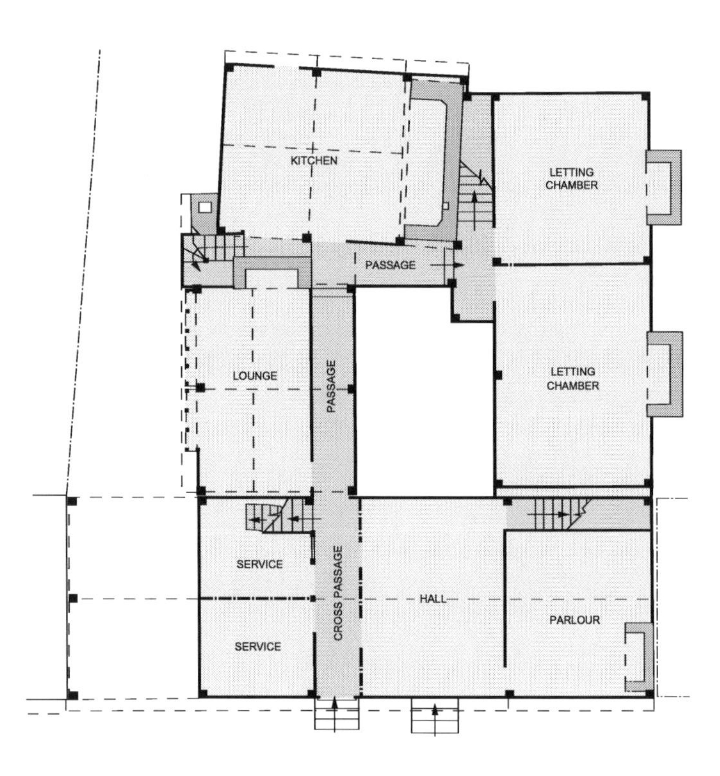

Fig. 12.57
The Mermaid. Remains of support to toilet seat within garderobe.

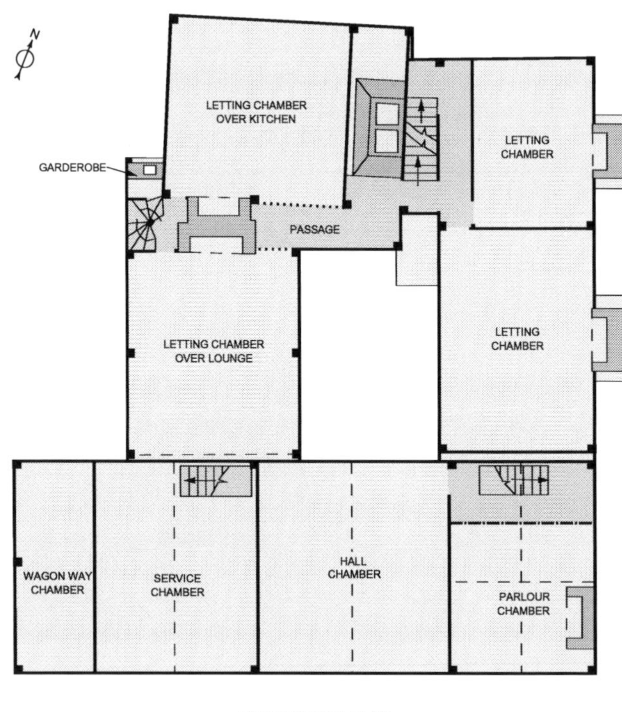

Fig. 12.58 (Right)
The Mermaid. Reconstructed plans.

fully moulded, large glazed windows flanked at ceiling level by clerestory lights, and flush under-plastered ceilings (removed) supported by narrow, deep joists set with their soffit flush with the tiebeams and girders. It is likely that the walls were panelled. The roofs over both chambers are reached from the main staircase and are of clasped-side-purlin construction. Both roofs have open trusses with collars which are acutely cambered in order to improve headroom. That over the rear parlour is windbraced: if windbraces were included over the kitchen chamber they have been removed.

Fig. 12.59
The Mermaid. Ceiling joists in phase-3 range. The joists were intended to be hidden by a plaster ceiling.

Fig. 12.61
The Mermaid. Shoulder-arched fireplace surround in phase-3 range.

Fig. 12.60
The Mermaid. Clasped-side-purlin roof over late 16th-century range showing windbracing.

Phase 4 (c.1580). The next and final phase of alterations followed on very rapidly from the first and involved major expansion giving four extra high-quality heated letting chambers plus one long garret chamber. The new work entailed demolishing the until now retained eastern end of the early rear service block and replacing it by a new three-bay eastern range enclosing a small central courtyard. The layout of the new range was identical on both the ground and first floor: a two-bay southern room and chamber with a smaller northern room and chamber beyond. As is to be expected within an inn of this calibre, all the letting rooms were independently accessed. This was achieved by extending the passage within the earlier western range eastwards along the southern wall of the kitchen range, utilizing in part the already existing small lean-to outshut. A short return at the eastern end allowed both of the new ground-floor letting rooms to be reached, whilst the first-floor chambers were accessed by squeezing a stair into a link between the rear wall of the kitchen chimney and the new range (Figure 12.58). From the head of these stairs a passage was contrived down the side of the northern letting chamber allowing the southern letting chamber and garret stairs to be reached. Apparently, it also gave improved access (via a lean-to outshut) to the two principal letting chambers built as part of the previous phase of alterations.[21] The passage, which was formed by introducing a panelled partition into the northern bay, was lit by one of the clerestory windows in the north wall.[22]

All four of the new letting chambers were of similar high status to those built during the previous phase. They were each fitted with shouldered stone fireplaces of typical 'Rye' design and had panelled walls, flush plastered ceilings, and generous up-to-date fenestration incorporating clerestory lights.[23] The roof over the new range is similar to those over the earlier phase, being of clasped-side-purlin construction with collar trusses. It is fully windbraced throughout its three-bay length. Of particular interest are the link roofs which connect to the earlier parts of the building. Both of these use 'medieval style' paired-rafter-and-collar construction, this method apparently having been chosen for reasons of economy.

By the completion of its 16th-century enlargement The Mermaid had grown to incorporate no less than ten chambers plus a series of lesser-status garret areas. It had developed a courtyard plan with enclosed passages allowing independent access to all six of its principal letting rooms. Some sections of these passage areas were incorporated within the width of the main ranges, others were contrived within a complex lean-to outshut arrangement built against the side wall of the courtyard. In the 1662-1664 hearth tax returns Michael Cadman, Jurat innholder, was assessed 11 flues for this property (but *see* [71] above). In 1660 his resident adult household consisted of himself, his wife, two male servants and one female servant.[24] *[ESRO HBR/1/0506]*

73. 40-41 Mermaid Street, 13 West Street —
16th C or earlier (Not Illustrated)

All information about this house, which was almost totally rebuilt in the middle years of the 19th century, comes from a letter dated 7th March 1864, written by William George Lamb to Thomas Frewen of Brickwall in Northiam, in which he informed Frewen that he wished to give to him a large piece of old furniture, at that time standing in Lamb's hall, but formerly from this property.[25] Regarding the house, he wrote as follows:

> 'At the corner of Mermaid Street ... I recollect standing a very ancient large straggling mansion inhabited

by a very old man and his wife, who appeared to have little intercourse with the outer world; in the course of years the old people died, and the house being little more than a ruin was condemned to be pulled down and ... for the first time access was obtained for those who, from curiosity or otherwise might wish to visit the interior.'

'I now found that the house forming the corner of the street had in fact two fronts, one in Mermaid Street aforesaid and the other in what is now called West Street and also a front door in each. On entering one of these doors, you found yourself in a passage, which leading to the centre of the building took a turn at right angle & led to the other door: thus you will see that at the turning an elbow was formed, which was filled up by a closet, appropriated to all appearances to the purpose of hanging coats etc. out of the way. However on examining the ... closet a spring was discovered, on touching which, the side opened in [the] form of a door & you entered a spacious room of a good height: this room was covered with handsome oak panels and the piece of furniture of which I have spoken, was let in one side; there was a stone fireplace, which showed evidence of having been at sometime gilded; the light was obtained from the lower part of a handsome oriel window, on approaching which a small door was discoverable in the wainscoting, which opened into a back yard: on the side near the fireplace, a door presented itself opening on a flight of stairs, by which you ascended to a room above of the same dimensions, but not of equal height with the room below nor ornamented in the same way, but lighted by the upper part of the Oriel window.'

Although mostly rebuilt, the layout of the present structure retains within it the footprint of the large room referred to by Lamb, set back from and built parallel to Mermaid Street. Beneath it is a basement which, because of the slope of the land, is mostly above ground towards the rear yard. To the east it abuts the truncated southern end of 14 West Street. In common with some other buildings in Mermaid Street, the layout referred to by Lamb, and implied by the present building, is that of a house with its principal rooms set back from the street in order to allow the frontage to be used for commercial purposes.

13 THE HOUSES TO *c.*1660 SUMMARIZED: CHURCH SQUARE, WATCHBELL STREET AND TRADER PASSAGE

74. 6 Church Square — *1490 +/-25; 1535 +/-25*
(Figures 13.1 - 13.3)

Phase 1 (c.1490). What survives is a single-bay hall entered by an overshot cross passage with a single-room (rather than two-room) service area beyond. The spered screen between hall and cross passage is of 'developed' form, incorporating two, rather than one large opening. This house most likely represents an example of alternate rebuild, alternating about the hall's high-end truss (Figure 13.2). Beyond the high end of the hall now stands 8, 10 Church Square [75], a two-cell, fully-floored early 16th-century house, but there is evidence for a blocked doorway (with draught spere) at the rear end of the dais partition, apparently leading south towards a 'missing high end'. This same configuration has been noted at 12 Lion Street [47], which was not constructed with a high-end bay, but which had open ground beyond its dais partition. However, at 6 Church Square it is known that something stood to the south of the hall, for the infill to the dais partition shown in Figure 13.1 is set flush with the hall face of the truss, leaving the crossbeam, tiebeam and principal posts projecting proud of the wall infill on the opposite side — not a configuration used in an external wall. The southern face of the truss (visible within 8, 10 Church Square [75]) contains no redundant joints, so the possibility of a contemporary end bay demolished early in the 16th century to make way for 8, 10 Church Square [75] is not an option. Therefore, whatever stood to the south of the hall was separately framed and most likely of earlier date. It is of

Fig. 13.1
6 Church Square. First-floor section of the hall's high-end partition showing close studding and crownpost set flush towards the hall.

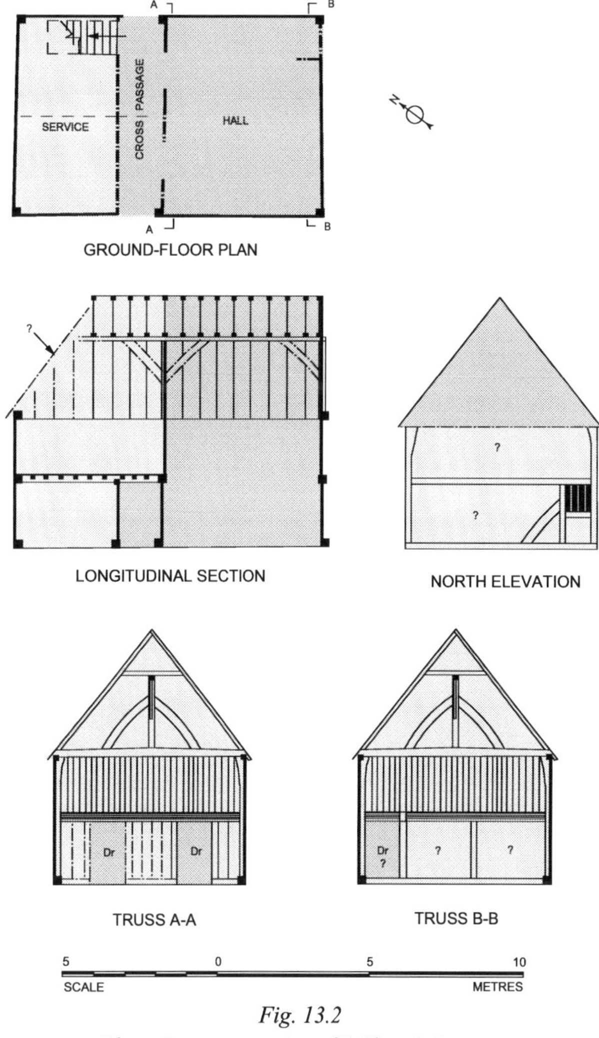

Fig. 13.2
Phase 1 reconstruction of 6 Church Square.

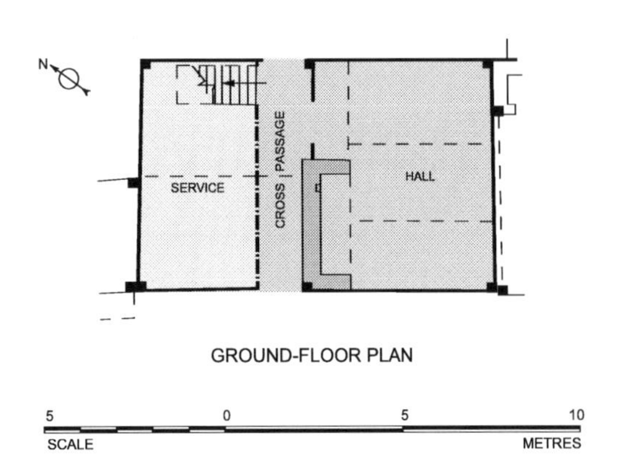

Fig. 13.3
Phase 2 reconstruction of 6 Church Square showing inserted floor and chimney.

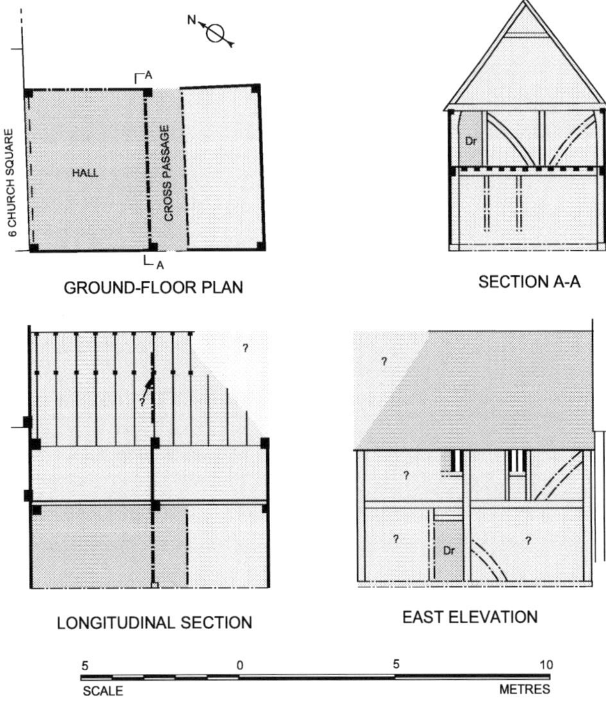

Fig. 13.4
Phase 1 reconstruction of 8, 10 Church Square.

course impossible to tell whether that separately-framed structure formed part of 6 Church Square or functioned as an entirely separate dwelling. The apparent doorway in the dais partition implies the former of the two options, but it could have been included in the expectation that the builder would be able in the future to acquire vacant possession of the neighbouring house, and thereby complete his dream of a three-unit layout.

Phase 2 (c.1535). Phase 2 is represented by the insertion of a floor and two-flue chimney into the open hall, and perhaps the addition of a ceiling within the newly-formed hall chamber. As Figure 13.3 shows, the chimney is traditionally located backing onto the cross passage. *[ESRO HBR/1/0888]*

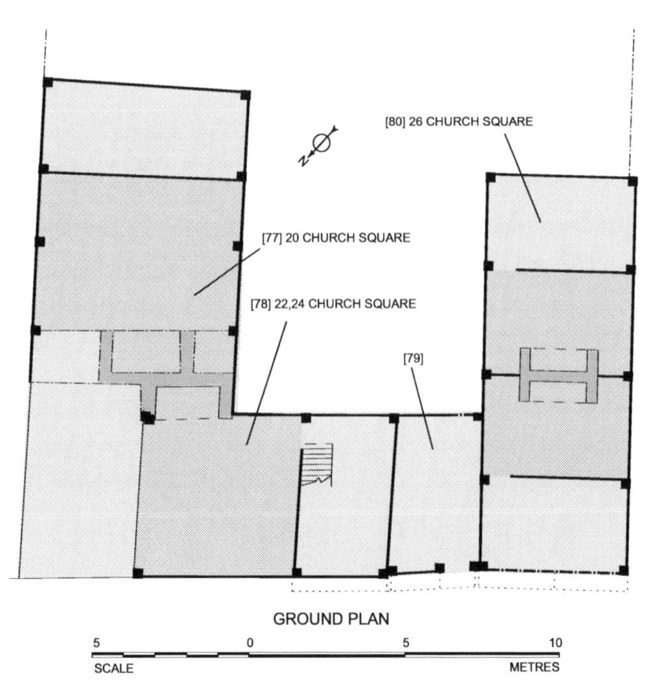

Fig. 13.5
Reconstruction plan showing 20 , 22, 24, 26 Church Square [77 - 80] as in c.1560.

75. 8, 10 Church Square — *1525 +/-25; 1550 +/-25.*
(Figure 13.4)

Phase 1 (c.1525). A two-cell early 16th-century building constructed with a floored-over hall. At 7.60 metres (24'11") long by 5.00 metres (16'4") wide, it is smaller, narrower, and less substantially built than its neighbour to the north (6 Church Square [74]) against which it is open framed. The area to the south of the house was open land, giving access to the rear of the plot: it was not until the 18th century that the building was extended to abut against 12 Church Square [76]. When first built the plan was of near 'textbook' type with an entrance passage within the low-end bay, though this passage seems to have been more fully divided from the hall than in most earlier examples. The two first-floor chambers (one within each bay) were linked by a doorway within the dividing partition. The only serious problem of interpretation the building presents is its total lack of heating.

Phase 2 (c.1550). The present four-flue chimney built against the rear wall of the hall was added when a rear range was built: both the chimney and rear range block windows within the phase-1 rear wall. *[ESRO HBR/1/0618]*

76. 12 Church Square — *16th C?*
(Not Illustrated)

A two-bay hall built parallel to the street with both bays of near equal length. Beyond this the internal layout is uncertain. There are no surviving old chimneys. *[Not surveyed]*

77. 20 Church Square — *c.1560*
(Figure 13.5)

Almost certainly this dwelling was formed by dividing off the service bay of the adjacent 'Wealden' hall house (22, 24 Church Square [78]) and augmenting its floor area by

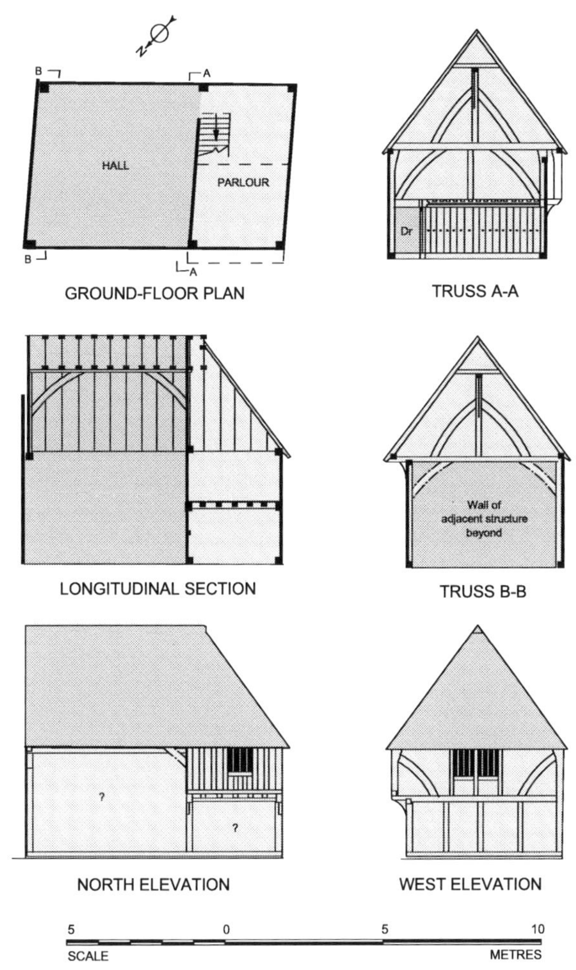

Fig. 13.6
Phase 1 reconstruction of 22, 24 Church Square.

Fig. 13.7
22, 24 Church Square. Dais panelling at the high end of the open hall (Truss A-A)

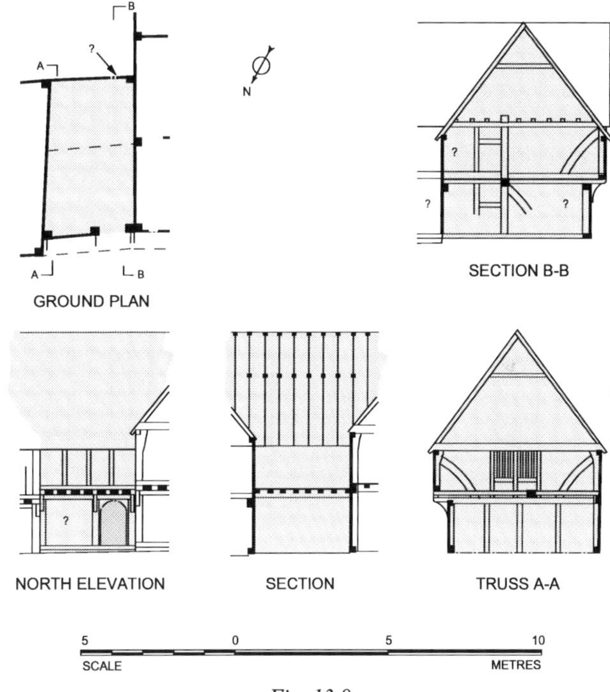

Fig. 13.8
Reconstruction of Pt.24 and Pt.26 Church Square.

the construction of a substantial rear range built overlapping the rear of the medieval hall. This allowed both the new house and the hall of the 'Wealden' to be heated by a shared chimney. This suggests, but does not prove that both parts remained in common ownership at this time. *[ESRO HBR/1/0801]*

78. 22, 24 Church Square —
1475 +/-25; 1545 +/-25; 1560 +/-25.
(Figures 13.6 & 13.7)

Phase 1 (c.1475). A late medieval 'Wealden' hall house. In its present form it consists of a long single-bay hall with high-end accommodation to its west. As shown in Figure 13.7, the high-end wall of the hall still retains its dais panelling set beneath a moulded dais beam. The eastern end wall of the hall is formed by an open truss, indicating that it was built against an earlier structure on the site of 20 Church Square [77]. Now rebuilt, most likely 20 Church Square represented the service bay of the 'Wealden's' predecessor, retained when the hall and parlour were reconstructed. It is therefore likely that 20, 22, 24 Church Square represent an example of 'alternate rebuild'.

Phase 2 (c.1545). When a floor was inserted into the hall an area at the eastern end was left open as a smoke bay. Most likely this backed onto a cross passage within the part which is today occupied by 20 Church Square.

Phase 3 (c.1560). The hall was now heated by a shared chimney built within the new rear range of 20 Church Square [77] which was by this time divided off to form a separate dwelling (*see* above). *[ESRO HBR/1/0800]*

79. Part 24, Part 26 Church Square — *1530 +/-25*
(Figure 13.8)

A structure which may not have been built as a house and which, despite its extremely small size, could have been in dual occupation. It fills the 2.65-2.95 metre (8'8"-9'8") gap between the parlour bay of the 'Wealden' 22, 24 Church Square [78] on the east and the semi-detached pair of tiny hall houses (26 Church Square [80]) on the west. It blocks windows in the walls of both buildings. Whether this indicates that 22, 24 Church Square [78], 26 Church Square [80] and this site were all in the same ownership at this time is a moot point, but the likelihood is that it does.[1]

The building in question is the same width and height as the 'Wealden' and is simply built — a front and rear wall, jettied first floor and roof only: there are no trusses, the timbers being jointed into those of the neighbouring buildings. The ground floor had its own front doorway and could have served either as a domestic room or shop. There are no indications of heating and no apparent location for a stair, though the possibility of a former stair trap having been carefully infilled cannot be ruled out. Today the ground floor has an access passage thrust through it with the remainder of the space thrown into neighbouring number 24, though it was originally separate from it. The chamber above now forms part of number 26 and is accessed through the side wall of its hall chamber. What is unknown is whether this has always been the case. Almost certainly the infill structure predates the flooring over of the hall within number 26, though there is no reason why the chamber could not have been reached from the hall by means of a stair ladder rising through the intruded doorway. So, the infill building could have been designed as an unheated one-up-one-down dwelling, it could have been a shop with store/workshop above, or it could have been a ground-floor shop built for separate letting with the upper chamber used to augment the accommodation within adjacent number 26. *[ESRO HBR/1/0599]*

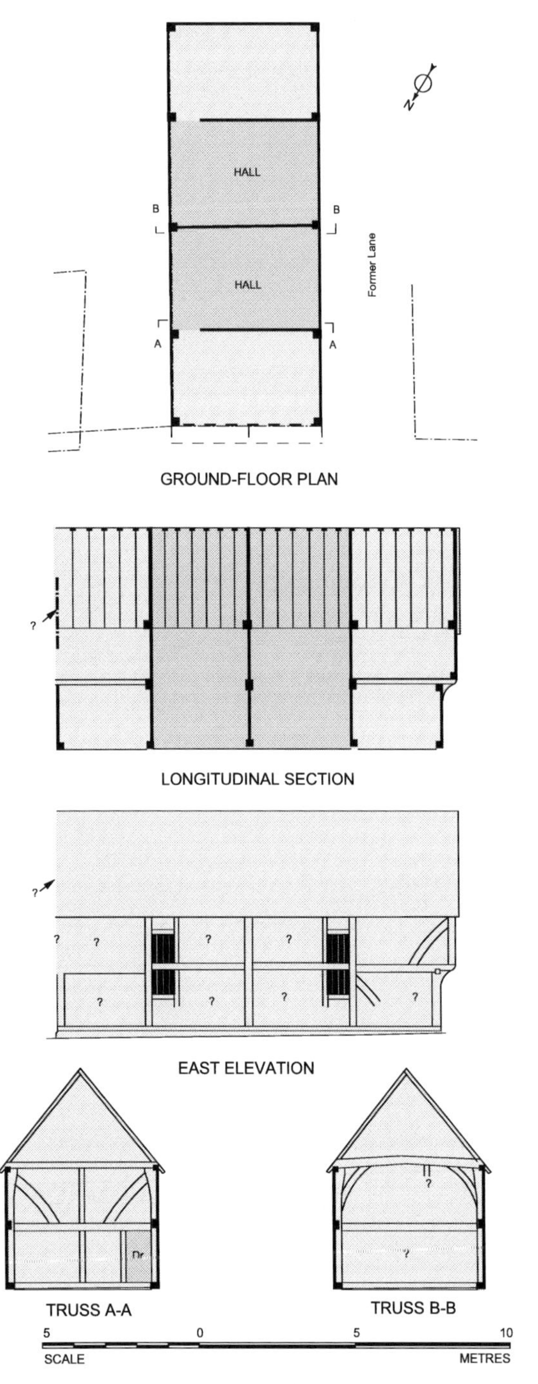

Fig. 13.9
Phase 1 reconstruction of the semi-detached pair of hall houses now known as 26 Church Square.

Fig. 13.10
Rear (eastern) wall of the southern of the semi-detached hall houses [80] showing the blocked upper light of the double-height hall window in the centre of the picture, beneath the later high-level window.

80. 26 Church Square — *1520 +/-25; 1540 +/-20*
(Figures 13.9 - 13.11)

Phase 1 (c.1520). A handed semi-detached pair of houses with open halls. Of the town's medieval halls, these are probably the lowest in status; certainly they are the smallest. Even so, they are competently built, despite the use of small-scantling timbers. Measuring only 3.10 metres long x 4.70 metres wide (10'2" x 15'4") internally, the single-bay halls are tiny and entirely unadorned. They were presumably entered direct from the narrow lane which once ran along the west elevation, but it is now impossible to tell whether these doorways were located against the shared party wall or adjacent to the floored-over end bays.[2] Nor is it known whether there were doorways in the rear (eastern) wall — the pair could have been built backing directly onto the rear garden of the adjacent house. If the rear wall did incorporate doorways they must have been against the party wall, for the hall windows within this elevation were located at the opposite end, hard against the internal doorways leading into the floored-over bays. The blocked upper part of one of the hall windows is shown in Figure 13.10, complete with its diamond-section mullions still *in situ*. This arrangement of window and door locations is interesting, for usually hall windows are sited towards the high end, rather than the low end, implying that the floored ends served as high-end accommodation. This would certainly be consistent with the locations of the doorways which led into them — against the rear posts rather than positioned at centre span, as in normal service ends. But, given the small size of these houses, perhaps it is wrong to consider the halls as having defined high and low ends, and likewise wrong to be contemplating whether the floored bays were used as services or private accommodation. Perhaps the families who occupied this modest pair of cottages were sufficiently low down the social scale to neither bother nor care about such social niceties!

Phase 2 (c.1540). When floors were inserted into the open halls of these houses, the most economical means of heating them was to add a back-to-back axial chimney astride the party wall, providing a fireplace to each cottage (Figure 13.11). *[ESRO HBR/1/0598]*

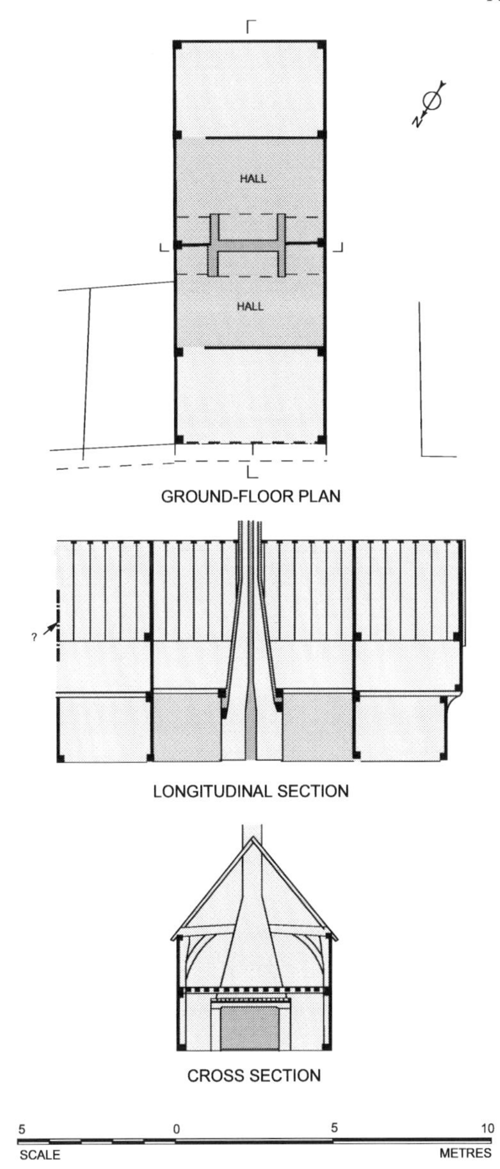

Fig. 13.11
26 Church Square. Phase 2 reconstruction showing inserted floor and chimney

Fig. 13.12
Early 20th-century photograph of 30 Church Square looking north along line of former lane. The house in the background is 28 Church Square which was rebuilt larger in the late 18th or 19th century, extending across the former entrance to the lane off Church Square

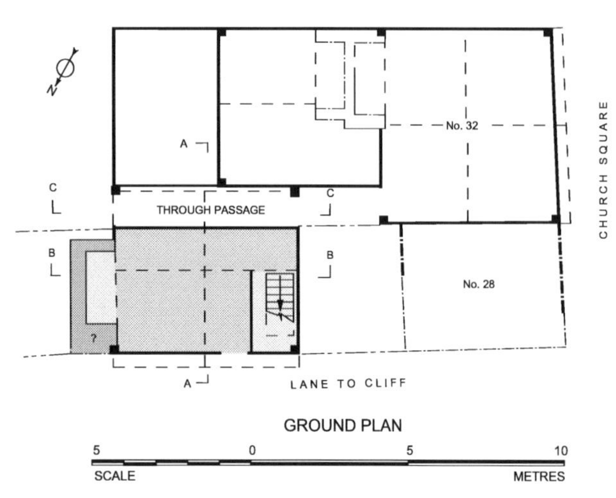

Fig. 13.13
Reconstructed plan of 30 Church Square showing its context in relation to 28 and 32 Church Square

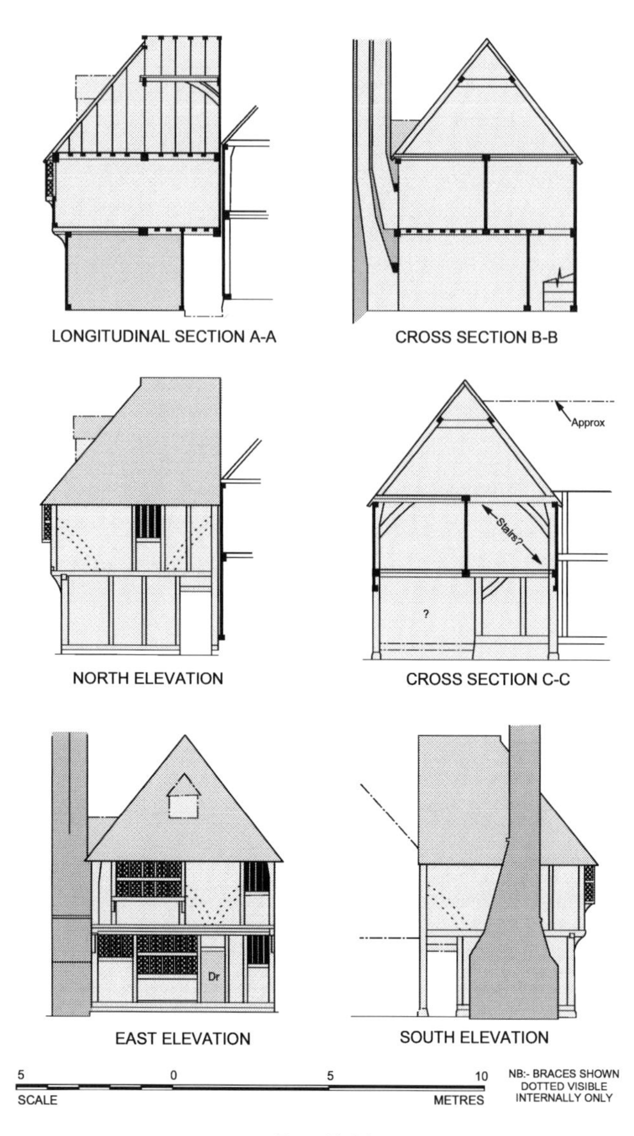

Fig. 13.14
Reconstruction of 30 Church Square

81. 30 Church Square — *1565 +/-25*
(Figures 13.12 - 13.15)

An off-street tenement measuring 5.00 metres east-west by 6.10 metres north-south (16'5" x 20'0"). It projects forwards at right angles to the side wall of No. 32 [82], presenting a hipped end to the lane. Despite its back-lands location, the facade not only incorporates a jetty, but display fenestration, including a projecting first-floor oriel window (Figure 13.12). Abutting the side wall of No. 32 [82], on the ground floor the available floor area was reduced by the need to incorporate a through passage. As Figure 13.13 indicates, there was originally no doorway linking the passage to 30 [81], and thus it served solely as a right of way for No. 32 [82]. The building's only means of access was from the lane via a doorway in the jettied eastern end wall. It led into a single room taking up the entire ground-floor space, though the north-eastern corner was partially screened off to accommodate the stairs with a small storage area beneath. A chimney built against the south wall heated the main area. All windows at this level faced the lane but, whereas those serving the main part of the room were glazed, that lighting the storage area was of unglazed type (Figure 13.14).

On the first floor the building was divided into two chambers by an axial partition located beneath the central girder of the ceiling. The northern of the two chambers doubled as a large landing: it not only housed the main stairs, but also a flight leading up to the roof area. It was lit by two small unglazed windows: one in the front wall and another in the northern side wall. In comparison, the southern chamber was luxurious in that it was heated by a round-backed fireplace against the south wall and was lit by a large projecting oriel window located within the jettied eastern facade. Additional space was provided within the roof which, surprisingly, was fitted with a hipped end — a gable would have been far more practical. Perhaps the hip was necessary in order not to rob 26 Church Square (on the opposite side of the lane) of light. Located centrally within the hip is a dormer window which, although now altered, is shown in a sketch made by Van Dyck in 1634 (*see* Figure 13.15). It is therefore likely to be an original feature.

The roof itself is of typical clasped-side-purlin construction with a collar truss and one-way windbracing. The frame beneath is of traditional construction incorporating large panels with inset, concealed footbraces. Despite its diminutive size, it is not a poor building — glazed and moulded windows, moulded principal ceiling beams within the main room, an external jetty and a side-built two-flue brick chimney are all features associated with houses of reasonable status. Although unglazed windows serve the lesser rooms, all three were fitted with sliding shutters. *[ESRO HBR/1/0798]*

82. 28, 32 Church Square — *Medieval; 1500 +/-25*
(Figures 13.16 & 13.17)

Phase 1 (Medieval). Visible as a weathering ghost on the present (phase-2) hall, the phase-1 building measured 5.05 metres (16'7") wide and had walls approximately 3.40 metres (*c.*11'2") to eaves. When the (assumed) open hall was rebuilt the small, low eastern service end was retained. This retained service end (28 Church Square) was evidently extended subsequently, but was not rebuilt until the

Fig 13.15
Detail from drawing by Van Dyck dated 1634 showing 30 Church Square with dormer window in end hip.
[© Gabinetto Disegni e Stampe delgi Uffizi, Florence, Italy]

early 19th century.

Phase 2 (c.1500). The new hall block has good quality moulded ceiling beams (*see* Figure 13.17) supporting a hall chamber which is ceiled from the roof space in order to give garret storage. It measured 6.00 metres (19'8") wide overall the front jetty and had much loftier walls standing 4.80 metres (15'9") to eaves. It is heated by either a three-flue or a four-flue chimney built into its rear wall, positioned so as to also serve a parlour within a contemporary rear range. Probably because of the contemporary garret, 32 Church Square does not have a crownpost roof, but instead makes use of clasped-side-purlin construction with full windbracing and jowled heads to its diminished principal rafters. Confirmation of the sequence of construction is to be found within the western gable wall which not only shows close studs in its western face, but also contains a window lighting the garret; these facts leave no doubt that this end of the house was designed as an external wall with nothing built against it.

Given that the rebuilt section lacks services of its own and bearing in mind that a rear lean-to service area was later added, it seems logical to suggest that the entire building was still in single occupancy at the date when the hall was rebuilt, though it was subsequently divided. However, there is no guarantee of this, nor is there a guarantee that the much lower service end did not remain in the same occupation as the rebuilt part until the late 18th or 19th century (when the present 28 Church Square replaced it) though this seems very unlikely. The most likely scenario is that the medieval service area was initially retained because of lack of money and was divided off during the middle of the 16th century in order to make an extra dwelling, at which date a lean-to service area was added to the rear of 32 Church Square in order to compensate for the loss of storage space. If both 28 and 32 were still in single occupancy when No. 30 was constructed in the back yard there seems no reason why a through passage

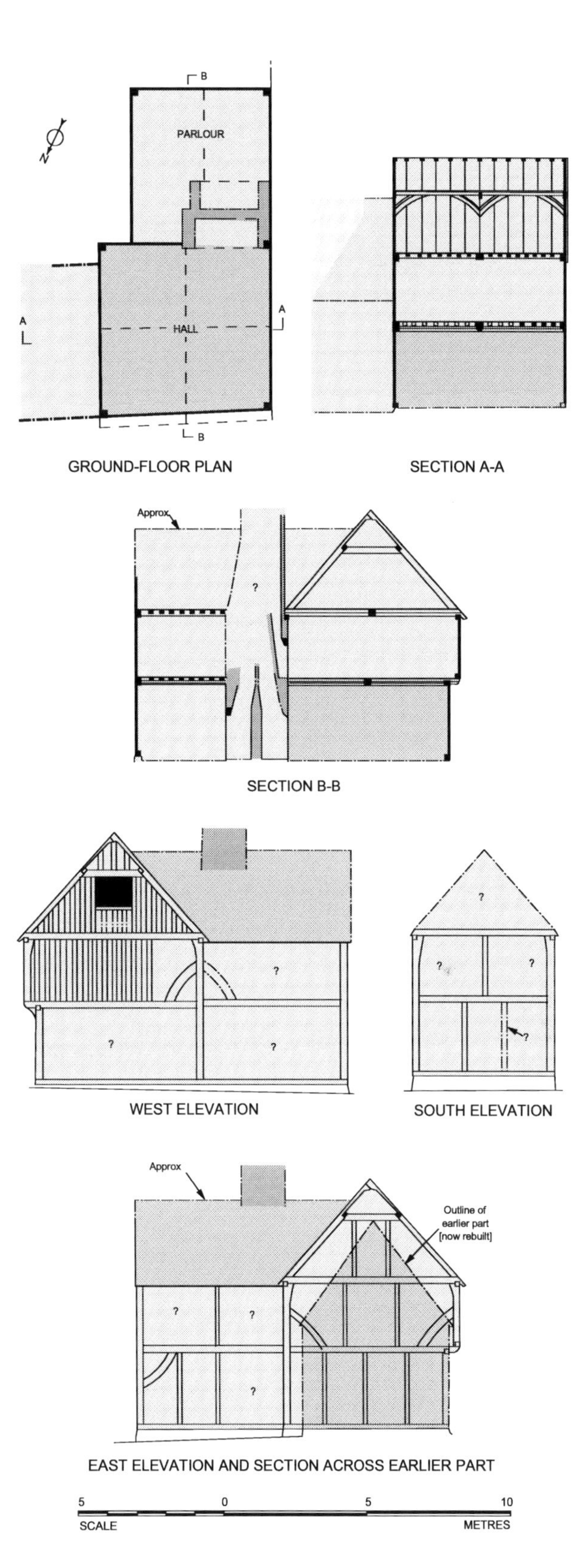

Fig. 13.16
Phase 2 reconstruction of 32 Church Square.

Fig. 13.17
32 Church Sq. Moulded timbers in hall ceiling, phase 2.

was incorporated in order to serve as a right of way through No. 30 [81] (*see* Figure 13.13). *[ESRO HBR/1/0799]*

83. 34, 36 Church Square — *1515 +/-25; 1565 +/-50. (Figure 13.18)*

Phase 1 (c.1515). Number 34, 36 is a continuously-jettied house, adjacent to 32 Church Square [82], standing hard against its western wall, totally blocking the latter's end window. Given the design of its earlier neighbour, the surprise in 34, 36 Church Square is that not only are the floor joists of medieval scantling, but the first-floor chambers were initially open to the roof, which was of totally traditional crownpost type. The floor plan is simple — two large, near equal-sized rooms (probably linked by a doorway) with a pair of interlinked chambers above. The original stair position is not known, nor is the initial heating system — if, indeed, it was heated. One of the two chambers is inexplicably crossed by an open truss without a crownpost. In the other chamber there is no such intermediate truss, though the first-floor joisting does incorporate an intermediate crossbeam. The intended use of the rooms and chambers is not known and it must be accepted that the building may not initially have been designed as a dwelling.

Phase 2 (L16th C). When a single-storeyed rear outshut was added a three-flue chimney was built into the eastern bay against the rear wall, with a central-newel staircase to its side. The modifications cannot be closely dated. *[ESRO HBR/1/0720]*

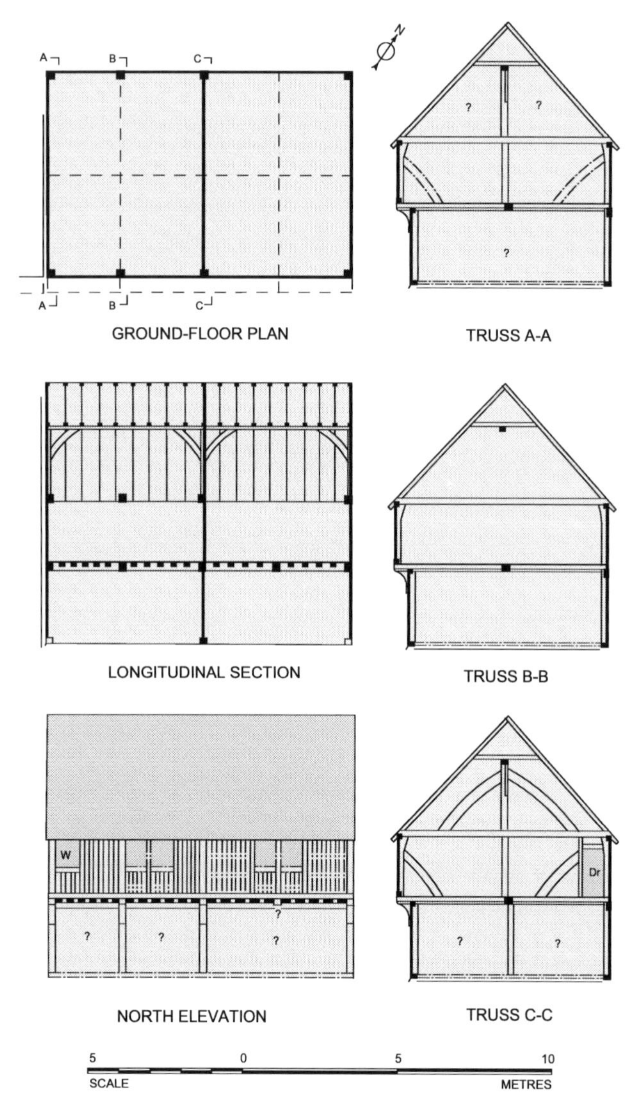

Fig. 13.18
Phase 1 reconstruction of 34, 36 Church Square.

84. 42 Church Square — *1540 +/-25 (Figures 13.19 - 13.21)*

A house fitted into a sliver of a gap, which at the street frontage measured just 2.70 metres (8'10") wide, increasing slightly to 3.05 metres (10'1") at the rear (Figure 13.21). As Figure 13.19 makes very plain, fitting a usable house into such a narrow gap was a challenge. The resultant building extends back 10.30 metres (33'9") from the street and follows a predictable two-cell design with a two-bay hall to the front and a central axial chimney pushed hard to one side in order to give access to an unheated rear room. It is not known where the stair was located, but presumably it was in the rear bay. Not surprisingly, both chambers were open to the roof, which was of simple paired-rafter-and-collar design.

It is equally unsurprising to note that the side walls of the house are formed by the external walls of the two adjacent

Fig. 13.19
Principal first-floor chamber, 42 Church Square.

Fig. 13.20
Terracotta 'peep' window, 42 Church Square.

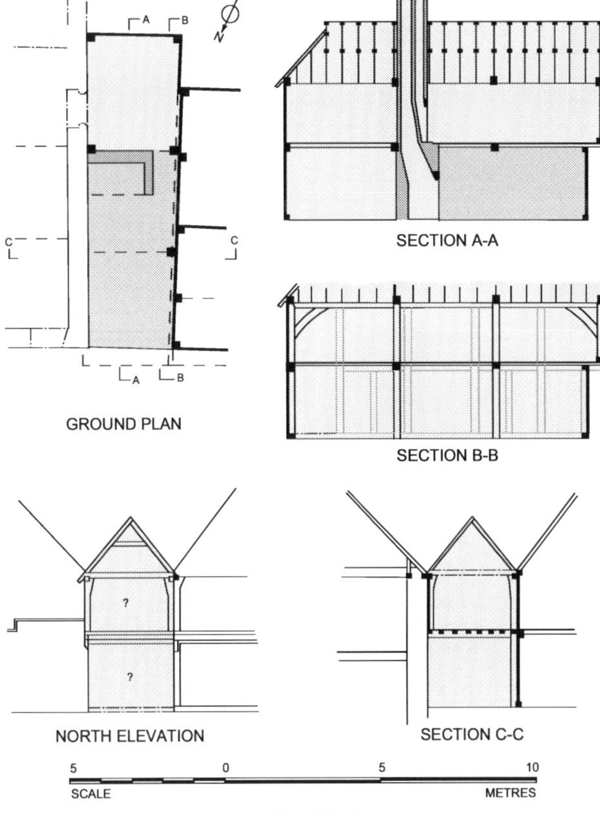

Fig. 13.21
Reconstruction of 42 Church Square.

buildings — there was no room to waste space constructing new walls. On the western side, against the timber-framed 44 Church Square [85], there is an open frame consisting of principal posts, wallplate and arch braces, not dissimilar to the arcade of an aisled building. Down the opposite side, where the stone wall of the late 13th-century 40 Church Square stands (for which *see* Chapter 4), the ends of the crossbeams are built into the masonry and support stilted principal posts. The street elevation is timber framed and jettied, with the upper storey projecting forwards slightly from the front wall of the adjacent stone house. The resulting narrow side panel is not infilled with daub, but with tiny 'Flemish' bricks incorporating a 'peep' window of terracotta with pierced tracery (*see* Figure 13.20). The window allows a good view down the street! *[ESRO HBR/1/0825]*

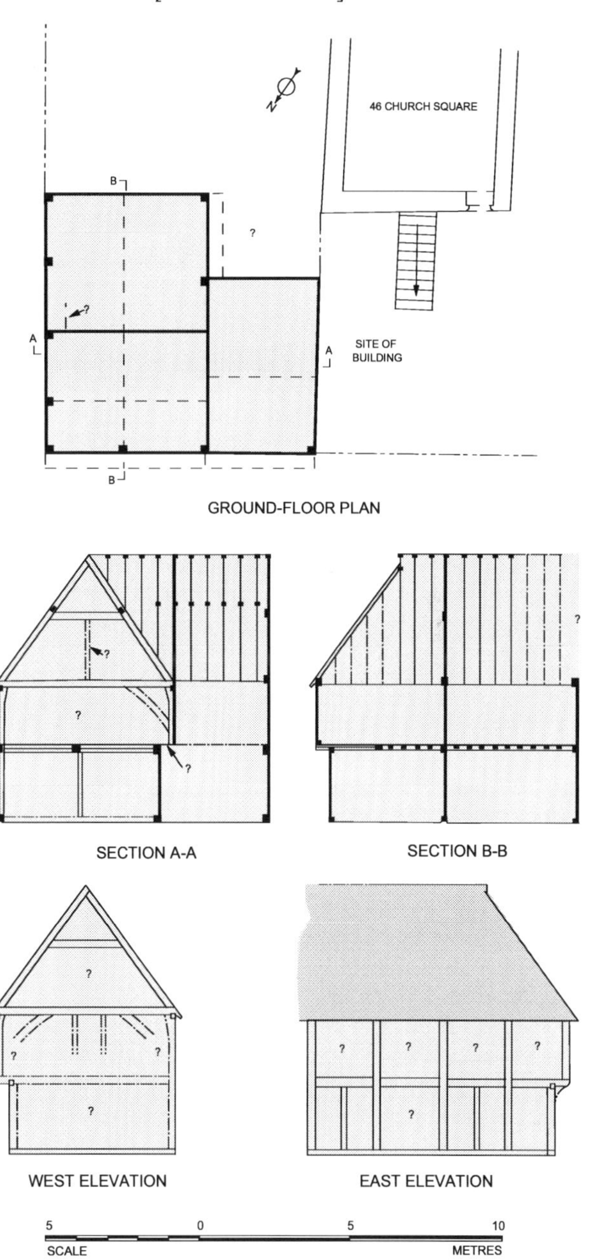

Fig. 13.22
Reconstruction of 44 Church Square.

85. 44 Church Square — *1525 +/-25*
(Figure 13.22)

This small, crosswinged building's room layout (shown in Figure 13.22) falls into no recognizable pattern. Furthermore, the ground- and first-floor parts of the crosswing's western side wall do not align one over the other, and there are no indications of original heating. The building was continuously jettied to the street and contained two principal ground-floor rooms within its crosswing, which may be truncated at its southern end. The larger of the two rooms is at the rear: the crosswing's front room could have served as a shop. Not only may the crosswing have been truncated, but the same may apply to the main range: if so, like 64 Church Square [52], this may have been part of a much larger complex, in this instance encompassing the adjacent building called The Store House, 46 Church Square [86] to the west. *[ESRO HBR/1/0826]*

86. 46 Church Square — *1400 +/-50.*
(Figures 13.23 - 13.25)

Despite the fact that much detail was lost when extensively restored in 1898, this building remains one of the most intriguing houses within the town. Set back at right angles to the street and built over a vaulted cellar (for which *see* Chapter 6), it is one of the town's very few stone-built structures and ought to be early. Made red by fire, the superstructure walls are reputed to predate the disastrous French raid of 1377. This may be the case, though the details of the replacement crownpost roof (*see* Figure 13.24) and of the stone entrance doorway in the west wall (*see* Figure 13.25) are more consistent with an early 15th-century date, so perhaps the building escaped the French, only to be severely damaged by a subsequent fire.

In its present form the house is a two-cell structure consisting on the ground floor of a two-bay open hall with, to the south, what is assumed to have been a room with a chamber above (Figure 13.23). It is into this room, not the hall, that the main entrance in the west wall led. It is tempting to see this as a standard entrance area and service room sited at the low end of the hall, but such an interpretation does not fit the other evidence: the hall windows are located towards this end, and the larger of the hall's two roof bays is also at this end. Both these features imply that this southern end of the hall was the more important — not the reverse. It is also clear that, despite the stone structure apparently being complete (there are no visible wall scars) it is not the entire building — something to the north has been demolished: there must originally have been a (presumably timber-framed) structure occupying the open space between the extant stone section and Church Square.[3] This missing element was quite large and was perhaps (at least in part) put to commercial use. In this respect (and bearing in mind the vaulted cellar) this building is comparable to the specialized designs found in some of the larger towns, where the domestic accommodation was relegated to the rear of commercial space. Even so, the principal means of access to the stone-built part appears to have been via a side street running back to the cliff edge, rather than via a cramped private alley or internal access.

The now lost, assumed timber-framed northern part of the complex apparently still stood in the early 16th century when adjacent 44 Church Square [85] was built. Indeed, if the

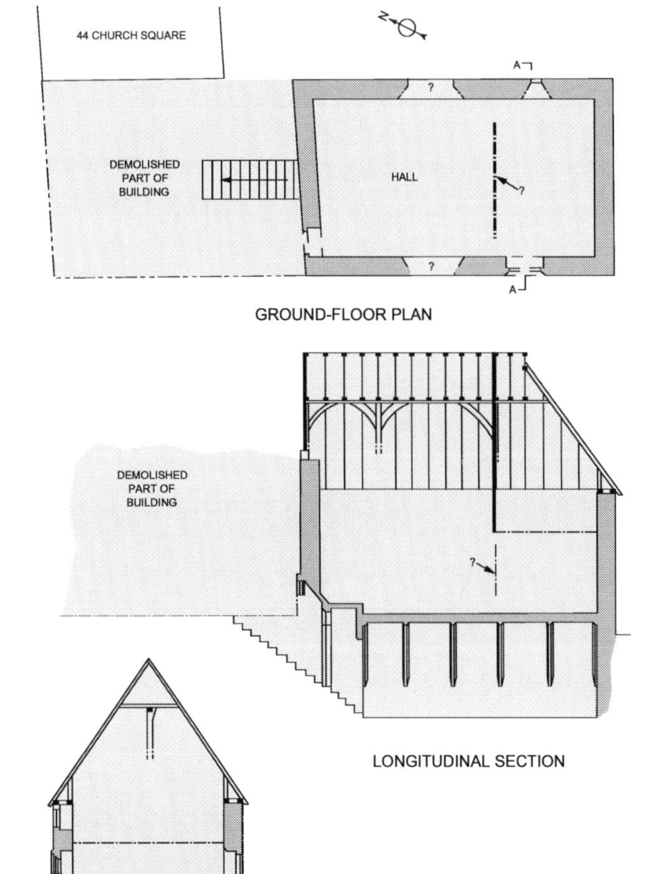

Fig. 13.23
Reconstruction of 46 Church Square.

Fig. 13.24
Remains of freestanding crownpost at 46 Church Square

Fig. 13.25
Exterior of 46 Church Square from the south west. Note the original entrance doorway (now blocked).

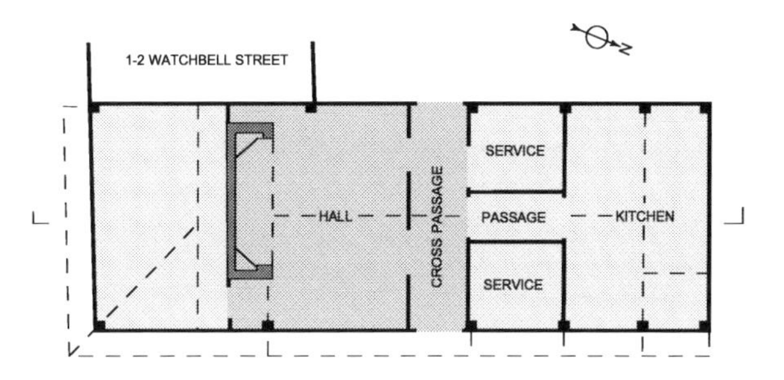

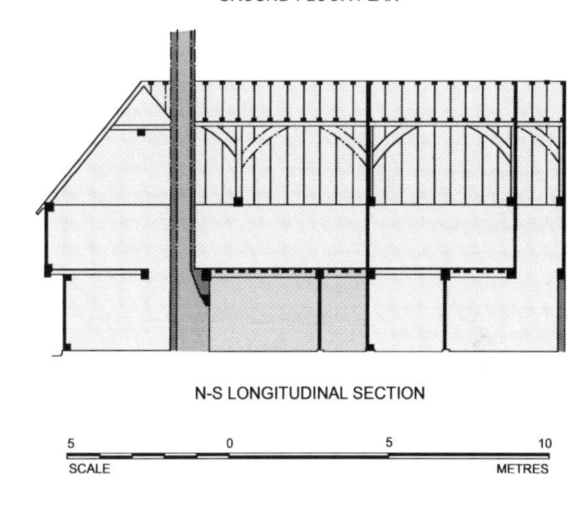

Fig. 13.26
Reconstruction of St Anthony's, Church Square..

street range of 44 has been truncated, these two buildings may have formed part of the same rambling 'U'-planned structure, though perhaps always in more than one occupation. *[ESRO HBR/1/0727]*

87. St Anthony's, Church Square — *1490 +/-25*
(Figures 13.26 - 13.28)

A large and imposing house which either dates from the late 15th or very early 16th century, probably built by John Jervase (Jarvis) — *see* Chapters 6 and 7. Its 16.30 metre (53'6") street frontage has a two-bay kitchen beyond its otherwise 'textbook' three-cell plan. The kitchen was reached from the hall via a central passage which extended through the service bay, between the two service rooms (Figure 13.26). The hall is heated by a contemporary high-end chimney, whilst the kitchen is served by its own smoke bay. There is evidence within the front facade which could be interpreted as indicating that the high-end room was intended for commercial use, though this is far from proven. The heavy joisting in this area supports a ceiling formed of timber boards.

The structure is of one build, occupies a corner plot, and is of 'L' plan. However, the return range was designed from the outset as a separate house (for which *see* 1-2 Watchbell Street [90] below) and was probably built for let. Despite St Anthony's having a floored-over hall from the outset, the second dwelling within the structure had an open hall, was of two-cell type, and incorporated a 'Wealden' recessed front.

Fig. 13.27
Exterior of St Anthony's, Church Square.

Deeds suggest that during the late 16th century the northern end of the main dwelling may have been divided off to form a separate house. An intruded doorway inserted between the two original houses shows that these two southern parts became merged sometime during the late 16th or 17th century and it is possible that at this period the entire structure was occupied as one dwelling. Regardless of whether this was so, by 1860 the building was in four separate occupancies (two facing Watchbell Street and two facing Church Square). Today the entire building is a single house. *[ESRO HBR/1/0356]*

88. 54, 56 Church Square — *1550 +/-25; 1565 +/-25. (Figures 13.29 & 13.30)*

Phase 1 (c.1550). A two-cell house built onto the service end of the medieval 'Wealden' known as Grene Hall (now 58, 60 Church Square [89]). It was probably constructed by Robert Gaymer, the owner of Grene Hall.[4] To the south, where 52 Church Square now stands, there was a gap in the built-up street frontage, and in consequence 54, 56 [88] was built with a hipped terminal at its southern end. In its initial form the structure presents considerable problems of interpretation. It is of four bays, consisting of a narrow bay (now, and perhaps always housing a chimney) a larger floored bay, another narrow bay (apparently once housing a chimney) with yet another larger floored bay beyond. There was at least one first-floor doorway within the rear wall, so there must have been a structure (or structures) built against this wall, but whether a lean-to outshut or turret/turrets is unknown. The two chambers always had first-floor ceilings. A further peculiarity is the storey heights — a lofty 2.75 metres (8'11") on the first floor, but only 2.25 metres (7'5") on the ground floor. The craftsmanship throughout is of good quality. Was this structure built as some form of specialized building, or could it have been built as a pair of tiny, good-quality single-cell dwellings? Both are possible, though neither fits all the available evidence.

Phase 2 (c.1565). Whatever the initial form of the building, the (assumed) southern chimney was quite quickly removed, the trimmed openings in the first floor and attic floor blocked, and the area in question incorporated into the northern room and chamber, thereby giving a two-cell house of standard layout. Whether the present chimney within the narrow northern bay is original to the initial build or was built during the phase-2 alterations is unclear, though it certainly belongs to the mid/late 16th century. The wide ground-floor fireplace has a heavy and relatively plain timber lintel which, despite its depressed, chamfered four-centred arch, has plain pyramidal sunk spandrels. In contrast, the first-floor fireplace is of stone with a shouldered arched head and spandrels carved with shield and tendril-like foliage, all capped by a frieze incorporating decorative modallions above an ovolo-moulding

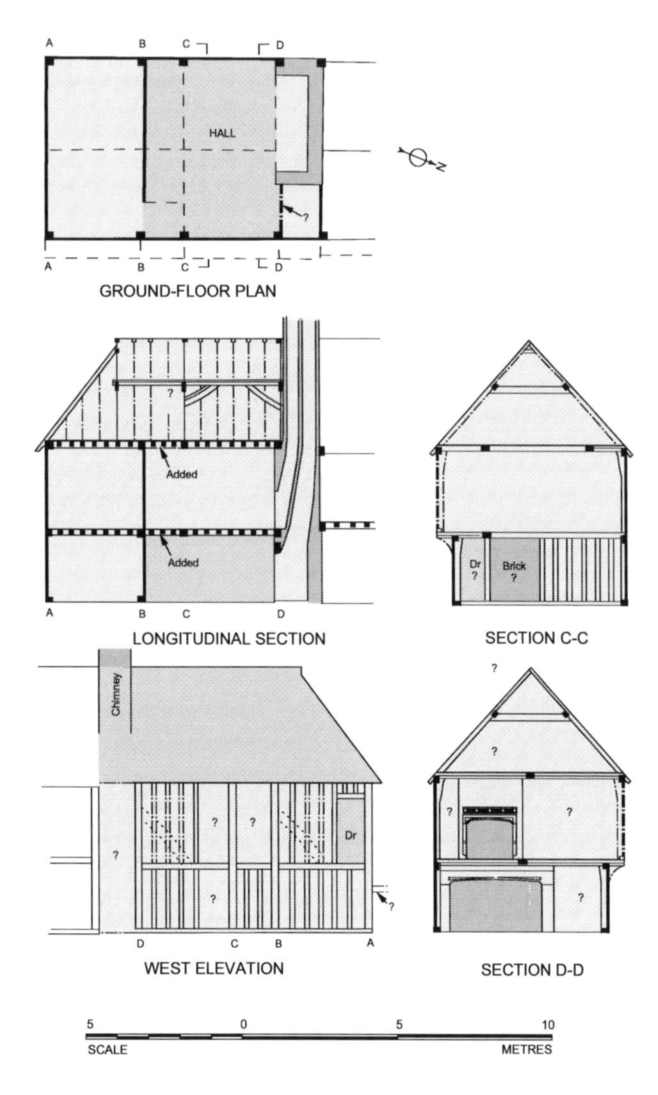

Fig. 13.29
Phase 2 reconstruction of 54, 56 Church Square.

Fig. 13.28
St Anthony's, Church Square. Fireplace in hall.

Fig. 13.30
Phase 2 fireplace in hall chamber, 54, 56 Church Square.

enriched with egg-and-tongue ornamentation (Figure 13.30). The whole shows signs of having been skimmed with a plaster wash, either partially or entirely painted. A number of similar fireplaces dating from the second half of the century exist within the town, including one added into the parlour of adjacent 58, 60 Church Square [89].[5] *[ESRO HBR/1/0805]*

89. 58, 60 Church Square — *1500 +/-25; 1565 +/-10. (Figures 13.31 - 13.38)*

By the middle of the 17th century this large house was occupied by Thomas Greenfield, jurat, 'his majesties searcher for the port of Chichester and members thereof': because of this the house is today known as The Old Customs House. It stands opposite John Shurley's mansion, on the corner of

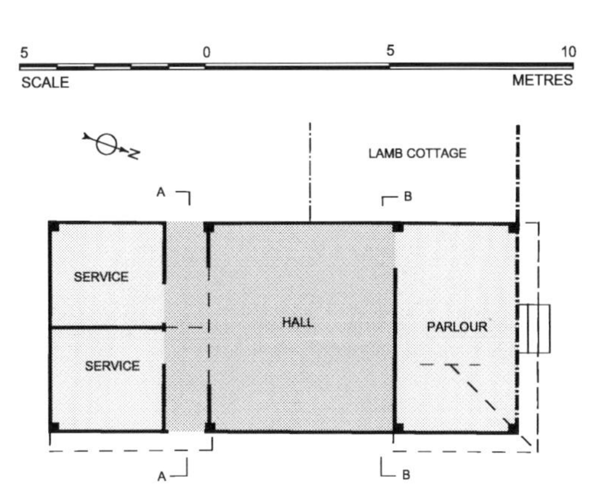

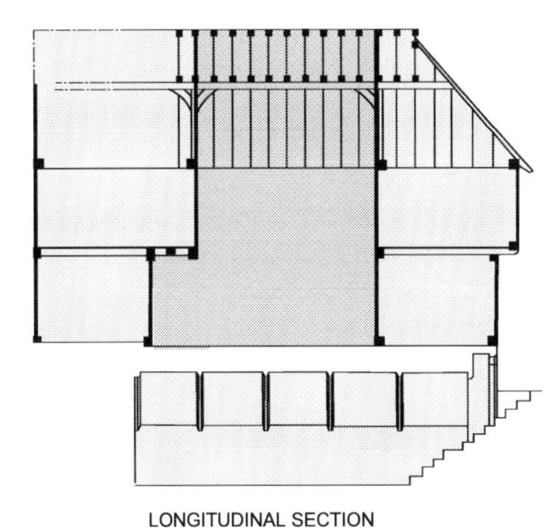

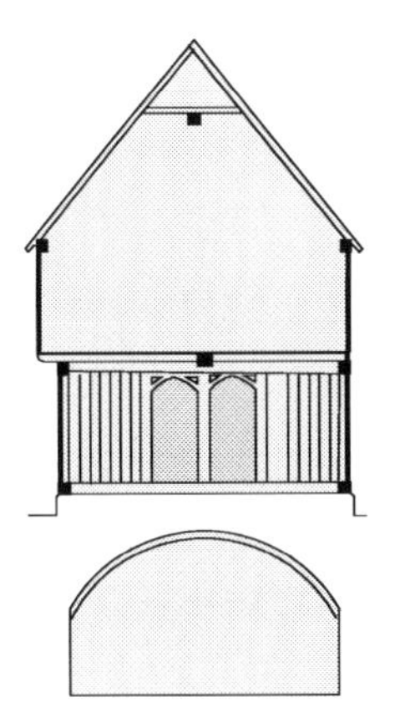

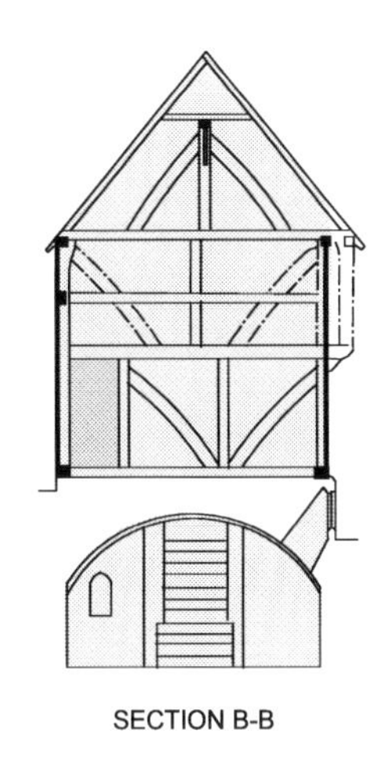

Fig. 13.31
Phase 1 reconstruction of 58, 60 Church Square (chimney assumed to be phase 2, therefore not shown)

Fig. 13.32
Hall roof, 58, 60 Church Square

Fig. 13.33
Hall fireplace, 58, 60 Church Square

Fig. 13.34
Service doorways, 58, 60 Church Square

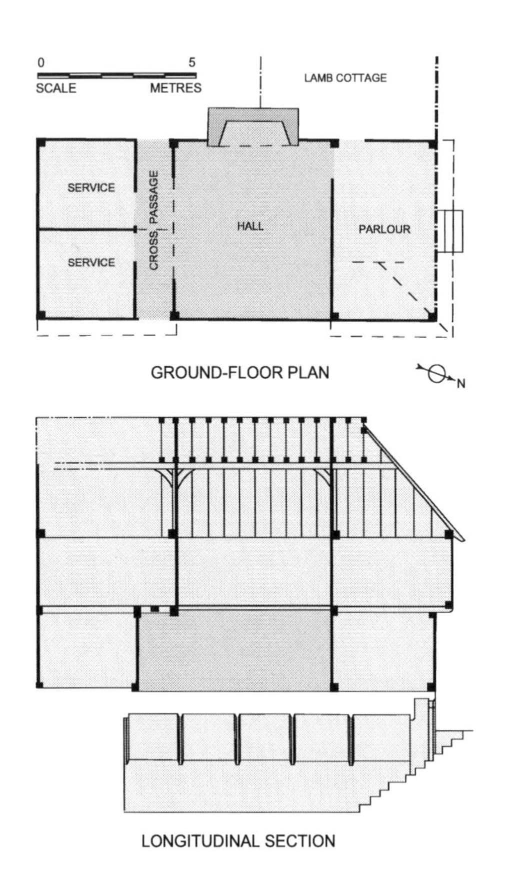

Fig. 13.35
Phase 2 reconstructions of 58, 60 Church Square after insertion of hall floor and chimney

Fig. 13.37
58, 60 Church Square [89]. Detail of doorway to cellar, leading through back of chimney

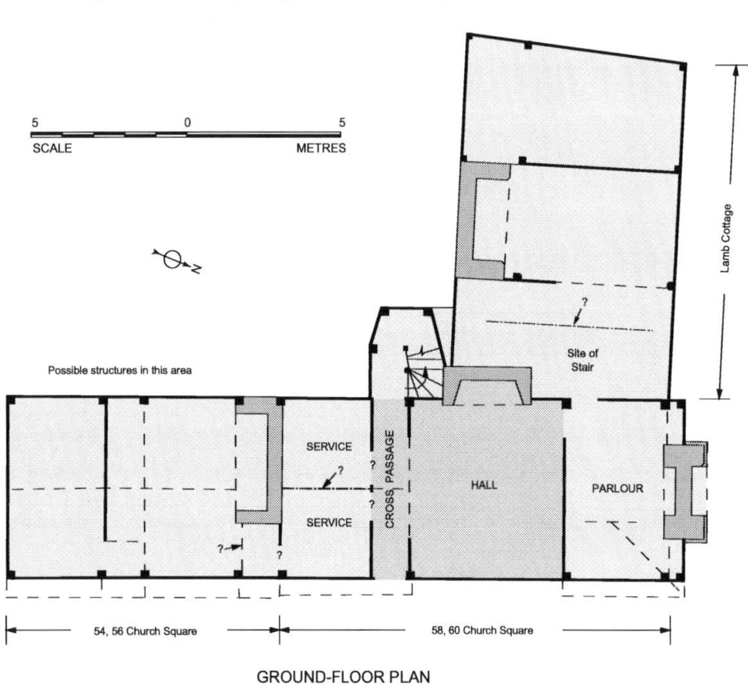

Fig. 13.36
54, 56, 58, 60 Church Square [88, 89] and Lamb Cottage, West Street [53]. Reconstructed plan of complex in the time of Thomas Greenfield.

Fig. 13.38
60 Church Square showing late 16th-century chimney with entrance to cellar.
The roof was originally hipped.

Church Square and West Street, and once formed part of first Shurley's and then the Wymond family's estates within the town.

Phases 1 and 2 (c.1500). As first built this was a house of textbook three-cell plan with a recessed 'Wealden' type front. Elevated over a probably contemporary vaulted cellar (for which *see* Chapter 6) the front jetty beyond the high end of the hall was returned around the end of the house. As indicated by Figure 13.32, there is little or no soot on the timbers and partitions within the roof of the hall, suggesting that it was either built with a fireplace from the outset, or (more likely) had one added very soon afterwards, perhaps before the hall was floored over. Given that this house was one of those owned by John Shurley, this could be the 'chymney with lyme, sande and breke' which he instructed to be built 'in the house that John Pende dwelleth in' in 1504.[6] The fireplace, shown in Figure 13.33, has a stone surround with four-centred arched head and pyramidal sunk spandrels very similar in detail to the heads of the service doorways illustrated in Figure 13.34. Regardless as to whether the chimney is original or was added soon afterwards, if the fireplace heated an open hall this is a very unusual combination locally, as too is the fact that the entire house is elevated slightly above the street, upon the barrel-vaulted cellar. The cellar and house were not interconnected, and thus both could, if required, be let separately.

Phase 3 (c.1565). Alterations were made to the main part of the building, most noticeably the addition of a stair turret to the rear of the medieval cross passage and the upgrading of the parlour by the addition of panelling and the construction of a chimney of novel design, incorporating within it a flight of steps descending from the street into the vaulted cellar (Figures 13.37 and 13.38). The fireplace which heats the parlour has a typical 'Rye-style' stone surround with shouldered arch and enriched frieze.

Phase 4 (Late 16th and 17th C). Once called 'Grene Hall' the seven-flue assessment for this house in 1663 is interesting in that it indicates that the mansion (if that is what it can be termed) was by that time an amalgamation of three earlier houses — the late 14th-century single-aisled Lamb Cottage [53], Grene Hall itself, (this property) and 54, 56 Church Square [88] immediately to its south. Six flues are accounted for within the complex: two within 54, 56 Church Square [88]; three within 58, 60 Church Square [89]; one within Lamb Cottage [53] (Figure 13.36). The location of the seventh flue listed in 1662 is not known — perhaps it was within a detached building, or perhaps it served a since demolished range at the rear of 54, 56 Church Square, within the rear wall of which is evidence of a first-floor doorway (*see* [88]). Bearing in mind the slump in population which occurred within the town in the early 17th century, it is tempting to suggest that the amalgamation of these three properties into one was in response to this. However, tradition has it that this is where Elizabeth I was entertained by its then owner, Henry Gaymer, jurat (and at that time Mayor of the town) when she visited in 1573.[7] If this is correct, surely this was already a house of considerable status by that date, a point which supports the notion that the amalgamation may have occurred relatively early. *[ESRO HBR/1/0359]*

90. 1-2 Watchbell Street —
1490 +/-25; 1510 +/125; 1540 +/-25
(Figures 13.39)

Phase 1 (c.1490). A 'model' example of 'textbook' two-cell type, not least because there can be absolutely no doubt that it always lacked accommodation beyond the high end of its hall — the area beyond the hall is occupied by the large continuously-jettied house known as St Anthony's [87]. In common with half Rye's surviving hall houses, 1-2 Watchbell Street was built with a recessed 'Wealden' front. Despite incorporating only two cells, the house is of good size, measuring 9.90 metres (32'5") in length and having a roof span of 6.10 metres (20'1") to the front of its jetty. Beyond the western end wall was open ground (in separate ownership until 1519) explaining why the western roof terminal is hipped.[8] As Figure 13.39 shows, the house has an open hall of wholly traditional type, entered at the low end by an overshot cross passage partially screened from the main body of the room by draught speres. The service bay is slightly longer than in the majority of examples and it is at present impossible to tell whether it was divided on the ground floor into the usual two service rooms, though the likelihood is that it was. The large first-floor area over the services and cross passage is unusual in that it was divided from the outset into two chambers by an axial partition which rose up through the roof to collar-purlin level. The chamber at the front was initially open to the roof, but that at the rear appears always to have had a ceiling, presumably allowing the rear half of the

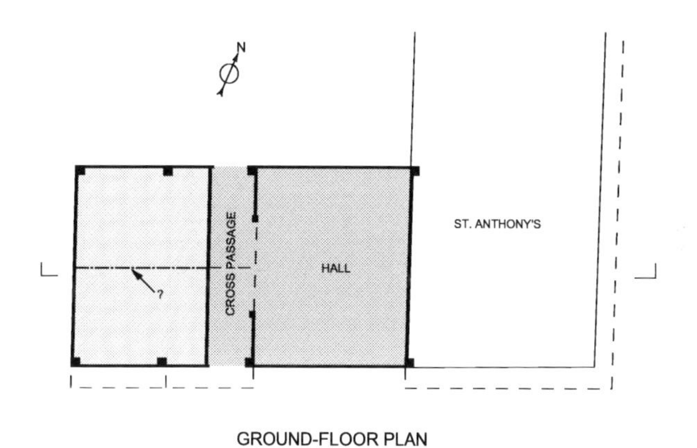

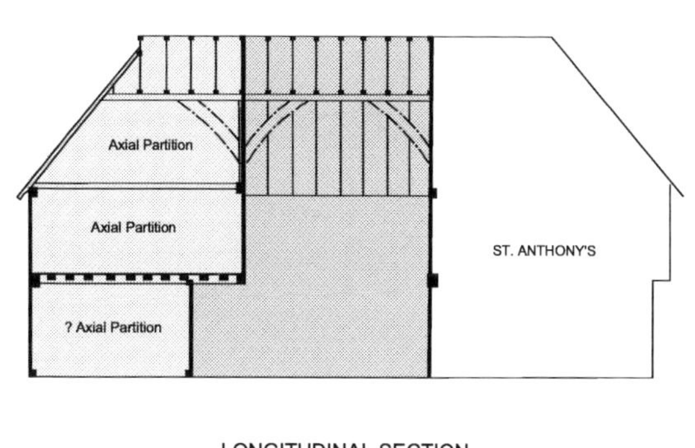

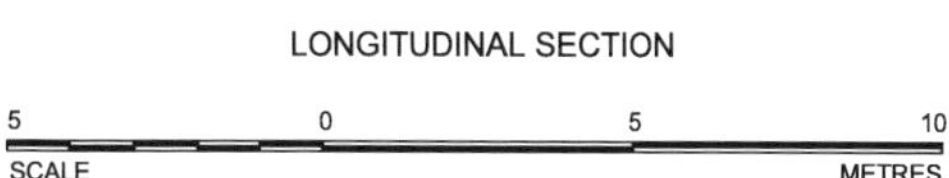

Fig. 13.39
Phase 1 reconstruction of 1-2 Watchbell Street.

roof to be used as storage space.[9]

Phase 2 (c.1510). Very quickly a floor with moulded central girder supporting 160 mm wide stop-chamfered joists was inserted into the hall. The girder is deliberately off-centred towards the rear and there are no stops at the rear end of the joists, features which suggest that they extended into an aisle-like rear lean-to outshut added behind the hall at the same date so as to increase the width of the hall. There are no indications at this date of a heating system serving the hall.

Phase 3 (c.1540). When the present two-flue chimney was added to heat the hall it was built within what is assumed to be the phase-2 outshut. The stack is constructed using small, light pink/buff 'Flemish' brick. *[ESRO HBR/1/0682]*

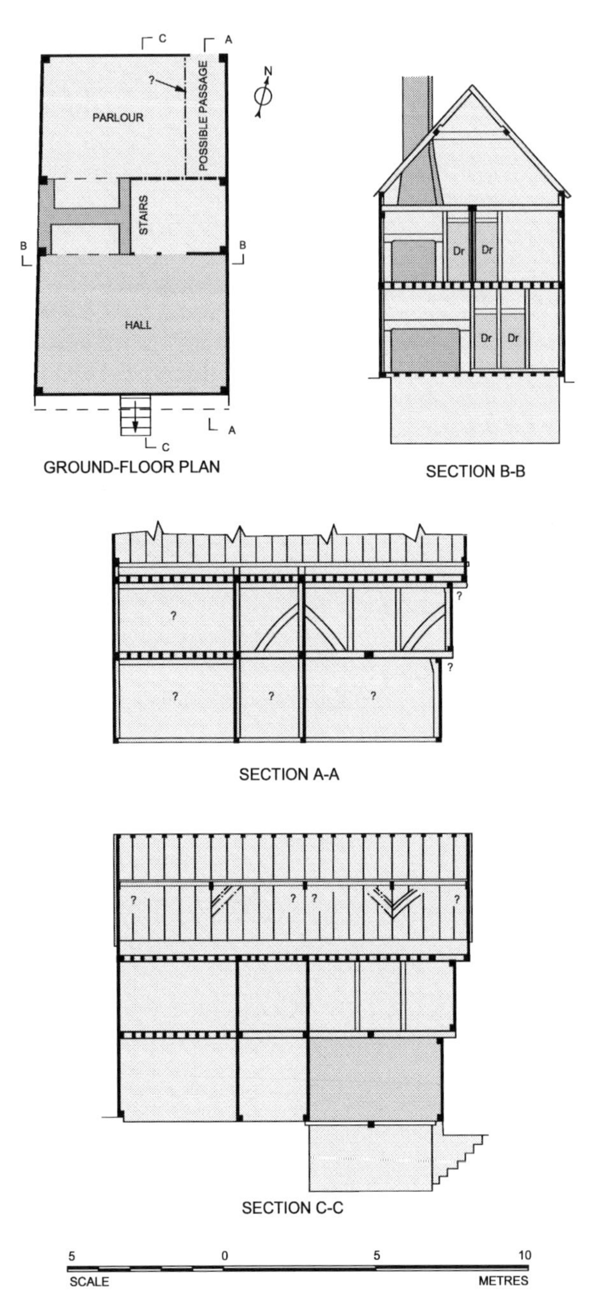

Fig. 13.40
Reconstruction of 4 Watchbell Street.

91. 4 Watchbell Street — *1556x1560*
(Figure 13.40)

This plot, immediately to the west of Nos. 1-2 Watchbell Street [90], was in use as a garden in 1500 when it was acquired by the King's bailiff, John Shurley. Shurley, who lived part time in a mansion to the northwest of the Church (7-9 West Street/62 Church Square [51]), was a speculator who held considerable property within the town, including Grene Hall (present day 58, 60 Church Square [89]) to the north of St Anthony's. It is presumed that he purchased the garden with a view to building upon it. Certainly it was large enough for that purpose: it had a street frontage of 37 feet (11.30 metres) and stretched back 47 feet (14.30 metres) from the street. If that was his intention he never got around to doing so, for nineteen years later he sold it (still described as a garden plot) to John Jarvis, the owner of St Anthony's. And so the land was laid into St Anthony's and remained part of that property until 1556, when Francis Terry, the then owner of St Anthony's, sold the westernmost part, with a street frontage of 20 feet (6.10 metres) to Robert Melidad of Rye, fisherman.

Within four years there was a house upon the plot, occupied by Nicholas Knaplock.[10] The house which Malidad built occupies the entire 6.15 metres (20'0") street frontage and extends 11.00 metres (36'2") down the 14.30 metre (47 foot) plot. The restricted street frontage meant that the two-cell layout required a three-bay frame constructed at right-angles to the street. Both rooms — hall at the front and parlour at the rear — are heated by a central four-flue brick-built chimney located hard against the western wall, leaving room to the east for a staircase and circulation space leading through to the parlour. The location of a rear doorway at the extreme eastern end of the rear wall suggests that a through passage may, as now, have been divided off down the eastern side of the parlour in order to allow the back yard to be accessed without passing through the parlour. As Figure 13.40 indicates, both hall and parlour were lit by windows in the front and rear walls.

Beneath the hall at the front of the house is a spacious cellar independently accessed from the street by a flight of centrally-placed steps. Above this the street facade was jettied at both first-floor and attic-floor levels, with an overhanging gable above. In essence the ground-floor layout was repeated on the first floor, though at this upper level the front bay was sub-divided by an axial partition located beneath the central girder. The two chambers thus formed were independently accessed from the staircase landing within the central bay. The staircase continued up to attic level, where the walls rise above the floor in order to increase usable floor space — in this instance the top of the wallplate is elevated 450 mm (1'6") above the floor. Thus, this house can be described as being of two-and-a-half storeys in height. The attic was a single large space extending the length of the house. As at 110 High Street [31], the frame relies upon the crossbeams which support the attic floor to prevent spreading, there being a complete lack of intermediate tiebeams.

Being firmly dated to within four years (1556x1560) 4 Watchbell Street is extremely useful in 'confirming' the typological dates given to other houses within the town. This is particularly important given that the construction sequences established within some buildings suggest dates earlier than would normally be given for similar buildings located in a rural or village context. Indeed, had the construction date for this house not been known it seems likely that a date in the final two decades of the 16th century would have been hypothosised. True, the wall infill is of footbraced large-panel design (rather than incorporating midrails) and the clasped-side-purlin roof is windbraced, but (because of the low walls of the attic rooms) the internal trusses lack jowls to their principal posts, a feature which gives the construction a late appearance. Furthermore, all ceilings were designed to be flush underplastered: they are supported by narrow, deep, joists of equal depth to the crossbeams and girders. The storey heights too are generous — 2.55 metres (8'4") measured from floor to ceiling on the ground floor and a more modest 2.15 metres (7'11") on the first floor, though lofty storey heights are a feature found in a number of Rye houses even during the first half of the 16th century. *[ESRO HBR/1/0957]*

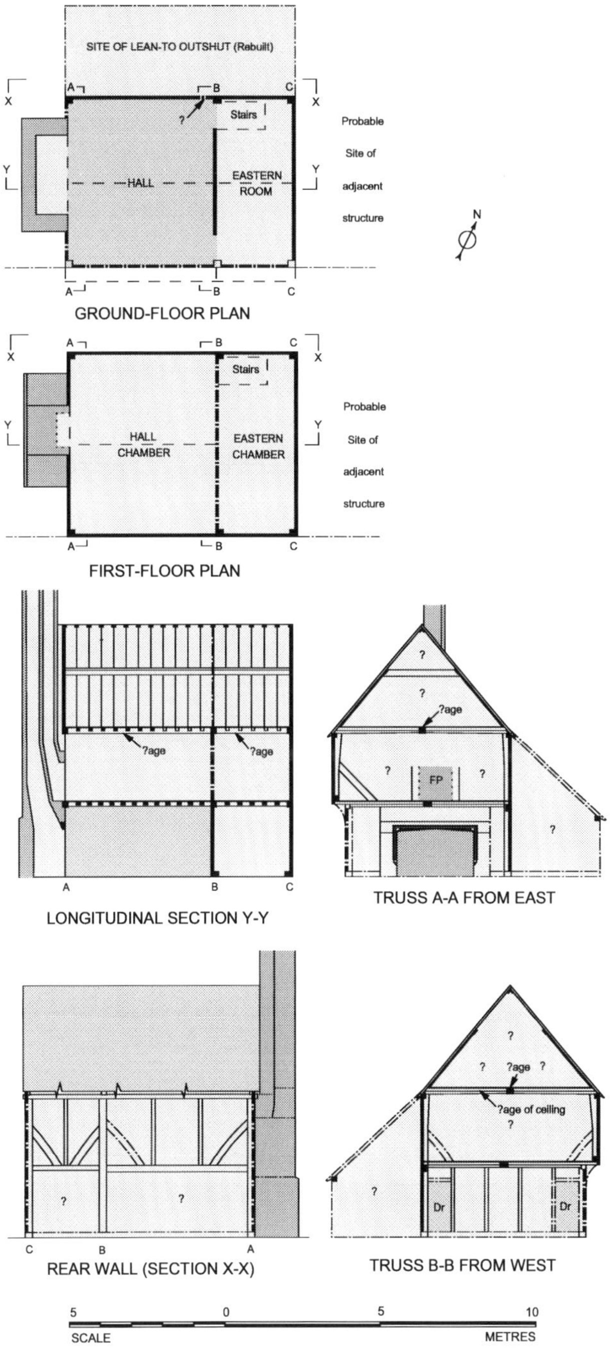

Fig. 13.41
Reconstruction of 9 Watchbell Street.

92. 9 Watchbell Street — *1550 +/-25*
(Figures 13.41 - 13.43)

A house of two unequal bays with a room in each bay on both the ground and first floors, creating spaces of markedly different sizes. The evidence as to the age of the ceilings within these chambers is inconclusive, but favours them having been inserted later. It is therefore likely that both chambers were initially open to the roof. The principal ground-floor room, the hall, is heated by an externally-built end chimney (in this instance probably enclosed within some form of perhaps very low attached structure). A significant feature of this house is its contemporary rear lean-to outshut (now

Fig. 13.42
Hall fireplace, 9 Watchbell Street.

Fig. 13.43
Hall fireplace, 9 Watchbell Street.
Detail of lefthand spandrel.

largely rebuilt) which probably housed a ground-floor service room (or rooms).

Despite its small size, the house is of good quality with a lofty 2.35 metres (7'8") ground-floor storey height and an exceptionally good fireplace serving the hall. The fireplace incorporates moulded stone jambs and a fully moulded and carved timber lintel. Stops on the jambs are enriched with carved geometric patterns, whilst the spandrels on the lintel are enriched with carved decoration which incorporates both foliage and geometric designs (Figures 13.42 and 13.43). *[ESRO HBR/1/1574]*

93. 10 Watchbell Street — *Late 16th C*
(Not Illustrated)

A two-and-a-half storey building of standard width, and very similar in design to 42 Church Square [84], 11 Market Street [41] and 4 Watchbell Street [91]. *[Not surveyed]*

94. 11-13 Watchbell Street — *1550 +/-25*
(Figure 13.44)

A three-bay structure with a two-bay rear range projecting from the centre of the main range. It had a relatively shallow pitched, fully windbraced roof with collar trusses. The roof trusses in the street range did not coincide with the bay divisions of the main frame. The street facade was continuously jettied and this elevation was apparently close studded and incorporated a large central window flanked by high-level clerestory lights. In contrast, the walls elsewhere are of footbraced large-panel framing and, although designed to be glazed, the windows lighting the central rear range were of standard design.

Observations made during building works indicate that there were no doorways linking the eastern bay to the central room and chamber. Thus, unless the eastern bay was accessed from the building's central rear range via a now lost rear outshut, the eastern and central bays of this building were presumably in different occupancies at ground- and first-floor levels. Even so, there was not a partition at this point at roof level and thus one or other of the two (assumed) tenancies appears to have had access to the entire roof garret.

Is there any way of evaluating how likely it is there was once an inter-connecting rear outshut? Unfortunately the eastern bay of the building was entirely rebuilt in the 19th century and thus there is now no way of checking the design of its rear wall. A glance at Figure 13.44 suggests such an outshut would have been very unlikely because of the location of the chimney and the position of the windows in the side wall of the central rear range. However, here too there is a problem in that the chimney either represents a later insertion or was not allowed for when the frame was fabricated: the design of the frame had to be modified in order to accommodate it. If the present four-flue chimney was not initially present a doorway linking to a rear outshut of similar design to that on the western side of the rear range is entirely possible. *[ESRO HBR/1/0787]*

95. Hope Anchor/16-17 Watchbell Street —
Medieval; 15th C
(Figures 13.45 - 13.47)

Phase 1 (Medieval). Plain barrel-vaulted cellar under 16 Watchbell Street (*see* Chapter 6, including Figures 6.3, 6.4, 6.9).

Phase 2 (15th C). A fragmentary three-cell hall house occupying a corner plot with its high-end (Hope Anchor)

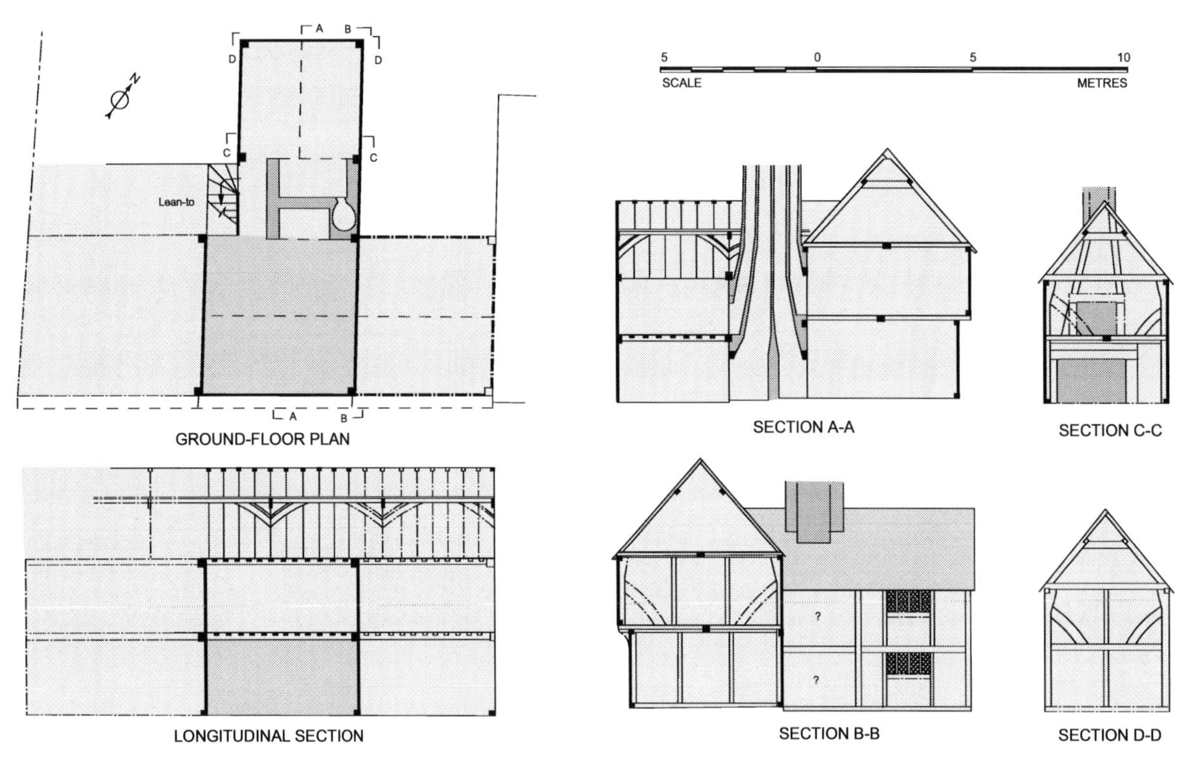

Fig. 13.44
Reconstruction of 11-13 Watchbell Street.

within the western end bay, which returned around the corner as an integrated crosswing. The best preserved part is the wall between the hall and the high-end bay, which retains its moulded dais beam (*see* Figure 6.27). It should be borne in mind that, as at St Anthony's [87]/1-2 Watchbell Street [90] at the opposite end of the street, this corner building may always have incorporated two dwellings, in which case the part which survives (16-17 Watchbell Street) would equate to 1-2 Watchbell Street [90], being a two-cell house with hall and services. *[ESRO HBR/1/0851]*

96. 19 Watchbell Street — *1475 +/-25; 1530 +/-25 (Figures 13.48 & 13.49)*

Phase 1 (1475). The smallest of Rye's three-cell 'textbook' hall houses: its very cramped street frontage meant

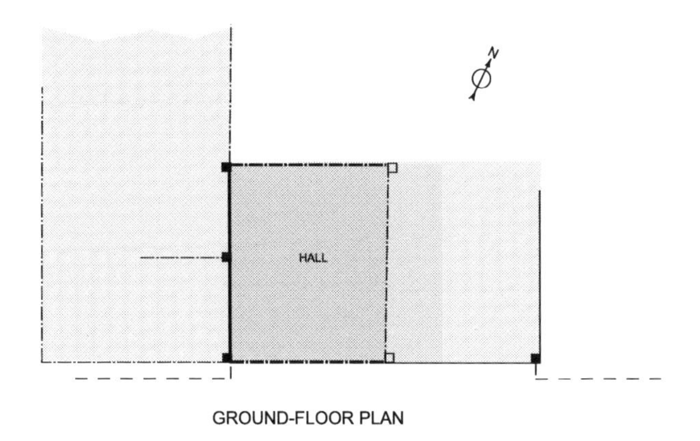

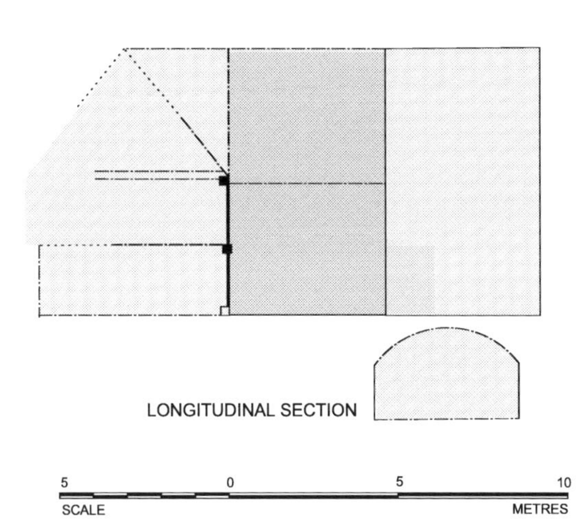

Fig. 13.45
Phase 2 reconstruction of 16-17 Watchbell Street.

Fig. 13.47
Hope Anchor/16-17 Watchbell Street. Phase 2 dais beam.

Fig. 13.46
Hope Anchor/16-17 Watchbell Street.
Upper part of dais partition viewed from hall.
The notch in the plate above the post is the dovetail for the tiebeam of the rebuilt crosswing/return range.

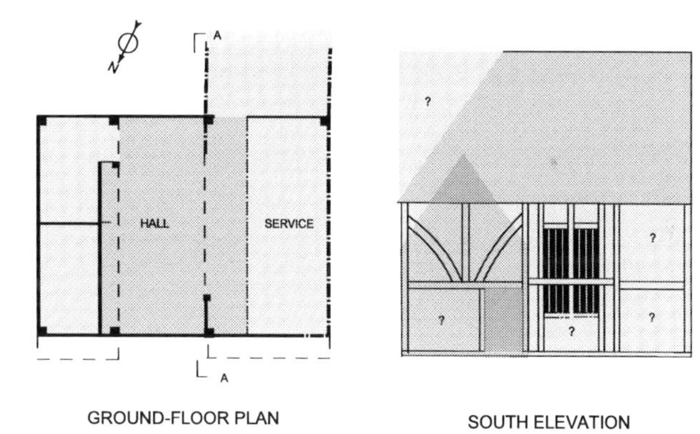

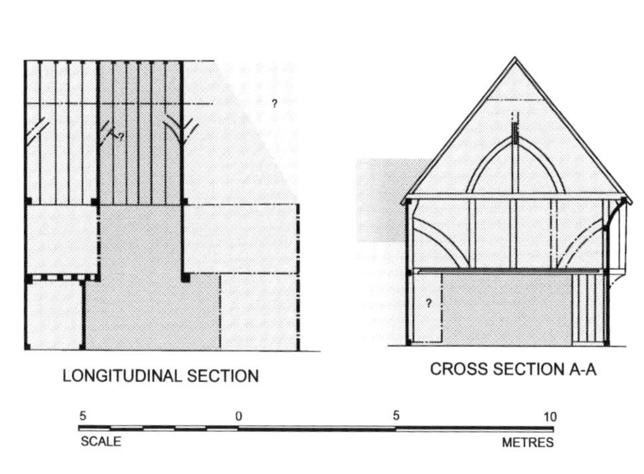

Fig. 13.48
Phase 1 reconstruction of 19 Watchbell Street.

major concessions were necessary to achieve a three-cell plan (Figure 13.48). Later partial rebuilding means that it is not known whether the service area was divided into two rooms or whether it was a single undivided space. However, sufficient survives to indicate that entry was by means of an overshot cross passage, partially shielded from the hall by a panelled draught spere located adjacent to the front door (and perhaps another adjacent to the rear doorway). Because of the confined nature of the site the open bay of the hall measures only 2.50 metres (8'2") long — insufficient to give a practical, usable floor area. To overcome this, the ground-floor section of the high-end 'dais partition' encroached by 540 mm (1'9") into the parlour bay, with the dais bench recessed back from the wall above, giving it a canopied effect. Usually described as an 'internal jetty' such a feature is relatively common in some parts of England (for example, in Surrey) though only occasional examples are found in the High Weald of Kent and East Sussex, where they occur in both urban and rural contexts. When used in rural houses there can be little doubt that it was adopted for aesthetic reasons, but at in this instance it was a practical solution to the problem of space.

The adoption of an 'internal jetty' in this instance had interesting repercussions, for although it gave both the hall and the high-end first-floor chamber larger floor areas than would otherwise be possible, the ground-floor high-end room was decreased in size to a narrow strip measuring 6.15 metres (20'2") long by 1.65 metres (5'6") wide internally: this area was divided by a partition and had to include the staircase giving access to the high-end first-floor chamber.[11] Such a small space was surely unusable as a private withdrawing chamber/bedchamber, but the use to which it was put remains a matter of speculation. The contracted street frontage of the plot should not be seen as an indicator of low status: the builder of the house had sufficient available funds to incorporate a recessed 'Wealden' front within the street facade. Furthermore, the available floor space within the house was increased by the inclusion of a contemporary rear range (since rebuilt) behind the service bay. It was a relatively narrow (3.20 metre - 10'6") range and, because of the adjacent cliff, could not have extended very far down the plot: nevertheless, it would have given useful additional space. The range was sited in the traditional location for an attached kitchen, but in an urban context such a use cannot automatically be assumed.

Phase 2 (c.1530). A back-to-back axial chimney with four flues was incorporated when this tiny 'Wealden' hall house was divided into two dwellings (Figure 13.49). This is a rare instance where the subdivision of a house into tenements can be recognized and dated, though subdivision of this type must have been relatively common within the town during the first half of the 16th century. The recessed front was converted to continuously-jettied type as part of the alterations and the new section of front wall incorporates a good window with arched heads. *[ESRO HBR/1/0809]*

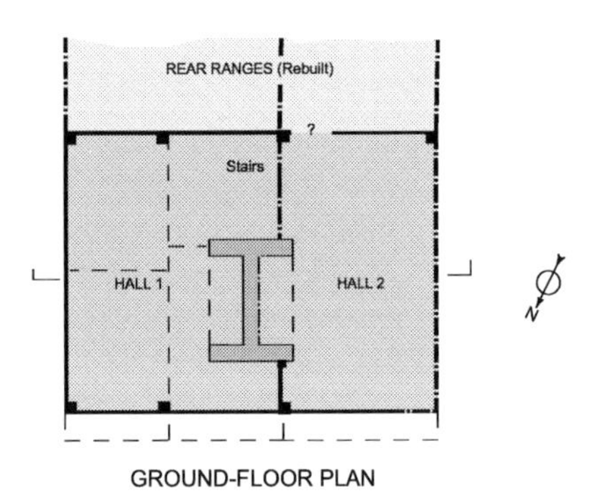

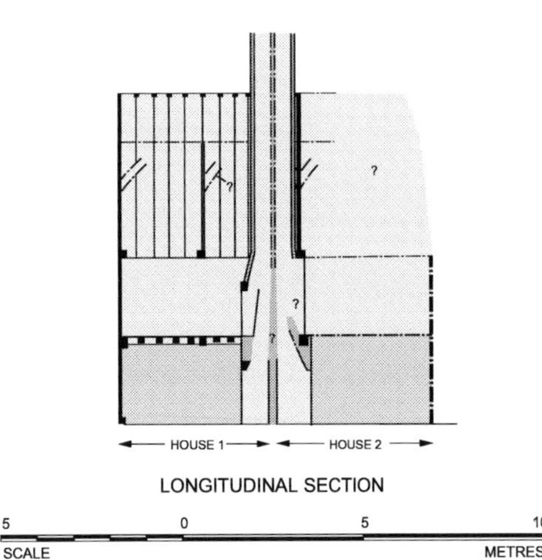

Fig. 13.49
Reconstruction of 19 Watchbell Street following insertion of floor and chimney (phase 2) in order to convert the building into two dwellings.

97. 20 Watchbell Street — *? 15th or 16th C*
(Not Illustrated)

All that survives upon this site is an un-vaulted stone-walled cellar of probably 15th- or 16th-century date. *[ESRO HBR/1/0827]*

98. 20A, 21 Watchbell Street — *1550 +/-25*
(Figure 13.50)

A mid 16th-century, three-bay, continuously jettied building with an 11.15 metre (36'7") street frontage. In addition to the main range there are rear wings and, although today these are effectively of late 18th- or 19th-century date, they incorporate sufficient earlier work to show that they replace two earlier ranges of which at least one (and probably both) were original to the build.[12] If so, this house was built to a double-pile plan with a full compliment of rooms behind the street range on both floors The eaves of these rear wings were much lower (about one metre — 3'3") than those of the street range, though this in itself is hardly surprising given the lofty storey heights of the latter — 2.75 metres (8'11") on the ground floor and 2.30 metres (7'7") on the first floor.

The builder of 20A, 21 Watchbell Street seems to have had very clear views with regards the use and size of the rooms he required within his new house. Furthermore, these requirements were different on the ground and first floors. In consequence, the two ground-floor partitions do not align with those on the first floor, the latter of which are located about 450 mm (1'6") further west than the former. To achieve this it was necessary to make modifications to the traditional design of the frame and this is particularly noticeable within the rear wall. As Figure 13.50 illustrates, both ground-floor partitions

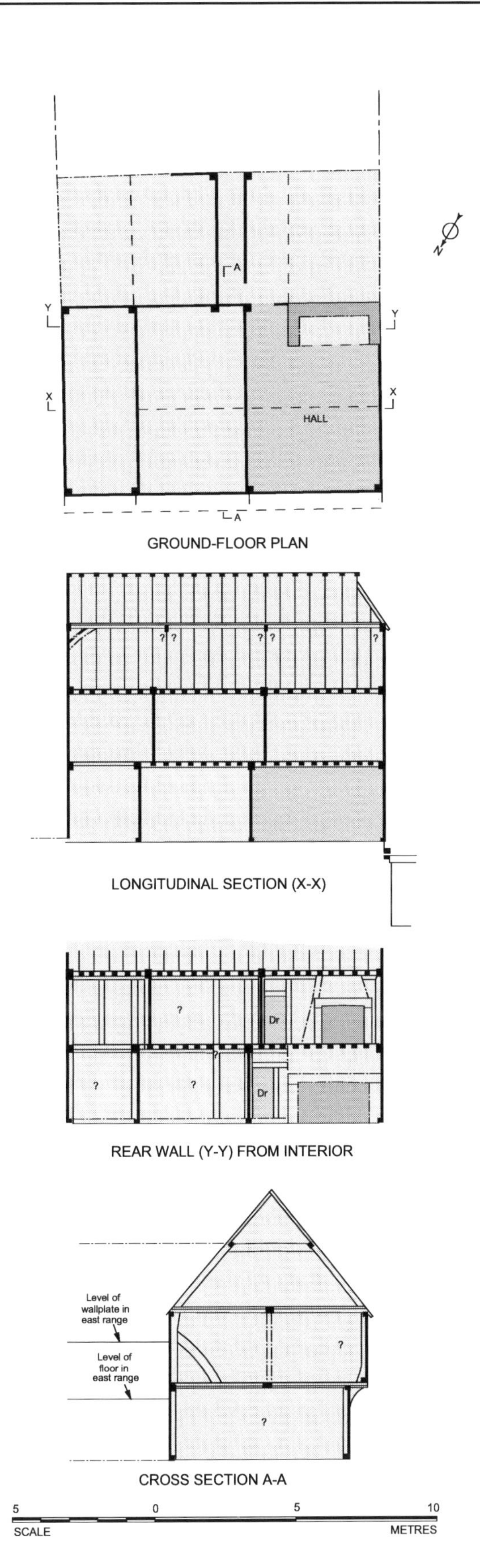

Fig. 13.50
Reconstruction of 20A, 21 Watchbell Street

are positioned beneath crossbeams, these in turn being jointed into jowl-less full-height posts incorporated into the rear wall. The offset first-floor partitions are supported by floor joists and are jointed at the head into tiebeams which are located 450 mm (1'6") to one side of the jowl-less main posts within the rear wall. Despite this, the carpenter incorporated jowled posts beneath the tiebeam: these do not extend down to ground but are instead supported upon the side girts which carry the ends of the first-floor joists. This is a feature only rarely encountered at this period. Locally, outside Rye, examples have been recorded at 25-27 High Street Robertsbridge, Sussex and Smallhythe Place, Kent (both built during the early 16th century) and at Ponts Farm and Westdown (both in Burwash, East Sussex, and both mid 16th century).[13] In Rye itself examples exist in The Mint at Nos. 39-40 [14] and at 29 Watchbell Street [101].

The offset partitions do not cause the same problem within the front wall because here the posts do not rise through both storeys, being naturally 'broken' by the continuous front jetty. For additional strength, the first-floor posts within this wall incorporate jowls at the feet rather than the head, thereby helping to transfer the load back to the inset ground-floor wall — a nice detail!

From what survives, it is now impossible to guess the uses to which the owner put the two eastern ground-floor rooms, the eastern one of which was surprisingly narrow for the period. Usually the central room would have been the hall, but not in this instance. Here the hall was in the larger western room and was heated by a chimney built against the rear wall. The reason for off-setting the first-floor partitions seems clear — it was to provide a larger, more usable eastern chamber. The windbraced clasped-side-purlin roof is framed in near equal bays and as a result the eastern of the two internal collar trusses is not located above a tiebeam. The eastern terminal is gabled, but the western end has a steeply-pitched half hip elevated above the formerly much lower roof of adjacent 20 Watchbell Street [97].[14] As in so many of Rye's houses at this period, the entire roof area formed a single space, probably for storage. *[ESRO HBR/1/0812]*

Fig. 13.51
26 Watchbell Street, viewed from west prior to demolition

99. 26 Watchbell Street — *Date unknown*
(Figure 13.51)

Now demolished, but known from a drawing and from an early photograph. The building is significant for the lowness of its eaves, which could indicate a relatively early date.

100. 27-28 Watchbell Street — *Date unknown*
(Not Illustrated)

Not viewed internally, but reputed to incorporate an early fireplace and some substantial ceiling beams, despite its present late-looking external appearance.

101. 29 Watchbell Street — *1550 +/-25; 1600 +/-25*
(Figure 13.52)

Phase 1 (c.1550). A house with two cells aligned parallel to the street, with the first-floor chambers open to the roof. Although now incorporated into a continuously built-up section of street frontage, when erected it occupied a corner-plot with Watchbell Street passing along its continuously-jettied northern facade and a short lane passing its eastern end wall, extending back to the cliff edge. As a mark of quality, both these elevations were infilled with close studding. Projecting from the eastern end wall was a chimney, almost certainly of timber-framed construction, but since rebuilt in brick. As Figure 13.52 shows, the ground-floor plan is classic, being divided into two unequal rooms with the large eastern room — the hall — heated by the end chimney.

Atypically, the first-floor joisting which forms the ceiling of these two rooms is not framed in two bays but as a single exceptionally long bay. The components forming the ceiling over the eastern room are chamfered, but those over the western room are unchamfered, reflecting its lesser status. The reason for this unusual floor-framing arrangement was the owners requirement of two unequal-sized rooms on the ground floor, but two equal-sized chambers at first-floor level. Thus, the first-floor partition is not located over that on the ground floor. This is a feature only rarely encountered at this period. For other examples *see* [98] above.

Phase 2 (c.1600). A rear range was added extending along the eastern lane, but little of this now remains. *[ESRO HBR/1/0893]*

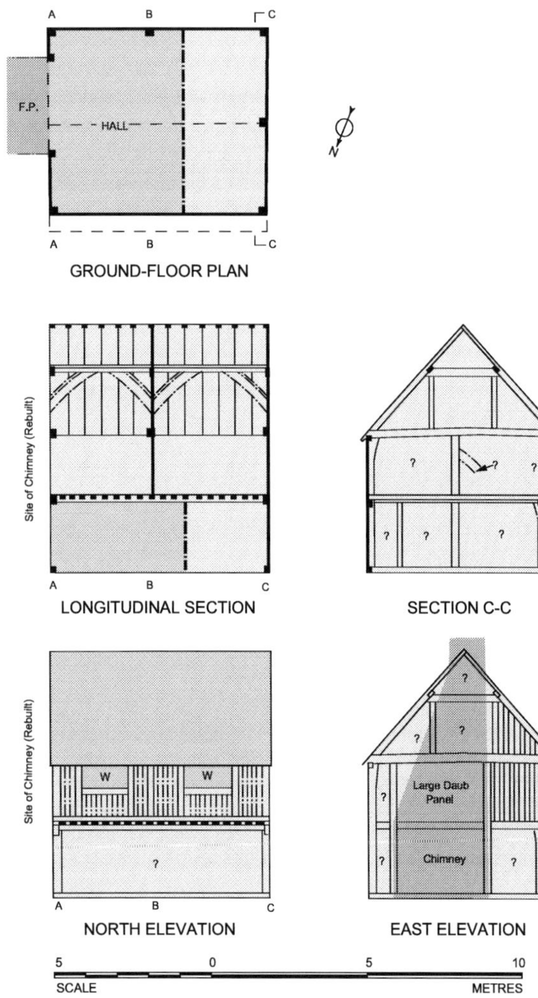

Fig. 13.52
Phase 1 reconstruction of 29 Watchbell Street.

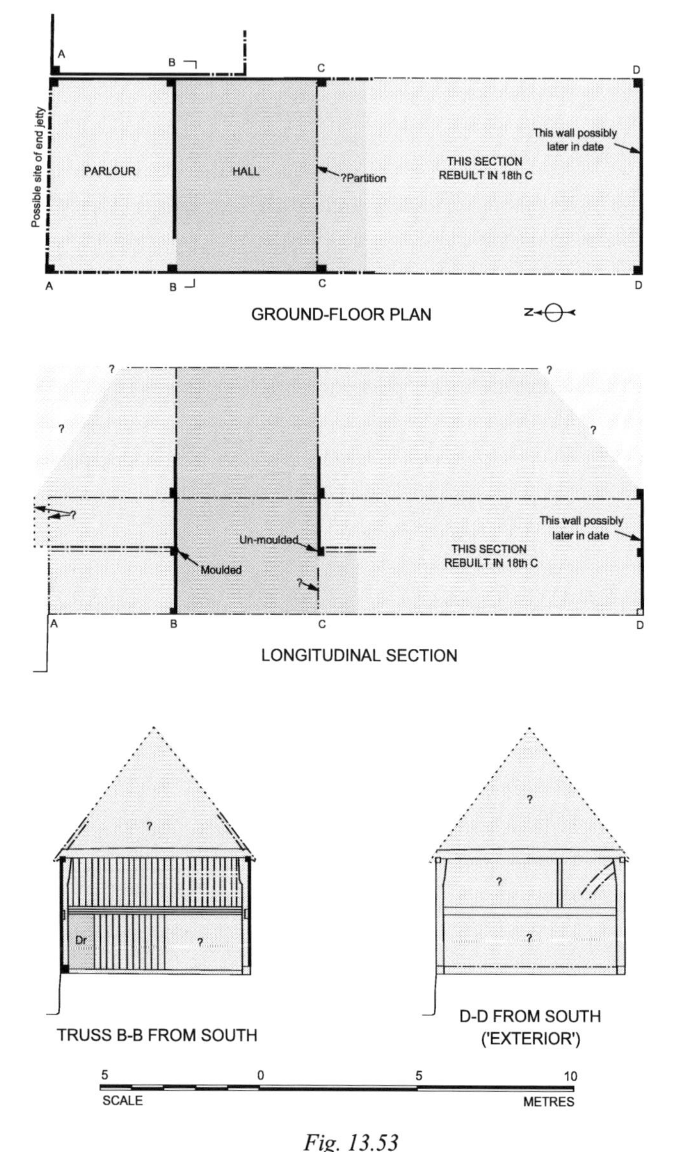

Fig. 13.53
Phase 1 reconstruction of Oak Corner and Oak House.

102. Oak Corner, Trader Passage — *1485 +/-25; 1510 +/-25; 1600 +/-25*
(Figures 13.53 - 13.55)

Phase 1 (c.1485). A two-bay house occupying a corner plot, with a single-bay open hall fronting Trader Passage and a high-end bay (now all but rebuilt) adjacent to Mermaid Street. At the low end of the hall, where the services should be, is a separate taller and much later house of similar length. Oak Corner clearly once extended onto the site of this taller house,

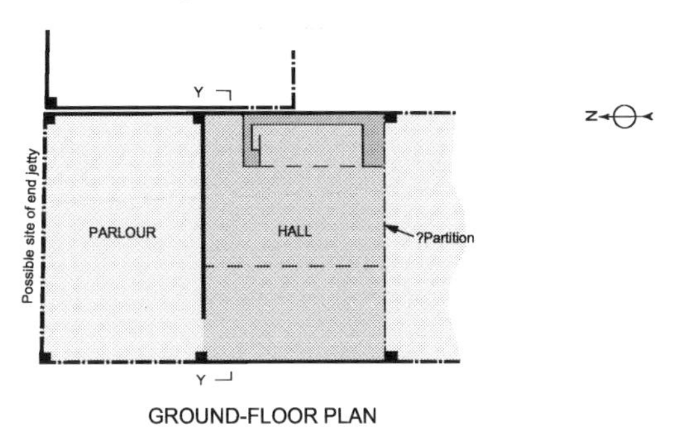

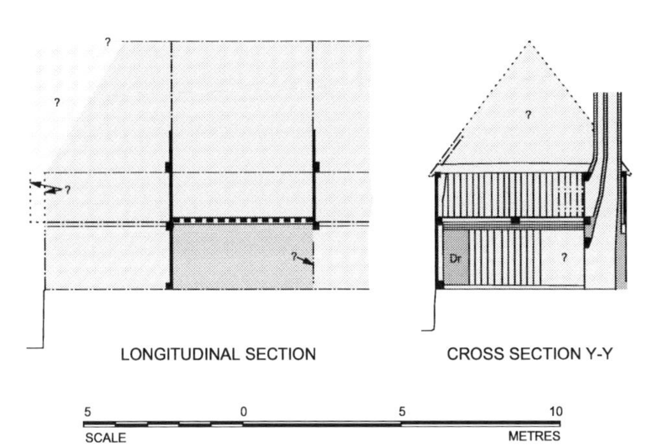

Fig. 13.54
Phase 2 reconstruction of Oak Corner, Trader Passage showing inserted floor and chimney.

Fig. 13.55
Oak Corner, Trader Passage. The hall showing moulded central girder and medieval-style joists added into hall (phase 2) with inserted fireplace built against the rear wall.

for not only is the infill to the end wall of its hall set flush towards the hall, but in addition there are joist mortices in the reverse face of the crossbeam. It would be logical to suggest that the service bay of Oak Corner was at some time demolished to make way for the longer, taller adjacent house, which was built extending southwards onto previously undeveloped land. But there is a problem: trapped within the far end wall of the taller house is the truss of a building the same width and height as Oak Corner (Figure 13.53). Insufficient of this truss is visible for it to be dated accurately, but it could be the same date. If so, Oak Corner was originally a very long structure and could have been built as a semi-detached pair of un-handed two-cell hall-houses without services. Alternatively, it could have been a long, substantial, four-cell dwelling consisting of a high-end bay, open hall, and service bay with an attached kitchen beyond. As has already been demonstrated, such an arrangement is known to exist in Rye, at St Anthony's [87]/ 1-2 Watchbell Street [90], so a house of this type is certainly possible. There is yet another option — a standard three-cell house which was later lengthened in order that the enlarged building could be converted into two equal-length dwellings, the southern of which was subsequently rebuilt taller. Any one of these scenarios is possible.

Phase 2 (c.1510). The medieval-scantling joists used within the floor inserted into the hall indicate the early date at which the phase-1 house was converted to fully-floored type (Figures 13.54 and 13.55). Because of lack of space, the two-flue chimney is built against the hall's rear wall: it has foliage carving on the spandrels of the hall's fireplace lintel.

Phase 3 (c.1600). The only recognizable work of this period relates to the front wall of the hall chamber, which was rebuilt taller incorporating a large central window flanked by clerestory lights. Given the eaves were raised, the likelihood is that the central window projected and was capped by an overhanging front gable. *[ESRO HBR/1/0680]*

103. Old Trader/Trader Cottage — *1425 +/-50; 1525 +/-25*
(Figures 13.56 - 13.58)

Phase 1 (c.1425). A single-aisled three-cell hall house of which the aisle has been destroyed. It has an exceptionally

Fig. 13.56
Old Trader/Trader Cottage. Crownpost and partition within truss B-B

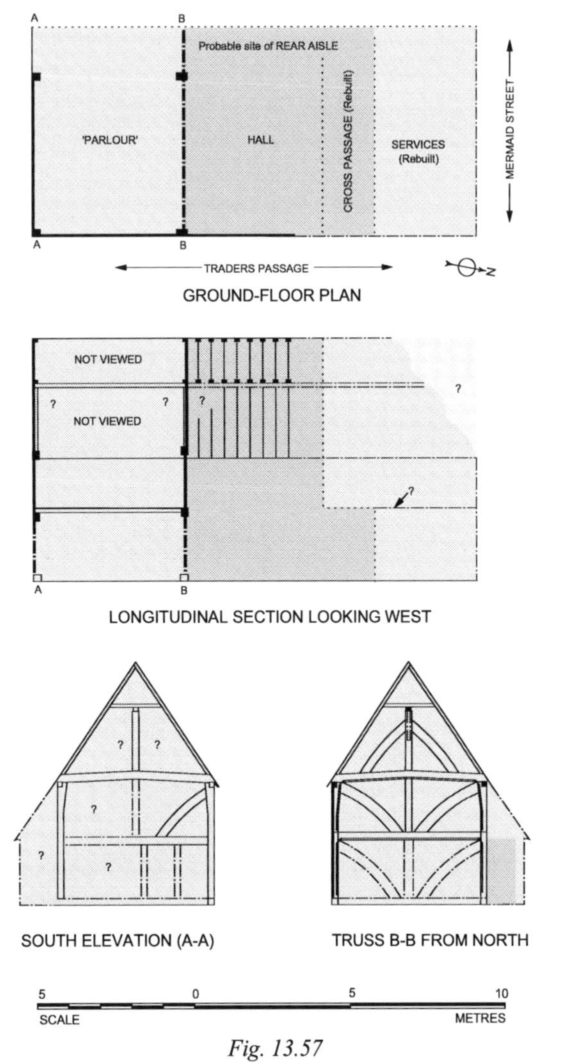

Fig. 13.57
Phase 1 reconstruction of Old Trader/Trader Cottage

Fig. 13.58
Old Trader/Trader Cottage. Detail of rose-and-foliage carving on fireplace lintel

long floored-over high-end bay, but seems otherwise to have been similar to the other 'textbook' examples, with a single-bay hall served by an overshot cross passage with services beyond (services now rebuilt). The front wall shows large-panel framing with long footbracing.

Phase 2 (c.1525). Insertion of a first floor and chimney into the hall, the later apparently sited backing onto a cross passage (passage now destroyed). The central-girder floor is neatly formed using 110 mm wide stop chamfered joists, whilst the hall fireplace is of equal high quality, having dressed stone jambs and a moulded timber lintel, the spandrels of which are elaborated with rose-and-foliage carving (Figure 13.58).

When the house was leased out for 60 years by the Churchwardens of Rye in 1543 it had already been divided into three tenements. The new tenant, Adrian Arnold, tailor, was to spend £10 on 'building and repairs' within the first three years of the lease. The reference to three tenements seems to relate to a straightforward subdivision of the medieval building during the early years of the century. Although the 1543 lease could indicate the date at which the hall was floored and the chimney inserted, it is hard to understand how the house could have been divided into three occupancies whilst it still had an open hall. Therefore, it is more likely that the phase-2 modifications were undertaken earlier, prior to the division of the building into tenements — this would certainly explain the high quality of the phase-2 work. A reference to a tenement and garden then divided into three dwellings amongst the town's concealed lands in 1585 probably relates to this property: if so, it was still in three occupancies at that date. By 1860 it was one dwelling and included an extension which forms the present day Borough Arms, but the complex is now once more divided into three.[15] *[ESRO HBR/1/1612]*

14 THE HOUSES TO *c.*1660 SUMMARIZED: EAST CLIFF AND THE SUBURBS

104. The Dormy House, East Cliff —
1500 +/-50; 1575 +/-25; 1600 +/-25 (Figures 14.1 - 14.6)

Phase 1 (c.1500). The early remains in this building are fragmentary due to dramatic remodelling in the 18th-century as its gentry owners strove to modernise their aging mansion. Within the main range the fragments of the northern end bay are all that seem to have survived subsequent phases of rebuilding. They indicate a substantial timber-framed house measuring 7.60 metres (25'0") wide, set back from and at an angle to the street, with a yard in front. As Figure 14.2 indicates, by 1821 this yard was at least partially enclosed and infilled by buildings, but whether or not this duplicates an earlier arrangement is unclear. Equally unclear is whether a continuously-jettied wing built at right angles across the end wall of the main range, facing Turkey Cock Lane, originally formed part of the main house or was intended to be occupied separately.

Phase 2 (1575) and Phase 3 (c.1600). Substantial extensions were added to the front and rear of the main range, carried out in two phases (Figure 14.1: additions depicted in darker grey). In part, these may have been carried out by Robert Farley, a wealthy Rye merchant who not only dealt in the export and import of glass but also acted as agent for London clothiers.[1] It was most likely he who added the two-and-a-half storeyed front range, canted at an angle to the main house in order to fit the cramped site, avoiding 1-4 East Cliff [105], built *c.*1557. The range, which has a windbraced side-purlin roof and an extensive cellar beneath it, has been truncated at its eastern end, towards the highway.

It was more likely Robert Farley's successor who either built or rebuilt the substantial 'kitchen' range to the rear in *c.*1600. As Figures 14.3 and 14.4 indicate, the kitchen has good detailing, including a coffered ceiling with plain but effective ovolo-moulded girders and crossbeams and a borrowed light over the entrance infilled with early-style balusters. The room is dominated by a massive, 3.65 metre (11'11") wide fireplace with heavy cambered and chamfered timber lintel. Above, the kitchen chamber (now divided into two) likewise has ovolo-moulded ceiling beams, and here the wallplates are similarly moulded. The walls are panelled, as too are the entrances to the closets which flank the fireplace. As with the front range, the roof is of windbraced clasped-side-purlin construction.

By 1646 the house had been acquired by Anthony Norton and in 1660 it was occupied by his son, Richard Norton, gent., who lived there with one male and one female servant. He was assessed for the house at 8 flues in 1662, as well as 5 flues for an empty house nearby. Two years later he had left town and the mansion had been let to John Martin. It

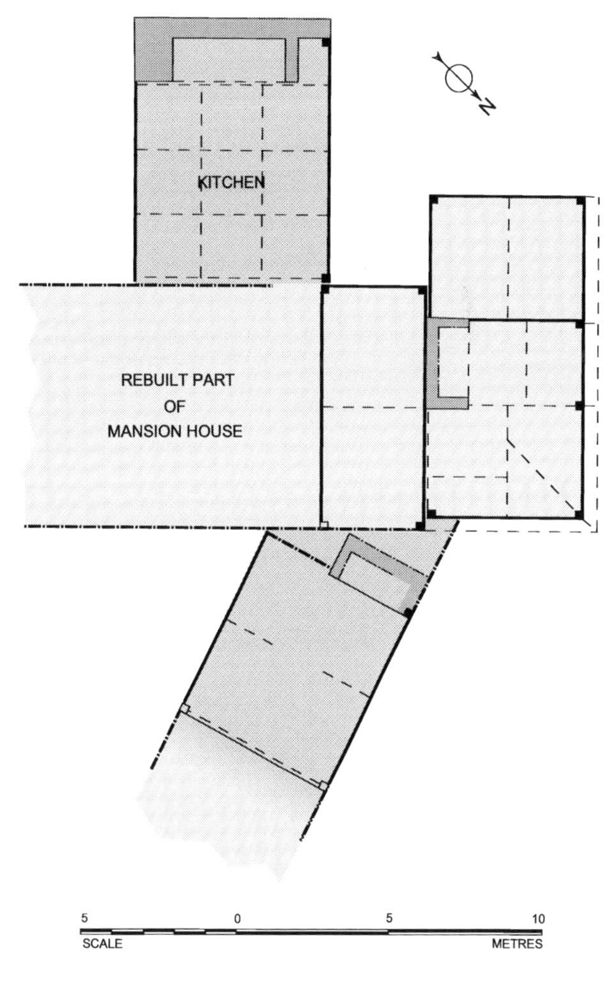

Fig. 14.1
Reconstructed plan of Dormy House, as in phase 2

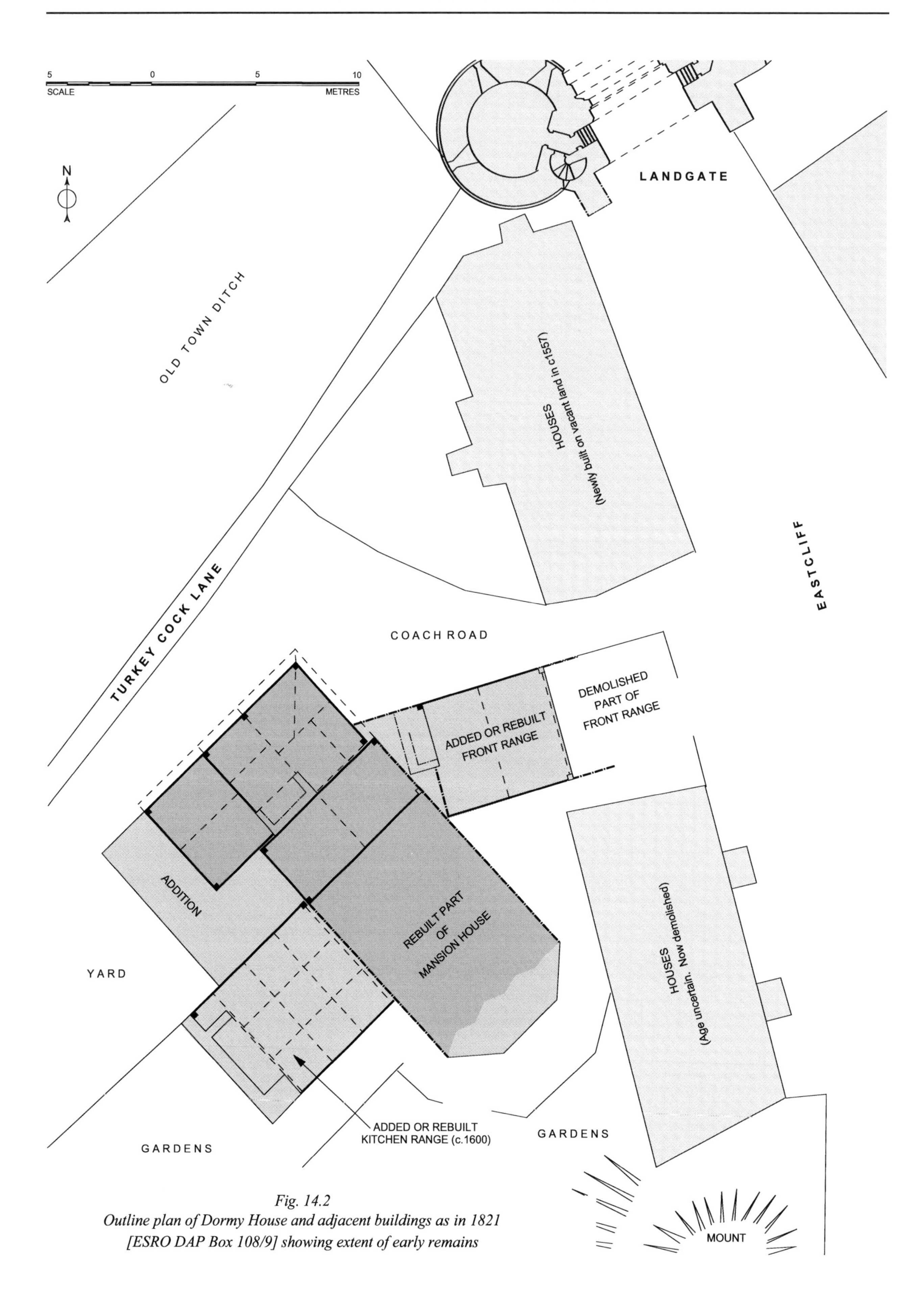

Fig. 14.2
Outline plan of Dormy House and adjacent buildings as in 1821 [ESRO DAP Box 108/9] showing extent of early remains

remained tenanted until *c.*1711 when the then owner, Ralph Norton, returned to the town. He died aged 84 in 1750 and it was his daughter and co-heir, Catherine, wife of Thomas Owen, who remodelled the house. Despite this upgrade, it narrowly escaped demolition during the following century, being described by the Rye historian, Holloway, in the 1860s as a 'sad wreck of a house, with broken windows, and bearing every distressing feature of ruin and decay, while a piece of waste land, immediately adjoining, completes the picture of misery'.[2] *[ESRO HBR/1/0629]*

Fig 14.3
Dormy House. Phase 2 kitchen showing fireplace and coffered ceiling

Fig 14.4
Dormy House. Borrowed light over former doorway leading from hall into kitchen

105. 1-4 East Cliff — *1557*
(Figures 14.7 - 14.11)

An important building on account of the documentary date for its construction. In 1557 John Ford received a grant of this property from the Corporation. In the grant, which included other land in the area, it is described as a plot on which Ford had then recently built a house within the Northgate, abutting east on the street, north on a footway measuring 7 feet (2.15 metres) wide between the town walls and the premises, and south, west onto other lands owned by Ford.[3]

Unfortunately the structure was much altered in the 18th century when it was brick encased, extended at the rear and converted into four dwellings, only one of which has been viewed as part of this project. Even so, the information which can be gleaned is informative. It was evidently built as an identical handed semi-detached pair of two-cell units flanking a central four-flue axial chimney built of small red 'Flemish' bricks (*see* Figure 14.7). There are cellars. Measuring only 4.55 metres (14'11") wide on the ground floor, the building

Fig. 14.5
Detail from a drawing by S H Grimm, c.1785 showing Dormy House viewed from the north with the chimneys of the kitchen range (right) and the front range (left) clearly visible and the cap of the main range chimney just visible between the two, peeping over the ridge. The structure on the left is the western tower of Land Gate
[© The British Library Board. Add Ms 5670 f.16 [30]]

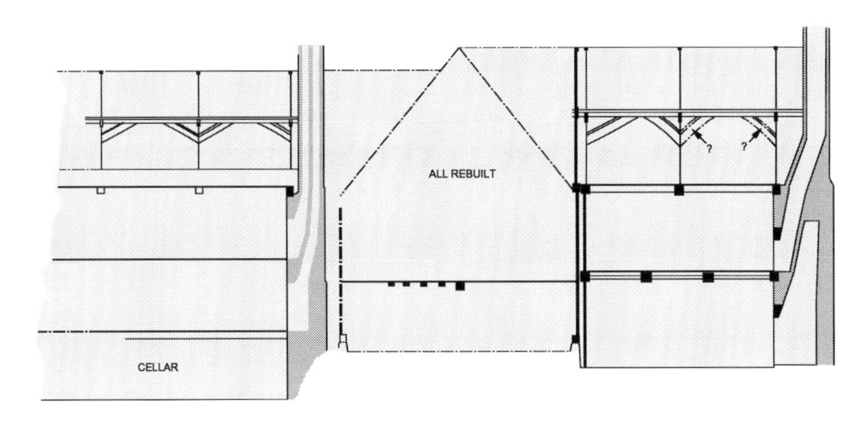

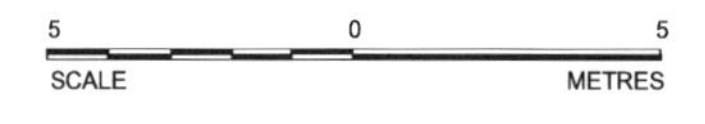

Fig. 14.6
Dormy House.
Reconstructed section through front range (left), main range (centre) and kitchen range (right), as in phase 2

was originally fully timber framed and incorporated a continuous front jetty, as shown by the dovetailed joint in the crossbeam, next to the later street facade (Figure 14.8). Given the mid 16th-century date, the first-floor partition within the hall chamber is something of a surprise: it has rough exposed staves and a central stud flanked by footbraces of very irregular curvature. An indication of the partition's appearance is given by Figures 14.9 and 14.10. The chamber had lodged ceilings from the outset and thus the roof area was utilized, though being fully hipped, it was probably intended for storage only. The construction of the roof is also of interest — windbraced clasped side purlins with collar trusses which do not coincide with the bay divisions within the main frame of the building. Outside the environs of Rye such roofs are usually 17th century in date, though a number of other such examples are found within the town which (based on other typological dating evidence) ought to belong to the period 1540-1590 — *see* Chapter 7. To have such a date 'confirmed' by documentary evidence is significant.

The building is illustrated in one of the mid-1630s sketches made of Rye by the artist Van Dyck. As Figure 14.11 indicates, it is the rear of the property which is shown by him. By this date a rear range incorporating a chimney had been added to the northern dwelling and the accommodation within the southern dwelling had been augmented by a rear lean-to outshut. These additions have since been replaced by four adjacent rear ranges of much later date extending along the entire length of the rear wall. *[ESRO HBR/1/1615]*

Fig. 14.7
'Flemish' bricks, hall fireplace, 1-4 East Cliff

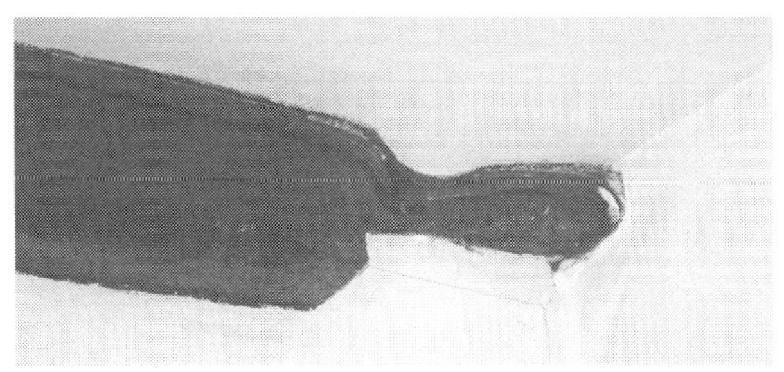

Fig. 14.8
Dovetailed joint for former jetty plate. 1-4 East Cliff

106. 1 Landgate

House not viewed, but it is shown looking very much as it does today in a drawing made by Van Dyck in the 1630s (*see* Figure 14.13).

107. 24 Landgate — *1525 +/-25; 1590 +/-25*
(Figures 14.12 - 14.14)

Phase 1 (c.1525). A well built, fully-floored, three-bay building, measuring 10.40 metres x 5.95 metres (34'2" x 19'6"), with a large two-bay hall. When first built the ground-floor plan conformed to a standard two-cell layout, with a pair of service rooms beyond the low end of the hall. However, on the first floor were four chambers — one each within the service bay and low-end hall bay, with two smaller chambers (divided from one another by an axial partition) over the hall's high-end bay. The stairs appear to have been within a rear outshut, since destroyed. Untypically for the period, all four chambers were fitted with ceilings, allowing use to be made of the roof space, presumably for storage purposes.

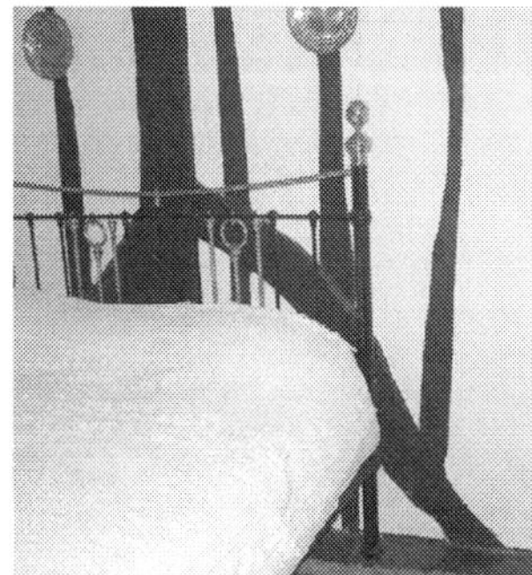

Figs. 14.9 and 14.10
End wall of hall chamber, 1-4 East Cliff

Fig 14.11
Detail from a Van Dyck drawing made in the mid 1630s showing the rear of 1-4 East Cliff (central) viewed from the west (rear). Land Gate is on the left and the northern range of Dormy House on the right
[Private collection]

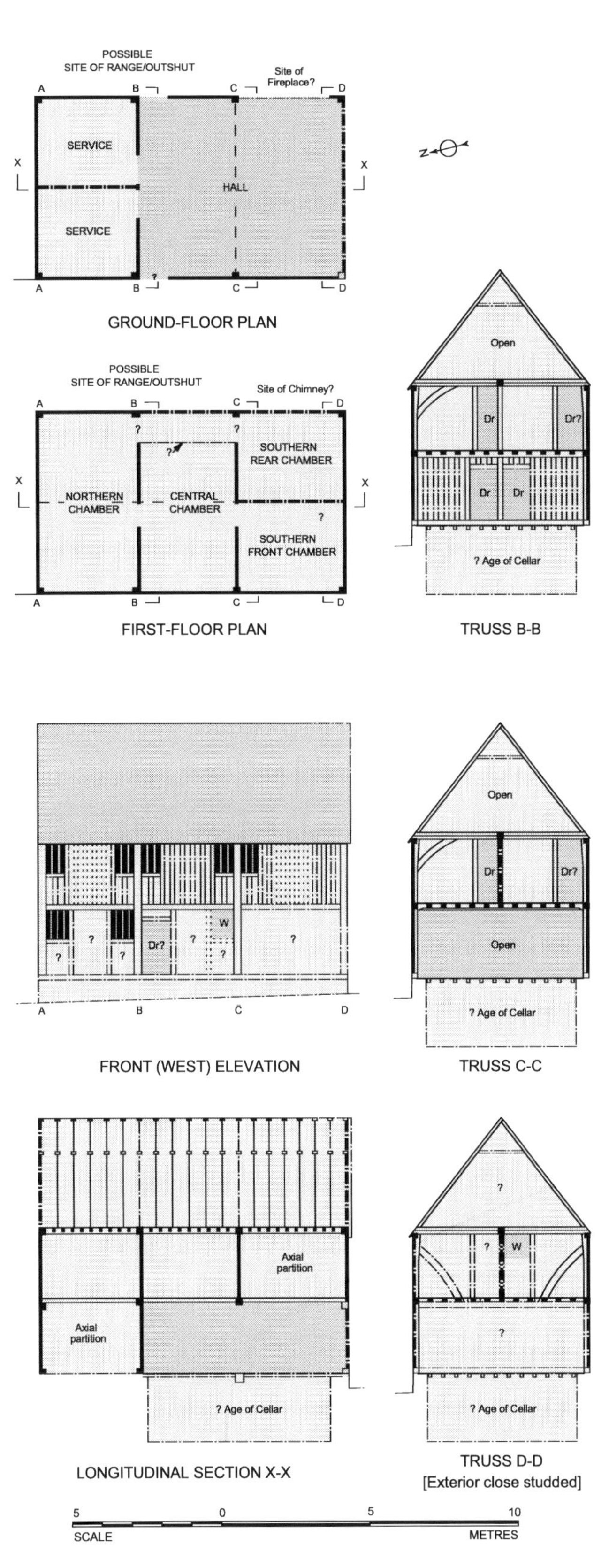

Fig. 14.12
Phase 1 reconstruction of 24 Landgate

Fig. 14.13
24 Landgate viewed from Tower Street, as drawn by Van Dyck in the 1630s. Detail with 1 Landgate visible on the left and the front tower of the Land Gate on the right.
[Private collection]

Phase 2 (c.1590). Possibly as a result of the subdivision of the property, rear ranges were added, the northern heated by a side stack and the southern by a chimney located to the rear of the hall. This latter chimney also heated the high-end bay of the hall. It was totally removed in the late 20th century and it is therefore impossible to prove that this was not an early single-flue chimney against which an extra fireplace was added during this phase. If not, the phase-1 hall was unheated.

When surveyed in 2004 this phase of alteration was interpreted as nothing more than a response to the need for increased floor area, though it was noted that the two-bay hall had been divided into two rooms by the insertion of a partition beneath the crossbeam. A superficial trawl through the documentary record gave no reason for doubting such an interpretation. In 1664, when the building was in the owner occupation of Benjamin Martin II, he was assessed in hearth tax at six flues. This fits the house well — two flues in the northern rear range and four in the main chimney to the south.[4]

The true history of occupation within the house is revealed by the deeds, for in 1658 when John Martin conveyed his interest to his brother, Benjamin II, it was described as a messuage purchased by his father, Benjamin I, 'by the name of two messuages, two gardens and a parcel of land' by deed dated 1612 (*see* Chapter 7). This qualification was evidently necessary in order to clarify the apparent contradiction between the then current situation and that given in the earlier deeds. From this data it seems clear that the late 16th-century alterations did not merely increase the size of the building, but were made in order to facilitate the subdivision of the house into two. Upon Benjamin I's acquisition of the property in the early 17th century he returned it to single occupancy. The house is shown in its altered form in a Van Dyck sketch of the mid 1630s, though whether it was at that date in two occupations or had been returned to one is impossible to tell (*see* Figure 14.13). *[ESRO HBR/1/1569]*

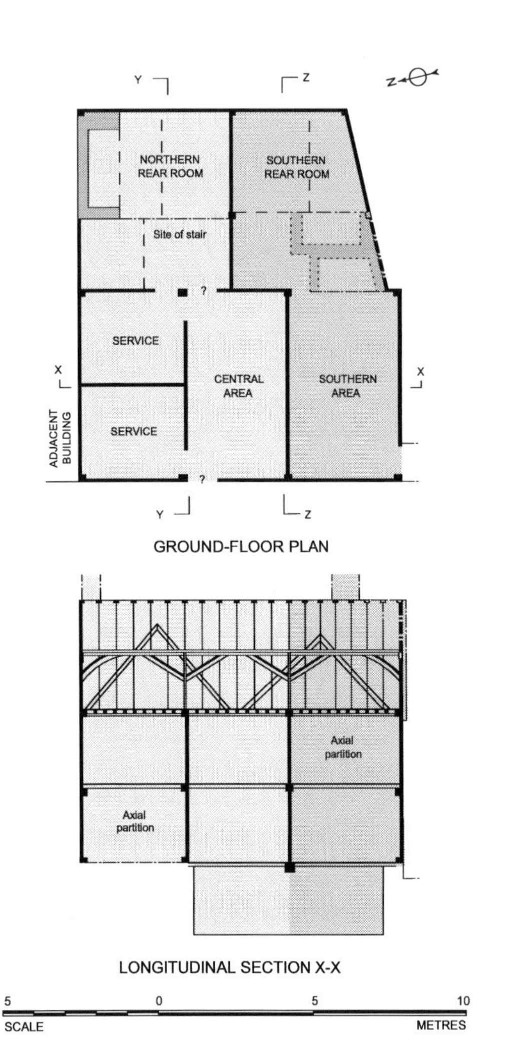

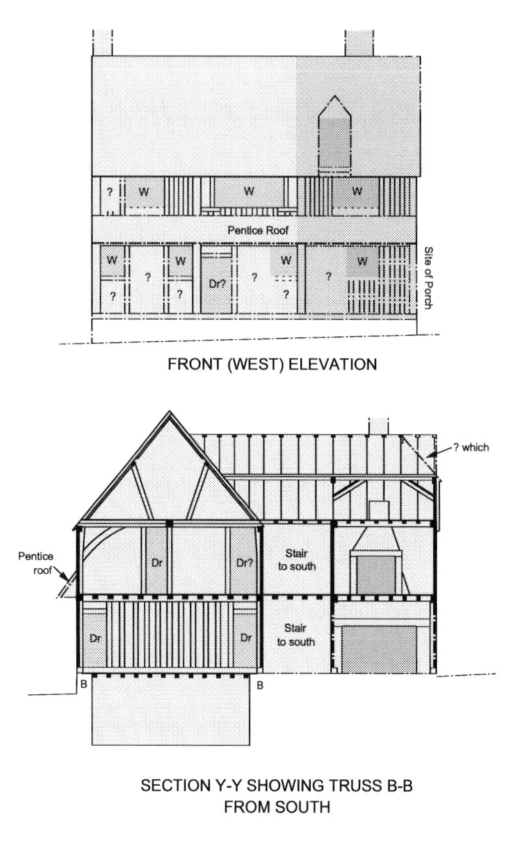

Fig. 14.14 (left and above)
Phase 2 reconstructed details of 24 Landgate showing alterations associated with division of the building into two occupations (depicted by light and darker grey shading)

108. 18-23 Landgate — *1575 +/-25*
(Figures 14.15 & 14.16)

A terrace of six houses, all of very standard design — a hall and small inner room, repeated on the first floor, with a two-bay attic space (probably for storage) above. The roof is of clasped-side-purlin construction, partially windbraced, with raking struts supporting the purlins at centre span of each attic area. No details are known regarding the design of the infill framing within the street facade, but otherwise all walls are of footbraced large-panel framing and all evidenced windows were designed to be glazed from the outset. When first built each cottage incorporated but one fireplace — serving the hall — but others have been added subsequently. Windows within the rear wall of the terrace of the six houses confirm that neither rear ranges nor rear outshuts originally existed within this terrace, though they were added later.

The details of construction suggest that the terrace is likely to have been built at a time when Rye was beginning to stagnate in economic terms. Given this fact, it is particularly disappointing that the circumstances which gave rise to the construction of this speculative venture are not known. Nor is it known whether the terrace was construction upon a virgin site. A map of the town and its environs drawn by John Prowze (a resident of the town) in 1572 shows this section of street frontage built up, though, bearing in mind the date, it is not known whether the terrace already existed at that date or whether the structures shown are its predecessors.

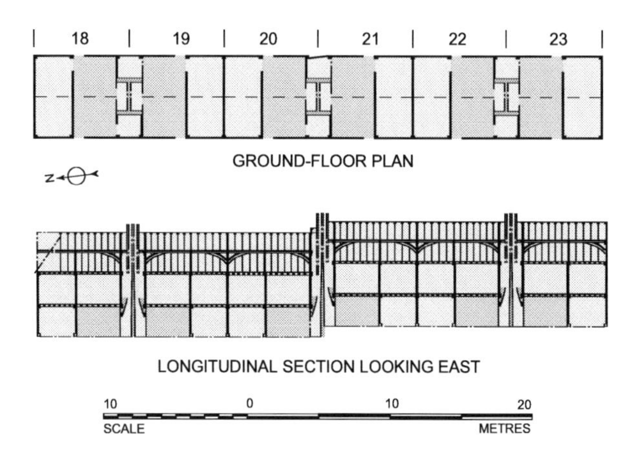

Fig. 14.15
Outline reconstruction of 18-23 Landgate, a terrace of six two-cell houses

Number 23, at the southern end, is built hard against the end wall of 24 Landgate [107], built *c.*1540 but there appears to have been a gap in the built-up frontage beyond the northern end. In order to compensate for the downward slope

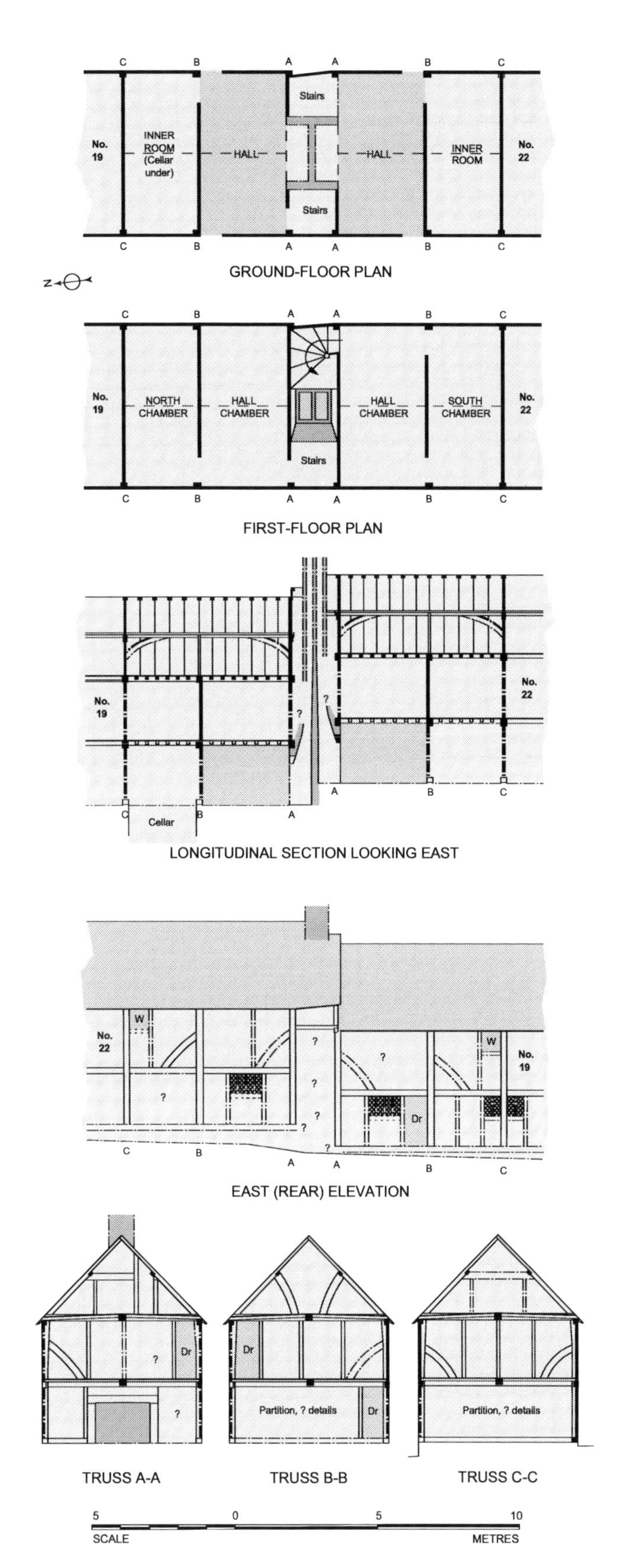

Fig. 14.16
Reconstruction of 20-21 Landgate

Fig 14.17
Detail from a Van Dyck drawing of 1633 showing Landgate Square viewed from the north. The building in front of it (bottom left) is the Almshouse. Land Gate is visible top left [© The Pierpont Morgan Library, New York. III, 178. Not to be reproduced without the express permission of the Trustees of the Pierpont Morgan Library]

on the street the terrace was framed in two parts with a *c.*750 mm (*c.*2'6") step in roof level halfway along the length. In plan the terrace is designed as three handed pairs with a shared axial chimney occupying the central bay of each pair. These chimney bays appear also to have housed the staircases, with the stairs of one cottage located on the street side of the chimney and the other stair to the rear. Because of the step in levels, the central bay within the terrace (housing the central chimney) was not prefabricated but was instead constructed on site. Hence the terrace is made up of two identical prefabricated frames of seven bays, each linked by a bay fabricated around the central chimney. *[ESRO HBR/1/1567; ESRO HBR/1/1572]*

109/110. Landgate Square (*see* also separate entries below) *(Figure 14.17)*

These off-street tenements are far less typical than others in Rye in that the buildings are arranged around a courtyard and, furthermore, this courtyard most likely incorporated a mix of buildings of different usages. The courtyard may have developed in front of a medieval house, which at this period was incorporated into the rear range of the yard. The complex is depicted by Van Dyck in 1633 (Figure 14.17) and on Jeake's map of 1667 as a quadrangle entered direct from the street. The same configuration is shown in the 1771 town map, though what survives today is about half, the street range (probably a late addition — it appears not to be shown by Van Dyck) and the north range have been demolished. The depiction by Van Dyck gives a good impression of the complex's form and appearance in 1633. It must surely be relevant that the north range (which had a lean-to outshut running along its northern side) is shown entirely devoid of chimneys, whilst the west range had a chimney at its extreme southern end only. Thus, at least by this date, these parts were most likely in use either as storehouses or workshops, or both. This is consistent with documentary evidence which suggests that by the 1660s the square was the focus of the Burwash family's tannery business.[5] In contrast, the southern end of the west range and the entire southern range were in domestic use.

109. 1-3 Landgate Square — *1565 +/-25; c.1600 +/-25 (Figures 14.18 & 14.19)*

The southernmost range of the complex is divided from the west range by a narrow gap in the southwestern corner of the square. It has had a complex evolution, being of at least two, probably three, and perhaps four separate builds (Figure 14.18).

The easternmost element consists of a three-bay un-jettied two-and-a-half storeyed structure aligned east-west and perhaps originally having a rear lean-to outshut running behind at least one of its bays. To the rear of the two western bays is a single-bay range framed at right angles and incorporating a rear jetty. The central part of the complex is occupied by a two-bay, two-and-a-half storeyed crosswing with front jetty and a massive rear chimney. Finally, at the western end is an east-west aligned two-storeyed, single-bay jettied range with rear lean-to outshut. All parts appear to date from the last quarter of the 16th century or perhaps — in the case of the western element — to the opening decade of the 17th century.

Although small, the complex incorporates evidence of projecting oriels and clerestory windows, and good quality chimneys, one of which is embellished with detached diamond-section shafts. Thus the small size of the individual parts should not be taken as indicators of low status.

It is difficult to know how the separate elements of the building should be interpreted. Although it is now divided into three separate dwellings, in the mid 17th century the entire range appears to have been in use as a single house associated with the adjacent tannery. The question which needs to be asked is, prior to that period had this always been the case? Is the haphazard, unplanned design of the complex the result of the progressive piecemeal expansion of a single dwelling, or do the individual parts represent separate dwellings which were only later combined to form a single unit once population pressures with the town diminished?

The cut-in nature of the two doorways shown in Figure 14.19 intruded through the western wall of the central crosswinged unit cannot be used to argue the case either way because this unit predates the western one and thus the structural evidence would be the same whichever was the case. Likewise, the inclusion of a separate external front door leading into the (apparently unheated) western addition could reflect an 'office' function, perhaps associated with the tannery business. Alternatively the apparent lack of heating could be explained by the removal of a rear stack without leaving any visible evidence. At present, these questions remain unresolved. *[ESRO HBR/1/0953; ESRO HBR/1/0609]*

110. 5-6 Landgate Square — *1475 +/-50*

A very fragmentary building, incorporated into the western range of Landgate Square. This building has only briefly been viewed and extends northwards into the adjacent house. What survives are the fragments of one truss and part of a crownpost roof with heavy (200 mm wide) joists to the north and smaller joists to the south, suggesting either an extension or a floored-over open hall. Whether the medieval

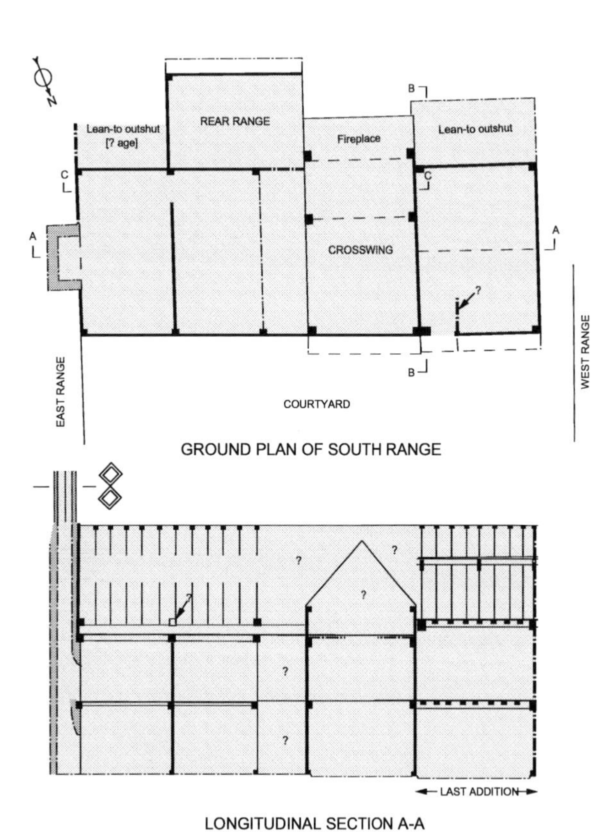

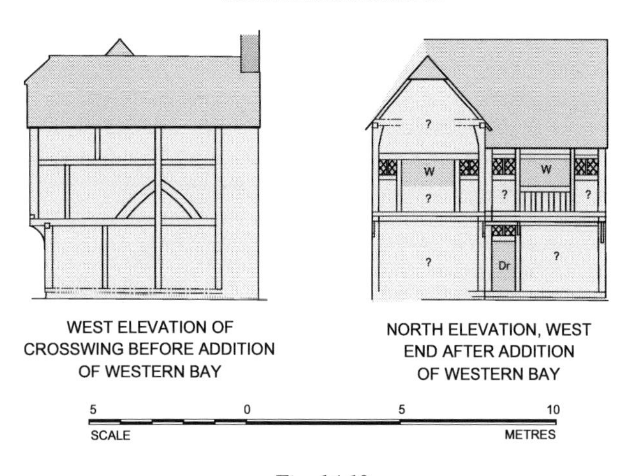

Fig. 14.18
Reconstruction of 1-3 Landgate Square

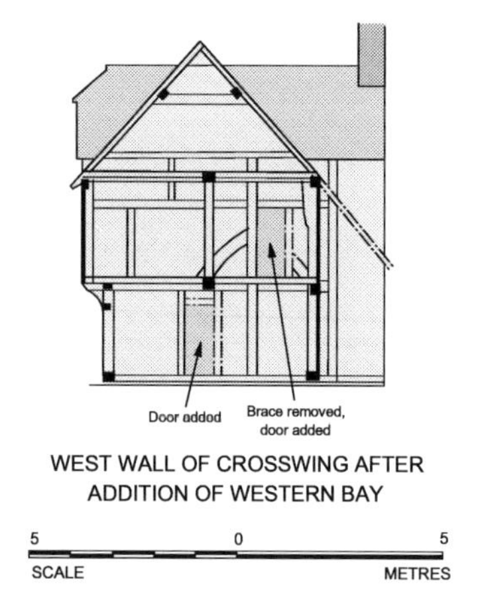

Fig. 14.19
Side wall of 2 Landgate Square after addition of No. 3

frame is *in situ*, or has been re-erected upon its present site is uncertain. There are no buildings shown in this immediate area in Prowze map of 1572. If *in situ*, its importance lies in the fact that it is the only medieval house known in the suburb (excluding a vaulted cellar further south) and it is set well back from the street.[6] *[ESRO HBR/1/0850]*

111. The Crown, Ferry Road — *1565 +/-25*
(Figure 14.20)

An off-street tenement, built as a house about 1565. This could be one of the 15 dwellings erected by Robert Sheppard on the edge of St. Mary's Marsh between 1555 and 1572.[7] Despite the (assumed) general poverty of this part of town, it should be emphasized that it is well built. As Figure 14.20 shows, it is of two bays and (excluding its end chimney) measures 7.05 metres x 5.30 metres (23'1" x 17'4"). Its layout is typical of the 'standard' two-cell houses. Following the normal pattern, the hall occupies the larger (northern) of the two bays with a small room beyond, and this layout is repeated on the first floor. An externally-built chimney (now removed) heated both the hall and hall chamber.

The clasped-side-purlin roof is hipped at one end and gabled at the other and, unusually, the hip is located at the same end as the former external chimney — normally the reverse was the case. There is one-way windbracing and the central truss is of collar type and was always open. Thus, as in many of the town's other houses which incorporate an attic area, the entire two-bay roof void formed a single space and was probably used for storage. In order to increase usable floor space the wallplates of the building are elevated above the level of the attic floor, though admittedly not by very much — the top of the wallplate is 400 mm (1'4") above the floor. Often the internal tiebeams within this type of building were either omitted altogether or trimmed in order to allow easy access along the length of the roof. Probably because of the exceptionally low level of the attic walls, in this instance this was not the case — instead the tiebeam had to be stepped over.

All other features in the house are standard for the period: the walls, for example, are of footbraced large-panel design. The one evidenced window — lighting the hall chamber — was of unglazed type and, bearing in mind that this was the principal chamber, this was probably the case with all the windows within the structure.

Despite its present ownership as part of The Crown, the building is perhaps better located by reference to Cinque Port Street, to which it is historically associated. It is set back about seven metres from the street and is orientated at right angles to it, with a 19th-century house (almost certainly a reconstruction of an earlier building) occupying the intervening space. Access is via an alley which steps down from the street and passes the eastern side of the building.

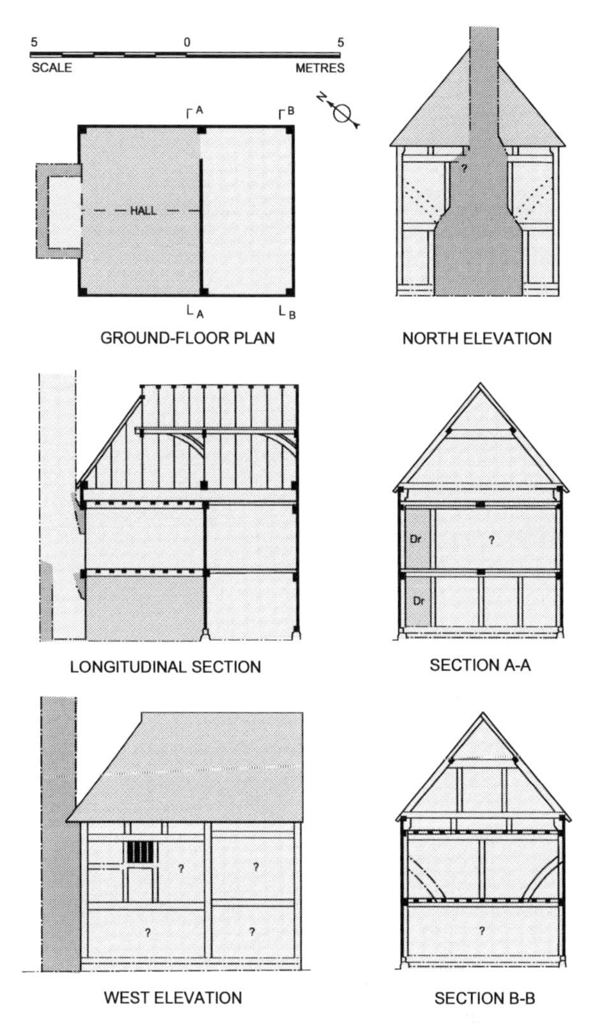

Fig. 14.20
Reconstruction of former house at the rear of The Crown

It should be stressed that there is no absolute guarantee the structure did not originally form part of the house fronting Cinque Port Street, though the available evidence suggests it served as a dwelling in its own right, representing back-garden development. It is significant that it is the only 16th-century building known to survive within the once populous, though relatively poor suburb known as Wishe Ward, an area all but depopulated as a result of the town's 17th century period of contraction (*see* Chapter 5). *[ESRO HBR/1/1072]*

NOTES AND REFERENCES

ABBREVIATIONS

ASE	Archaeology South-East
BL	British Library
CCR	Calendar of Close Rolls
CChR	Calendar of Charter Rolls
CPR	Calendar of Patent Rolls
ESRO	East Sussex Record Office
HBR	Historic Building Record
HMC	Historic Monuments Commission
OD	Ordnance Datum
SAC	Sussex Archaeological Collections
SRS	Sussex Record Society
TNA	The National Archives
VCH	The Victoria History of the Counties of England
WSRO	West Sussex Record Office

NOTES AND REFERENCES

1 — INTRODUCTORY OVERVIEW

1 *VCH Sussex* **9**, 185. Also *see* Biddle *et. al.* 2001.

2 For the town of Winchelsea *see* Martin & Martin 2004.

3 Eddison 2004, 1-4; Gardiner 2000, 76, 89; *VCH Sussex* **1**, 391; Martin 1993, 73-78.

4 Eddison 2004, 3; *VCH Sussex* **9**, 49.

5 *VCH Sussex* **9**, 36.

6 Sylvester 2004, 9, 200; also Stenton, D.M. (Ed.). 1940. 'The Great Roll of the Pipe, the Sixth Year of the Reign of King John, Michaelmas 1204 (Pipe Roll 50)' *Pipe Roll Society* **18**, p.218. As Sylvester notes, the 1204 assessment is not without its problems as it either omits ports or includes them under the totals of other ports. Hastings is not listed and may have been included under Winchelsea's total. The Cinque Port of Hythe is likewise absent from the return. The tax is not a reflection of all exports, but focuses principally on wool and hide exports. For further details *see* Lloyd, T.H. 1977. *The English Wool Trade in the Middle Ages*. Cambridge: CUP, pp.11-13.

7 *VCH Sussex* **9**, 49, 168-9; Vidler 1954, 125-156. It should be noted that the part of Rye parish to the west of the town was not owned by Fécamp Abbey, but by the wealthy Etchingham family. *See also* TNA SC11/649; SC12/15/51; ESRO ACC 7024.

8 Draper 2009; Eddison 2004, 3-5; Britton, C.E. 1937. *A Meteorological Chronology to AD 1485*. London: HMSO, pp. 90-125; CPR 1261; Eddison 1998; ESRO RYE 45/13-15.

9 Eddison 2004, 4, 6; Britton 1937 (*op. cit.*), 124; BL Add. Ch. 20169. Recent geomorphological fieldwork undertaken by Martin Waller and others indicates that some of the previously held views with regards to a hypothisized lack of a break in the shingle bank in the area of Winchelsea are likely to be in error. The debates continue as to the locality of the early mouth of the Rother, as does the debate as to whether during this early period the Brede and Tillingham flowed into the Rother (as now) or had their own separate estuary which served the ports of Rye and Winchelsea. Although the debate is of considerable importance, the resolution is not of direct relevance to this present architectural study. For further discussion *see* Draper 2009.

10 *VCH Sussex* **9**, 40, TNA SC6/1032/7.

11 CPR 1361-64, 440.

12 *VCH Sussex* **9**, 40, including note 25.

13 Unless stated to the contrary, this brief summary of the town's medieval economy is based upon *VCH Sussex* **9**, 54-56, and Sylvester's account in the Winchelsea volume (2004). Although the latter deals principally with Winchelsea, much is included about Rye for the purpose of context. *See also* Draper 2009.

14 Sylvester 1999, 140, Table 4.2.

15 *SAC* **73**, 74, 77.

16 As note 13 above.

17 For Defences *see* Chapter 3; for work on the church *see* Chapter 4; and for the construction of domestic buildings *see* Chapter 7. Regarding corporate income *see VCH Sussex* **9**, 50.

18 This summary is based upon Mayhew 1987, 11-54, unless stated to the contrary.

19 Mayhew 1987, 235.

20 Mayhew 1987, 235, 242, Table 40. Although the table in Mayhew relates specifically to shipments of wood and timber, the fact that such shipments represent a relatively constant percentage of total shipments indicates that a substantial rise occurred in trade generally during the period 1490/1 to 1497/8, a rise which thereafter continued to increase through to 1531/2.

21 Mayhew 1987, 234-235; Hipkin 1998-9, 108.

22 Martin and Martin 2004, 103.

23 *SRS* **56**, 164-166; Mayhew 1987, 81. In Martin and Martin 2004, 22, the total of Rye aliens in 1524/5 is incorrectly given as 32, the result of an incomplete photocopy of the return, which excluded the entries on p.165.

24 Mayhew 1987, 16.

25 Hipkin 1998-9, 109; Mayhew 1987, 236. Sandwich was at this time suffering a period of depression — Clarke *et. al.* forthcoming, Chapters 7 and 8.

26 Clarke *et. al.* forthcoming, Chapter 7. Of the 420 households in Sandwich at that date, 291 were English and 129 Dutch, most of the latter having arrived after 1560.

27 Mayhew 1987, 14-17.

28 Mayhew 1987, 18.

29 Martin and Martin 2004, 21-23.

30 TNA SP 12/38 f.28.

31 Mayhew 1987, 19.
32 Hipkin 1998-9, 108.
33 Mayhew 1987, 24, 27.
34 Kent's east-coast port town of Sandwich experienced a similar phenomenon, but in that instance it was Dutch protestants, rather than French, who took shelter. Furthermore, unlike at Rye during this initial wave, many of those arriving at Sandwich stayed, with Dutch families accounting for almost a third of the town's population (expressed as households) in 1565 (Clarke *et. al.* forthcoming, Chapters 7 and 8). It was not until after 1565, following renewed persecution, that French refugees took up long-term residence in Rye. By then the native population may already have been on the wane, giving at least some of the new resident French unoccupied houses in which to live. As at Sandwich, it seems likely that during the final decades of the century the percentage of foreigners within the town accounted for a high proportion of the resident population.
35 Mayhew 1987, 79-90.
36 For detailed discussion relating to this period *see* Mayhew 1987 and Hipkin 1998-9. *See also* Brent 1975.
37 ESRO XA3/16 (microfilm) — Rental of Battle, dated 1652; Brent, C. 2004. *Pre-Georgian Lewes c.890-1714: The Emergence of a County Town.* Lewes: Colin Brent Books.
38 ESRO RYE 82/82. *See also* Chapter 5.

2 — INFRASTRUCTURE

1 Sea levels changed over time, even within the historical period. In 1940 the high water for equinoxial tides was 3.9 metres (12.7 ft) O.D.: mean high water for spring tides 3.2 metres (10.5 ft) O.D., and mean high water for neap tides 2.3 metres (7.5 ft) O.D. — Green, R. D. 1982. *Soils of Romney Marsh.* Harpenden: Agricultural Research Council, Soil Survey of Great Britain: England and Wales, Bulletin 4, p.2 fn. To be safe from inundation, sea defences had to be considerably higher than this in order to cope with occasional tidal surges resulting from high tides associated with unfavourable weather conditions in the channel.
2 Holloway 1863, 23.
3 ESRO RYE 132/15 — Map of Rye by Samuel Jeake, copied 1728 by William Wybourn.
4 1771 town map (Rye Museum); Vidler 1934a, 121. We are grateful to Jo Kirkham for alerting us to the flood in 1875.
5 Draper 2009, Chapter 9.
6 ESRO RYE 132/15 — Map of Rye by Samuel Jeake, copied 1728 by William Wybourn. At a later date steps descended from just inside Landgate and from the junction of East Street and Market Street, but neither of these are depicted in 1667, nor in the 1771 town map held by Rye Museum, which likewise omits those indicated in 1667.
7 1771 Town Map held by Rye Museum. Not shown in the 1667 map. *See also* Draper 2009, Chapter 9.
8 Mayhew 1987, 14 and 289, fn.3.
9 *VCH Sussex* **9**, 151.
10 For a summary of the current thinking on town layouts *see* Hindle, P. 1990. *Medieval Town Plans*, Princes Risborough: Shire Publications.
11 Street widths scales from the 1st edition (1871-2) 1:500 Ordnance Survey plan.
12 Martin and Martin 2004, 29.
13 ESRO RYE 132/15 — Map of Rye by Samuel Jeake, copied 1728 by William Wybourn.
14 Vidler 1934a, 45. Holloway 1847, 364, states "Persons ascended and passed over the wall then standing, and long since, into the town".
15 Vidler 1934a, 47; Clark 1861, 29. Market Road is used as a one way street leaving town. Likewise, the traffic within High Street is one way, leaving at The Strand. Local traffic is permitted to flow along Mermaid Street in either direction, though the street is little used by vehicles.
16 Johnson 1998. No trenches corresponded with the projected alignment of this possible street.
17 ESRO RYE 33/20.
18 ESRO RYE 132/15 — Map of Rye by Samuel Jeake, copied 1728 by William Wybourn.
19 For Le Pygge Lane *see* ESRO RYE 136/49 and 53, ESRO RYE 124/3; Schytbourglane *see* ESRO RYE 136/112; Lane leading to M[i]lnerstrete *see* ESRO RYE 136/86; Merstret *see* ESRO RYE 136/29; Potepiriestrete *see* ESRO RYE 136/60.
20 Buildings appear to be shown in this area in a drawing of 1633 by Van Dyck (*see* Figure 2.3), but are not shown in the Jeake map of 1667 (ESRO RYE 132/15).
21 Draper and Meddens *et. al.* forthcoming, Chapter 3.
22 Martin 1993, 73-80.
23 *VCH Sussex* **1**, 375, 391.
24 In this general area, between Mint House and the rear gardens of properties in Mermaid Street, there is a terrace cut deeply into the hillside, held back by a retaining wall. The date of this could be relatively recent (perhaps 18th century) but, equally, it could be the result of early quarrying. Even so, its location is such that it is away from the alignment of any westward projection of the straight section of High Street and does not, therefore, seem to be the reason for the double curve in the street's lower section.
25 Draper 2009.
26 Holloway 1847, 288.
27 CPR 1348-50, p.93.
28 Vidler 1934a, 42, 44.
29 ESRO RYE 130/5-8. Erosion in this area was still occurring in the 17th century. In 1634 a tenement in Longer Street (High Street) abutted Ockmans Lane on the south, but by 1673 the same tenement lay north of the cliff, formerly ... Ockmans Lane (ESRO ACC 516; catalogue entry relating to ESRO AMS 6440).
30 ESRO RYE 130/9; ESRO W/C11.50. It is possible that a further seven houses and a cellar stood on the opposite side of the lane (ESRO RYE 139/51) though these could be the same houses as already mentioned standing on the south side.
31 ESRO RYE 131/1-2. John Forde was at this time the owner of the mansion house just within Land Gate (later Tower House and now Dormy House) which he had purchased in 1544 from James Sutton, son and heir of Nicholas Sutton (d.1524) for £45 (Vidler 1934a, 59).
32 ESRO RYE 135/5 (dated 1515) and 135/7 (dated 1559).
33 ESRO RYE 1/4/129r, 145v, 223; ESRO RYE 47/6/47.
34 Mayhew 1984, 113.
35 *Pers comm.* Martyn Waller.
36 ESRO RYE 136/99; An earlier reference to the same mill is found in 1330 — *see* ESRO RYE 136/67. 'La Nesse' should not be confused with other nesses in the vicinity of the town. For instance, in its 1568 version the Customal refers to the hanging of criminals 'upon the Saltness on the east side of town, behind the salt water of the town', whilst in 1692 the harbour entrance included a shingle projection known as Ness Point.
37 ESRO RYE 136/80. The house was to be re-erected between two other houses, but whether these were in the same area is uncertain. Was the house being dismantled because it was in danger from slippage? Persons with the surname 'atte La Nesse' are regular witnesses to Rye deeds at this period.
38 TNA SC6/1028/8; TNA SC12/15/73 (three entries); ESRO RYE 136/25; 136/34; 136/64; 136/97.
39 *VCH Sussex* **9**, 57-61. Both Nairn and Pevsner 1965, 594-596, and Norwich 1985, 637 are noncommittal over a close date, and merely state 'Norman', but neither says anything to indicate they suspected it to be earlier than the 12th century.
40 In Domesday the Fécamp manor of Rameslie is recorded as having five churches, of which Rye was most likely one. It should be noted that an area of open land south-east of the church, next to Baddings Tower *otherwise* Ypres Tower, is marked on Jeake's map of 1667 (ESRO RYE 132/15) as 'old

churchyard' and it is also referred to as such in some late 17th and 18th-century documents. Confirmation of two churchyards at Rye comes from the glebe terrier of 1635 (WSRO EpII/17/1-238) which states that, apart from the Vicarage House and its kitchen garden, there is no glebe, although the vicar 'has the two churchyards'. The existence in the mid 17th century of an 'old churchyard' has caused some to speculate that the first church in Rye was located not where it is today, but in this area. If this were so, it is surprising that no references to the old churchyard can be found before the 17th century, despite good deed coverage, with boundary clauses. A likely explanation for this apparent contradiction comes from a deed dated 1588 to an empty plot of land (59 ft. by 15 ft.) in the Baddings area. The south abutment of the plot is given as the 'new churchyard called Baddings', with streets to its north and west (ESRO RYE 130/43). This is clearly different from the churchyard around the church, to which there are many references in the boundary clauses of deeds throughout the 16th century. The 'new churchyard' appears, from its location, to be synonymous with Jeake's 'old churchyard'. Could it be the plot of land in Baddings Ward (assumed by Vidler as intended as a garden) which the vicar, Thomas Sewell, clerk, acquired from William Stonacre in 1502 and to which he subsequently added an 18 ft. wide lane leading from the street to the town wall? (Vidler 1934a, 47, 48). And is it a coincidence that in 1517 Sewell was leasing from Newbury a barn with a garden 'next to the [Ypres] tower, in the very area the 'old churchyard' was later located? (ESRO RYE 124/17). Whether this is coincidence or not, the suggestion is that this area of unused land was commissioned as a new, overflow churchyard at some point in the 16th century, probably following one of the major plagues known to have hit the town, and that this overflow churchyard remained in use in 1635, but by 1667 had become abandoned — hence 'old' as in former use, no longer used, and/or derelict.

41 CPR 1348-50, 98, quoted in *VCH Sussex* **9**, 40.

42 CPR 1361-4, 327, quoted in *VCH Sussex* **9**, 61.

43 Vidler 1934a, 16, 17, 25 and others. For a list of known rectors and vicars *see* Vidler 1934a, 156-157.

44 ESRO RYE 130/1.

45 *VCH Sussex* **9**, 61; Luxmoore, L. A., 1963. *A Glance at Rye's Old Documents*. Rye: Adams, p.23. No land is described as owned by the Bishop of Winchester in the 1860 poor return, ESRO PAR467/38/1.

46 ESRO RYE 136/122.

47 ESRO RYE 132/15 — Map of Rye by Samuel Jeake, copied 1728 by William Wybourn.

48 ESRO RYE 132/15. Because of the lack of detail shown in Jeake's map, and bearing in mind that it is known to show some distortions of scale, it leaves doubt as to whether Vicarage Lane ran to the north or south of Fletchers House (1-2 Lion Street) – it can be shown that there were once lanes on both sides of Fletchers House, though only that on the south now remains and this only as a blind passage. The doubt is resolved by a deed of 1642 (ESRO AMS 5729/80) relating to a house abutting the highway (Lion Street) east, Vicarage House west, and Vicarage Lane south. No. 3 Lion Street never abutted westwards onto the Vicarage (*see* ESRO DR/B/28/1), and thus the deed in question must relate to Fletchers House and Vicarage Lane must be represented by the blind passage which still extends along its south side. The north abutment to the property is given as John Crouch's house, indicating that by 1642 the lane between Fletchers House and 3 Lion Street had been stopped up. This is consistent with the 17th-century date of the southern extension to 3 Lion Street, which is built over the alignment of the former lane.

49 ESRO RYE 130/2.

50 WSRO EpII/17/1-228. The vicarage land at that date amounted to 20 perches and was in two adjoining parts – the Vicarage House and out-kitchen on the east and, 'behind the house' on the west a kitchen garden. The abutments to the house and out-kitchen are given as the churchyard on the south and east, a lane giving into the butchery on the east and north, and a lane leading to the tenement of John Crouch on the north. The kitchen garden bounded the tenement of John Kemp (64 Church Square) on the south and west, the lands of John Crouch on the north, and the churchyard south. The south and west abutments for John Kemp are explained by the substantial chimney which projects out into the corner of the kitchen garden, whilst the abutments of the vicarage house south and east onto the churchyard suggests that (unlike the situation both earlier and later) the sites of 68, 70, 72 Church Square then formed part of the churchyard. This latter interpretation agrees with a statement by Luxmoore to the effect that the vicar was allowed to sell land between his vicarage and the top of Lion Street in order to pay for the reconstruction of the vicarage (Luxmoore 1963, 22). Given that it was church land, it should not be surprising that the vicarage retained its 1635 boundaries in 1860, when it was measured as amounting to 0a.0r.14p, a little short of the size given in the terrier (ESRO PAR 467/38/1 — plot 1239).

51 ESRO RYE 136/144; ESRO RYE 137/21.

52 Subsequent to 1635 this area firstly became a churchyard and then the garden of the vicar, before eventually being sold by the vicar to assist in the reconstruction of the vicarage.

53 Examples are Winchelsea, Battle, Hastings and Mayfield. Contrary to some accounts, Abbey Green at Battle was not the site of the town's medieval market place: the market place was a small square which occupied an area beside the junction of High Street and Mount Street.

54 ESRO RYE 60/9. Some (or perhaps all) of these entries could relate to rents reserved to the Corporation when they sold properties off at an earlier date.

55 ESRO AMS 5729/80.

56 ESRO DAP Box 42 — 2nd property listed in a deed to lead to the use of a fine, dated 11th May 1723.

57 ESRO PAR 467/38/1 and ESRO DR/B/28/1, plots 1228-1232.

58 For example, *VCH Sussex* **9**, 49-55; Mayhew 1987, 91-138; Hipkin 1995; Draper 2009.

59 Vidler 1934a, 32, 42, 50; Mayhew, 1987, 35, 178; ESRO RYE 124/1-13 and 18; Bagley, G. S. and Clark, K. M. 1978. *The Story of the Ypres Tower and Rye Museum*. Rye: Rye Museum, p.3. Proof that the tower was in use as a court hall in 1421 is found in an order of that date which states that all persons summoned to the Tower and not attending should pay 12d (Vidler 1934a, 32). Vidler also notes that in 1481 the Corporation purchased new keys for the 'door of the tower, "for Sergeant to go in and out with prisoners"' (1934a, 42). He suggests that, as the Corporation did not own Ypres Tower at this date, this entry probably relates to Land Gate, though it would be unusual to refer to that building as "the tower" rather than the Land Gate or North Gate. An alternative possibility is that the Corporation was by then already leasing Ypres Tower from its then-absentee owner. In the 1450s and 1460s it was in the ownership of James Hyde who, like Ypres, being a Rye man could have lived within the tower. However, in 1477 Hyde's heirs sold to an outsider, Lord Stanley, and so from that date it was almost certainly leased out. It was conveyed by Stanley to John Newbury (another outsider) in 1492 and he in turn conveyed his interest to the Corporation in 1495, though other members of the Stanley family appear to have retained interests and, in consequence, the Corporation did not acquire the full title until 1517. Specific reference to Ypres Tower in use as a courthouse is found in ESRO RYE 1/4/24r which refers to 'Courthouse called Baddings Tower', whilst the same source refers to the Courthouse/prison in 1577. However, in 1559 it was decreed that 'all such prisoners [for which named persons were responsible] to be kept in Landgate' – ESRO RYE 1/2/25r.

60 TNA SC12 15/73 1r.

61 Mayhew 1987, 92.

62 ESRO RYE 60/4 321v-323r; ESRO RYE 60/5 7r, 10r; Mayhew 35. A documentary reference is quoted in A. F. de P. Worsfield. 1925. 'The Court Hall, Rye', *SAC* **66**, 208 as relating to 'a tenement called The Court House' sold by Robert Jackson to the Corporation in 1572, but this is a misquote: the document (ESRO RYE 126/4-5) relates to the sale of a tenement behind the court hall. The abutments make it clear that it was located between the court hall and the cemetery wall. It is probably the same piece of land granted to Anthony Boniface at an annual rent of 3s.4d. and described as a 'Piece of ground behind the Court hall on the north 41ft. 6ins., east-west 29 ft.' (ESRO RYE 1 /4, 370v).

63 Vidler 1934a, 96.

64 ESRO RYE 47/39/26.

65 Mayhew 1987, 41. Because Mayhew did not take into account the possibility of changes in location over time, some of his statements as to location seem to be suspect and need to be used with care.

66 ESRO RYE 126/2; SAC 66, 208; Mayhew 1987, 35.

67 Vidler 1934a, 17, 21.

68 ESRO RYE 1/3/192v; ESRO RYE 1/7/474v-475; Mayhew 1987, 92.

69 ESRO PAB 4. In 1695 the western part of The Queen's Arms, measuring 86 ft by 40 ft, was sold off to form a separate property. It had upon it two stables, a slaughterhouse and a gatehouse.

70 Medieval sources (early 14th century) mention Westwish, The Longeswish, The Kaneswish, and Kingswish, but it is clear that these were on the fringes of Rye. The area known as Kingswish was on the northern side of the town, but much further east, behind the properties on the western side of the Landgate suburb — *see* abutments in a deed relating to a house outside North Gate (Landgate) dated 1390 (ESRO RYE 136/134). It may be no coincidence that Landgate was called King Street until about 1900. Another deed, of 1363, refers to Kingswish as a meadow — ESRO RYE 136/107. The others two appear to be meadows to the north of Rye.

71 The only investigation carried out in this area was trial trenching in Blackman's Yard, to north of Wish Street, carried out in 2002 (ASE Report No. 1522) Three trenches were cut: none were taken to any depth.

72 Mayhew 1987, 205; ESRO RYE 130/36.

73 ESRO RYE 130/27, 130/30, 130/32, 130/35, 131/3, 131/5; ESRO RYE 1/4/228.

74 ESRO RYE 60/6/91-114; Mayhew 1984 113; ESRO RYE 131/8.

75 We are grateful to Frank Palmer for bringing this photograph to our attention.

76 *VCH Sussex* **9**, 48; ESRO HBR/1/0942; ESRO RYE 131/8.

77 ESRO RYE 60/6/91-114; Mayhew 1984, 113.

78 ESRO RYE 33/7 fo. 10r.

79 Vidler 1934a, 34.

80 Mayhew 1987, 26. In 1485 £11.8s.10d. was spent on building new shops at the Strand (Vidler 1934a, 44). In 1473 a grant was made by the Corporation of vacant land, 75 ft x 24 ft 'outside the Watergate at the Strand' abutting east on town land, south opposite the town walls and 'on the common Quay', west on 'the Strand' and north on 'town lands called the common Strand'. (ESRO RYE 130/3 and 4) This appears to be in the northern area marked as 'The Strand' in 1667. In 1498 a parcel 23½ ft by 12 ft 'at the Strand' was described as 'near the Fishmarket place', abutting east on the town shops, north on land of the heirs of Crouch, west on the market and south on town land (ESRO RYE 130/10). Despite reference to the Strand, this was in the area marked by Jeake as the Fish Market. Likewise, in 1506 a feoffment by the Corporation of vacant parcel, part of 'The Dock at the Strand', 62 ft by 23 ft. The abutments are given as east on the street [i.e. Wish Ward], south on 'a way from that street to the market place at the Strand' [as marked by Jeake], west on town land [i.e. other part of The Dock, measuring 15ft by 10 ft, granted out by the Corporation in 1517], north on a footway from the market place to 'cokyngstole'. The deed includes endorsements, including an agreement that the grantee will keep clear the water running from the town dyke and horsepit to the said dock, and a further annotation that the deed relates to 'Mr Burchets shops'. (ESRO RYE 130/13 and 18). The site was immediately south of The Wishe, to the south of what is now Wish Street. Similarly in 1535 a vacant plot 'at the strand' abutting west onto 'common land near the Fishmarket' (ESRO RYE 130/26) There are other deeds of recently erected shops (often described in plural) and plots for the building of shops at the Strand in 1507, 1515, 1516, 1517, 1518, 1524, 1529 (ESRO RYE 130/14, 16-21, 23). The grants continue throughout the 16th century.

81 Mayhew 1987, 123.

82 Mayhew 1987, 26, 28; Vidler 1934a, 55.

83 ESRO RYE 33/20.

84 *Ibid.* For the storehouse *see* WSRO Wiston 2255 (deed of 1574).

85 Mayhew 1987, 40.

86 ESRO RYE 1/5/113; Mayhew 1987, 103.

87 ESRO RYE 1/6; ESRO RYE 130/45.

88 Mayhew 1987, 28-29.

89 ESRO RYE 60, fo.60v.

90 Mayhew 1987, 166.

91 Mayhew 1987, 234.

92 Mayhew 1987, 268; ESRO RYE 1/6/324v-325r, 412; WSRO WISTON 224; ESRO RYE 130/45.

93 ESRO RYE 132/15.

94 ESRO RYE 33/7, fo.10r.

95 TNA SP 12/254, 75.

96 Mayhew 1987, 43, 283.

97 ESRO RYE 127/6, 7.

98 Capt. H. Lovegrove, R.N., 'Remains of two old vessels found at Rye, Sussex' in Mariners Mirror. *J. Soc. Nautical Research* **50**, 115-122.

99 *Pers. comm.* Alan Tyler.

100 Collard 1978, 36.

101 Mayhew 1987, 28.

102 Summarized from Mayhew 1987, especially pp.30-31, 48-49.

103 Martin and Martin 2004, 33-35.

104 Summarized from Mayhew 1987, especially pp.29-30; 178-179.

105 Martin and Martin 2004, 39-40.

106 Parish, Rev. W. D. 1957. *A Dictionary of The Sussex Dialect.* Bexhill: Gardner's of Bexhill Ltd, p.14 — 'BUDGE [Bouge, *French] A cask placed on wheels for carrying water (see* Bodge and *Bouge*)'.

107 Summarized from Mayhew 1987, especially pp.42-44, 47, 218. For waste disposal in Winchelsea, where cess pits have been excavated, *see* Martin and Martin 2004, 173-176.

108 *Pers. comm.* Alan Dickinson.

3 — TOWN DEFENCES

1 Barley, M. W. 1975. 'Town Defences in England and Wales after 1066' in *The Plans and Topography of Medieval Towns in England and Wales.* CBA Research Report No. 14, pp.57-70; Draper and Meddens forthcoming; Martin, D., Martin, B. and Whittick, C. 1995. *An Archaeological Interpretative Survey of The Old Town Wall, Hastings, East Sussex.* ESRO HBR/1/1234; Clarke *et. al.* forthcoming.

2 The approximate length of the wall, measured from west cliff (just south of Strand Gate) to east cliff (east of Land Gate) is 575 metres, whilst the length of the cliff top from one end of the wall to the other measures approximately 770 metres, including a length of cliff-top wall flanking the Ypres Tower.

3 Cal. Papal Reg., I, 111; CChR 1, 321-322, 15th May 1247; Close Rolls of the reign of Henry III, A.D.1242-1247, London 1916, 45. We are grateful to Susanne Jenks and Christopher Whittick for looking up and checking these references for us.

4 Renn 1979. In Renn's words Savoy was to 'fortify the castles of Hastings and la Rye'; CCR, Hen III, 5, 45; CChR 1, 321.

5 CPR, Hen III, 4, 50.
6 Colvin, H. M., Allen Brown, R. and Taylor, A.J. 1963. *The History of the King's Works: The Middle Ages*. London: HMSO.
7 CCR 1242-7; 30 H3; 436. Bertram de Criol of Westenhanger, Kent, was at that time Constable of Dover Castle and Lord Warden of the Cinque Ports: he was also Sheriff of Kent. (Hasted, E. 1799 *The History and Topographical Survey of the County of Kent*, **8**. Institute of Historical Research. Reproduced 1972, pp.63-68).
8 For the defences at Winchelsea *see* Martin and Martin 2004, Chapter 5. With respect to Rye, in 1272/3 one Denis (*Dyonisis*) de Stonewall is named as the tenant of land in the Rye Bailiff's account (TNA SC 6/1028/8), whilst in *c.*1285 Wymund atte Wall witnessed a Rye deed (ESRO RYE 136/13). The rental of the reign of Edward I (1272-1307) also refers to a *walle lapidee*, i.e. stone wall (TNA SC12/15/73).
9 TNA C47/2/48.
10 Vidler 1934a, 157.
11 *VCH Sussex* **9**, 40b.
12 ESRO RYE 134/2. The only archaeological section across the town ditch was cut in this very area (*see* Hadfield 1981).
13 CCR 1377-81, 3R2, 288; *VCH Sussex* **9**, 40.
14 Many towns struggled to build their walls and progress could be slow. Some were never completed, as was the case at Winchelsea, where in the early 15th century a new defensive circuit of lesser circumference was abandoned (*see* Martin and Martin 2004, 46-48). That the town walls at Rye were indeed built at this period is indicated by the boundary clauses in 15th-century deeds, for example ESRO RYE 136/18/3 (1427); ESRO RYE 136/19 (1441, 1455 and 1482); ESRO RYE 137/14 (1448); ESRO RYE 130/3/4 (1473). The abutment to the deed of 1427 relates to the isolated southern length of town wall adjacent to the Ypres Tower; the others refer to the main section of wall extending from the Strand round to the wall's end at Land Gate.
15 CPR 1381-85, 8R2, 519, 525, 532.
16 Vidler 1934a, 36.
17 HMC **V**, 490-494; *VCH Sussex* **9**, 40, including note 25; Vidler 1934a, 38. This same concern to watch and defend against the French is expressed at New Romney between 1385 and the 16th century. Here the town accounts cover a longer period than those of Rye, and the references in the accounts to purchases of weaponry such as 'bows and arrows for Common House' and two guns with six chambers are echoed in the unusual finds of lead shot and a powder-measure cap on the New Romney sea front.
18 Mayhew 1984, 114.
19 *VCH Sussex* **9**, 185; Mayhew 1984, 114 and note 39.
20 Mayhew 1984, 115.
21 For a detailed report on Camber Castle *see* Biddle *et. al.* 2001. *See also VCH Sussex* **9**, 185.
22 Mayhew 1984, 111 and note 25.
23 Mayhew considered the threat to have been from the north, due to inundation of St Mary's Marsh, but even with this area inundated it seems highly unlikely that a ship of any draught would have been able to enter this area, even at exceptional high tides. Furthermore, even if it was possible it would have either been a very foolish or desperate enemy who would attempt such a manoeuvre as they would very easily have been trapped there.
24 Mayhew 1984, 111-116.
25 Vidler 1934a, 47. At Winchelsea, not just the walls but also the gates were limed in this way, and the same had probably been the case at Rye: certainly there is evidence of a lime covering at Ypres Tower.
26 ESRO RYE 130/15.
27 Mayhew 1984, 111-115.
28 Mayhew 1984, 111-115; Mayhew 1987, 35.
29 Mayhew 1984, 114-115.
30 Mayhew 1987, 283; ESRO RYE 127/12-13; 130/38-44.
31 ESRO RYE 132/15.
32 Vidler 1934a, 55, 97, 103; Holloway 1847, 77, 288-9.
33 ESRO RYE 132/15.
34 Recent accounts of Ypres Tower have been based upon earlier work, mostly without provenance, and upon un-referenced hearsay. In an attempt to re-assess the structural evidence, in 1996 Rye Museum Association (the present owners) commissioned Archaeology South-East to undertake a new archaeological survey of the building. This was programmed to coincide with repairs being made by the then owners, Rother District Council, thereby allowing information to be recorded during the temporary opening-up of the roof structure for essential repairs. Further targeted recording work was undertaken by Archaeology South-East as part of a programme of limited alterations and repairs undertaken in 2005-2007. A copy of the full report, upon which this summary is based, is held at East Sussex Record Office (ESRO HBR/1/1295 (Revised)). The commissioned work excluded documentary research.
35 Martin and Martin 2004, 41-66.
36 Renn 1979, 197, Figure 3.
37 The eastern window is today blocked and although the opening is visible internally, there are no visible traces of its external surround, and thus the design is uncertain. The external surround is shown in Van Dyck's view from the east drawn in 1633/4, though the details are too indistinct to be of help: it is not even certain whether the opening was in use or blocked at that time.
38 Writing in Victoria County History (*VCH Sussex* **9**, 41-42) J. W. Bloe does not commit himself to a date for the tower, although the accompanying plan does give the main fabric as '13th century'. Renn, in support of his 13th-century castle theory, cites as parallels other 13th-century towers with corner turrets, but all are foreign (Renn 1979). The only exception — where the argument is rather strained — is Clifford's Tower, the keep of 1245-72 at York Castle where Renn straightens the walls of a shell keep in order to make the comparison. Furthermore, in size Clifford's Tower is a very different building from the diminutive Ypres Tower.
39 Martin and Martin 2004, 165-172.
40 ESRO RYE 136/137, 153; ESRO RYE 136/139. For further details *see* Draper 2009.
41 Vidler 1934a, 32.
42 ESRO RYE 124/1.
43 ESRO RYE 124/3-18.
44 Mayhew 1987, 180.
45 ESRO RYE 124/1-13 and 18. Other members of the Stanley family appear to have retained interests and, in consequence, the corporation did not re-acquire the full title until 1517.
46 HMC **V**, 493-6.
47 Vidler 1934a, 42, 50; Vidler suggests that, as the corporation did not own Ypres Tower at this date, this entry probably relates to Land Gate, though, if so, it would be unusual to refer to that building as 'the tower' as opposed to the Land Gate or North Gate. Specific reference to Ypres Tower in use as a courthouse is found in ESRO RYE 1/4/24r which refers to 'Courthouse called Baddings Tower', whilst the same source refers to the Courthouse/prison in 1577. However, in 1559 it was decreed that 'all such prisoners [for which named persons were responsible] to be kept in Landgate', showing that Land Gate was, at least on occasions, used for this purpose (ESRO RYE 1/2/25r).
48 Mayhew 1987, 35, 178. The former town sergeant's furnishings (described as 'waynescott work, portalls and a small bedsteddle') for which the corporation paid 46s.8d are mentioned within the courthouse in 1577 (Mayhew 1987, 178).
49 Renn 1979, 196, states that Van Dyck illustrates the roof as being gabled. This statement is in error, for although Van Dyck's view from the south-east appears to show a gable with a doorway in it, this is the result of poor perspective. What appears to be a doorway is the chimney, whilst Van Dyck's drawing of the tower viewed from the south-west very clearly shows the roof as being

fully hipped.

50 Vidler 1934a, 57, quoting from the Chamberlain's accounts. That the roof replaced an earlier structure is indicated both by the location of its wallplates and by a recess for an earlier wallplate recorded during building works carried out in 1996: it had been blocked using 'Flemish' bricks.

51 Vidler 1934a, 55, 97.

52 TNA S.P.Dom 46/36 1 MPF 1/3; BL Add Mss 5670, fo.16 (undated, 1780s).

53 ESRO RYE 1/4/223; ESRO RYE 60/3, fo.32; Mayhew 1984, 111-115.

54 TNA SC12 15/73; ESRO RYE 136/57, 64 and 73; *VCH Sussex* **9**, 40-41. Thanks are due to Christopher Whittick for pointing out an error in the catalogue entry relating to one of the above — the document refers to a property as *extra portum* (outside the gate) rather than *extra portas* (outside the gates) as given in the catalogue.

55 *VCH Sussex* **9**, 41.

56 The wall is of rubble masonry and contains a pair of low-level, blocked loop lights with, above them, a blocked, trefoiled ogee-headed light: all face east. A wall in this approximate location is shown in a Van Dyck illustration (Figure 2.3) but this projects less far and is located further to the east than the present structure. More significant, the wall is not shown in S. H. Grimm's drawing made in the 1780s (Figure 3.12), nor in drawings of the gate made by Moore (1798) and Munn (1823).

57 Vidler 1934a, 41; Mayhew 1984, 114.

58 A later stone staircase around the south side of the drum of the east tower now rises to the first floor of the gateway.

59 Mayhew 1984, 34, 114.

60 Slightly over 10 metres O.D. near Land Gate to just over 7 metres O.D at the foot of Conduit Hill.

61 It is not clear what the vegetation shown on the bank is: it might be rough grass, but is more likely bushes, which would have the effect of visually exaggerating the height of the bank.

62 Martin and Martin 2004, 42-66; Martin, D., Martin, B. and Whittick, C. 1995. *An Archaeological Interpretative Survey of The Old Town Wall, Hastings, East Sussex.* ESRO HBR/1/1234.

63 Hadfield, J. 1979. 'Excavations at 1-3 Tower Street, Rye, including Town Wall and Town Ditch', *Rescue Archaeology in Sussex,* 29-30; Hadfield, J. 1981 'An excavation at 1-3 Tower Street, Rye, East Sussex', *SAC* **119**, 222-225.

64 No heights above ordnance datum are given on either the drawn section or in the published accounts, so the level of this deposit cannot be determined with any precision: based upon known street levels it appears to have been at about 2.5 metres (c.8'3") O.D.

65 The present street level at this point is at 4.9 metres O.D., but bearing in mind this is roughly two and a half metres above the top of the silt layer and the Van Dyck drawing shows no major drop from the road into the ditch, it seems likely that the level was raised when the track was upgraded to the status of a street and subsequently metalled.

66 Top located at roughly 4.5 metres above O.D.

67 Clark 1861, 23; Vidler 1934a, 95, 104, 117. Writing from first-hand experience in 1817, Stockdale refers to surviving gates, some ruinous (indicating the survival at that time of more than one ruinous gate) — Stockdale, F.W.L. 1817. *A Concise Historical and Topographical Sketch of Hastings, Winchelsea and Rye.* Hastings: Powell.

68 Rye Museum, Town Plan of Rye, 1771.

69 TNA MPF 1/212 (ex SP12/254 (751)); TNA SP 46/36 (1), MPF 1/3; ESRO RYE 132/15.

70 At what level within the wall the Postern Gate entrance was located is impossible to say: the street levels at the lower end of Conduit Hill could have been lowered when this section of town wall was removed in 1767, allowing vehicular traffic to use Conduit Street. Even if the intra-mural ground was at a higher level than now, the arch could have been positioned low down in the wall (as implied by the Jeake map — ESRO RYE 132/15) reached from the townward side by a cut-in ramp. Alternatively, the bridge could have crossed to a point quite high in the external face of the wall.

71 Mayhew 1984, 111, 114.

72 The ground here is at *c*.9.0 metres above OD. This could result from the ground level on the townward side having been raised subsequent to construction of the wall, as indeed can be shown to have occurred further west. That this is unlikely in this instance is indicated by archaeological investigations carried out in 2001-2005 at 59, 59a Cinque Ports Street. The investigations were carried out in three stages, all undertaken by Archaeology South-East. The work commenced with an evaluation undertaken by Simon Stevens in April 2001 (Stevens 2001) followed by a programme of excavation undertaken in November 2004 (yet to be written up, but for a post-excavation assessment *see* Stevens and Barber 2005) and a programme of recording undertaken on the exposed section of town wall by Neil Griffin in April/May 2005 (Griffin 2005). Bearing in mind that the post-excavation analysis is yet to be completed, the information contained within this present interpretation may be subject to revision. It is Archaeology South-East's intention to fully publish their investigations carried out within this part of the town in due course.

73 The intended design of the wall is indicated by the rough nature of its eastern face, compared to the neat face on the west. Given the known medieval ground levels immediately to the west of the wall scar, it seems likely that the construction of the wall involved a degree of terracing into the hill slope at this point.

74 Medieval ground level against the western face of the toothings was *c*.6.70 metres above OD: at a point 15 metres to the west it was *c*.6.00 metres above OD, less than 500 mm above the level on the extra-mural side. At this point the base of the wall's foundation was encountered at about 5.50 metres above OD.

75 The alignment of the wall in this area still survived as a boundary in 1771 — *see* Rye Museum Town Map — and thus it is likely that the wall itself still survived at that date. According to Clark there were steps over the wall at the bottom of Jarret's Yard (i.e. on the alignment of Market Road) in 1683, but it appears that this was later superseded by a doorway cut through the wall. Clark, writing in 1861, stated 'through which [doorway] I have heard the old inhabitants say they have often passed' (Clark 1861, 23). This implies that the wall was taken down within living memory of 1861.

76 At this point natural ground lies below 4.70 metres above OD.

77 Medieval ground surface was encountered at 8.55 metres above OD at a point just 10 metres back from the wall (Johnson 1998). It was not possible to establish early ground levels closer to the rear of the town wall in this area.

78 Immediately against the base of the wall the top of the berm varied from between 4.8-5.1 metres above OD at its lowest point to 5.50+ metres above OD towards the eastern end and 6.2 metres above OD at a distance of 71 metres to the west of Market Road. Probing at a point 56 metres to the west of Market Road and 8.5 metres in front of the town wall suggested that the bottom at this point might be located at a depth of 3.45 metres above OD (Stevens 2001; Knight 2004; Johnson 1999).

79 Vidler 1934a, 47. He specifically states that 'the first [point of] interest in the [16th] century was the making of a Ponde-garden. This was situated in what is now the Corporation yard in Cattle Market Road . . . . . It had a drain which led through the wall to the town ditch and was built of stone and brick and the drain needed frequent cleansing'.

80 Vidler 1934a, 47; Mayhew 1987, 12, 143, 177, 279. It seems likely that in drawing his conclusions Vidler was picking up on documentary references to the making or maintenance of drainage holes through the wall in this area and that he connected this with the making of a pond, though it is also possible that he had stumbled upon documentary references to the excavation of

the pit discovered during the 59, 59a Cinque Port Street excavations. Vidler, of course, did not have the advantage of the archaeological investigations to assist him. The additional data suggests a more obvious alternative: that the drains were intended to rid this wet area of unwanted, perhaps seasonal accumulated surface water.

81 It varies from 6.9 metres above OD at a high point near the end of Ferry Road, falling to 4.8 metres a little to the north of the Strand Gate, before rising slightly to the site of Strand Gate itself. These are modern surface levels, after backfill of the town ditch.

82 Holloway 1847, 288-9. We know from notes made by Vidler that Holloway made a note dated 3rd April 1856 stating that the bastion had 'lately been pulled down', though 'one of the embrasures had been preserved and placed in the west wall and the stone with the circular hole in the north wall [?but of what]. Some of the stones have been used in the foundation of the house now building at the south-east end of the row now belonging to John Pain under the cliff opposite the wool warehouse at Landgate, which is the building mentioned at p.596 in my History of Rye, the called the old warehouse'. Vidler's note is contained within a specially printed annotated copy of his own book, now held at Rye Museum. We are grateful to Jo Kirkham for making this reference available.

83 It is over this that the much later western wall of Sharps Pottery is built.

84 Very disappointingly, access to the flat which incorporates the upper part of the wall was denied, and thus interpretation of this element relies upon the evidence contained within the ground floor of 54 The Mint, from the face exposed to view within Wishe Ward, and from aerial photographs. The gable wall of 54 The Mint is stepped back a considerable distance from the extra-mural face of the wall, indicating that the parapet walkway is likely to survive.

85 Platt *et. al.* 1975, 83-85.

86 For an illustration of the town wall at King's Lynn as it survived in the year 1800 *see* Higgins, D. 2001 *The Antiquities of King's Lynn from the sketchbooks of the Rev. Edward Edwards.* King's Lynn: Phoenix Publications, p.13.

4 — RELIGIOUS, EDUCATIONAL AND WELFARE BUILDINGS

1 Draper 2009; Mayhew 1987.

2 For a detailed discussion regarding Rye's chantries *see* Draper 2009, Chapter 6.

3 Draper 2009, Chapter 6.

4 Draper 2009, Chapter 6; *VCH Sussex* **9**, 43; ESRO HBR/1/0792.

5 Martin, D. and Martin, B. 2005. 'Archaeological Interpretative Survey of the Standing Building' in Thomas, G. 'Refining the biography of a marketplace tenement', *SAC* **143**, 173-204.

6 Draper 2009, Chapter 6. *See also VCH Sussex* **2**, 96-97.

7 Martin and Martin 2004, 73, 88-90.

8 Draper 2009; ESRO RYE 60/5, f.140. There have been considerable variations to the height of walls since the dissolution, associated with new roofs. As illustrated in Figure 4.26, the eaves were originally located a little above the heads of the windows in the south wall — the change in masonry is still clearly visible. Van Dyck's illustration reproduced in Figure 4.30 shows a small square-headed window above the arched window in the east gable. It is the opinion of Gerald Moody of the Trust for Thanet Archaeology that this was related to an upper floor inserted as part of the reconstruction of the building into alternative use after the dissolution (*pers. comm.* Gerald Moody (Deputy Director of the Trust for Thanet Archaeology).

9 There are the remains of a series of blocked openings in a fairly regular series to be seen on the north side of the chapel of the chapel. The plan shown in *VCH Sussex* **9** does not show this door in the north-west end of the chapel as it was obscured by a heavy wooden staircase whose treads were partly chased into the frame of the door. The door frame is in stone but mouldings on each side do not match and part of the east side seems to have been repaired with parts of a window ledge. The joint in the arch does not meet properly as if half an original frame was repaired leaving too narrow a gap and breaking the curve of the arch. (*pers. comm.* Gerald Moody (Deputy Director of the Trust for Thanet Archaeology)).

10 Holloway 1847, 592.

11 The buildings shown in the Van Dyck drawing may have been freestanding — certainly they were not keyed into the wall of the chapel — though this could be explained either by the fact that they were erected later in the sequence of construction (as with, for example, the straight-jointed internal walls at Bodiam Castle, East Sussex) or the lack of wall-scars could indicate that the cloistral buildings were of timber-framed construction and were thus butted against the chapel wall. However, it should also be noted that Van Dyck seems to show a gable which crosses the roof line of the chapel where the east range meets the chapel building. Unfortunately, here too the configuration does not prove either a difference in date or that the two buildings did not adjoin one another, as not all medieval buildings constructed against and at right angles to another structure incorporate integrated roofs with valleys. It should be noted that no evidence was found in the Trust for Thanet Archaeology's evaluation excavation to indicate scars of any abutting walls or joints with the foundation courses. Based upon the above information, the hypothesis preferred by the archaeologist working on the friary is that the buildings shown as standing to the north of the chapel in Van Dyck's illustration were of post-dissolution date. We are still to be convinced by this theory, as it seems surprising that the (assumed reasonable-quality) monastic buildings would have been destroyed in order to make way for replacement structures constructed on a similar footprint. It is worth bearing in mind that this is a late monastic foundation and was always small: its chapel does not conform to a standard friary plan. Until further site investigations have been undertaken it must be admitted that either of the two suggested interpretations mentioned above could be correct. We are grateful to Gerald Moody, Deputy Director of the Trust for Thanet Archaeology for discussing his thoughts with us.

12 Draper 2009, Chapter 6.

13 For the full survey of 1670 (including acreages and abutments of the individual blocks of land) *see* ESRO DAP 1/3; CKS U455 M53, and for a sketch plan of the land (but not the site of the manor house) of 1673 *see* ESRO NOR 15/79 (formerly SAS/HC 181). The history of the hospital is discussed in full in the chapter devoted to Religious Rye in Draper 2009, which also discusses the possible sites of the hospital. *See also VCH Sussex* **2**, 104-105.

14 WSRO Ep/I/1/2, f.80v.

15 ESRO RYE 111/1; *VCH Sussex* **9**, 61; Holloway 1863, 46; Mayhew 1987, 32. *VCH Sussex* **9** gives the date erroneously as April 1550.

16 Mayhew 1987, 32, 176.

17 Mayhew 1987, 32.

18 Holloway 1863, 47.

19 Mayhew 1987, 32.

20 Kirkham, J. with a foreword by G. Mayhew. 1989. *Schools.* Rye Memories Series **XI**. Thomas Peacocke Community College Local History Group; Draper, G. 2008 'The education of children in Kent and Sussex: interpreting the medieval and Tudor ways', *Nottingham Medieval Studies* **52**, 222, 224-26, 237.

21 Mayhew 1987, 53.

22 Worsfield, A.F.de P. 1925. 'Peacock's School, Rye, Sussex,' *SAC* **68**, 199-209; *VCH Sussex* **9**, 46.

5 — POPULATION, HOUSEHOLD DENSITY AND OCCUPATIONS

1 Martin and Martin 2004, 100-102.
2 TNA SC12 15/73. For an in-depth discussion of the rental *see* Draper 2009.
3 TNA SC 6/1032/7; SC 6/1032/10; Martin and Martin 2004, 196-7.
4 Deeds of the 1350s (ESRO RYE 136/96; 136/10/2) and 1390 (ESRO RYE 136/13/4) indicate houses outside the Land Gate, on the west side of the street, and Extra Portam suburb is shown well populated in the early 15th century half-scot and scot. Some houses are still mentioned in the 1440s (ESRO RYE 135/1; 136/19) but by this period there are also references to empty plots and vacant ground (ESRO RYE 135/1; 136/15/4). After that date the documents are silent until land in this area once more started to be granted out by the corporation during the early 16th century, though even then housing on this western side of the street remained very limited. Given the number of persons living in Extra Portam, it seems likely that at one time the eastern side of the street was also built up, but was perhaps abandoned as the land on this side eroded. It was not until the 16th century that people felt confident to build in this area again. For the eastern end of High Street *see* ESRO RYE 130/5-9.
5 ESRO RYE 136/71; 136/113; 136/126. The area known as Halton was given to the Austin Friars by the corporation in 1378: it is bounded today by properties against East Cliff (east), properties against High Street (south), Conduit Hill (west) and Turkey Cock Lane (north).
6 ESRO RYE 77/1 and 77/2. The undated scot was made during the same mayorality as that of 1414, though the mayor in question is known to have served more than one term. There is close correlation between the two returns, implying little time-lag between the two. Internal evidence suggests that the undated return was prepared later than dated half-scot.
7 ESRO RYE 130/5-9.
8 ESRO RYE 77/3; ESRO RYE 15/1; ESRO WIN 440.
9 Foreign-sounding names in the 1491/2 sesse include Moreis Hous, Cornelis Irescheman, John Overhous, Martyn Spaynard. For the list of aliens see TNA E 179/230/200C. The three names identified in both the 1483 alien subsidy and the 1491/2 sesse are John George, John Dirrikson and Anthony Lameson.
10 Vidler 1934a, 52.
11 ESRO RYE 130/9.
12 Mayhew 1987, 140. The method used to differentiate between heads of exempt households and relatives, servants and apprentices within assessed households is not stated.
13 Examples are 101-102 High Street [26], St Anthony's, Church Square and 1-2 Watchbell Street [87, 90], 26 Church Square [80].
14 There appear to have been five shops with chambers above them incorporated within the street frontage of the Shurley mansion, and these could have been let to tenants as shops with habitable chambers over, though shops with storage above seems more likely. An example in the nearby port town of Hastings is to be found at the butchery in High Street where there were 5 butchers' shops with 10 chambers over them (*SRS* **36**, 33, 180-81). In the case of the Hastings example there was probably independent external access to the chambers, rather than access through the shops.
15 In the 1660 poll tax, households headed by widows accounted for 14 per cent of the total — many of these lived alone and were exempt from hearth tax — *see* ESRO RYE 82/82 and ESRO RYE 83/5. Widows listed in 1491/2 account for only 6 per cent of the total. Using the percentage for 1660 to calculate the number of widows in 1491/2 gives 24 which, making allowance for the nine widows taxed, gives 15 possible widow households exempt through poverty. If a similar number is used to calculate destitute males, the total calculates at 209 households, at the low end of the 200-240 households quoted in the text.
16 There is one assessment at 15s. 0d., but this is an exception. The entry for the document in the Historical Manuscript Commission catalogue to the Rye corporation archive states that the highest valuation is £400, but this is in error: Oxenbridge's £500 valuation seems to have been overlooked. Even this £500 assessment is a downward 'correction' of the original valuation, replacing an initial entry of £600. We are grateful to Christopher Whittick for verifying the £500 valuation and for identifying the value of the erased total.
17 The data for Richard Swan, in Fisherstreet Ward, is contradictory — two figures appear to be given against his valuation (£100 and £20) but he paid only 1s.8d. in tax, the equivalent of a £10 valuation. In calculating the statistics used from this point onwards within this chapter Swan's tax of 1s.8d. has been used to indicate a valuation of £10.
18 The figures quoted above include the three persons who head the tax return and who are not allocated to a ward (and therefore do not appear in Figure 5.2). Excluded are the five persons for which valuations are given, but are not included within the tax return, and therefore their ward of residency is unknown.
19 The ownership of St Anthonys is known from summarized transcripts of the deeds to the property made by the Rye historian, L.H Vidler. The transcript includes abutments. For the two rich widows *see* ESRO RYE 136/199 and for the properties at the eastern end of High Street, granted to persons assessed in Market Ward *see* ESRO RYE 130/5-9.
20 ESRO RYE 1/3, fos.43r-48r.
21 Mayhew 1987, 280. *See also* ESRO RYE 139/32.
22 More deeds are likely to exist, but it has not proved possible within the present project to search through the extensive corporation records for this period contained within ESRO RYE to check for enrolled deeds.
23 Mayhew 1987 generally, especially 233-262 and Table 36.
24 Mayhew 1987, 235-6.
25 *See* Chapter 1, note 23.
26 TNA SP12/38 f.28.
27 Hipkin 1998-9, 108.
28 Mayhew 1987, 22-23.
29 Mayhew 1987, 47.
30 These numbers in themselves must surely be significant for, based upon 530 households in 1565, this represents 1 birth per annum per 5 households.
31 For custom returns *see* Mayhew 1987, Table 36; for Chamberlains' income *see* Mayhew, Appendix 2. The summarized analysis given here ignores those annual figures inflated by income from sesses.
32 For more detail *see* Chapter 1 and Mayhew 1987, 79-90.
33 An enhanced transcript of the 1576 sesse, together with the ward descriptions, is given in Mayhew 1987, Appendix 4.
34 Hipkin 1998-9, 110.
35 Mayhew 1987, 145. Most of the foreigners (8 out of 13, being 3 merchants, a mercer, a surgeon, a glazier and a locksmith) resided in Landgate ward. Two merchants and a sailor lived in Middlestreet ward, another merchant in Market ward and a baker in Baddings ward. Although some of these men could have been refugees who had taken up residence, the town is always likely to have included a small resident alien population, as indeed the 1483 Alien Subsidy *(see* note 9 above) and the 1524/5 lay subsidy returns illustrate.
36 Mayhew 1987, 141-143.
37 Mayhew 1987, 141-143.
38 ESRO RYE 1/5/56; Mayhew 1987, 147.
39 Mayhew 1987, 150, 153.
40 Mayhew 1987, 151-152.
41 Martin and Martin 2006, 34.
42 ESRO RYE 124/17; ESRO RYE 135/5-7; ESRO RYE 126/3.
43 ESRO NOR 13/81— Land usage assessment for the parishes of Playden and Iden.
44 Mayhew 1987; Brent 1975.

45 ESRO RYE 82/82; ESRO RYE 83/1-5; ESRO RYE 132/15.
46 ESRO RYE 83/1. Although this return does not list the houses by ward, most persons named are identifiable in the poll tax return of 1660. The return for 1664 (ESRO RYE 83/5) is incomplete in that exempt and empty houses in Baddings ward are missing.
47 ESRO RYE 132/15; WSRO WISTON 22/41; Holloway 1847, 325-6.
48 1801 Census Summary (BPP).
49 National census returns; *VCH Sussex* **2**, 228.

6 — RYE'S MEDIEVAL HOUSING

1 For cellars in towns generally *see* Faulkner, P. A. 1966. 'Medieval Undercrofts and Town Houses', *Archaeological Journal* **123**, 120-135. For Oxford *see* Munby, J. 1992. 'Zacharias's: A 14th Century Oxford New Inn and the Origins of the Medieval Urban Inn', *Oxoniensia* **57**. We are grateful to Julian Munby for supplying the statistical data relating to the town. Regarding Sussex examples outside Rye and Winchelsea, at Lewes, *VCH Sussex* **7**, 10-46, mentions vaulted cellars at 72 High Street, The Town Hall in High Street, and Anne of Cleves, Southover High Street. Also mentioned is a medieval cellar (no reference to vault) at 74 High Street. For surveys of the cellars at Town Hall and Anne of Cleves *see* ESRO HBR/1/1394 and HBR/1/1655 respectively. The known cellar in Battle is beneath 33-35 High Street (ESRO HBR/1/905), that in Eastbourne is beneath The Lamb Inn, High Street (ESRO HBR/1/1314) and that in Mayfield is beneath London House, *etc*, High Street (ESRO HBR/1/1363). For reports on the cellar in Seaford *see* ESRO HBR/1/1193. All three Lewes examples are barrel vaulted, but the others have ribbed quadripartite or similar vaults.
2 ESRO HBR/1/708. Architectural report of 8-10 High Street, Rye, by Alan Dickinson.
3 Faulkner 1975, 118.
4 We are grateful to Alan Dickinson for making the example at 29, 30 High Street known to us. He viewed the cellar in December 1993.
5 The survival of medieval houses in Kent is discussed in Pearson 1994. As yet unpublished research relating to the rural parts of the Rape of Hastings suggests a survival rate of around 10 per cent, though it should be noted that the rate within individual parishes varies markedly, with some parishes entirely devoid of standing medieval houses, and others (such as, for example, Northiam) having an above-average number.
6 This estimate is based upon existing medieval houses for which the early 16th-century ownership is known and for which the owners can be identified in the 1524-25 Lay Subsidy Returns (*SRS* **56**), correlated with the number of persons paying similar totals and the known/approximate number of houses which existed in the individual Hundreds of the Rape. The figures, as currently calculated, are by necessity very approximate and are likely to be subject to revision once further research has been completed.
7 BL Add Mss 45194.
8 Martin and Martin 1999.
9 Examples are Sandhills, Warbleton (ESRO HBR/1/0501); Tyles, Warbleton (ESRO HBR/1/0524); 11,13,15 High Street, Robertsbridge (ESRO HBR/1/0001); Watermans, Ewhurst (ESRO HBR/1/0330); and Cleaves, Peasmarsh (ESRO HBR/1/0681).
10 It should be noted that crosswings are more common in parts of Kent than in East Sussex (for the distribution of crosswings in Kent *see* Pearson 1994, 122-134, 147, especially Figure 138 on p.122.
11 As exemplified by ESRO NOR 13/81.
12 For towns in general *see* Quiney, A. 2003. *Town Houses of Medieval Britain*. New Haven and London: Yale University Press; for a specific example (Sandwich, Kent) *see* Clarke *et. al.*, forthcoming.
13 Martin and Martin 2004, 89.
14 Martin, D. and Martin, B. Forthcoming. *Hastings Old Town*.
15 For Burwash *see* ESRO HBR/1/0029, HBR/1/0610; for Winchelsea *see* ESRO HBR/1/1375; for Bexhill *see* ESRO HBR/1/0363, and for New Romney *see* Martin, D. and Martin, B. 2004. *An Archaeological Interpretative Survey of 3-4 West Street, New Romney, Kent*. Unpublished ASE Report, Project 1911.
16 Alcock *et. al.* 1996, G20.
17 For Bexhill *see* ESRO HBR/1/0363; for Salehurst *see* ESRO HBR/1/0078; for Winchelsea *see* ESRO HBR/1/1375; for Uckfield *see* ESRO HBR/1/1274; for Lewes *see* ESRO HBR/1/1655; for Alfriston *see* ESRO HBR/1/1185 and HBR/1/1186.
18 Barnwell and Adams 1994. *See also*, Martin and Mastin 1974, 12-23, particularly 19-21; Martin and Martin 1977-80, 69-70; Martin and Martin 1981, 54-56; Martin and Martin 1989, 21-23, 27.
19 The ground floor areas of the halls have been calculated from measurements taken from end wall to end wall (including the widths of any overshot cross passage, which in some instances have had to be estimated) and between the internal faces of soleplates and principal posts. The exact floor area of 99-100 High Street depends upon whether or not this building incorporated a wealden facade — the figure quoted is an average of the two possible widths. The smallest open hall currently known in Hastings in Dickens Cottage, 112 High Street (*see* ESRO HBR/1/254 (revised)) which has a floor area of 13m^2, equal to those at 26 Church Square Rye.
20 The twelfth example, at 9-10 East Street/13-14 Market Street [42], is too damaged to warrant illustration, but the surviving elements are similar to those at 16 East Street [34] and Lamb Cottage, West Street [53].
21 *Pers. comm.* Joan Harding, Domestic Buildings Research Group (Surrey). For examples in the local towns of Hastings and Battle *see* Martin, D. and Martin, B (forthcoming) *Hastings Old Town* and Martin, D. and Martin, B. (forthcoming) *Battle Town*.
22 TNA PRO PROB 2/141.
23 The emergence of fully-floored houses in the late 15th century is now well documented, but it is always interesting to note examples with and without open halls built side-by-side. In the town of New Buckenham, Norfolk, Yellow Cottage/Oak Cottage has two full storeys, an axial multi-flue chimney, and oriel windows on the first floor. It was previously thought to date from the 1520s, but has now been tree-ring dated to 1473 (Longcroft 2005, 171-175, 205-206).
24 ESRO AMS 5742/2; ESRO XA 24/2; ESRO RYE 33/20, 135/8, 135/10, 139/31; ESRO DAP Box 42; Privately held deeds transcribed by Vidler.
25 TNA PRO PROB 2/141.
26 ESRO HBR/1/0222; ESRO HBR/1/0152.
27 TNA PRO PROB 2/141.
28 For details of local wall construction in medieval houses *see* Martin and Martin 1989 and Barnwell and Adams 1994, 76-87.
29 Martin and Martin 1989, 43-47.
30 For details of local doorway design and construction *see* Martin and Martin 1991, 120-141, and Barnwell and Adams 1994, 88-102.
31 In Devon, John Thorpe has convincingly argued that the dais beam was kept low in order to inflate the stature of the owner sitting against the wall. Linked to this, he has noted a number of buildings in which the hall narrows towards the high end, thereby exaggerating the size of the hall (Devon Vernacular Architecture Group conference, Spring 2008). The generous depth of the dais beams in many Sussex examples may indicate a similar desire.
32 For details of local window design and construction *see* Martin and Martin 1991, 2-59, 73-111, and Barnwell and Adams 1994, 103-111.

33 The window at Fletcher's House, 1-2 Lion Street is no longer visible but is described on page 45 in *VCH Sussex* **9** (1937) as 'a former two-light window in the front wing with moulded mullions'.
34 Martin and Martin 1991.
35 For the use and construction of jetties in the local area *see* Martin and Martin 1989, 20-21, and Barnwell and Adams 1994, 39-43. No detailed analysis has yet been undertaken on floor joisting in the area, but for joist layouts see Barnwell and Adams 1994, 17-22, 73-74; for a study of joist patterns within the East Sussex village of Robertsbridge *see* Martin and Mastin 1974, 46-48.
36 The three surviving medieval joists at 17 West Street were not measured, but photographs show that they are at the small end of the range.
37 No detailed analysis has yet been undertaken of the medieval roofs in Eastern Sussex, but those in Kent (which are all but identical in form and detail) have been fully analysed in Barnwell and Adams 1994, 46-63, 75.; for a study of the roofs within the East Sussex village of Robertsbridge *see* Martin and Mastin 1974, 38-40; for medieval roofs over East Sussex agricultural buildings *see* Martin and Martin 2006, 81-92.
38 The same type of construction is found in some early roofs of much wider span, but no examples are known in Rye.
39 Mayhew 1987, 177.
40 A similar slackening of pitches over time has been recognized within local barns where both the early steep roofs and the more shallow-pitched later roofs are thatched in similar proportions — *see* Martin and Martin 2006, 81-82. It is possible that a move from thatch to tile in newly-built high-status houses and a consequent reduction in pitch to facilitate this meant that lower pitches became thought of as fashionable, even in those houses built to be thatched. The important point is that a lower-pitched roof cannot be used as proof that a roof was not thatched.
41 For chimneys and fireplaces in general *see* Wood 1981, 257-291. For chimneys in Southampton *see* Faulkner 1975 and for the town of Winchelsea *see* Martin and Martin 2004, 165-172. The exceptions with regards to rural houses are houses built by magnates, monastic houses and the upper tier of the gentry. Local rural examples are at Bodiam Castle, built by Sir Edward Dallingridge under licence date 1385 (*VCH Sussex* **9**, 159-162), the chimney of 1372-3 serving the crosswing of Battle Abbey's manor house at Great Maxfield, Guestling (ESRO HBR/1/0806), a 14th-century fireplace in the principal chamber of the prior's lodgings at Michelham Priory, Arlington (ESRO HBR/1/1056) and those of *c.*1400 serving the chapel and private chambers in the Oxenbridge mansion at Brede Place (ESRO HBR/1/0381), and to Southampton and Winchelsea.
42 To judge from the Rye inventories which survive from the 16th century, painted cloths were by that date common (*see* Chapter 7). There are no reasons for thinking them a new innovation within ordinary houses.
43 The known examples are 99-100 High Street [25]; 16 East Street [34] (internal and external); 4-6 Lion Street [45]; 10-11 Mermaid Street [64]; The Mermaid, Mermaid Street [72]; 22, 24 Church Square [78]; St Anthony's, Church Square [87].
44 For the use of combed daub locally *see* Martin and Martin 1977-80, 30-34; Barnwell and Adams 1994, 122-123; Martin and Martin 1989, 79-81.

7 — RYE'S POST-MEDIEVAL HOUSING

1 Johnson 1993.
2 TNA SP12/254 75.
3 Mayhew 1987 and deeds in ESRO RYE generally. A number of persons, both resident within the town and living elsewhere, acted as rentiers, holding small estates of properties which were let out. In each individual case care is needed as it is often difficult to ascertain whether the estate of an individual represents the development of an individual property into a number of letable tenements, or whether the estate was scattered across the town — in some instances it was a mixture of both. Even so, sufficient of the entries refer to the subdivision of existing houses or to houses built upon a single property to show that this practice was widespread. To quote just one good example, the inventory of Peter Adrian made in 1577 refers to the lease of 'one tenement and close or garden divided into four messuages' which he held of the churchwardens by 60 year lease dated 1543 (ESRO RYE 35/31). There are many similar descriptions.
4 Mayhew 1987, 175-6.
5 ESRO RYE 82/82 — 1660 Poll Tax.
6 ESRO RYE 82/82; ESRO RYE 83/1-5.
7 Mayhew 1987, 35-6, 123.
8 ESRO RYE 33/20.
9 Mayhew 1987, 44, 219, 257-8, 277.
10 Holloway 1863, 57.
11 To judge from the order of the entries in the 1660 poll tax (ESRO RYE 82/82) and the various hearth tax returns (ESRO RYE 83/1-5), the house appears to have been assessed at only 5 in 1663, when it was in the occupation of Thomas Miller, gentleman. However, there are problems. By the 1670s the owner is known to have been Thomas Palmer (*see* Draper 2009) who in the early 1660s was likewise assessed under Middlestreet ward, where he had a seven-flue house. From the position of his entries in the returns, his house seems to have been in another part of the ward, but this assumes the returns were assessed in topographical order, which is not known for certain. A further complication is the fact that 31 Mermaid Street fits neither of the assessments in that it has only four flues, though the possibility — even the likelihood — of a detached outhouse must be borne in mind. From the point of view of wealth, it is irrelevant whether the house was occupied by Miller or Palmer in 1660, for both were amongst Rye's wealthiest men: to judge from the figures included in the poll tax, Miller was the more wealthy of the two, being amongst the half-dozen highest assessed residents.
12 Hunter, M. & Gregory, A. 1988. *An Astrological Diary of the Seventeenth Century: Samuel Jeake of Rye 1652-1699* Oxford: Clarendon Press, p.150.
13 TNA PROB 2/328.
14 Mayhew 1987, 123.
15 Vidler 1934a, 52; Mayhew 1987, 123; 175.
16 Mayhew 1987, 191-199.
17 The most up-to-date study of shops and workshops for the period under discussion is Barnwell, P.S., Palmer, M. and Airs, M. (Eds) 2004, *The Vernacular Workshop: From Craft to Industry, 1400-1900.* York: Council For British Archaeology, in particular Alston, L, 'Late medieval workshops in East Anglia', pp.38-59. See also Clark, D. 2000. 'The Shop Within? An Analysis of the Architectural Evidence for Medieval Shops', *Architectural History* **43**, 58-87, and Stenning, D.F. 1985, 'Timber-Framed Shops 1300-1600: Comparative Plans', *Vernacular Architecture* **16**, 35-9.
18 Keene, D. 1985. *Survey of Medieval Winchester.* Winchester Studies **1**. Oxford: OUP, 149, 164; Alston, L. 2004 'Late medieval workshops in East Anglia' in Barnwell *et. al.* 2004 *op. cit.*
19 Alston 2004, 38-59.
20 Mayhew 1987, 25, 84-85,111; Hipkin 1995, 247-248.
21 Mayhew 1987 attempted this in Appendix 4, in which the non-victualler shopkeepers are annotated 'S'. The procedure has been repeated as part of the present study, allowing a few additional identifications to be made. In all 30 non-victualling shopkeepers could not be identified in the 1576 sesse. In 6 instances this is due to the use of non-specific names — 'the bookbinder', 'the French tinker', 'the French joiner', 'the French shoemaker', 'the French turner', 'the hookmaker,' — but in the others the people are not listed on the sesse, either because they were exempt, or occupied a message on a larger holding the entry for which was

paid by the occupier of the capital messuage, or the property was paid by a landlord who was not a Rye resident.

22 Mayhew 1987, 147 and note 6 on p.300.

23 Mayhew 1987, 35. No specific reference is given to underpin his statement.

24 ESRO RYE 60/9, fo.59r (Rental of town property). For the wards in which Marshe and Harry lived see Mayhew 1987, Appendix 4.

25 Mayhew 1987, for instance, 42-43.

26 For John Clarke *see* Mayhew 1987, 182; for the occupiers of the town's shops *see* ESRO RYE 60/9; ESRO RYE 1/4/228; Mayhew 1987, 277-284.

27 ESRO RYE 139/59.

28 Alston 2004, 38-59.

29 ESRO RYE 139/18.

30 We are indebted to Dave Stenning for sharing with us his observations regarding the normal size range of early shops in England.

31 Alston 2004, 38-59; Stenning, D.F. 1985. 'Timber-framed shops 1300-1600' *Vernacular Architecture* **16**, 35-39. Stenning's later work remains unpublished: comments contained here are based upon a paper given to Essex Historic Buildings Group at Chelmsford in 2008.

32 Clarke *et. al.* forthcoming.

33 *See* Part 2 of this volume: building reference numbers 1, 3, 4, 5, 9, 50, 65, 67, 68, 69, 104.

34 Vidler 1934b, 151.

35 An example of the fluidity of inn names is the village of Robertsbridge, where there were six inns in 1567. However, the Pied Bull of the 17th century was not on the site of The Bull which existed in 1567, whilst over time three different buildings have borne the sign of The George. The building which was The Tonne of 1567 has traded under no fewer than four different signs, firstly as The Tonne, then The George, subsequently The One Star and finally The White Horse (Martin and Mastin 1974, 8-9).

36 Mayhew 1987, 36, 279.

37 The location of The George when it was in Market Street is known from a rental of 1671 which includes abutments (Holloway 1847, 325). By that date the building was no longer trading and was divided into tenements, but an earlier owner is given in the rental as John Prowze, who is listed in the 1576 sesse as an innholder and scorer living in Market Ward (Mayhew 1987, 278). For further details *see* entry for house number 40 in Part 2 of this volume.

38 ESRO RYE 65/5 and Mayhew 1987, Appendix 4. In his text (pp.152-153) Mayhew gives a slightly different breakdown of the occupations, illustrating the multiplicity of occupational tags people could use.

39 ESRO RYE 65, Great Book, entries for beer tipplers, Midsummer Quarter, 1575. Many of the names can be identified in the 1576 sesse, for which *see* Mayhew 1987, 277-284.

40 Mayhew 1987, 36. As Mayhew notes, 'The figure for 1588 when there were 28 licensed premises was only 55 beds, but this latter figure leaves blank some of the details of the principal inns ...'.

41 Mayhew 1987, 36.

42 Mayhew 1987, 36.

43 Mayhew 1987, 57.

44 ESRO RYE 33/20. Enrolled deed dated 9th February 1658. This is another example of a sign which has changed location, for in 1581 The Swan was located in the Butchery, near the church (Mayhew 1987, 37).

45 Probate inventories of the 1560s indicate that painted cloths were at that time very common in the houses of Kent (*see* 'Probate Inventory Register of Canterbury Archdeaconry, from September 1565', a selection of which have been transcribed by Richard Harris in an unpublished report entitled 'Houses and Inventories in Kent', being a combined text of lectures given to the Wealden Building Study Group on 31st May 1989 and The Regional Furniture Society/Vernacular Architecture Group Conference in Oxford, 8th September 1991).

46 Mayhew 1987, 115-116, 176. By the middle years of the 16th century the building had come into the possession of the Wymond family, who had been prominent within the town since at least the late 15th century and who, during the 16th century, boasted no fewer than three generations of Rye jurats amongst their ranks. However, by 1582 the then owner, Robert Wymond of Midhurst in West Sussex, had leased the mansion to the Rye merchant, James Milles. Milles was himself a man of considerable substance within the town: he not only had a virtual monopoly on the wood and timber trade of the port, but also dealt in other goods, including the importation of hops and Flemish bricks.

47 ESRO PAR 467/38/1; ESRO DR/B/28/1. For further details *see* entry for house number 70 in Part 2 of this volume.

48 Mayhew 1987, 36.

49 ESRO RYE 35/42 — Inventory of James Pearsall, gent., deceased, 3rd January 1593.

50 Inventory of Francis Daniell, ESRO RYE 47/46/10. Both Daniell's and Pearsall's inventories list a hall, a great and little parlour, a kitchen, two butteries, and an entry, together with six chambers. Those in Daniell's inventory are given as over the hall, buttery, two over the entry and two over the kitchen. Both inventories list a hayloft. Despite these similarities, the furnishing in both inventories are of very different quality and thus, if they do relate to the same building, Pearsall's proprietorship must have seen a marked improvement in the standards of the inn. Reference to Daniell as a butcher makes it likely that the building was in Market Ward — in Rye this was where the butchers habitually dwelt.

51 Mayhew 1987, 186.

52 Mayhew 1987, 36.

53 Mayhew 1987, 174.

54 The post-medieval domestic houses and non-proven inns which had parlours are 11 High Street [2], 13-14 High Street [3] (heated), 31 High Street [10] (heated), 41 The Mint [15], 42-43 The Mint [16] (heated), 67-69 The Mint [19] (heated), 5-6 West Street [50], 15 West Street [56] (heated), 16-16a West Street [57], 31 Mermaid Street [69] (heated), 28, 32 Church Square [82] (heated), 34, 36 Church Square [83], St Anthonys, Church Square [87], 58, 60 Church Square [89] (heated), 4 Watchbell Street [91] (heated), Dormy House, East Cliff [104] (heated), 24 Landgate [107] (heated). The following are doubtful examples: 39-40 The Mint [14] (heated, but perhaps a kitchen), 103-103a High Street [27], 3 Market Street [37], 7 Mermaid Street [62] (heated, but perhaps a kitchen), 34 Mermaid Street [71].

55 The buildings in which the present chimneys are of later date are 4 High Street [1], 34 The Mint [12], 45-46 The Mint [17+], 103-103a High Street [27], 8 East Street [33*], 1-2 Lion Street [43*], 12 Lion Street [47], 5-6 West Street [50], 16-16a West Street [57], 14-15 Mermaid Street [65], 35-38 Mermaid Street [72*], 8, 10 Church Square [75*], 34, 36 Church Square [83*], 44 Church Square [85] and 1-2 Watchbell Street [90+]. In those marked * the evidence is compelling, and in those marked + it is only a little less convincing.

56 Martin and Martin 2006, 147-154.

57 Identified examples of integrated kitchens are 39-40 The Mint [14] (mid 16th century), 9-10 Market Street [40] (*c.*1600), 7-9 Lion Street [46] (mid 16th century), The Mermaid [72] (16th century), St Anthony's, Church Square [87] (*c.*1490), 11-13 Watchbell Street [94] (mid 16th century), Dormy House, East Cliff [104] (*c.*1600) and perhaps 7 Mermaid Street [62] (early 16th century).

58 To repeat Mayhew's findings within the present volume would be pointless: what has been concentrated on here are the complete (or likely complete) inventories. Explain all this with

references, which are Mayhew 1987, 174, 180-188.

59 Mayhew 1987, 174.

60 Mayhew 1987, 180-183.

61 ESRO RYE 47/51/39; Mayhew 1987, 174.

62 TNA PROB 2/323; Mayhew 1987, 179, 182-183.

63 ESRO RYE 47/13/7; Mayhew 1987, 181-182, 184-186, 188, 282.

64 ESRO RYE 35/31; Mayhew 1987, 182-183 Peter Adrian is not listed in the 1575/6 sesse, so it must be assumed that either the sesse on the property was paid by somebody else (perhaps his landlord, or possibly a tenant of another part of the property) or he moved into the town subsequent to the sesse being assessed — he is unlikely to have escaped payment through poverty.

65 ESRO RYE 47/58/16; Mayhew 1987, 183-185, 187.

66 ESRO HBR/1/0942.

67 Martin and Martin 1989; Martin and Martin 1991.

68 For roof pitches in local agricultural buildings *see* Martin and Martin 2006, 81-82. The situation with regards to houses is similar.

69 For an overview of the form and development of doorways in the area *see* Martin and Martin 1991, 120-163.

70 For a full analysis of window forms and construction details in the region *see* Martin and Martin 1991, 1-119.

71 Mayhew 1987, 177-178.

72 For photographs of the joists at Laughton Place *see* ESRO HBR/3/R264/1A-2A — the joists measured 85 mm x 270 mm in section; for Brede Place *see* ESRO HBR/1/0381. The structural history of floors in the area has yet to be written, but a number of examples of deep floor joists supporting entirely flush under-plastered ceilings are included in the HBR archive in ESRO.

73 No detailed analysis has yet been undertaken of the post-medieval roofs in Eastern Sussex; for a study of the roofs within the East Sussex village of Robertsbridge *see* Martin and Mastin 1974, 38-40; for post-medieval roofs over East Sussex agricultural buildings *see* Martin and Martin 2006, 81-92.

74 Roberts 2003, 27-37, particularly Figure 3.9.

75 The sample of 22 early 16th-century crownpost or paired-rafter-and-collar roofs includes 16 buildings (11 crownpost, 5 paired rafter) with 'post-medieval' scantling floor joists, whilst in 3 other buildings the joists are hidden, so their type remains uncertain.

76 Even in East Sussex very occasionally a medieval open hall was built with a clasped-side-purlin roof, though to date only three examples have been recorded in the Rape of Hastings and all are of late date — for reports on these *see* ESRO HBR/1/0115, 0227, 0364.

77 Raking struts occur within alterations and extensions of *c.*1590 at 24 Landgate [107] and next door, in the open trusses in the row of six late 16th-century two-cell houses at 18-23 Landgate [108].

78 Good examples of roofs in which the trusses are not located over the tiebeams are 15 High Street [4] (*c.*1590), 24-25 High Street [5] (*c.*1560), Flushing Inn, 4-5 Market Street [38] (rear addition of *c.*1565), 54, 56 Church Square [88] (*c.*1550), 4 Watchbell Street (built 1556-1560), 11-13 Watchbell Street [94] (*c.*1550) and 1-4 East Cliff [105] (1557). Roofs of this type are found in the hinterland, but they are later in date, mostly mid 17th century and after.

79 Notched principal rafters occur at 13-15 High Street [3] (*c.*1600), in the main range at 15 West Street [56] (*c.*1575), 30 Mermaid Street [68] (*c.*1550) and at 4 Watchbell Street [91] (built between 1556 and 1560).

80 The examples of garrets with raised wallplates are 13-14 High Street [3], 15 High Street [4], 24-25 High Street [5], 41 The Mint [15], 54 The Mint [18], 98 High Street [24], 107 High Street [30], 110 High Street [31], 14 Lion Street [49], crosswing at 15 West Street [56], 16, 16a West Street [57], 31 Mermaid Street [69], 4 Watchbell Street [91], Front range at Dormy House [104], Crosswing at 1-3 Landgate Square [109] and The Crown, Ferry Road [111]. Other examples are known which date from after the close of the present study.

81 Mayhew 1987, 176-177.

82 ESRO RYE 7/1-4. *See also* Mayhew 1987, 176-177.

83 *See* note 82 above.

84 Mayhew 1987, 176.

85 Mayhew 1987, 177-178.

8 — CONCLUSIONS

1 Nairn and Pevsner 1965, 594.

2 TNA SP12/36 (14), Southampton; (28) Sussex Rapes of Pevensey and Hastings; SP12/37 (11), Sussex Rapes of Lewes and Bramber, (12) Sussex Rapes of Chichester and Arundel. For the Kent return *see* BL, Stowe MS 570, ff.216-19, discussed in Gibson, J. M. 1993. 'The 1566 Survey of the Kent Coast', *Archaeologia Cantiana* **112**, 341-353.

3 TNA SP12/36 (28), Sussex Rapes of Pevensey and Hastings; ESRO BAT 42.

PART 2

10 — HIGH STREET AND THE MINT

1 It is difficult to see how the earlier rear range, even if single storeyed, could have avoided partially blocking the rear window in the rear wall of the street range, but it is equally unlikely that the cellar was not capped by a building, particularly as it stood partially proud of the adjacent ground.

2 No. 24 High Street now trades as 'The White Vyne' and was formerly known as Holloway House, whilst No. 25 High Street is today occupied by Boots the Chemist.

3 ESRO DR/B/28/1 — map of 1860. For the associated schedule *see* ESRO PAR 467/38/1.

4 The available evidence suggests that the hall was truncated and its low-end truss removed when the adjacent bay was demolished. This is not an unusual phenomenon, a good example being the hall house from Sole Street, Crundale, near Canterbury (now re-erected at the Weald and Downland Open Air Museum).

5 Pearson 1994, 89; ESRO HBR/1/976; Martin and Martin 2004, 141.

6 The hall was totally rebuilt late in the 16th century, so there is the outside possibility that this area initially housed a short hall with a floored-over bay beyond. If so, this house was built as a three-cell, rather than a two-cell house. However, given that the present hall occupies this entire space, this is not considered to be likely.

7 It has not been possible to undertaken a full survey of 54 The Mint — indeed, no details are known regarding the first-floor chambers and the roof area has been viewed in photographs only. Despite these restrictions, on account of the building's significance it is considered of sufficient importance to warrant brief discussion.

8 Holloway 1863.

9 Martin, D. and Martin, B. 2004. *An Archaeological Interpretative Survey of 3-4 West Street, New Romney, Kent.* Unpublished ASE Report, Project 1911.

10 The partition in question is currently the party wall between the two properties within the building, but this is not the case on the ground floor, where the party wall is further to the west. It is impossible to tell the date at which the division was made, though it appears to have been in antiquity.

11 — EAST STREET, MARKET STREET AND LION STREET

1 Schofield, J. (Ed.). 1987. *The London Surveys of Ralph Treswell.* London Topographical Society Publication **135**.
2 Vidler 1934b.
3 ESRO RYE 33/20.
4 We are grateful to Alan Dickinson for making available to us details of the features recorded by him during the building works.
5 In 1662, the five-flue assessment 'For the George' is listed with the entries for Strandgate ward, rather than Market ward (ESRO RYE 83/1).
6 Holloway 1847, 325; Mayhew 1987, 159, 278.
7 ESRO RYE 130/11.
8 ESRO RYE 132/15.

12 — WEST STREET AND MERMAID STREET

1 Martin and Martin 2004, 129-136.
2 Vidler 1934a, 52.
3 ESRO HBR/1/1304 (Isfield Place), Historical Background; TNA PROB 11/23.
4 ESRO RYE 139/20.
5 ESRO RYE 33/20.
6 ESRO RYE 82/82, Poll Tax Return.
7 ESRO RYE 83/1.
8 ESRO PAB/4.
9 ESRO RYE 132/15 — Copy of 1728.
10 Rye Museum, 'An Accurate Survey of the Town of Rye, 1771' reproduced in Bagley, G. S. 1982. *The Book of Rye.* Buckingham: Barracuda Books.
11 The only slight doubt concerning the layout of this building relates to the precise location of the ground-floor partition at the high end of the hall — there is the slight possibility that, as at 19 Watchbell Street [96] the section of partition at this level was recessed back slightly from the upper part.
12 ESRO RYE 33/20. Enrolled deed dated 9th February 1658.
13 Despite the small scale of the stair turret's replacement, it blocks an original window in the rear wall of the main range, confirming the tiny size of the original turret.
14 Much of the detail is hidden by plaster, so the evidence for windbraces could be hidden from view.
15 Hunter, M. & Gregory, A. 1988. *An Astrological Diary of the Seventeenth Century: Samuel Jeake of Rye 1652-1699* Oxford: Clarendon Press, p.150.
16 *Ibid.,* 196, 203.
17 It is possible that the staircase and (assumed) service area were located within a rear lean-to outshut. If so, there would have been no opportunity to include an additional first-floor chamber.
18 Mayhew 1987, 125.
19 Mayhew 1987, 36, 125, 258.
20 Mayhew 1987, 280.
21 Much of the structural detail in this area is currently hidden from view, but there seems little point to this lean-to section unless it was intended to access the chambers.
22 There is no evidence to prove that the partition is an original feature: it could have been intruded a little later. However, given the class of clientele, it seems highly unlikely that a quality letting chamber would have been provided through which the majority of other guests had to pass in order to reach their rooms.
23 The rooms have now been much 'restored'. The two ground-floor letting rooms have been thrown into one in order to provide a large dining room, the plaster ceilings have been removed to reveal the utilitarian joists, crossbeams and girders, much of the panelling has been stripped away and some of the windows have been blocked. The fireplaces are in poor condition and, although of antiquity, that heating the northern ground-floor room differs from the others in design and probably replaces a damaged original.
24 ESRO RYE 82/82.
25 Transcript of a letter from William George Lamb to Thomas Frewen dated March 7th, 1864. Document held at Rye Museum. We are grateful to Pauline Kingswood for drawing this document to our attention.

13 — CHURCH SQUARE, WATCHBELL STREET AND TRADER PASSAGE

1 Caution is needed as cases are known in Rye in which neighbours fell out over infringement of rights. For examples *see* Mayhew 1987, 173-199.
2 The orientation of the building has since been revised, with doorways cut through the eastern wall, accessed via an intruded alley called Hucksteeps Row.
3 The cellar beneath the building is accessed through the stone-built northern end wall via a central flight of steps which extends well beyond the envelope of the present superstructure. This northern end wall incorporates the remains of a narrow ground-floor doorway (now blocked) entering the hall at the northwestern corner. More convincing still, the details of the hall's northern roof truss indicate that it was never intended to be external.
4 Robert Gaymer is an abutment on the 1556 deed relating to 4 Watchbell Street [91].
5 For details *see* Chapter 7, '*Chimneys*'.
6 ESRO RYE 33/7/159; Mayhew 1987, 176.
7 *VCH Sussex* **9**, 44; Mayhew 1987, 35-36.
8 In 1519 John Shurley sold the plot of ground to the west of 1-2 Watchbell Street to John Jarvis, the owner of St Anthony's/1-2 Watchbell Street. The plot, 37 ft along the street by 47 ft deep, was then described as a garden. Subsequently, in 1556, part was sold off for the construction of 4 Watchbell Street, though the eastern part remained with St Anthony's *etc* — Transcript of deeds in private hands.
9 A similar, though even more unusual, arrangement existed at The Pilgrims Rest, Battle, where the rear service room was open from ground floor to roof and evidently served as a kitchen — ESRO HBR/1/207 (revised 2002).
10 *See* note 8 above. The relevant deed is dated 1560 and relates to adjacent 5 Watchbell Street. It gives the eastern abutment of No. 5 as 'The tenement and garden of the heirs of Robert Merilad, late of Rye, Fisherman, in which Nicholas Knaplock now lives'.
11 *See also* 42-43 The Mint [16]. There is the very slight possibility that a similar arrangement once existed at 10-11 Mermaid Street [64], but otherwise this is the only overshot dais known in Rye. If 10-11 Mermaid Street did follow this pattern, its high-end bay is sufficiently large to have still given a usable ground-floor room within the high-end bay. In a similar example at Dickens Cottage, 112 High Street, Hastings, the length of the high-end room is of similar size to that at 19 Watchbell Street, being *c.*1.75 metres x 4.25 metres (*c.*5'9" x 13'11") internally — *see* East Sussex Record Office HBR/1/254 (revised 2004).
12 A main post has been purposely incorporated into the frame of the front range, apparently to achieve a structural join between it and the rear ranges. There is the outside possibility that this post has something to do with a lost chimney, though, if so, this does not explain the existence of a first-floor doorway in the same wall.
13 For 25, 27 High Street, Robertsbridge *see* ESRO HBR/1/0007; for Smallhythe Place *see* Martin, D. and Martin, B. 2005. *An Archaeological Interpretative Survey of Smallhythe Place, Kent.* Unpublished ASE Report, Project 1967; for Ponts Farm and Westdown *see* ESRO HBR/1/0094 and ESRO HBR/1/0035.

14 No. 20 has since been rebuilt to the same height and width as 20A, 21 Watchbell Street and now has the external appearance of being part of that building.

15 In 1860 the entire plot (shown as plot 1523 in the 1860 plan, ESRO DR/B/28/1) was occupied by one house called 'The London Trader Inn and yard', owned by Mrs Meryon and occupied by James Crowhurst (*see* entry for plot 1523 in ESRO PAR 467/38/1).

14 — EAST CLIFF AND THE SUBURBS

1 Mayhew 1987, 44, 219, 257-8, 277.

2 Holloway 1863, 57.

3 ESRO RYE 131/2.

4 Even this 'fit' is not as perfect in that for the year previous Benjamin Martin was assessed in the same part of town at 8 flues — ESRO RYE 83/4-5.

5 ESRO RYE 127/22 (abutments to land associated with the almshouse); ESRO RYE 82/82 (entry under 'Landgate Ward' for Alice, widow of William Burwash, jurat [and tanner] and entry in the same ward for George Burwash, tanner); ESRO RYE 83/1-5 (entries under 'Landgate Ward' for George Burwash and Alice Burwash). *See also* ESRO RYE 91/3; ESRO RYE 91/8.

6 We are grateful to Alan Dickinson for making this information available to us.

7 TNA SP 12/254 75.

BIBLIOGRAPHY

ABBREVIATIONS

ASE Archaeology South-East
HBES Historic Buildings in Eastern Sussex
RCHME Royal Commission on the Historic Monuments of England
SAC *Sussex Archaeological Collections*

Alcock, N. W., Barley, M. W., Dixon, P. W. and Meeson, R. A. 1996. *Recording Timber-Framed Buildings: An Illustrated Glossary.* York: Council for British Archaeology.

Barnwell, P. S. and. Adams, A. T. 1994. *The House Within: Interpreting Medieval Houses in Kent.* Swindon: RCHME.

Biddle, M., Hiller, J., Scott, I. and Streeten, A. 2001. *Henry VIII's Coastal Artillery Fort at Camber Castle, Rye, East Sussex.* Oxford: Oxford Archaeological Unit for English Heritage.

Brent, C. 1975. 'Urban employment and population in Sussex between 1550 and 1660', *SAC* **113**, 35-50.

Clark, H.P. 1861. *Clark's Guide and History of Rye To Which Is Added Its Political History.* Rye: H.P.Clark

Clarke, H., Pearson, S., Mate, M. and Parfitt, K. Forthcoming. *Sandwich: 'The Completest Medieval Town in England': A Study of the Town and Port from Its Origins to 1600.* Oxford: Oxbow

Collard, J. 1978. *A Maritime History of Rye.* Rye: J. Collard.

Draper, G., with contributions by Martin, D., Martin, B. and Tyler, A. 2009. *Rye: A History of a Sussex Cinque Port to 1660.* Chichester: Phillimore.

Draper, G. and Meddens, F. with Armitage, P., Egan, G., Goodburn, D., and Jarret, C. Forthcoming. *The Sea and the Marsh: the Medieval Cinque Port of New Romney.* Pre-Construct Archaeology Monograph.

Eddison, J. 1998. 'Catastrophic changes: The evolution of the barrier beaches of Rye Bay', in Eddison, J., Gardiner, M. and Long, A. (Eds.). *Romney Marsh: Environmental Change and Human Occupation in a Coastal Lowland.* Oxford: Oxford University Committee for Archaeology Monograph No. 46.

— 2004. 'The Origins of Winchelsea', in Martin, D. and Martin, B. *New Wincheslea, Sussex: A Medieval Port Town,* King's Lynn: Heritage Marketing and Publications.

Faulkner, P. A. 1975. 'The Surviving Medieval Buildings' in Platt, C. and Coleman-Smith, R. *Excavations in Medieval Southampton 1953-1969: Volume 1, The Excavation Reports.* Leicester: Leicester University Press, 56-124.

Gardiner, M. 2000. 'Shipping and trade between England and the Continent during the eleventh century', *Anglo-Norman Studies* **22**, 71-93.

Griffin, N. 2005. *An Archaeological Recording Brief at 59 Cinque Ports Street, Rye, East Sussex.* Unpublished ASE Report, Project 2005.

Hadfield, J. 1981. 'An Excavation at 1-3 Tower Street, Rye, East Sussex', *SAC* **119**, 222-225.

Hipkin, S. 1998-9. 'The maritime economy of Rye, 1560-1640'. *Southern History*, 20/21, 108-42.

— 1995. 'Buying Time: Fiscal policy at Rye 1600-1640', *SAC* **133**, 241-254.

Holloway, W. 1847. *The History and Antiquities of the Ancient Town and Port of Rye.* London: John Russell Press.

— 1863. *Antiquarian Rambles through Rye.* Reprinted from local newspaper articles.

Johnson, C. 1998. *An Archaeological Evaluation at the Site of the Former Winter's Dairy Site, Cinque Ports Street, Rye, East Sussex.* Unpublished ASE Report, Project 416.

— 1999. *A Watching Brief at The Former Winter's Dairy Site & Monitoring of Engineering Test-Pits at The Old Market Dairy Site, Cinque Ports Street, Rye, East Sussex.* Unpublished ASE Report, Project 1127.

Johnson, M. 1993. *Housing Culture: Traditional Architecture in an English Landscape.* London: UCL Press.

Knight, S. 2004. *An Archaeological Watching Brief at The Former Central Garage, Cinque Port Street, Rye, East Sussex.* Unpublished ASE Report, Project 1697.

Longcroft, A (Ed.). with contributions from Sue Brown, Michael Brown, Jennifer Maughan, David Luckhurst, Ian Tyers, David Durrant and Paul Rutledge. 2005. 'The Historic Buildings of New Buckenham', *Journal of the Norfolk Historic Buildings Group* **2**.

Martin, D. 1993. 'The development of Old Hastings', in D. Rudling and L. Barber, 'Excavations at the Phoenix Brewery Site, Hastings, 1988', *Sussex Archaeological Collections* **131**, 73-113.

Martin, D. and Martin, B. 1977-80. *Historic Buildings in Eastern Sussex* **1**. Robertsbridge: Hastings Area Archaeological Papers.

— 1989. *Domestic Building in the Eastern High Weald, 1300-1750: Part 1, Wall Construction, HBES* **5**. Robertsbridge: Hastings Area Archaeological Papers.

— 1991. *Domestic Building in the Eastern High Weald, 1300-1750: Part 2, Windows and Doorways, HBES* **6**. Robertsbridge: Hastings Area Archaeological Papers.

— 1999. 'Adapting houses to changing needs: Multi-phased medieval and transitional houses in eastern Sussex', *SAC* **137**, 121-132

— with contributions by Jill Eddison, David Rudling and David Sylvester. 2004. *New Winchelsea, Sussex: A Medieval Port Town.* King's Lynn: Heritage Marketing and Publications.

— 2006. *Farm Buildings of the Weald, 1450-1750.* King's Lynn: Heritage Marketing and Publications.

Martin, D. and Mastin, B. 1974. *An Architectural History of Robertsbridge.* Robertsbridge: Hastings Area Archaeological Papers.

Mayhew, G. 1984. 'Rye and the Defences of the Narrow Seas: A 16th-century town at war', *SAC* **122**, 107-126.

— 1987. *Tudor Rye.* Falmer: Centre for Continuing Education, University of Sussex.

Norwich, J. J. 1985. *The Architecture of Southern England*: London, MacMillan.

Pearson, S. 1994. *The Medieval Houses of Kent: An Historical Analysis.* Swindon: RCHME.

Platt, C. and Coleman-Smith, R. 1975. *Excavations in Medieval Southampton 1953-1969: Volume 1, The Excavation Reports.* Leicester: Leicester University Press.

Roberts, E. 2003. *Hampshire Houses 1250-1700: Their Dating and Development.* Southampton: Hampshire County Council.

Renn, D. 1979. 'The Castles of Rye and Winchelsea', *Archaeological Journal* **136**, 193-202.

Stevens, S. 2001. *An Archaeological Evaluation at 59 and 59a Cinque Ports Street, Rye, East Sussex.* Unpublished ASE Report, Project 1364.

Stevens, S. and Barber, L. 2005. *59 & 59a Cinque Port Street, Rye, East Sussex: Post-Excavation Assessment and Project Design.* Unpublished ASE Report, Project 1763.

Vidler, L. A. 1934a. *A New History of Rye.* Hove: Combridges.

— 1934b. 'The Fifteenth Century House in Rye now known as The Flushing Inn', *Sussex Notes and Queries* **V**, 147-151.

INDEX

This index excludes endnotes. Illustrations are listed under the page number upon which they occur and are not separately identified from text references. Places and subjects relate to Rye except where stated to the contrary. Houses within the town are indexed under the street in which they are located. Domestic room usuage is not generally indexed within part II